EXPLAINING EMOTIONS

TOPICS IN PHILOSOPHY

1. Stephen P. Stich (ed.), *Innate Ideas*, 1975
2. John Perry (ed.), *Personal Identity*, 1975
3. Amélie Oksenberg Rorty (ed.), *The Identities of Persons*, 1976
4. Robert J. Swartz (ed.), *Perceiving, Sensing, and Knowing*, 1976
5. Amélie Oksenberg Rorty (ed.), *Explaining Emotions*, 1980

EXPLAINING EMOTIONS

15675967

Edited by

AMÉLIE OKSENBERG RORTY

UNIVERSITY OF CALIFORNIA PRESS
Berkeley   Los Angeles   London

BF
561
E95

University of California Press
Berkeley and Los Angeles, California

University of California Press, Ltd.
London, England

Library of Congress Cataloging in Publication Data

Main entry under title:

Explaining emotions.

(Topics in philosophy; 4)
Bibliography: p. 537
1. Emotions.   I. Rorty, Amélie.
BF561.E95   152.4   78-62859

ISBN 0-520-03921-1

Printed in the United States of America

4 5 6 7 8 9 0

The paper used in this publication meets the minimum requirements of
American National Standard for Information Sciences—Permanence of
Paper for Printed Library Materials, ANSI Z39.48–1984.   ∞

CONTENTS

INTRODUCTION   1
Amélie O. Rorty

I   SENSORY AND PERCEPTIVE FACTORS IN
EMOTIONAL FUNCTIONS OF THE
TRIUNE BRAIN   9
Paul D. MacLean

II   EMOTION AND ANXIETY: SOCIOCULTURAL,
BIOLOGICAL, AND PSYCHOLOGICAL
DETERMINANTS   37
James R. Averill

III   BIOLOGICAL AND CULTURAL CONTRIBUTIONS
TO BODY AND FACIAL MOVEMENT IN THE
EXPRESSION OF EMOTIONS   73
Paul Ekman

IV   EXPLAINING EMOTIONS   103
Amélie O. Rorty

V   THE RATIONALITY OF EMOTIONS   127
Ronald de Sousa

VI   CHARACTER AND THE EMOTIONS   153
Adam Morton

VII   FUNCTIONALISM AND THE EMOTIONS   163
Georges Rey

VIII   OVERDETERMINATION AND THE EMOTIONS   197
Graeme Marshall

IX   A CASE OF MIXED FEELINGS: AMBIVALENCE
AND THE LOGIC OF EMOTION   223
Patricia S. Greenspan

X   EMOTIONS AND CHOICE   251
Robert C. Solomon

XI   SELF-DECEPTIVE EMOTIONS   283
Ronald de Sousa

XII ON PERSONS AND THEIR LIVES 299
Richard Wollheim

XIII INTELLECTUAL DESIRE, EMOTION, AND
ACTION 323
Michael Stocker

XIV RITUAL AND THE RELIGIOUS FEELINGS 339
Gareth Matthews

XV NATURAL PRIDE AND NATURAL SHAME 355
Arnold Isenberg

XVI PRIDE 385
Gabriele Taylor

XVII MASTER PASSIONS 403
Annette Baier

XVIII JEALOUS THOUGHTS 425
Jerome Neu

XIX JEALOUSY, ATTENTION, AND LOSS 465
Leila Tov-Ruach

XX AGENT REGRET 489
Amélie O. Rorty

XXI COMPASSION 507
Lawrence Blum

XXII EMOTION, PRACTICAL KNOWLEDGE AND
COMMON CULTURE 519
Roger Scruton

BIBLIOGRAPHY 537

CONTRIBUTORS 544

ACKNOWLEDGMENTS

Paul D. MacLean, "Sensory and Perceptive Factors in Emotional Functions of the Triune Brain" originally appeared in L. Levi, *Emotions— Their Parameters and Measurement,* New York: Raven Press, 1975.

James R. Averill, "Emotion and Anxiety: The Sociocultural, Biological and Psychological Determinants" is an excerpt from a longer paper, "The Sociocultural, Biological and Psychological Determinants of the Emotions" originally published in *Emotions and Anxiety: New Concepts, Methods, and Applications,* edited by Marvin Zuckerman and Charles Spielberger, New York: LEA-John Wiley, 1976.

Paul Ekman, "Biological and Cultural Contributions to Body and Facial Movement in the Expression of Emotions" is an excerpt from a longer paper, "Biological and Cultural Contributions to Body and Facial Movement," published in *The Anthropology of the Body,* edited by John Blacking, London: Academic Press, 1977.

Amélie O. Rorty, "Explaining Emotions" originally appeared in the *Journal of Philosophy,* 1978.

Ronald de Sousa, "The Rationality of Emotions" originally appeared in *Dialogue,* 18 (1979).

Robert C. Solomon, "Emotion and Choice" originally appeared in *The Review of Metaphysics,* XVII, i (September 1973).

Ronald de Sousa, "Self-Deceptive Emotions" originally appeared in *The Journal of Philosophy.*

Gareth Matthews, "Ritual and the Religious Feelings" is a revised version of a paper entitled "Bodily Motions and Religious Feelings," published in the *Canadian Journal of Philosophy* 1 (1971).

Arnold Isenberg, "Natural Pride and Natural Shame" originally appeared in *Philosophy and Phenomenological Research* 10, 1 (September 1949).

Roger Scruton, "Emotion, Practical Knowledge, and the Common Culture" is a revised version of a paper entitled "The Significance of Common Culture," published in *Philosophy,* 1979.

INTRODUCTION

Amélie Oksenberg Rorty

Emotions do not form a natural class. After a long history of quite diverse debates about their classification, emotions have come to form a heterogeneous group: various conditions and states have been included in the class for quite different reasons and on different grounds, against the background of shifting contrasts. Fear, religious awe, exuberant delight, pity, loving devotion, panic, regret, anxiety, nostalgia, rage, disdain, admiration, gratitude, pride, remorse, indignation, contempt, disgust, resignation, compassion (just to make a random selection) cannot be shepherded together under one set of classifications as active or passive; thought-generated and thought-defined or physiologically determined; voluntary or nonvoluntary; functional or malfunctional; corrigible or not corrigible by a change of beliefs. Nor can they be sharply distinguished from moods, motives, attitudes, character traits.

Some emotions can be induced physiologically, controlled chemically, and are characteristically behaviorally identifiable even when the person is not aware of his condition. Other emotions are strongly intentional in character: a person's beliefs and perceptions, the descriptions under which he views the objects of his attitudes are essential to the identification and the individuation of the emotion. The general description of the objects and behavioral expression of some emotions (e.g., anger) are cross-culturally invariant in origin and expression; others (e.g., Japanese *amae*) are strongly culturally and even subculturally variable. Emotions that are closely associated with pleasures and pains can be mapped on a scale of aversion-attraction to their objects; such emotions (e.g., fear) are often directly motivational because they are ingredient in a person's apprehension of what is to be pursued or avoided. Because they presuppose beliefs about objective satisfactions, they are thought to be capable of being evaluated for their rationality as well as for their appropriateness. Other emotions (e.g., nostalgia) are relatively motivationally isolated: their connections with a range of appropriate actions are commensurately distant, even when they are normally expressed in characteristic sounds, gestures, or facial configurations. Such emotions are standardly evaluated for their appropriateness rather than for their rationality. Some emotions are relatively easy to change or to correct by changes in beliefs and perceptions. Others are far more resistant to straightforwardly rational correction, evincing such strong conservation that they distort perception and attention. Some emotions are strongly dispositional, explained by and indicative of a person's constitution and character; others are episodic, explained primarily by their immediate contextual causes.

An investigation of the emotions might be thought, then, to produce a taxonomy: a classification of varieties of emotions along a number of parameters, a schematic diagram placing varieties of emotions on a number of scales (passivity/activity, voluntary/nonvoluntary, behaviorally/intentionally defined).[1] But a number of difficulties stand in the way of such an enterprise. The general class, *emotions,* cannot, with its varieties, be contrasted with other classes: *motives* and *cognitive attitudes.* There are, moreover, enormous differences within each emotion-type: some angers are etiologically and functionally closer to indignation than to rage. The problems that beset analyses of the emotions are symptomatic of deeper problems in philosophical psychology. The dichotomies that have been the stock in trade of psychologists and philosophers are highly suspect: these are the working dichotomies between physical and psychological processes, between activities and passive responses, between voluntary and nonvoluntary behavior, between cognition and other psychological activities. What makes the placing of emotions along a schema of these various parameters problematic is that the meanings and force of these dichotomies have themselves shifted. They were terms of art, introduced at very different periods in the history of the subject, to perform quite different functions. The contrast between activities and passive responses, for example, has an extremely muddled history: its place in relation to the contrast between voluntary and nonvoluntary actions is a matter of substantive disagreement.[2] Behind the debates about whether specific emotions are (for instance) cognitively corrigible stand yet further disagreements about the characterization of cognition and its relation to affect. In short, it becomes clear that a proper account of the emotions requires a revision of the whole map of psychological processes and activities, and of their complex interrelations.

The subject of our study may evaporate as a natural kind, contrasted with other natural kinds. We should have done a large service to further investigation if we succeeded in making that plausible. Naturally this is not the sort of claim that can be demonstrated: at best it can be grounded in detailed discussions of the problems that arise in identifying, explaining, characterizing those various conditions that are commonly classified as emotions. The explosion of a subject sometimes generates considerable light.

One might think that, at least in principle, all this could be bypassed. We could take some range of emotions as central, abstract and analyze the functioning of the variables that seem to explain them, and construct our analysis to develop a general theory. If the theory does not readily apply to cases for which it was not expressly designed, those cases can be classified as nonemotions and left for analysis elsewhere. Or else charges of self-deception can be brought into play: the errant or anomalous cases could be claimed really to conform to the theory, appearances and first-person denials to the contrary. Rather than being explained, they are explained away.

As long as we are quite clear about the reconstructive and legislative character of such an enterprise, careful not to confuse the surgery necessary to elegant theory construction with Procrustean butchery, there is no harm in this. After all, splendid theories have emerged from a carefree disregard of the muddles that come from staying too close to the descriptive ground. Precisely because our vocabulary *is* in disarray, it might be thought fruitful to abstract from common beliefs and characterizations, moving as sharply as possible toward a technical or even formally constructed terminology. The difficulty is, however, that legislative analyses often also present themselves as simply and straightforwardly descriptive. They therefore tend to be taken as being in a polemical disagreement with other theories that began with quite different cases as central for their analyses and constructions, focusing on quite different sorts of questions, going in a different direction from a different starting point. But such alternative accounts need not conflict at all, any more than a Beethoven variation on a theme from Mozart conflicts with a Brahms variation on the same theme (let alone a Brahms variation on a theme from Haydn). A theory that takes fear as the central example of emotion will take a quite different form from one that abstracts from regret or nostalgia as central cases. Conflicts between the two theories may appear to be profound; but they will be largely perspectival and verbal.

Without legislating against legislative theories, these essays are enterprises of another sort. They attempt to describe and preserve the phenomena, presenting distinct approaches to the emotions, raising questions that do not claim to preempt the field. The authors are committed to remaining close to the descriptive ground, even at the cost of elegance and simplicity. An adequate account of the emotions requires research in quite different fields. It is too early to construct a unified theory, even too early for a single inter-disciplinary account of the approaches whose contributions are required to explain the range of emotional conditions. The vocabu-laries of neurophysiologists, psychologists, anthropologists, biolo-gists, and philosophers have not been uniformly or consistently established in a reliable form. Even workers within a single disci-pline often turn out, on close examination, to be talking at cross purposes. At this stage, we still need to become informed of the work in a number of fields which can illuminate problems in our own, even when such work cannot directly be applied to solve these problems.

All too often, philosophers take strong stands on issues without informing themselves of the results of relevant empirical investiga-tions: and all too often empirical researchers remain naive about the assumptions built into their conceptual apparatus. It would be an advance to formulate and to distinguish some questions and to collect and compare work from different fields.

This anthology presents papers from several disciplines. All the essays presuppose the rehabilitation of the emotions. They take it for granted that emotions are not irrational feelings, disturbances, or responses to disturbances. They also take it for granted that emotions are not merely proprioceptive states, identified and indi-viduated by introspective insight or by a physiological description.

The authors assume that emotions play an important part in our lives, that having an emotion can not only be functional but also informative. Recent strategies of philosophers arguing that the emotions are not intrinsically irrational (or arational) concentrate on showing that the emotions can themselves be evaluated for their rationality: the beliefs they presuppose can be judged true or false, validly or invalidily inferred.[3] Most of the papers in this volume construe the reconciliation of the emotions and rationality more broadly, without reconstructing the intentional component of an emotion as a judgment in propositional form.

The best way to characterize the essays is give an account of the various questions they address. In "Sensory and Perceptive Factors in Emotional Functions of the Triune Brain," MacLean reports research into the respective functions of the three layers of the brain, discovering that "Although the three brain types are extensively interconnected and functionally dependent, there is evidence that each is capable of operating somewhat independently." He discusses the correlation of various sorts of emotional disorders with lesions in specific parts of the brain, with spatiotemporal disorientation, and with characteristic sensory and perceptual disorders.

In "The Sociocultural, Biological, and Psychological Determinants of Emotion," Averill analyzes some of the ways in which the plasticity of the biological determinants of emotion allow for social and individual specification and formation. Influenced by early Darwinist theory and the seminal work of Silvan Tomkins, Averill is interested in the adaptive advantages of the expression of the emotions to communicate environmental dangers and benefits, and to form bonds among group members.

In "Biological and Cultural Contributions to Body and Facial Movement in the Expression of Emotions," Ekman maps the facial configurations that express specific emotions, investigating patterns that are culturally invariant even when there are cultural and conventional variations in the contexts and proprieties of expression, as variations in their significant symbolic functions.

Rorty and de Sousa analyze the causal functions of the intentional components of the emotions, arguing that they form organized patterns of attention and focus, rather than beliefs in propositional form. This is one of the reasons that the correction or change of emotions involves restructuring habits of perceptual or conceptual organization and salience.

The papers by Norton and Rey place the attribution of emotions in the more general context of psychological theory. Morton discusses the psychological theories implicit in the attribution of psychological traits, the ways in which emotions are located within a person's general character structure, suggesting that emotions are identified not only by their causal history but also by their place in a system of clustering and contrastive traits.

Rey suggests that by focusing on the psychological effects of our constitutions and social histories, a study of the emotions could solve some of the problems of functionalist theories whose identification of psychological states by their causes, effects, and roles leaves them open to the charge of being too broad and too intellectualistic. An adequate account of the emotions should provide constraints for functionalism.

Marshall analyzes the objects and causes of complex emotions, asking whether complex emotions can have multiple and distinct causal histories without thereby fracturing into several conjoined emotions. Greenspan argues that some cases where fracturing does occur—cases of ambivalence or contrary emotions with the same object—need not involve irrationality, as cognitive conflict presumably would.

Solomon explores the relation between a person's characteristic range of emotions and his conception of what is essential to his identity. Strongly influenced by Sartre, Solomon claims that a person's choice of his emotions constitutes a choice of self-identification or definition. He takes emotions to be voluntary judgments, ways of seeing or interpreting one's modes of being in the world. In a new appendix, he sets more stringent limits on his account of the voluntary character of psychological states.

In his account of self-deceptive emotions, de Sousa investigates the ways we acquire our emotional repertoires from early "paradigm scenarios." Since we also learn the meanings of terms that refer to emotions from such paradigm scenarios, identifying the cognitive component of emotions requires understanding their formation. De Sousa analyzes some strategies for evaluating and changing the "ideological" force of emotions.

In "On Persons and their Lives," Wollheim examines the ways

in which the affective interpretations and reconstructions of memories influence—and are in turn influenced by—a person's conception of the unity of his life, his sense of its forming a whole. Experiential memory, affective interpretation, and personal identity are mutually constitutive.

Stocker attacks the divisions standardly drawn between emotions and other psychological activities, arguing that emotional dispositions are not only presupposed by but also are expressed directly in intellectual investigations. The sharp distinctions between cognition, connation, and motivation prevent our understanding how emotions and character traits direct inquiry, their style entering into the determination of the outcome.

Like Stocker, Matthews is interested in breaking down the distinction between emotions and other sorts of cognitive and interpretive attitudes. He investigates the ways in which at least some emotions are characteristically ingredient in, and expressed by a person's posture, words, thought, rituals of behavior. He holds that such rituals not only express but compose the character of some religious feelings and attitudes.

Isenberg, Taylor, Baier, Neu, Tov-Ruach, Rorty, and Blum investigate particular sets of emotions and emotional attitudes. They raise the questions: In what does the emotion consist? What are the characteristic thoughts, anticipations, causes, and objects of the emotion? How is it related to neighboring and opposing attitudes? What range of attitudes—especially attitudes toward oneself—does it presuppose and express? What sorts of behavior and actions are characteristic of the emotion? How are particular instances evaluated as appropriate or inappropriate, rational or irrational? Can the emotion be evaluated for its moral force, and moral arguments advanced for strengthening or redirecting the emotion? To what extent and how can a person control or correct such attitudes?

Scruton discusses the cultural transmission of patterns of emotions, particularly through poetic and literary works that come to form our descriptions of events. By being embedded in our perceptions of states of affairs, emotions form our judgments and expectations of appropriate actions.

NOTES

1. See J. de Rivera, "A Structural Theory of the Emotions," *Psychological Issues* (1977).

2. See H. Frankfurt, "Identification and Externality," *The Identities of Persons,* ed. A. O. Rorty (Berkeley, Los Angeles, London: University of California Press, 1976); G. Marshall, "On Being Affected," *Mind* (1968); I. Murdoch, *The Sovereignty of the Good* (London, 1970).

3. See the articles by Bedford, Pitcher, Thalberg, Pears, Kenny, and Wilson listed in the Bibliography.

I

SENSORY AND PERCEPTIVE FACTORS
IN EMOTIONAL FUNCTIONS
OF THE TRIUNE BRAIN

PAUL D. MacLEAN

In the world of literature and the fine arts there are countless illustrations of the importance that introspective human beings place on the role of sensation and perception in the generation of emotional feelings. Add to this what has been written on the subject in such fields as religion, philosophy, psychology, and medicine, and the amount of information would choke the output of an ordinary computer. Imagine, however, a computer search in which the three words sensation, perception, and emotion were tied to brain function. Suddenly the outflow of substantive references would be reduced to a mere trickle!

But even this mere trickle would be more than we could cope with within the limits of this presentation. If, for example, we were to examine "first causes," we would need to analyze the extensive literature on receptors, as well as to review the effects of sensory deprivation of whatever origin on emotional experience and expression. I will therefore set arbitrary limits on the ground to be covered and deal mainly with the unanswered question of how sensory and perceptive mechanisms exert their influence on forebrain structures believed to be involved in emotion. In attempting an orderly approach to this problem, I shall deal successively with the three main evolutionary formations of the forebrain. Somewhat like an archaeological dig, I shall begin at the surface with the most recent formation and proceed toward the most ancient. For reasons to be explained, I shall focus particular attention on the limbic system, which phylogenetically represents an inheritance from lower mammals. Then in conclusion, I shall call attention to some seldom asked questions that are possibly relevant to functions of the major counterpart of the reptilian forebrain in mammals.

In constructing a piece of writing we use words both as building materials and tools for thought. Because of the lack of unanimity about the meanings for psychological terms employed in this chapter, it will be worthwhile to read the fine print of the following "contract" regarding the use of certain key words such as sensations, perceptions, and emotions.

DEFINITIONS[1]

It is the element of subjectivity that most clearly distinguishes psychological from other functions of the brain (MacLean, 1960). Even so-called unconscious processes probably require the existence of the subjective state. The case of sleep presents no exception because introspection reveals that a feeling of subjectivity is pervasive in dreaming. Subjectivity refers to the awareness associated with various forms of psychological information. A philosopher such as Kant might have called it an a priori "form of consciousness." To paraphrase Spencer (1896), objective psychology begins with subjective psychology. In addition to what we vaguely recognize as awareness or consciousness, introspection reveals five main classes of psychological information that will be here considered under the provisional categories of sensations, perceptions, propensions, emotions, and intellections. All these elements of the psyche are of themselves no more than information. As Wiener (1948) stated more succinctly than Berkeley and Hume, "Information is information, not matter or energy." At the same time, it is empirically established that there can be no communication of information without the intermediary of what we recognize as *behaving entities.* The statement of this invariance might be considered as a law of communication.

Information itself is regarded as orderliness or, in other words, the order that emerges from a background of disorder. The greater the ratio of order to disorder, the greater is the amount of information. In this respect immaterial information lends itself to a quantification. (In information theory the word information is used in the strict sense to refer to a numerical quantity that is the measure of uncertainty in a communications system. In the present context it is used in the broad sense to refer to anything meaningful.)

The derivation and communication of information in animals depends upon behaving entities of the nervous system. Although introspection per se can give no clue as to the workings of these behaving entities (see MacKay, 1970), it is, as already stated, the first step in making an investigation. How shall we define sensations and perceptions? As a beginning, we may say that sensation represents the raw feelings that, under normal circumstances, depend upon the initiation of impulses resulting from activation of intero- and exteroceptors. In Sherringtonian terms, sensations fall into two broad classes of interoceptions and exteroceptions. They are distinguished in terms of quality (modality) and intensity. Individually, or in combination, sensations become more informative as they are appreciated in terms of time and space. In such transformation they are introspectively recognized as perceptions.

Sensing and perceiving, vis-à-vis mentation. With the exception of certain pathological conditions, it is characteristic of sensations and perceptions that they depend on incoming signals to the brain from specific afferent systems and cease to exist after the termination of such activity. Contrast this situation with what applies to the three other main classes of psychological information, namely, propensions, emotions, and intellections. The latter are distinguished from sensations and perceptions by their capacity to occur "after-the-fact." The unexplained process that makes this possible is referred to as mentation. In terms of a behaving nervous system, one might say that mentation involves self-regenerating neural replica of events either as they first occurred or in some rearrangement. How the original ordering of the events is preserved (i.e., memorized) or recorded (i.e., imagined or conceived) remains a mystery.

Of the three psychological terms in the title of this chapter we have yet to consider the definition of emotions. It is usual to speak of both the expressive and subjective aspects of emotion. I will use the word "affect" to refer to the subjective state. Only we as individuals can experience affect. The existence of affects in another individual must be inferred through some form of verbal or nonverbal behavior. In the sense that originally inspired its use by Descartes (1967), the word emotion is an appropriate designation for such behavior.

The affects differ from other forms of psychological information by being imbued with a "physical" quality that is neither agreeable or disagreeable. There are no neutral affects because, emotionally speaking, it is impossible to feel unemotionally. As illustrated in figure 1, the agreeable and disagreeable affects can be subdivided into three main categories, which I have labeled basic, specific, and general.

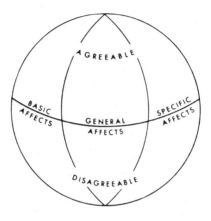

Fig. 1. A scheme for viewing the world of affects (from MacLean, 1970).

The basic and specific affects are first-order affects insofar as they are immediately dependent, respectively, on interoceptions and exteroceptions. The basic affects derive from interoceptions signaling different kinds of internal states associated with basic bodily needs—namely, the needs for food, water, air, sexual outlet, sleep, and those associated with various emunctories. The specific affects apply to exteroceptions and perceptions immediately generated by activity in a specific sensory system. Some are unlearned, whereas others are conditioned. The latter include aesthetic affects identified with agreeable and disagreeable aspects of music and various art forms. Examples of unlearned specific affects are ones associated with repugnant odors, startling sounds, and intense flashes of light.

The general affects are second-order insofar as they originally derive from the first-order affects, but which through mentational processes mentioned above may persist or recur "after-the-fact." I call them general affects because they may apply to feelings aroused by other individuals, situations, or things. All the general affects may be considered from the standpoint of self-preservation and the preservation of the species. Those general affects that are informative of threats to the self or the species are disagreeable in nature, whereas those that signal the removal of threats and the gratification of needs are agreeable.

Exclusive of verbal behavior, there are six main types of animal and human behavior that we identify in varying degree with affective experience and emotional expression. These behaviors are recognized as (1) searching, (2) aggressive, (3) protective, (4) dejected, (5) gratulant, and (6) caressive. Corresponding words that would be broadly descriptive of the associated affective states are desire, anger, fear, sorrow, joy, and affection. Symbolic language and the introspective process make it possible to identify many variations of these affects, but in investigations on animals inferences about emotional states must be based largely on these six general types of behavior.

There are several behaviors that, at first, might not seem to fit these categories but turn out to be amenable to such classification. Primary among these are obsessive-compulsive, repetitious, ritualistic, superstitious, deceitful, and imitative behaviors.

EVOLUTIONARY CONSIDERATIONS: THE TRIUNE BRAIN

Given these psychological and behavioral definitions, we next consider how the three main evolutionary formations of the forebrain participate in the sensory and perceptive aspects of emotional processes. In its evolution the primate forebrain expands along the lines of three basic patterns that may be characterized as reptilian, paleomammalian, and neomammalian (fig. 2). There results a remarkable linkage of three cerebrotypes which are radically different in

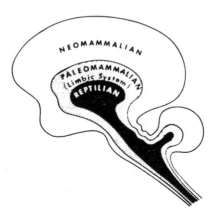

Fig. 2. In evolution the human brain expands in hierarchic fashion along the lines of three basic patterns referred to in the diagram as reptilian, paleomammalian, and neomammalian. As indicated in parenthesis, the limbic system conforms to the paleomammalian pattern. Since the limbic system has been shown to play an important role in emotional behavior, I have given particular attention to the question of how it is influenced by sensory and perceptive mechanisms. (From MacLean, 1967, *J. Nerv. Ment. Dis.* 144, 374-82.)

chemistry and structure and which in an evolutionary sense are eons apart. There exists, so to speak, a hierarchy of three-brains-in-one, or what I call, for short, a *triune* brain (MacLean, 1970, 1973*c*). It is inferred that each cerebrotype has its own special kind of intelligence, its own special memory, its own sense of time and space, and its own motor and other functions. Although the three brain types are extensively interconnected and functionally dependent, there is evidence that each is capable of operating somewhat independently.

The major counterpart of the reptilian forebrain in mammals includes the corpus striatum (caudate plus putamen) globus pallidus, and peripallidal structures.[2] The paleomammalian brain is represented by the limbic system, a designation that I suggested in 1952. Most of the phylogenetically old cortex is contained in the limbic lobe which surrounds the brainstem (fig. 3) and conforms somewhat like a mold to the corpus striatum (see fig. 2 in MacLean, 1972*a*). The neomammalian brain is represented by the rapidly evolving neocortex and structures of the brainstem with which it is primarily connected.

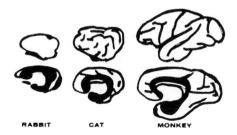

RABBIT   CAT   MONKEY

Fig. 3. The limbic lobe, which was so named by Broca because it surrounds the brainstem, contains most of the phylogenetically old cortex. Indicated by the dark shading, it is found as a common denominator in the brains of all mammals. The neocortex which undergoes great expansion relatively late in evolution is shown in white (after MacLean, 1954).

ROLE OF THE NEOMAMMALIAN BRAIN

It has long been recognized from clinical observations that specific areas of the neocortex are respectively related to the somatic, auditory, and visual systems, and that these cortical areas are essential for normal sensation and perception. The evolutionary ascendancy of these systems indicates that the neocortex is primarily oriented toward the external environment. As I have commented elsewhere, "...the signals to which these three systems are receptive are the only ones that lend themselves to electronic amplification and radiotransmission. Smells, tastes, and interoceptions have no such avenue for communication" (1972b). Anatomical and electrophysiological studies have demonstrated that an orderly projection exists between receptors and thalamus and between thalamus and neocortex, resulting in a "point-to-point," topographical relationship. The evoked potential technique has made it possible to subdivide the somatic, auditory, and visual areas into a number of subareas, with the recognition thus far of the first, second, and third visual areas; the first, second, and third auditory areas;[3] and the first, second, and supplementary somatosensory areas.

With encephalization, it is evident that in spite of the many redundancies of the nervous system, the neocortex becomes more and more crucial for sensation and perception, and that indeed there is hierarchical ordering within the neocortex itself. Higher primates, for example, are for all intents and purposes blind without the primary striate cortex. This is the extreme opposite of what Snyder and Diamond (1968) have recently observed in the tree shrew, an animal that is presumed to represent an antecedent of primates. "With a complete removal of the geniculo-striate system," they report, "tree shrews retain form and pattern vision as well as the capacity to localize visual objects in space." Even after removal of all the known visual areas of the neocortex, these animals are capable of differentiating between horizontal and vertical stripes.

The work of Diamond and his colleagues (Harting, Hall, Diamond, and Martin, 1973) has also added to the accumulating knowledge of the anatomical course of other than the classical sensory pathways to the neocortex. They have demonstrated a collicular-pulvinar-temporal pathway that presumably accounts for sparing of visual function in the tree shrew after ablation of the striate cortex (Snyder and Diamond, 1968). In an abstract in 1963, Myers had described collicular projections to the inferior pulvinar in the monkey. I shall refer to this pathway again when discussing limbic connections.

Electrophysiological studies have identified a number of functional properties of the neocortical sensory areas that are presumed to be involved in the perception of form. The "inhibitory surround" detected in testing receptive fields of cells in the somatosensory (Mountcastle, Davies, and Berman, 1957) and visual areas (Hubel and Wiesel, 1962), for example, is believed to be of fundamental importance in this respect. Studies of individual cells of the visual system have revealed units that respond specifically to edges, contrast, orientation, directional movement, color, and so on. The findings have tended to generate a magical jargon in which reference is made to "sophisticated neurons" that are "edge detectors," "motion detectors," and the like, somewhat as though they possessed subjective properties of Leibnitz's monads and were especially constituted to recognize only one or two types of stimuli, when in actuality it is the neural network to which they belong that accounts for the selective response. Curiously enough, as Michael

(1969) points out, the retinas of such animals as the frog, ground squirrel, and rabbit have the capacity for discriminative functions that take place only in the visual cortex of higher mammals—specifically the detection of edges, orientation, and direction of movement.

In neurophysiological studies of mechanisms of perception it is usually implicit that the primary goal is to learn how animals achieve the recognition of well-defined patterns, as though this aspect of perception was what mattered most to the organism. As yet, little consideration has been given to a fundamental question of the opposite sort—namely, what is it that makes an animal reactive to environmental apparitions, including ill-defined partial representations of an object or animal, that are conducive to propensive and emotional behavior, serving also, in ethological terms, as "releasers" of specific forms of behavior? Of the many examples, one of the best known is that of infants responding to crude, partial representations of the human face. I shall return to this question in discussing the limbic system and the major mammalian counterpart of the reptilian forebrain.

During neurosurgical procedures it has been learned that crude sensations may result from stimulation of the somatic, auditory, and visual cortex (see Penfield and Jasper, 1954). In attempting to locate epileptogenic foci, Penfield has found that in some individuals brain stimulation of the so-called association areas of the temporooccipital cortex may induce auditory and visual illusions or hallucinations (Penfield and Perot, 1963).

But neither clinical nor experimental observations have made it possible to trace the neural circuitry by which verbal or nonverbal information derived through the visual, auditory, and somatic systems generates affective states. Of the *specific* affects, pain has received foremost attention. In their analysis of disturbances associated with thalamic lesions, Head and Holmes (1920) noted that sometimes simple tones, like various somatic stimuli, aggravated the sense of pain on the affected side of the body. In addition, they described a curious situation that is somewhat the reverse of the one we are considering. No one seems to have recognized, they pointed out, that states of emotion may evoke different sensations on different sides of the body. "One of our patients," they continued, "was unable to go to his place of worship because he 'could not stand the hymns on his affected side.'" Cases of this kind led them to infer that the optic thalamus was the wellspring of emotion.

PROLEGOMENON TO THE CONSIDERATION OF THE LIMBIC AND REPTILIAN FORMATIONS

Von Economo (1931) singled out more ventral loci as being of primary consequence in emotional experience. In his monograph *Encephalitus Lethargica* he concluded that the tegmentum, the basal and posterior walls of the third ventricle, and the region of the aqueduct were the "favorite target" of the disease. He emphasized the relevance of these findings to the observation that among the persisting symptoms "the difficulty of arousing emotion... is above all a primary defect." He pointed out that some patients may feel hungry but take no pleasure in eating, or recognize the sensation of cold without experiencing the usual feeling of cold. In general, they may complain that they "feel like a spent volcano."

It is to be noted that the structures particularly mentioned by Von Economo lie in the region fed by the perforating vessels of the interpenduncular fossa (see Mettler, 1955). Thanks to recent investigations that can trace part of their "ancestry" to Von Economo, it is now known that there are dopamine-containing neurons in this region that innervate the corpus striatum, including the so-called olfactory striatum. In view of the profound influence of these ascending systems on spontaneous behavior of animals, we may wonder in retrospect to what extent the emotional blunting emphasized by Von Economo was due to the destruction of dopamine-containing cells of the substantia nigra, as well as those of the network spanning the interpenduncular fossa (groups A9 and A10 of Dahlström and Fuxe, 1964). Let me give two unpublished illustrations: We have found that destruction by 6-hydroxydopamine of these cell groups in the squirrel monkey results first in catalepsy followed by a picture of parkinsonism. The cataleptic signs can be detected before the monkey fully recovers from anesthesia. In retrospect, it would appear that the catalepsy that Ingram, Barris, and Ranson (1936) observed in cats following lesions between the mammillary bodies and the third nerve may have resulted from damage of these cell groups. The incapacity produced by lesions in this region is to be contrasted with the mobilizing effect of apomorphine which is believed to act on dopamine receptors. A comparative survey has revealed that in such diverse species as the parrot, turkey, opossum, and squirrel monkey apomorphine induces aimless, increased activity. The turkey, for example, will run aimlessly in and out of the flock for three to four hours. The two opposing conditions that have been described would support other kinds of evidence that the ascending dopaminergic systems exert an "energizing" influence on an animal's behavior.

In extrapolating from animal experiments by Ranson (1939) and others, one might go further than Von Economo and say that the main avenues for the expression of the basic personality pass through the ventral diencephalon, with the lateral and the medial forebrain bundles, respectively, being two major fiber systems leading to and from striatal and limbic structures. The lateral forebrain bundle includes the ansa and fasciculus lenticularis, as well as the nigrostriatal and striatonigral pathways. The ansa lenticularis sweeps out of the rostromedial part of the globus pallidus like the swish of a mare's tail, with both compact and diffuse components coursing through the dorsolateral part of the hypothalamus and becoming partly entangled with the medial forebrain bundle. It is curious in rereading the literature to find how investigators have either discounted or overlooked the significance of the compact and widely diffuse portions of the *ansa,* as well as the fasciculus lenticularis. This may be in part due to Ranson's (1939) conclusion that these striatal connections probably did not play an important part in the emotional changes observed in rhesus monkeys with bilateral lesions of the lateral hypothalamus. Yet at the same time he pointed out that lesions of the ansa resulted in complete disappearance of the neurons in the medial segment of the globus pallidus. Parenthetically, it should be noted that the ansa is not simply a pallidofugal pathway. It is now evident that like the medial forebrain bundle, it contains ascending fibers (Carpenter and Peter, 1972). Jacobowitz and I (unpublished), in experimental material on the squirrel monkey, have found that it contains ascending dopamine fibers, some of which run through the hypothalamus just lateral to the fornix.

Experimental findings in animals attest to the fundamental role of the lenticular pathways in the expression of an animal's "charac-

ter.'' In connection with investigations of brain mechanisms of
species-typical behavior of the squirrel monkey (see below), I have
had occasion to produce large bilateral lesions in the ventral diencephalon involving the central ansal system and part of the medial
forebrain bundle. As the result of careful nursing, a number of
monkeys have survived the acute postoperative period. Although
there is a recovery of locomotion and an ability for self-feeding, the
striking thing about these monkeys is the complete lack of what one
might call their animality. They have, so to speak, a zombielike
behavior which is distressing to observe.

THE LIMBIC SYSTEM

With this background we turn next to the limbic system which represents an inheritance from lower mammals. The best evidence of
the role of the limbic system in emotional behavior is derived from
clinical observations. Neuronal discharges in or near the limbic cortex of the temporal lobe may trigger a broad spectrum of vivid,
affective feelings. The *basic* and *general* affects are usually of the
kind associated with threats to self-preservation (MacLean, 1958).
More rarely, there may be affects of an agreeable or ecstatic nature,
possibly reflecting a spread of the seizure to other subdivisions of
the limbic system.

  The *basic* affects include those of hunger, thirst, nausea, and
feelings associated with the emunctories. *Specific* affects include
unpleasant tastes and odors and somatic sensations such as pain
and tingling (see also below). Among the *general* affects are feelings of fear, terror, sadness, wanting to be alone, familiarity, un-
familiarity, and (very rarely) anger. The feeling of fear is commonly referred to the epigastric region and may give the impression
of rising in the chest to the throat. As I have emphasized elsewhere
(1952), the *general* affects are usually "free-floating" insofar as
they are not identified with any particular person or situation. One
of the more common affective experiences is the so-called déjà vu.
Significantly, as Penfield and Erickson (1941) have noted, the
patient may experience *only the feeling* that accompanies the act of
remembering. A similar situation applies to auras conveying
eureka-type feelings expressed by such words as "This is it, the

absolute truth," "This is what the world is all about" (MacLean, 1970, 1973*b*). Ironically, it would seem that the ancient limbic system provides free-floating, strong affective feelings of conviction that we attach to revelations and beliefs, regardless of whether they are true or false!

Case histories of limbic epilepsy also indicate (1) that the limbic system is basic for affective feelings of the reality of the self and of the environment (MacLean, 1972*b*) and (2) that ictal disruptions of its functions may result in changes of mood, distortions of perceptions, feelings of depersonalization, hallucinations, and paranoid delusions (MacLean, 1973*c*).

The affective aspects of one's experiences—as illustrated by the déjà vu—seem to be an important requisite for memory (MacLean, 1969*a*). One of the consequences of limbic seizures is the amnesia that is temporally related to the termination of the aura and the onset and duration of the automatism. Sometimes the automatism involves activities that almost certainly require a functioning neocortex.

Feelings triggered by epileptogenic foci may involve any one of the sensory systems. There may be olfactory, gustatory, visceral, and genital sensations; sounds may seem unusually loud or faint; parts of the body may seem swollen to large proportions; there may be the condition of micropsia or macropsia in which objects seem unusually small or large.

Sensations, perceptions, affect—there is no clinical entity other than limbic epilepsy which combines these three psychological aspects of our topic in its symptomatology. What is the neural basis for these and other manifestations that have been summarized?

In the "visceral brain" paper of 1949, I elaborated upon the Papez (1937) theory of emotion by suggesting that impulses from all the intero- and exteroceptive systems find their way to the hippocampus via the hippocampal gyrus. The hypothetical pathways were schematized in figure 3 of that paper. The hippocampal formation was visualized as a mechanism that combined information of internal and external origin into affective feelings that found further elaboration and expression through connections with the amygdala, septum, basal ganglia, hypothalamus, and the principal reentry circuit to the limbic lobe that has become known as "the Papez circuit."

Prior to discussing the question of inputs to the limbic cortext, two other important considerations require mention. First, the pathological studies of Sano and Malamud (1953) and of Margerison and Corsellis (1966) have revealed that Ammon's horn sclerosis is, in Malamud's words (1966), the "common denominator" in cases of psychomotor epilepsy. Since the sclerosis often extends to other medial temporal structures, Falconer, Serafetinides, and Corsellis (1964) prefer to use the term "medial temporal sclerosis." That such sclerosis or other medial temporal lesions are responsible for epileptogenic foci is strongly supported by two series of 100 cases of epilepsy in which Falconer (1970) resected the offending temporal lobe in one block, a procedure that not only affords removal of all or most of the damaged tissue but also allows complete pathological examination.

Second, it is a remarkable fact that seizure discharges originating in or near the limbic cortex have a tendency to spread in and be largely confined to the limbic system. It is probable that the hippocampus is almost always involved, with the discharge either originating in it or spreading to it from related structures. Simultaneous recordings from the neocortex may show little change during such seizures except for a generalized desynchronization. For such reasons I have referred to the potential "schizophysiology" (MacLean, 1954) of limbic and neocortical systems and suggested that this situation may partly account for conflicts between what we affectively "feel" and what we "know."

Except for olfaction with its representation in the piriform lobe, and the less certain evidence of the representation of gustatory and visceral sensation in the limbic part of the insula, it has not been at all clear how various sensory and perceptive phenomena are generated by limbic discharges. There is experimental evidence that limbic seizures do not appreciably change the bioelectrical activity of the primary sensory areas of the neocortex. Acoustic stimuli, for example, continue to be effective in evoking potentials in the auditory area during propagating hippocampal seizures (Flynn, MacLean, and Kim, 1961; Prichard and Glaser, 1966).

In the 1949 paper mentioned above, I hypothesized that somatic, auditory, and visual information was channeled to the hippocampal gyrus by transcortical connections from the primary receiving areas. Subsequently, Pribram and I reported strychnine neuronographic findings in the cat (MacLean and Pribram, 1953) and monkey (Pribram and MacLean, 1953) that would be compatible with this hypothesis. Three years ago, Jones and Powell (1970) described an experimental anatomical study in the macaque which not only revealed the possibility of stepwise cortical connections from these areas to the hippocampal gyrus, but also to the limbic cortex of the anterior cingulate gyrus and posterior orbital area (see also recent anatomical study by Van Hoesen, Pandya, and Butters, 1972).

After a brief recapitulation of earlier electrophysiological findings, I shall summarize a series of microelectrode studies that indicate, on the basis of response latencies, that visual, auditory, somatic, and visceral information reaches respective parts of the limbic lobe by rather direct subcortical pathways. At the same time, I shall mention supporting anatomical evidence.

In a study reported in 1952 (MacLean, Horwitz, and Robinson, 1952), we found that gustatory and noxious somatic stimulation resulted in rhythmically recurring olfactorylike potentials in the piriform area. Sometimes rhythmic potentials appeared in the hippocampus following olfactory or gustatory stimulation. In pursuing this lead, Green and Arduini (1954) showed that various forms of sensory stimulation evoked rhythmic theta activity in the hippocampus of unanesthetized animals. Such effects were observed in macrosmatic animals but not in primates and were regarded as nonspecific in nature.

In continuing the investigation of limbic inputs we have employed microelectrode recording of evoked unit responses in chronically prepared, awake, sitting squirrel monkeys. Such experimentation avoids the depressant effects of anesthesia on neural transmission and, in contradistinction to the technique for recording evoked slow potentials with macroelectrodes, makes it possible to be sure of the locus of the neural response. Thus far we have tested more than 7,500 cerebral units, of which about 2,500 (33%) were located in the limbic cortex. We have explored all of the cortex of the limbic lobe except for the posterior orbital and piriform areas. I shall now summarize briefly our published findings on the results of visual, auditory, and somatic stimulation.

VISUAL STIMULATION

Virtually all photically responsive units were located in the posterior hippocampal gyrus (see fig. 4), the parahippocampal cortex of the lingual gyrus, and the retrosplenial cortex near its junction with the striate cortex (MacLean, Yokota, and Kinnard, 1968). The conditions of the experiment made it impractical to plot receptive fields and to do more than to test with moving patterns. The regularity and character of the photic responses, as well as the latency values, were suggestive of a subcortical, rather than transcortical, pathway. Evidence in support of this inference was obtained in a neuroanatomical study in which improved techniques for demonstrating fine fibers were used to trace degeneration from lesions in the lateral geniculate body and pulvinar (MacLean and Creswell, 1970). Lesions in the ventrolateral part of the lateral geniculate nucleus resulted in degeneration in that part of the optic radiations known as Meyer's loop, which makes a temporal detour and enters the core of the posterior hippocampal gyrus. Some fibers could be traced to the photically responsive limbic cortex and adjoining neocortical areas. A coarser type of degeneration was seen in the posterior hippocampal gyrus and contiguous areas following lesions of the inferior pulvinar. The pulvinar projections are contained in a

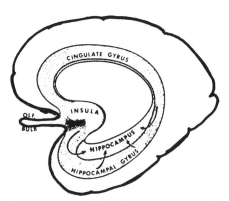

Fig. 4. Shaded areas show main areas of the limbic lobe referred to in the review of microelectrode findings on inputs from intero- and exteroceptive systems. The insular cortex overlying the claustrum is limbic by definition because it forms part of the phylogenetically old cortex surrounding the brainstem (from MacLean, 1970).

band of fibers just lateral to the optic radiations. These observations will recall the discussion in Section C of recently described connections between the superior colliculus and the inferior pulvinar.

About one-half the cells in the posterior hippocampal gyrus gave a sustained on-response to ocular illumination, raising the question of their possible role in states of wakefulness, alerting, and attention, or in the regulation of neuroendocrine functions affected by diurnal and seasonal changes in light.

Some cells in the retrosplenial cortex responded only to stimulation of the contralateral eye, suggesting that they may receive their innervation from the primitive temporal monocular crescent, the part of our retina through which we become aware of objects moving in from the side or rear. As witness the blinders used for horses, unexpected movements in the peripheral visual field may induce startle and alarm. I recall a patient with psychomotor epilepsy whose aura began with a feeling of fear that someone was standing behind him. If he turned to see who it was, the feeling became intensified, and he might have a generalized convulsion. He learned that by resisting the impulse to turn that he could usually prevent a generalized seizure. Horowitz, Adams, and Rutkin (1968) have reported clinical cases in which stimulation with electrodes presumably in "posterior hippocampal areas" was more apt to result in visual imagery than stimulation at other sites in the temporal lobe.

The insular cortex overlying the calustrum (fig. 4) is by definition limbic because it forms part of the phylogenetically old cortex surrounding the brainstem. We encountered a few units in the limbic cortex of the insula, that responded with a brisk discharge to an approaching object. This finding recalls observations by Penfield and Jasper (1954) that discharges in the parainsular region may result in macropsia, a condition in which objects appear to become larger.

SOMATIC AND AUDITORY STIMULATION

Responses to somatic and to auditory stimulation were elicited only in the limbic cortex of the insula (Sudakov, MacLean, Reeves, and Marino, 1971). The receptive fields of the somatic units were usually large and bilateral. Units responding to auditory stimulation were located somewhat more caudally. There were two main types, one of which discharged with short latencies ranging from 7 to 15 msec. Latencies of this order suggest the possibility of direct connections from the medial geniculate body. As discussed in the original paper, both anterograde and retrograde degeneration studies indicate that the insular cortex overlying the claustrum receives projections from the medial geniculate body. The anatomical evidence is conflicting in regard to somatic projections.

GUSTATORY STIMULATION

While exploring the insula, we also tested the responsiveness of units to gustatory stimulation. Responsive units were located anteriorly in the same region from which Benjamin and Burton (1968) recorded evoked potentials upon stimulation of the chorda tympani in the squirrel monkey. Other units in this same region were activated by mechanical stimulation of the oral cavity, including the pharynx.

VAGAL STIMULATION

Somewhat surprisingly, units of the cingulate cortex (see fig. 4) are virtually unresponsive to visual, auditory, and somatic stimulation (Bachman and MacLean, 1971). In a further attempt to discover the nature of inputs to the cingulate cortex we have investigated the possibility of visceral projections by testing the effects of vagal volleys on unit activity. These experiments have been performed on awake, sitting squirrel monkeys previously prepared with electrodes chronically implanted on the cervical vagus or at the site where the vagus enters the jugular foramen (Bachman, Katz, and MacLean, 1972b). Of more than 300 units thus far tested, a little more than 20 percent have been responsive, with the ratio of initially excited to initially inhibited units being about 2 to 3. Most of the responsive units have been located in the middle portion of the gyrus. The response latencies of the excited units have been as short as 15 msec suggesting a fairly direct pathway. In a parallel study we have attempted to mimic natural stimulation of visceral receptors by injecting micro-amounts of 5-hydroxytryptamine (serotonin) through an indwelling catheter in the superior vena cava (Bachman,

Katz, and MacLean, 1972*a*). Of 82 tested units in the supracallosal cingulate cortex, 18 percent were affected, with two-thirds showing an increased firing rate and one-third a decrease. These units were also located in the midportion of the gyrus. The anatomical studies of Morest (1961) suggest the possibility of an ascending pathway from the nucleus solitarius to the dorsal tegmental nucleus of Gudden, from which impulses might ascend via the mammillary peduncle system to the anterior ventral nucleus of the thalamus and the cingulate cortex. The findings in histofluorescence studies (e.g., Fuxe, 1965; Jacobowitz and Kostrzewa, 1971; Olson and Fuxe, 1972) are not incompatible with the interesting possibility of an ascending norepinephrine system from the nucleus solitarius. The anterior ventral nucleus of the thalamus has numerous fine norepinephrine terminals, and such terminals are also found in the cingulate gyrus. In a comparative histofluorescence study including the pygmy marmoset and squirrel monkey Jacobowitz and I (unpublished) have found that the organizational pattern of all of the recognized aminergic systems have been preserved with remarkable consistency in the evolution of primates.

Among other limbic areas we hope to explore in the monkey for vagal responses are the posterior orbital and anterior insular areas which correspond to a region in the cat from which a number of investigators recorded changes in spontaneous activity (Bailey and Bremer, 1938) or evoked potentials (Dell and Olson, 1951*a*, *b;* Korn, Wendt, and Albe-Fessard, 1966) with vagal stimulation.

SENSORY INTEGRATION

In prefacing the question of sensory integration I would like to emphasize that in our own experiments no hypothalamic units responded to photic and somatic stimulation, and only a few were affected by auditory stimulation (Poletti, Kinnard, and MacLean, 1973). This would suggest that sensory information affecting the hypothalamus is first integrated and processed in related structures such as the limbic cortex.

In our initial studies in monkeys anesthetized with alpha-chloralose we found a few limbic cortical units that showed convergence of sensory inputs. But it is remarkable that in the awake, sitting monkey all responsive units appear to be modality specific, indicating a high degree of selectivity. This raises the additional question as to how information reaching the limbic cortex from the intero- and exteroceptive systems is integrated and processed? Or metaphorically stated, where do the "viewers" reside in the limbic system? One likely place is the entorhinal cortex of the hippocampal gyrus which receives connections from the frontotemporal cortex (posterior orbital, anterior insular, piriform, and temporal polar areas) and from the caudally lying parahippocampal cortex (fig. 4). The entorhinal cortex forms an extensive area in man. From the entorhinal area information would be fed forward through the perforant and alveolar pathways to the hippocampus (fig. 4). The anterior hippocampus also receives connections from the frontotemporal region, and there are afferent connections to the posterior hippocampus from the cingulate gyrus via the cingulum, as well as from the lamina medullaris superficialis. These latter pathways might transmit information of vagal origin (see above). In the hippocampus the Schaffer collateral system would provide one means of interrelating information from the various sensory modalities.

The septum, which receives connections from the hypothalamus, is another presumed source of interoceptive information reaching the hippocampus. The septal projections are believed to terminate in the stratum oriens, possibly on the basal dendrites of the hippocampal pyramids, whereas the perforant pathway terminates on the apical dendrites. In an intracellular study of hippocampal neurons in the awake, sitting monkey we found that septal stimuli elicited excitatory postsynaptic potentials associated with neuronal discharge, whereas the stimulation of the olfactory bulb generated EPSP's but never spikes (Yokota, Reeves, and MacLean, 1970). In terms of classical conditioning, impulses from these respective exteroceptive inputs might be compared to unconditional and conditional stimuli. Brazier (1964) has reported photically evoked slow potentials in the hippocampus of patients undergoing diagnostic tests for epilepsy.

LIMBIC OUTPUTS

It is beyond the scope of this chapter to deal with output mechanisms of the limbic system, but a few salient points deserve mention. Microelectrode studies have shown that fornix volleys or hippocampal afterdischarges inhibit unit responses in the caudal intralaminar region to potentially noxious stimuli of the fifth nerve (Yokota and MacLean, 1968). In a recent paper (Poletti et al., 1973) we have reported that hippocampal volleys elicit responses in a large proportion of units in *certain* structures of the basal forebrain, preoptic region, and hypothalamus. In each case more than 80 percent of the responsive units showed initial excitation. Hippocampal afterdischarges also more commonly excited than inhibited units. Following afterdischarges, units showed changes in their firing patterns that lasted from 1 to 11 minutes. These latter findings may help to explain the prolonged "rebound" behavioral and autonomic changes seen following hippocampal afterdischarges, including agitated states on the one hand and enhanced pleasure and sexual reactions on the other.

As seemed evident from the electrophysiological findings, a parallel neuroanatomical study showed for the first time in a primate that the fornix projects to the medial preoptic area and to the perifornical region (Poletti et al., 1973). The work of Hess and Brügger (1943) implicated the perifornical region (the so-called intermediate zone of Hess) in the expression of angry behavior. The medial preoptic area has become of increasing interest not only because of its participation in the control of gonadotropic activity and genital function but also because of its role in sexual differentiation in certain macrosmatic animals.

A few fibers could also be traced to the tuberal region where the electrophysiological study had shown a cellular response to hippocampal volleys. In view of this and other findings, attention should be called to the accumulating evidence that hippocampal stimulation, depending on the physiological state at the time, may have a facilitatory or inhibitory effect with respect to ACTH release, cardiovascular reflexes, and visceral responsiveness (see Poletti et al., 1973, for references). The results of our own microelectrode studies would indicate that in the awake, sitting monkey there is leeway for attributing a range of inhibitory, excitatory, and modulating functions to the hippocampus.

Poletti, Sujatanond, and Sweet (1972) have since shown that, following sections of the fornix, hippocampal volleys were still effective in eliciting unit responses in the structures examined in the preceding study but with a longer latency. It seems probable that the impulses are transmitted via the amygdala, which represents one of the major avenues for projections from the frontotemporal division of the limbic system.

Clinically, as well as experimentally in animals, the hippocampal formation has been implicated in dreaming and other manifestations of REM sleep. This is a matter relevant to our topic because of the strong affective component of dreaming. The subject has recently attracted additional interest because aminergic systems have been implicated in mechanisms of sleep (see Jouvet, 1972, for review). As we reported in 1957 (Paasonen, MacLean, Giarman, 1957), the cellular parts of the hippocampus, as well as its closely associated nuclei, the amygdala and the septum, contain relatively large amounts of serotonin, and the work of Fuxe (1965) has demonstrated the presence of norepinephrine terminals in the radiate layer.

In summary, the work that has been reviewed suggests mechanisms by which information of intero- and exteroceptive systems can interact in the hippocampal formation and influence hypothalamic and other brainstem structures involved in emotional behavior.

STRIATAL COMPLEX

There remains the question of the role of the striatal complex in sensory and perceptive aspects of emotional behavior. Here we are obliged to sound even greater depths of ignorance than in the case of the neomammalian and limbic formations. Evidence has accumulated in recent years that most parts of the neocortex and limbic cortex project to the corpus striatum. The observed degeneration, however, appears to be rather scant. From an evolutionary point of view, it would appear to be of special significance that the limbic lobe conforms to the corpus striatum somewhat like a mold. The seemingly obligatory relationship between the two is reflected by the way the head of the caudate is drawn out into a long tail that is enfolded by the temporal part of the limbic lobe.

In addition to reciprocal connections with the substantia nigra, the corpus striatum (caudate plus putamen) projects to the globus pallidus which in turn establishes connections with the ventral part

NOTES

1. This section is based on previously published material (MacLean, 1960, 1969*b*, 1970) and a book in preparation.
2. "Peripallidal structures" applies to the variously named structures closely associated with the globus pallidus, including the substantia innominata, basal nucleus of Meynert, nucleus of the ansa peduncularis, and entopeduncular nucleus.
3. Auditory "area IV" overlaps the limbic cortex of the insula (see below).

REFERENCES

Albe-Fessard, D., Rocha-Miranda, C. E., and Oswaldo-Cruz, E. 1960. Activités évoquées dans le noyau caudé du chat en réponse à des types divers d'afférences. II. Etude microphysiologique, *Electroencephalogr. Clin. Neurophysiol. 12*, 649-661.

Bachman, D. S., Katz, H. M., and MacLean, P. D. 1972*a*. Effect of intravenous injections of 5-hydroxytryptamine (serotonin) on unit activity of cingulate cortex of awake squirrel monkeys, *Fed. Proc. 31*, 303.

———. 1972*b*. Vagal influence on units of cingulate cortex in the awake, sitting squirrel monkey, *Electroencephalogr. Clin. Neurophysiol. 33*, 350-351.

Bachman, D. S., and MacLean, P. D. 1971. Unit analysis of inputs to cingulate cortex in awake, sitting squirrel monkeys. I. Exteroceptive systems, *Int. J. Neuroscience 2*, 109-113.

Bailey, P., and Bremer, F. 1938. A sensory cortical representation of the vagus nerve, *J. Neurophysiol. I*, 405-412.

Banjamin, R. M., and Burton, H. 1968. Projection of taste nerve afferents to anterior opercular-insular cortex in squirrel monkey (Saimiri sciureus), *Brain Res. 7*, 221-231.

Brazier, M. A. B. 1964. Evoked responses recorded from the depths of the human brain, *Ann. N.Y. Acad. Sci. 112*, 33-59.

Carpenter, M. B., and Peter, P. 1972. Nigrostriatal and nigrothalamic fibers in the rhesus monkey, *J. Comp. Neurol. 144*, 93-116.

Dahlström, A., and Fuxe, K. 1964. Evidence for the existence of monoamine-containing neurons in the central nervous system. I. Demonstration of monoamines in the cell bodies of brain stem neurons, *Acta Physiol. Scand. 62*, 5-55.

Dell, P., and Olson, R. 1951*a*. Projections thalamiques, corticales et cérébelleuses des afférences viscérales vagales, *C.R. Soc. Biol. 145*, 1084-1088.

———. 1951*b*. Projections "secondaires" mésencéphaliques, diencéphaliques et amygdaliennes des afférences viscérales vagales, *C.R. Soc. Biol. 145*, 1088-1091.

Descartes, R. 1967. *The Philosophical Works of Descartes*, Vols. 1 and 2, translated into English by E. S. Haldane and G. R. T. Ross, Cambridge.

Falconer, M. A. 1970. Historical review: The pathological substrate of temporal lobe epilepsy, *Guy's Hosp. Rep. 119*, 47-60.

Falconer, M. A., Serafetinides, E. A., and Corsellis, J. A. N. 1964. Etiology and pathogenesis of temporal lobe epilepsy, *Arch. Neurol. 10*, 233-248.

Flynn, J. P., MacLean, P. D., and Kim, C. 1961. Effects of hippocampal afterdischarges on conditioned responses. In *Electrical Stimulation of the Brain*, ed. D. E. Sheer, Austin.

Fuxe, K. 1965. Evidence for the existence of monoamine neurons in the central nervous system. IV. Distribution of monoamine nerve terminals in the central nervous system, *Acta Physiol. Scand. 64* (Suppl. 247), 37-84.

Green, J. D., and Arduini, A. A. 1954. Hippocampal electrical activity in arousal, *J. Neurophysiol. 17*, 533-557.

Harting, J. K., Hall, W. C., Diamond, I. T., and Martin, G. F. 1973. Anterograde degeneration study of the superior colliculus in *Tupaia glis:* Evidence for a subdivision between superficial and deep layers, *J. Comp. Neurol. 148*, 361-386.

Head, H., and Holmes, G. 1920. Part IV. The brain. Sensory disturbances from cerebral lesions. Chapt. II. Sensory disturbances associated with certain lesions of the optic thalamus. In *Studies in Neurology,* ed. H. Head, vol. 2, London.

Hess, W. R., and Brügger, M. 1943. Der Miktions und der Defäkationsakt als Erfolg zentraler Reizung, *Helv. Physiol. Acta 1*, 511-532.

Horowitz, M. J., Adams, J. E., and Rutkin, B. B. 1968. Visual imagery and brain stimulation, *Arch. Gen. Psychiatry 19*, 469.

Hubel, D. H., and Wiesel, T. N. 1962. Receptive fields, binocular interaction and functional architecture in the cat's visual cortex, *J. Physiol. 160*, 106-154.

Ingram, W. R., Barris, R. W., and Ranson, S. W. 1936. Catalepsy: An experimental study, *Arch. Neurol. Psychiatry 35*, 1175-1197.

Jocobowitz, D., and Kostrzewa, R. 1971. Selective action of 6-hydroxydopa on noradrenergic terminals: Mapping of preterminal axons of the brain, *Life Sci. 10*, 1329-1342.

Jones, E. G., and Powell, T. P. S. 1970. An anatomical study of converging sensory pathways within the cerebral cortex of the monkey, *Brain 93*, 793-820.

Jouvet, M. 1972. Veille, sommeil et reve: le discours biologique, *Rev. Médecine 16*, 1003-1063.

Korn, H., Wendt, R., and Albe-Fessard, D. 1966. Somatic projection to the orbital cortex of the cat, *Electroencephalogr. Clin. Neurophysiol. 21*, 209-226.

MacKay, D. M. 1970. Perception and brain function. In *The Neurosciences,* ed. F. O. Schmitt, New York.

MacLean, P. D. 1949. Psychosomatic disease and the "visceral brain." Recent developments bearing on the Papez theory of emotion, *Psychosom. Med. 11*, 338-353.

———. 1952. Some psychiatric implications of physiological studies on frontotemporal portion of limbic system (visceral brain), *Electroencephalogr. Clin. Neurophysiol. 4*, 407-418.

———. 1954. The limbic system and its hippocampal formation. Studies in animals and their possible application to man, *J. Neurosurg. 11*, 29-44.

———. 1958. Contrasting functions of limbic and neocortical systems of the brain and their relevance to psychophysiological aspects of medicine, *Am. J. Med. 25*, 611-626.

———. 1960. Psychosomatics, *Handbook of Physiology*. In *Neurophysiology III,* American Physiological Society, Washington.

———. 1964. Mirror display in the squirrel monkey, *Saimiri sciureus, Science 146*, 940-952.

———. 1969a. The internal-external bonds of the memory process, *J. Nerv. Ment. Dis. 149*, 40-47.

———. 1969b. The hypothalamus and emotional behavior. In *The Hypothalamus,* eds. W. Haymaker, E. Anderson, and W. J. H. Nauta, Springfield.

———. 1970. The triune brain, emotion, and scientific bias. In *The Neurosciences Second Study Program,* ed. F. O. Schmitt, New York.

———. 1972a. Cerebral evolution and emotional processes: New findings on the striatal complex, *Ann. N.Y. Acad. Sci. 193*, 137-149.

———. 1972b. Implications of microelectrode findings on exteroceptive inputs to the limbic cortex. In *Limbic System Mechanisms and Autonomic Function,* ed. C. H. Hockman, Springfield.

———. 1973*a*. Effects of pallidal lesions on species-typical display behavior of squirrel monkey, *Fed. Proc. 32,* 384.

———. 1973*b*. The brain's generation gap: Some human implications, *Zygon Journal of Religion and Science 8,* 113-127.

———. 1973*c*. A triune concept of the brain and behaviour; Lecture I. Man's reptilian and limbic inheritance; Lecture II. Man's limbic brain and the psychoses; Lecture III. New trends in man's evolution. In *The Hincks Memorial Lectures,* eds. T. Boag and D. Campbell, Toronto.

MacLean, P. D., and Creswell, G. 1970. Anatomical connections of visual system with limbic cortex of monkey, *J. Comp. Neurol. 138,* 265-278.

MacLean, P. D., Horwitz, N. H., and Robinson, F. 1952. Olfactory-like responses in pyriform area to nonolfactory stimulation, *Yale J. Biol. Med. 25,* 159-172.

MacLean, P. D., and Pribram, K. H. 1953. Neuronographic analysis of medial and basal cerebral cortex. I. Cat, *J. Neurophysiol. 16,* 312-323.

MacLean, P. D., Yokota, T., and Kinnard, M. A. 1968. Photically sustained on-responses of units in posterior hippocampal gyrus of awake monkey, *J. Neurophysiol. 31,* 870-883.

Malamud, N. 1966. The epileptogenic focus in temporal lobe epilepsy from a pathological standpoint, *Arch. Neurol. 14,* 190-195.

Margerison, J. H., and Corsellis, J. A. N. 1966. Epilepsy and the temporal lobes: A clinical, electroencephalographic and neuropathological study of the brain in epilepsy, with particular reference to the temporal lobes, *Brain 89,* 499.

Mettler, F. A. 1955. Perceptual capacity, function of the corpus striatum, and schizophrenia, *Psychiatr. Q. 29,* 89-111.

Michael, C. R. 1969. Retinal processing of visual images, *Sci. Am. 220,* 104-114.

Morest, D. K. 1961. Connexions of dorsal tegmental nucleus in rat and rabbit, *J. Anat. 95,* 1-18.

Mountcastle, V. B., Davies, P. W., and Berman, A. L. 1957. Response properties of neurons of cat's somatic sensory cortex to peripheral stimuli, *J. Neurophysiol. 20,* 374-407.

Myers, R. E. 1963. Projections of the superior colliculus in monkey, *Anat. Rec. 145,* 264.

Nauta, W. J. H., and Mehler, W. R. 1966. Projections of the lentiform nucleus in the monkey, *Brain Res. 1,* 3-42.

Olson, L., and Fuxe, K. 1972. Further mapping out of central noradrenaline neuron systems: Projections of the "subcoeruleus" area, *Brain Res. 43,* 289-295.

Paasonen, M. K., MacLean, P. D., and Giarman, N. J. 1957. 5-Hydroxytryptamine (serotonin, enteramine) content of structures of the limbic system, *J. Neurochem. I,* 326-333.

Papez, J. W. 1937. A proposed mechanism of emotion, *Arch. Neurol. Psychiatr. 38,* 725-743.

Penfield, W., and Erickson, T. C. 1941. *Epilepsy and Cerebral Localization,* Springfield.

Penfield, W., and Jasper, H. 1954. *Epilepsy and the Functional Anatomy of the Human Brain,* Boston.

Penfield, W., and Perot, P. 1963. The brain's record of auditory and visual experience. A final summary and discussion, *Brain 86,* 596-696.

Poletti, C. E., Kinnard, M. A., and MacLean, P. D. 1973. Hippocampal influence on unit activity of hypothalamus, preoptic region, and basal forebrain in awake, sitting squirrel monkeys, *J. Neurophysiol. 36,* 308-324.

Poletti, C. E., Sujatanond, M., and Sweet, W. H. 1972. Hypothalamic, preoptic, and basal forebrain unit responses to hippocampal stimulation in awake sitting squirrel monkeys with fornix lesions, *Fed. Proc. 31,* 404.

Pribram, K. H., and MacLean, P. D. 1953. Neuronographic analysis of medial and basal cerebral cortex. II. Monkey, *J. Neurophysiol. 16,* 324-340.

Prichard, J. W., and Glaser, G. H. 1966. Cortical sensory evoked potentials during limbic seizures, *Electroencephalogr. Clin. Neurophysiol. 21,* 180-184.

Ranson, S. W. 1939. Somnolence caused by hypothalamic lesions in the monkey. *Arch. Neurol. Psychiatr. 41,* 1-23.

Sano, K., and Malamud, N. 1953. Clinical significance of sclerosis of the cornu ammonis. Ictal "psychic phenomena," *Arch. Neurol. Psychiatr. 70,* 40-53.

Snyder, M., and Diamond, I. T. 1968. The organization and function of the visual cortex in the tree shrew, *Brain, Behav. Evol. I,* 244-288.

Spencer, H. 1896. *Principles of Psychology,* New York.

Sudakov, K., MacLean, P. D., Reeves, A. G., and Marino, R. 1971. Unit study of exteroceptive inputs to claustrocortex in awake, sitting, squirrel monkey, *Brain Res. 28,* 19-34.

Van Hoesen, G. W., Pandya, D. N., and Butters, N. 1972. Cortical afferents to the entorhinal cortex of the rhesus monkey, *Science 175,* 1471-1473.

Von Economo, C. 1931. *Encephalitis Lethargica. Its Sequelae and Treatment,* translated by Newman, K. O., London.

Wiener, N. 1948. *Cybernetics, or Control and Communication in the Animal and the Machine,* New York.

Yokota, T., and MacLean, P. D. 1968. Fornix and fifth-nerve interaction on thalamic units in awake, sitting squirrel monkeys, *J. Neurophysiol. 31,* 358-370.

Yokota, T., Reeves, A. G., and MacLean, P. D. 1970. Differential effects of septal and olfactory volleys on intracellular responses of hippocampal neurons in awake, sitting monkeys, *J. Neurophysiol. 33,* 96-107.

II

EMOTION AND ANXIETY: SOCIOCULTURAL, BIOLOGICAL, AND PSYCHOLOGICAL DETERMINANTS

JAMES R. AVERILL

The purpose of this chapter is to provide a theoretical framework for the interpretation of emotion. If the chapter has a central theme, it is this: *emotions are social constructions.* That is, emotions are responses that have been institutionalized by society as a means of resolving conflicts which exist within the social system. In elaborating upon this theme, the biological and psychological—as well as the sociocultural—determinants of emotions will require examination. Hence, the chapter is divided into four sections. The first section examines the nature of emotion, with an emphasis on the cognitive structures or "rules" that govern emotional expression. The next three sections deal with the sociocultural, biological, and psychological determinants of emotion, respectively.

THE NATURE OF EMOTION

The term *emotion* is derived from the Latin, *e + movere*. It originally meant to migrate or transfer from one place to another. It also was used to refer to states of agitation or perturbation, both physical (e.g., the weather) and psychological. It is this latter, somewhat metaphorical usage, that gave the term *emotion* its modern meaning. It is important to note, however, that the widespread application of the term *emotion* to psychological states is a rather recent development. For approximately two thousand years, from the ancient Greeks to the middle of the eighteenth century, it was common to speak of emotions as "passions." The term *passion* is derived from the Latin, *pati* (to suffer), which in turn is related to the Greek *pathos*. Also derived from *pati* are such expressions as *passive* and *patient*. At the root of these concepts is the idea that an individual (or physical object) is undergoing or suffering some change, as opposed to doing or initiating change. Thus, in ordinary discourse, we speak of being "gripped," "seized," and "torn" by emotion. Stated more formally, emotions are something that happen to us (passions), not something we deliberately do (actions).

KINDS OF EMOTION

There are three main sources for the experience of passivity during emotion, and these help define three main kinds of emotion. First, most "standard" emotional reactions (e.g., anger, love, jealousy, hope, and the myriad of other emotions recognized in ordinary language) are responses the initiation of which has become dissociated from consciousness. Stated differently, emotions of this kind involve a restricted insight into the sources of one's actions. The domain of this limited self-awareness may be called the phenomenal self or ego. It is the *I* and the *Me,* the subject and object, of experience. During stated emotional reactions, ego-boundaries are so narrowly drawn that the phenomenal self is perceived as the passive recipient (the *Me*) rather than the active initiator (the *I*) of the response. This state of affairs is somewhat analogous to the hallucinated images and peculiar responses which sometimes are experienced by hysterical and psychotic patients. Patients typically describe themselves as being assailed or gratified by such experiences, as being passive in relation to them; but, of course, the images and responses are ultimately the person's own doing.

Standard emotional reactions are not the same as hysterical reactions, but the two kinds of response do share many features in common. In both instances, the experience of passivity is an illusion. It is an illusion, however, with identifiable antecedents and consequences. In the case of hysterical reactions, the experience may represent a kind of defense mechanism: By shrinking the awareness of self-responsibility, the hysteric can help alleviate distress. In the case of standard emotional reactions, we must look to social norms and customs, in addition to intrapsychic processes, for an explanation of the experience of passivity. These are matters which will be taken up in detail in the sections on Sociocultural Determinants and Psychological Determinants of this chapter.

While standard emotional reactions presume well established but restricted ego-boundaries, there is a second kind of emotion that involves the dissolution of such boundaries. For example, through psychological conflict, physical trauma, the use of drugs, unusual stimulation, and the like, the cognitive structures that help define the phenomenal self may be disrupted. When this occurs, there can be no action, only passion. Experiences of this type may be called "transcendental," first, because they have their source in a transcendence of the ego and, second, because the quality of the experience tends to be indefinite, nebulous, and ineffable.

There is still a third source for the experience of passivity during emotion. Certain kinds of responses, such as startle to a sudden noise, feeling uneasy when looking over the edge of a tall building, and attacking the source of pain, are largely determined by biological predispositions. We cannot help but experience such reactions because it was biologically adaptive for our primate ancestors to be wary of strange sounds, to withdraw from high places, and to attack when hurt. This kind of response often has been taken as the paradigm for emotion in general. However, one of the basic contentions of this chapter is that the traditional view of emotions as biologically primitive is misleading. Biologically determined responses form a relatively small class of emotional reactions. Their primary importance is that they may be incorporated as elements into other kinds of emotion.[1]

EMOTIONS CONCEPTUALIZED AS COGNITIVE SYSTEMS

In this chapter, emotions will be conceptualized as cognitive (information processing) systems or rules of behavior. To use an analogy drawn from linguistics, it might be said that emotions have a "grammar"; and like the grammatical structures studied by linguists, emotional systems cannot be identified with any specific set of behaviors. For example, there are an indefinite number of ways in which a person may express his anger, just as there are an indefinite number of ways in which any particular proposition may be expressed in language. Thus, an angry person may physically assault another with his bare hands; he may attack from a distance using sophisticated weapons; he may indicate his wrath with verbal insults, letters to the editor, or even subtle forms of wit; he may withdraw affection or "smother" with kindness; and so on ad infinitum. In short, we must focus not on the concrete expressions of emotion; but, rather, on the rules that govern emotional expression.

When emotions are conceptualized as rules of behavior, the major problem addressed by the present chapter can be posed as follows: What is the relationship of emotional systems to broader rule-systems defined at the sociocultural, biological, and psychological levels of analysis? Or, more specifically, how are the rules governing emotional expression related to, say, legal and moral systems on the sociocultural level, to adaptive systems of behavior on the biological level, and to the individual's own system of self-concepts on the psychological level?

THE STRUCTURE OF THOUGHT

Having defined emotions as cognitive systems, it might be helpful to have some overview of the relationship between emotions and other types of cognitive activity.

One way in which cognitive activities can be compared is in terms of levels of structuralization, how loosely or tightly organized a system of thought happens to be. Figure 1 depicts different types of cognitive activity arranged along a spiral. The vertical axis of the spiral represents increasing degrees of structuralization while the horizontal swing represents the degree to which behavior is experienced as deliberate and self-initiated.

At the very lowest level of structuralization are the transcendental emotional states (e.g., anxiety, mystical experience). These shade into systems of thought which frequently are considered emotional but which also bear some resemblance to ordinary patterns of thought. Examples of such states are hyponogogic reverie, dreaming, creative activity, and the like. In psychoanalytic terms, this range of experience—where boundaries between cognitive systems are relaxed and highly permeable—is referred to as "primary process."

Ascending further along the spiral depicted in figure 1, we come to everyday discursive thought (inductive and deductive reasoning), or what in psychoanalytic terms is called "secondary process."

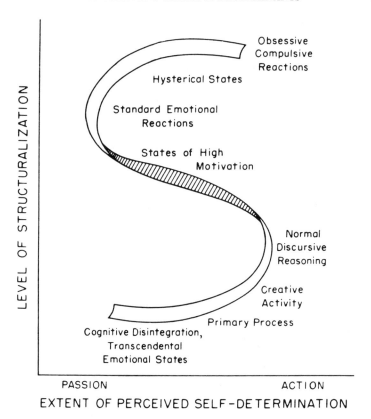

PASSION   ACTION

EXTENT OF PERCEIVED SELF-DETERMINATION

Fig. 1. Types of cognitive activity arranged in the form of a spiral from low to high levels of structuralization (vertical axis) and from low (passion) to high (action) perceived self-determination or responsibility (horizontal axis).

This level of structuralization is characteristic of normal problem solving and coping responses, examples of which may range from such simple activities as avoiding commonplace dangers (e.g., an oncoming automobile) to complex attempts at mastery (preparing for a doctorate examination, starting a new job, getting married, and the like). Under optimal conditions, such coping is purposive, reality oriented, and flexible; and when need satisfaction is involved, such satisfaction is achieved in an ordered and tempered way rather than in an overriding, all-or-none fashion. (For a more detailed discussion of normal coping activity and its relationship to stress and emotion, see Lazarus, Averill, & Opton, 1974).

As efforts at problem-solving become more focused and directed, we may speak of states of high motivation. These states deserve special comment because they have been the subject of considerable research ostensibly dealing with anxiety. Much of this research has stemmed from Hull-Spence behavior theory in which a learning factor (habit strength) combines multiplicatively with a generalized drive factor to determine the excitatory potential of a response (see Spence & Spence, 1966). One implication of this theory is that at high levels of drive, behavior becomes rigid and stereotyped because dominant habits are not easily displaced from their position in a habit-family hierarchy. When Taylor (1953) introduced the Manifest Anxiety Scale as a measure of drive in humans, a marriage of convenience was effected between anxiety and learning theory. Two points need to be noted with regard to the body of research which was propagated by this marriage. First, the Taylor Manifest Anxiety Scale was not developed with anxiety as its primary concern, and a variety of other measures of motivated states (e.g., repression-sensitization, hostility, etc.) would have served the same purpose. Second, from the standpoint of this chapter, states of high motivation are not conceived in terms of drive variables at all; motivated behavior does not become rigid *because* of high drive; rather, a rigidity of cognitive structures is part of what we mean by a "state of high motivation." In short, the problem of motivation from a cognitive standpoint has to do with the structure of thought and not with the energizing of behavior (cf. Breger, 1967; Dember, 1974; Klein, 1967).

Returning now to figure 1, states of high motivation blend into standard emotional reactions (e.g., anger, fear, envy, hope, etc.), and these in turn shade into hysterical states at still higher levels of structuralization. The term "hysterical" is used here to refer to a large and heterogeneous set of responses which are lumped together primarily because they tend to be unusual or idiosyncratic. Their common characteristic is that they involve a rather severe dissociation of consciousness and tend to be highly rigid and stereotyped. Because hysterical reactions reflect many of the features of standard emotional reactions, albeit in exaggerated and unusual form, they frequently will be used for illustrative purposes in subsequent discussion.

At even higher levels of structuralization, hysterical reactions tend to become fractionated and the affective component drops out, leaving only a part response which may symbolize the underlying conflict. Obsessive-compulsive reactions perhaps best exemplify this stage of structuralization. Often it is difficult to distinguish an obsessive-compulsive response from normal problem-solving activity, except that it is rigid and reality distorting rather than flexible and reality oriented (consider, for example, the delusional system of a paranoid).

With the main features of emotion now before us, let us turn to an examination of the major determinants—sociocultural, biological, and psychological—of emotion.

SOCIOCULTURAL DETERMINANTS OF EMOTION

As noted in the introduction, the central theme of this chapter is that emotions are social constructions. That is, they are fashioned, organized, brought about—in short, *constructed*—according to rules of culture. When approached in this fashion, the study of emotion bears some resemblance to the field study commonly known as the "sociology of knowledge." Traditionally, however, the sociology of knowledge has been concerned primarily with such matters as ideology, religion, science, and similar abstract systems of thought. In a sense, then, this chapter is an attempt to extend the sociology of knowledge to the ostensibly mundane topic of emotion. To avoid confusion, it must be emphasized that the present discussion is limited primarily to standard emotional reactions. This is not a great limitation, however, for standard emotional reactions are by far the most numerous of the three kinds of emotions outlined above. Moreover, only with an understanding of standard emotional reactions can other kinds of emotion (including anxiety) be viewed in proper perspective.

SOME CULTURE-SPECIFIC EMOTIONAL SYSTEMS

Since there is a strong bias toward viewing emotions as biologically basic and pan-cultural, it might be helpful to begin this section with a description of some emotionlike syndromes in which the influence of culture is readily apparent.

Newman (1964) has described an emotionlike syndrome among the Gururumba, a horticultural people living in the New Guinea highlands. This syndrome is called by the natives, "being a wild pig." There are no wild (undomesticated) pigs in the area of the highlands where the Gururumba live and the analogy is to domesticated pigs which have escaped their masters, running wild and attacking other animals. The Gururumba do not understand why domesticated pigs sometimes run wild, but they believe that such behavior is only a temporary state. Through proper procedure and ritual, the animal can be redomesticated. And so it is with a person who becomes a wild pig: he has temporarily broken away from human control and must be reintegrated into society.

The individual who is afflicted with "being a wild pig" may engage in a variety of aggressive acts, including looting, shooting arrows at bystanders, and the like. These "attacks," however, seldom result in serious harm. Such behavior may continue for several days, until the affected individual disappears into the forest where he destroys what he has taken (usually inconsequential objects left for him to steal). He may then return in a normal condition, neither remembering anything of his previous behavior nor being reminded of it by the villagers. Alternatively, he may return still in a wild state. In this case, he is captured and treated in a ceremony similar to that performed for pigs that have gone wild. He is held over a smoking fire until he returns to normal and is publicly rubbed all over with pig fat. This is not punishment, however, for a small pig is killed in his name by a prominent person and he is presented with a sumptuous collection of cooked tubers and roots.

In interpreting this syndrome we may consider first the explanations offered by the Gururumba themselves and then examine the underlying sociocultural determinants. The Gururumba believe that "being a wild pig" is the result of being bitten by the ghost of a person who has recently died. These ghosts are malevolent, destructive entities; they reflect the qualities of men before the achievement of advanced culture, that is, before men lived in social groups, had domesticated plants and animals, and so forth. The Gururumba view of human nature is hardly that of the "noble savage." On the contrary, primeval men attacked, stole, and raped on whim. The Gururumba believe they would behave likewise if it were not for social control. When bitten by a ghost, such control is lost and more primitive impulses are set free.

In short, "being a wild pig" is recognized by the Gururumba as a human action. The ghost does not possess the man or use his body for its own goals; it only triggers the response through its bite. On the other hand, the man is not responsible for his actions for he did not choose to be bitten. The response of the Gururumba is to let the reaction run its course, subtly directing it into nondangerous channels, and then to reintegrate the individual back into society.

On a deeper and less well-articulated level, the Gururumba seem to recognize that it is not just a ghost which causes the reaction, but also frustrating circumstances created by society and the inability of the individual to cope with those frustrations. Only males between the ages of approximately twenty-five and thirty-five exhibit the syndrome; it is not tolerated in other age groups. The twenty-five—thirty-five year age period is an especially stressful time for the Gururumba male. He must forego the considerable freedom of his youth and accept economic and social obligations related to marriage (prearranged and often unstable at first) and other group coordinated enterprises. His success in these ventures determine not only his personal prestige and power but also that of his clan.

According to Newman (1964), "being a wild pig" is a way of calling attention to one's difficulties in meeting social obligations. Following an episode, members of the society apparently reevaluate the individual's ability to meet his obligations, and expectations are adjusted accordingly.

Salisbury (1966a, 1967) has reviewed numerous other cases of amoklike reactions in various New Guinea societies. He points out that in some groups the response occurs in females as well as males (although called by a different name), and in different age groups. He believes that while stress and conflict may be a necessary precondition for the response, this does not explain why only certain individuals are affected. Salisbury notes that New Guinea highland societies are very closely knit. Communal living and cooperative enterprises require a great deal of conformity. An individual cannot play different roles on different occasions; rather, a person is expected to show continuity and consistency in all aspects of his behavior. This makes it difficult to make a decision that is not in keeping with past performance or group expectancies. Salisbury argues that reactions such as "being a wild pig" are ways of "announcing" to the group that a nonconforming decision has been made, without the individual having to assume responsibility for the decision. For example, if one wished to move to another location, get rid of a wife, renounce certain obligations, and the like—actions which might be blocked by the group under normal circumstances—being bitten by a ghost is one way of dramatically underscoring the decision. As support for his argument, Salisbury reports that affected individuals may deliberately (unconsciously or consciously) place themselves in situations where ghosts can reasonably be expected to "bite," for example, a person may chase a pig into the woods at night or walk past a grave.

IMPLICATIONS FOR THE STUDY OF EMOTION

"Being a wild pig" and related syndromes are not emotions in the ordinary sense; nevertheless they exhibit many of the features of standard emotional reactions. For example, these behaviors are experienced passively. The person who becomes a wild pig cannot control his actions; typically, he cannot even recall the episode after it has happened. And because of this lack of voluntary control, the affected individual is not considered completely responsible for his actions. The experience of passivity often has been taken as a sign that emotions are biologically primitive or instinctive. Certainly, this assumption is made by the Gururumba, at least as far as "being a wild pig" is concerned. The name itself implies the presumed animallike qualities of the response; and the Gururumba believe that the behavior involved is similar to that of their progenitors before they became socialized. Nevertheless, it is clear from the preceding discussion that "being a wild pig" is a consequence of— and not antecedent to—socialization. No child or infrahuman animal could engage in such complex behavior, only a highly socialized adult.

Elsewhere (Averill, 1974), I have argued that the view of emotions as biologically primitive is primarily a value judgment. It stems from the unfavorable contrast between emotional behavior and certain values esteemed by Western cultures, especially rationality and self-control. That is, within the Western intellectual tradition, rationality and freedom of will have been considered the hallmarks of humanity; irrational and compulsive responses have therefore tended to be viewed as animallike, brutish, and the like.

But value judgments such as these are, of course, not limited to Western societies; no group could long endure if in practical matters of survival it emphasized the irrational and the whimsical. One might, therefore, expect emotional behaviors to be viewed as primitive in most, if not all, cultures. One of the basic arguments of this chapter is that, no matter how widespread the assumption that emotions are biologically primitive, the fact of the matter is that most standard emotional reactions are socially constructed or institutionalized patterns of response.

For a response to become institutionalized, it must serve some social function. From Newman's analysis of "being a wild pig," we might almost view this emotionlike response as a form of community mental health. That is, when societal pressures become too great for an individual to handle, "being a wild pig" offers an acceptable means of communicating the difficulty. This, in turn, allows the group to reevaluate the needs and capabilities of the individual, bringing expectancies more in line with reality. Thus, by proving an involuntary "out," the society can maintain pressure on individual members to conform voluntarily to social expectancies. Of course, if the "out" is to serve its function, it must be used sparingly and only in extreme cases. Therefore, although in one sense accepted, "being a wild pig" definitely is not condoned.

The above considerations do not depend for their validity on Newman's particular explanation of "being a wild pig." One might well question the exact function of this and similar syndromes. For our present purposes, however, it is not important what particular function these syndromes serve. Indeed, their functions probably vary somewhat from one group to another, depending upon differences in social organization. And even within a single group they may be multifunctional. Thus, one might ask why (according to the local interpretations of the behavior) a person acts like a wild pig after being bitten by a ghost, rather than after some other event. To answer this question, an examination would have to be made of the role played by ghosts in the total cultural configuration. The ghosts in question are primarily of recently deceased kinsmen. They may be either benevolent or malevolent, depending upon the quality of the relationship before death. Thus, if a person quarrels with a kinsman before he dies, his ghost may seek retaliation. This helps maintain amiable social relationships, especially toward the elderly who sometimes threaten younger persons that their ghost will haunt them if they do not act properly (see Langness, 1965).

"Being a wild pig" and related syndromes provide a concrete illustration of emotionlike responses in which sociocultural determinants are quite evident. The remainder of this section will be devoted to a presentation of theoretical constructs necessary for an analysis of the social construction of emotional behaviors.

A SYSTEMS APPROACH TO THE STUDY OF EMOTIONS

As a point of departure, let us consider the classical problem posed by the sociology of knowledge—what is the existential basis of thought? Most persons would agree that knowledge is determined by some underlying "reality"; there is, however, little agreement as to what this underlying reality actually is. For the sociologist of knowledge, reality is to be found in social activity. This existential relationship has been expressed in a variety of ways, but the Marxian concepts of "superstructure" and "substructure" can be taken as representative. The superstructure (thought, consciousness) is a reflection of the substructure (labor, economic activity). But what exactly is the superstructure. To say "thought" or "consciousness" is not very helpful, for this can mean many different things. Traditionally, the sociology of knowledge has focused on theoretical systems of thought, such as mythology, religion, and science. If we had to settle on a phrase to summarize the superstructure in this sense, the *cultural system* would perhaps be the most appropriate. And what about the substructure? Marx considered this to be economic activity in a very broad sense. Other theorists have proposed alternate possibilities, but most emphasize the way interpersonal interactions are structured, whether in terms of social classes, division of labor, and so on—in short, the *social system*.

In identifying the superstructure with the cultural system and the substructure with the social system we are following the suggestion of Parsons (1961, p. 989). In so doing, however, it would seem that we have made the sociology of knowledge irrelevant to the problem of emotion. As long as the superstructure is defined vaguely in terms of "thought" or "consciousness," one might intuit its relevance for emotion. After all, thought and conscious experience are as fundamental to emotion as to any other type of behavior. However, one rightly balks at treating emotion as a part of the cultural system.

To clarify this potential source of confusion, we must follow Parson's systems approach a little further. We can then return to the sociology of knowledge and examine its relevance for the study of emotion.

Systems of action. Parsons (1959; Parsons & Shils, 1962) has developed a conceptual scheme for the analysis of behavior which he calls a "theory of action." To be an "action" a behavior must be analyzable in terms of (1) its goal orientation or anticipated state of affairs toward which it is directed; (2) the situation in which it occurs; (3) its normative regulation, for example, whether it is expressed in a reasonable or acceptable manner; and (4) the expenditure of energy or effort required for its occurrence. Actions in this sense are not isolated bits of behavior but occur in organized constellations or systems. Parsons distinguishes four general systems of action, which represent modes of organization on cultural, social, personality, and biological levels of analysis.

The cultural system is the organization of values, norms, and symbols which guides and limits the types of interactions which may occur among individuals. As such, the cultural system is not made up of concrete actions, but of abstractions that help guide behavior. These abstractions may, however, be encoded in physical symbols (e.g., books, flags, religious artifacts) and may thus be transmitted and acted upon.

The social and personality systems, in contradistinction to the cultural system, are made up of the actions of individuals, in fact, the same actions in both cases. The two systems are differentiated on the basis of their organization. The social system consists of actions organized around roles and role expectations; stated differently, the social system is constituted by the regulated interaction of two or more individuals. With regard to the personality system, however, actions are organized with respect to other actions on the part of the same individual.

Finally, the biological system—the "organism" in Parsons's terms—consists of that aspect of physiological functioning which interacts with the personality and other systems of action. Parsons does not give much consideration to the biological system, and below we shall define it differently than he, focusing primarily on the evolutionary adaptive significance of certain behavior patterns.

It is important to note that the systems of action outlined by Parsons are analytically, not concretely, separable. That is, all are abstractions or ways of analyzing behavior. There could be no cultural system if there were not systems of social interaction to support it. Similarly, there could be no social system without individual personalities to enter into relationships. And, of course, there could be no personality system without a biological organism. What differentiates the systems is their foci of organization, i.e., the aspects of behavior which are being related to one another.

Emotions can be treated as actions in Parsons's sense. That is, they are directed toward some goal (i.e., have objects), occur in concrete situations, are normatively regulated, and involve some expenditure of energy (physiologically speaking). This means that emotional reactions can be analyzed in terms of the four systems delineated by Parsons. This is perhaps most easily done if we view the emotions themselves as complex systems, or more precisely, as subsystems of personality. As any system, the emotions consist of related but semiautonomous elements—cognitive, behavioral, and physiological. When we examine any particular emotion in terms of cultural, social, personality, or biological systems, we are taking certain elements of the entire emotion (or perhaps certain aspects of different elements) and relating them to other elements within the particular system under consideration. On the biological level, for example, the focus might be on physiological elements and their relationship to other subsystems of the organism, such as the cardiovascular system. On the social level, one might focus on those aspects of emotional responses which involve the interaction among individuals and their relationship to certain institutions, for example, courts of law. Similar considerations apply to the personality and cultural levels of analysis.

Perhaps these remarks will be more meaningful if we take a concrete example, say, the emotion of guilt. On the cultural level, the symbolic aspects of guilt, or what might be called moral guilt, may be considered in relation to the system of norms and standards by which conduct is evaluated. On this level, the guilt of the Jew, for example, is to be understood in terms of the beliefs and attitudes which collectively make up the Jewish religion and culture. In this respect it may be said that the guilt of the Jew is different from the guilt of the Christian, or that the guilt of the Japanese is different from the guilt of the American (see Schneiders, 1968). On the social level, the judiciary is perhaps the institution most relevant to guilt. That is, in their roles as judge and jurors, certain individuals pass sentence on others whom they consider responsible for criminal activity. In a fully integrated society undergoing little change, there generally will be a high correspondence between moral guilt, on the cultural level, and legal guilt, on the social level. However, cultural norms may at times change more rapidly than social institutions, and vice versa. This may create a disjunction between moral and legal guilt. In such an instance, a person may break the law, be legally guilty, in order to obey a "higher commandment," that is, to avoid moral guilt. Similarly, one may conform "to the letter of the law, but not its spirit," that is, incur moral but not legal guilt.

On the level of the personality system, an analysis of guilt might focus on the feelings of negative affect experienced by the guilty person, the defense mechanisms designed to ward off such feelings, retributive behavior, and the like. Of course, there may be a disjunction between psychological guilt, on the one hand, and legal and moral guilt, on the other. The criminal psychopath is an example of a person who may be legally and morally guilty, but not psychologically so. The neurotic racked with guilt for no "objective" reason (cultural or legal) is an example of the other extreme.

Finally, one might examine elements of guilt on the biological level. Here the data is very meager and speculative. But, following Darwin (1873), analysis could be made of such physiological responses as blushing and eye-aversion; these, in turn, might be related to some broad adaptive system such as attachment or the need for group cohesiveness.

The above remarks indicate how elements from a single emotion can enter into the various systems of action defined by Parsons. The important point is that we are dealing with aspects of the *same phenomenon,* regardless of level of analysis. Thus, when we speak of guilt as part of the cultural system, we are not suggesting that it can somehow be disembodied and exist independently of the individual. But *aspects* of guilt can be *abstracted* and treated independently of any particular individual, regardless of level of analysis. With this in mind, it is not difficult to see how social and cultural systems, as well as personality and biological systems, can help constitute emotional reactions—elements of the behavior (albeit sometimes different elements) enter into all four systems. In this way, the values and norms of society may become constitutive parts of an emotion in as real a sense as, say, biological predispositions.

Now let us return to the original formulation of our problem regarding the sociology of knowledge and the superstructure/substructure dichotomy. If we take the social system to be the substructure, what is the superstructure? Within the tradition of the sociology of knowledge, we would say the cultural system. However, if we turn to the "symbolic interactionist" tradition (e.g., Mead, 1934) the answer might be the personality system, that is, the individual personality is a product of social interaction. Both answers would in a sense be correct. But why give the social system the privileged position of substructure, which seems to imply that it somehow has greater reality or is more fundamental than the cultural, personality or biological systems. Why not consider the biological system as substructure and social system as superstructure? This appears to have been the position of McDougall (1936), about whom we shall have more to say in a subsequent section. Other candidates for the substructure also exist. Most contemporary social psychologists would probably consider the personality system as basic to the social, while the Sapir-Whorf hypothesis (which makes the perception of reality dependent upon linguistic systems) would seem to make culture the substructure.

In short, if we stick to the problem as originally formulated, we are in a quagmire. No one system is substructure to any other, but all may be viewed as fundamental in one sense or another. Moreover, emotion does not "belong" to any one of the various systems we have discussed, but has elements which may enter into each. What we must ask, then, is how did these systems come about, and how do they interrelate with one another? In approaching this problem we shall follow Berger and Luckmann (1966) in their dialectical approach to the sociology of knowledge. This is not to imply that we have exhausted the relevance of a systems approach to the study of emotion. Quite the contrary: In the section following this one, we shall return to an examination of the manner in which biological systems contribute to the construction of emotional behavior.

A DIALECTICAL APPROACH TO THE STUDY OF EMOTION

Berger and Luckmann (1966) focus on the *process* by which everyday social reality is constructed, rather than on the structure of pre-established systems. This skirts the very difficult question of how the various systems (cultural, social, personality, biological) interact and influence one another. Systems are, after all, only abstractions; they may be distinguished in an analytical sense, but in no other. The question of their interaction therefore arises only within a particular analytic framework. When looked at in terms of process, rather than structure, the problem of interaction between systems is greatly simplified. This is because there is little need to even speak of distinct systems, as opposed to the continuous unfolding of human behavior and its various products. The question of interaction then becomes one of *feedback;* that is, how do the results of one type of human activity (e.g., religious theorizing) serve to influence other aspects of behavior (e.g., experience of guilt).

Berger and Luckmann postulate three essential characteristics of the social world: *society is a human product; society as an objective reality;* and *man is a social product.* This characterization assumes an ongoing dialectical process between man and society. The three moments or aspects of this dialectical process, corresponding to the three characteristics of society, are *externalization, objectivation,* and *internalization.*

The characterization of society as a human product stems largely from the tradition of Hegel and Marx. The mechanism by which this occurs, externalization, is assumed to be a biological necessity. That is, human beings are by nature "world-open"; the plasticity of their biological makeup does not provide the means for stable conduct. This means that the structure of any particular society must be the product of human activity, with only general restrictions imposed by biological and environmental necessities.

The second characteristic of society—that it is an objective reality—was originally stated most forcefully by Durkheim (1950), who considered the "first and fundamental rule" of sociological method to be: *"Consider social facts as things* [p. 14]." The process by which social facts come to be perceived as concrete realities ("things") is objectivation, the second moment in the dialectical process. Like externalization, objectivation is a basic human propensity. It is especially evident in young children, who tend to view the world of their parents as overwhelmingly real. The externalized products of human activity are capable of objectivation in a variety of ways, most importantly through the use of language, but also through many other symbols, signs, and artifacts. Thus, anger may be objectivated in the weapons used to express aggression and in the terminology used to describe and explain the behavior. Through objectivation, the externalized products of human activity become available as objective facts both to their producers and to others as elements in a common world.

The third characteristic of society is that man is a social product. This completes the dialectical process wherein man is both the producer and the product of a social world which he nevertheless perceives as having an objective reality independent of himself. Internalization is the presumed mechanism by which man becomes a social "product." During the course of socialization the infant "takes over" and internalizes the objectivated social world into which he is born.

It goes without saying that externalization, objectivation, and internalization are continuously ongoing processes. Internalization, for example, does not stop with childhood. Moreover, no person is ever completely socialized into a preestablished order; there is always some "slippage" during transmission, so that each individual contributes through externalizations to the construction of his own reality. It should be noted too that objectivation admits of varying degrees, depending upon the individual and the society. We have already pointed out that children are more prone to objectivation than adults. To the child, the world could not be other than it is. Most adults, on the other hand, recognize the arbitrariness of at least certain social institutions, although this varies considerably from one culture to another (compare, for example, a theocracy with a secular democracy). In general, the more an institution or societal norm permeates everyday behavior, the more it will tend to be objectivated. The extreme of objectivation is *reification,* where the human origins of the behavior pattern are obscured. In such a case, the behavior may be perceived as following some divine law, or for the more secularly inclined, some biological necessity.

The institutionalization of emotion. Given the tripartite dialectical process of externalization, objectivation, and internalization,

Berger and Luckmann (1966) illustrate how social reality is continuously being constructed, layer upon layer, from the simplest interpersonal behaviors to great religious and scientific representations of the universe. We will only sketch in barest outline the general nature of their argument and indicate its relevance for a constructivist view of emotion.

The first step (figuratively, not literally) toward the construction of social reality involves the *habitualization* of activity. Behaviors which are repeated more than once tend to fall into a pattern, thus providing a certain economy of action. If the behavior in question is observed by another, or is reflected upon by the actor, it may be categorized as a certain type. Language is the main vehicle for this *typification*. By naming a behavior (or a person, or inanimate event or object) we give it a certain degree of distance or anonymity. That is, other actions or persons could fill the same category. *Institutionalization* occurs when there is reciprocal typification of both actions and actors, that is, where role relationships are established so that actions of type X can be performed by actors of type X. Everyday social reality is apprehended in a continuum of typifications that become progressively anonymous the further removed they are from the face-to-face situation. The institutional structure is the sum total of these typifications and the recurrent patterns of activity established by them.

With regard to emotion, it is important to note that the institutionalizing process of reciprocal typification is inherent in any interaction between two or more persons. I apprehend another's emotional reactions in terms of typificatory schemes. For example, if I believe that a person is angry with me, I will expect certain reactions to follow on his part; moreover, I will base my own actions on this typification, for example, by becoming contrite, defensive, fearful, and so on, depending upon whether I believe his anger to be justified and on his ability to carry out retribution. Compare the typification of anger among Americans with the typification of a similar emotional state—*to nu*—among the Kaingang Indians of Brazil. According to Henrey (1936), when a Kaingang says, "I am angry [*to nu*]" it means, "I am *dangerous toward* you." That is, the concept of *to nu* implies a desire to hurt or kill regardless of perceived wrong. "With this background" Henrey observes, "we can understand why telling a Kaingang you are angry with him, or even

using the intonation associated with anger will make him angry
with you. If you say to A, 'I am angry with you,' his reaction is not
contrition or repentance, or any kind of 'negative self-feeling,' but
rage.''

It is apparent from the above description that ''anger'' is not a
very exact translation of the Kaingang term *to nu*. Indeed, from the
present perspective it may be said that anger and *to nu* refer to *two
different emotions,* albeit both may have aggressive components in
common. This follows from the fact that emotional reactions are,
in part, a function of their typification.

Reciprocal typifications of behavior are built up during the
course of a shared history. With the acquisition of a history, behavior may come to be experienced as nonarbitrary and even inevitable. ''Everyone knows that is the way it is done.'' But simply knowing *how* a thing is done is not enough. Inevitably, people also are
interested in knowing *why* it is done. The *why* of behavior is its
legitimation.

Berger and Luckmann distinguish four levels of legitimation. On
the first level, legitimating explanations are built into the terms
used to typify a response. For example, to describe a response as
''angry'' is already to impose an interpretation on it. The second
level of legitimation contains theoretical propositions in rudimentary forms, for example, proverbs, moral maxims, and the like.
These are highly pragmatic and directly related to actions (e.g.,
''Two things a man should never be angry at: what he can help, and
what he cannot help.'') Legitimations on the third level contain
explicit theories in terms of a differentiated body of knowledge (cf.
the frustration-aggression hypotheses). Finally, the fourth level of
legitimation consists of symbolic universes or theoretical traditions
that integrate different provences of meaning. On this level, for
example, human anger might be related to the ''wrath of God,''
thus placing it within an overarching, theological frame of reference. (For a detailed analysis of the relationship between anger and
religious systems, see Stratton, 1923.)

As a further illustration of these levels of legitimation, we might
consider the syndrome of ''being a wild pig'' described earlier. The
name itself implies a rudimentary explanation of the syndrome—
one has broken the bonds of social control, like a domesticated pig
gone wild. We can also imagine that the Gururumba have maxims

or sayings about being a wild pig, although none are specifically mentioned in the ethnographic account. On the third level of legitimation, there is an explicit theory about the origins and causes of "being a wild pig," that is, the affected person has been bitten by a ghost and this has released primordial impulses. Finally, the idea of being bitten by a ghost places the behavior in a general cosmological framework, entailing notions about death and the afterworld, and so on.

It will be noted that the fourth level of legitimation described by Berger and Luckmann bears certain similarities to the cultural system described by Parsons. Also, their notion of an institution as the product of reciprocal typifications and recurrent patterns of interaction is similar to Parson's notion of a social system. These similarities, however, are perhaps misleading. Berger and Luckmann explicitly reject the idea that institutions cohere to form systems. The "inner logic" which institutionalized activity possesses is primarily a secondary outcome of legitimation, and the latter process occurs on all levels from the simplest typifications to the most grandiose symbolic schemes. But this is not the place to debate the issue. Suffice it to note that no matter how one approaches the topic—on a structural level in terms of interpenetrating systems, or on a dynamic level in terms of ongoing dialectical processes—the conclusion is similar as far as the social construction of emotional behavior is concerned: There is no invariant core to emotional behavior which remains untouched by sociocultural influences. The latter view (that there is an invariant core) is essentially *a reification of emotion into a biological given.*

This last statement requires a consideration of the biological determinants of emotion. We shall then be in a better position to see how the legitimation of an emotional response may, through the process of internalization (socialization), help construct that response.

BIOLOGICAL DETERMINANTS OF EMOTION

Historically, there has been a tendency to treat emotions as biologically primitive, instinctive response patterns. It is against this backdrop that the concept of emotions as social constructions must be viewed. It has, of course, long been recognized that emotional *expression* and *eliciting conditions* are subject to cultural influence. Nevertheless, theorists have tended to treat cultural differences in emotion as superficial variations imposed on basic biological substrata. This position is epitomized by McDougall (1936), who built his social psychology on the emotions. The structure, however, was very one sided. While emotions helped shape society, the reverse was not true, at least not on a fundamental level. According to McDougal (1936), "emotional excitement . . . is the only part of the total instinctive process that retains its specific character and remains common to all individuals and all situations in which the instinct is excited" (p. 29).

Although the doctrine of instinct has gone out of vogue, the above statement couched in different terminology would reflect the attitudes of many contemporary theorists (e.g., Izard, 1971; Plutchik, 1962). That is, there is some "core" aspect of emotional behavior, identifiable in terms of neurological circuits and/or subjective experience, which is biologically given and hence pan-cultural. By contrast, a basic assumption of the present chapter is that there are no core aspects of emotion which are not intrinsically and essentially influenced by sociocultural factors. But an adequate analysis of emotion must avoid the Scylla of cultural relativism as well as the Charybdis of nativism. The course between the two lies in the recognition that emotions come into being only through the interaction of biological and sociocultural systems. The biological contribution to that interaction is the subject of the present section.

BIOLOGICAL SYSTEMS OF BEHAVIOR

In the previous section, we outlined briefly four systems of action as defined by Parsons. These were, namely, the cultural system, the social system,[2] the personality system, and the biological system. We noted then that each of these systems may contribute elements to a particular action pattern. We must now attempt to define more precisely what is meant by a biological system, and to indicate how such systems contribute to emotion. Our definition of a biological system will not, however, follow that of Parsons, who focuses primarily on physiological homeostatic mechanisms (e.g., the cardiovascular system). The conception of biological system adumbrated here is based primarily on ethological analyses of behavior.

We will begin this discussion with a description of cliff-nesting in the Kittiwake, a species of gull (see Cullen, 1957; Tinbergen, 1960). This example illustrates well what is meant by a biological system. Unlike most gulls, the Kittiwake lives in the open sea outside of the breeding season; and, when it does visit the land to breed, it nests on tiny cliff ledges which are sometimes only four inches wide. Some additional ways in which the Kittiwake differs from other species of gull are:

1. Claws and foot musculature are well developed.
2. Females sit down during copulation.
3. Nests are solidly constructed with deep cups.
4. An average of only two eggs are laid, and these hatch asyncronously.
5. Chicks do not run when approached by strangers.
6. Chicks face the wall of the cliff.
7. Appeasement movements are a common response to threat.
8. There is a special "twisting" technique of fighting.
9. Males use a "choking" display to attract females.
10. Nest material is frequently stolen.
11. Empty nests are guarded.
12. Food is incompletely regurgitated when feeding chicks.
13. Parents lack a food call.
14. Chicks do not stretch their neck in a "pumping" fashion to attract parents.
15. There is no personal recognition of chicks by parents.

Although many of these characteristics might at first seem quite unrelated, they actually form a coherent system related to one major adaptation—cliff-nesting as a defense of the young against predation. Characteristics 1 through 6 help prevent falling off the cliff. Appeasement movements (7) reduce intraspecific fighting, which otherwise would be common in such close quarters. Twisting movements while fighting (8) are a means of throwing an intruder off the cliff. Since the male Kittiwake's territory is little more than his nest site, choking movements (9)—which are probably displaced elements of nest-building activity—suffice as a display in attracting a mate. Stealing of nest material (10) is related to the scarcity of such material on cliffs, while the guarding of empty nests (11) is a protection against theft. Incomplete regurgitation of food (12) prevents fouling of the nest, which chicks do not leave until they can fly. Also, since the chicks are always in the nest, parents do not need to call them for food (13), nor do the chicks need to attract their parents' attention by "pumping" (14). Indeed, the parents do not even recognize their chicks individually (15), since the nest site identifies the brood.

There are other characteristics peculiar to the Kittiwake which can be viewed as the relaxation of antipredator defenses common in other gulls. Thus, Kittiwakes do not attack predators, alarm calls are rare, chicks are not camouflaged, and egg shells (which attract predators) are not removed from the nest.

The defense of the Kittiwake against predation illustrates a number of features of biological systems. First, a biological system consists of a variety of semiautonomous responses and the "rules" for the organization of those responses. Second, any particular response may be an element in more than one system. Third, a biological system is not activated as a unit; rather, it is a complex series of responses, some of which may occur, others not, depending upon the circumstances. Fourth, a biological system is defined in terms of its "goal." The ultimate goal of a biological system is, of course, the preservation of the species. But this ultimate goal can only be achieved through a series of intermediate steps of subgoals. The delineation of a biological system can thus be made at different levels of generality. The antipredator system of the Kittiwake has been defined at a very general level. It could be broken down into subsystems serving more proximate goals, for example, nest building, pair formation, mating, parental behavior, and so forth.

A fifth feature of biological systems—indeed, of any type of system (see Hall & Fagen, 1968)—is that they undergo progressive *segregation* in the absence of maintenance inputs. That is, the individual elements gradually become more loosely connected and independent (compare the relaxation in the Kittiwake of antipredator defenses common in other gulls). The opposite of segregation is *systematization,* that is, the strengthening of preexisting relations and/or the addition of new elements and relationships to a system. In biological systems, segregation may result from such genetic processes as mutation, independent assortment, recombination, and the like, while natural selection acts as the major systematizing influence. Natural selection is not, however, the only means of systematization; even in lower organisms, individual experience in a particular environment is an important factor in determining the manner in which response elements will become coordinated into an organized whole (Eibl-Eibesfeldt, 1970). And as we ascend the phylogenetic scale, biological systems become increasingly segregated on a genetic level, with individual experience assuming greater importance as a systematizing factor.

As an example of biological system on the human level we may consider Bowlby's (1969) analysis of the attachment of an infant to its mother. According to Bowlby, attachment is a biological adaptation to protect the infant from danger, especially attack from predators. In this respect attachment could be considered a human analogue of cliff-nesting in the Kittiwake. Attachment consists of a set of responses, such as sucking, clinging, crying, and smiling, which are so organized and activated that a child tends to be maintained in proximity to its mother. The whole process can be analyzed, according to Bowlby, as the operation of a complex control system. The essential features of a control system are an internal reference against which external input can be compared, and feedback regarding how successful a response is in reducing any discrepancies between environmental conditions and the internal reference.

It will be noted that the notion of a biological system bears some resemblance to the older notion of instinct. If by instinct is meant an unlearned, stereotyped response pattern, then a biological system definitely is not an instinct. If on the other hand, one means by instinct only the potential to develop certain patterns of responses which contribute to species survival, then a biological system may be termed "instinctive." When interpreted so broadly, however, the term *instinctive* is not very informative and, because of the connotations it has accrued historically, it is perhaps better dropped altogether.

The relationship between biological systems and emotions may now be set forth in the following five propositions:

1. It is meaningful to speak of biological systems only on the species level. Some theorists (e.g., Plutchik, 1962) have argued that there are distinct biological systems corresponding to various "primary" emotions, and that each system fulfills a basic adaptive function evident at various phyletic levels. Carried to its logical extreme, this view leads Plutchik to conclude that there are eight primary human emotions (fear, anger, joy, grief, acceptance, disgust, surprise, and expectation), each of which ultimately is trace-

able to processes observable in the amoeba. Grief, for example, is related to food deprivation—a proposal which certainly would seem far-fetched if it were not for the long-standing habit of thinking of the emotions as biologically primitive.

Of course, there are occasions when it may be useful to treat broad adaptive functions in the abstract. However, as the examples of nest-building in the Kittiwake and attachment in the human indicate, the same adaptive function (i.e., protection of the young) can be achieved by very different biological systems. And what is true of biological systems is even more true of emotional reactions, which involve sociocultural as well as biological determinants. This means that one must be very cautious in making inferences about human emotions from observations made on the infrahuman level. Indeed, for reasons which will become apparent below, concepts which describe human emotions can be applied only metaphorically to infrahuman animals.

2. An indefinite number of biological systems can be identified, depending upon the purpose of the investigator and the level of generality desired. For example, in discussing reproduction as a biological system, one might limit consideration to copulation and immediately related behaviors. For other purposes, however, one might wish to include courtship as well as copulation, or even the entire sequence of courtship, copulation, gestation, and child rearing. Moreover, since the same behavior elements may be shared by more than one system, different systems can shade into one another without any sharp demarcation. In other words, the distinction among biological systems is inherently somewhat arbitrary. There is thus little point in debating the kind or number of biological systems and attempting to relate these to so-called primary emotions.

3. As we ascend the phylogenetic scale, biological systems become increasingly segregated on a genetic level and individual experience assumes a greater importance as a systematizing factor. In discussing the effects of infantile deprivation on primates, Mason (1968) has observed:

> All these observations suggest that the number and variety of discrete motor acts, and the tendency to combine such acts spontaneously into new and more complex patterns, increases progressively from monkey to man. One of the pathways toward human behavior thus seems to be a "loosening" of motor patterns, and we can already see the process at work in the great apes. That a similar change has occurred in the internal mechanisms that govern behavior

seems most likely. . . . In my own work with young chimpanzees I have found it necessary to speak in terms of a generalized motivational state, because more specific motives—fear, aggression, hunger, sex—do not seem to be able to provide a satisfactory account of their behavior. [P. 99]

Rather than speaking of a "generalized motivational state," as Mason suggests, we prefer to speak of biological systems that have undergone a high degree of segregation. In man, elements from these behavior systems may be incorporated into specific emotions on the basis of cultural prescriptions and individual experience. The process by which such systematization occurs (i.e., externalization, objectivation, and internalization) has been discussed in the previous section, and will be taken up again in the next section when we consider the psychological determinants of emotion.

4. It follows from the above propositions that there is no simple relationship between emotions and biological systems. Depending upon the cultural context, a variety of different emotions may be fashioned from the same biological system; conversely, elements from several different systems may be incorporated into a single emotion. Consider the case of attachment. This biological system contributes to a variety of specific emotions depending upon the cultural context. For instance, the Japanese seem to have molded from attachment an emotion, *amae,* which is experienced by them as extremely basic and fundamental (Doi, 1962). There is no equivalent to *amae* in European languages, although "dependency" (without its negative connotations) carries some of the meaning. The constructivist view of emotion being presented here would further suggest that people with a European background *do not experience* an emotion equivalent to *amae.* This does not mean that attachment is biologically less important for westerners, only that different types of response patterns are constructed from it. Romantic love, for example probably has elements of attachment as well as sexual behavior associated with it. These are combined into an emotional system (love) which fulfills certain functions within society (such as getting couples to marry when economics and other inducements are weak—see Greenfield, 1965; Rosenblatt, 1967).

5. The various human emotions differ in how closely they are related to biological systems. This fact was alluded to in the first section when a distinction was made between standard emotional

reactions and biologically based responses (e.g., startle to a loud noise, attacking the source of pain, and the like). We can now see that this distinction does not represent a true dichotomy. Rather, standard emotional reactions vary along a continuum, one end of which is anchored in biological systems, and the other end of which is anchored in sociocultural systems. The important point to emphasize is that this continuum does not represent a hierarchy, with social emotions being complex mixtures of more fundamental biological emotions. Neither end of the continuum is more fundamental than the other in the sense that it better represents what an emotion "really" is. Certainly, a response is not more emotional simply by virtue of the fact that it is closely related to a biological system.

We have now sketched in broad outline some of the sociocultural and biological determinants of emotion. Let us examine next how these become manifest in the psyche of the individual actor.

PSYCHOLOGICAL DETERMINANTS OF EMOTION

Recent psychological approaches to the study of emotion (e.g., Arnold, 1960; Lazarus, 1966) have emphasized the role of appraisal in the determination of emotional responses. Every emotional reaction is a function of a particular kind of appraisal, i.e., the emotion of anger is based on one kind of appraisal, fear on another, sorrow, and joy on still different ones, and so forth. One of the major problems for the study of emotion is thus the elucidation of the appraisals on which the various emotions are based. Since much of the research on appraisal has been reviewed elsewhere (Averill, Opton, & Lazarus, 1969; Lazarus, Averill, & Opton, 1970, 1974), this aspect of the psychology of emotion will not be considered in the present chapter. Rather, we will focus attention on another core feature of emotional behavior, namely, the experience of passivity.

An individual not only responds according to his appraisal of a situation, he also monitors his own response and evaluates how it should be interpreted—e.g., as an action or as a passion. In other words, the experience of passivity during emotion is, in a sense, an interpretation of one's own behavior. The reasons why certain behaviors are experienced passively is thus a central problem for the psychology of emotion.

THE SELF-ATTRIBUTION OF EMOTIONAL EXPERIENCE

As previously noted (see the first section), the experience of passivity during standard emotional reactions presumes a limited self-awareness, a restricted insight into the sources of one's actions. The person may realize that he is behaving in a particular manner, but does not interpret the behavior as deliberate or self-initiated. Earlier, this state of affairs was compared to the hallucinated images and peculiar responses sometimes experienced by persons "suffering" from hysteria. Let us pursue that analogy further with a concrete example.

Mahl (1969) has described the case of a young woman, Edie, who came to psychoanalysis for the treatment of an eating problem. Edie's problem began during adolescence. Whenever she attempted to eat with boyfriends, she would become nauseated and fearful of choking. Fortunately, she met a young man who nursed her with his own cooking. Following their marriage Edie's eating problem became sporadic and seemed to fluctuate in accordance to her sexual relationships with her husband. She started psychoanalysis after the problem had become intensified for a few months, a period during which she was not enjoying an adequate sex life.

Edie had been raised to believe that all sexual activity not directly related to procreation was sinful. Nevertheless, Edie did have strong sexual desires, and these became the occasion for considerable guilt and distress. According to Mahl, eating became symbolic of sexual activity; thus, when sexual desire became intense, so did the desire to eat. However, this subterfuge eventually became a source of anxiety and guilt in its own right, resulting in an inhibition of eating.

The case of Edie illustrates several features of emotional reactions which are important for the present analysis. The first thing to note about Edie's eating problem is how two generally independent biological systems—eating and mating—became fused into a single emotional (hysterical) system of unusual character. Edie's behavior was unusual, however, primarily in the sense that eating is not a culturally organized and fostered response to sexual arousal. Rather, Edie's behavior developed idiosyncratically in response to her own peculiar needs and past history.

In Edie's case, eating and mating were not simply fused—the former actually came to stand for the latter, its original significance then being dissociated from consciousness. In this way, the original impulse (sexual arousal) could be satisfied, albeit in a substitute and disguised manner. Behaviors of this type typically have been classed as defense mechanisms, which has tended to focus attention on their negative as opposed to their positive functions. But as Schafer (1968) has emphasized, a defense mechanism is a means of gratifying an impulse as well as defending against it. It is because eating could offer Edie a vicarious means of sexual gratification (symbolic intercourse, according to Mahl) that it too became the object of conflict.

In short, although Edie's behavior was a serious source of distress to her, it nevertheless did have functional significance when viewed in the context of her entire being. In this respect, it is useful to compare the type of idiosyncratic response displayed by Edie with the culture-specific emotional syndromes described in the second section. Thus, "being a wild pig" is not acceptable behavior among the Gururumba, yet it is maintained because it helps resolve certain conflicts with the social system. Moreover, the significance of the behavior is not recognized, but is symbolically transformed to fit the overall cosmology of the culture (i.e., one becomes a wild pig after being bitten by a ghost). Similar considerations apply to most standard emotional reactions. These are behaviors which frequently are condemned by society and yet which are maintained because they serve useful (but disguised) functions within the sociocultural system.

The precise function served by standard emotional reactions differs, of course, from one emotion to another. The function of anger, for example, is not the same as the function of romantic love. Nevertheless, the underlying principles are similar: society has established conflicting norms which simultaneously encourage and discourage a particular kind of behavior. The conflict is resolved by allowing the responses to be symbolically transformed and its initiation dissociated from consciousness. An individual may thus perform the act without incurring responsibility—he cannot help himself if he is "overcome" by emotion. Take anger as a case in point.[3] There is general cultural proscription against intentionally harming another; however, under certain circumstances (which will be discussed more fully below) retaliation may be expected and even demanded; it must, however, be carried out in such a manner that the individual does not *willingly* violate the general cultural norm against injuring another. Being "overcome" by anger is one way of meeting this dual standard.

SUMMARY AND CONCLUSION

The psychology of emotion is a complex area of inquiry, and that complexity has been reflected in this chapter. We began with an analysis of everyday emotional concepts, noting that what is common to various emotions is a sense of passivity, of being "gripped" and "overcome." This experience of passivity may arise from three main sources, and these help define three main classes of emotion. The first class, which we have called standard emotional reactions, are socially constructed response patterns, the initiation of which has been dissociated from consciousness. Such dissociation represents a way of resolving conflicting demands placed upon the individual by society. The second class of emotional reactions is comprised of states in which the boundaries of the self have been transcended or broken down—through physical trauma, intrapsychic conflict, lack of social input, and so on. Anxiety is one example of a transcendental emotional state. A third class of emotion-like responses have their origin in man's phylogenetic past. Responses of this type are experienced passively because it was of evolutionary advantage for our hominid ancestors to respond quickly and automatically to certain natural dangers and rewards.

Until recently, it has been customary to treat biologically based responses as though they were paradigmatic of emotion in general. For the most part, however, biology only contributes elements to, and set limits upon, the social construction of emotional behavior. The present analysis thus rejects the traditional disjunction between emotion and cognition. Standard emotions are as much a product of complex cognitive processes as are such other cultural products as religion, art, science, and the like. This means that investigation into the sociocultural determinants of thought (e.g., the sociology of knowledge) is relevant to emotional processes also.

From a psychological point of view, the experience of passivity which characterizes standard emotional reactions can be viewed as a kind of interpretation of one's own behavior. This interpretation or self-attribution of emotion is based on a variety of cues, the most important of which is the anticipated or actual outcome of a response. The self-attribution of emotion allows the individual to abjure, to a limited extent, the responsibility for the consequences of his actions. The dynamics of this process is in some respects similar to the dynamics underlying hysterical reactions. A person suffering from hysterical blindness, for example, may be greatly troubled by his affliction and go to great lengths to seek help. On a deeper level of analysis, however, the blindness is a product of his own intrapsychic conflicts. It is a way of coping which the person cannot recognize or condone as such, and yet which fulfills a definite function in maintaining intrapsychic equilibrium. By analogy, standard emotional reactions might be viewed as hystericallike reactions on a sociocultural as opposed to an individual level of analysis. Thus, although an emotion such as anger may be discouraged and even condemned in terms of explicit cultural values, it may at the same time be encouraged as a way of coping with certain conflicts inherent within the sociocultural system.

There is a fundamental difference between standard emotional reactions and the state of anxiety. Specifically, while the former class of emotions presuppose highly structured cognitive systems, a cardinal feature of the latter is cognitive disintegration. The possibility for anxiety is inherent in man's world-openness and his capacity for symbolic constructions. Through the dialectical processes of externalization and internalization, man constructs his world in the image of himself and himself in the image of his world. But the cognitive structures which a man creates are never completely secure; anxiety is one manifestation of their impending or actual collapse.

This, then, is our framework for the interpretation of emotion and anxiety. Like any framework, it is incomplete in itself. Hopefully, however, it may help place some old problems in new perspective.

ACKNOWLEDGMENTS

Preparation of this chapter was supported, in part, by a grant (NEG-00-3-0139) from the National Institute of Education, Department of Health, Education, and Welfare.

NOTES

1. There are, of course, behaviors other than emotions which are experienced passively, including well-ingrained habits, reflexes, deficit states such as hunger and thirst, and even perception in general. An attempt to distinguish emotion from these other passively experienced behaviors would be beyond the scope of the present chapter (but see Peters, 1969).

2. In subsequent discussions, it generally will not be necessary to make a distinction between social and cultural systems. For the sake of convenience, therefore, reference will be made simply to "sociocultural" systems.

3. Space obviously does not allow an examination of the social function of a wide variety of different emotions. The present analysis focuses on aggressive syndromes because the underlying dynamics are more easily illustrated with these than with other emotional reactions. However, it is not difficult to extend the present analysis even to the case of positive emotions (Averill, 1973a).

REFERENCES

Arieti, S., and Meth, J. M. Rare, unclassifiable, collective, and exotic psychotic syndromes. In S. Arieti, ed., *American Handbook of Psychiatry*. Vol. 1. New York: Basic Books, 1959.

Arnold, M. B. *Emotion and personality*. 2 vols. New York: Columbia University Press, 1960.

Averill, J. R. Grief: Its nature and significance. *Psychological Bulletin,* 70 (1968), 721-748.

――――. Why are there not more positive emotions? Paper presented at the meetings of the American Psychological Association, Montreal, August 1973a.

――――. The dis-position of psychological dispositions. *Journal of Experimental Research in Personality,* 6 (1973b), 275-282.

――――. An analysis of psychophysiological symbolism and its influence on theories of emotion. *Journal for the Theory of Social Behavior,* 4 (1974), 147-189.

――――. A semantic atlas of emotional concepts. JSAS *Catalog of Selected Documents in Psychology,* 5 (1975), 330 (Ms. No. 421).

Averill, J. R. DeWitt, G. W., and Zimmer, M. The self-attribution of emotion as a function of success and failure. Unpublished manuscript, 1975.

Averill, J. R., Opton, E. M., Jr., and Lazarus, R. S. Cross-cultural studies of psychophysiological responses during stress and emotion. *International Journal of Psychology,* 4 (1969), 83-102.

Bedford, E. Emotions. *Aristotelian Society Proceedings,* 57 (1957), 281-304.

Berger, P. L., and Luckmann, T. *The Social Construction of Reality.* New York: Doubleday, 1966.

Bowlby, J. *Attachment and loss.* Vol. 1. *Attachment.* New York: Basic Books, 1969.

――――. *Attachment and loss.* Vol. 2. *Separation.* New York: Basic Books, 1973.

Breger, L. Function of dreams. *Journal of Abnormal Psychology Monograph,* 72 (1967), 1-28.

————. *From instinct to identity.* Englewood Cliffs, N.J.: Prentice-Hall, 1974.

Bronowski, J., and Bellugi, U. Language, name and concept. *Science,* 168 (1970), 669-673.

Carpenter, E. S. Witch-fear among the aivilik eskimos. *American Journal of Psychiatry,* 110 (1953), 194-199.

Cullen, E. Adaptations in the kittiwake to cliff-nesting. *Ibis,* 99 (1957), 275-302.

Darwin, C. *The expression of emotion in man and animals.* London: Murray, 1873.

Dember, W. N. Motivation and the cognitive revolution. *American Psychologist,* 29 (1974), 161-168.

Doi, L. T. Amae: A key concept for understanding Japanese personality structure. In R. J. Smith and R. K. Beardsley, eds., *Japanese culture: Its development and characteristics.* Chicago: Aldine, 1962.

Durkheim, E. *The rules of sociological method.* Glencoe, Ill.: The Free Press, 1950.

Eibl-Eibesfeldt, I. *Ethology: The biology of behavior.* New York: Holt, 1970.

Fromm, R. *Escape from freedom.* New York: Holt, Rinehart & Winston, 1941.

Goldstein, K. *The organism.* New York: American Book, 1939.

————. On emotions: Considerations from the organismic point of view. *Journal of Psychology,* 31 (1951), 37-49.

Greenfield, S. M. Love and marriage in modern America: A functional analysis. *Sociological Quarterly,* 6 (1965), 361-377.

Hall, A. D., and Fagan, R. E. Definition of systems. In W. Buckley, ed., *Modern systems research for the behavioral scientist.* Chicago: Aldine, 1968.

Hallowell, A. I. Fear and anxiety as cultural and individual variables in a primitive society. *Journal of Social Psychology,* 9 (1938), 25-47.

————. The social function of anxiety in a primitive society. *American Sociological Review,* 6 (1941), 869-881.

Henrey, J. The linguistic expression of emotion. *American Anthropologist,* 38 (1936), 250-256.

Izard, C. *The face of emotion.* New York: Appleton-Century-Crofts, 1971.

Klein, D. F. Delineation of two drug-responsive anxiety syndromes. *Psychopharmacolgia,* 5 (1964), 397-408.

Klein, G. S. Peremptory ideation: structure and force in motivated ideas. In R. R. Holt, ed., *Motives and thought.* New York: International Universities Press, 1967.

Kumasaka, Y. A culturally determined mental reaction among the Ainu. *Psychological Quarterly,* 38 (1964), 733-738.

Laing, R. D. *The divided self.* Baltimore: Penguin Books, 1965.

Langness, L. L. Hysterical psychosis in the New Guinea highlands: A Bena Bena example. *Psychiatry* (1965), 258-277.

Lazarus, R. S. *Psychological stress and the coping process.* New York: McGraw-Hill, 1966.

Lazarus, R. S., and Averill, J. R. Emotion and cognition: With special reference to anxiety. In C. D. Spielberger, ed., *Anxiety: Current trends in theory and research.* New York: Academic Press, 1972.

Lazarus, R. S., Averill, J. R., and Opton, E. M., Jr. Towards a cognitive theory of emotion. In M. Arnold, ed., *Feelings and emotions.* New York: Academic Press, 1970.

————. The psychology of coping: Issues of research and assessment. In G. V. Coelho, D. A. Hamburg, and J. E. Adams, eds., *Coping and adaptation: Interdisciplinary perspectives.* New York: Basic Books, 1974.

LeVine, R. A. *Culture, behavior, and personality.* Chicago: Aldine, 1973.

McDougall, W. *An introduction to social psychology.* 23d ed. London: Methuen, 1936.

McKellar, P. The emotion of anger in the expression of human aggressiveness. *British Journal of Psychology*, 39 (1949), 148-155.

Mahl, G. F. Conflict and defense. In I. L. Janis et al., *Personality: Dynamics, development, and assessment.* New York: Harcourt, Brace, & World, 1969.

Mason, W. A. Early social deprivation in the nonhuman primates: Implications for human behavior. In D. C. Glass, ed., *Environmental influences.* New York: Rockefeller University Press, 1968.

May, R. *The meaning of anxiety.* New York: The Ronald Press, 1950.

Mead, G. H. *Mind, self, and society.* Chicago: University of Chicago Press, 1934.

Miller, W. B., Geertz, H., and Cutter, H. S. G. Aggression in a boys' streetcorner group. *Psychiatry,* 24 (1961), 282-298.

Newman, P. L. "Wild man" behavior in a New Guinea highlands community. *American Anthropologist,* 66 (1960), 1-19.

Noyes, R. Dying and the mystical consciousness. *Journal of Thanatology,* 1 (1971), 25-41.

———. The experience of dying. *Psychiatry,* 35 (1972), 174-184.

Parker, S. The wiitiko psychosis in the context of Ojibwa personality and culture. *American Anthropologist,* 62 (1960), 603-623.

Parsons, T. An approach to psychological theory in terms of the theory of action. In S. Koch, ed., *Psychology: A study of a science.* Vol. 3: *Formulations of the person and the social context.* New York: McGraw-Hill, 1959.

———. Introduction to part four: Culture and the Social System. In T. Parsons, E. Shils, K. D. Nagele, and J. R. Pitts, eds., *Theories of Society.* New York: Free Press, 1961.

Parsons, T., and Shils, E. A., eds., *Toward a general theory of action.* Cambridge, Mass.: Harvard University Press, 1962.

Perkins, R. M. The law of homicide. *Journal of Criminal Law & Criminology,* 36 (1946), 391-454.

Peters, R. S. Motivation, emotion, and the conceptual schemes of common sense. In T. Mischel, ed., *Human action: Conceptual and empirical issues.* New York: Academic Press, 1969.

Plutchik, R. *The emotions.* New York: Random House, 1962.

———. Emotions, evolution and adaptive processes. In M. B. Arnold, ed., *Feelings and emotions: The Loyola symposium.* New York: Academic Press, 1970.

Richardson, F. *The psychology and pedagogy of anger.* Baltimore: Warwick & York, 1918.

Rosenblatt, P. C. Marital residence and the functions of romantic love. *Ethnology,* 6 (1967), 471-480.

Rubel, A. J. The epidemiology of a folk illness: *Susto* in Hispanic America. *Ethnology,* 3 (1964), 268-283.

Salisbury, R. Possession on the New Guinea highlands: Review of literature. *Transcultural Psychiatric Research,* 3 (1966a), 103-108.

———. Possession among the Siane (New Guinea). *Transcultural Psychiatric Research,* 3 (1967b), 108-116.

———. Reply to L. L. Langness. *Transcultural Psychiatric Research,* 4 (1967), 130-134.

Schachter, S. The interaction of cognitive and physiological determinants of emotional state. In C. D. Spielberger, ed., *Anxiety and behavior.* New York: Academic Press, 1966.

———. *Emotion, obesity, and crime.* New York: Academic Press, 1971.

Schafer, R. The Mechanisms of defense. *International Journal of Psycho-Analysis,* 49 (1968), 49-62.

Schneiders, A. A. The nature and origins of guilt. *Transactions of the New York Academy of Sciences,* 30 (1968), 705-713.

Schutz, A. On multiple realities. In C. Gordon and K. J. Gergen, eds., *The Self in social interaction.* Vol. 1. *Classic and contemporary perspectives.* New York: Wiley, 1968.

Scott, J. P. The development of social motivation. In D. LeVine, ed., *Nebraska Symposium on Motivation.* Vol. 15. Lincoln: University of Nebraska Press, 1967.

Spence, J. T., and Spence, K. W. The motivational components of manifest anxiety. Drive and drive stimuli. In C. D. Spielberger, ed., *Anxiety and behavior.* New York: Academic Press, 1966.

Spielberger, C. D. Theory and research on anxiety. In C. D. Spielberger, ed., *Anxiety and behavior.* New York: Academic Press, 1966.

Spiro, M. E. Ghosts: An anthropological inquiry into learning and perception. *Journal of Abnormal and Social Psychology,* 48 (1953), 376-382.

Stratton, G. M. *Anger: Its religious and moral significance.* New York: Macmillan, 1923.

Taylor, J. A. A personality scale for manifest anxiety. *Journal of Abnormal and Social Psychology,* 48 (1953), 285-290.

Tinbergen, N. Behavior, systematics, and natural selection. In S. Tax, ed., *Evolution after Darwin.* Vol. 1: *The evolution of life.* Chicago: University of Chicago Press, 1960.

Vygotsky, L. S. *Thought and language.* Cambridge, Mass.: MIT Press, 1962.

Wolfgang, M. E. and Ferracuti, F. Subculture of violence—a socio-psychological theory. In M. E. Wolfgang, ed., *Studies in homicide.* New York: Harper & Row, 1967.

Yap, P. M. The latah reaction: Its pathodynamics and nosological position. *Journal of Mental Science,* 98 (1952), 515-564.

———. Koro—a culture-bound depersonalization syndrome. *British Journal of Psychiatry,* 111 (1965), 43-50.

III

BIOLOGICAL AND CULTURAL CONTRIBUTIONS TO BODY AND FACIAL MOVEMENT IN THE EXPRESSION OF EMOTIONS

PAUL EKMAN

(This is a section of a larger work,[1] in which the author develops a taxonomy for analyzing the significance of nonverbal actions that are informative about a person's psychological state, even if they are not intended to communicate that state. He distinguishes varieties of: emblems [symbolic actions, typically used intentioally, which have a verbal meaning], body manipulator actions [movements that are not performed intentionally but which are interpretable because they are characteristically associated with particular psychological conditions such as nervousness, anxiety, deference], and illustrators [gestures that accompany speech and help to disambiguate and interpet it]. Following Darwinian hypotheses, he treats emotional expressions as a category of informative bodily and facial movement: he argues that the universality of patterns of expression is compatible with cultural variation in forms of coding.)

INTRODUCTION

There is no agreed upon single name for the range of facial or bodily activities I will describe. Part of my purpose will be to suggest that there should *not* be, for this is not one phenomenon but many. Terms such as nonverbal behavior, nonverbal communication, kinesics, kinetics, expressive behavior, body language, and the like, have been used by one or another author to refer to some activity of the face and/or body. It has not always been clear whether actions that seem to have some instrumental purpose, such as pencil sharpening or push-ups, were included. If not then why did they include head scratching? Is the phenomenon restricted to movement or does it include static position of body or face (postures)? If limited to movements, it has not always been clear whether those too fast or too small for visibility under normal circumstances have been included. No matter. While a single suitable term[2] would be a boon when writing about the face and/or body, it could further confuse study of the phenomena, adding to the tendency to ignore or gloss over fundamental differences in what a person does with his face and body.

Some of those who study nonverbal behaviors (kinesics, expressive behaviors, etc.) have argued for an evolutionary perspective. They sought and found universals. Others, arguing for the utility of a linguistic model or the perspective of cultural relativism, sought and found extraordinary differences among cultural groups. Both studied the nonverbal, but it is likely that each examined entirely different activities: activities that differ in origin (how the behavior became part of the repertoire), in coding (the relationship between movement and what it signifies), and in the circumstances of usage. Perhaps because the phenomena are all the result of muscular action, or because vision is the means for perceiving these activities, or the camera the method of recording, investigators may have expected to find but one type of activity, just one principle of organization, just one type of function, just one major determinant. There are many.

EMBLEMS

We have employed Efron's (1941) term *emblem* to refer to symbolic actions where the movement has a very specific verbal meaning, known to most members of a subculture or culture, and typically is employed with the intention of sending a message. The head nod "yes" or "no" are examples of emblems. The person performing the emblem takes responsibility for having communicated, for having said something with his face or body. He can be held accountable for his message. The person who sees an emblem considers it was performed for his benefit, to tell him something. Not so with many other actions that nevertheless can be informative. The viewer may infer nervousness when observing a high incidence of body manipulator actions (e.g., scratching, rubbing, picking, etc.), but he will not consider these movements were performed to tell that to him. The knowledge gained from such body manipulator actions is stolen; the message provided by the emblem is given.

Emblems are often used when we could speak but choose not to. For example an emblem may be employed when recognizing a friend seated across the aisle during a theatrical performance, or an emblem may be used to avoid the likelihood of being caught in an extended dialogue when hoping to pass quickly a colleague in a corridor. Of course emblems are also used when verbal discourse is just not possible; for example, because of noise (see Meisner & Philpotts [1975] study of emblems among sawmill workers).

Emblems occur also during conversation, by either speaker or listener. When speaking an emblem may replace a word entirely, or repeat the message spoken in a word, or comment or qualify what is being said in words. When emblems repeat what is said in words, they may precede, accompany, or follow the verbal statement of the message. Depending upon what is being said, how it is said, the speaker's stance toward what he is saying, there may or may not be latitude about where an emblem must be placed in relation to the word whose message it repeats.

Emblems are the most languagelike of the facial and body movement activities. They are symbolic. What a movement symbolizes is learned in a culturally variable fashion. The movements are employed specifically for the purpose of communicating. In all these respects emblems are like language and different from the other nonverbal activities we will describe next. Emblems also differ quite considerably from language. Words are typically employed during conversation in strings or sequences, governed by a syntax. Emblems are usually not employed during conversation in strings, but singly.

Many of the most important questions relevant to an understanding of emblems require developmental study. There has been only limited, usually incidental study of the ontogeny of emblems. Are the emblems first shown likely to be similar for all infants, due to common limitations in capacity, needs, and problems in communicating with a caretaker? What are the ages when various emblems become established in the repertoire? How are they acquired? Do they develop out of intention movements, or instrumental acts, or are they specifically taught? Are there emblems used by children but not by adults? Do children recognize emblems before they can utilize them to communicate to another?[3] When bilinguals switch language do they switch into a different emblem vocabulary? What about male/female differences in usage of emblems? In New Guinea we found that there were emblems referring to sexual activity, menstruation, and pregnancy utilized and known only by women.

This is only a partial list of the variety of questions that need to be investigated. Elsewhere (Ekman, 1976), I have discussed these issues in more detail, raised other questions, and reported findings on how emblems vary with psychopathology and with interpersonal deceit. Let us turn now to a second type of facial or body movement, a type of movement that in almost all respects is maximally different from emblems.

BODY MANIPULATORS

Body manipulators are movements in which one part of the body does something to another body part. Scratching the head, picking the nose, wringing the hands, licking the lips are examples. Also included would be the use of a prop in other than an instrumental act; for example, playing with a pencil, twisting a book of matches, using a paper clip to scratch an ear.

It is important that actions are not classified as body manipulators just because there is contact among body parts. In some cultures putting the forefinger to the temple is an emblem for thought and so it would be classified. If while speaking about how hard it was to look at something a person illustrated his speech by putting his hand in front of his eyes it would not be classified as a body manipulator, but as a kinetic illustrator (discussed later). The very same action if not illustrating what is being said would be called a body manipulator.

Another problem in defining the boundaries of body manipulators activities is what to do with instrumental actions. Taking off a shoe is not a body manipulator, but playing with a shoelace is.

Striking a match to light a cigarette is not, but fingering the match is a body manipulator. Our treatment of grooming activities as body manipulators may seem to contradict such a distinction. It might be argued that rearranging the hair which changes overall appearance should not be called a body manipulator, and only when the hand to hair movement results in no enhancement of appearance should it be classified as a body manipulator.

Our studies suggest that people are usually not aware of engaging in these body manipulator actions. If you ask the person to repeat what he has just done, he often won't remember. There is little reason to expect that these movements are ever used deliberately to transmit a message to another (other than by an actor or perhaps a psychopath). This does not mean that people do not gain information when observing these behaviors. We have found that observers characterize people who show many body manipulator actions as awkward, tense, and untrustworthy (correlations between .50 to .75; Ekman and Friesen, 1974; Ekman, Friesen and Scherer, 1976). As mentioned earlier, the observer of the body manipulator action does not believe the action was performed to provide a message. In contrast, just that presumption is made about the emblem.

Parents, of course, hold their child accountable for body manipulators, but it is for being uncouth, impolite, and the like, not for having said something with this type of activity. Despite such attempts to suppress these activities, they are more common in adults than one might expect. What we seem to learn is not to look when the other person cleans his ear, picks his nose, scratches his crotch, and so on. The disattending seems unwitting, but quite consistent. Rudeness seems to reside as much in watching someone engage in these bathroom behaviors, as in performing them.

Another difference between body manipulators and emblems is in regard to the specificity of what is signified. Emblems are movements that have quite precise meanings, well known to all members of a culture or subculture. The meaning of a body manipulator is more vague, imprecise, and not necessarily agreed upon. As mentioned earlier, the occurrence of body manipulators does influence how a person is perceived, but it is in global terms. Generally, they are interpreted as signs of discomfort, nervousness, and so on. Indeed, our studies have found that while the absolute frequency varies from individual to individual body manipulators do increase with discomfort.[4] Paradoxically body manipulators also increase when the person is quite relaxed and not engaging in any censorship over these actions. Certain types of body manipulators have specific meaning but not as precise as an emblem. We found that scratching occurred more often with patients judged by their psychiatrists to have problems with hostility. Eye covering occurred more often among patients judged to suffer from guilt (Ekman and Friesen, 1968, 1974).

EMOTIONAL EXPRESSIONS

Emotional expressions have received the most attention of all the nonverbal behaviors, and are the subject of continuing controversy. Most of the discussion has been of facial movements (facial expressions), with less attention to body movement.[5] At issue is whether there are universals in facial expression or whether that which is signified by each facial movement varies from culture to culture. There have been persuasive but contradictory reports from the two sides: those claiming universals (e.g., Darwin, 1872; Eibl-Eibesfeldt, 1972; Izard, 1971; Tomkins, 1961) and those claiming cultural differences (Birdwhistell, 1970; Klineberg, 1938; LaBarre, 1947; Leach, 1972; Mead, 1975). The difference in what has been found may have been owing in part to differences in what has been examined. Facial movements can be recruited into a variety of quite different activities, which may have little to do with emotion. For example, such a symbolic gesture as a wink can be made with the face; or a brow movement can be made to punctuate speech.

The contradictory observations of the relativists and universalists can be resolved, in part, if we presume that the relativists were describing the cultural variations in the nonemotional facial activities and not distinguishing these from the universals in emotional expression. Conversely, the universalists may have focused on the emotional expressions to the exclusion of recognizing cultural variations in other facial actions unrelated to emotion.

Avoiding such confusions not only requires a conceptualization that allows for a number of differently organized facial activities but also much more careful description of facial movement itself. The facial musculature allows for an extraordinary number of visibly and anatomically different movements which may on first impression seem similar to the untutored eye. Terms like frown, smile, play-face, and even brow-raise are much too gross. Each could cover dozens of different behaviors that may or may not have the same function. Such imprecise descriptions increase the likelihood that two observers would needlessly argue because their descriptive language does not reveal that they are each talking about a different facial action.

The Facial Action Coding System that Friesen and I have devised to describe anatomically based facial movement offers more precision and distinctions than may actually be needed, so that empirical results can determine which visible distinctions should be disregarded. The Facial Action Coding System allows description of both the configuration (the "expression") and the timing of facial movement. Even when exactly the same muscles were to be involved in two facial actions, they may differ in the onset of movement, in the duration at apex, and in the time it takes to disappear.

The contradictory reports on facial expression have not just been due to a difference in focus, abetted by reliance on imprecise descriptions of the face. It reflects a fundamental difference in interests. One side has been primarily interested in evolutionary explanations, in the biological contributions to behavior. While cultural influence is acknowledged, it is seen as an overlay, and only lip-service is paid. The other side has been interested in the power of culture in determining social behavior. It borrows from a linguistic model and emphasizes what is different in each culture. While biological contributions were acknowledged, biology was seen as only providing the equipment that was shaped by culture.

The core of the confusion about facial expression is probably the failure by both sides to specify what they have meant by emotion.[6] Most shied away from describing internal processes or even distinguishing emotional from nonemotional behavior or situations. Each side took for granted that others knew what they meant by emotion. Such vagueness concealed oversimplified models about the biological and social influences on emotional behavior. It allowed each side to gather evidence that failed to change the other side's view or force revision or expansion of their theoretical model. Instead, contradictory evidence has fueled the argument, which has spilled over into false disputes about what counts as evidence and what credentials are required to investigate.[7]

To resolve the dispute, or at least clarify its basis, I will go out on a limb, describing different aspects of the phenomenon we term *emotion*. What follows is not a theory of emotion, but only a discussion of those matters that need to be considered to deal with the contradictory evidence and to show where both relativists and universalists have been right, and wrong, in their claims. Many issues central to a theory of emotion are not discussed here but left for presentation elsewhere (Ekman and Friesen, in prep. a).

A NEUROCULTURAL ACCOUNT OF EMOTION[8]

The term *neurocultural* emphasized our interest in both biological and social determinants of emotion. I will start with a characterization of emotional responses, both observable and nonobservable responses. This characterization will require that I hypothesize internal mechanisms—an *affect program* that directs emotional responses, and an *appraisal system* that determines when the affect program becomes operative. *Elicitors* will be described as those events that are appraised quickly as the occasion for one or another emotion. *Display rules* for managing the appearance of the face in various social contexts, and efforts to *cope* with the source of emotion will also be described. This account will allow *one* answer to the question of what is emotion, and how we know when emotion is occurring. It will provide the basis for discussing pitfalls in cross-cultural research on emotion, for integrating seemingly contradictory findings, and for describing the many ways emotional expressions vary with culture.

This account of emotion, however, risks a good deal. It is too long, perhaps, for this paper, and certainly too short to be complete. It deals with nonobservables reaching beyond data to explanatory mechanisms that may help in understanding the data. It may seem wrong, misguided, mechanistic, full of jargon, and the like. Nevertheless, it should provide the terms and raise the issues for exposing the *variety* of points for possible disagreement which have too long laid hidden.

Emotional Responses are brief, often quick, complex, organized, and difficult to control. Let us consider each of these characteristics. Emotions can be very brief. It is not uncommon to be angry or afraid or happy for only a few seconds. Surprise is always brief, while the other emotions vary in duration depending upon the circumstances. If an emotion lasts for many hours, or days, the language of everyday life would utilize mood terms rather than those of an emotion. The person is said to be irritable or hostile, not just angry; blue, not just sad, and so on. A full discussion of the difference between mood and emotion would take us far afield, yet there is probably some merit in the notion that typically emotions have fairly brief durations, shorter than moods, attitudes, traits, or many beliefs or values.[9]

Quickness refers just to the onset of an emotion. Emotions can become aroused in a fraction of a second. Not that they always must be aroused so quickly, but as will become apparent later, the potential for speed in onset time, for a very quick response, is important in explaining and distinguishing emotional from other kinds of behavior.

Emotion is complex, entailing a number of different response systems. Only some of them can be directly observed. There are skeletal muscle responses such as flinching, thrusting forward, turning away, overall relaxation, and others. Facial responses include the expressions I will describe in detail later, as well as vascular and muscle tonus changes. Vocal responses include sounds such as screams or groans, as well as a tensing of the vocal apparatus, with consequent changes in voice quality. These are all likely to be very quick, initial responses. Somewhat longer and more elaborated are the coping behaviors directed at whatever has set off the emotion. Included would be fighting, fleeing, denying, apologizing, and so on. Specific changes in the autonomic and central nervous system are also involved, in ways I will not detail here.

The subjective experience of the emotion, usually neglected by modern psychology, is another important emotion response system. The subjective experience includes—but may not be limited to —sensations that are the result of feedback from changes occurring in the already named response systems. Also subsumed are memories, images, and expectations associated with one or another emotion, and with the very specific circumstances of the occasion for an emotion. One important characteristic of the subjective experience of emotion is the awareness that the changes occurring are not easy to control consciously. I will return to this point later.

The various response systems mentioned are organized in two ways. The activity in each response system is interrelated rather than independent. *And* the changes occurring within each (or most) response systems are distinctive for one as compared with another emotion. In a preliminary study we (Ekman, Malmstrom and Friesen, 1971) found different patterns of heart rate acceleration and deceleration to occur simultaneously with different patterns of facial movement. This study showed organization within each response system and in the interrelationship between response systems. Admittedly, there is little evidence one way or another for such interrelationships among all the response systems we propose. And the evidence for distinctive patterns for each emotion is presently limited to facial expression.

Affect Program. For there to be such complexity and organization in various response systems, there must be some central direction. The term *affect program* refers to a mechanism that stores the patterns for these complex organized responses, and which when set off directs their occurrence. I am not concerned with where in the brain this program is located. (Lower areas must be involved, but I do not presume either a single location or involvement of only one neural mechanism.) Instead, I will describe what is assumed about how such an affect program must operate.

The organization of response systems dictated by the affect program has a genetic basis but is influenced also by experience. The skeletal, facial, vocal, autonomic, and central nervous system changes that occur initially and quickly for one or another emotion, we presume to be in largest part given, not acquired. For example, habits would be unlikely to determine just which pattern of impulses are transmitted to the facial nerve, although we will later describe how habits, what we term display rules, develop to interfere with the operation of these responses dictated by the affect program. Experience of course plays an important role. The emotional response systems change with growth, disease, injury, and the like. They are not constant through life.

Through experience, with sufficient time and learning, habits become established for how to cope with each emotion. I do not believe that such coping behaviors are part of the given affect program. These habitual ways of coping may become so well learned that they operate automatically and quickly in conjunction with specific emotions. Given our lack of knowledge about the operation of the central nervous system, it matters little whether I say that those habitual ways of coping become governed by the affect program, or that they operate automatically in conjunction with it. Memories, images, expectations associated with one or another emotion are, like coping, not given but acquired, and can similarily become habitual, automatically involved when the affect program is set off.

Thus, I postulate that when the affect program is set off, a number of other things happen in addition to the responses immediately governed by the program. Memories, images, and expectations associated with the emotion and the circumstance come into play. Coping behaviors associated with the emotion begin, and habits directed at managing emotional behavior may become operative. All these related changes can occur automatically with great speed, rather than deliberately.

Management of the responses governed by the affect program is usually not easy and not always entirely successful. Some of the responses under the command of the affect program begin to change in fractions of a second. Deliberate or habitual interference is more successful with some of the emotional responses governed by the affect program than with others. For example, it is far easier to inhibit or squelch a facial movement than to change respiration or heart rate. The difficulty experienced when trying to interfere with the operation of the affect program, the speed of its operation, its capability to initiate responses that are hard to halt voluntarily is what is meant by the out-of-control quality to the subjective experiences of some emotions.

I have been working backward in time. I started with a description of the brevity, complexity, and organization of emotional responses. Then I described an affect program that directs those responses. Now I must take a further step back, to consider what happens to call the affect program into operation. There must be an appraiser mechanism that selectively attends to those stimuli (external or internal) which are the occasion for activating the affect program. Otherwise the complex organized emotional responses directed by the affect program would occur randomly. Since the interval between stimulus and emotional response is sometimes extraordinarily short, the appraisal mechanism must be capable of operating with great speed. Often the appraisal is not only quick but it happens without awareness, so I must postulate that the appraisal mechanism is able to operate automatically.

Automatic appraisal mechanism. It must be constructed so that it quickly attends to some stimuli, determining not only that they pertain to emotion but to which emotion, and then activating the appropriate part of the affect program. The automatic appraisal may not only set off the affect program and the responses it directs but also may initiate the processes that evoke the memories, images, expectations, coping behaviors, and display rules relevant to the emotion.

Appraisal is not always automatic. Sometimes the evaluation of what is happening is slow, deliberate, and conscious. With such a more ponderous appraisal there may be some autonomic arousal, but perhaps not of a kind that is differentiated. The person could be said to be aroused or alerted but no specific emotion is operative. Cognition plays the important role in determining what will transpire. During such ponderous appraisal the evaluation may match the selective filters of the automatic appraiser, and the affect program may be set off. It need not be, however; the experience may be diffuse rather than specific to one emotion. I suspect that if the emotion is not specific, if the affect program is never involved, there are limits to how intense the more general emotion arousal state may become.

When the automatic appraiser responds to a stimulus, sets off the affect program that directs a particular complex, organized set of emotional responses, appraisal does not necessarily stop. The event may continue to unfold, new stimuli may be emitted which again are subject to automatic appraisal → affect program → emotional responses. The same emotion may be repeatedly triggered, or a number of different emotions may be triggered sequentially or simultaneously. If the event does not continue to unfold, as in a near miss car accident, the person will usually realize and consider what has happened. He may realize there was no "need" to have become emotional and struggle to stop the operation of the affect program. Or, the realization of having had an emotional response may itself become the occasion for another emotional response. For example, responding to a criticism immediately and automatically with anger once realized may be the elicitor for shame or disgust with oneself. Or, the situation may become ambiguous and the ponderous appraisal system may work in trying to figure out what is happening and going to happen next.

Elicitors. One farther step backward leads to the elicitors of emotion, what characterizes the events appraised as emotional. There is variation in the particulars of what elicits a given emotion, yet there are also common features in what are identified as elicitors for an emotion. We use the term *elicitor* to refer only to those stimuli that are identified by the automatic appraiser as specific for one or another emotion. Elicitors call forth emotion quickly, but what occurs is not a reflex arc. The connection between specific stimulus and response is not given, and it is not fixed. Probably there is no emotion for which there is a universal elicitor, uniform in its specific details, which always calls forth the same uninterruptible set of emotional responses.[10] Certainly there is no empirical evidence of such. One possibility would be that the sight of a missile traveling directly toward the eye at a given speed would be automatically appraised so as to set off the fear affect program. Even here interference or interruption of the fear response is probably possible. At best there would be only few if any such innately wired elicitors.

Cultural anthropology is replete with accounts of great variety in the specifics of what elicits one or another emotion. Most of the specific elicitors for emotion are variable, learned through different experiences. If you see a disgust facial expression (nose wrinkled, upper lips raised, etc.) you cannot know what made the person disgusted; it depends on his personal experiences. What is disgusting varies within as well as between cultures. Yet you could know something about the other responses likely to occur since you can see from his face that he is disgusted. For example, he is more likely to say something sounding like "uuchk" than "mmh," more likely to move backward or away than to approach, more likely to describe his experience using gustatory images than explosive ones.

While the specific elicitors for emotion vary with individual experience, there is also some commonality apparent in the general outline of what elicits, through automatic appraisal → affect program, the emotions. Disgust elicitors share the characteristic of being noxious rather than painful; and, in all cultures taste stimuli are among the elicitors of disgust. Surprise depends upon the details of what would be unexpected for a particular person in a particular situation, yet surprise elicitors share the characteristics of being unexpected, novel and usually sudden rather than gradual. People learn how to recognize impending harm, to avoid danger. While the specific stimuli so identified as potentially harmful will vary, fear elicitors share the characteristic of portending harm or pain. One of the common characteristics of some of the elicitors of happiness is release from accumulated pressure, tension, discomfort, and the like. Loss of something to which one is intimately attached might be a common characteristic of sadness elicitors. Interference with ongoing activity might be characteristic of some anger elicitors.

These are but tentative examples. My point is that the elicitors for each emotion share some characteristics. I propose that the automatic appraiser is sensitive to these general characteristics. With experience such sensitivity may become sharpened and more precise.

To point to similarities in what elicits surprise, fear, and the like, does not mean that those characteristics will be found for every elicitor for every emotion, only that some will be similar. Through repeated experience specific elicitors become identified by the automatic appraiser as relevant to one or another emotion. We expect that many but not all of these specific elicitors will share common characteristics.

Recall that I have been describing as elicitors only those stimuli that are identified by the automatic appraiser. There are many other more complex and variable stimulus situations which are not so identified but instead become subject to the more ponderous appraisal process. Perhaps it is just because they do not obviously share one of the common elicitor characteristics (or because they combine elements of too many elicitors) that such stimulus configurations are subject to ponderous rather than automatic appraisal.

What is emotion? It certainly is not any one of the elements I have described: response systems, appraiser, program, or elicitors. Nor is emotion just the combination. Instead emotion refers to the process whereby an elicitor is appraised automatically or in a ponderous fashion, an affect program may or may not be set off, organized responses may occur, albeit more or less managed by attempts to control emotional behavior. What gives an emotion its particular flavor, is the particulars of the elicitor, the appraisal, the part of the affect program set off, and those parts of the response systems which go unmanaged or managed.

Is there a sine qua non for emotion? I disagree with past theorists who would say it is visceral reactions, or cognitive appraisal, or facial responses. My answer that there must be an appraiser, a program, and response systems more or less capable of action for emotion to occur, is only to say that the organism is alive. If the affect program is not set off, if the appraisal is only of the ponderous not of the automatic kind, it is still emotion but not the same as when those things do happen. If the anger part of the affect program is set off, for example, but there is interference with the activity of the facial muscles, it is still anger, but not the same anger as when facial activity is not so squelched.

Looking from the outside, without access to know what is occurring in the central nervous system, how can an observer tell when emotion is present? The estimate that emotion is present is more likely to be correct when:

—The response system changes are complex, when it is not just a facial, or skeletal, or vocal, or autonomic, or coping response, but a combination;

—the changes are organized, in the sense of being interrelated and distinctive for one or a combination of emotions;

—the changes happen quickly;

—some of the response system changes are ones common to all people;

—some of the responses are not unique to Homo sapiens.

This is *not* the only time emotion occurs, but when an observer's estimate is *most* likely to be safe.

I will now explain more about display rules and coping behaviors, to provide the background necessary for then discussing the pitfalls in cross-cultural observations of emotional expression.

Display Rules. When an elicitor is automatically appraised, the affect program is set off, and organized complex emotional responses begin, interference is still possible. The emotional responses may be interrupted, diminished, amplified, or masked with the appearance of another emotion. Some emotional response systems may be more difficult to manage than others (e.g., heart rate more than facial movement), but people often try to control their emotional behavior.

We coined the phrase *display rule* to refer to the conventions, norms, and habits that develop regarding the management of emotional responses.[11] A display rule specifies who can show what emotion to whom, when. These rules are often learned so well that they typically operate automatically, noticeable only in the breach. For example, the prohibition against showing anger, or the rule to substitute sadness for anger, is learned so well by some middle-class American girls, that later, if liberated, it requires some struggle to "get their anger out." Other display rules are learned more by example, by observing what others do or following implicit instructions of those who manage events when emotion is made the occasion for public ceremony. The performance for such display rules may not be as good, but errors are usually overlooked. An example of this type of display rule is that at beauty contests a winner may cry but not the losers. At funerals, one can note almost a "pecking order" of grief expressions based on the rights to mourn. A man's secretary cannot look sadder than his wife unless she intends to state something quite different about the true nature of their relationship.

There are also *personal display rules,* habits learned about managing emotional expression which do not reflect a cultural norm, but more individualized experience. The extent to which one follows a cultural display rule may depend upon the extent to which it conflicts with a personal display rule. For example, a woman may have the personal display rule never to show her feelings of distress, which depending upon her culture, could put her in conflict in the mourning situation if just such expressions are required by the widow.

The management of emotional responses may occur also by deliberate choice of the moment, for a particular advantage, rather than as part of a long standing personal or cultural display rule. Then the person is more aware of what he does and is likely to be rather slow and inept.

Note that although the origin differs—cultural or personal display rules or deliberate choice of the moment—management of emotional expression may be either the product of well-learned habit or a more deliberate process. This has implications for what we have termed "leakage" (Ekman and Friesen, 1969b), when the emotional responses escape attempts to conceal them. When the management is deliberate (either because of choice of the moment or when following cultural rules never practiced so as to become habitual), it is likely that some of the emotional response systems governed by the affect program may be noticeable at least briefly, unless the person was alerted ahead of time and prepared himself. When the management is habitual due to a culturally shared or personal display rule, the management efforts may be set into operation just about as quickly as the emotional responses dictated by the affect program. Better concealment should occur.

Some emotional responses may be more subject to modification and disguise than others. Furthermore, display rules, personal or cultural, may focus more upon one response system than another. We (Ekman and Friesen, 1969b, 1974) have suggested that there is usually more management of words spoken than of voice, more of voice than facial movement, more of facial movement than body movement. We attribute such differences in what is managed to differences in the amount of attention that is typically paid by others to what a person does. While we have some evidence to support our hypothesis that there is more leakage in body movement than in either words or facial movement, it is limited to middle-class Americans. There are individual variations and there may be cultural differences in which emotional responses are most subject to management attempts. Even though facial expressions are managed, mistakes are made, and leakage may be detected (Ekman and Friesen, 1975, chap. 11).

Coping. This term refers to attempts to deal with the emotion felt and its source; to increase, diminish, or sustain what is occurring. Coping includes various cognitive activities as well as such organized behaviors as attacking or fleeing. As the system where learning contributes the most, coping is the most elaborated of the emotional response systems.

Compare with coping the initial skeletal muscle response directed by the affect program when an anger elicitor has been identified by the automatic appraiser. The immediate skeletal muscle response might be a slight movement forward. Coping could vary—attack, flight, denial, appeasement, and so on. We discover how to cope with our emotions, what is likely to be successful, proper, or improper. When angry, our likelihood of fighting or scratching our face, depends upon what we have learned about dealing with the particular kind of anger elicitor.

Once coping techniques have been acquired, they can become so well learned that they operate automatically and are called forth when the affect program is set off. They are notoriously difficult to change. Coping also occurs when ponderous appraisal is the manager. Then, more alternatives and flexibility in coping may be possible.

Biology may provide some predispositions affecting the likelihood of one versus another type of coping behavior being developed for an emotion. For example, the skeletal muscle response for anger suggests that attack may become more frequent for coping with anger than flight. Yet, this predisposition is relatively fragile. Experience can overcome such predispositions and institute diametrically opposite coping. Coping involves a wide range of elaborated activities, and biology at best gives only a tap in a direction. Culturally and individually variable learning is the overwhelming contributor to coping.

Pitfalls in Cross-Cultural Research on Facial Expressions. Before turning to describe facial expression let me describe some pitfalls that await the observer of facial expression who does not consider variations in elicitors, display rules, and coping. Suppose different facial expressions are observed at funerals in two different cultures (e.g., Labarre). In one culture let us say, the mouth corners are down and the inner corners of the brow are drawn up and together, while in the other culture the lip corners are pulled up obliquely, causing crowsfeet to appear at the side of the eyes. To conclude that this proves facial expression is culture-specific, would be to ignore the elicitor pitfall. Funerals are not necessarily a universal elicitor of grief, sadness, distress, or any such feeling. If it is not an elicitor for such an emotion in two cultures, then the observation of different facial actions does not prove cultural determination of the emotional expression. Paradoxically, it was those who were wedded to a culturally relativistic viewpoint who sought evidence that culture was the sole determinent of facial expression, who were the most "biological" in assuming that the elicitor for an emotion was standard across the cultures compared. Many of the observations of differences in facial expression in the same situation across cultures are ambiguous because there was no independent evidence that the situation evoked the same emotion in each culture.

Suppose there was. Suppose it was known that the death of a child was an elicitor for sadness in each culture. Would the observation of different facial expressions by the mourners in two cultures prove that facial expressions are only arbitrarily associated with emotion? Only if we ignore the display rule pitfall, by failing to recognize that the cultures could differ in their norms about masking facial expressions of emotion. The different facial behaviors observed might not mean that the down-cornered mouth is associated with sadness in one culture while upturned mouth is associated with sadness in another, but only that one culture has the display rule to cover sadness with a happy mask at a funeral. Again, it was those who viewed facial expression as an arbitrary set of movements whose relationship to emotion was solely determined by culture, who treated the facial expressions as if they were reflexes, not capable of management by habit or choice.

In a similar fashion cultural variations in coping can lead to another pitfall. The association of the same facial response with different coping activities does not mean ipso facto that the facial expression is arbitrary, solely determined by culture.

The elicitor, display rule, and coping pitfalls admittedly make it more difficult to obtain conclusive evidence to prove the arbitrary nature of facial expression of emotion. It would be necessary to verify by some means independent of the face that the situation compared in two cultures elicited the same emotion, that in neither culture was there a display rule to disguise the emotional expression, and that the emotion was associated with the same coping behavior. Only then would evidence of quite different facial expressions unambiguously suggest that the emotion signified by a facial movement is totally arbitrary, different from culture to culture. No such evidence exists, but just the opposite. In an experiment I will report shortly, the universal facial expressions first occurred and then disappeared when culturally different display rules came into operation, disguising facial expression more in Japan than in the United States.

Facial Expressions. In contrast to coping, there is a major biological contribution to facial expressions of emotion. Biology has shaped the affect program, determining which facial movements are likely to occur with one or another of the emotions, and perhaps also the timing of those movements. The particular combination of facial movements and the corresponding changes in visual appearance are not arbitrarily associated with each emotion but, for at least some emotions, are the same for all people. Shortly I will review the evidence for that assertion. First, let us consider just why it might be that one set of muscle actions rather than another occur with a particular emotion. Why is it that the lip corners go up not down with happiness, that the brows lift not lower with surprise, and so forth?

The biological contribution may be extensive, involving an innate association between muscle movements and emotion, or more modestly biology may only predispose the organism to acquire these associations through common learning experiences. Species constant learning as the explanation for universals in emotional expression was suggested by Allport (1924). Let us consider the example of the raised brow (inner and outer strands of the *frontalis* muscle) in surprise. All that biology may contribute is how the face is constructed. Raising the brows does increase perception of the top part of the visual field. Infants encounter unexpected events in which they would raise their brow to see what is happening above them. (One could even argue that the unexpected is more likely to be above than below the infant.) Over time, perhaps abetted by the signal value of the movement, brow raising and surprise would become associated. In the strictest version of this explanation the infant would have to learn, presumably by trial and error, that brow raising increases his visual field. Alternatively, that might be given, and what he learns is to make this movement when trying to see what has unexpectedly happened. To grant even more to biology, the infant could be born equipped to raise his brows when visually scanning unexpected sudden *visual* events. What he needs to learn is to generalize this response to *any* unexpected event, regardless of whether it is visual. The more extreme innate explanation would be that as a consequence of evolutionary processes, humans are constructed so that brow raising is built into the affect program for elicitors automatically appraised as pertaining to surprise.

These explanations differ in a number of ways: in how much emphasis they place on ontogeny as compared to phylogeny; on whether current adaptive function is relevant; and whether signal value is implicated in development. I have not described completely any one explanation, nor all the explanations that are possible. My purpose is to show that there is more than one way in which biology could contribute to facial expression. In all likelihood, more than one such explanation is relevant to account for the different universal facial expressions. It is even possible to design studies that could help choose among these explanations for particular emotions, for example, studies of early development in blind and sighted infants.[12]

Quite apart from which way biology contributes, the evidence I will now describe of a universal association between emotion and particular facial expressions can only be explained by acknowledging a major substantial biological basis to facial expression of emotion.

Evidence of universals in facial expression. One type of evidence is based on studies in which people in different cultures were shown faces and were asked to interpret the emotion shown in each face. If what a facial expression signifies is totally arbitrary, variable from culture to culture, then the interpretations so obtained should also be variable. This type of study has been carried out by more than a half dozen investigators, the majority of whom were trying to prove that facial expression is culture specific. In thirteen different countries, where nine languages were used, the same emotional interpretation was obtained for the emotional expressions (see reviews of these studies in Ekman, Friesen and Ellsworth, 1972, chap. 19; Ekman, 1973, chap. 4).

One problem with this evidence is that all the people who interpreted the facial expressions were members of literate cultures subject to mass media influences. It was possible to argue that these people might have totally different facial expressions but had learned how to interpret one another's unique expressions. Or, they have different expressions but had all learned to recognize the stereotyped expressions shown in the theater. or, they have the same facial expression because they had all learned their facial expressions from cinema, television, and magazines.

To meet this criticism we carried out studies with more visually isolated people in the South Fore of New Guinea (Ekman, Sorenson and Friesen, 1969; Ekman and Friesen, 1971). Studying only those who had not seen any mass media and few outsiders, we found that they interpreted faces as showing the same emotions as did the people from the literate cultures. The one exception was that fear and surprise faces were not distinguished from each other, although they were each distinguished from anger, sadness, happiness, or disgust. Another type of study was conducted with the

South Fore in which members of this culture were asked to show on their own face how they would look if they felt one or another emotion. The expressions they showed were once again the common universal expressions, with the exception of surprise and fear which showed elements of both emotions. We studied spontaneous facial expressions in Japan because the popular notion of the inscrutability of the Oriental. We hoped to demonstrate that this was due to display rules about masking negative affect in the presence of authorities. Another reason for choosing Japan was that Lazarus et al. (1966) had previously determined through psychophysiological measurement that certain stress films had a similar impact on the Japanese as they did on Americans. Thus, we could avoid the elicitor pitfall by utilizing an elicitor known to produce some similar effects in two cultures. We avoided the display rule pitfall by videotaping when the subjects thought they were completely alone and unobserved.

The identical experiment was performed at Waseda University in Tokyo and the University of California in Berkeley.[13] Subjects came into a laboratory and watched both a travelog and stress-inducing films while measurements were taken of their skin resistance and heart rate. The videotapes taken with a hidden camera unknown to the subjects were later measured by persons not knowing which film was seen when the facial expressions occurred. We found a better than .90 correlation in the particular facial movements shown by the Japanese and by the Americans. Virtually the same repertoire of facial movements occurred at the same points in time. We believe this is definitive evidence that facial expressions of emotion are not limited to simulations, but do occur spontaneously as well.

Later in this same experiment, we brought a research assistant into the room, garbed in white coat, to sit with the subject while he watched a stress film. Now we expected that display rules for managing facial expression in the presence of an authority figure should be operative, more so in Japan than in the United States. Measurement showed that the facial movements were no longer the same. The Japanese looked more polite, showed more smiling than did the Americans. Examining these videotapes in slow motion it was possible to observe sometimes the actual sequencing in which one movement (a smile for example) would be superimposed over another muscle action (such as a nose wrinkle, or lower lip depressor).

If only the latter part of the experiment had been performed, if we had studied Japanese only when they knew we were doing so (likely conditions in many anthropological studies) and we did not do micromeasurement to look for the possibility of masking, we would have been misled. Instead, guided by our theoretical formulation about emotion we were able to arrange an experiment to show the biological basis of facial expression and how cultural influences modify expression. When alone, Japanese and Americans showed virtually the same facial expressions. When in public, due presumably to display rules, Japanese more than Americans controlled and masked negative expressions. Taking the evidence I have summarized, together with the observations of Eibl-Eibesfeldt (1972), studies of blind infants and children, expressions in young infants, and work tracing facial expressions phylogenetically, we can conclude there is *some* universal association between emotion and facial movements.

The evidence is consistent with our neurocultural account of emotion outlined earlier, although it does not establish all that was proposed. Some such explanation, positing both biological and social factors in emotional expression, is required to deal with the evidence. Now let me delimit the universality of facial expression by describing, on the basis of our theory, some of the ways in which culture moulds the biologically based facial expressions of emotion.

CULTURAL INFLUENCES ON FACIAL EXPRESSION

Most of the cross-cultural evidence supporting universality was about expressions that were manifest across the entire face. The faces were instances in which muscular action produced a distinctive appearance in the forehead, eyelid, and mouth areas. This need not always happen. Often only part of a total expression may occur, muscle groups acting in only one part of the face with the rest of the face not active. Friesen and I (Ekman and Friesen, 1975, chap. 11) have hypothesized that such *partial* facial expressions may occur when a person attempts to control or manage facial appearance. Such attempts to control can be the product of choice of the moment, long established personal display rules, or cultural display rules. As discussed earlier, display rules should vary across cultures.

Another reason for partial facial expressions of emotion would be learning which has emphasized one part of an expression more than another. Families may pay attention to and otherwise reinforce one part of a facial expression of emotion more than another. The child may learn that one part of the facial signal brings forth more response from others, and he may see that part of the expression more often on the faces of those around him. Based on such experiences one or another part of the biologically based total facial expression could become more prominent in the person's repertoire. There is little reason to expect uniformity across cultures in these experiences.

Still a third reason for partial facial expressions is the possibility that when emotion is felt only slightly it may register in only some muscle groups rather than across the entire face. There is no evidence as yet whether this is so. If it is, we do not know whether slight versions of an emotion tend to recruit consistently the same muscles. For example, in slight fear would it be the *frontalis* and *corrugator* affecting the brow, or the *risorius* and *platysma* affecting the cheek and mouth, or the upper eyelid levator, which would most likely act? Are there consistencies for a given person across such slight fear experiences, across persons within a social grouping across groupings within a culture?[14]

Cultural differences in facial expressions of emotion may also be apparent in the most common *blends* of emotion. A blend is a compound facial expression in which the muscular actions for two or more emotions combine in a single facial expression. Blends sometimes occur because the elicitor calls forth more than one emotion. For example, a surprising event may be also frightening, or the surprising event may be pleasing. Blends also happen because of habits that associate one emotion with another. One such habit is affect-about-affect; for example, one person may always feel disgusted with himself when he feels anger, another may habitually feel afraid of his own anger. Another type of habit relating affects is mixture of two feelings toward a class of elicitors; for example, one person may habitually feel disgusted by what makes him angry, another may habitually feel afraid of whatever makes him angry. Owing to either type of habit a single elicitor of anger may result in one person showing an anger/disgust blend, while another shows an anger/fear blend. These habits associating two emotions may become established through individually idiosyncratic learning, or through learning experiences common among some social group.

Cultural variations in facial expressions manifest in blends could be the result of differences in the likelihood of encountering elicitors which call for a particular blend; or, variations in experiences leading to habits associating one emotion with another. Even if the same blend is shown in two or more cultures, it may not always have its own linguistic label. For example, facial expressions showing blends of happiness/anger or happiness/disgust, might occur, but not every culture need have a single word label for them, such as "smug." We are planning to test some of these hypotheses about cultural differences in partial and blend expressions. For now they rest only upon casual observation and logic.

The evidence of universality in emotional expression is limited to the emotions of happiness, surprise, fear, anger, disgust, and sadness. We expect that there are also universal facial expressions for interest and, perhaps, shame. There may be other emotions for which there is also a universal facial expression, but probably not many. Presumably, there are emotions for which there is no specific facial expression consistent within a culture; or for which there is a consistent expression in one culture but not in another. Take the example of contempt. We suspect that the expression for this emotion will be different in some cultures. In still other cultures there will be no consistent expression at all. There may not even be a verbal label in every culture with the denotation and connotations of contempt. It is reasonable to presume that contempt, and any other emotions for which there is no universal distinctive facial expression, is not the product of the automatic appraisal → affect program process outlined earlier. Contempt might still be related to certain types of stimuli, but appraised more slowly, with a less direct linkage with simultaneous changes in other emotion response systems. Alternatively, it is possible that an emotion without any distinctive facial emotional response may still be part of the automatic appraisal → affect program system. There is no data to provide a basis for choosing between these possibilities.

Let us return to those emotions for which there is evidence of a universal expression—happiness, surprise, fear, anger, disgust, and sadness. Just because there is one (or more) universal facial expression for each of those emotions does not prevent additional culture specific facial expressions for each of these emotions. For example, in addition to a universal facial expression of fear, there might be additional facial expressions for fear common in one culture but not apparent in another. Acquired culture specific facial expressions for an emotion might receive sufficient attention in a particular culture to become more frequent than the universal expression for that emotion. Theoretically, the culture specific expression for an emotion should not be as quick to occur as the biologically based expressions.

All the sources of cultural variations in facial expression so far mentioned have been about the *morphology* of facial expression, not the *timing*. So little is known about the timing of facial expression that it is difficult to speculate about whether there would be much variation across persons within a culture or between cultures. Is there a fixed *onset* time for the actions involved in any of the universal facial expressions to reach the point of maximum muscular action (*apex*)? Or, does onset vary with the particulars of the elicitor, cognitive appraisal, and the like? What about the duration of the apex? Is there any fixed minimal length of time the action must remain on the face before decaying (*Offset*)? Does apex duration vary from emotion to emotion, or is it solely a function of the particular elicitor, appraisal, and so on? Is offset time fixed, or does it too reflect differences in circumstance, display rules, and so forth? The timing of facial expressions of emotion has not been investigated within a given culture (with the exception of the startle, see footnote 9), let alone across cultures.

Another aspect of timing has to do with the sequence of muscular actions during onset or offset. Take the example of raising the brows (*frontalis*), drawing them together (*corrugator*), and raising of the upper eyelid (*levator palpebralis superioris*) in a partial fear expression. Does *frontalis* always start before *corrugator* or vice versa? Or does it depend upon the person, the specifics of the elicitor, or other? We suspect that there is probably some biological contribution to timing, both to onset, minimal apex, offset, and to sequencing, but that as with morphology the biological contribution is modifiable by experience. It is only now that precise methods for measuring facial movement have been developed these questions about timing can begin to be examined.

Having taken some time to explain a number of different ways in which culture and various experiential factors could shape facial expressions, let me say that I don't think there is complete plasticity. For example it would be unlikely for the *zygomatic* muscle (involved in the smile) to become a culture specific expression for sadness. It seems unlikely that experience will be organized and maintained directly in opposition to biological predisposition. However, there is ample room for enormous cultural difference in emotional expression because of:

—variations in the specifics of the elicitors, display rules and coping;

—variations in partial or blend expressions;

—additional nonuniversal expressions for emotions for which there is also a universal expression;

—some emotions having no universal expression but only culture specific, if any, consistent facial expression;

—variations in timing (onset, apex, and offset, as well as sequencing), of facial actions.

There is also ample need for research to explore and document how these cultural differences might develop.

CONCLUSION

Hinde (1972) has suggested that we should expect similarities among cultures in signals that concern the personal or the emotional, and we should expect differences in movements that take the place of words, which symbolize aspects of culture or which depend on languages. His interpretation agrees with our view that nonverbal communication is not a unitary phenomenon, but a term used to cover a number of different phenomena, activities that differ in origin, usage, coding, and in the relative contribution of biological and social factors.

Discussion of the interplay of biological and social factors in facial expression makes apparent that these are not single forces operative by but one mechanism. A variety of nonexclusive processes may be at work. It is to all these complexities that we should attend.

NOTES

1. The preparation of this report was supported in part by a grant from NIMH, MH 11976, and from the Harry F. Guggenheim Foundation. The research described was supported by those grants and by grants from ARPA, AF-AFOSR-1229 and by a Career Development Award and Research Scientist Award MH 6092. Wallace V. Friesen has collaborated on all the research and in the development of the theoretical framework.

2. There are problems with all the terms used to refer to the study of facial and body movement:

Nonverbal behavior: that implies that what distinguishes the phenomenon is that it isn't words, and that is not necessarily what motivates much of the interest or theory; further, it is strange to use a term that defines a phenomenon by what it is not.

Motor behavior: that implies an interest in skills.

Kinesics: that is identified with but one theoretical and methodological viewpoint (Birdwhistell, 1971).

Expressive behavior: that term implies the action is a manifestation of some internal affective state or personality characteristic, which is probably appropriate for only some facial or body movements.

Visually observed behavior: awkward and odd to define a range of phenomena by how they are sensed by the observer.

See discussion of terminology by Sebeok (in press) and Ekman (in press).

3. Kumin and Lazar (1974) began work on the decoding of emblems, but they only attempted to show that more emblems are decoded at later than earlier ages.

4. Although using different terms to describe the activity a number of other investigators have also found that body manipulators are related to negative affect (Freedman and Hoffman, 1967; Knapp, Hart and Dennis, 1974; Mahl, 1968; Mehrabian, 1971; Rosenfeld, 1966).

5. We agree with Hinde's (1974) criticism of our earlier formulation that restricted emotional expressions to the face. In our current formulation we have also included vocal changes and body movement among emotional expressions.

6. Tomkins's theory of *Affect, Imagery and Consciousness* (1962, 1963), is a notable exception. Paradoxically, the very complexity and length of his theory may have discouraged others from any such attempt.

7. Margaret Mead (1975), in reviewing a book I edited, entitled *Darwin and Facial Expression* (Ekman, 1973), raised a number of such pseudo-issues. The argument about universality of facial expression of emotion is *not* between:

—anthropologists and psychologists; an interest in the biological basis of behavior is found in both disciplines, and advocates of each side hold credentials in each field;

—quantitative and qualitative methods; both types of evidence have been gathered by advocates on each side;

—naturalistic and experimental methods; again, both types of studies have been cited by each side;

—those spending a few months and those spending a few years in another culture; both are found on each side.

—those "who are more interested in validity and reliability than in what they are actually studying" (Mead, 1975:211); everyone is interested in his observations being correct and repeatable.

8. Although not the same, the theory of emotion we propose shows the influence of Silvan Tomkins, who first considered many of these issues, although he did not

resolve them all in the way we propose. The term "Affect Program" is Tomkins's, and the description of emotional responses is similar to his account. Our formulation shares certain features with Izard's (1971) formulation that was also influenced by Tomkins.

9. To distinguish emotions from moods is not to imply that moods are bereft of emotion. Quite the contrary; moods are highly saturated with one or another emotion. Someone is said to be in a hostile mood if he shows anger very frequently, or very easily, or seems ready to become angry. In a similar fashion, while I do not consider jealousy as an emotion, jealousy is characterized by strong emotions (anger, fear) within a particular interpersonal context.

10. The startle response seems to be an exception, and for that reason, I question whether it should be considered an emotion. The early work of Landis and Hunt (1939) showed that a sudden loud noise (e.g., gunshot) anticipated or not, resulted in highly regular changes in facial and body movement despite attempts to prevent those responses. While their work was not cross-cultural, their studies strongly suggested that uniformity would be found.

11. When we originally proposed this phrase it was meant to apply just to the management of facial expression. Now we broaden its reference to include habits about managing *any* aspect of emotional behavior, posture, body movement, what is said, etc.

12. If blind infants do not show the brow raise to sudden expected sounds or touches, then at least we could assume that the brow raise is not wired in for surprise, nor for scanning if the eyes are not operative. Unfortunately the data is equivocal (Charlesworth, 1970; Eibl-Eibesfeldt, 1972; Goodenough, 1932).

13. We are grateful to Richard Lazarus, University of California, Berkeley; Masatoshi Tomita, Waseda University; Ned Opton, Wright Institute; and Jim Averill, University of Massachusetts, for their help and cooperation in making this study possible.

14. My discussion of partial facial expressions assumes that the affect program sets off a total expression, involving a number of different muscles, and that experience can limit how many of those muscles act. An alternative possibility is that the affect program sets off a number of different muscles, and that experience determines whether they come to be recruited together or not. Cross-cultural developmental studies of facial expression would be relevant to determining whether one or both of these possibilities actually happens.

IV

EXPLAINING EMOTIONS

AMÉLIE OKSENBERG RORTY

Sometimes our emotions change straightaway when we learn that what we believed is not true. The grieving husband recovers when he learns that, because she missed her plane, his wife did not die in the fatal plane crash. But often changes in emotions do not appropriately follow changes in belief. Their tenacity, their inertia, suggests that there is *akrasia* of the emotions; it reveals the complex structure of their intentionality.[1]

I want to examine the strategies we use to explain cases of unexpected conservation of emotions: those that seem to conflict with a person's judgments and those that appear to have distorted our perceptions and beliefs, making them uncharacteristically resistant to change or correction.[2] I shall begin with complex cases, so that we will be forced to uncover layers of explanation that need not normally be brought into play in what are taken to be the standard cases. When people act or react in ways that can be explained by reasonable beliefs and desires, we tend to suppose that these beliefs and desires are the causes of their behavior. We then try to construct our explanations of the more complex cases, using only what was necessary to explain the simple ones. Not surprisingly, we often then find that we are left with bizarre cases at the margins of our theory: self-deception, *akrasia,* and the irrational conservation of emotions. By beginning with fringe cases, we may find the more complex structures that underlie the apparently straightforward cases but which are difficult to discern when everything is going as we expect. One of the difficulties of our enterprise is that of specifying the psychological principles that rationalize a person's beliefs and desires, his interpretations and responses. When an emotion appears to be anomalous, and its explanation requires tracing its etiology, it is difficult to identify the intentional object of the emotion without constructing its rationale, if not actually its justification. But accurately describing a person's beliefs and attitudes, especially when they involve *akrasia* or the apparently inappropriate conservation of the emotions, often involves attributing false beliefs, apparently irrational intentional sets.[3] Sometimes it is implausible and inaccurate to explain an inappropriate attitude by attributing a belief or desire that would rationalize it, because the apparently anomalous emotion is embedded in a system of other inappropriate attitudes or false beliefs. Yet explaining a person's condition requires tracing its causal history, reconstructing the details of a ramified, gradually changing intentional system of attitudes, beliefs, habits of attention and focusing. Constructing the causal history often involves reconstructing a rationale: the problem is to determine at what point in that history to apply some modified version of the principle of charity.[4] Often it is accurately applied only quite far back in the person's psychological history, to explain the formation of prepropositional but intentional habits of salience, organization, and interpretation. It is these which, through later intervening beliefs and attitudes—many of them false and inappropriate—explain the conservation of emotions. When so applied, the principle of charity is modified: it accounts for the coherent appropriateness of the *formation* of a person's intentional system without maximizing agreement on the number of true beliefs. It is not the belief or emotion that is rationalized, but a person's coming to have it.

Emotions do not form a natural class. A set of distinctions that has generally haunted the philosophy of mind stands in the way of giving good descriptions of the phenomena. We have inherited distinctions between being active and being passive; between psychological states primarily explained by physical processes and psychological states not reducible to nor adequately explained by physical processes; distinctions between states that are primarily nonrational and those that are either rational or irrational; between voluntary and nonvoluntary states. Once these distinctions were drawn, types of psychological activities were then parceled out *en bloc* to one or another side of the dichotomies. That having been done, the next step was to argue reclassification: to claim that perception is not passive but active, or that the imagination has objective as well as subjective rules of association. Historically, the list of emotions has expanded as a result of these controversies. For instance, the opponents of Hobbes, wanting to secure benevolence, sympathy, and other disinterested attitudes as counterbalances to self-interest, introduced them as sentiments with motivational power. Passions became emotions and were classified as activities. When the intentionality of emotions was discussed, the list expanded still further: *ressentiment,* aesthetic and religious awe, anxiety and dread were included. Emotions became affects or attitudes. As the class grew, its members became more heterogeneous; the analysis became more ambiguous; and counterexamples were explained away by charges of self-deception.

When we focus on their consequences on behavior, most emotions can also be described as motives;[5] some—but not all—emotions can also be described as feelings, associated with proprioceptive states. The objects of some emotions—exhuberance, melancholy—are difficult to specify; such global states verge toward being moods.[6] Still other emotions come close to being dispositional character traits: we speak of vengeful or affectionate persons. But when we speak of a psychological state as an emotion, contrasting it to feelings, motives, moods, or character traits, we focus on the ways we are affected by our appraisals, evaluative perceptions, or descriptions.[7]

The causal history of our emotions, the significant events that form our habits of response, affects our conceptions of their objects. There are three closely interwoven strands in that causal history: (1) the formative events in a person's psychological past, the development of patterns of intentional focusing and salience, habits of thought and response; (2) the socially and culturally determined range of emotions and their characteristic behavioral and linguistic expressions; and (3) a person's constitutional inheritance, the set of genetically fixed threshold sensitivities and patterns of response. Because the social and genetic factors were assumed to be shared or invariable, their effects always appearing within a person's psychological history, we have treated them, when we focused on them at all, as fixed background conditions. But they are essential to the full account, and often critical in explaining apparent anomalies: their contribution to that explanation does not simply reduce to a variant of individual psychological explanation.[8] I shall, however, abstract from the social and genetic factors, and concentrate on the intentional components in the formation of a person's individual emotional dispositions.

CAUSES, OBJECTS, TARGETS

Jonah, a newswriter, resents Esther, his editor, whom he thinks domineering, even tyrannical. But as bosses go, Esther is exceptionally careful to consult with the staff, often following consensus even when it conflicts with her judgment. His colleagues try to convince Jonah that Esther's assignments are not demeaning, her requests not arbitrary. Jonah comes to believe he was mistaken in thinking her actions dictatorial; he retreats to remarking that she derives secret pleasure from the demands that circumstances require. Where his colleagues see a smile, he sees a smirk. After a time of working with Esther, Jonah realizes that she is not a petty tyrant, but he still receives her assignments with a dull resentful ache; and when Anita, the new editor, arrives, he is seething with hostility even before she has had time to settle in and put her family photographs on her desk. Although many of the women on the secretarial staff are more hard-edged in mind and personality than either Esther or Jonah, he regards them all as charmingly endowed with intuitive insight. He patronizes rather than resents them.

To understand Jonah's plight, we need distinctions. We are indebted to Hume for the distinction between the object and the cause of emotions. But that distinction needs to be refined before we can use it to understand Jonah's emotional condition. In the case of the husband who believed his wife had been killed in a plane crash, the precipitating or immediate cause of the man's grief is hearing a newscast announcing the fatal crash of the plane his wife intended to take. But of course the newscast has such a powerful effect on him because normally such news stories are themselves effects of the significant cause of his grief: her death in the fatal plane crash. Often when we find emotions puzzling, it is because we do not see why the immediate cause should have such an effect.

The significant cause of an emotion is the set of events—the entire causal history—that explains the efficacy of the immediate or precipitating cause. Often the significant cause is not in the immediate past; it may be an event, or a series of events, long forgotten, that formed a set of dispositions which are triggered by the immediate cause. Tracing the full causal story often involves more than locating initial conditions or identifying immediate causes: it requires analyzing the magnetizing effects of the formation of our emotional dispositions, habits of thought, as well as habits of action and response.[9] Magnetizing dispositions are dispositions to gravitate toward and to create conditions that spring other dispositions. A magnetized disposition to irascibility not only involves a set of specific low thresholds (e.g., to frustration or betrayal) but also involves looking for frustrating conditions, perceiving situations as frustrating. It not only involves wearing a chip on one's shoulder but involves looking for someone to knock that chip off. Magnetizing dispositions need not by themselves explain actions or attitudinal reactions: they can do so indirectly, by characterizing the *type* of beliefs, perceptions, and desires a person is likely to have. Such traits determine actions and reactions by determining the *selective* range of a person's beliefs and desires.[10] The genesis of a magnetizing disposition need not always lie in an individual's particular psychological history; such dispositions are often acquired, along with other characteristically culture-specific intentional sets and motives, as part of a person's socialization. It is because significant causes often produce magnetizing dispositions that they are successful in explaining the efficacy of the immediate causes of an emotion: they explain not only the response but the tendencies to structure experience in ways that will elicit that characteristic response.

In order to understand the relation between the immediate and the significant cause, we need refinements in the account of the objects of the emotions. The immediate object of an emotion is characteristically intentional, directed and referring to objects under descriptions that cannot be substituted *salva affectione.*[11] Standardly, the immediate object not only is the focus of the emotion but is also taken by the person as providing its ground or rationale. The immediate target of the emotion is the object extensionally described and identified. I shall refer to a person's emotion-grounding description of the target as *the intentional component of the emotion,* to his having that description as his *intentional state,* and to the associated magnetized disposition as his *intentional set.* Of course a person need not be able to articulate the intentional component of his emotions. Ascriptions of emotion, like ascriptions of belief, are inferences to the best explanation.[12]

A person's intentional set may fail to ground the emotion because the target does not in fact have the relevant properties, or because it does not have them in the configuration with the centrality that would ground the emotion, or because it does not in fact exist: the description does not succeed in referring. The difficulties of ascribing intentional states and those of referring in opaque contexts are no more (and no less) devastating in ascribing emotions than they are elsewhere.[13] When an otherwise perceptive and reasonable person widely and persistently misdescribes matters or persistently responds in a way that apparently conflicts with his beliefs, we first try standard strategies for explaining misperceptions and errors. Sometimes, indeed, we persuade a person that his emotion is unfounded; and sometimes this is sufficient for the emotion to change.

When an emotion remains intractable or an anomalous intentional set persists, we suspect that the emotion is rooted in habits of selective attention and interpretation whose activation is best explained by tracing them back to the significant causes of a magnetized disposition.[14] The causal story of that formation can take several forms. For instance, we might suspect that Jonah resents Esther because he now is, or once was, resentful of his mother. In such cases his mother may be the (acknowledged or unacknowledged) target of his emotions, and Esther only the front for that target. But Jonah's mother need not be the explanatory target—acknowledged or not—of Jonah's emotion; she may simply have been a crucial part of the significant cause of Jonah's magnetized disposition to structure and interpret situations by locating some female figure whom he sees as hostile and domineering, a figure who, so seen, grounds his resentment. Which of the various alternatives best explains Jonah's condition is a matter for extended investigation; we would have to examine a wide range of Jonah's responses, interpretations, and emotions under different conditions. In any case, our best explanatory strategy is: When in doubt about how the immediate target and precipitating cause explain the emotion, look for the significant cause of the dispositional set that forms the intentional component of the emotion.[15]

HABITS AND INTENTIONAL SETS

To see how finding the significant cause can help us reconstruct the rationale of the intentional component of the emotion, we need to examine the composition of the significant cause. An important part of the history of Jonah's condition will show us what we need.

Not only does Jonah regard women in high places with resentment and hostility, but he also suffers from nightmares and, sometimes, from obsessive terrors. Both have a recurring theme: his mother is trying to kill him. Moreover, he loathes scarves, refusing to wear them even in the coldest, dampest weather. No matter what wonderful things have just happened to him, he breaks into an anxious sweat when he walks through the scarf section at Woolworth's. His mother, a gruff, brusque woman, used to swathe him in scarves that she knitted herself. But she always bought the itchiest wool imaginable; and when she bundled him up in winter, she used to tie the scarf with a swift harsh motion, pulling it tightly around his throat. She had never come close to trying to kill him. She was in fact an affectionate woman, but an awkward one. Certainly she was occasionally ambivalent, and sometimes exasperated and angry. It was because Jonah was sensitive to the negative undertones of her attitudes (a sensitivity that had an explanation of its own) that he felt the pressure of the scarf as painful rather than as reassuring or comforting.

To understand what has happened to Jonah, we must examine several components of the significant causes of his nightmares, phobias, terrors. When children remember events as attacks, they may be picking up genuine undercurrents in the behavior of those around them. Adults often behave with hostility without attacking, seductively without trying to seduce. Because children are unable to place the undercurrents they discern in the context of a person's whole psychological character, they magnify what frightens them. But the "fantasy" often rests on something perceived. Perception, magnified or distorted interpretation, and fantasy shade off into one another, often in ways that can only be distinguished with the benefit of theory-laden hindsight.

But let us suppose that what Jonah's mother did would not in itself have been sufficient to form his emotional dispositions. His perceptions of the attitudes that determined her manner toward him are essential ingredients in the causal story of his condition. There were not two events, two significant causes: the tying of the scarf and the tying of it in a way that pained Jonah. In such situations it is often necessary not only to identify the significant cause by an extensional description (scarf tied at speed so-and-so, pressure so-and-so), but also to see it through the eyes of the beholder. When we understand that both components of the significant cause —the scarf tightly tied and Jonah's feeling that tying as painful— are fused in the forming of Jonah's emotional dispositions, we can see how locating the significant cause can help us reconstruct the emotion-grounding description that links the intentional component of Jonah's emotion to its immediate cause and target.

Because the intentional component of the significant cause and the intentional component of the apparently anomalous emotion do not always fall under the same description, it is not always as easy to spot the significant cause as, in this post-Freudian age, it has been easy to locate, almost without stopping to think, the significant cause —and even in this case, the explanatory target—of Jonah's emotion. Nor need the significant cause involve a particular set of events that fused and formed the person's magnetized dispositions, the patterns of salience and attention. The causal story is likely to involve idiosyncratic beliefs and associations, many difficult to recover or articulate. In any case, our motto can now be made more precise: When in doubt about the rationale of an emotion, look for the intentional component of the significant cause of the dispositional set that forms the intentional component of the emotion.

But we are not yet through explaining Jonah's condition, for we do not yet have an account of his tendency to focus on the minimally harsh manner of his mother's scarf-tying ways, his interpreting her actions as hostile. It might seem as if we have reintroduced our original problem—the problem of explaining an anomalous emotional reaction—at an earlier stage. Jonah's perceiving his mother as hostile is an essential part of the significant cause of his phobias and his troubles with lady bosses. Nevertheless, if only Jonah and not his brother Abednego has this intentional set, although Abednego was also tightly swathed in itchy scarves, we have not got the significant cause in all its glory: though our explanation is fuller, it is not yet complete.

To understand why the usually perceptive Jonah so misperceived his mother's attitudes, I must tell you more of his story.

Jonah was the eldest of the children. During his childhood, his father the Major was given army leave only to return home for short visits. At an appropriate time after one of these visits, Abednego was born. Since his mother was on her own at the time, Jonah was sent off to stay with his adored grandfather while his mother was in the hospital. Now the truth of the matter is that the adored grandfather loathed his daughter-in-law, whom he saw as a domineering angry woman, the ruination of his son. Without intending to do so, Jonah's grandfather conveyed these attitudes to Jonah, who at that time was apprehensive of losing his mother's affections. Susceptible to the influence of a figure who represented his absent father, he found in his grandfather's attitudes the confirmation and seal of what might have been a passing mood. His grandfather's perspective became strongly entrenched as his own.

We now have an account of why a reasonable person might, in a perfectly reasonable way, have developed an intentional set that, as it happens, generates wildly askew interpretations and reactions.[16] But have we found a stopping place, thinking we've explained an anomalous attitude simply because we have come to a familiar platitude? Perhaps: that is a risk explanations run; but if we have stopped too soon, at a place that requires further explanation, we can move, whenever the need arises, farther back in the causal story. And indeed, we may want explanations of reactions that are not at all anomalous: we can ask why an accurate perception or a true belief has the form it does, why a person focused on matters *this* way rather than that.

The principle of charity is now seen to be very general in scope. Characteristically, it is best applied to the intentional components of the significant causes of magnetizing dispositions, where it accounts for a range of attitudes and beliefs (without necessarily maximizing agreement on truth), rather than to individual episodic beliefs. Moreover, its use presupposes not only that we have a certain gravitational attraction toward truth but that we are also endowed with a wide range of psychological dispositions that determine the ways in which we acquire and change our beliefs and attitudes. These dispositions are quite varied: some are neurophysiological determinants of perceptual salience (e.g., red being more salient than gray under standard background and contrast conditions); others are psychological in character (e.g., the dominance order of emotions under standard conditions: fear displacing and reorganizing the emotional field in characteristic patterns); still others are psychosocial (e.g., the effects of mass hysteria or the presence of a schizophrenic on a person's schema of intentional sets). In short, when we try to apply the principle of charity to those places where it best explains and identifies the range of our attitudes, its canonic formulation is so modified as to disappear as a special principle.

But having come to the end of Jonah's story, have we come to the end of an account of how we explain emotions? Our questions seem now to multiply: Will we, in tracing the significant cause to an appropriate stopping point, always still introduce an intentional component of the significant cause? Are we to interpret young Jonah's tendency to take on the intentional set of a figure who stands in a certain relation to him as itself an intentional set? Or do significant causes of magnetizing dispositions sometimes have no intentional component of their own? We do not know enough about the neurophysiology and psychology of early learning to know what constraints should be set on our philosophical theory. In any case, an account of the etiology of the intentional components of emotional dispositions is nestled within a general psychological theory: it is inseparable from theories of perception and theories of motivation. The holistic character of mental life makes piecemeal philosophical psychology suspect.

Since air-tight arguments have vacuous conclusions, it would be folly to stop speaking at the point where we must start speculating.

There are good, but by no means conclusive, reasons for recognizing a gradation between beliefs or judgments in propositional form and quasi-intentions which can also be physically or extensionally identified. Let us distinguish:

(1) beliefs that can be articulated in propositional form, with well-defined truth conditions;

(2) vague beliefs in sentential form whose truth or satisfaction conditions can be roughly but not fully specified ("It is better to have good friends than to be rich." "Men in Islamic countries tend to have sexist attitudes.");

(3) specific patterns of intentional salience that can be formulated as general beliefs (A pattern of focusing on aspects of women's behavior construed as domineering or hostile rather than as competent or insecure might in principle be treated as a set of predictions about the behavior of women under specific conditions.);

(4) intentional sets that cannot be easily formulated as beliefs (A pattern of focusing on the military defensibility of a landscape, rather than on its fertility or aesthetic composition, cannot be so easily formulated as a set of predictions about the benefits of giving priority to military defense over fertility or aesthetic charm. Nor can such patterns of salience be translated straightforwardly as

preference rankings. For instance, a painter can focus on patterns of color in a landscape rather than on its compositional lines, but the patterns and habits of his attending are quite distinct from his painterly preferences.);

(5) quasi-intentional sets that can, in principle, be fully specified in physical or extensional descriptions (e.g., other things being equal, painful sensations are standardly more salient than pleasurable ones).

For such intentional sets—patterns of discrimination and attention —the question of whether the significant cause of a magnetized intentional set has an irreducibly intentional component is an open one. Such quasi-intentional components form patterns of focusing and salience without determining the description of that pattern. A quasi-intentional set (patterns of perceptual salience under standard conditions of contrast and imprinting) can be given both physical and intentional descriptions; in some contexts, the physicalistic descriptions can function in an explanation, without any reference to the intentional description. But in other contexts, particularly those that move from functional explanations toward interpretive or rational accounts, the intentional description is essential. Often the intentional and the quasi-intentional component of the significant cause of magnetized interpretive dispositions is ambiguous in this way: we tend to read the intentional component back into the significant cause when doing so helps rationalize the person's responses. But the intentional set that is introduced at that stage often bears a causal rather than a directly logical relation to the magnetized set produced. (The quasi-intentional set that made Jonah prone to adopt his grandfather's interpretations at just that time bears a causal but not a logical relation to the intentional set he acquired as a result of this sensitivity. But the connections between the intentional set he acquired from his grandfather and the intentional set that leads him to see Esther as domineering are logical as well as causal.)

In such cases there are physiological generalizations about the quasi-intentional states under their extensional descriptions. Although the opacity criteria for intentionality do not yet apply, it is useful to recognize that such selective sensitivities are oriented to a stimulus under a description that later does function in its fully intentional form. Holistic considerations influence us: the wider the range and the greater the complexity of behavior that is best explained by the intentional set in its fully intentional form, the more likely we are to treat the significant cause as having that intentional component, even though it need not, in its original appearance, have then functioned in its fully intentional form. (For instance, a child can be frightened *by* a clap of thunder without initially having an intentional set to interpret such sounds as danger signals. If he is ill and feverish, hearing loud sounds is painful, and, if he is generally in a weak and fearful condition, he can develop a fully intentional sensitivity, becoming frightened *of* thunder because he had been frightened *by* it.)

OBJECTIONS

One might wonder: Why do we need these distinctions descending like a plague to devour every living thing, transforming a once fertile plain into a desert? Why can't we explain intractable, inappropriate emotions more simply and elegantly by specifying the relevant belief that fixes the description of the target? Perhaps what explains Jonah's resentment is that he thinks figures in authority are likely to be, or to become authoritarian. Although such beliefs or judgments are occasionally interesting and true, it is sometimes difficult to ascribe the appropriate plausible belief. Jonah does not resent Abe Zloty, the editor-in-chief, though Zloty is far more peremptory than Esther. It seems more plausible to ascribe to him the belief that when women are in a position of authority, they become insufferably authoritarian. But Jonah is a skeptical sort of fellow, who rarely leaps to generalizations, let alone wild ones. Often when we don't understand an emotion, or its intractability, we also don't understand why the person should have and hold the belief that is its intentional component. The belief "explains" the emotion only by subsuming its intentionality in a more general frame.

But our objector persists, claiming that in tracing the etiology of an emotion, intentional sets and quasi-intentions are unnecessarily complex ways of talking about beliefs or evaluative judgments. If we judge emotions for their rationality, they argue, then some belief must either be presupposed by, or embedded in, the emotion. The correction of emotions generally involves the correction of the mistaken belief.

Certainly many cases do follow such a pattern; and certainly some emotions can be identified by the full-blown beliefs that are also a part of their causal explanation. But the issue is whether the intentional component of an emotion always is a belief, and whether there are emotions that are more properly evaluated as inappropriate or harmful than as irrational.

If the intentional component of an emotion is always a belief, then the conservation of an emotion after a change of belief would always involve a conflict of beliefs. Now this may indeed sometimes occur; but often the only evidence that the person retains the abandoned belief is his emotional state. One of the reasons for resisting assimilating all intentional components of emotions to beliefs is the difficulty of stating *what* the belief is. There is sometimes no non-question-begging way of formulating a proposition *p,* where "inserting *p* in the sentence '*S* believes that ——' would express the fact that the subject was in that state."[17]

A person may not only deny having the abandoned belief but (with the exception of the episode in question) consistently act in a way that supports the denial. On the view that emotions always involve beliefs, it becomes necessary to suppose that the person is massively successful in deceiving himself about the conflict between the belief embedded in the emotion and the belief implicit in the rest of his conduct. This is certainly a recognizable and even common phenomenon. It seems implausible, however, to assimilate all cases of the conservation of emotions to cases that involve a self-deceptive denial of such conflicts. No doubt much conservation is to be explained by ambivalence, and at least some ambivalence is to be understood as involving conflicting judgments, with the person deceiving himself about at least one side of a divided mind.[18] But unless the claim is to be question-begging, the conservation of emotions cannot *automatically* count as grounds for attributing self-deception. Characteristically, self-deception involves quite distinctive behavior: signs of facial malaise, frozen features, certain sorts of systematic failures in action.[19]

Even if it were the case that—in a much revised and extended sense of belief—the intentional components of emotions were

beliefs, the distinctions we have drawn would have to be reintroduced to differentiate the ways in which a person accepts or uncharacteristically ignores or refuses counterevidence. The phenomena
of the conservation of emotion would then reappear as the anomalous conservation of belief. To explain such conservation, we would
once again have to return to the ravenous hordes of distinctions
between the immediate and the significant causes of magnetized
intentional states; we would have to introduce beliefs that could not
be attributed in propositional form. Explaining the anomalous conservation of belief, or its resistance to considerations or observations that would characteristically change it, would lead us to
exactly the same sort of schema of causal explanation that we use in
understanding the conservation of emotions.

There are objections from other quarters. Nowhere does the
mind-body problem raise its ugly head with a stiffer neck than in
the analysis of the thought component of the emotions. In some
cases, it might be said, the significant cause isn't significant at all.
It casts no light on the rationale of the intentional component of an
emotion because there is no rationale. [In the narrative epilogue at
the end of *War and Peace,* Tolstoi describes the emotional condition of the aged Countess Rostoff. She needs, he says—and he suggests that this is also a physiological need—to become angry, melancholy, merry, peevish, to express the cycle of her emotional repertoire every few days. Usually the family manages to arrange matters in such a way so as to give her emotional life an air of appropriateness. But sometimes this cannot be done, and she becomes peevish in a situation in which she is normally merry. Tolstoi remarks
that in infancy and old age (and we might add: in adolescence) the
apparent reasonableness that we believe really conditions our adult
emotional life wears thin, and emotions reveal a rhythm and pattern of their own. Tolstoi does not, unfortunately, go on to speculate whether the independent rhythm of the emotions is merely disguised in our prime, indiscernible beneath our bustling intention-
directed activity, or whether it is precisely this difference that
makes the emotional life of infants and the senile different from
our own, that their emotions are merely coincidentally associated
with the appropriate intentions.] When a person suffers from a
hormonal imbalance, his emotions have one target after another,
none intentionally linked to the intentional component of a signifi-

cant cause. When we look for the explanation of a recalcitrant in-appropriate emotion, there is sometimes no need to look deeply into the etiology of the intention: the state of the person's endo-crine system is explanation enough.[20] The best thing to do with this objection is to accept it gracefully. It is after all true.

But we must be careful not to conclude too much. From the fact that the best explanation of a person's emotional state may some-times be that he suffers glandular malfunction, it does not follow that, under standard conditions, explanations of emotions can be given without any appeal to beliefs or intentional states.[21] Most physicalistically oriented theories fill in their accounts by tracing the causal interaction between the *sorts* of physical states that are associated with being in an emotionally charged condition (gener-ally metabolic states) with the sorts of physical states that are asso-ciated with a person's having propositional attitudes (generally brain states).[22] Such physicalists do not, however, claim to be able to identify the propositional content of a person's attitudes solely by reference to physically described brain states. On this view, we would not expect to find strict physicalistic laws distinguishing Jonah's perceiving-Esther-as-Slavic and his perceiving-Esther-as-Semitic.

The zealot hard-core physicalist goes farther: he proposes to identify "psychological" states as states whose descriptions elimi-nate all reference to intentional states and their propositional con-tent, distinguishing Jonah's believing Esther to be bossy from his believing her to be vain, by specifying the differences in the brain states that constitute the two beliefs. It seems at the very least pre-mature to present the results of what is an extended and only pro-jected program of research as having provided the explanations we need, especially as hard-core zealot physicalists have yet to give us an account of how to proceed with the reductive analysis. So far, all we have are science-fiction stories about possible worlds in which the reductive analysis has taken place, "what Scientists somehow discovered" already become part of the popular culture. Until the theory is established, all the physicalist account of the emotions adds to the intentional account is the important observa-tion that, when the best explanation of a person's emotional state is primarily physiological, then raising questions about the causal force of the intentional object may produce arbitrary ad hoc answers. There may be a revealing pattern in the immediate causes or objects of an adrenally charged person's various aggressive angers, but sometimes that pattern is best explained by tracing the effects of chemical changes on perception and attention.

This suggests that, for at least these sorts of cases, the physicalist and the intentionalist accounts of anomalous emotions are perfectly compatible and perhaps even complementary, physicalistically oriented theories explaining why a person is in *that* state, intentionalistically oriented theories explaining why the emotion has *that* intentional object. They appear to be at odds only when both theories get reductionally ambitious: when, denying overdetermination, each tries to explain all phenomena at all levels. Certainly if the intentional accounts deny that a person's hormonal state ever enters into the explanation, and if the physicalistic account denies that intentionality is ever required to explain or identify the emotional states, the two approaches will clash in an unilluminating struggle whose sterility will be masked by the parties goading each other to dazzling displays of ingenuity.[23]

Does it follow that both levels of explanation, the physiological and the intentional, are necessary but neither sufficient? The situation is (un)fortunately more complex. The physiological and the intentional aspects of our emotions do not enter into all emotions in the same way. The difference between a distaste for malicious gossip in departmental politics and the terror of waking after a nightmare whose drama one has already forgotten, the difference between nostalgia-for-the-lilacs-of-yesteryear and fear in the face of a powerful danger, are differences in kind.

Some emotions are primarily associated with physical states largely affected by metabolic imbalance: malfunctions of the pituitary or adrenal glands are associated with highly specific emotional disorders, leaving the rest of a person's emotional dispositions relatively intact. Other, quite different sorts of emotional disorders are associated with some sorts of brain damage rather than with endocrinological malfunction.[24] Still other sorts of emotions—such culturally variable ones as nostalgia or Sunday melancholy—seem difficult to associate with any particular physical condition. While the introduction of intentional apparatus seems forced in some cases, the introduction of physiological determinants is forced in others.

EXPLANATION, CHANGE, AND RATIONALITY

> We can expect three things from the study of history: the sheer pleasure of knowing particulars; useful precepts for the important matters of life; and furthermore because the origins of things recur in the present from the past, we acquire the best understanding of all things from a knowledge of their causes.
>
> —Leibniz, Preface to *Accessiones Historicae*

The conservation of emotions has its explanation in the conservation of habit, especially of those magnetized dispositions involved in selective attention and focused interpretation. We have concentrated primarily on that aspect of a person's psychological history which explains the formation of his characteristic intentional habits. But social and genetic factors also contribute to the causal story; the full account of the conservation of emotional habits would have to introduce these determinants as well. The three layers of explanation—the individual, the social, and the genetic—are closely interwoven. A person's constitution—his threshold to pain and to various sorts of stimuli, the structure of his glandular and nervous systems—affects the development of his intentional sets, his habits of interpretation and response. Constitutional factors (for instance, metabolic rate) influence the social roles and settings in which a person is cast; this in turn also affects the formation of his intentional sets. Sociocultural factors structure the interpretations of a person's experiences: a range of emotional responses is formed by such interpretations.[25] The full explanation of a person's emotions requires not only an analysis of the causal contribution of each of the three strands but also an account of their interactions.

(But what goes without saying may need to be said: we would not be misled by talk of interaction, layers, or strands, to suppose that we are dealing with distinct variables whose causal interaction can be traced. What is variable in a theory need not be independently variable in fact. At this stage, we are still using metaphors; we are not yet entitled to suppose we have detached them as a technical vocabulary. "Biological limits" or "constraints" to sociocultural variation, physiological "determinants" of psychological or intentional processes, cultural "forms" of biological "givens": all these expressions are borrowed from other contexts. Our vocabulary of the "interrelation" of these "domains" is crucially in the formative stage; talk of separate but interwoven explanatory strands must be treated as provisionary to a developing explanatory scheme—heuristics without ontology. We have here a clear example of the encroaching constitutive character of early terminological raiding. Perhaps eventually, by tracing these sorts of "borrowings," we shall be able to see the rewards—and the costs—of theft that cannot be distinguished from honest toil without the benefit of a program.)

It might be thought that my suggestion that emotions are not only explained but often also identified by their causal histories must be either trivial or exaggerated. No one would deny that we require more than the immediate occasion to understand the exact shades of Jonah's resentment: the images and thoughts, sensations and anticipations, the evocation of associated emotions that constitute just *that* condition. But it doesn't follow that we need a causal account to identify his condition as a case of resentment, and to explain it by his perception of Esther.

Certainly emotions are often identified in a rough way without tracing their causal histories; one need not always know why a person is angry to recognize his condition. The contexts in which they occur, their expression in speech and behavior are sufficient to identify them; their immediate contextual causes are often quite sufficient to explain them. There is, however, a rough and unexamined, but nevertheless quite specific folk psychology that stands behind, and informs such standard explanations.[26] The explanatory strategies that I have sketched make explicit the stages and assumptions embedded in our ready and quick contextual identifications of emotions and their intentional objects. It is because we supply the standard causal history of emotion-types that we readily identify tokens of that type.

But instances of emotion-types differ markedly from one another in their origins, their expressions in speech and action, and in their psychodynamic functions. To bring order into these heterogeneous classes, we need a much finer taxonomy of the varieties of (e.g.) anger, melancholy, envy. Such a taxonomy can be constructed by distinguishing varieties of causal histories of the intentional component of these emotions. Differences in the characteristic causal histories of their intentional components helps to explain why different instances of the same emotion-type often have different tonal and behavioral expressions. But we have been too impressed by the multiplicity of instances of emotion-types, and so have tended to distinguish different instances of the same type by the differences in their *particular* intentional objects. Certainly if we want an account of their individuation, especially in cases of overdetermination, this is necessary.[27] When we identify and explain a particular emotion without tracing its etiology, however, we are implicitly classifying it as a standard instance of a *variety* of the emotion-type; in doing so, we are relying upon the characteristic causal story that distinguishes that variety from others. If we thought that the causes of a person's condition conformed to none of the standard histories, we would doubt the attribution.

If this analysis is correct, then an account of how people succeed in changing emotions that they judge inappropriate or irrational closely follows the more general explanation of how people change their habits. The difficulties involved in bringing about such changes—the deep conservation of emotional habits—make the claims that emotions are choices or voluntary judgments seem implausible.[28] Sometimes—rarely—it is possible for some people—a happy few—to take steps to restructure their intentional sets, to revise their emotional repertoire. Sometimes secondary emotions—emotions about emotions—play a crucial role in such transformations. For instance, someone who thinks that the objects he fears are indeed dangerous, may nevertheless reasonably judge that he is too afraid of being afraid. He may think that he should not go as far as he does in order to avoid situations where there is only a remote possibility of danger. It is this secondary fear ("We have nothing to fear but fear itself.") that impels responses the person might judge inappropriate; and it is this, rather than the first-level fear, that he might wish to change. Or it might go the other way: a person might underwrite a second-level emotion, and wish to change its first level.[29]

Shifts in emotional repertoires can often take quite subtle forms: someone might wish to check the standard expression or behavioral consequences of either a first- or a second-level emotion without wishing to change the habits or intentional set of having it. Although some tendency to action, often taking the form of posture or expression, is "part" of many first-level emotions, it is often possible to restrain or mask the behavior without changing the emotional set.[30] One of the ways of doing this is to distinguish more sharply between the varieties of instances of an emotion-type. A person might learn to discriminate between appropriate and inappropriate responses by coming to see that different instances of the same type cluster together because they have the same causal history. They form a variety defined by its etiology. If he tackles his problem of identifying and overcoming inappropriate resentments separately each time, Jonah is unlikely to make much headway by learning not to resent Esther, and then learning not to resent Anita, and then Sarah, ... and each and every woman in authority. Because he thinks some cases of resentment are perfectly justified by their causes and objects, he is unlikely to solve his problem by setting himself the task of avoiding resentment altogether. By understanding the special etiology of the variety of resentments of which his resentment of Esther is a particular instance, he can at least begin to be alert to the situations that trigger magnetized dispositions he regards as inappropriate.

The analysis of the causal history of our emotions suggests that judgments of the appropriateness of the emotions must be made on a number of different levels. It may be not only irrational but inappropriate for someone to be frightened of lions in a zoo, but it is not inappropriate to be frightened before one has had time to be reasonable, so constructed that one's fear is not immediately eradicated by one's more considered reactions. It may be irrational for Jonah to take on his grandfather's attitudes without testing them, irrational for him to reinterpret all the evidence that might correct his attitudes. But it is also beneficial for children to tend to absorb the intentional dispositions of the crucial figures around them, even at the cost of generating confusion and conflict. What is maladaptive in a particular case, need not be so typically; it may be highly beneficial for habitual responses to dominate rational considerations, and for them to be changed by rational considerations only with considerable difficulty. It is part of the discomforting character of our emotional life that the genetic programming and the social formation of emotional dispositions are not respecters of the rationality or the comfort of individual persons.[31]

NOTES

1. The contrast between voluntary actions and involuntary passions is generally too sharply drawn. For an account of the degrees in the voluntary control and redirection of the emotions, see Iris Murdoch, "The Idea of Perfection," in *The Sovereignty of the Good* (London: Routledge & Kegan Paul; New York: Schocken Books, 1970).

2. Russell Dancy and Nancy Cartwright suggested an emotion need not be irrational or inappropriate to be anomalous: it may simply be out of character. Identifying an emotion as anomalous can, but need not, presuppose a normative judgment. Michael Stocker convinced me that even apparently appropriate and rational responses can be baffling: the question "Why did he do *that?*" always has a purchase.

3. A person's emotion is irrational if correcting the belief presupposed by the emotion fails to change it appropriately *or* if the person uncharacteristically resists considerations that would normally lead him to correct the belief. But an emotion can be irrational even if the presupposed belief is true; for the true belief presupposed by an emotion need not be its cause, even when the person does genuinely hold it. The emotion may be caused by beliefs or attitudes that bear no relation to the belief that would rationalize it, quite independently of whether the person does in fact also have the rationalizing belief. The rationality or irrationality of an emotion is a function of the relation between its causes and the beliefs that are taken to justify it. But irrational emotions can sometimes be perfectly appropriate to the situation in which they occur; and an emotion can be inappropriate when there is no irrationality (if, for instance, it is too strong or too weak, out of balance with other emotions that are appropriate). Both judgments of rationality and of appropriateness involve conceptions of normality that have normative force. Disagreements about the classification of an emotion often disguise disagreements about what is wholesome or right.

4. Cf. W. V. Quine, *Word and Object* (Cambridge, Mass.: MIT Press, 1960), pp. 57-61; Donald Davidson, "Belief and the Basis of Meaning," *Synthese,* XXVII, 3/4 (1974): 309-323. For some modifications of the principle, see Richard E. Grandy, "Reference, Meaning and Belief," *Journal of Philosophy,* LXX, 14 (August 16, 1973): 439-452; and Colin McGinn, "Charity, Interpretation, and Belief," ibid., LXXIV, 9 (September 1977): 521-535.

5. Cf. William P. Alston, "Feelings," *Philosophical Review,* LXXVIII, 1 (January 1969): 3-34; and "Emotion and Feeling," in Paul Edwards, ed., *Encyclopedia of Philosophy* (New York: Macmillan, 1967). See also R. E. Lazarus, "Emotions and Adaptation: Conceptual and Empirical Relations," *Nebraska Symposium on Motivation,* 1968; P. T. Young, *Motivation and Emotions* (New York: Wiley, 1961); and Magda Arnold and J. A. Gasson, "Feelings and Emotions as Dynamic Factors in Personality Integration," in Arnold, ed., *The Nature of Emotion* (New York: Penguin Books, 1968). This anthology—and Arnold's *Emotion and Personality* (New York: Columbia, 1960)—contain an excellent selection of papers, surveying current psychological theories of the emotions.

6. But cf. Michael Tanner, "Sentimentality," *Proceedings of the Aristotelian Society,* LXXVII (1977): 127-147, who describes a range of objectless (and sometimes pointless) emotions.

7. J. de Rivera, "A Structural Theory of the Emotions" (New York: International Universities Press, 1977).

8. For discussions of genetic and physiological determinants of emotions, see

Charles Darwin, *The Expression of the Emotions in Man and Animals* (New York: Appleton, 1896); and D. Hamburg, "Emotions in the Perspective of Human Evolution," in Peter Knapp, ed., *Expression of the Emotions in Man* (New York: International Press, 1963). See also: Paul Ekman, "Darwin and Cross-cultural Studies of Facial Expression," in his *Darwin and Facial Expression: A Century of Research in Review* (New York: Academic Press, 1973); Ekman, Friesen, and Ellsworth, *Emotion in the Human Face* (New York: Pergamon Press, 1972); and Ekman, *Unmasking the Face* (Englewood Cliffs, N.J.: Prentice-Hall, 1975; Silvan A. Tomkins, *Affect, Imagery and Consciousness,* vols. 1 and 2 (New York: Springer, 1962-63); and C. E. Izard, *The Face of Emotion* (New York: Appleton-Century-Crofts, 1971). For discussions of cultural and social factors, see John Middleton, ed., *From Child to Adult: Studies in the Anthropology of Education* (New York: Natural History Press, 1970). The essays by Margaret Mead, Meyer Fortes, and Dorothy Eggan are especially useful for an account of the socialization of the emotions. See also Hildred Geertz, "The Vocabulary of the Emotions," *Psychiatry,* XXII (1959); and Jean Briggs, *Never in Anger* (Cambridge, Mass.: Harvard, 1970). For a controversy about the priority of social structure and "basic" human sentiments, see Rodney Needham, *Structure and Sentiment* (Chicago: University of Chicago Press, 1962); and George Homans, *Sentiments and Activities* (New York: Free Press, 1962). For a general discussion of the genetic and the social determinants of emotions, see James Averill, "The Sociocultural, Biological, and Psychological Determinants of Emotion," chap. 3 of this book.

9. This terminology is meant to be neutral between competing analyses of causality and of the logic of dispositional terms. I shall speak of dispositions and habits interchangeably; but I want to examine the relation between the cause of a disposition and its triggering conditions, and to alert us to the possibility that the component "elements" of a disposition may be quite heterogenous. I would hope that the account of dispositions—as it finally emerges from the specialists concentrating on that issue—will show us why and how some dispositions have a magnetizing momentum of their own: the more they are acted upon, the more likely it is, the easier it becomes, to fall into that way of responding.

10. For an excellent account of how traits dispose a person to have characteristic *sorts* of beliefs and desires, see N. Hirschberg, "A Correct Treatment of Traits," unpublished manuscript.

11. Cf. G. E. M. Anscombe, "On the Grammar of 'Enjoy'," *Journal of Philosophy,* LXIV, 19 (October 5, 1967): 607-614; Anthony Kenny, *Action, Emotion and Will* (New York: Humanities, 1963), chs. 1-3; D. F. Pears, "The Causes and Objects of Some Feelings and Psychological Reactions," *Ratio,* IV, 2 (December 1962): 91-111; George Pitcher, "Emotion," *Mind,* LXXIV, 295 (July 1965): 326-346; Irving Thalberg, "Constituents and Causes of Emotion and Action," *Philosophical Quarterly,* XXIII, 90 (January 1973): 1-14.

12. Cf. Gilbert H. Harman, "Knowledge, Reasons, and Causes," *Journal of Philosophy,* LXVII, 21 (November 5, 1970): 841-855. Harman's solution to the Gettier problem provides an analogue to my account of the conservation of the emotions. But, as Brian Skyrms pointed out and as Bas C. van Fraassen has shown in "The Pragmatics of Explanation," *American Philosophical Quarterly,* XIV, 2 (April 1977): 143-150, the phrase 'inference to the best explanation' is incomplete: apparently competing claims are sometimes compatible because there are different questions at issue. For instance, sometimes we want to know why a person has that emotion (is resentful rather than hurt) and sometimes we want to know why his emotion is directed to that object (why he is angry with his son rather than his boss).

13. Cf. Keith S. Donellan, "Reference and Definite Descriptions," *Philosophical*

Review, LXXV, 3 (July 1966): 281-304; and Saul Kripke, "Naming and Necessity," in Davidson and Harman, eds., *Semantics of Natural Language* (Boston: Reidel, 1972), esp. pp. 269-272, 301-303.

14. Cf. H. Hartmann, "Ego Psychology and the Problem of Adaptation," in *Essays on Ego Psychology* (London: Hogarth, 1964); and Hartmann, E. Kris, and R. Lowenstein, *Papers on Psychoanalytic Psychology* (New York: International Universities Press, 1964).

15. One might worry that this involves the sort of circularity that is supposed to trouble claims that the reasons that sometimes cause actions also identify them. But Davidson, among others, has made headway in answering these objections by distinguishing action-types and action-events. These solutions can be transposed to emotion contexts. Cf. Davidson, "Actions, Reasons, and Causes," *Journal of Philosophy,* LX, 23 (November 7, 1963): 685-700; and Anscombe, *Intention* (Ithaca, N.Y.: Cornell, 1958), pp. 11, 45-46. A different solution is proposed by Alvin Goldman, *A Theory of Human Action* (Englewood Cliffs, N.J.: Prentice-Hall, 1970).

16. Cf. Rousseau, *Fragments pour 'Emile':* "Nos passions sont des instruments spirituels dont la nature arme nôtre coeur pour la defense de nôtre personne et de tout ce qui est necessaire à nôtre bien être. Plus donc nous avons besoin de choses étrangères, plus d'obstacles peuvent nous nuire, plus aussi nos passions sont nombreuses et éxaltées; elles se mesurent naturellement sur les besoins de nôtre coeur."

17. Cf. Stephen Stich, "Beliefs and Subdoxastic States," unpublished manuscript, p. 16. Stich gives excellent arguments for the necessity of postulating intentional states that are not beliefs. Though he is primarily concerned with perception, the argument can be generalized.

18. Cf. Robert C. Solomon, "The Logic of Emotion," *Noûs,* XI, 1 (March 1977): 41-49. For an excellent discussion of ambivalence, cf. Patricia Greenspan, "A Case of Mixed Feelings: Ambivalence and the 'Logic' of Emotion," in chap. 9 of this book.

19. As part of his general program of mapping the facial configurations characteristic of particular emotions, Paul Ekman has begun to specify the configuration of facial muscles associated with various forms of deception. Cf. Ekman, Friesen, Schever, "Body Movement and Voice Pitch in Deceptive Interaction," *Semiotica,* XVI (1976).

20. It is common in such circumstances to deny the attribution, saying of an adrenally charged person, "Oh, he isn't angry; it's just glands." Sometimes, at any rate, we shy away from attributing an emotion because the person's condition hasn't got the right sort of causal history.

21. Cf. Jerome Singer and Stanley Schacter, "Cognitive, Social and Physiological Determinants of Emotional States," *Psychological Review,* LXIX, 5 (September 1962): 379-399. Following Cannon, they argue that, as the same visceral changes occur both in a variety of emotional states and in nonemotional states, our perception of these changes cannot identify distinctive emotions. They also hold that "cognitions arising from the immediate situation as interpreted by past experience provide the framework within which one understands and labels feelings" (380). It is, they argue, the cognition that determines whether the state of psychological arousal will be labeled "anger," "exhuberance," "fear." Their experiments led them to conclude that "emotional states may be considered a function of a state of physiological arousal and a cognition appropriate to that arousal" (398). But, "given a state of physiological arousal, for which an individual has no immediate explanation, he will label that state and describe his feelings in terms of the cognitions available to him" (398). The subject's reports of his emotions, and sometimes his behavior, can be manipulated by exposing him to modeling behavior or by misinforming

him about the drugs administered to him. These classical experiments have been subjected to a variety of criticism, ranging from criticisms of experimental design to criticisms that the data do not warrant the conclusions. In any case, Singer and Schacter do not discuss whether the psychological factors they introduce can be redescribed in physical terms.

22. William James, *The Principles of Psychology,* II (New York: Holt, 1893), 499: "The bodily changes follow directly the perception of the exciting fact . . . and our feeling of the same changes as they occur *is* the emotion." It is very difficult to establish whether or to what extent James can be called a physicalist. On the one hand, he seems to hold that particular perceptions can be distinguished from one another by their felt qualities. On the other, he does not reduce the content of propositional attitudes to extensionally described brain states.

23. Cf. the controversy in John O'Connor, ed., *Modern Materialism: Readings on Mind-Body Identity* (New York: Harcourt, Brace & World, 1969).

24. Cf. Paul MacLean, "Sensory and Perceptive Factors in the Emotional Functions of the Triune Brain," and "The Triune Brain, Emotion and Scientific Bias," in F. O. Schmitt, ed., *The Neurosciences: Second Study Program* (New York: Rockefeller University Press, 1970). Cf. also P. Black, ed., *Physiological Correlates of Emotion* (New York: Academic Press, 1970).

25. Cf. Clifford Geertz, "Deep Play: Notes on the Balinese Cockfight," in his *The Interpretation of Cultures* (New York: Basic Books, 1973), esp. pp. 448-453.

26. Cf. Adam Morton, "Framing the Psychological," unpublished manuscript, with an illuminating account of how we attribute and explain psychological states in ordinary contexts.

27. Cf. Graeme Marshall, "Overdetermination and the Emotions," chap. 8.

28. Cf. Solomon, "Emotions and Choices," chap. 10, and Jean-Paul Sartre, "Bad Faith," in *Being and Nothingness* (New York: Philosophical Library, 1956). Of course it might also be useful to think of choices and voluntary judgments as the expressions of certain sorts of habits, and so as also evincing the problems of conservation. Sartre constructs an ontological explanation for the conservation of habits of choice: consciousness' evasion of its own nonbeing. More naturalistic explanations are given by Melanie Klein, "On the Development of Mental Functioning," *Envy and Gratitude* (New York: Delta, 1975), pp. 236-246; and by John Dewey, *Human Nature and Conduct* (New York: Modern Library, 1930), part III, pp. 172-210.

29. The distinction that Harry Frankfurt has made between first-order desires and their second-order evaluations can be applied to the emotions. Cf. "Freedom of the Will and the Concept of a Person," *Journal of Philosophy,* LXVIII, V (January 14, 1971): 5-20. There is, however, much more latitude in second-order emotions than there is in second-order attitudes toward desires. A person can enjoy being afraid, be angry at being afraid, regret being afraid, fear being afraid, etc.

30. I am grateful to Sara Ruddick for this point, and to Jerome Neu for his discussion of it in "Jealous Thoughts," chap. 18.

31. Many people contributed to the writing of this essay. Ernest Loevinsohn and Adam Morton helped shape an early draft. Jonathan Bennett and Georges Rey showed me how to eliminate some unnecessarily Baroque elaborations; Mark Johnston and Graeme Marshall gave me some distinctions when I needed them most.

V

THE RATIONALITY OF EMOTIONS

RONALD DE SOUSA

Ira brevis furor, said the Latins: anger is a brief bout of madness. There is a long tradition that views all emotions as threats to rationality. The *crime passionnel* belongs to that tradition: in law it is a kind of "brief-insanity defense." We still say that "passion blinds us"; and in common parlance to be philosophical about life's trials is to be decently unemotional about them. Indeed many philosophers have espoused this view, demanding that Reason *conquer* Passion. Others—from Hume to the Emotivists—have appeared to reverse this hierarchy ("reason is and ought to be nothing but the slave of the passions"). But those philosophers who refuse to join in the general denigration of emotion as irrational usually share the presupposition that the role of rationality is limited to the calculation of means. Insofar as emotions (often confused with desires) are concerned with the determination of ends, they remain, on this view, beyond the pale of rationality. Modern decision theorists have worked out schemes to assess the rationality of desires, as well as actions, against the background of beliefs and other desires.[1] But these schemes leave no room at all for emotions, except, by implication, as disrupters of the rational process.

Yet there is also another streak. Plato, for example, whose views are often given as paradigms of the first tradition, in fact held a subtler position. Although he assigned emotion, or *thumos,* to a part of the soul which it is the business of the Rational part to rule and control, *thumos* is also said to be generally the *ally* of the rational part; and besides, Plato sometimes questions the value of the rational too narrowly construed: "the greatest goods come to men through madness," says the *Phaedrus* (244). Some have suggested that emotions have their *own* logic: "Le coeur a ses raisons que la raison ne connaît pas," said Pascal. Common sense is quite ready to assess particular emotions as reasonable or unreasonable. And several philosophers, from Spinoza on, have emphasized the *thought-dependence* of emotions. The connection is not always easy and direct: but the process of psychoanalysis—of all schools and versions—is based on the existence of such connections even where they are not easily accessible. Without it a "talking cure" aimed at emotional change would make no sense.[2]

Such considerations have inspired existentialist attempts to show that emotions are judgments or courses of behavior directly liable to assessments of rationality.[3] The implausibility of these attempts lies in their extremism: they leave no room for any accommodation with the dominant view. We need a perspective capable of assimilating the grounds of both traditions. My aim here is to make a beginning at sorting out the issues involved.

RATIONALITY

It would be convenient to start with an analysis of rationality. But this is such a fundamental concept that what is proffered as analysis generally turns out to be ideological manifesto. So I shall try to make do without such an attempt. Nevertheless, we need some idea of what has to be true of states that can be assessed for rationality. I shall formulate three theses, for which I give only the barest arguments. They entail plausible constraints on the objects of rationality assessments, and I shall proceed on the assumption that they are true. But the reader who finds them contentious can take them simply as circumscribing the notion of rationality which I am presupposing. If this notion turns out to be helpful in the present context, that will be so much in its favor. In formulating these theses, I am guided by what seems true of the paradigm objects of rationality assessments: actions, beliefs, and wants. Later I shall examine their applicability to emotions.

Teleology: cognitive and strategic. Rationality is always a teleological concept. Anything that we speak of as rational or irrational, we so designate in the light of some function or end. An *act* is irrational if it tends to frustrate its ostensible or ultimate goal, or the agent's. A *want* can be said to be irrational in the light of other wants claiming precedence in a hierarchy of wants and ends. A *belief* is irrational if it is unlikely to be true, or if it was arrived at in a way that in general is not conducive to the acquisition of true beliefs (or the avoidance of false ones).

This way of putting things with regard to belief presupposes that we can make sense of something like *epistemic utility:* in terms of this we assess the rationality of judgments as if they were acts. This is a well-explored and useful point of view;[4] but it is not incompatible with the fact that our "epistemic ends" have, programmed into us by nature, a measure of autonomy from other ends. Evolution is a rule-utilitarian, not an act-utilitarian process. The value of truth—epistemic utility—is no doubt in general subordinate to less abstract biological ends; but in particular cases it is not assessed in terms of any direct common measure with those ends. I propose to mark this relative independence by labeling two sorts of rationality: the *cognitive,* applicable directly to judgments and beliefs, and the *strategic,* applicable primarily to actions or wants.

Intentionality. Appropriateness to a goal is not a sufficient condition of rationality. For consider organs of the body: they are, by and large in thriving species, appropriate to their function. And if there were a god it would have been rational of it to endow animals with lungs and livers if it intended that they should thrive. But that does not make the functioning of lungs and livers rational, nor does it make it rational *of* those organisms to have those organs. It is primarily individuals who are assessed for rationality, and it is in respect of their *intentional states* that they are so assessed. This is my second thesis: the teleology implied in rationality applies only to *intentional states.*[5]

Here it may be objected that acts, which are among my paradigms of entities assessable for rationality, are not intentional states. True, insofar as acts are not states. So let us modify the prescription to read: "intentional states *or events.*" Acts are at least intentional *events,* in this sense: any act, if it is to be distinguished from a mere occurrence befalling the "agent," must be characterized in terms of intentional states: in terms, that is, of the beliefs and intentions in the light of which it is the act that it is claimed to be.

Minimal Rationality. It is precisely in connection with this aspect of actions that my third thesis is most readily explained. It is this: Any intentional state amenable to criticism in terms of canons of rationality must be described by some true description that represents the state as rational. I shall refer to this as the condition of minimal rationality. It needs some explanation and defense.

The case is clearest with respect to actions. To label an event an action is to attribute to it a want set and a belief set as determining factors. The want set determines the goal of the act (even if the act is done "for its own sake") and the beliefs pertain to the circumstances and the likelihood of the end being attained by performing that particular act (or some "basic" act that underlies it) under those conditions. If the description of the act is sufficiently circumscribed, no distinction can be made at that level of description between the act's teleological structure—which is indispensable for it to be called an act at all—and its rationality. It is only when we enlarge the context to include other beliefs and wants, as well as the arguments that have served to bring them into existence, that the charge of irrationality can be made to stick.

It is frequently pointed out that in "Man is a rational animal," the word must be taken in a categorial sense for the dictum to come out true: taken in the evaluative sense, it is clearly false. The evaluative sense presupposes the categorial sense: to be either rational or irrational (evaluatively) is to be rational (categorially). In terms of this familiar distinction, the thesis of minimal rationality is this:

It is a necessary condition of an intentional state or event's being describable as rational (categorially), that there be some true description under which it can properly (though perhaps vacuously) be said to be rational (evaluatively).

Two overblown but well-known dogmas are related to the application of this thesis to belief and to wanting. The dogma of phenomenalism aims to pare down the existential claims involved in (perceptual) beliefs until they are "incorrigible." The Platonic doctrine that no one desires the bad, or that desire is always *sub specie boni,* also depends on abstracting from the circumstances that make an actual want be of something really good or not. In both doctrines the grain of truth is this: each intentional state has a "formal" or "proper object"—respectively truth and goodness. For a state to *count* as a belief, it must consist in the positing of a given (intentional) object as belonging to the proper object of belief —that is, being true; for it to count as a want, it must consist in the positing of an intentional object as belonging to the proper object of wanting—that is, being good.[6] In that minimal context, wants and beliefs have the structure of states that are categorially rational, but the restriction of context insulates them from any considerations in terms of which they can be said to be irrational. They are therefore (evaluatively) rational under those minimal descriptions.

Quine has offered a principle of translation which can be seen as an application of the present point of view. Why should I not allow myself to translate a native belief as something of the form '$p \& p$'?[7] Because an explicit contradiction could not intelligibly be posited as true. Such a proposition lacks the condition of minimal rationality, and therefore cannot be the content of any belief. The Freudian analysis of parapraxes can be viewed in the same light. Why are Freudian "slips" not merely accidents? Because they *can* be seen as having the structure of minimally rational acts: if enough abstraction is allowed from the realistic circumstances in which the parapraxis occurs, and if certain assumptions can be made about the existence of a certain context of beliefs and wants, the event can be fitted into that context and ascribed the minimally rational structure that is definitive of an *act*. It does not matter that in a broader context the act is irrational.

THREE LEADING QUESTIONS

Each of the above theses suggests a question to be raised in regard to the emotions:

1. Which sort of rationality can emotions aspire to? If, as Sartre has suggested, they were acts intended to effect a magical transformation of reality, they would presumably come under the category of strategic rationality. But Solomon (also inspired by Sartre) has recently suggested that they are species of judgment: if so they might be expected to fall under a cognitive criterion.[8]

2. What are the objects of emotions, and what are their "formal objects"—if indeed they have any?

3. What application can be made to emotions of the principle of minimal rationality?

These questions are more easily separated in the asking than the answering. For we need to know something about the nature of objects of emotion before we can classify judgments of rationality with cognitive or strategic ones, or pin down cases of minimally rational emotions. Nevertheless, I shall start in a preliminary way with the first question.

The category of cognitive rationality calls for a further distinction. I have written as if it were judgments or beliefs in themselves that were up for assessment; but I have also indicated that the assessment is likely to be made in terms of the way that the belief was arrived at. Should we then, properly speaking, ascribe rationality to the belief itself, or to the argument or other process that has led up to it?

INTRINSIC RATIONALITY: THE PROBLEM OF OBJECTIVITY

There is some temptation to think that rationality properly applies only to *transitions*. These, however, can only be assessed in the light of something like the probability of adequacy which they confer to the resultant state. In the case of inferences, "adequacy" is simply truth. We do not rate a transition—an argument or inference—rational if and only if it leads to true belief, but we do require at least that it be of a sort that generally tends to increase the likelihood of truth. It is therefore useful to stipulate the following extension of the notion of rationality: call "intrinsic rationality," or more briefly *success,* the property of the end state which rational transitions make more probable. In the case of actions, "success" is generally called just that: success. In belief it is called *truth*. In wants, success is actual desirability or goodness. I propose to extend this to emotions, and to call the success of an emotion "appropriateness." Plato, who first claimed that pleasure and pain, and emotions generally, could be assessed in a dimension of success separable from mere pleasantness, seems to have shocked practically everybody by calling it truth. The idea I want to defend is not so different;[9] but for two reasons I won't speak of the *truth* of emotions. One is that I have no wish to be unnecessarily provocative. A more important reason is that I do not want to beg the question whether the dimension of rationality appropriate to emotions is the cognitive, rather than the strategic, or whether it is in some important way different from both. The answer to that question will eventually emerge. So I shall stick with "appropriateness." And I shall say that

an emotion is appropriate, if and only if the evoking object or situation *warrants* the emotion.[10]

This immediately suggests an objection: is there anything objectively in a situation—as opposed to the mere heart of the emoter—that can be said to *warrant* the emotion? The implied analogy is with perception: but in the case of perception there is a distinction between objective correctness and illusion. What is there, in the case of emotion, to correspond to this?[11] The objection may get additional impetus from remembering that the whole point of the Emotivist Theories of Ethics was to remove moral judgments from the realm of the factual. This was agreed on both by its advocates, who saw it as a virtue, and by its opponents, who rejected Emotivism on precisely that ground.

Let us then explore the parallel with perception. Consider the quality of redness. To be sure, it depends in part on the character of our receptors; in this sense redness, as a "secondary quality," differs from mass. The measurement of mass depends on our instruments and ultimately on our senses, but the property itself can be defined independently of any reference to our senses. This is not the case for red. On the other hand, red is not simply "in the mind": it is not a matter of fantasy, an arbitrary projection from my consciousness. Nor can the quality of being red be defined exclusively in terms of an experience, a sensation: for in order to pinpoint the sensation of red, we need a reference to standard conditions of observation by standard observers: the sensation of red is that caused by the sight of blood, by daylight, in a normal observer.[12] To this extent we might therefore say that colors, while they are monadic properties, depend for their existence on some relational ones. But there is no reason why such properties, any more than straightforwardly relational ones, cannot be objective. To claim otherwise is to confuse a property that depends for its existence on certain other, relational, ones, with one that is assigned without criteria at the whim of a subject. The latter would be really a property of the subject itself; of its purported bearer it would only be an intentional property, that is no property at all. The former, on the other hand, even if it were claimed to be *really* (covertly) dyadic, can quite legitimately generate a monadic property by dint of holding the second term (the "subject") constant. The normal observer in normal conditions plays just this role. This disposes of the claim that secondary qualities are less objective than primary ones.

A just objection, however, does remain: At best what has been said so far clears the way for there to be objective correlates of emotions: it does not establish that there must be some. But to make that further point, we cannot continue to discuss the nature of emotional rationality—our first "leading question"—in isolation from the other questions. I shall rest my hope of progress on two sets of considerations. The first is intended to make plausible the idea that there is a biological *point* to emotions, just as there is a biological point to our capacity to discriminate colors (in spite of the fact that from the physical or scientific point of view colors are very unimportant: they reveal absolutely nothing of the essential properties of matter).[13] I shall offer some speculations about what that biological point might be, and this will tell us something about the nature of emotional appropriateness. In the second set of considerations, I shall offer some thoughts about the origins and development of our capacity for emotional discrimination: this will involve characterizing the paradigm cases in which, in abstraction from context, the existence of a given emotion is a sufficient condition of its rationality. Thus each set of considerations will connect with one of the other two leading questions I have posed: the first, with the question of appropriateness, or the nature of the formal object of emotions, and the second, with the application of the principle of minimal rationality. We shall be led, in conclusion, to consider some essential limitations of a purely biological approach. Realizing the nature of these limitations—the dependence of emotions on the process of socialization—will round out the proffered sketch of the rationality of emotions.

WHAT ARE EMOTIONS FOR?

"What are emotions biologically for?" may seem an odd question to ask. But it is, I think, a question all the more urgent because of the prevalence of the view of emotions as disrupters rather than collaborators of rational activity. From the point of view of evolution, it is a question that is always appropriate: though it may not get a positive answer in every case. "Chance genetic drift," an answer that amounts to rejecting the question, may well explain something harmless such as the prevalence of a certain eye color in a population. But when we are talking about something so often thought destructive, we must ask: how did we come by it? Why are we not the better off without it? and if we are, how come we're still here with it?

Let us try to imagine what it would be like to be without emotions. It is not easy to make the supposition clear in view of the close connection between emotion and motivation: it must not be confused with the supposition that we might be without wants. For I am still speaking of agents. I see two forms for this speculation to take. A being without emotion would either be some kind of Kantian monster with a computer brain and a pure rational Will, or else a Cartesian animal-machine, an ant, perhaps, in which every "want" is preprogrammed and every "belief" simply a releasing cue for a specific response. My hunch here is that it is because we are neither one nor the other, "neither beast nor angel," that we have emotions as well as beliefs and desires. But a hunch is not an explanation.

What is it that animal-machine and Kantian angel have in common? I submit that it is *complete determinacy:* on the one hand by mechanisms, on the other by reason. In fact, of course, both are equally mythical beings: there are no animal-machines of the sort described, because of the fact of biological variability. Two individual ants, two individual viruses even, won't do exactly the same thing under every condition. But close enough: close enough in particular so that individual ants have no need of special clues to tell them how, from a repertoire of equally probable alternatives, other ants are likely to react. Ants, unlike primates, have no need for communicativeness of emotional expression. If ants emote, they need not know it of one another. But the more interesting impossibility concerns the angel. There, full predictability does not elude us because of angelic variability, but because there is no such thing as fully determinate rationality.

Consider the epistemic level. There are many issues on which logic gives no unique prescription. Logic suggests that in consistency we should avoid false beliefs and pursue true ones: "Don't believe an inconsistent set," but "Believe the consequences of your beliefs." Plausible as they are, these principles are not always compatible in their application, nor do they prescribe their own ordering. Thus even at the lowest level we require "policies that seem reasonable" to supplement hard logic. But the most important areas of indeterminacy have to do with what subjects to investigate, and what inductive rules to adopt. No logic determines *salience:* what to attend to, what to inquire about. And no inductive logic can make a strictly rational choice between, say, the extremes of "soft headedness" and "hard headedness." The terms are borrowed from the *Theaetetus:* you will recall that Plato (at 191 c) describes two sorts of "tablets" in the mind: soft ones that easily take impressions but lose them as fast, and hard ones that are difficult to scratch, but once imprinted hard to erase. Plato's problem was what statisticians now call the problem of the choice of *significance level:* how probable must it be that your hypothesis is true on the evidence, and how improbable must it be that it should be false on the evidence, before it is rational to accept it? Inductive logic does not tell us, and statistics offers only sophisticated rules of thumb.

The same goes for choices of strategies in the light of existing desires: there are choices that no rational calculation can make, because they are between alternatives that on rational calculation turn out the same. An obvious example is the choice between a minimax and a maximax strategy. In a situation where I can either act, with much to lose and as much to gain, or refrain, with nothing to gain or lose, the probabilities involved may be such that the expected desirabilities of the two are identical. Yet there is clearly a perceptible difference between the two options: minimize losses, or maximize gains. One can make up a principle here, of course, as one can for consistency or for induction. But no principle can claim to be dictated by rationality alone.

This suggests a hypothesis: the function of emotion is to fill gaps left by (mere wanting plus) "pure reason" in the determination of action and belief.

Consider how Iago proceeds to make Othello jealous. His task is essentially to direct Othello's attention, to suggest questions to ask: "did Michael Cassio, when you woo'd my lady—Know of your love?'' and then to insinuate that there are inferences to be drawn without specifying them himself, so that Othello exlaims:

> By heaven, thou echoest me
> As if there were some monster in thy thought
> Too hideous to be shown. . . .
>
> [III iii]

Then more directly Iago advises: "Look to your wife." Once attention is thus directed, inferences which on the same evidence would before not even have been thought of are experienced as compelling: "Farewell, the tranquil mind . . ."

In this example, the emotion is changed via the manipulation of attention. But such manipulation is not always possible. It can be blocked by the grip of a preexisting emotion. Even where an emotion is already regnant, however, the order of causal accessibility of emotion and attention is not fixed; it depends in part (for reasons I will sketch below in "Paradigm Scenarios"), on the historic origins of an individual's experience of and capacity for the emotions involved. As commonsense "psychologists" we learn to "play on" people's emotions—sometimes the more abusively for being more shrewd. Iago is a master psychologist in that sense: a con man, which is to say, a sophist of the emotions. The con man and the sophist differ in the emphasis they place on different methods, but there is some of the other in each. A sophist needs to divert attention from his most slippery arguments, and one way to do it is by manipulating emotion (the art of the political orator.) But a con man must also be, like Iago, adept at "passing" bad arguments by making them look plausible. In the light of this example, the hypothesis for exploration can be restated thus:

Emotions are determinate patterns of salience among objects of attention, lines of inquiry, and inferential strategies.

Before asking how this hypothesis can help with my three questions, let us survey a sample of applications, just to get the feel of what it is I am suggesting.

Item: The hypothesis can help us to see the importance of the expression of emotion among members of a species whose behavior is not highly stereotyped. To read the emotional configuration of another's body or face is to have a guide to what they are likely to believe, attend to, and therefore want and do. Such dispositions tend to be given different names depending in part on their duration: a short one is an emotion, a longer one a sentiment, and a permanent one is called *character*. (Psychoanalysts recognize both the difference and the connection between such long and short term dispositions by distinguishing two sorts of pathology: "neurosis," and "character neurosis.")

Item: We can also see why it has been tempting to assimilate emotions both to judgments and to desires. On my view, emotions ask the questions which judgment answers with beliefs: but as every committee chairman knows, questions have a good deal to do with the determination of answers: the rest can be done with innocuous facts. In this way emotions can be said to be judgments rather in the way that scientific paradigms might be said to be "judgments": they are what we see the world "in terms of." But they cannot be articulated propositions. Much the same reasons motivate their assimilation to desire (which is itself sometimes classed as an emotion). For as long as we presuppose some basic or preexisting desires, the directive power of "motivation" belongs to what controls attention, salience, and inference strategies preferred where logic leaves a choice.

Item: Emotions are often described as guiding the processes of reasoning—or distorting them, depending on the describer's assessment of their appropriateness. Indeed, this is in great part what all good novels are about. In extreme cases we think of reasoning as being distorted into self-deception: but there is seldom a sharp mistake in logic of which the self-deceiver can be accused. If my account is right, self-deception is not different in kind or mechanism from normal cases of reasoning about matters of concern. The difference may largely rest in the relation of a piece of reasoning to what is expected in the circumstances.

Consider for example the way that we are wont to discount experience for distance in space, time, or affection. It seems reasonable to do this, within vague bounds: but there are no rules of rationality that prescribe the rate of discount. The thought of our own death is subject to this discount, but in certain ("emotional") moments our attention shifts; we feel our mortality in a different way. These are rare moments of experience when we feel the truth of a commonplace, which is as different from what we call knowing it as the vision of waters upon the earth is different from the delirious vision of the water which cannot be had to cool the burning tongue.[14]

They illustrate that shifts of emotion are primarily shifts of salience.

Item: Although emotions are manipulators of reasoning, the experience of emotion tends to be an "intuitive" one: it is not easy to formulate reasons for one's shifts of attention. To be sure, there are great differences between types of emotion on this point: it applies least to indignation, or perhaps to embarrassment: but many emotions find it hard to give their own reasons, even though they produce reasons of their own. This applies not just to the most diffuse or least "thought dependent," such as joy or depression: but also to those, like love or mistrust, that are specific in their targets and sometimes even loquacious about their propositional objects. Even these are often not given to much pretense of having been brought about by reasons: "I can't explain: he just gives me the creeps." An explanation sometimes offered for this is that emotions are somatic phenomena; that they consist largely in autonomic reactions, of which the phenomenological component consists in dim awareness. A preferable explanation can be given in terms of the model I have sketched: paying attention to certain things is a source of reasons, but comes before them. Similarly, scientific paradigms, in Kuhn's sense,[15] are better at stimulating research in certain directions than at finding compelling and fair reasons for their own adoption. They are too "deep" for that, too unlike specific, easily formulated beliefs.

Item: Emotions have a very variable degree of adaptivity. Hence of course their reputation for being disruptive. There is bound to be a good deal of atavism, of various levels of antiquity, in the determinants of our emotions. And this means that they will be variously well adapted to the circumstances in which they are now likely to arise. On the present account this is to be expected: to be inclined to look to certain things may have a very different utility in different circumstances. Here as elsewhere, the overall usefulness of some device of nature is quite compatible with its noxiousness in particular cases. This is a point that was made by Descartes:

The utility of all the passions consists in their fortifying and perpetuating in the soul thoughts which it is good it should preserve.... And again, all the harm which they can cause consists in the fact that they fortify and conserve these thoughts more than necessary. (Passions of the Soul, 74)

Descartes here explicitly links the variable utility of emotions with what one might call their *inertia*.[16] But inertia is not, as on Descartes's view it should be, the general case. What we get instead are variable patterns of continuity and transformation between emotions. Here are some examples:

(a) In some cases, the discovery that an emotion was premised on a false belief, instead of simply canceling the emotion, will transmute it into another. Indignation can turn into remorse upon finding that it was unjust; and we have all seen a parent punish a lost child when, on finding it, anxiety turned to anger. In such cases the focus of attention is not changed by the mere change of belief: so there is a kind of inertia of attention. But since the facts are now different, new features of the situation naturally become salient to the same attentive set, in turn provoking shifts in the dominant patterns of concern.

(b) In other cases, the emotion's habit of looking for certain sorts of facts and facilitating certain sorts of inference will simply look for more: thus when Mrs. Farebrother learns that Lydgate is not the natural son of Bulstrode, she does not take this to be sufficient ground for ceasing to think ill of Bulstrode: "the report may be true of some other son."[17] Here the emotion can be clearly seen as a disposition to ask certain questions.

(c) Conversely, there are cases where something comes to change that disposition without any change in the object or in any directly relevant belief. A friend of mine felt intimidated by a woman he met, apparently because of her character. Later he discovered that the woman had been his student: though not claiming to perceive any difference in her character, "I'm not afraid of her any more," he said, "because I have this maxim that you can't be afraid of students." From the point of view of a teacher, signs of intellectual threat are not salient, nor are they easily inferred. The story is a good illustration of the fact that emotions operate at the meta-level with respect to beliefs.

Item: These facts about emotional change are related to a more general point, about the voluntariness of emotions. In spite of the "irrationality of emotion" tradition, we commonly hold people responsible for their emotions. This seems to presuppose that emotions are at least to some extent in our power. The hypothesis I have offered suggests an explanation for the limited extent to which this is true.

Emotions, I have said, are in part patterns of attention. Therefore one might expect a change in patterns of attention to entail a change in emotion. I can't be very angry any more, if I notice none of your misdeeds, nor even infer to any when there is a doubt to be resolved.

Now attention, to some degree, is in our power. But among the limitations to this control is a logical one, which results in its being a lot easier to attend at will than to withdraw one's attention at will. I can clearly keep in mind a target to be avoided: but if the avoidance sought is *inattention,* my efforts will be self-defeating. (This is the starting point of some of the notorious puzzles of self-deception.) So we may expect great difficulty in trying to get rid of an unwanted emotion, but more success in working ourselves *into* one. And indeed, these are familiar facts. It does me no good to tell myself how foolish I am to miss her: for the thought is an enemy agent, as it were, calculated to fix my thoughts on just what I should forget. I should forget her smile, her eyes, her perfect breasts.... The best course is to fall in love with someone else: "it'll take my mind off her." Or failing that, to hate her: directing my attention onto her betrayal, her levity, her heartlessness.... And the same goes for self-love: "Il est facile de se haïr," said Bernanos, "Le difficile est de s'oublier."

I have been expanding and illustrating the idea that our emotions underlie our rational processes. This claim—this model of emotions and what at the most general level they are *for*—was introduced to make it plausible that there is some objectivity, related to biological significance, to the proper objects of emotions. But it is time to address the question directly. For it might well seem that the way emotions have been claimed to underlie rational processes does not argue for their susceptibility to rational assessment for themselves: either "intrinsically" or "in transition." Have I not shown merely that emotions are nonrational supplements to rationality, serving merely to ensure that rational processes will have determinate outcomes?

Yes, but not only that. It seems to be so only because we are strongly tempted to assume that only propositional states of the kinds familiar from the formulations of belief and desires can be assessed for rationality. But I have resisted the assimilation of emotions either to mere judgments or to desires: their formal or proper objects are different in kind, and their intentional objects may be too. This requires some explanation.

PARADIGM SCENARIOS

Classical writers on the emotions, from Descartes on, are fond of making lists of primitive emotions, then going on to show how the more complex are built out of those. The diversity in the resulting lists is warning enough that this is an unpromising strategy. And yet it cannot be denied that there are, in other animals as in human babies, modes of behavior that we take to express something like human emotions. The determination of salience and preferred inference patterns cannot afford to wait for the development of fullfledged rationality. I think we can understand, in principle, how our repertoire of emotions gets built up, without positing a set of "primary emotions" that get combined like basic blocks or even mixed like primary colors. We do need a repertoire of primitive instinctual responses, but emotions are not mere responses. I suspect it works like this:

We are made familiar with the vocabulary of emotion by association with *paradigm scenarios,* drawn first from our daily life as small children, later reinforced by the stories and fairy tales to which we are exposed, and, later still, supplemented and refined by literature and art. Paradigm scenarios involve two aspects: first a paradigm situation providing the characteristic *objects* of the emotion (where objects can be of various sorts, sometimes more suitably labeled "target," or "occasion"), and second, a set of characteristic or "normal" *responses* to the situation. It is in large part in virtue of the response component of the scenarios that emotions are commonly held to *motivate:* though this is, in a way, back-to-front: for the emotion often takes its name from the response disposition and is only afterward assumed to cause it. There is little doubt that a child is genetically programmed to respond in specific ways to the situational components of some paradigm scenarios. An essential part of education consists in identifying these responses, giving the child a name for them in the context of the scenario, and thus teaching it that it is experiencing a particular emotion.[18]

The essential thought-dependency of certain emotions, and the lesser extent of that dependency in some of the more "primitive" ones (such as lust or terror) is easily explained in terms of the kinds of paradigm scenarios to which they are related. If the paradigm scenario cannot be apprehended without complex linguistic skills, for example, we shall not expect to find in whoever lacks those skills an emotion specifically tuned to that scenario. That is why, as Iris Murdoch has put it,

> the most essential and fundamental aspect of culture is the study of literature, since this is an education in how to picture and understand human situations.[19]

On the other hand, scenarios that involve primitive responses such as flight or attack can subsist to define so-called primitive emotions, fear and rage, retaining their power even over individuals whose repertoire has been expanded by experience and literature to include the most "refined" emotions. We can all bear witness to such survivals, if not in ourselves, at least in our best friends.

The way that paradigm scenarios fit into my central hypothesis should be obvious. Learning to "gestalt" situations in terms of such scenarios is learning to attend differentially to certain features of an actual situation, to inquire into the presence of further features of the scenario, and to make inferences that the scenario suggests.[9] Armed with the notion of paradigm scenarios, then, we can now return to the questions asked at the conclusion of our discussion of rationality.

APPLICATIONS TO OUR LEADING QUESTIONS

To start with the last: there is an obvious application to the question about *minimal rationality*. Since emotions are learned in terms of these paradigms, they cannot, at least within a given social context, be criticized for inappropriateness if they occur in response to the paradigm situation. Though we must here carefully distinguish the emotion itself from the response in behavior which the scenario might involve: it does not follow from the rationality of the emotion evoked that the stock response will continue to be seen as rational. Where the response is an action or strategy, it needs to be assessed in its own terms. It may be that a further narrowing of the context is needed before the minimal rationality of the behavior is guaranteed. A spouse witnessing sexual intercourse between their spouse and another person may react with jealousy and rage, and insofar as the situation belongs to the paradigm scenario for jealousy, the emotion must be counted appropriate. But even if the original scenario, *as learned,* involves the response of murdering the parties, this will not necessarily make the action rational. That act will have its own minimal rationality as an extreme act of revenge: but the mere existence of the scenario will not determine whether extreme revenge is rational in cases of jealous rage.

Nevertheless, this account raises a problem. It appears to suggest that the rationality of an emotion is fixed irretrievably by its origins in socialization, and that nothing can affect the appropriateness of an emotion provided the evoking situation fits the paradigm. What then of the changes in emotional dispositions that we call "maturing emotionally"? And what of the possibility of striving for greater emotional rationality? Can we not repudiate certain scenarios altogether in an effort, for example, to be rid of sexist attitudes and emotions?

This objection amounts to much the same as the charge, justly laid against a certain kind of "Oxford philosophy" a couple of decades ago, of misusing the notion of paradigm. But that a concept is learned in a given context is not the end of the matter. It does not mean that the concept cannot be revised and refined; that our understanding of it cannot be deepened to the point where we are able to ask without contradiction whether it is appropriate to the paradigm itself. The smiling bride was the paradigm of a free agent: we might well teach the concept in terms of this example. But that should not prevent us from analyzing the concept and then applying it from a broader perspective to the paradigm itself: but is she *really* free? When the paradigm is questioned in this way, it is invariably in the light of a wider range of considerations than are available when the case is viewed in isolation. The concept of minimal rationality does not require that the state or event in question be describably as (evaluatively) rational in the light of all wider perspectives. Paradigms can be revised in the light of other, competing paradigms that are seen *also* to be applicable to the situation at hand: though the emotion will retain its basic intelligibility (its minimal rationality) provided it can be seen in the light of its own, narrowest, proper scenario. Further, a scenario can become completely inert, obsolete: this will take place if every situation that fitted the original scenario comes to be seen as fitting another (set of) scenario(s), one that is preferable or more congenial when the situation is viewed from a more comprehensive perspective.[21] The attempt to restructure one's emotions by "consciousness raising" is based on this possibility—without which, I suspect, there could be no such thing as moral development.

Nevertheless, an objector might insist, in what sense can we maintain that the process of one paradigm's being supplanted by another is rational? And to what extent can it be maintained that there is any *objectivity* involved here? Am I not saying that attitudes, dispositions, and habits may change unaccountably, since what leads to change—what one might barbarously call "emotional regestalting"—is simply beyond the pale of rationality? Do emotions not remain as subjective after as before such changes?

Mostly, no. Again the tendency to think so springs from an unrealistic picture of the rationality of belief changes, and from unwarranted standards for "objectivity." I said that an emotion is appropriate (or minimally so) in a given situation if and only if that situation is relevantly similar to, can accurately be "gestalted" as, the situation of a suitable paradigm scenario. But there is no requirement that situation and response not also be similar to some other scenarios. Indeed, such a requirement would be incoherent. Emotions, like other perceptual Gestalts, are not necessarily compatible: hence although there are cases where emotions mix, in varying proportions, we can also expect a class of cases where one Gestalt, one emotion, crowds out another. To be sure, what can be seen as similar to a given scenario admits of a certain amount of leeway. Can the complicated friendships of sophisticated Bloomsburyites adequately be seen as instantiating "the Eternal Triangle," for example, or would that scenario be truly stifled, in those circles, by the meta-scenario in which it appears as *vulgar*? To this extent, emotions and their adequacy to their objects, or rationality, cannot be assessed with mathematical precision. But on the other hand not just anything goes, either, as those have learned to their regret, who have attempted to "rationalize" their lives in terms of invented scenarios insufficiently rooted in human nature and the facts of life. True irrationality of emotion involves the perception of a situation in terms of a scenario which it does not *objectively* resemble: in such cases we are well advised to see unconscious links and transformation rules that have turned one situation into another. Emotional irrationality is a matter of muddled scenarios: a loss of *reality,* intensified in neurosis and extreme in psychosis. The minimal rationality of those emotions must be sought in terms of the scenario unconsciously evoked: thus psychotherapy typically looks for clues to the transformation in free association; and it is a sound principle of therapy not to rest in the search for the original scenario until the emotion inappropriately evoked is in this way accounted for as minimally rational.

At this point yet another objection may occur to you. What I have tried to describe under the names of "adequacy," "success," "appropriateness," clearly belongs in the cognitive rather than the strategic category of rationality. But I distinguished two kinds of cognitive rationality, and what I have said has clear application only to what I called rationality by extension, or "success." It is the analogue of *truth,* not of *validity* of argument. It has also been said to underlie transitions between beliefs and/or desires by selecting the inductive rules involved in such transitions. But can the term *rationality* really apply to transitions from one *emotion* to another?

I think it can: and I have already given examples of such "transitions." But it must be pointed out that in this regard emotional rationality is more akin to the strategic kind. For just as there are no strategic arguments that consist exclusively in premises and conclusions referring to wants (for there must also be factual premises, or ones that are relevant to belief), so emotions do not reason to other emotions without more conventionally cognitive premises. The reason for this is that the chief instrument of criticism with respect to emotions, consists in the working out of consequences of the application of a given scenario, in confrontation with others that may also be applicable. And these consequences as well as the applicability of different scenarios, are matters of empirical fact in a common-or-garden sense. This is analogous to the way we debate about wants: we examine what, under the prevalent conditions, would be the effects of acting on some of our wants, with relation to our other wants. In this way we work out hierarchies—some temporary, just for the purposes of an occasion of deliberation, and some more permanent—among our wants and values. So with emotions: the chief task of establishing rational transitions between emotions, and rational emotional responses to situations where several alternatives compete, involves determining hierarchies among applicable scenarios. To pick another example from a rich mine, consider how Will Ladislaw

> felt that his dislike was flourishing at the expense of his gratitude and spent much inward discourse in justifying this dislike.

Part of that inward discourse goes like this:

> He was much obliged to Casaubon in the past, but really the act of marrying his wife was a set-off against the obligation. It was a question whether gratitude which refers to what is done for one's self ought not to give way to indignation at what is done against another.[22]

The hierarchies and orders of precedence among emotions are, in a given culture, fixed to a great extent. They represent that aspect of the ideology of a culture which prescribes dispositions of character as *virtues*—often different for different social classes, ages, and sexes.[23] For this reason, one who has succeeded in modifying the usual hierarchy may find herself not merely vilified as immoral by those who make the conventional assumptions, but literally not understood. Thus *Ms. Magazine* recently reprinted an item, from a counseling column, in which a doctor advised:

> Mothers who force weaning early and abruptly may experience anger at the loss of the intimate relationship with the nursing child. Some women may express this anger by returning to work or taking a vacation.[24]

Of course, in such cases, the allegation of lack of understanding is mutual: which is what we should expect from parties interpreting a situation in terms of different ideologies or scenarios. The application of a scenario to a real situation makes the "reasonable" hierarchy of emotions seem so obvious, that the likely mutual charge is not merely misunderstanding but *self-deception*. The fact that it is mutual, however, in no way implies that there is not correctness in the matter.

SUMMARY

It is time to recapitulate and conclude. I began by offering, with little argument, what I take to be plausible theses about the conditions for ascription of rationality. These conditions suggested three "leading questions," which could not be easily separated in the course of the discussion, but to which I can now summarize one by one the answers that have emerged.

1. The first question was whether the rationality of emotions was of the cognitive or the strategic kind. On this I conclude that it is sufficiently close to the cognitive type in admitting a close analogue of *truth,* a distinct species of intrinsic "success"—claims about the subjectivity of emotions notwithstanding. Their mode of objectivity is, to be sure, one that is relative to human nature, its characteristic inclinations and responses. This objectivity is grounded in paradigm scenarios that are at the origin of our capacity for specific emotions. I speculated that their biological function is to take up the slack in the rational determination of judgment and desire, by fixing salience of objects of attention and inquiry, and preferred inference patterns. In this way emotions remain *sui generis:* they are not to be identified with a species of judgment. Indeed, although their mode of rationality is closely analogous to the cognitive in respect of their intrinsic "success," the rationality of *transitions* among emotions is more akin to the strategic kind. This view therefore nicely accounts for, while still resisting, the opposed temptations to assimilate emotions to something else, namely beliefs or desires.

2. The second question concerned the objects of emotions and their relation to proper or formal objects. I have thrown a blanket, quite deliberately, over the complications of the analysis of objects, by the use of the term *evoking situation*. But I have attempted to explain the role of the *formal* objects of emotions by reference to the paradigm scenarios in terms of which emotions are learnt. It is

in terms of the relation between the evoking situation and the formal object—the quality that is tied to the paradigm situation—that the appropriateness or intrinsic rationality of an emotion is assessed.

3. The detail of how this is done is subject to the condition described in answer to the third question:

I claimed that for any intentional state amenable to assessment for rationality, it must be possible to circumscribe the context of the state to such an extent that it appears "minimally rational." The application of this to emotions is this: in terms of the paradigm scenario alone, the emotion that fits it is by definition rational. But the "all-things-considered" assessment of an emotion is determined in a complicated way: first, by determining whether the evoking situation is actually an instantiation of the paradigm, and secondly, by confronting it with other applicable paradigms and working out the relations of compatibility, incompatibility, and hierarchic dominance between the relevant scenarios. This complicated process is at the center of our moral life.[25]

NOTES

1. See Richard C. Jeffrey, *The Logic of Decision* (New York: McGraw-Hill, 2965.) The view of emotions as disruptive of normal capacities and activities is not confined to philosophers. For an attack on this conception in psychology, by a psychologist, see R. W. Leeper, "A Motivational Theory of Emotion to Replace 'Emotion as Disorganized Response,'" *Psych. Rev.* vol. 55 (1948), excerpted in M. B. Arnold, ed., *The Nature of Emotion* (Harmondsworth: Penguin, 1968).

2. See Jerome Neu, *Emotion, Thought, and Therapy* (London: Routledge & Kegan Paul, 1978).

3. See J.-P. Sartre, *The Emotions: Outline of a Theory* (New York: The Philosophical Library, 1948), and Robert C. Solomon, *The Passions* (Garden City: Doubleday Anchor, 1976).

4. The approach goes back at least to W. Clifford, "The Ethics of Belief" and W. James, "The Will to Believe." Both are reprinted in W. Kaufman, ed., *Religion from Tolstoy to Camus* (New York: Harper Torchbooks, 1964).

5. See D. Dennett, "Intentional Systems" (*Journal of Philosophy,* vol. 68 [1971] for the distinction between the explanatory stance that attributes goals and beliefs to a *person,* and the "design stance," which while it may attribute "goals" or "functions" to organs or mechanisms, does so only in an extended sense and without reference to person or self. The distinction must be made for cognitive no less than for strategic rationality. For in some sense all biological processes might be called "cognitive," in that they involve differentiated responses to complex signal systems. But the teleology involved in processes below the level of the "intentional" is so called only by analogy: it is the outcome of evolutionary process, not of individual mental-

ity. I have tried to clarify this distinction in "Instincts and Teleology" (forthcoming).

6. The notion of "formal object" for beliefs and wants, and the differences between them, are explored in R. de Sousa, "The Good and the True," *Mind* 68 (1974), 534-551.

7. W. V. Quine, *Word and Object* (New York and London: Wiley, 1960), chap. 2. Note that Quine's principle is weaker than the related "principle of charity" espoused by Davidson and recently criticized by Colin McGinn in "Charity, Interpretation, and Belief" (*Journal of Philosophy* 74 [1977], 521-535, which see for references to Davidson). That principle requires that the work of interpretation begin with the assumption that the subject's beliefs are mostly true; mine requires only that they be supposed *not absurd.* "You appreciate the reasonableness of an action by putting yourself into its agent's shoes, not by forcing him into yours" (McGinn, p. 522).

8. Sartre, *The Emotions;* Solomon, *The Passions.*

9. I have tried to explicate and defend Plato's view in "True and False Pleasures in the *Philebus*" (forthcoming).

10. Some reasons will later become apparent for speaking of "evoking situations." But one reason must be acknowledged right away: it is that I do not propose in this paper to give a typology or analysis of *objects* of emotion. The phrase "evoking situation" leaves matters intentionally vague in this regard.

11. The view that emotions are purely *subjective,* and thus lack objective correlates and can be assessed for rationality only in the strategic sense, is curiously coupled with the view that they are *judgments* in Solomon, *The Passions.*

12. For a most illuminating elaboration of this line, showing how it helps to dispel some of the temptations of phenomenalism, see W. Sellars, "Phenomenalism," in *Science, Perception, & Reality* (London and New York: Routledge, Kegan Paul, and Humanities Press, 1963). For the point made in this paragraph, see also David Wiggins, "Truth, Invention, and the Meaning of Life" (Annual Philosophical Lecture, British Academy, 1976).

13. It should not be thought that this remoteness from the essential properties of nature is necessarily linked with the status of color as a secondary property. For (macroscopic) shape is, in general, equally irrelevant to the deep nature of things (except in crystals). Yet it is among Locke's typical primary qualities because its characterization in a particular case does not depend on any particular features of our sensory receptors.

14. George Eliot, *Middlemarch.*

15. See Thomas Kuhn, *The Structure of Scientific Revolutions* (Chicago, 1962).

16. For a discussion of inertia or "emotional akrasia" and of the variable adaptivity of emotions, see A. O. Rorty, "Explaining Emotions" (*Journal of Philosophy* 75, 3 [March 1978], 139-161). I have derived much help from this paper, as from many conversations with its author.

17. Ibid.

18. Hence, as Aristotle knew, a central part of moral education has to do with learning to feel the right emotions. (*Nicomachean Ethics* II-6).

19. I. Murdoch, *The Sovereignty of Good* (London: Routledge & Kegan Paul, 1970), p. 34. There are difficult and fascinating questions here, about the extent to which literature can *invent* scenarios that when applied to one's own life result in "authentic" emotions. Sociobiology and psychoanalysis are both, from different points of view, concerned with this question. The first asks: how many of the familiar scenarios can be traced to genetically programmed dispositions, and how much

does this matter to the malleability of human emotions and social organization? The latter asks: what is "genuine" sublimation, and what "mere" defense mechanism?

20. Inference-making on the basis of appropriate scenarios is an important part of the psychoanalyst's art. But note that such inferences can be made in two ways: one consists in fitting the situation of the patient into a plausible scenario ("an oedipal problem," for instance), and making "by the book" the inference that this implies. The other way involves *feeling* an emotion that seems to spring from a certain scenario, and allowing inferences to be guided by that emotion in the normal way. The second method is the one every good analyst strives for, though it obviously involves great risks if the therapist has not been "successfully analyzed." It is called "working with the transference and the countertransference."

21. This suggests an analogue of Donald Davidson's "principle of continence": "Let your emotions be appropriate to the widest possible range of available scenarios" (see D. Davidson, "How is Weakness of the Will Possible?" in J. Feinberg, ed., *Moral Concepts* [London: Oxford University Press, 1969]). The complications of working out what this would mean in general, however, are enormous: because the emotional level of rationality is the deepest, that is, the most inclusive. some of these complications are hinted at in the text below.

22. Eliot, *Middlemarch.*

23. See *Meno,* 71e.

24. "No Comment," *Ms. Magazine* (December 1977), p. 97.

25. On the role of the emotions in the moral life, see B. A. O. Williams, "Morality and the Emotions," in *Problems of the Self* (Cambridge, 1973), and Gabriele Taylor, "Justifying the Emotions," *Mind* 84 (1975), 390-402.

The research for this paper was generously supported by a Canada Council Leave Fellowship, 1977-1978.

VI

CHARACTER AND THE EMOTIONS*

ADAM MORTON

Emotion is a category into which we put states for which we have no more revealing title, as long as they have some not too indirect role in motivation and not too explicit propositional content. There need be no natural unity in this pile, in all these passing traits of character, infusions of feeling, colorings of consciousness. I am going to argue that there *is* a unity to some of these things, or at any rate that they are part of a body of concepts which serve a particular function in our talk about people. This unity is more a matter of the way the concepts enter into patterns of attribution and explanation than of the nature of the facts behind their application. It consists in the coincidence, the very nonaccidental coincidence, of a certain indirectness in their attribution, most easily revealed in the way we can't avoid metaphor in saying what emotion, mood, character attaches to someone, and on the other hand a specific way in which these concepts govern routine psychological explanations. The only aim of this paper is to describe this coincidence.

SUBVERTING EXPLANATIONS

Consider, to begin, the attribution of depth of character to people. One says of someone that they have hidden depths or that the apparent depth of their feeling is illusory, or that some particular part of their character, perhaps their loyalty to some ideal, is deep. To say just this would be banal and uninformative, so one usually decorates the image to fit the particular person. The made-to-order metaphors one then comes up with are still governed by a general understanding of how the image of depth works. Deep is persistent; it is down where passing changes do not get at it. So deep motivation is stubborn and tends to underlie more fluctuating desires.

Deep is hidden, too, away from the surface of sociality. So deep thoughts and attitudes may be hard to express, and may evolve in ways that are hidden and hard to explain.

What is the use of describing through these images? One use is to serve as a corrective to more explicit description. A story: *A* says of *B* "It's pretty clear why she ditched George; his influence was no longer any use to her, and there was Simon, with all those stories and friends she could weave into her work." And *C* denies the explanation, without denying the attributions, saying "No, she is as opportunistic as you think, and she does use her friends like that, but in a deeper way; she starts her thinking from the very bottom with reactions to her friends and to their reactions to their friends, and I suppose the thing with George has dried up to the point where it can give her only anecdotes, and not these basic reworkable intuitions. But if she then replaced him with Simon it wasn't because of the number and influence of Simon's friends but because he is tied to them in such interesting peculiar ways." *C* would have difficulty making this comment without the image of deeper and shallower levels of *B*'s use of people. *C* is denying no attribution that *A* is making of *B,* but *C* is denying the explanation *A* makes of *B*'s actions.

The phenomenon I want to discuss is this. Given all the things that any person believes and wants, and all the things that can easily be said of that person, there is a great range of explanations that can be given of their actions. Some of them will apply, but most of them will be just wrong of *that* person, *then.* If one knows which of the formally correct explanations actually does say why someone did something, one knows a pretty basic fact about what that person is like. To express, and think out, these basic facts of people's particular natures we need a vocabulary that cuts across the usual vocabulary of psychological explanation, which can select those particular explanations that apply to a particular person. It is for this reason that we have our highly metaphorical vocabulary of character, mood, and emotion.

THE INVENTION OF PERSONALITY

There are far less problematic impressions of personality, that take the form of explicit literal beliefs that someone's character or mood is of some determinate sort. We think of people as hasty, kind, stupid, frantic, and we qualify our expectations of what they may do accordingly. And there is nothing notably metaphorical about most uses of these terms. If we could make do with just these descriptions we wouldn't have to have any dealings with diffuse images or inarticulate impressions. I think, though, that the two are inextricably connected, that one cannot use concepts of character, mood, or emotion without acknowledging that what one is trying to do with them may sometimes require less tidy attributions.

The function of concepts of character in psychological explanation is, as I indicated, to block, qualify, or emphasize the connections between the beliefs and desires that an explanation appeals to and the actions it explains. The idea is essentially that the use of these concepts has an overriding aim, that of fitting general patterns of explanation to the quirks of the particular case. This makes them inevitably quirky themselves: irregular, resenting regimentation. The first point to make is their resistance to being characterized in behavioral terms.

The point is this: if a character term, say "haste" characteristically serves to pick out a class of intentions from which the person to which it applies may act (e.g., haste rules out the motives for double-checking what one does and reinforces the motives of speed and efficiency) then the range of *actions* in whose explanation it can figure may not have any simple unity at all. The range of actions associated with such a term may in fact not characterize the term at all; they may for example be the same as the actions associable with some other term. Perhaps every action that can be done from haste can be done from care, and vice versa, given suitable variations in the accompanying beliefs and desires.

The difficulty is familiar enough in its general form; behavioral characterizations of psychological terms run afoul of the fact that it is complexes of states rather than individual states that lie behind action. The position of terms of character in the connection of complexes of states with actions is rather special. Their purpose is not to be simply states among the other states that motivate action, but to operate at another level, as indicators of which complexes actually will connect with which actions. The ultimate perfect character term would thus give a paradoxical behavioral quality to the whole scheme. A set of states S and the term t would jointly hold only when one of a defining range of actions was performed, and given an action there would be a set of combinations of S and t which could account for it. This is impossible; at any rate it is beyond the wildest aims of the kind of explaining we actually do. What we seem to do, in practice, is to use fixed patterns of explanation in terms of beliefs, desires, and other well-behaved states, which get us as near as we can to this ultimate end, and then to let free use of the "holes" left in these patterns for attributions of character (mood, emotion) take up as much of the slack as they can.

The result is clearly very imperfect. To have the concept of a character concept, though, is to share something of its hopeless aim; one wants to be able to capture in one's ascriptions of character the reasons why this particular person, at this time, is moved by these motives. And so we invent a labyrinth of character terms, interacting in their effects and stratified in complicated ways, to capture more and more of the particularity of people.

To understand about character concepts must be, then, to have mastered much of the concept of mind of socialized adults in one's culture. Here is a very schematic picture of a possible sequence of stages by which these concepts might be acquired.

To begin, one has a crude grasp of the more literal terms of character and mood. At this stage they may be understood in terms of characteristic patterns of behavior. Angry people curse and kick and move abruptly; sad people move slowly, don't notice much, and cry. A child who understands these as their meanings is on the right track. These can coexist with a grasp, at this stage more a simple skill than any kind of knowledge, of the modulability of one's own perception and behavior, and of other people's styles of action, of a kind that is revealed in childish mimicry. There is no very evident connection between these things at this stage. Nothing here tells one what someone else's sorrow or anger is like (or one's own for that matter), and nothing generates the idea of a thing, experience, which both one and others have.

And then one bright day, one bright year perhaps, hitherto unintelligible parts of the culture begin to make sense as an awareness of the more subtle algebra of psychological explanation combines with a more developed knowledge of the facts of consciousness and of imitation; one realizes that the three elements of the first stage are not unrelated. Most importantly, the two ineffabilities, ineffable in part because they were not at all propositional, those of the control of one's own manner of behavior and those of others individual styles, connect, via the connections each has with the application of terms of character.

Several things have to fit into place for this transition to occur. The simplest of them is just the correlation of terms of character with styles both of one's own and of other people's actions. One needs to have made this correlation in order to, for example, act according to verbal instructions, or fake an emotion one does not have (knowing what emotion it is one is faking). I would imagine this element to be prepared for by one's becoming aware of the same factors in the control of one's own behavior and in one's imitation of others'. A considerably more subtle element is the realization of the variety of explanatory schemes that the culture affords one. One learns that one has to pick the right one for a particular person at a time, and one learns that, within very imprecisely set limits, one can play variations on standard forms of explanation to make them fit particular cases. And one learns that terms of character indicate some of these modulations of explanation. I imagine that a crucial step toward this is the understanding of the role terms of character play within the allowable patterns of explanation.

A final, consolidating, element is the discovery that one can partially represent the ways people seem to one and the ways one is trying to act, in terms of the classes of explanations that would be appropriate and thus eventually in terms of traits of mood and character. A result of the consolidation, and a test of its having occurred, is the arrangement of character concepts in dimensional schemes of the kind social psychologists uncover. Such schemes can have little intelligibility to a purely behavioral understanding of character terms. Presumably they reflect the connections of character concepts with underlying models of mind implicit in the explanatory patterns in which they eventually find their home.

METAPHORS AND EXPLANATIONS

One test of the way one has come along this route, the sophistication one has acquired, is the use one makes of metaphor as a glue to hold together structured explanations, graspings of character, and management of oneself. The metaphorical devices we use here have various degrees of sophistication.

One device, not a very profound one, we use to pick out a range of explanations appropriate to a particular person is to project a characteristic of some of the person's actions into a feature of their personality. So we describe people as clumsy, hasty, meticulous, abrupt, and use these labels to justify our explanations of actions that are not themselves clumsy, hasty, meticulous or abrupt. What one is saying in describing a person as abrupt is, roughly, "think of an action performed abruptly, imagine what it takes to act that way, and now keep this imagined state in mind while thinking what one might do in the following situation." With the right characteristics of action to project, and the right inobtrusiveness at insinuating them beyond their area of literal application, the trick works. We get some increase in understanding of what people are likely to do and what their motives may be.

A rather more subtle device, also for projecting from a class of actions to a class of explanations, is to construe the deliberation, practical reasoning, motivational process, whatever it is that one takes to lie between the beliefs and desires and the action, in terms of the same concepts that one applies to action. In effect, one describes deliberation as covert action. We say of someone that their delicacy is pervasive, that their thinking is like the manipulation of some fragile material which breaks if one bends it too quickly or ties it too tight, or that the movement of their desire is like the response of a creature made of glass, breakable both by resistance to the forces on it and by a too abrupt response to them.

There is something evidently mechanical about these action-to-attribute and action-to-motivation projections. No such easy picture of what is going on will lay out any of the really fine and powerful metaphors. Often, as when we use one of the images of depth, construing the mind as a nested system of fields of action or as concentric shells of the permanence of desire, the use we make of the image or model we produce is so delicately imbedded in the context of description and in the details of the explanation being challenged, endorsed, or qualified, that just stating some general pattern that it conforms to will miss the force that it has in the particular case.

The metaphors of depth have a particular versatility, I think. On different occasions they can introduce combinations of a great variety of considerations into psychological explanations. Let me mention five. (a) There is the difference in permanence and changeability between superficial and profound motives and beliefs, and roughly correlated with this the different intelligibilities of different beliefs. The metaphor presupposes that more permanent, "deep-seated," states will be harder to state and less confidently ascribed. (b) There is the fact that thought is as much effect as it is cause, that thinking like action results from other thinking and from other states of the person. And so we try to represent thought as action, with its own field of action and its own mechanisms of articulation and execution. Inevitably, the result is that we conjure up a stratification of fields of action, since thoughts-as-actions are produced by further thoughts-as-actions, and so on, with each level having its own field of action. (c) We use the same style of imagery often to represent the different degrees of social accessibility or directness that different people exhibit at different times. Much more complicated attitudes and motives are assimilated to the sketch of a pretentious person with layers and layers of makeup, clothes, wigs, and medals, presenting a persona defined only by the social significance of the show.

The usefulness of images of stratification and depth is increased also by their natural congruence with other metaphorical schemes, which are not based on literally spatial imagery. (d) We speak of thoughts and thinkings as being wounds and woundings, searches and hidings, attacks and protections, describing them in terms of physical actions. It is significant in comparison with (b) that we do this most readily when the action to which the thought is assimilated is one whose domain is spatial. (e) We describe processes of deliberation and decision as if they were the play of opposing teams of subsidiary selves. We speak of debates and struggles in the head and heart. Sometimes the selves or teams occupy loci in the space of their struggle; sometimes their opposition is less embodied, and the positions and resolutions themselves are formed into strata and hierarchies.

In any particular case one can combine implications of all these kinds. The sense one intends one's ascription to have, and the sense it is taken to have, is determined not only by the details of the image one presents and of the context in which one presents it but also by the structure of the explanation at issue. Spatial imagery construed as with (a) supports the attribution of motives at apparent odds with an evident pattern of action; (b) serves to motivate the application of blocking considerations, reasons why a motive did not have the effect one might have otherwise supposed it to have; (c) works in the relevance of new motives and subverts that of others; (d) provides a vocabulary for describing processes that would otherwise be hard to capture in the overall scheme of motive, belief, and attempt; and (e) allows one to use inconsistent sets of beliefs and desires, suitably partitioned, to explain the details of a series of actions.

THE REALITY OF EXPLANATIONS

The attempt to give a systematic commentary on our explanations, to spell out the conditions under which they will succeed, and to adapt them to these conditions is by its very nature a business with few fixed rules. One takes the motives that are claimed to underlie the action, and one tries to be as exact as one can about the relations they may have to the facts of the case. Sometimes one can work one's commentary into and around the explanation, treating personality like character, mood, and emotion, and we have formal devices for doing this. Sometimes one cannot, and there are occasions when one can just endorse or deny the explanation, appealing to one's authority as someone who knows the agent.

It is also by its nature a business that must often fail. For the facts, the real psychological facts, about an agent's state of mind and relation to the surroundings, are what makes an explanation apply. A scattered set of true ascriptions of beliefs and desires can rarely be expected to capture enough of these facts, even when these beliefs and these desires are in some other person responsible for a similar action. And mechanical ways of working in attributions of character, mood, and emotion are not always going to suffice, to summon the particularity of people. We can continually find new ways of capturing further facts, further sources of particularity, in our formal patterns of explanation, though, primarily by finding more subtle ways of talking about character, emotion, and mood.

But however ingenious we are, it seems certain that the dialectic continues, that as formal explanation becomes more subtle further regions of intuition of personality become available as inexplicitly conceptualized, tacit, knowledge. The inexpressible is always one step ahead.

This might be a disappointing fact if one were to expect that our modes of psychological explanation could ever be completely autonomous, working according to stated general laws from literally construed ascriptions. The fact that this is not so is reassuring, though, if one's concern is with the reality of the explanations that we use. One might worry that the standard forms of psychological explanation that our culture affords us provide rationalizations rather than real explanations, that they allow one just to weave some words around an action so as to make it seem unsurprising, rather than in any more substantial sense explaining why it happened. Explanation is *not* always merely formal. We can be fairly sure of it because of the presence of concepts, of emotion, mood, character, whose main function is to force a general pattern of explanation to confront the details of each particular case. The presupposition in their use is that there are underlying facts of mental life, and that in any way we can we must connect what we say about people to these facts. Our successes here are a tribute to the accuracy of our culture's psychological lore; our recurrent inevitable failures attest to the danger that any explanation may just not appeal to the right facts, may be hollow.

NOTE

*This is an adaptation of a chapter from the draft of a book on psychological explanation. My appreciation of issues about the emotions is due to conversations with Ronald de Sousa, Amélie Rorty, and Alan Spiro. The immediate impetus for this paper came from thinking that a theory of the particularity of psychological explanation like that of Sartre in Part Four of *Being and Nothingness* fits far better with a realism about psychological states (a modern realism, like, for example, Fodor's) than it does with Sartre's own definite antirealism about states of mind.

VII

FUNCTIONALISM AND THE EMOTIONS

GEORGES REY

A common reaction to the suggestion that machines might someday be persons, or that persons might all along be machines, is that it's absurd, since machines can't have "feelings" and persons obviously do.

There is probably much in this reaction which is confused and mistaken. People too often have in mind very primitive machines—adding machines, or perhaps even the most advanced computers yet developed—about which no defender of mechanism need make any feeling claim. If we are machines, we are surely *very* complicated ones, of a sort yet to be understood in any but the most general way. Sometimes, too, people are wedded to traditional metaphysical ideas regarding the "soul," or some special "mental substance," that is not supposed to be producible by arrangement of mechanical or electrical materials alone, but for which, however, independent evidence is still wanting. There are other mistakes as well. I do not want to dwell on the mistakes here. It seems to me that persons *are* machines, of a sort we might even someday build, but that there is nonetheless something odd about the usual ways we think about this possibility, and that we are presently more in danger of dismissing the common reaction too lightly than of falling into its familiar errors. (Consider, for example, the disturbing ease with which many people seemed to accept the story of HAL in the film *2001*.) I should like to examine here just what might be the grain of insight in the common reaction. In particular, I should like to consider the role of the emotions, and what the emotions might plausibly involve, within the general framework of a mechanical, or what has come to be called a "functional" theory of mind. What manner of phenomenon is an emotion? What are the sorts of conditions under which a person, and possibly a machine, might properly be said to be "having" or "experiencing" one? Consideration of the nature and role of the emotions seems, moreover, all the more urgent in view of outstanding, independent problems besetting the functionalist theory of mind: it has been noted that this view seems to have some wildly unintuitive consequences, and is badly in need of constraints. The emotions conceivably may provide some of the constraints we need.

In the first section of this paper, I shall set out, quite roughly and generally, what I take a functionalist view of mind to be, some of its virtues and appeal, and some of the problems philosophers have raised in regard to it. This shall lead me to consider also what I shall call the "cognitivist" tradition in the philosophy of mind, which provides much of the plausibility for functionalism, but also may be the source of some of its problems. In the second section I shall consider just what sorts of states the emotions might be, proceeding in section three to place these considerations in the context of the functionalist view. For reasons that I will advance in the course of that discussion, I shall not have a great deal conclusive to say here. I do believe that we are led, by the considerations I raise, to place greater importance upon the role of aspects of our physiology in our psychology than we have traditionally been encouraged to do. However, as I shall conclude, these considerations do not in the end undermine a functionalist view of many central features of mind, nor even the still real possibility that machines might someday be persons, or that persons might all along be machines.

I

Ned Block has recently pointed out[1] that theories of the nature of mind generally run two opposite, although not mutually exclusive risks: either they are too "chauvinistic," excluding as intelligent things that would patently appear to be so, or they are too "liberal," including things that patently are not. These defects are hardly mere philosophical quibbles: an extreme form of liberalism is animism; and a particularly vicious form of chauvinism is racism.

The "functionalist" view of mind, as it has come to be called in the Anglo-American philosophical literature of the last twenty years,[2] developed partly out of reaction to these kinds of defects with the two traditional materialist theories of mind, physicalism and behaviorism. Physicalism, identifying types of mental state with types of physical state, seemed to be too chauvinistic, excluding perfectly intelligent, even passionate creatures that were simply made of nonhuman material; and Behaviorism, identifying types of mental state with types of behavioral (disposition) state, seemed both too chauvinistic *and* too liberal: some machines might (have the dispositions to) behave intelligently without really being so; and some intelligent creatures might not be disposed to manifest it at all (they might be paralyzed, or utterly terrified of so behaving). I don't wish to rehearse these arguments here. Suffice it to say that philosophers gradually came to find mental states inextricably intertwined, in such a way that no one state could properly be identified without mention of the others, no one of them, therefore, being "reducible" to nonmental terms.

Particularly important examples of this interdependence are afforded by the states involved in beliefs and preferences. These states seem rightly ascribable to an object chiefly on the basis of what might be regarded as "rational" relations that obtain both among themselves and with stimulations and behaviors: there seem to be, for example, interesting inductive relations between stimulations and beliefs (stimulations from objects commonly lead people to believe there to be objects before them); inductive and deductive relations among beliefs (the belief that p and the belief that q often give rise to the belief that p and q); and practical, means-ends relations among beliefs, preferences and behaviors (people tend to do what they believe will best secure what they most prefer). It is insofar, and perhaps only insofar, as an object (or its parts) enters into at least some of these relations that it would seem to be creditable with beliefs or preferences at all. And since something like beliefs and preferences are the states implicated in the paradigmatic mental activities of thinking and decision making, it would seem that entering into at least some of these relations is what is essential to an object's having a mental life. If this is so, then the material out of which the object happens to be made, and the behavior that it happens to exhibit, would be inessential. A whole system of these states might be *realized* in one or another sort of physical (or perhaps even some special mental) stuff, and parts of that system might *rationalize* particular behaviors; but there is no reason to think that parts of the system (e.g., a particular belief or preference) might be type-wise identifiable with the stuff in which it happened to be realized, or with (a disposition to) a particular sort of behavior to which it happened to give rise. Mentality seems to involve what Aristotle regarded as the "form," not the "matter" (much less the behavior) of mental things. An individual mental state should, then, be individuated by what might be called its "functional" role in those rational relations, or within the whole of a person's psychology.

There are at least two forms this "functionalism" assumes. There is a quite *general* form, which consists in applying a specific logical technique for explicating theoretical terms in general to the particular mentalistic case. This is a technique, originated by Frank Ramsey and lately revived and refined in the work of David Lewis,[3] whereby theoretic terms are defined by their specific theoretic and/ or causal role. A particular sort of mental state, for example, might be identified by its typical kinds of causes and effects, or by whatever nomological role a true theory of that state prescribes. I shall not be concerned with this form of functionalism here. Even though it may be especially appropriate for a macro-science like psychology, it raises some very general issues in the philosophy of science that are indifferent to psychology, and, as we shall see, independent of the specific issues that we shall be considering.

The form of functionalism that shall concern me here (and to which I shall restrict the term) is what might be called "computational functionalism." It consists of a substantial, and controversial, empirical hypothesis to the effect that *psychological processes can be perspicuously understood as involving the execution of encoded algorithms.*[4] An algorithm may be intuitively thought of as a sequence of completely "obvious," unambiguous instructions, each of which could be *plainly* executed by an entirely "mechanical" device. Thus, "Print a stroke; move to the left" is an algorithm, while "Determine whether Goldbach's conjecture is a theorem of arithmetic; compose a tender love song" is (as yet) not. Recipes are sometimes algorithms, as are typical mathematical functions; it is often by our *consciously following* them that we manage to cook geese and extract cube roots. Machines can be constructed to execute algorithms; but they obviously don't do so ordinarily by consciously following them. Instead, what they do is *encode* them: operations in the machine correspond systematically to the instructions in the algorithm, and the machine's ability to compute the algorithm is explained by reference to this correspondence. The claim of computational functionalism is that mental organisms may be understood to be such machines, that particularly the activities of thinking and decision-making can be perspicuously explained as the execution of sequences of mechanical instructions that are encoded in the organism's nervous system, and give rise to the beliefs, preferences, and rational relations that the organism (and/or its parts) appear to satisfy. (Notice that the claim is *not,* and does not at all entail, the claim that organisms *consciously follow* algorithms, as they indeed sometimes do, but which would hardly *explain* the astonishing fact that they do.)

The "functionalism" of computational functionalism emerges most clearly from its more formal characterization. One standard such characterization is in terms of a "Turing Machine." This is an entirely abstract object that consists of a set of interdefined states and an infinitely long "tape" (or memory capacity): each state operates on the tape in a fashion entirely determined by a specification of an input, and a consequent output and succeeding state. State S_1, for example, might be individuated by the fact that, when given input i_1 (say, a stroke on the tape), it emits output o_1 (erases the stroke, prints a dash, and moves right) and proceeds to state S_2, which, in turn, is individuated by the fact that, when given input i_2 (say, a dash on the tape) it emits output o_2 (erase the dash, print a stroke, move left) and proceeds back to state S_1. According to what appears to be the immensely plausible "Church-Turing Thesis," all intuitively algorithmic processes are computable by one or another Turing Machine. In particular, for every intuitively computable mathematical function there exists some such machine for which, if the input to the initial state represents a value in that function's domain, then the portion of the output printed on the tape in the end (or halting) state represents the corresponding value in the range. An especially interesting Turing Machine is the "Universal Turing Machine": for it, the inputs are numerical representations of other Turing Machines and of *their* inputs, and the outputs are representations of their outputs. Most modern, "programmable" computers can be regarded as realizations of just such a Universal Turing Machine, restricted, however, simply by the finitude of their "tape" (or memory capacity). The claim of computational functionalism could be said more formally to be the claim that thinking and decision-making organisms can be understood as realizations of Turing Machines—more plausibly, of a Universal Turing Machine—with what appears to be an only finite tape.[5] Such a claim captures the functionalist intuition that what matters about a mental state is its form by characterizing mentation in terms of machine states that are identified purely in terms of their inputs, outputs, and relations to one another. It would seem to avoid the chauvanisms of both physicalism and behaviorism by not confining a mental state to any particular kind of material or behavior, and it would seem also to avoid the excessive liberalism of behaviorism by requiring a mental state to have the right sort of internal structure. Put another way: it is neither necessary nor sufficient for something's being a realization of a particular Turing Machine that it be made of a particular kind of material or that it (superficially) behave in any particular sort of way; all that is important is that it realize the right internal relations. And this is precisely the kind of analysis that seems appropriate for mental states.

But the plausibility of computational functionalism is not based merely upon its satisfaction of these fashionable functionalist intuitions. It also derives importantly from consideration of the representational properties of many mental phenomena, and from the evident capacity of many existing algorithmic devices to deal with those properties. Representations are, paradigmatically, things like words, sentences, and (on some views) ideas, images, propositions. That mental phenomena seem to involve representations has been widely noted. There is the familiar "intensionality" of many mental states: beliefs and preferences appear to be relations that creatures bear not (on pain of violating Leibniz's Law) to the world *directly,* but rather to some or other kind of representation of the world, into which corepresentational expressions cannot be substituted *salva veritate.* Furthermore, the rational relations into which beliefs and preferences themselves enter also seem to be relations *between* representations: deductive relations are relations among sentences or propositions, and the practical and inductive relations (to the extent that we have any clear idea of the latter) appear to be so as well. Now, the best account we have to date of these relations between representations, indeed, of the nature of representations themselves, are *formal* or *syntactic:* it is in virtue of its form that one representation is a logical consequence of another, that a representation is the representation it is. The spectacular achievement of modern logic has been to show how deductive relations can be regarded as formal transformations of formal representations; and I take it that it is a hope of "Inductive Logic" and "Decision Theory" to show how inductive and practical relations can be so regarded as well. Insofar as that hope is realized, and insofar as thinking and decision-making consist of beliefs and preferences in these rational relations, it would seem promising to regard thinking and decision-making as just such formal transformations of representations.

It is precisely here that algorithms, and explanations in terms of them, seem peculiarly apt. Algorithms seem to present an especially perspicuous way of characterizing formal transformations of representations. A Turing Machine itself can rather naturally be regarded as engaged in precisely such a process: it computes a particular arithmetic function, for example, by "mechanically" transforming a stroke representation of a value in the domain of the function to a stroke representation of the corresponding value in the range. The actual computer that keeps track of things at my bank quite mechanically transforms representations of my balance; and a computer that plays chess (being a realization of a finite Universal Turing Machine) mechanically transforms not only representation of positions but also representations of algorithms themselves (e.g., strategies) as well. What is rational seems to be representational; what is representational seems to be formal; and what is formal seems to be algorithmic and thereby mechanical. Or, anyway, that's the hope. In a way, algorithms could be regarded as the beginning of a real solution to the mind/body problem: on the one hand, they seem to be able to account for key properties of mentation, and, on the other, they seem to do so in a way that is clearly mechanically realizable. They provide at least one example of a way that "dumb" matter might give rise to intelligent mind.

These considerations are, to be sure, far from conclusive. They are intended only to be suggestive of the kinds of reasons philosophers and psychologists have for beginning to take computational functionalism seriously as a hypothesis about the nature of mind. I do not wish to further defend or dispute this claim as a hypothesis about thinking and decision making. Its further plausibility depends, to my mind, largely upon the success of the still nascent enterprises, for example, cognitive psychology, computer science, linguistics, a success which I suspect is, if available at all, still many centuries away. What I want to consider here are some of the consequences of the view, were it true, for our more general conception of mind, and particularly for our concept of a person, those supposed paragons of mind.

There is a long tradition in the philosophy of mind—I shall call it the "Cognitivist Tradition"—which regards persons as "rational animals" (res cognitans, thinking things) which characteristically engage in the kinds of activities that are the focus of functionalism: thinking or problem solving, and decision making. Of course, as our understanding of other animals has grown richer, it has become increasingly likely that mere thinking is not quite the distinguishing mark of persons: most animals seem to engage in it just in getting from here to there (improvising routes, using tools). So there have been a great many efforts to isolate a particular form of thought as peculiar to persons. Philosophers have called attention to our use of language; to our possessing a certain form of self-consciousness; to our having "second-order" beliefs and preferences (beliefs and preferences about beliefs and preferences); to our understanding moral reasoning. In the spirit of D. C. Dennett's recent, and elegant paper, "Conditions of Personhood,"[6] which brings many of these efforts together, one might say that a central idea that emerges from the Cognitivist tradition is the conception of a person as an "n-order intentional system": a system capable of having beliefs and preferences about beliefs and preferences about beliefs and preferences . . . to any arbitrary nesting. Such a system could surely be "self-conscious" (have beliefs and preferences about its *own* beliefs and preferences), and could quite manage the baroque intentions Grice and Schiffer have located as conditions of language use;[7] and I see no reason to suppose that it would not therefore also be capable, insofar as it was supplied also with moral categories and generalizations ("moral laws"?), of genuine moral reasoning: seeing an action from different points of view, taking into account different "interests" in arriving at a conclusion regarding what it "ought" to do. At any rate, I think Dennett is right in thinking that n-order intentionality is lacking in most animals, but present in most human beings.

However, it seems to me that this condition, while certainly illuminating, is still inadequate for personhood. Moreover, I am inclined to think that not only it but any purely *cognitive* condition will inevitably be inadequate, for reasons that emerge from considering the consequences of the functionalist hypothesis. For, if the functionalist hypothesis is correct, then cognitive processes can be characterized *extremely abstractly,* more abstractly than may initially be evident. In particular, the "inputs," "outputs," relations between the states, and even the "tape" (or memory capacity) can be characterized *completely independently* of the material, if *any,* in which these things happen to be realized. This was the very virtue that led us from chauvinistic materialism to computational functionalism in the first place. One might say that it's this fact that makes the computing business so lucrative: you can make intelligence out of *anything*. But do we really want to allow that a *person* can be made out of just anything, that anything that realizes the Turing Machine description of thinking and decision making would qualify as a being with rights and responsibilities, deserving our sympathy and concern, counting for moral purposes exactly as much as those of us that happen to be made of flesh and blood?

Some of the problems of so allowing begin to emerge if one just begins to consider how relatively easily such a condition as n-order intentionality might be realized by existing computational machinery. There is, for example, a computer program called the "Believer System" being developed in the work of Geoffrey Brown, and Charles Schmidt at Rutgers University,[8] which, insofar as it is intentional at all, would appear to be capable of nested intentions of a depth limited only by its memory capacity. What it does, essentially, is to extract from descriptions of various actions of an agent, "plans" and "motivations" that bear (what I have called) practical rational relations to those descriptions: at any rate, included in its "motivational rules" are such things as an agent's performing an action he believes will result in a beneficial outcome for himself, or for someone whose benefit he desires, and performing actions that satisfy some "normative" (e.g., ethical) rule. Thus, from descriptions of someone gathering together some logs and rope and thereafter building a raft, the program extracts the motive that the agent wanted to build a raft, and a plan to the effect that he believed gathering together some logs and rope was the best available means of doing so. There are a number of constraints the program places upon admissable beliefs and motivations: some, but not just any beliefs may be derived from others, and some motivations subordinated to others, in chains of plausible inductive, deductive, and practical reasoning. But the program is hardly very subtle. Of course, neither are we very much of the time when we ascribe beliefs and preferences to an agent on what appears to be a very similar basis (indeed, it is the near vacuity of at least much of what ordinarily passes for such mentalistic explanation that has made so many philosophers and psychologists wary of it as a whole). The somewhat surprising moral of this example seems to be that *if a system were to be intentional at all, it would be a very small matter to render it n-order intentional.* It need only be capable of ascribing this "Believer" program itself, and of ascribing such ascriptions, and such ascriptions of ascriptions to any depth of nesting, to an agent as part of his "plan": if the program provides a basis for ascribing beliefs and preferences, it could in this way provide a basis for ascribing beliefs and preferences about beliefs and preferences to any depth of nesting. Such a simple recursive computation is well within the capabilities of even existing machines, the only limitation being the size of the memory needed to store arbitrarily deep nestings (although they would probably be far better at keeping track of these nestings than we are). Thus, if any existing machine were to qualify as intentional at all—were it, itself, sufficiently to satisfy the rational relations so as to qualify for the ascription of beliefs and preferences—it would be a small matter to supply it further with this recursive Believer program and so, on the Cognitivist criterion, render it a person. (Remember that such nested intentionality seems to be sufficient for "self consciousness," language use, and—particularly since the Believer system relies also on "normative" rules of motivation—for moral reasoning.) Now, it's not entirely clear whether any existing machines actually do qualify as even first-order intentional. Let us grant that some of them nearly do. But surely they don't just as nearly qualify as *persons.* Surely we are not so nearly morally constrained, for example, not to unplug them, to count their preferences equally with those of human beings, to treat them with sympathy and respect, and so forth. What this particular mechanical example seems to suggest, then, is that even such conditions as nested intentions, self-consciousness, language use, and moral reasoning are not sufficient for something's being a person.

Perhaps there are further, finer cognitive conditions that would be a little harder to satisfy. But that they still probably wouldn't be sufficient for something's being a person may be brought out by considering still further examples that would be consequences of *any* merely cognitive conditions and the functionalist hypothesis. In the same discussion of the perils of chauvinism and liberalism, Ned Block points out that, on the functionalist hypothesis regarding at least intelligence, not only would a rightly programmed electronic computer qualify as intelligent but all manner of odd entity might qualify as well. One of Block's more colorful examples involves what might be a kind of festival in China: all the billion or so Chinese might arrange themselves in such a way as to realize the Turing Machine description of some actual human being's cognitive system. The "inputs" and "outputs" might be realized simply in the raising and lowering of red flags of one individual to another, the "tape" as some subset of the people with whom certain of these raising and lowerings are retained. (Or, for simplicity, one might imagine them raising and lowering the flags precisely on the contingencies on which the billion or so neurons in some actual human brain emit a "spike.") On a Cognitivist view of persons, if the right arrangement is realized, the result—that is, the whole of China—would count as a person. Moreover, if we were to abstract from the standard characterization of inputs and outputs as physical signals, we would be faced with an even greater diversity of systems. For example:

> Economic systems have inputs and outputs, e.g. influx and outflux of credits and debits. And economic systems also have a rich variety of internal states, e.g. having a rate of increase of GNP equal to double the prime rate. It does not seem impossible that a wealthy sheik could gain control of a small country, e.g. Bolivia, and manipulate its financial system so as to make it functionally equivalent to a person, e.g. himself. You don't think this is possible? Remember that the economic states, inputs, and outputs designated by the sheik to correspond to his mental states, inputs, and outputs, need not be "natural" economic magnitudes. Our hypothetical sheik could pick any economic magnitudes at all— e.g. the fifth time derivative of the balance of payments. His only constraint is that the magnitudes he pick be economic, that they be inputs, outputs, and states, and that he be able to set up a financial structure that realizes the intended causal structure.[9]

Now, there's clearly something going wrong here. In particular, there's surely something wrong with the form of argument that runs "anything that realizes a Turing Machine description of a $\emptyset$ is itself a $\emptyset$," since clearly anything that realizes, say, a Turing Machine description of an economic system is not itself an economic system (one might run the above example backward, from an economy to a human brain). But it's very difficult to say just what. There seems to be some need of a *concrete* constraint on the extreme abstractness of functional descriptions. But it's hard to see how such a constraint could be imposed in the case of mentality without running up against the very chauvinism we were originally concerned to avoid.

Block, himself, concludes (tentatively) that the sorts of examples he produces vitiate functionalism as an account of psychological states. Functionalist theories save themselves from chauvinism only at the cost of a still worse liberalism. At any rate, he seems to believe that a full psychology needs to include also reference to "qualia," or the qualitative feels of experience, which, he argues, are independent of functional descriptions, as well as to "a certain sort of connection between the world and [a system's] inputs and outputs." Alternatively, he suggests that qualia and connections with the world might not be regarded as in the domain of *psychology*.

I should like to explore a still different conclusion: let the psychological states involved in thinking and decision making be functional states; and let even any realization of those functional states instantiate also those psychological states and processes: for example, let the sheik's manipulations of the Bolivian economy instantiate the sheik's cognitive life. Still, we need not regard the Bolivian economy as a person on, as it were, the same footing as the sheik, since a person may be something more than merely a cognitive system, more than merely a thinking and decision-making thing. That is, instead of (or possibly in addition to) abandoning functionalism as an account of cognition, we might abandon cognitivism as an account of the notion of a person.

As perhaps we already saw in the case of the "Believer System," such a move is not without its independent motivation. Indeed, it is here that we might begin to find something right in the common reaction to the suggestion that a machine might be a person: these devices just don't seem to have any *feelings,* any emotional lives. And it is for that reason it is hard to see why we should *care* about them at all, much less accord them the moral status of persons. Even if the Bolivian economy, or China, or the "Believer" machine at Rutgers can be rightly regarded as engaged in thinking and in making intelligent and moral decisions, still if these entities don't *feel* in something like the way we feel—if they don't form personal attachments, grieve, feel remorse, experience fear, pride, anger, embarrassment, frustration, humiliation, depression, fall in love, empathize, feel warmth, grow resentful—if they don't enter into *any* of these kinds of states and relations, then it is surely difficult to regard them as full members of the moral community, about which *we* ought to feel any sympathy or concern, and to which we ought to accord any rights and responsibilities.[10] If moral feeling without reason is blind, moral reasoning without feeling seems empty, pointless. And so, for all the prodigious moral reasoning in which these various entities might be thought to engage, it seems empty and pointless to regard them fully as persons.

But perhaps we're wrong in denying them any feelings. To be sure, they don't ordinarily engage in anything like *our* customary emotional histrionics; but then neither all the time do we. Perhaps they have "hidden" feelings, feelings they can only blandly report on, which they are tragically unable otherwise to express, feelings hidden away in all that thinking and decision making, or perhaps in other of their computational states. To assess this possibility we need to have a firmer grip than yet we have on what an emotional state might be.

II

There seem to be at least seven different sorts of considerations that philosophers and psychologists have claimed enter into the ascription of emotional states, what I shall tentatively regard as seven components of emotional states: the *cognitive,* the *qualitative,* the *behavioral,* the *physiological,* the *contextual,* the *etiological,* and the *relational.* They doubtless overlap; I shall be concerned with setting them out only as they contrast with one another, proceeding after that to appraise their relative importance.

The cognitive component is essentially that portion of mentality that we have already considered, with which most emotional states seem to be involved as well. At any rate, most emotional states seem to be importantly connected to, roughly speaking, the beliefs and preferences of the person in the state. Thus, *fear* that some event is going to happen is usually connected to a (usually high) preference that the event not occur, and a belief that it is likely to occur; embarrassment about having said something foolish is usually connected to the belief that one has said something foolish, the preference that one hadn't, and the belief that others noticed. It would appear to be by virtue of these connections that many—although not all—emotions exhibit the intensionality that, we noted earlier, is characteristic of cognitive states: one may fear demons that don't exist (because one may *believe* they do); and one might be sad over the departure of a friend, yet not over the beginning of a better life for him, with which the departure might be identical (since one might *prefer* the beginning to occur, but not the departure). —Notice, though, in at least one natural reading, if one *loves* the kindly father who happens also to be a brutal soldier, one thereby loves the brutal soldier too.— In dealing with the intensionality of many emotions, however, it is important to distinguish, as many philosophers have, between the *cause* and the *object* of the emotion: it may be merely the suddenness of the appearance of an unfamiliar face that is the cause of the fear whose intensional object becomes the unfamiliar face itself. It is this intensional object, not the cause, that at least appears to be traceable to the intensional object of the cognitive component of the emotion.

One thing should be obvious: a typical emotional state is not *analyzable* as merely the cognitive component of the state, since one may have the beliefs and preferences without the emotions, and the emotions sometimes without the beliefs and preferences. Thus do some people "overcome their fear of death," without however in any way transforming their belief that they are going to die or their preference not to do so; and thus do others suffer from "free-floating" anxiety, and from "objectless" elations and depressions. (*Moods* might be regarded as enduring emotional states that lack in just this way particular intensional objects.) It is perhaps the failure of any obvious sort of analysis of an emotion into its cognitive components that might lead one to be doubtful of the emotional states of the merely cognitive devices that we have considered.

One sort of thing that many people take to be necessary to an emotional state in addition to, and even in the absence of, the appropriate cognitions is the "qualia," or "inner feels" by which emotional states are often introspectively identified. There is "the lump in one's throat" in many cases of sorrow and frustration, the "butterflies in one's stomach" in expectant anxiety, and just plain "feelings of," for example, fear, embarrassment, affection, hope, joy. They seem to be the sorts of things someone might regard as the objects of the "knowledge of what it's like" to be afraid, to feel lust, to experience a friendship of a great many years. I shall refer to at least the kinds of phenomena that lead people to posit such objects in the case of emotions as the *qualitative* component of an emotion.

A reason for hedging in regard to qualia has to do with the multitude of problems traditionally and still surrounding them. It is at least controversial whether they can be identified with physiological states, or are ontologically additional. Usually they are posited not with respect to the emotions, but with respect to *sensations* of for example, touch, sight, hearing; and it is quite unclear whether the two sorts ought really to be considered together. Sensations do seem more readily identifiable merely on the basis of introspection. Identification of an emotion would seem to depend much more upon some of the very other components we are presently considering. Emotional qualia, however, would seem to share to some extent in the traditional "problems of other minds" that many have thought arises for sensations: at any rate, if one is worried about possible, undetectable reversals of the sensations of red and green, or about their possible, undetectable absence altogether, then one might also worry about similar possible reversals and absences in the case of emotional qualia (and one might come to worry about such possibilities not only with regard to others but even with regard to oneself). Consideration of the emotions in this way might lead us, as considerations of the sensations in this way led Ned Block, to regard functionalist accounts of mind as inadequate. But I do not want to take that route here. For, a not implausible alternative route in either or both of those cases would be to disbelieve in qualia altogether: one might, for example, believe that they involve some sort of illusion, or false, but tempting belief and that "they" shouldn't be thought of as objects at all. But it is not, I take it, equally plausible to similarly disbelieve in emotional states.

And so it is worth considering the problems the emotions might pose for functionalism quite independently of these problems that might be posed for qualia. By adverting merely to what I take to be an ontologically neutral "qualitative component" I hope to keep that independence clear.

While the qualitative component certainly seems to be very important in the ascription of emotion, it does not seem always to be necessary. People seem to be capable of being depressed, angry, afraid, sometimes without "feeling so," even without being able to introspect that they are. There are the now fairly familiar "defenses" and "repressions," by means of which people may conceal from themselves feelings that they prefer they didn't have. And then there is just simple lack of introspective acuity: many people are simply rather poor at discriminating their inner life, confusing sadness with depression, envy with resentment, affection with lust, love with merely an evening's tempting titillation. Indeed, as reading Proust can often remind us, we are all probably much poorer at introspection than we ordinarily suppose. Moreover, it is surely not impossible that, as we learn more of the details of the other components of the emotions—as we learn more about exactly which beliefs and preferences inform them, and about their physiology— we might discover that much of our existing vocabulary for the emotions misclassifies them, or is otherwise inadequate. We might find, for example, that the differences among sorrows are as great as the differences between sorrows and joys; or that grief was much closer to frustration than to depression; or that "affection" covers a motley assortment of states that don't really belong together; and that new terms ought to be introduced to mark the newly drawn, more appropriate distinctions. If this were to occur, it would mean that we were in an important way presently mistaken about much of our emotional lives, at least insofar as we sort them out introspectively.

Ordinarily, when we reject the deliverances of introspection, what we appeal to instead is *behavior*. This term gets bandied about a bit much in psychology, blurring a great many distinctions, not least among which is that between behavior subject to voluntary control and behavior that is not. The latter I should like to consign to the physiological component, to be discussed shortly. And among the voluntary behaviors, we ought to distinguish those that, either naturally or culturally, are *typical* of a particular emotional state: thus, in sadness the features tend to be drawn down, the body relatively immobile; in joy just the reverse; in passion we languish; in fright we tense. Not all behaviors that can be indicative of a particular emotional state, however, are so by virtue of being *typical* of it. Silence and a smile are by no means typical of contempt, but in a particular conversation they may be a powerful indication. And people generally have their idiosyncratic ways of indicating, for example, affection—some with a monstrous hug, others with a quiet glance. In general—indeed, even in the case of the typicalities —the inference from behavior to an emotional state would seem to be just another instance of "inference to the best explanation" (of the behavior and of whatever other details) that appears to be characteristic of the rational acquisition of belief in nearly any domain.

It is this fact that tends to undermine the efforts of behaviorists to identify a particular emotional state with a particular form of behavior: there just doesn't seem to be any really dependable connection between particular behaviors and the particular emotional states inferred as the best explanations of them. The best explanation of someone behaving as though she were grief-stricken might be that she merely wished to appear that way and actually felt nothing of the sort; or someone might in fact be grief-stricken, but not behave in any of the ways typical of being so, for fear of the exposure, or out of a sense of decorum. What the Behaviorists tend generally to confuse is especially confused here, namely the *evidence* for a particular state with the *nature* of that state. Nevertheless, they are surely right in calling attention to the often striking typicalities in our behavior. Despite how sometimes undependable and inessential they may be, these particular, voluntary behaviors that are typical of an emotional state might be usefully regarded as comprising the *behavioral component* of the state.

All the components of the emotions so far considered might, of course, be thought of as physiological: cognitions, qualia, and voluntary behavior all pretty surely involve activity in the nervous system and the striated musculature. But many emotions seem fairly systematically connected to activity in other parts of the body as well, for example the circulatory system, the viscera and smooth musculature, and especially the endocrine system. Thus, there is the blush of embarrassment, the perspiration of fear. As introspection alone suggests, and recent research seems to confirm, many specific emotions are accompanied by quite specific visceral changes.[11] And, increasingly, endogenously produced hormones and neuro-regulators are being causally implicated in a wide range of emotional states: for example, the presence of testosterone seems to be necessary to many forms of aggression;[12] secretion of epinephrine is associated with "inwardly directed anger," and of norepinephrine with anger more "outwardly directed,"[13] as well as with excitement and anxiety;[14] and the depletion or deactivation of norepinephrine is highly correlated with depression.[15] The degree to which specific emotional changes can be tied to such specific hormonal and other chemical processes is, however, a matter of considerable controversy: in a famous (but as yet unreplicated) experiment of Schachter and Singer's,[16] it was found that high levels of epinephrine could induce in subjects a wide variety of emotional (or "seemingly emotional") states, depending upon the details of the subject's cognitive state. It would appear to be the cognitions that provide the fine differentia of emotional states. But, whether the associations are general or highly specific, there seems to be little doubt that such hormonal and other physiological processes are intimately bound up with a person's having any emotional reactions at all: they seem to be involved in the functioning of the limbic system, the part of the brain that appears to be associated with emotional activity.[17] Such processes need, then, to be regarded as a still further component of emotional states, the *physiological component.*

There are at least three other, interrelated sorts of considerations that recent philosophers have raised with respect to the emotions in such a way as to suggest that they ought to be regarded as components. These are the *contextual,* the *aetiological,* and—what I shall argue is the important residue of the two—the *relational.*

Emphasis upon contextual considerations in the identification of psychological states in general arises especially in the later work of Wittgenstein. There is one particular sequence of passages in the *Investigations* in which he addresses specifically emotional states, and the ways in which he takes them to be inextricably embedded in what he elsewhere calls "the stream of life." Some of the sequence is worth quoting at length not only for the exquisiteness of the prose:

An expectation is embedded in a situation, from which it arises. The expectation of an explosion may, for example, arise from a situation in which an explosion *is to be expected.* . . .

Could someone have a feeling of ardent love or hope for the space of one second—*no matter what* preceded or followed this second? What is happening now has significance—in these surroundings. The surroundings give it its importance. And the word "hope" refers to a phenomenon of human life. (A smiling mouth *smiles* only in a human face.)

Now suppose I sit in my room and hope that N.N. will come and bring me some money, and suppose one minute of this state could be isolated, cut out of its context; would what happened in it then not be hope? —Think, for example, of the words which you utter in this space of time. They are no longer part of this language. And in different surroundings the institution of money doesn't exist either.

A coronation is the picture of pomp and dignity. Cut one minute of this proceeding out of its surroundings: the crown is being placed on the head of the king in his coronation robes. —But in different surroundings gold is the cheapest of metals, its gleam is thought vulgar. There the fabric of the robe is cheap to produce. A crown is a parody of a respectable hat. And so on.[18]

I take it what we're being asked to notice is that a state like *hoping that someone will come with money* is not simply a *state* of a particular person at a particular time, in the way, say, that having a depleted level of norepinepherine might be; rather, it is a "phenomenon of human life," involving both the hopeful person *and* much that happens in other places, afterward and before, in quite the way that the dignity of a coronation can seem to involve much more than merely the moment, however solemn, at which the king is crowned. Where such additional factors are essential to the identity of an emotional state, they might be regarded as comprising the *contextual component* of the state.

A related, but rather more specific claim is advanced by Amélie Rorty in her recent article, "Explaining Emotions."[19] She considers how the identification of a particular emotion *as* a specific kind of emotion might depend upon details of its causal history, much in the way, one supposes, that the identification of a picture as a *genuine Rembrandt print* depends crucially upon the details of how it came to be produced. As an example, she constructs a story of how someone might on a variety of occasions find himself resenting women in positions of authority over him, as a causal consequence (unbeknownst to him) of his childhood perceptions of his mother's ambivalent intentions toward him. In order to respond appropriately on such occasions, it might be important that he come to recognize these otherwise isolated resentments as sharing this common source. That is, it might be important that he classify the isolated resentments as resentments of this particular etiological kind. I'm not sure any of our ordinary vocabulary for the emotions does classify them this way, but where the history of an emotional state is essential to its being an emotional state of a specific kind, we might then speak of the *etiological component* of that kind.

There are a good number of distinctions that need to be made in dealing with both of these latter components. First of all, as we already noticed with regard to the behavioral component, we need to distinguish the *evidence* for the ascription of a state from the *nature* of the state, the conditions by virtue of which the state is the sort of state it is. Thus, the words that someone might utter while he sits in a room hoping for money may furnish excellent evidence of his hope for money, but they are surely not necessary conditions of his so hoping. Consequently, the fact that in other surroundings these words might no longer have the same meaning, that they might no longer even be part of the same language, is quite irrelevant to the question of whether in those different surroundings the "minute of this state" would still be hope. Similarly, one would want to distinguish, as Rorty does, between cases in which someone's history might provide evidence and explain his emotional state from those that interest her in which the history might furthermore be essential to that state being the sort of state it is.

Secondly, we need to distinguish this *nature* of a state from the *identity* of the state itself. This is a general distinction: it may, for example, be part of the nature, insofar as it is a defining condition, of someone's being Smith's murderer that Smith in fact be dead, but this doesn't make Smith's death somehow part of the *identity* of his murderer ("Smith's murderer" doesn't refer to *inter alia* Smith's death!). In a more psychological, but (I hope) still innocuous vein, someone might correctly be said to know that Hannibal crossed the Alps only if Hannibal in fact did so; but that doesn't imply that so knowing cannot be just a state of that person, that it must instead be some sort of phenomenon having as parts both that person *and* Hannibal and/or the crossing. It may just be a state of that person that is correctly *described* as "knowing that Hannibal crossed the Alps" only if Hannibal did indeed cross the Alps. Wittgenstein's claim that "hope" refers not to a state of the hoper, but to a "phenomenon of human life" seems to be based upon a confusion of just this sort. (Rorty nowhere makes a similar claim, but it is worth noting that etiological dependencies call for the same distinction: that a picture is a print may depend upon the steps of its production; but the steps are not therefore *part* of the print since presumably *it* came into existence only after some of the steps were completed.)

Thirdly, in considering particularly the etiological component, it is important to distinguish etiology as it might pertain to the *character* of an emotional state from etiology as it might pertain merely to the identification of its intensional object. A number of recent writers on reference have plausibly argued that the reference of many terms depends crucially upon the etiology of their tokens; and such an argument could conceivably be extended to include terms that are used (or mentioned) in citing the intensional object of a particular emotional state. Thus, on this view, someone might properly be said to be sorrowful about Nixon's present isolation only if she (and/or a relevant one of her representations) stood in the appropriate historical relation to the man (she couldn't, for instance, have felt sorrowful about *him* before he happened to be born). This may be what is plausible about Wittgenstein's concern that there be or at least have been, an institution of money if someone is going to hope for some. But it does not seem to be all that Rorty has in mind in her concern with classifying resentments. For this latter involves not merely identifying the *content* of the resentments, and so, possibly, the etiology of the representations expressing that content, but identifying in addition the common etiology of the resentments, as kinds of states, themselves. If, as I have proposed, the cognitive component of an emotion can be regarded as the source of the emotion's intensional object, then the former etiological dependencies could be regarded as merely a feature of that specific component. But these latter etiological dependencies cannot obviously be handled in a similar fashion, and so provide reason for insisting, at least in some cases, upon an independent etiological component.

Lastly, and perhaps most importantly, one needs to remember that psychological states are indeed intensional; that is, as we noted earlier, they involve relations not to the world directly but to repre-

sentations of the world. In particular, what is important about the
"surroundings" of, say, someone's expecting an explosion or hoping for money are not the surroundings *themselves* but, rather,
what the hopeful or expectant person *takes* or *believes* or *notices*
the surroundings to be. And a person may take, believe, or notice
the surroundings to be quite other than they are. Someone might
fail to expect an explosion in a situation in which an explosion is to
be expected, and may expect one where one is not, as a result of
some *mistake*. In at least cases like these it seems just wrong to
claim that the expectation is "embedded" in the situation *itself;* if
it's embedded anywhere, it's embedded merely in the person's
mind. Similarly, one might hope that N. N. will come and bring
some money entirely in a dream or other delusional state: the actual
surroundings might be a hospital or desert island or faraway planet,
at a time, moreover, when the institution of money had entirely
died out. And the common source of someone's resentment toward
women need not be any *actual* childhood encounter with his
mother, but merely an *imagined* one (Freud observed that very
often the pivotal "seduction scenes" of childhood never actually
took place, but were merely believed by the child to have, as a result
of a wish that they do). All that *perhaps* need obtain outside the
expectant, hopeful, or resentful person's mind is, as we've already
noted, that he stand in the right causal relation to for example,
explosions, N. N., money, or women in order for it to be about
explosions, N. N., money, or *women* that he has his various expectations, hopes, or resentments. But surely this causal relation
hardly deserves to be called "the surroundings." As these examples
suggest, it is probably an abstract relation, one, moreover, that,
after perhaps an initial worldly encounter, would appear to be realizable entirely in the person's mind, particularly in his memory,
completely independently of any particular surroundings at all.
Thus, Wittgenstein's comparison of an emotional state to a coronation, in which the *actual* complex of surroundings (perhaps the
entire history of the kingdom) are doubtless essential to its dignity,
seems inapt and misleading. Emotional states may not be merely
qualitative, introspectable states, as Wittgenstein is often right to
remind us; but that doesn't mean that they are spread all over the
countryside. They may often simply be states of the person that are
not entirely, or maybe not at all, qualitative or introspectable, but

are nonetheless psychological, intensionality, and contained entirely within his skin. In view of this intensionality, and of the former distinctions, one might wonder whether there is any specifically contextual, apart from a cognitive and from an etiological component, to emotional states at all.

There is this consideration. There is surely something right to Wittgenstein's suggestion that someone couldn't have a feeling of hope or ardent love for the space of one second no matter what, at any rate, preceded it. Especially if one takes the "couldn't" here as not merely a logical "couldn't," then there surely couldn't be a moment of hope or ardent love without there at least being a rudimentarily intact psychological being there beforehand. Indeed, there are probably numerous conditions included among some of the components of the emotions we have so far mentioned (prior to the contextual) that are necessary conditions for particular emotional states (we shall return to discuss some of them in a moment). And there are other dependencies, not included in any of the previous components, of which Wittgenstein's claim can remind us. There are particularly dependencies *among* emotional states: one probably couldn't be said to feel ardent love toward someone if one didn't also feel positively disposed toward them; one couldn't feel jealousy toward one person without attachment to another; feelings of grief surely involve at least imagined feelings of prior affection. Many emotions, that is to say, may come in networks of relations with one another, from which no single one could with integrity be abstracted. However, it would still be odd (to my ear) to regard such interrelations as part of the *context* or *surroundings* of an emotional state, particularly in view of Wittgenstein's persistent interest in this regard in affairs outside of one's skin. Indeed, in view of the confusions we have so far encountered in talk of a contextual component, it would seem more perspicuous to regard these dependencies that one emotional state may have upon another as comprising a separate component of the emotions, the *relational component*. This component can be taken to absorb not only what seems plausible in the supposed contextual component but also at least most of what seems plausible in the etiological one as well: for an etiological relation is just one among many relations between one another that emotional states may enjoy.

We are left, then, with at least five principal components of emotional states: the cognitive, the qualitative, the behavioral, the physiological, and the relational. In view especially of Wittgenstein's innuendos about some necessary conditions for some emotional states, we might wonder about the relative importance of each of these components, which are essential, which inessential and, indeed, about just what the nature of an emotional state might be.

It is important to be clear about the nature of such inquiries into the natures of things. I see no reason to suppose that our wondering about the nature(s) of emotional states is any different, epistomologically, from our wondering about the nature of many seemingly natural kinds of phenomena: we want to discover the conditions whereby the phenomenon is the natural kind of phenomenon we take it to be, the conditions whereby all that we know about the phenomenon hangs together, the conditions that, all things considered, can be regarded as *defining* of the phenomenon. As recent (and some traditional) philosophers have argued,[20] this inquiry involves *inter alia* finding those conditions that play a central role in the *explanation* of the various facts and properties that we associate with the phenomenon, in particular, the conditions that emerge from the taxonomies in our best theories of the phenomenon and of other phenomena in the same domain. Thus, to cite the sorts of examples current in the literature, the nature of water might best be regarded as H_2O, that of gold, *the element with atomic number 89.* Examples perhaps closer to our inquiries are afforded by some diseases. Measles is not merely a bodily state involving fever and red spots on the skin, since (as mischievous children know) you can have the fever and the red spots without really having the disease. The nature of the disease is more aptly defined by the active presence in a person's body of a particular sort of virus, which presence causes in a specific way the red spots and the fever. As all these examples serve to indicate, such inquiries into the natures of things are hardly the sort that can be conducted entirely a priori: all the things that need to be considered in properly defining a phenomenon are not the sorts of things that are known or knowable a priori. Some of them, particularly conditions that are relatively "hidden" from view (such as the presence of a virus) are only discovered by careful empirical research, by constructing a posteriori theories and taxonomies of the phenomenon and its domain.

Unlike the cases of some diseases, we have nothing approaching a satisfactory theory or taxonomy of any of the emotions: we remain ignorant as yet of their specific natures. But we are in a position to speculate on trends. Of the components of the emotions we have isolated here, the ones that would appear to cluster together as very nearly essential are the cognitive, the qualitative, and the physiological. The relational component seems to impose additional conditions only upon certain specific emotions that need to come in clusters; and, as we have already observed, the behavioral component seems to be entirely inessential to an emotional state. Indeed, memory reports of people who have been wholly paralyzed by curare strongly suggest that emotional states can exist without any muscular activity whatsoever.[21] We have noticed, however, that for all their evident centrality to emotional states, neither the cognitive nor the qualitative component appear to be in all cases essential either. Perhaps the heart of the matter is to be found in our physiology.

Not just any parts of our physiology, not even parts that undergo change with change of emotional state, can be regarded as essential to emotional states. Contrary to the famous James-Lange theory of emotions, which proposes that an emotion consists of the experience of the bodily changes produced by a particular cognition, it appears that at least the peripheral mechanisms of the body—for example, the viscera and musculature—are quite inessential to emotional states: some persons with lesions fairly high up on the spinal cord, and insensitive therefore to stimuli originating in most of their peripheral bodily organs, seem to be able to experience a normal range of emotional states—grief, joy, displeasure, affection—with no evident change in personality or character. In some people there does appear to be a decrease in the *intensity* of what nevertheless appear to be normal states, although, interestingly enough, there appears to be an *increase* in the intensity of the "sentimental" emotions (e.g., those elicited by a "tear-jerking" movie).[22]

The portions of our physiology that do seem to be emerging as essential to emotional states are those involving the secretion of hormones and neuroregulators. In particular, all the examples mentioned above, regarding the role of testosterone, epinephrine, norepinephrine, are examples taken by many researchers to demonstrate the real dependence of for example, depression upon depletion of norepinephrine, and of "outwardly directed anger" upon its increased secretion. Even in the Schacter and Singer experiments, the presence of epinephrine seemed to be essential to the states being at least *emotional* states: it was just their specific character that seemed to depend upon the specific character of the cognitive component. What appears to be the case is that the character of the functioning of the limbic system—the portion of the brain that seems to be essential to emotional activity—depends to some extent not only upon cognitions but also upon the secretion of these hormones and neuroregulators.

A tentative hypothesis about the nature of emotional states which would seem to be consonant with what we've noted here might be that they are, typically, complex states involving nomological interactions between cognitions, qualitative states, and physiological processes (should qualitative states come to be reduced to eliminated in favor of physiological processes, the interactions would of course be only between the cognitive and the physiological). For example, a specific cognition, or constellation of cognitions, might be linked nomologically to specific qualitative and physiological states, which might be linked to further cognitions, which in turn might be linked to further qualitative and physiological states, and so forth; a given emotion might be regarded as some commonly occurring segment of just such a sequence. A crude but not impossible instance might be, say, depression over the collapse of one's career: this might be identified as the sequence beginning with the belief that one's career has indeed collapsed, the quite strong preference that it hadn't, a consequent depletion of norepinephrine, the effects of that depletion upon the nervous system, consequent further changes in cognition (e.g., the belief that nothing any longer is worthwhile, decreased preferences for doing anything at all), followed by still further depletions of norepinephrine, and further effects of this still greater depletion, various portions of this sequence being accompanied, perhaps, by that unmistakable qualitative feel. Some emotions, of course, might consist of shorter, simpler sequences; and others, of ones still more complex (particularly those emotions, like jealousy and grief, that seem to involve a relational component might also involve interactions with the particular emotions to which they are related). Of course, insofar as we oftentimes refer to a kind of emotional state without referring to any intensional object, as we do when the physiological effects are particularly distinctive or when there is no intensional object to be had, then the appropriate segment begins, as it were, at the second place of the sequence, after the initial cognitive component. Thus are people described as merely angry, upset, sad, joyous: they are being described in a way that simply abstracts from the cognitive component (which, where it exists, may nevertheless still be causally and psychologically important).

An emotion, on this view, is more a process than a state, a process rather like digestion, or respiration, or metabolism, which also seem to involve complexes of common nomological interactions. Like those processes, too, an emotion would not be defined in terms of the interactions in the body of any particular individual, no matter how nomological those interactions in that body might be; rather, they are defined by reference to the standard interactions in a standard, perhaps idealized human physiology. Thus, even if someone were regularly to get a headache whenever they were annoyed, the headache would not count as part of the annoyance, since this effect is not by any means sufficiently widespread, nor an effect to be expected as part of a standard interaction in a standard psychophysiology. Of course, if these latter conditions were different—if headaches accompanying annoyance became widespread, and their previous absence were explained by the presence of, say, a particular pollutant in our air, then it would seem to have turned out that headaches were indeed part of the state, or process, of being annoyed.[1]

The comparison with other physiological processes is useful in another way. In both emotions and, for instance, digestion, an appeal seems to be made to inner processes that, for all their public interest, are by and large inaccessible to ordinary public view (including by and large our own). Moreover, having a particular emotion seems to involve, as does digestion, undergoing a particular kind of process shared by, or at least standard to, other human physiologies. And so, for all our intimacy with our innermost feelings and emotions, it would appear that our position in coming to understand them is not much better than our position in coming to understand such a process as digestion: their precise nature is just as much a matter of systematic empirical investigation. So the comparison serves to remind us of what so often in the case of the mental it is easy to forget, that we are not anything like incorrigible experts about even our own emotional lives. Our minds, in an important way, are no more transparent to us than are our bodies.

III

. We are perhaps now in a slightly better position to consider the emotional life of some machines. We began with the functionalist hypothesis, which seemed plausible for its antichauvinistic abstraction of at least our cognition from our embodiment. But we then noticed that this abstraction threatened to go too far. It seemed to commit us to an amazing plethora of different sorts of entities as realizations of our cognitive lives; and this, given the notion of a person that emerges from the Cognitivist tradition, seemed to commit us to regarding this same plethora of entities all as persons. So it seemed prudent to supplement the Cognitivist tradition with the claim that, in addition to the appropriate cognitions, persons must also have some semblance of human emotional life. But our recent discussions of human emotional life suggest that having some semblance of it requires having as well some semblance of human physiology; in particular, having at least something like our system of hormones and neuroregulators. We seem to need to retreat from the abstractness of computational functionalism back down to matters of our material embodiment. But perhaps the actions and interactions of the system of hormones and neuroregulators with the system of our cognitions can, themselves, be perspicuously understood in a computationally functional way.

I have no conclusive argument that they can't be. But there is the following consideration. As we discussed earlier, the immense plausibility of computational functionalism as it applies to our cognition, to thinking and decision making, derives from the fact that those processes seem essentially to involve only rational relations. What is rational seems to be representational; what is representational, formal; and what is formal, in particular what involves formal transformations of representations, seems to be most perspicuously understood algorithmically. That is, computational functionalism seems to be plausible with regard to explaining systems of rational relations. With regard to other sorts of phenomena it is not ordinarily plausible at all. With regard to phenomena involving merely causal relations that aren't also rational relations among representations, algorithmic explanations can often seem inappropriate, even wrong. Osmosis across a cell membrane, for example, doesn't seem to involve *representations* of, say, differential salinity on either side, the membrane somehow *encoding* an algorithm that transforms those representations so that the salinity on both sides is equalized. We could, of course, discover or construct membranes that *would* in fact work this way. I take it that it's just a plausible empirical hypothesis that ours don't, that the differential salinity works "directly" upon the membranes, unmediated by representation. And so an algorithmic explanation of osmosis, an explanation that describes it as involving the encoding of an algorithm for the transformation of representations of salinity, seems inappropriate, even wrong.[24]

It seems to me that we so far have no reason whatever to believe that the actions and interactions of the hormonal with the cognitive system involve any rational relations among representations at all. The relations that do obtain appear to be *merely causal* ones, in this respect like those involved in osmosis. A belief that one's career has collapsed, or that one's situation is entirely hopeless, would seem to cause only "directly" a depletion of norepinephrine; and secretion of epinephrine would just seem to be involved again merely "directly" in various excited emotional states. There at least does not appear to be any mediation of these interactions by representations. If this is so, then we have no reason to think that an algorithmic explanation of these interactions would be in the least appropriate; as in the case of osmosis, they might even be wrong. And so we would have no reason to believe that these interactions could be perspicuously characterized by a Turing Machine, and no reason to suppose, therefore, that at least this aspect of our mental life could be understood in merely the abstract terms of inputs, outputs, and relations between states. Certain straightforwardly physical properties of our embodiment just may be, likely as not, essential to our minds. In particular, we would have no reason to suppose we could abstract away from those purely chemical properties of, for example, our hormones and neuroregulators by virtue of which they interact with our cognitions to produce our emotional states and processes.

Perhaps an algorithmic explanation, and a Turing Machine characterization of our emotional lives, would be appropriate in some other way, for some other reasons. This form of explanation is fairly novel, its manifold forms and uses not yet fully understood (although in this regard notice that such explanation seems to be in need of greater restraint, if we are to block, as we earlier noted we ought to block, the move from something's satisfying a Turing Machine description of a ϕ to something's actually being a ϕ). But, in any case, the burden of proof surely rests now with the defender of computational functionalism.

We might conclude, then, at least tentatively, that only an entity possessing (in its parts) the emotionally relevant chemical properties of our hormones and neuroregulators would qualify fully as a person. And neither the nation of China, the economy of Bolivia, not the computers at Rutgers or even at M.I.T., so far as I have heard, possess any such properties. Consequently, we are not threatened, as we otherwise seemed to be, by their excessively liberal inclusion as persons in our moral community. Pure (computational) functionalism seems to be inadequate as a complete account of our psychology; we seem to need, here and there, to return to some more straightforward materialism. And this, then, would seem to be the grain of truth in the common reaction that machines can't be persons: they don't have our feelings because they don't possess our relevant physiology.[25]

It might be protested that while machines may not have *our* feelings, still they might have feelings of a kind all their own. And, of course, one can't rule this possibility out entirely a priori. But there is a danger of a certain illusion here, an illusion for some reason peculiarly enticing in thinking about mind. One wouldn't suppose, equally, that there might be machines that engaged in digestion, but of a form quite unlike any such processes that take place in humans and animals. If, for example, the process they underwent for production of their energy was something more like the processes of an internal combustion engine, then surely that wouldn't count as *digestion* (cars don't *digest* gasoline). What gets called digestion depends upon its resemblances, in natural respects, to what gets called digestion *around here.* Similarly, what gets called an emotion depends upon its resemblances to what gets called an emotion around here, the best examples of which are also afforded by human beings and animals. But, moreover, even if they did have emotional states of a kind all their own, still there would be a matter of showing these emotions to be of a morally relevant sort, relevant to including these beings as persons in a moral community. Not just any emotions might do.

It might also be tempting here to cite science fiction on behalf of functionalism. After all, there is HAL in *2001,* who certainly appears to have feelings: he seems forlorn at the prospect of his final dismantlement, and seems to implore his dismantler—movingly, some say—to desist. Or, anyway, so his speech behavior leads us to believe. And, to be sure, speech behavior is ordinarily good evidence of emotional, as of other, psychological states. But this is so ordinarily only in the case of human beings, about the nature of whose physiology we also have reliable independent clues. Tape recorders can emit moving speech, but presumably without themselves being moved. One wants to know more about the etiology of HAL's speech behavior, whether it is caused by the same sorts of internal states that cause our emotional reports. And this, I submit in view of our discussion, ought to lead us to consideration of, *inter alia,* his hormones (or the general functional equivalents thereof), which, again, I doubt that any present machine secretes in anything like the manner that we do.

Of course, we might someday build just such a machine. If we did, and the machine also possessed our cognitive capacities, then I see no reason not to regard it then as a kind of person; nor, insofar as we operate like it, ourselves as a kind of machine.

NOTES

1. N. J. Block, "Troubles With Functionalism," in *Minnesota Studies in the Philosophy of Science,* Vol. IX, ed. C. W. Savage (Minneapolis: University of Minnesota Press, 1979).

2. Although functionalist views of mind can be traced back to Aristotle, the contemporary resurgence of interest in them seems to have begun with Hilary Putnam's "Minds and Machines," first published in 1958, reprinted with many other papers that discuss the view in his Collected Papers, Vol. II, *Mind, Language, and Reality* (Cambridge, 1975). Other treatments can be found in J. A. Fodor, *Psychological Explanation* (New York: Random House, 1968) and Gilbert Harman, *Thought* (Princeton: Princeton University Press, 1973), especially pp. 43-46.

3. See, e.g., David Lewis, "How To Define Theoretical Terms," in *Journal of Philosophy* (1970), and "Psychophysical and Theoretical Identification," in *Australasian Journal of Philosophy* (December 1972).

4. This form of functionalism is most robustly advanced by J. A. Fodor in his *The Language of Thought* (New York: Crowell, 1976), esp. chap. 2.

5. A fuller account of Turing Machines could be found in almost any second-year logic text. A particularly rich discussion may be found in Marvin Minsky, *Computation: Finite and Infinite Machines* (Englewood Cliffs, N.J.: Prentice-Hall, 1967), chaps. 6 and 7. Notice none of the claims in this discussion entails that any Psychological state may be *analyzed* in any way as a machine state of a Turing Machine. Reasons for finding this latter claim false are advanced in N. J. Block, and J. A. Fodor, "What Psychological States Are Not," *Philosophical Review* (1972).

6. D. C. Dennett, "Conditions of Personhood," in *Identities of Persons*, ed. Amélie Rorty (Berkeley, Los Angeles, London: University of California Press, 1976).

7. H. P. Grice, "Meaning," *Philosophical Review* (1957), and S. Schiffer, *Meaning* (Oxford: Oxford University Press, 1972).

8. G. Brown, "The Believer System," technical report RUCBM-TR-34 (July 1974), Dept. of Computer Science, Rutgers University; see also Schmidt and D'Addami, "A Model of the Common Sense Theory of Intention and Personal Causation," in *Proceedings of 3rd International Joint Conference on Artificial Intelligence* (Stanford: Stanford University Press, 1973), pp. 465-471.

9. N. J. Block, "Troubles With Functionalism."

10. I am grateful to Marcia Aufhauser for emphasizing this point to me, both in some papers of her own and in several discussions out of which the present paper grew.

11. See e.g., D. H. Funkenstein, "The Physiology of Fear and Anger," in *Scientific American* (May 1955).

12. See e.g., R. M. Rose, I. S. Bernstein, and T. P. Gordon, "Androgens and Aggressive Behavior: A Review and Recent Findings in Primates," in *Primate Aggression, Territoriality, and Xenophobia*, ed. R. L. Holloway (New York: Academic Press, 1976).

13. Marianne Frankenhaeuser, "Experimental Approaches to the Study of Catecholamines and Emotion," in *Emotions: Their Parameters and Measurement*, ed. Lennart Levi, M.D. (New York: Raven Press, 1975), p. 218.

14. D. A. Hamburg, B. A. Hamburg, and J. D. Barchas, "Anger and Depression in Perspective of Behavioral Biology," in Lennart Levi, *Emotions*, p. 261.

15. Frankenhaeuser, "Experimental Approaches," p. 219.

16. S. Schachter and J. F. Singer, "Cognitive, Social, and Physiological Determinants of an Emotional State," in *Psychological Review* (1962).

17. For a discussion of the role of the limbic system in emotional activity, see R. I. Isaacson, *The Limbic System* (New York: Plenum Press, 1975).

18. L. J. J. Wittgenstein, *Philosophical Investigations*, 3d ed., trans. G. E. M. Anscombe (London: Blackwell, 1967); part I, sections 580, 583, and 584 (p. 153e).

19. Amélie Rorty, "Explaining Emotions," in *Journal of Philosophy* (March 1978), reprinted in this anthology.

20. See e.g., Hilary Putnam, "The Meaning of 'Meaning,' " in idem, *Mind, Language and Reality*, but also John Locke, *An Essay Concerning Human Understanding* (London: Dent, 1961), Book III, chap. vi, sect. 6.

21. See G. C. Davidson, "Anxiety Under Total Curarization: Implications for the Role of Muscular Relaxation in the Desensitization of Neurotic Fears," in *Journal of Nervous and Mental Diseases* (1966).

22. N. Lader and P. Tyrer, "Vegetative System and Emotion," in Levi, *Emotions*, p. 130.

23. I owe the objection to which this last point is a reply to Jerry Fodor.

24. This, of course, does not imply that an explanation of e.g., osmosis, as of any "mechanical" process, cannot be *set out* as an algorithm: any explanation can be regarded as an algorithm where the states and their transitions mirror the laws, and the inputs and outputs correspond to the initial and resulting conditions. That is, algorithms can be *used* to explain things. The point here is that it is only in the explanation of certain sorts of phenomena that they can *also* be *mentioned* in the explanation, in particular, imputed to a device whose operation involves an encoding of it.

25. Note that what has been said here has been directed only against *computational* functionalism; none of it in the least undermines the still real possibility of what I earlier called the "general form" of functionalism, of the sort proposed by, e.g., David Lewis. Indeed, I would expect that what is relevant about our hormones with respect to our emotions is, as the general functionalist urges, the properties of them by virtue of which they interact with the rest of our psychological embodiment (all I have claimed is that these interactions do not seem computational). Substances other than hormones could, conceivably, possess just those properties. And so organisms other than human beings could, on my account, still qualify as persons, if their embodiment included such substances.

26. I am grateful to Marcia Aufhauser, Ned Block, Joseph Levine, Daniel Osherson, Amélie Rorty, and Sylvia Weir for discussions of earlier drafts of this paper. I am particularly indebted to my colleague, Richard Davidson, for his patience and lucidity in explaining to me the rudiments of the physiology of the emotions that I've mentioned here, and for directing me to appropriate articles.

VIII

OVERDETERMINATION AND THE EMOTIONS

Graeme Marshall

I

It is a commonplace now that our emotional lives are overdetermined. In that case, their explanation is philosophically problematic. The overdetermination of particular events is not serious if it is not usual or common, but if it is to be expected over a whole class of events or states then it is a question whether there can be any understanding of such events or states at all since it is unclear what the adequacy conditions could be for explanations of them and what the relations between these explanations are. Either there is no adequate explanation for any event of that sort or each explanation is as good as any other or a conjunctive explanation alone is adequate.[1] The first alternative is prima facie objectionable because it seems to make pointless the whole enterprise of attempting adequate explanations and hence of attempting explanation at all. Who would bother to explain even his own apprehension if nothing he came up with would, quite nonskeptically, do at all? The poet may object[2] that he does not need the scientist's thunder when he is his own lightning; but it would be a mistake to suppose that the form of his illumination is different from the scientist's. They each want to achieve adequacy. The second alternative is prima facie objectionable because it conflicts with the insight that to accept an explanation is presumptively to accept it as true, while there is no guarantee in advance that the different explanations available are not incompatible. It is not obvious, for example, that the explanation of a person's sexual promiscuity in terms of the excessive masculinity of his self-image is not incompatible with that in terms of his insecurity and inadequacy at close personal relationships. But how can both be acceptable? The third alternative is prima facie objectionable for the opposite reason that if the explanations for the event are properly independent, their conjunction is as scarcely intelligible as it is practically frustrating. Can one simply *add* to the explanation of a person's lightheartedness in terms of his having just finished an amusing novel a further explanation in terms of the beautiful day it is and another in terms of the prospect of an agreeable dinner, if these are genuinely independent explanations? And where should one stop? Why should there not be many more independent explanations than are dreamed of in our psychology?

To resolve these doubts and make clear what should count as an adequate explanation of experienced emotions, it needs to be established that the senses in which it is reasonable to say that our emotions are frequently overdetermined do not in the end prevent adequacy criteria from being stated and used. This requires an approach to emotional overdetermination (II), some discussion of the plausibility of some definitions of it (III), and the elucidation of consequent problems for adequate explanation (IV).

II

Overdetermination is a phenomenon that belongs to the particular case, to Napoleon's anger at a deserted Moscow, for example, or Boswell's amazement at Hume's calmness in the face of death. Most theories of emotion however, being theories, are concerned with the particular case only as instances of the general truths they purport to state or as more or less clear, perfect, or exact manifestations of the relations generally held to obtain within the whole class of objects that constitute the domain of the theory. Therefore, insofar as theories are concerned, *inter alia,* with the determination of the emotions, they can provide explanations of particular cases of overdetermined emotions only by being applied as it were twice over: the case is subsumed under more than one of the laws of the theory. So in the context of most theories, overdetermination is defined simply in terms of determination.

Consider, for example, how it would be done in Magda Arnold's Theory of the Emotions,[3] a recent instance of a cognitive psychological theory in the tradition that goes back to Aristotle by way of

Darwin, Hume, and Aquinas, and an instance that is, incidentally, probably the most comprehensive philosophically and experimentally to date. Arnold considers the cognitive appraisal of objects to be particularly important in the etiology of an emotion[4] and sees the sequence perception-appraisal-emotion as that which alone explains the conditions necessary for arousing it. She defines an emotion as "the felt tendency toward anything intuitively appraised as good (beneficial) or away from anything intuitively appraised as bad (harmful). This attraction or aversion is accompanied by a pattern of physiological changes organized toward approach or withdrawal."[5] The bodily changes may themselves be appraised when they are felt, particularly when the connection of the first appraisal with the emotion and autonomic changes has escaped attention because the person was otherwise occupied. A person's emotions, therefore, are, given his physiological organization, determined by the objects he perceives when he appraises them as affecting himself as good or bad. It would appear to follow that they will be overdetermined only if there occurs more by way of perception and appraisal than is needed to call them forth.

But what is more? "What is needed" has reference to norms that we cannot specify except too generally. All such talk must be secured by that part of the General Theory of Persons which makes it clear that certain emotions are appropriate for human kind because it is normal for beings with a certain range of properties to appraise certain objects when perceived in such a manner that they are affected in the right way by such objects. The trouble is, even leaving aside the enormous difficulties involved in spelling out "the right way" so as to avoid wayward causal chains, there is no theory of the Proper Objects of the Emotions adequate to a usable characterization of overdetermination. The reason is plain. In order to avoid tendentiousness and to make the theory widely enough applicable to be taken seriously, only the broadest categories of emotional response can be specified, the roughest limits of emotional intensity and the most conventional of appraisals. Am I too fond? Do I protest too much? Is he too hot? How much may one love? Should I rather pity than despise? Should she affect a cooler passion for her father? The theory can give only the most general answers to questions like these, and consequently overdetermination defined with respect to such a weak theory is too vague to be of much use. If the most that the theory can say is that jealousy was appropriate for Othello given what he believed and was made to believe about Desdemona, then clearly there is more to be said beyond that obvious truth. The lack of specificity in the theory sets low standards of adequacy for explanation in terms of it such that other explanations at least as satisfactory are also available from what is left out in the particular case. The weaker the theory, the weaker the requirements that adequate explanation must meet and hence the greater the incidence of overdetermination defined in terms of the theory.

What is at issue here is not the *truth* of any supposition in a theory of the Proper Objects of emotions, suppositions such as, perhaps, "One may love only that which one respects," "Recognized evil is the only proper object of hatred," or "The proper object of pride is the self." Neither is it a matter of hesitating over the moral overtones and equivocations that have sometimes crept into the notion of something being a "Proper" Object of an emotion. (Does lust have a proper object?) Half of life turns on the rod of that, which is not to say that moral questions should not arise about one's emotions. The question is rather how "overdetermination" is to be understood. The argument is that by virtue of the generality unavoidable in an account of the conditions under which emotions are properly determined, either too many actual emotions in particular circumstances are underdetermined (the generality being pushed by moral pressure toward an ideal), or too many are overdetermined. In either case, the mode of definition is inadequate.

The alternative is to locate a phenomenon sui generis. Since the terms *overdetermination* and *overinterpretation* are credited to Freud, it is reasonable to look to him for an explanation of them, the more so since evidence of overdetermination is to be expected rather in life and the clinic than the laboratory and the armchair.

The concepts were introduced in connection with the interpretation of dreams which was always for Freud the foundation of and the best exemplar of psychoanalytic theory and therapy.[6] Dreams, like neurotic symptoms generally, must be "overinterpreted" (or more strictly, interpreted in more than one way) if they are to be fully understood, since they, like all other psychopathological structures, regularly have more than one meaning. The different meanings are not just alternatives on the same level as it were, but are arranged in superimposed layers. This produces overdetermination in the different elements of the dream's content, the dream-thoughts, and the dream affects. The first are overdetermined in the sense that they have been "represented in the dream-thoughts many times over" and similarly the individual dream-thoughts themselves "are represented in the dream by several elements." "Associative paths lead from one element of the dream to several dream-thoughts and from one dream-thought to several elements of the dream."[7]As an example, Freud uses his own dream of Irma:

> She appeared with the features which were hers in real life, and thus in the first instance represented herself. But the position in which I examined her by the window was derived from someone else, the lady for whom, as the dream-thoughts showed, I wanted to exchange my patient. Insofar as Irma appeared to have a diptheritic membrane, which recalled my anxiety about my eldest daughter, she stood for that child and, behind her, through her possession of the same name, as my daughter, was hidden the figure of my patient who succumbed to poisoning. In the further course of the dream the figure of Irma acquired still other meanings, without any alteration occurring in the visual picture of her in the dream.[8]

Freud adds that this is not the only way in which a collective figure can be produced for purposes of dream-condensation.

Affects in dreams are overdetermined in that they are "fed from a confluence of several sources." "During the dream-work, sources of affect which are capable of producing the same effect come together in generating it."[9] Freud adds in a footnote that he has given an analogous explanation of the pleasurable effect of tendentious jokes. The results of such overdetermination can be variously seen in the detachment of the affect from "the idea which belongs to it," a suppression of affect, the reversal of affect in which a contrary affect instead is attached to a dream-thought, and the intensification of affect. Freud explains that a satisfaction, for example, "which is exhibited in a dream and can of course be immediately referred to its proper place in the dream-thoughts is not always completely elucidated by this reference alone. It is as a rule necessary to look for *another* source of it in the dream-thoughts, a source which is under the pressure of censorship."[10] An explanation along these lines is to be given too of "a striking feature in neurotic characters—the fact that a cause capable of releasing an affect is apt to produce in them a result which is qualitatively justified but quantitatively excessive."[11]

If we were to apply Freud's results to the emotions we experience in the ordinary course of life,[12] as Freud believes we may, we should expect to find, first, that our emotions had more than one object, the manifest object being related by associative paths to others, themselves manifest objects of related emotions experienced much earlier, and each of these others being similarly related to more than one manifest object of our more or less current emotions. The consequent associative net exhibits their complex meaning. Second, we should expect to find that our emotions were causally overdetermined, presenting as a reversal or an intensification of the emotion over what might be regarded as reasonable in the circumstances, or in general, as a *mismatch* of emotion and object.

These two expectations belong together; overdetermination with respect to meaning and overdetermination with respect to causality are but one and the same in the end. The associations of the first are a clue to the causal relations of the second which, when fully articulated, constitute the particular interpretation of the emotion experienced. Different associative networks, if such there be and they survive investigation, become in the end different causal chains and thereby different interpretations.

It might be thought that Freud has not after all provided us with an alternative to a definition of overdetermination in terms of determination. If mismatch is a sign of overdetermination, then we can recognize it as a phenomenon only if we know how the emotions and their objects should match up. But that part of a General Theory of Persons we said cannot be known with sufficient precision to give a usable definition of overdetermination. However, there remains a very significant difference. Instead of concentrating on the general conditions under which emotions are properly determined and leaving to our imagination what overdetermination is (which does require being more precise about proper determination than we can be), Freud focuses on overdetermination and leaves to our imagination the general conditions under which emotions are normally and properly determined. Thus overdetermination becomes a phenomenon sui generis. What begins by being described as a mismatch ends by being described as overdetermined without the route going through a theory that tells us how emotions and their objects should match. Freud's theories certainly presuppose an account of the Proper Objects of emotions, the more so since *all* emotions are proper to their objects and vice versa if one builds into the manifest object all the right associations. But all he requires for a beginning to an understanding of overdetermination, both in general and in the particular case, are the rough and ready intuitions that the emotions and the object are in some way mismatched. This does not need first to be made more precise because it will become so as the details of overdetermination are filled in. When they are, the phenomenon vanishes into history.

III

We can extract from Freud's not altogether clear or even consistent suggestions[13] at least three definitions of emotional overdetermination. Most generally:

> *OD1:* An emotion is overdetermined if and only if it has an historically layered composite object and is caused in its kind and degree by reinforcing causes each of which is capable by itself, together with standing conditions, of producing an effect of the same sort.

This simply summarizes the main material in the brief exposition. The object mentioned is, of course, the intentional object of the emotion, and employing that concept is a convenient way of bringing together those features of the thing, person, event, or situation which under our perception and appraisal trigger the emotion, and the other associated features of other things and events which under our remembrance and old appraisals fill out the emotion and overdetermine it. The perceiving and remembering and appraising of the object thus characterized is clearly a necessary part of the cause of the experienced emotion.

Since it makes sense to suppose that there can be, of a particular emotional response, different interpretations that exploit different associative networks and consequently differ at least in detail over the composite object of and causes assigned to the emotional experience, we have two further possibilities:

OD2: An emotion is overdetermined if and only if it conforms with OD1 and is such that if there are alternative interpretations of it they are independent of each other.

A less subtle interpretation, for example, may be given independently of a more subtle one and vice versa.

OD 3: An emotion is overdetermined if and only if it conforms with OD1 and is such that if there are alternative interpretations of it they are related either as parts of the same whole or by the deriveability relation under some ordering principle.

The less subtle interpretation, for example, may be inferred from the more subtle one together with redefinitions consonant with the more subtle theory of the less subtle terms.

To these we may add two further senses of overdetermination standard in the literature on causation[14] but not always explicitly distinguished:

OD4: An emotion is overdetermined if and only if there is for it a sufficient causal condition which would have been satisfied if the actual sufficient condition had not been satisfied.

OD5: An emotion is overdetermined if and only if there are actually satisfied for it at least two independent sets of sufficient conditions.

The question now is whether emotions can plausibly be said to be often enough overdetermined in any or all of these senses.

There is surely no doubt about the first. OD1 represents emotional overdetermination as belonging both to its object and its cause. It is the *characteristic complexity* of each which is necessary and together sufficient for overdetermination; it is not just the simple requirement that an emotion has both an object and a cause. If that were all that was needed, all emotions except possibly some pathological kinds and degrees, would be overdetermined since emotions characteristically have both objects and causes and can be both elucidated and causally explained. Indeed, if they are able to be elucidated then it *follows* that they are causally explicable. There either is or is not a need to explain why a certain emotion has the object it has. If there is no need, that is because a certain standard causal explanation is taken for granted. It is obvious why in present day American young blacks should feel angry at middle-class whites. If there is a need, then a causal explanation has to be provided. The sudden coolness in a good friend's behavior toward one is puzzling until one discovers that he has had weighty matters on his mind. In either case, the adequacy of the object explanation implies that there is an adequate causal explanation, whether it is in fact given or not. Freud, for example, often gives only the elucidation or interpretation, but the causal explanations are certainly there too in his metapsychology, though of course we need not, and perhaps had better not, follow him there.

Emotions, as OD1 requires, often spring from a "confluence of several sources," and *therefore* have a historically layered composite object. Evidence, though it cannot amount to proof, is provided by the very common mismatch of emotion and object which Freud above all others has brought to light. People are often said to overreact particularly with anger or eagerness: one kicks the very innocent cat and another treasures the polite interest shown by the overly respected superior. People invariably misplace their guilt: one may feel dreadful about taking up the time of another and the other may feel awkward about enjoying passing the time with someone so seductive. One may fear the approach of the smiling, welcoming natives and another weep at the honors bestowed upon him. Whether we deal with mismatches like these in a pre-Freudian way by trying to make the emotion fit the object or whether we take Freud's way of accepting the emotion as datum and look for a further and appropriate object for it, at least the mismatch has to be explained. The explanation shows the additional factors that helped determine the inappropriate emotion given the manifest object or the inappropriate manifest object given the emotion. In either case, it follows that the emotion had reinforcing causes. If the mismatch is one of degree of affect, which it most commonly is, then each cause is, together with the other necessary conditions, capable of producing an affect of the same sort as was produced, since either that affect was greater than might have been expected, in which case the same kind of affect *was* produced, or else it was less, in which case the cause is proved to be a negative condition for the production of that kind of affect that, as such, had better be satisfied along with the other conditions necessary for its occurrence.

In order to *conclude,* however, that the emotion thus caused has a historically layered composite object, we should have to take at least something like Freud's way with mismatch, otherwise we might explain it in terms of physiological organization or by supposing only misperception or eccentric appraisal of the manifest object, and these themselves are not to be explained only in terms of the perception and appraisal of other objects historically associated. Although one might wonder whether Freud's apparent failure to accept genuine eccentricity that results in eccentric and genuine appraisals shows a much too facile respect for rationality or on the contrary an inhibiting and reducing attachment to conformity, there is by now an enormous amount to be said for his way with mismatch. His *way* is not, however, to be confused with his *theories* about the other objects involved and their significance in a case history. We can accept his definition of overdetermination without accepting his use of it. Indeed, it is no longer much of a question of *whether* the objects of our emotional experiences are composite and historically layered, but of *how* they are and of the terms in which an illuminating account of the past in the present can be given. One is not committed to Freud's theories by OD1.

It is sometimes said that talking in terms of overdetermination in this sense is simply an excuse for avoiding a precise causal hypothesis. But this is false. Talking in such terms sets up the problem. It is the work of the clinical hypothesis (in clinical cases) to solve the problem in the particular case. The general theory will provide the terms and structure of the clinical hypothesis but will not, of course, dictate *it.*

This brings us to OD2 and OD3. OD2 is realistic enough. It does not seem implausible to suppose that one affect can be described in different ways and hence ultimately interpreted in the context of different associative networks. Jesus wept over Jerusalem. The conscience of the political reformer about to make trouble? The sentiments of a Jew contemplating patriotically the history of his people focused in that city? The apprehension of one bent upon self-destruction? Or the righteous sorrow of the Son of God? *Prima facie,* the four descriptions place the event in four different histories and different meanings or interpretations are given thereby to that event. It may be argued that which one chooses does not depend upon the truth of the matter determined independently of one's choice and the reasons for it, but rather upon the way in general one prefers to make human behavior and response, including particularly emotional response, intelligible. Some cannot use clinical and psychological descriptions at all, for example. Are they blind to a whole dimension of experience and theory? No more so, perhaps, than those who find unintelligible descriptions of emotional experiences in terms of spiritualistic auras, happenings and journeys and visions. Without indulging in the full excesses of unrestricted holism, one can with a great deal of plausibility lock the phenomena as *interestingly* classified into different theories or ways of interpreting the world so that as such they belong to only one theory. The identifying or uninteresting descriptions can be as common as one likes.

This is already discernible between or even within disciplines. The aggression seen by the social psychologist may be the enthusiasm seen by the social worker and the governable but ungoverned impulse seen by the judge and the propensity to vandalism seen by the jury. It is easy to believe that there is no truth of the matter outside the frame of reference of one's own and favored colleagues, only the subtle connections and relations that add up to different interpretations that cannot conflict with each other because they are so different. The lawyer cannot show that the psychologist is wrong; at most he can believe that he can show that he is irrelevant. On the other hand, one psychological theory may not cancel another out but allow for theoretical complementarity because they deal with the mind under different descriptions.[15] The existence of aspects is theory dependent: is there a truth of the matter about aspects? Implied by OD2 is a contention of the greatest importance: beyond the common chronicle, there lies nothing except a theory that gives us the words to use in the redescription of things and determines what aspects of things are to be redescribed.

The inclination to accept OD3 rather than OD2 arises from the very strong inclination to say that there is, after all and despite OD2, a truth of the matter. The inclination arises from two quite different sources: the old and familiar first person privilege and the a priori conviction that nothing short of a case-historical narrative will provide the proper descriptions and explanations. The former has taken an equally familiar beating over the course of the century, mainly of course due to Freud but also in no small measure to the behaviorists. But neither would say that there is not a truth of the matter; each would settle for his own way of determining it. We are back again with OD2. Hence the inclination toward the entire narrative.

One does not have to be a determinist to accept OD3 and believe that a particular person's behavior and responses are all of a piece and coherent over time. This is not to say that people do not change and it is not to suppose that a person does not have at any one time conflicting needs, desires, emotions, and beliefs. These are presumptions with which one looks at the data in the first place. The need to see a person's behavior as coherent over time is just the need to find it intelligible and to explain it. This is the same need that a history of anything satisfies. If a history is incoherent it is worthless. Like any historical narrative, case-historical narratives would be worthless if incoherent. The explanatory power of any narrative lies in its consistently tying together a wealth of material, including biographical material, into a coherent whole. What indeed the difference between OD2 and OD3 could be said to present is the difference between scientific and historical models for how this might be done. This is not to say that there might not be ultimately one model which they both share, but it is to say that they begin by looking very different. Prima facie, narratives given in the terms of at least certain behavioral and social sciences are obviously independent of one another in the way that different histories of the same events are equally obviously not.

Whether emotional responses, therefore, are taken to be overdetermined in the sense either of OD2 of OD3 is not an empirical matter to be decided by the production of evidence; it is a philosophical matter. Since a philosopher particularly should be concerned to preserve the possibility both of various scientific ways of understanding the diverse range of human behavior and response and of a historical understanding of individual cases, both OD2 and OD3 should apparently be accepted. The difficulties consequent upon doing so we shall consider in the final section of the paper.

Overdetermination in the sense of OD4 appears to abound at least where human resourcefulness is equal to human desires. One can safely say in many cases, both pathological and not, that the same emotional result would have eventuated even if its actual

proximate antecedents had been different. If either singing or dancing is equally pleasing to me and I want to be pleased, then it does
not matter whether I sing or I dance or, if prevented from doing
one, I do the other. It is equally true, all being well, that I would
have been just as pleased had I sung and not danced or had I
danced and not sung. Or seeking to be revenged upon my neighbors
for their noisy and late party last night, I played my hi-fi very
loudly early this morning, then I shall be equally satisfied if I exac-
erbated the younger son's headache or prevented the elder from
getting back to sleep. Or the child who *will* be at odds with the
world no matter what one does, would have been even if he had
been given a pear instead of an apple. In general, we are sometimes
sure enough that we would have been just as happy, sad, surprised,
exhilarated, satisfied, or bored had the determining cause been
other than it in fact was.

But emotions apparently overdetermined in this sense are not
quite as simple as their dependence on resources of one sort or another may suggest. First, though we might be sure enough sometimes that we would have felt the same if we had done this instead
of that or got this instead of that, what we are sure we would have
felt is roughly the same degree of the same *kind* of emotion that we
did feel, but certainly not the selfsame instance of it. The happiness
or sadness that we did feel, therefore, was not overdetermined in
any sense since *that* would not have occurred had the sufficient
conditions for it not been satisfied. There might be other sufficient
conditions for a certain degree of happiness or pleasure of some
sort which would, all being well, be satisfied if the sufficient conditions for the actual sort had not been, our desire for it and our
resourcefulness being what it is. But all that means is that we are
determined to be happy or pleased somehow, not that we are overdetermined to be happy or pleased as we are. The pleasures of singing and the pleasures of dancing, though both pleasures, are obviously not even the same sort of pleasure. Overdetermination
belongs not to kinds but to the particular case.

Second, if the appraisal of the object of an emotion is always
part of its cause, and if it is to be presumed that different objects
will not be appraised in exactly the same way, then how can it be
true that we should ever have been just as we in fact were had our
emotion had a different object and consequently a partially differ-

ent cause? The obvious answer is that the objects are not in the required sense different: if their specific features do not matter, their generic ones do. I am not indifferent to singing and dancing as *equal sources of pleasure* and it is the annoyance of either son, *as a member of my neighbor's family,* which is the object of my satisfaction. As for the child, it might have been the apple as fruit or as food or most probably as something which imposed upon him. One has to be careful here of course lest the object become so generalized that *anything* will do, for then it is a question whether the state can usefully be described as an emotion at all. But perhaps even this does not matter. Perhaps, indeed, it illuminates some of the hard cases of pathological depression or anxiety; it maybe is just what happens. What one must avoid, however, is the inference that the object under no description whatsoever had anything to do with the arousal and maintenance of the emotion since in that case it would be quite irrelevant to the emotion except as an occasion for its discharge, or expression. So on pain of confusing the real object of the emotion with the object that merely occasions its expression, there had better be some description such that had the object so described been different, we would have felt differently.

There is a fine line sometimes between the arousal of an emotion and the expression of an already existing one so that it is hard to distinguish between a real, composite, and historically layered object, the appraisal of which at some level features in the cause of the emotion directed toward it, and a merely convenient object that will, for some purposes such as expression and venting and maybe even confirmation, do as a temporary substitute. This difficulty is sometimes a good reason for suspecting the first although the case looks like the second.

Overdetermination in the sense of OD4, therefore, is simply apparent. If it is true that we would have felt just as we did had the object been different, it may be inferred that either the object under the identificatory description used is not the real object of the emotion, or it is not the object the appraisal of which is part of the cause of the emotion.

OD5 must be carefully interpreted. No two sets of causal conditions for an event are ever absolutely independent since a set of conditions is sufficient for an event only given the rest of the universe up until now. When there are at least two causal chains leading to events overdetermined in this sense, each is sufficient only given something that already includes the other. But the point that needs to be taken is that although in the actual case there are two causal chains, we know from our causal lore that there need not have been: an exactly similar event would have occurred had the conditions constituting either causal chain been fulfilled. The failure of the counterfactual referring to either set of conditions is characteristic of the events overdetermined in this sense. So the overdetermining conditions must be seen to be independent and sufficient only relative to whatever is presupposed by the counterfactuals. What that comes to is simply that the case is subsumable under two causal laws both of which hold, of course, only under the same normal conditions that the counterfactual presupposes. But, despite the overdetermination, that is the situation with the case in point. So OD5 should be understood as requiring the failure of the counterfactuals referring to each of the sufficient conditions, with the independence and sufficiency being construed as relative to what is presupposed by both counterfactuals.

The question is whether emotions are more than just occasionally, if ever, overdetermined in this sense. It is surely clear on a moment's reflection that it is implausible to suppose that they are. Would one have been exactly as surprised as one in fact was had one's long lost friend not suddenly appeared just as one's companion equally suddenly disappeared from view in a snowdrift? Or, indeed, if it had happened the other way round? Would one have taken against her quite as much as one did had she not both left one and destroyed what one most prized as well? It is extremely doubtful that the emotional reactions of even the most ostensibly unfeeling of people would have been just the same if one or other of the precipitating causes had not occurred. If her yellow hair, for example and with apologies to Yeats, figured prominently in his loving of her, then rather than his loving being for herself alone and independently for her yellow hair, it is better regarded as being a loving for herself alone *enhanced* by her yellow hair. If it were overdetermined in the sense of OD5, then his loving would have to have been the same if either herself or her hair had been different. The psychological implausibility of this inclines to the interpretation of the enhancement effect on affect.

The same conclusion holds generally. OD5 requires that there be satisfied two relatively independent sets of sufficient causal conditions for the arousal and maintenance of a particular emotional experience such that that experience would have been the same had one or other set of conditions not been satisfied. Taking it again that the appraisal of the object of an emotional experience is a necessary part of its cause, the arguments advanced in connection with OD4 apply to OD5 *a fortiori*. If we are sure enough that the same emotional experience would have occurred whether or not a certain appraisal of the object had been made, we know enough to conclude that the appraisal was no part of the cause and *a fortiori* no part of its overdetermined cause. If the absence of that appraisal would make no difference to the experience how could it be supposed that its presence does?

It may be replied that some emotional experiences do in fact exhibit the required asymmetry: they do not qualitatively alter when the perceived and appraised objects toward which they are directed quantitatively alter. It may be thought that moods supply cases in point. Already sad, excited, anxious, irritated, happy at some things, one is prone to be so for a while at others which feed the mood but neither intensify it nor are required for its continuation since it would have persisted anyway.

But the difficulty is to understand what appears to be an entirely useless "feeding." Either we know enough to say that the mood would have persisted in just the way it did without the object that "fed" it, in which case we also know enough to say that the object did not *feed* it at all, or we do not know what the mood would have been without the object that "fed" it. Of course, sometimes we can be sure enough; we have enough evidence without further objects. But in that case it is reasonable to believe that the mood would not have been just as it was had the *only* appraisal that caused it been that of the object that simply "fed" it. It is either enhancement or nothing.

It may perhaps seem that OD5 is still required for cases of complex reactions to undifferentiated objects and cases of ambivalence of a familiar sort where, for example, one both loves and hates another or is both excited by and apprehensive about a certain future happening. But it becomes quickly obvious that OD5 remains implausible. On the *post facto* analysis of a complex emotional response to a film, say, one may find that there were several intuitive appraisals of several objects that produced the same effect.

But that is described most simply as the enhancement effect again. And one clearly would not feel ambivalently if both appraisals were not made; each alone is not sufficient for that. There may be some underlying condition which makes the two appraisals likely but that is not to say that it renders either of them otiose.

The last remark, however, does point to what appears to be a more plausible case. An emotional response might be said to be overdetermined in the sense of OD5 if there are for one's intuitive appraisal itself more than one independent and sufficient reason or cause. (It is in this sense that philosophical and legal arguments are often from outside complained of for being overdetermined: if one reason is enough for accepting or rejecting a position, what need we of five?) For example, one may fear another because he is bad and mad; the appraisal that he is dangerous is supported by two sufficient reasons. Or one may be angry with another because he has added injury to insult, as Rousseau did to Hume by publishing his paranoid fancies about him. It is difficult, however, to find clear enough examples where the reasons are genuinely independent and do not lead to the enhancement effect. There is no denying that possibility in either of the above cases, for instance. And that is what we should in general expect and what we in general find with the emotions. Both the emotional responses and the terms of the appraisals which partly cause them admit and admit of degrees so that the possibility is naturally provided for the expression of variations in strength of judgment and conviction and in the number of reasons for it. Moreover, if the object of an emotion is, as earlier suggested, capable of being expressed in a complete sentence, our having multiple reasons for our appraisal that, say, the man is dangerous, rests on the predication of distinct properties of him and not the same property several times over. It is not surprising therefore, that talk of enhancement, confluence, and cumulative effects should be rationally preferred to descriptions conforming to OD5.

But such talk is in the terms used in OD1, which is a further reason for thinking that emotional overdetermination is properly defined by it. That is the conclusion toward which all the considerations of this part tend. If it is implausible to think that emotions are overdetermined in the sense of OD5 and if overdetermination in the sense of OD4 is merely apparent, then we are left with OD1 and the problem of deciding between OD2 and OD3.

Enhancement itself, however, is not overdetermination as given by OD1 because it is not overdetermination at all. But OD1 does define a kind of enhancement effect that occurs when there is *historical* complexity of cause and object. What distinguishes overdetermination of the emotions is the historical layering of their objects, not merely their complexity. That is what has emerged. Emotions are determined by the appraisal of things as perceived, no matter how complex it or they are, and are, as it were, the vectorial products of all that in the force-field of one's mind and body. Emotions are overdetermined when to that appraisal is added others in the remembrance of things past.

IV

Three consequences follow from what has been said so far for the issue of deciding between OD2 and OD3 with respect to explanations of emotional overdetermination. First, if OD1 gives the only remaining plausible sense of emotional overdetermination, then *all* explanations of the phenomenon will involve a historical narrative that continues up to the time of the emotion in question, which is therefore a necessary condition for an adequate explanation of that emotion. Second, if OD1 does not commit us to accepting Freud's theories about the terms that should feature significantly in the explanatory narrative, then there obviously is a choice of theory possible and necessary. That is, the chronicle, which is a simple, nonselective list of the events in a person's life in only chronological order, *underdetermines* the narrative. That is as it should be; otherwise, history would cease to be a discipline and become a trade. No chronicle is ever complete but it would still underdetermine the narrative even if, *per impossibile,* it were. No chronicle is ever quite nonselective either, but it should be as much as one's language and conceptual framework allows. No chronicle, finally, is easy to construct; it represents the greater part of the historian's labor and the clinician's work. The third consequence is that the question of whether OD2 or OD3 is to be preferred is the question of whether there is theoretical as well as empirical overdetermination: whether the different possible narratives are independent of one another or whether there is one true narrative of which they are parts or aspects; whether satisfactory explanation *requires* overinterpretation. To answer that question will be to give sufficient conditions for explanations of overdetermined emotions by way of giving, beyond the general conditions for any satisfactory explanation, the criteria for a true case historical narrative. The answer will be that a case-historical narrative is true when it is true enough.

It is necessary that for any case-historical narrative to be true enough there is a chronicle that underdetermines it. There is always something which is up for interpretation rather than the result of it, otherwise there is no possibility of disconfirmation and we reach John Wisdom's lands of the a priori "where there blow no winds of chance and *ipso facto* no breath of life." So there is a minimal truth of the matter without which there would be no way for different theorists to agree on what they attempt to explain differently.

But this does not take one very far. It is also necessary that a case-historical narrative treat of the matter of the chronicle in such aspects that it can coherently relate, otherwise there is no intelligibility. But the aspects of anything are discriminable and distinguishable ultimately because they are definable in the theoretical terms of some disciplined intelligibility scheme. Language discovers the properties because they are what get mentioned in the aspect-descriptions and the descriptions are intelligible only within some scheme or other; even, or perhaps especially, terms of art such as the historian's *resonance,* the critic's *felt life* and *moral seriousness,* and the philosopher's *paradigms.* There is a truth of the matter here too, of course, otherwise different experts in the same field could only argue a priori. But this truth of the matter consists in *conceptualized phenomena* and it is tedious to insist on the difference between realistic and nonrealistic interpretations of it. The place for realism is within a theory. There is indeed a strong feeling that there is *something* there to be conceptualized, but it is idle to say that it is the same thing that is captured in different conceptualizations. (Here lie the hopes and disappointments of interdisciplinary studies.) The terms in which the identity conditions are given are either common terms or they are not. If they are, the phenomena belong to what is given unilluminatingly by the chronicle itself. If they are not, they belong to the narrative as underdetermined by the chronicle and refer to its own conceptualized phenomena.

It follows from these two conditions that the chronicle can only show that the claims of a case-historical narrative are either false or not false; beyond compatibility it cannot confirm either it or them. The chronicle may be able to show, for example, that Poe was not the blackguard his first biographer made him out to be, sometimes by deliberate forgeries, and that the second, in rescuing his reputation, was somewhat too partial; but it will not decide that, in Patricia Highsmith's phrase, he was not a tosspot but a thimblebelly and possibly a diabetic, at least as far as the chronicle is yet determined. Like all "seeing as," the respects in which a narrative illuminates are extrinsic to what is given. Consequently, there must be further adequacy conditions to be met. These will of course include such conditions on any explanation: relevance, simplicity, utility, or whatever they may be. That is taken for granted here and set aside. The question concerns those conditions peculiar to explanation by way of case-historical narratives.

A narrative is determined by the application to the chronicle of two hypotheses: what I shall call the dominance hypothesis and the causal hypothesis.[16] One first of all finds what is dominant in the chronicle. There is really only one way in which this can properly be done: by abduction—forming a conjecture about it after surveying the chronicle. The dominance hypothesis accounts for the selectiveness of the narrative, supplies the terms in which the events emerging as significant are to be redescribed, and thus makes explicit the aspects to be dealt with. The hypothesis is named on analogy with what in decision-theoretic definitions of rationality has been called the dominance principle: x is to be preferred to y just in case it secures what y secures and more.[17] Something similar applies here. One dominance hypothesis is to be preferred to another just in case it secures more of the chronicle than another; with, however, the caveat that there is a favored point of view from which an investigator considers the chronicle and hence the size and constitution of the chronicle may to a degree be relative to the interests and consequent relevance orderings of each investigator. Even so, the more "don't cares" there are, the less acceptable the dominance hypothesis will be. That we critically use the dominance *principle* in this way is shown by our tendency to think that the dominance hypotheses provided by various social sciences are more or less acceptable to the extent that more or less human behavior as ordinarily described is incorporated into the phenomena in connection with which the hypothesis is formed. It seems reasonable to say, therefore, that one case-historical narrative will be better than another, insofar as its dominance hypothesis better accords with the dominance principle.

The causal hypothesis structures the narrative beyond its chronological ordering. It may be identical with the dominance hypothesis because that may, of course, be a certain causal hypothesis, as it probably is in Hume's case if he is to be believed when he says that his love of literary fame was the ruling passion of his life. The causal hypothesis brings together in a particular associative network things and events selected from the chronicle and thus gives them meaning. It can concern the person's reasons, purposes, or intentions, or his imagined economic preferences, or the functioning of his endocrine system, or whatever is favored. If it is not identical with the dominance hypothesis, it may, nonetheless, not be independent of it, though it may. In this hestiation lies, indeed, the rest of the answer. Consider, by way of illustration, Berlin on Tolstoy[18] and Freud on Dostoevsky.[19] Berlin's dominance hypothesis is that Tolstoy was constantly in contradiction with himself, "perceiving reality in its multiplicity but believing only in 'one vast, unitary, whole,' " and that the relation between his artistic vision and his moral teaching "can be seen as a titanic struggle between the monist and pluralist visions of reality." Hence, Berlin's narrative shows how "Tolstoy's 'lethal nihilism' led him to denounce the pretensions of all theories, dogmas, and systems to explain, order and predict the complex and contradictory phenomena of history and social existence" and how "the driving force of this nihilism was a passionate longing to discover one unitary truth encompassing all existence and impregnable to attack." Berlin's causal hypothesis, insofar as it is different from his dominance hypothesis, is that Tolstoy's art "can be understood only as a product of the same moral conflict as that experienced by the radical intelligensia."

Freud's dominance hypothesis for Dostoevsky is that "in little things he was a sadist towards others and in bigger things he was a sadist towards himself, in fact a masochist, that is to say, the mildest, kindliest, most helpful person possible." His causal hypothesis is of course provided by his own psychoanalytical theories. His narrative sketch mentions on the one hand Dostoevsky's great need of and enormous capacity for love "which is seen in the manifestations of exaggerated kindness and caused him to love and help where he had a right to hatred and revenge, as, for example, in his relations with his first wife and her lover''; and on the other hand in "his choice of material which singles out from all others violent, murderous and egoistic characters thus pointing to the existence of similar tendencies in his own soul," "his irritability, his love of tormenting and his intolerance even toward those he loved and which appear also in the way in which as an author he treats his readers." The narrative sketch explains this contradiction, his epilepsy and his gambling in terms of his oedipal guilt which Freud shows operating in various incidents throughout his life.

Both narratives are illuminating in distinct ways. Both writers place their subjects in a context which each uses to determine the dominance and causal hypotheses. Both have a theoretical ax to grind and we enjoy the sharpness of each. Both naturally enough are interested in applying their theories to a particular case; but while the cases are well chosen, they have their own features. Each is a particular case and not just an instance of the right kind and consequently each narrative is falsifiable by them. The dominance hypothesis in each narrative encompasses a great deal of what is known about their subjects and in neither case is the dominance hypothesis independent of the causal hypothesis. As admittedly fine examples of different kinds of case-historical narrative, there is nothing to choose between them.

But perhaps we should choose between both on the one hand and others on the other in which the dominance and causal hypotheses are independent of one another. To the extent that they are, it may be argued, the dominance hypothesis is more likely to be untendentious. There being no presumptions about how the events in the chronicle are related and hence no presumptions about their significant relative properties and hence no presumptions about the sortals to be used, the dominance hypothesis is more able to be determined by the ordinary properties of things and events that lie open to general view, and hence requires no special pleading for its acceptance. The dominance hypothesis is more nearly an inductive generalization and hence more nearly straightforwardly true or false. Hence the explanatory narrative determined by it is the more acceptable.

But this will not do. The dominance hypothesis by approaching an inductive generalization either carries the narrative with it, in which case the narrative becomes less explanatory,[20] or the narrative retains its explanatory power and the causal hypothesis increases in methodological importance. The first alternative is obviously to be avoided. To know of a person that it is usual or characteristic of him to act in a certain way is to make *that* he does so understandable but not why he should. Far from providing an explanation, it makes one more imperative. The second alternative is really incoherent. If we succeeded in making the two hypotheses independent in the way envisaged, we could only end up with a lot of events that had the wrong properties. We would not be able to relate them by our causal hypotheses at all and hence we would not be able to write an explanatory narrative. Consequently, a case-historical narrative will be a better explanation if its dominance hypothesis is more, not less, dependent on the favored and theoretically embedded causal hypothesis. That is what makes it explanatory at all.

But this makes the choice of narrative ultimately to turn on a "picture preference"[21] and stakes a lot on the variety of noncompeting pictures that can be presented of something or someone. To leave the matter there, it might be argued, is too much like coming to the end of one of those detective novels where one is presented with several different, entirely plausible, explanatory narratives without John Appelby to tell us what is really what. Should there not be some relation between the truth of the matter in its various aspects, some arguable, as opposed to a mere, preference for a certain kind of picture, perhaps, or some more satisfying overall picture?

But there is no great detective and we are on our own, with at least three inadequate answers to the question. We might try to use the dominance principle on the dominance hypotheses of the various candidate narratives. It should resolve the issue at least *within* a field. But we must remember that even there comprehensiveness is relative to a preferred point of view, and the question of whether something should or should not be included in the *chronicle* becomes more question begging as the issue of comprehensiveness gets more interesting. In the dating of an ancient text, for instance, what has to be interpreted is very often itself a matter of interpretation. Ancient putative memories are as difficult. Dominance won't decide between Freud and Berlin.

Second, we could try to put things together. But aspects cannot intelligibly be merely *summed,* unless the terms that pick them out are each definable in terms of a common language. This must be the language of the narrative itself, otherwise the coherence of the narrative will be lost. Nothing but confusion results from intruding, for example, psychological terms into an economic history, or into an account of how a thinker like Wittgenstein, say, arrived at his later views.

Or finally, there is always the possibility of reduction. The splendid aspirations of Unified Science aside, this may be quite acceptable in some cases, though there is always room for doubt and the argument needs to be made in each kind of case. Still, the argument can sometimes be made good. However, the criteria for adequacy in explanatory narratives, as with explanation in general, is independent of reduction since it does not follow from the successful reduction of one kind of explanatory narrative to another that the particular explanatory narrative one ends up with is adequate of its kind; and it does not follow from the mere failure of the reduction that the unreduced explanation is not adequate; only prejudice could have it otherwise. The most that could be claimed is that certain kinds of explanatory narrative are never adequate. But that is a matter of intrinsically inadequate dominance and/or causal hypotheses and is shown by the general considerations applicable to any explanation and not peculiar to explanatory narratives.

I conclude that OD3 is to be rejected, or, of course, used to define the goals of one of the sciences, in which case the different interpretations involved will all be in terms of one covering theory and therefore only one of the interpretations referred to in OD2. This is not a rejection of historical models but a clarification of them. In both science and history causal relations are asserted within some theory or other. But that is where all interesting facts are.

So an overdetermined emotion is adequately explained by being associated and causally linked by an adequate case-historical narrative with other objects and other times. Given the satisfaction of general conditions on explanation, the narrative is adequate just in case it is determined by coherent and well-supported dominance and causal hypotheses and is, with respect to the personal chronicle, not false. This allows as many adequate explanations as there are coherent and well supported dominance and causal hypotheses. But what should imagination require else?

NOTES

1. This is reminiscent of J. L. Mackie's trilemma of overdetermination: Neither a nor b caused c, so what did? Either a or b caused c, but what are disjunctive causes? Both a and b caused c, so each did alone! Remembered by Louis E. Loeb, "Causal Theories and Causal Overdetermination," *Journal of Philosophy* (1974), p. 531.

2. As Dylan Thomas did once about critics.

3. Magda B. Arnold, *Emotion and Personality*, 2 vols. (New York: Columbia University Press, 1960).

4. So do I. See G. D. Marshall, "On Being Affected," *Mind* (1968). It is interesting to observe that this makes emotion sentences amenable to Fregean semantics. The dependence on appraisals requires that the objects of emotions be expressed not by singular terms but by full sentences. What is loved, hated, or feared is not a person, thing, event, or state of affairs *as such,* but *its having, as we believe, certain properties.* This squares well with experience too. This observation began from one of Alan Donagan's insights.

5. Arnold, *Emotion and Personality*, 1:182.

6. S. Freud, *The Interpretation of Dreams,* trans. and ed. James Strachey, (New York: Avon Books, 1967).

7. Ibid., p. 318.

8. Ibid., p. 327.

9. Ibid., p. 518. Freud's text has emphasis.

10. Ibid., p. 517.

11. Ibid.

12. Amélie Rorty does something like this much more fully in her illuminating paper "Explaining Emotions."

13. Robert Wälder comments in a classic paper: "When it appeared overdetermination was explained by the fact that a psychic trend alone was not yet equivalent to psychic effectiveness. It is clear that this conception has been built up in analogy to those of the older neurology and it shows a logical difficulty: there can be a complete determination—natural science knows the concept of the necessary and adequate causes—and as long as one remains within the sphere of natural science, it is difficult to understand how far an occurrence should be determined more adequately. . . . The principle of multiple function is perhaps in a position to meet all these difficulties." "The Principle of Multiple Function," *The Psychoanalytical Quarterly,* 5 (1936), 50-52.

14. See, for example, the bibliographies cited in *The Nature of Causation,* ed. Myles Brand (Urbana: University of Illinois Press, 1976).

15. See John E. Gedo and Arnold Goldberg, *Models of the Mind* (Chicago: University of Chicago Press, 1973).

16. This is much simpler than Hayden White's schema and it may be oversimplified, even given the limitations imposed by case histories. There is more work to be done here. My "dominance hypotheses" include White's "emplotments" and my "causal hypotheses" include the "colligations" of his "contextualism." Perhaps we should use his finer (and grander) distinctions. Our conclusions, however, converge. See Hayden White, *Metahistory* (Baltimore: Johns Hopkins University Press, paperback, 1975), especially Introduction, pp. 1-42. I am grateful to the members of the Workshop in Psychoanalysis and Social Sciences of the Chicago Centre for Psychosocial Studies for this reference and discussion of these matters.

17. See, for example, David A. J. Richards, *A Theory of Reasons for Action* (Oxford, 1971), pp. 40 ff.

18. Derived from Aileen Kelly, "A Complex Vision: Isaiah Berlin and Russian Thought," *TLS,* 30 December 1977.

19. S. Freud, "Dostoevsky and Parricide" (1928), *Collected Papers,* vol. 5, ed. James Strachey (London: Hogarth Press, 1957).

20. The argument is due to C. S. Peirce, as is the term *abduction* itself.

21. John Wisdom's term. See "Gods" in his *Philosophy & Psychoanalysis* (Oxford: Blackwell, 1953).

IX

A CASE OF MIXED FEELINGS: AMBIVALENCE AND THE LOGIC OF EMOTION*

PATRICIA S. GREENSPAN

Traditional philosophical treatments of the emotions have usually emphasized questions of their *rationality;* and some philosophers have raised the related question whether they should be identified with *judgments,* or elements of cognition.[1] In contemporary literature, these questions are brought together by Robert C. Solomon, most recently in an article called "The Logic of Emotion," which argues that emotions have a logic of sorts which connects them quite firmly to judgments, and that they therefore are in many ways open to rational control.[2] Other current authors, though they may agree that emotions generally correspond to judgments, would apparently prefer not to *identify* the two; and some stress ways in which emotions are typically *ir*rational.[3] But there is one important fact about the emotions—indeed, a kind of logical fact—which none of them brings to bear on this dispute, although they may often be ready enough to grant it.[4] This is *the possibility of ambivalence:* contrary emotions with the same object in a basically rational person. Briefly: ambivalence seems to be possible in persons not so irrational as to hold genuinely contrary judgments.

I suppose that most people think of ambivalence in connection with some rather complex, and debatable, claims of psychoanalytic theory, like the claim that a child unconsciously hates a parent it consciously loves, where the parent is its rival in the Oedipal triangle. Indeed, if psychoanalytic theory is even roughly correct, the phenomenon of ambivalence is widespread and subtle enough to require an extended treatment. I shall not give it one here, however —our understanding of even the simplest emotions is just too fuzzy, at this point. Instead, I shall keep my argument close to common sense and focus on one very revealing yet relatively simple and uncontroversial example of ambivalence, an example roughly familiar to us as a case of "mixed feelings." I think I can extract this case from suggestions found in Spinoza, one philosopher who does make much of the possibility of ambivalence (besides anticipating Freud with some of his general views about knowledge and freedom).[5] In what follows, after constructing and defending my example (Section I), I shall show how it bears on the question whether emotions should be identified with judgments (II-III) and then draw out some implications for the tangled question of the rationality of the emotions (IV). (As my argument proceeds, I shall try to *un*tangle the rationality question somewhat by making a few rough distinctions.)

By putting "logic" in scare quotes much of the time, I mean to cancel out any suggestion that the logic of emotion is really analogous to that of judgment. In fact, I shall be arguing *against* that view, by stressing the logical differences between emotion and judgment, expanding on some of them (and raising further questions about them) in a long set of footnotes. At the same time, though, I think it may be useful to examine an artificial "logic" of emotion (a task I merely begin in this paper), just to see where the analogy must break down. For there *are* some significant parallels between emotion and judgment, which I shall point out, here and there, as my argument proceeds. Hence, even if the two should not be identified, I think we may be able to learn something interesting by exploring their interrelations. I shall explore them here, however—except in a few of my (optional) footnotes—just insofar as they bear on my case of mixed feelings.

I shall argue, then, that insofar as emotions have a "logic," it is one that tends to set them apart from judgments, though it also calls for a noncognitive assessment of their rationality. In my last section, on the second point, I shall present some initial thoughts on a subject that I do not think philosophers have dealt with sufficiently: the special motivational force of emotions, the pressure they exert on us to express them somehow in behavior. In a way, my argument will end with some questions about the nature of this special motivational force. We do not yet understand it fully; but I think we do know enough about it to question the familiar ideal of "philosophic detachment" from the emotions. Because of their motivational force, I shall argue, the emotions may often be useful to us—may play an essential role, for instance, in social communication—as long as we can control their behavioral consequences. In effect, then, my argument will bear out some of Solomon's more restrained comments on rational control of the emotions, while rejecting his central argument for them, which involves identifying emotions with judgments. But before I get to my critical points, I need to argue, using Spinoza, that ambivalence is indeed possible, and possible, moreover, without some sort of abnormal breakdown in reasoning.

I

In his treatment of the emotions in Part III of the *Ethics,* Spinoza allows for ambivalence—he calls it *fluctuatio,* or vacillation (p. 142) —as a result of a kind of transfer of emotions which he calls *imitatio,* imitation (p. 148). In his particular system, it seems to rest primarily on the resemblance of various possible objects of emotion. He introduces the subject of ambivalence in Proposition XVII:

> If we conceive that a thing, which is wont to affect us painfully, has any point of resemblance with another which is wont to affect us with an equally strong emotion of pleasure, we shall hate the first-named thing, and at the same time we shall love it. [P. 142]

Spinoza's claim here relies on his view that love and hate amount to the "primary" emotions pleasure and pain (*laetitia* and *tristitia,* often translated—more accurately, I think—as "joy" and "sorrow"), attributed to some object as cause (p. 140; see p. 138). I shall not attempt a scholarly account of Spinoza's overall system of the emotions; but this point should help us construct, in a moment, an example much more plausible than those Spinoza himself actually gives. In the quote above, the object of emotion is seen as causing both pain and pleasure—pain in its own right, and pleasure because of its resemblance to something else that causes pleasure in its own right. Spinoza does not tell us here what sorts of resembling "things" he has in mind; but his later remarks indicate that they would standardly be persons (or persons seen as experiencing pain or pleasure), including ourselves.

Proposition XXVII, his central proposition on imitation, runs as follows:

> By the very fact that we conceive a thing, which is like ourselves, and which we have not regarded with any emotion, to be affected by any emotion, we are ourselves affected by a like emotion. [P. 148]

The proof of XXVII adds:

> If, however, we hate the said thing like ourselves, we shall, to that extent, be affected by a contrary, and not similar, emotion. [P. 148]

Thus, on Spinoza's view, a kind of sympathy based on resemblance leads us to "imitate" others' emotions, or at least the emotions of others we do not hate. Taken by itself, XXVII may not seem to bear on the possibility of ambivalence, since it is apparently limited to objects toward which we have no contrary emotion, like hatred. But in light of Spinoza's further comments, it does suggest at least one way in which ambivalence might result from imitation.[6] If something like ourselves (another person, with whom we identify) causes us pain *by* gaining pleasure for itself—by getting something we would like to have ourselves, for instance—then according to Spinoza, it ought to cause us *both* pain and pleasure, and hence be an object of *both* hatred and love. Insofar as we imitate it, it causes us pleasure by virtue of the very same fact that simultaneously causes us pain: its fulfillment of our own competing desire. Thus, it is unaffected by XVII's exclusion of objects of prior hatred, and points toward situations of *rivalry* as one potentially rich source of cases of ambivalence.

Spinoza himself focuses on various other sorts of cases of ambivalence, as arising from the propositions I have quoted; and he does not make explicit any link to situations of rivalry.[7] But I think that the general connection he sets up between ambivalence and imitation would be most effectively illustrated by a case of rivalry. Cases of rivalry are emphasized, of course, in the discussions of ambivalence in psychoanalytic theory; but they should be especially interesting to us because, assuming that one does sometimes identify with others and share in their emotions, ambivalence toward a rival seems perfectly *rational,* even if by definition it involves a kind of inconsistency. Consider sibling rivalry, for instance: it seems quite *appropriate* to have "mixed feelings" toward a person one both to some extent identifies and competes with. I shall take up the question of "perfect" rationality in my last section; but for the moment, I think we may grant that ambivalence is at least compatible with what I shall call "basic" rationality. It is certainly not unreasonable, that is, even if it falls short of some higher rational ideal, like Spinoza's ideal of complete freedom from external emotional influence; for it need not involve any abnormal breakdown in reasoning.[8]

As they stand, however, Spinoza's comments do not seem to yield an intuitively compelling example of ambivalence, even once we turn to a case of rivalry. He seems to imply, for instance, that any rival would be sufficiently like ourselves to give rise to a sympathetic emotion; and this may certainly be doubted. We might even question his assumption, moreover, that emotions as strong as love and hatred (or for that matter, any conflicting emotions) are directed toward the rival himself, insofar as he causes both pleasure and pain. I think it would be better to concentrate on Spinoza's fundamental emotions of pleasure and pain (joy and sorrow, or positive and negative feeling; perhaps the most natural terms in common speech would be "happiness" and "unhappiness"), taken as directed toward some *facts involving* a rival. We should also restrict our attention to cases where we have some special reason (other than simple resemblance to ourselves) for identifying with a particular rival. For even if Spinoza is wrong about the extent of our identification with others, there clearly are some people (our close friends and relatives, for instance) whose happiness we sometimes participate in, because of love, perhaps, as he suggests in Proposition XXI (p. 145). Using this insight, then, but ignoring the details of Spinoza's system, I think we can construct a case of ambivalence which *is* intuitively compelling.

Instead of treating pleasure and pain as episodes of feeling, let us take the more modern view (not all that foreign to Spinoza himself), and consider those emotions as propositional pro and con attitudes—"being pleased" or (less naturally) "pained" (in common speech, being happy or unhappy) that something is the case; that a rival has won for himself the prize one was competing with him for.[9] Our initial question then becomes: could two statements ascribing contrary emotions with the same (propositional) object:

I am happy that he won (feel good about his winning).
I am unhappy that he won (feel bad about his winning).

both be true of me? I think they could, in a case where I am the rival of a close friend whose feelings I tend to share. Suppose that a friend and I are in competition for some honorific position; we both want to become chairman of the same department, for instance (to take a somewhat implausible example). What emotions might I feel, not toward my rival himself, but toward the fact that he turns out to win, when I hear it over the telephone, say? I think we might plausibly hold, in some conceivable cases, that I have mixed feelings. I feel both pleased (at least to some extent) and pained—happy "for" him (as we say)—since I know that he deserves the honor and has been hoping for it, but unhappy on my own account, since my own desire has been frustrated.

Perhaps in many such cases my unhappiness would vastly outweigh my happiness; and of course there may be cases where I would not really be happy for my rival, even if I said I was; where I would not really identify with him strongly enough for my negative feelings at losing out to be accompanied by any positive emotion, however weak. On the other hand, in many cases my ambivalence might extend beyond emotions directed toward my rival's victory to those directed toward my rival himself. But these possibilities do not affect my point here. I just want to make the rather weak claim that the two statements above might *sometimes* both be true of me to *some* extent—whatever else may be true as well—on the assumption that I am reacting reasonably. This claim results from what I take to be Spinoza's main insight on the subject of ambivalence— his view that we often "imitate" others' emotions, as applied to my case of friendly rivalry—and I think it provides us with a fairly ordinary and unproblematical example of ambivalence, one defensible without appeal to irrational forces like "the Unconscious," as in psychoanalytic theory.

Some further insights of Spinoza's should help us defend the example against various possible objections: attempts to deny that it represents a genuine case of ambivalence. For instance, someone might maintain that I could not really have contrary feelings toward my rival's victory at one and the same time; instead, I would waver between them, feeling happy at some times, unhappy at others. Spinoza would grant, I think, that this describes any pleasure and pain I actually experience—my emotions taken as episodes of feeling—since he uses the word *vacillation* for cases of ambivalence. Yet he clearly states that in such cases one has contrary emotions "at the same time" (p. 142). The point of his remarks should be evident: we may be said to have or exhibit a particular emotion (and indeed, I might add, to exhibit it consciously) over a span of time which includes, but is not limited to, the times (supposing there are some) when we are actually experiencing it. Thus, if I waver, over time, between happy and unhappy feelings about my rival's victory (I momentarily feel bad when I first hear the news on the phone, say; but then I immediately consider my friend's good fortune and momentarily feel good), we would reasonably conclude that I have "mixed feelings" throughout the overall time span involved, and not that I am continually changing my mind.[10]

But are my feelings really contrary emotions with precisely the same object? Someone might maintain that what I really feel bad about is not my rival's victory but my own loss. In the case as envisioned, however, my rival's victory entails my loss; so it would be natural enough for me to feel bad about both, even if I might sometimes manage to keep them rigidly distinct. Again, I am not claiming that ambivalence in such situations is inevitable, but only that it *can* occur in a basically rational person—a person whose reasoning comes up to the normal standards, even if it falls short of some ideal of perfect rationality. Someone might maintain, though, that the "contrary" emotions we attribute to that person do not really conflict in themselves, but simply happen to give rise to conflicting tendencies—to act, for example, or to feel. However, I think that, by grounding various pairs of emotions in the fundamental distinction between pleasure and pain, or positive and negative feeling, Spinoza in effect (whatever his intentions) stresses the genuinely contrary basis of many emotions. Emotions, or those amounting to pro and con attitudes, seem to involve taking "positions," of sorts, on their objects, and thus may be said to be capable of logical conflict.

Philosophers may try to dismiss their logical conflict by fiddling with the object of contrary emotions, building into it the reasons for a positive or negative reaction, so that contrary emotions may be taken as directed toward *different* objects. This is a legitimate move for certain purposes; but I think we should not let it keep us, here, from retaining our common sense description of cases of ambivalence. By varying my case of mixed feelings a bit, I think I can show that the reasons for an emotion certainly *need* not be taken as defining its object. Suppose that in fact I do not realize, at first, that my rival's victory frustrates any of my own desires; I have always fancied that I had no political ambitions, say, so I am initially quite surprised to find that I feel bad about the news I hear on the phone. Only after a moment of reflection am I able to discover the reasons for my emotion. Yet surely I might know what its object is—what I am unhappy *about*—before I discover its reasons; and it seems wrong just to insist that its object (in every sense of "object") must *change* as I come to understand my reaction to it. Nor need my increase in understanding in any way resolve the conflict between my positive and my negative feelings. (In fact, since both of them might seem appropriate to me upon reflection—I might accept my political ambitions once I become aware of them —I need not even try to resolve the conflict.) Intuitively, then, I think we can take my happiness and my unhappiness as contrary attitudes toward the same object, which conflict with each other quite apart from any tendencies they "happen" to give rise to. I shall try to explain how they could both be appropriate (and what it might mean to call them "contrary") in my third section; but first I want to go on to show how a basically rational person would handle contrary judgments. I shall argue that emotions differ from judgments in that they resist qualification and summing, moves we can normally make to resolve a conflict among judgments. On some interpretations, Spinoza himself seems to identify emotions, or those based on pleasure and pain, with certain sorts of judgments.[11] My ensuing argument will question this general view—though I shall now avoid any reference to Spinoza and consider the issue in its own right.

II

Should emotions be identified with judgments? I can think of two main sorts of judgments to which they might be said to correspond:

evaluations of the situations in which they arise; and their *grounds,* or the descriptions of those situations on which such evaluations would be based.[12] In the case where I have mixed feelings about my rival's victory, the grounds of both my positive and my negative feelings might seem to be the same: the judgment that my rival has won. So initially, at least, the first alternative looks more plausible. I shall return to the second alternative in my next section; but for the moment, let us consider some extremely simple evaluations as candidates for my contrary emotions in the case that concerns us:

> His winning is good.
> His winning is bad.

These, of course, are naturally interpreted as genuine (logical) contraries, judgments that conflict in themselves—apart from any tendencies they might or might not give rise to—since they cannot both be true at the same time. But would a basically rational person who does interpret them as contraries be likely to *hold* both of them at the same time? I shall argue that, even if his contrary emotions persist, he would sooner or later manage to resolve any such conflict among judgments, thus casting doubt on the identification of emotions with judgments.

Let us return, then, to the case where I waver in reaction to the news of my rival's victory, when I first hear it over the phone. Do I then believe both of the contrary judgments given above? Could two statements ascribing them to me as pro and con attitudes toward the same (propositional) object:

> I think it is good that he won (judge his winning good).
> I think it is bad that he won (judge his winning bad).

both be true at the same time?[13] Certainly they *need* not be true to support my mixed feelings; I might already have made up my mind (as I pondered my chances beforehand) that my rival's victory would be on the whole good, or on the whole bad, and yet feel both happy and unhappy about it when the news arrives. On the other hand, I might initially waver between the two contrary judgments, just as I waver between positive and negative feelings in reaction to them. In that case, however, I think we would reasonably conclude that I would not immediately make up my mind—that I *withheld* full assent for a moment or two, instead of according it to both judgments at once. Either of these possibilities cuts against the identification of emotions with judgments, or judgments of the sort now under consideration. But even if we ignore them, and grant that I might start out confused enough to accept two contrary judgments, my confusion would have to end rather quickly—or at any rate, more quickly than my ambivalence must—if I am to count as a basically rational person.

How would we normally handle such a conflict between judgments? First, I think, we would *qualify* both judgments, by building into them a description of the reasons for them. The resulting judgments, for instance:

> His winning is good in that it satisfies a desire of someone I identify with.
> His winning is bad in that it frustrates a desire of my own.

would no longer be genuine contraries, though they still might give rise to contrary emotions. I might continue to waver between happy and unhappy feelings about my rival's victory—though probably at longer intervals (experiencing *no* particular feelings much of the time)—once sufficient time has passed for me to resolve any conflict among judgments. Further, my contrary emotions need not "blend" into a single intermediate emotion, even after enough time has passed for me to *sum* their corresponding judgments: add them together, as a second step in their reconciliation, to form a single "all things considered" judgment, either:

> His winning is on the whole good.

or:

> His winning is on the whole bad.

Even if my feelings of unhappiness (say) are clearly much stronger than my feelings of happiness at my rival's victory, I still may continue to experience both, instead of opting entirely for those that are "overriding."

There may be some cases, of course, in which I am unable to make up my mind—to decide which of two contrary judgments is overriding, or even how they might be qualified. But then, supposing that I *am* convinced that they are genuine contraries, and hence that they could not be simultaneously true, I would treat the two judgments as merely *prima facie,* instead of giving my full assent to both—assuming, once again, that I am a basically rational person.

Belief in both judgments, even if not impossible, would seem to be unreasonable—to involve some sort of abnormal breakdown in reasoning—in a way that ambivalence does not. Even if it falls short of perfect rationality (the question I shall consider in my last section), ambivalence is at any rate *less* irrational than full assent to judgments one knows to be contrary. We cannot simply decide to treat emotions, like judgments, as merely *prima facie;* so "all-out" emotions may only correspond to *prima facie* judgments, since they resist the sort of qualification and summing that lets us reconcile contrary evaluations.

There are often limits, first of all, to the distinctions we can capture in feeling. A distinction, for instance, between unqualified happiness at my rival's victory and (say) happiness-for-him—an attitude that would not conflict with the unhappiness I feel on my own account—will not help us here; for reasons cannot just be "built into" emotions, in the way that they can be built into judgments. That is, even if I do feel happy for my rival, or happy about his winning *in that* it satisfies a desire of someone I identify with, I would normally still feel happy about his winning—*simpliciter*—so that my emotion cannot be said to be truly qualified. Hence emotions should not be identified with qualified evaluative judgments. (I say "should not," rather than "could not," here and elsewhere, because any such attempt at reduction *could* manage to swallow some counterintuitive consequences, in the interests of simplicity, say. I just mean to argue that this attempt does have counterintuitive consequences, in relation to cases of "basically" rational ambivalence.) Consider how qualification would *change* my initial contrary judgments, for instance: insofar as they both involve taking positions on some object, qualification weakens them, and thereby keeps them from conflicting with each other. But as I illustrated above, in dealing with questions about the object of my contrary emotions, my emotions may very well remain stable as I alter my conception of the reasons for them. It is perfectly conceivable that my unhappiness at my rival's victory should be completely unaffected—in object, quality, strength, and what have you—by the process of discovering the reasons for it and qualifying its corresponding judgment. If so, moreover, it certainly might still conflict with the happiness I feel because I identify with my rival as well as competing with him.

In general, then, it seems that a change in judgment, like the change it undergoes in being qualified, need not give rise to any change in the corresponding emotion; so intuitively, at least, emotions and judgments seem to be individuated somewhat differently.[14] Further, emotions need not change (except insofar as they naturally fade over time) at the second stage in our reconciliation of contrary judgments, as our qualified evaluations are combined to form a single "all things considered" judgment. Nor does there seem to be anything unreasonable about our failure to change them. For one thing, an emotion seems to be appropriate relative to a particular set of grounds, and not necessarily a unified evaluation of one's total body of "evidence." It is enough that it be justified by *some* (adequate) reasons, even if the overall *weight* of one's reasons favors a contrary emotion instead. Thus, emotions may persist, even when they are accompanied by stronger opposing feelings, in a basically rational person. In my next section, after considering another possible way of identifying emotions with judgments, I shall expand on this brief observation concerning the "logic" of the emotions. I shall conclude that it would be better to stick to our offhand (and much looser) characterization of emotions as *attitudes*—attitudes that generally correspond to judgments, but which seem to exhibit a logic of their own.

III

Instead of identifying emotions with evaluative judgments, someone might argue that they ought to be identified with judgments giving the grounds for a particular evaluation, what we would normally think of as the reasons for exhibiting the emotion in question, the facts that seem to make it appropriate. In the case where I have mixed feelings about my rival's victory, the reasons for my happiness and my unhappiness might seem to be identical with their common propositional object:

He won.

However, the discussion of qualified evaluations in my last section suggests a way of filling out this judgment to distinguish between my two emotions, at least where I am aware of the reasons for them. We can build the reasons into the judgment, and thus replace it with two:

He won, thereby satisfying a desire of someone I identify with.
He won, thereby frustrating a desire of my own.

Still, like the qualified evaluations in my last section, these judgments are not logical contraries—both, in fact, are true—though of
course they would be likely to give rise to contrary feelings. They
also fail to capture the positive or negative "point" of the emotions
—or at any rate, of the emotions I mean to be considering—since
belief in judgments like the two just above need not involve any pro
or con attitudes. Of course we could manage to interpret such belief
as involving *different* attitudes toward a common object. For
instance, in holding the second judgment, I might be made out as
applying a complex predicate to my rival—as judging that-he-won-
thereby-frustrating-a-desire-of-my-own—but this would not itself
amount to a con attitude. Rather, it would seem to give the reason
for one, for my negative reaction to the news I hear on the phone,
and if we want to preserve the force of this claim, we need to preserve some distinction between my emotional and judgmental
attitudes.

We can preserve the distinction by returning to the evaluative
judgments I discussed in my last section, by considering emotions
as analogous to them, but not identical. Thus we can speak of emotions as sometimes conflicting with judgments, in those all-too-
familiar cases of "head/heart" conflict, and as conflicting in a logical sense with one another. Since judgments like the two just above
do not conflict logically, it seems that any explanation of the possibility of ambivalence must refer beyond them. How is it that my
happiness and my unhappiness at my rival's victory can somehow
conflict in themselves, apart from any associated behavioral conflicts? So far, I have simply taken for granted our intuitive view
that these emotions *are* in some sense logical contraries; but now I
want to suggest a way of interpreting it. I suspect that the notion of
contrariety must be understood somewhat differently for emotions
than for judgments (relative, as I have suggested, to a particular
limited set of grounds), so that emotions can be identified with
judgments only at the cost of obscuring a logical distinction.

What I have in mind is this: contrary judgments are defined as
judgments that cannot both be true; but my case of friendly rivalry
makes it clear that we could not accept an analogous definition of
contrary emotions. Like judgments, emotions may or may not "fit

the facts," and above I have spoken of those that do as "appropriate." But appropriateness is not quite analogous to truth. For one
thing, it depends on the adequacy of certain reasons for an emotion, the facts that make it suited to its object (assumed to exist), as
in the two statements given just above.[15] For judgments, on the
other hand, questions of truth and justification are often distinct. I
shall let myself blur over the distinction, though, in the argument
that follows, since I take it that contrary judgments cannot both be
fully justified, any more than they can both be true. If we grant,
then, that appropriateness is the value for emotions which comes
closest to truth for judgments, we might expect contrary emotions
to be emotions that cannot both be appropriate. But we have seen
above that, in at least one case, contrary emotions might both be
appropriate for different reasons. Where I am in competition with
a close friend, happiness at his winning might be adequately justified by my identification with him, and unhappiness by my concern
for my own interests, even though each of these reasons would
seem to count as reason *against* exhibiting the contrary emotion.
Ambivalence is possible, then, in a basically rational person. But
how can we explain its possibility?

For emotions, I would suggest, support by some (adequate) reasons is enough for appropriateness; so contrary emotions might
both be appropriate and, hence, I take it, "basically" rational,
even if emotions are not under rational control to the extent that
judgments are. (I assume that, except in extreme cases, they are
under *some* control: we can usually avoid exhibiting emotions we
take to be *in*appropriate.) But even if they are both appropriate,
could contrary emotions be appropriate for exactly the same reasons? I think not—in which case contrary emotions might be
defined instead as emotions it would be inappropriate to exhibit *for
the same reasons*. The reason for an emotion is necessarily a reason
against its contrary, in short; and thus two contrary emotions may
be said to be contrary in a logical sense—to conflict "in themselves," as I have put it above. But however contrariety is defined
for emotions, we seem to treat them differently from judgments
when we evaluate them against their background of reasons pro
and con. The judgments of a person whose reasoning comes up to
the normal standards are justified in relation to the total background; but his emotions, even when they are appropriate, may

sometimes rest on particular limited portions of the background, if my treatment of the case of friendly rivalry is correct.

Thus, instead of identifying emotions with judgments, I think we should take both of them as attitudes of different sorts, and try to distinguish between them initially by describing differences in their logic—in how we "reason" with them, insofar as our reasoning comes up to the normal standards. I have sketched one such difference here, but I am sure there are many others (and a deeper explanation of the one I have sketched). Perhaps by describing them we can best explain the concept of an emotion (answer the philosopher's general question, "What is an emotion?") since the attempt to force emotions into some presumably clearer category (whether cognitive or noncognitive, mental or physical, physiological or behavioral) seems to have failed consistently.[16] The claim that emotions are attitudes is uninformative enough to be widely acceptable as a starting point; so perhaps we can make some progress toward understanding the emotions if we limit ourselves to asking what sorts of attitudes they are, how their logic differs, for instance, from that of judgments.

I have suggested that we treat emotions differently when we evaluate them against their background of reasons. Briefly: an emotion is appropriate as long as there are adequate reasons *for* it, whatever the reasons against it. My suggestion is meant to help explain how ambivalence is possible in what I have loosely termed a "basically" rational person. But does it also indicate that cases of ambivalence —and indeed, the emotions generally—involve a kind of *ir*rationality, in contrast to judgments, even though they do come up to the standards we think of as normal? Presumably, the normal standards are designed to fit beings who are subject to emotions—and subject to whatever irrationality emotions bring with them—so there may be a sense in which emotions are intrinsically irrational. Though we have *some* rational control over them, our control is limited; they are based on reactions to particular facts, as they come into consciousness, rather than consideration of all the relevant reasons. (Here, I think, is where a deeper explanation of basically rational ambivalence would lie.) However, I think we should be wary of applying to emotions the cognitive criteria for rationality in judgments, as we can see by trying to illustrate this argument with my case of friendly rivalry. Certainly—someone might maintain—

it would be *more* rational for me to reconcile my conflicting emotions as time passes. A perfectly rational person would come to take a detached view, and suppress any emotions that were not supported by the overall weight of his reasons. This argument may sound plausible; but I think that a closer look at my example will make us reject it. Emotions do involve irrationality in any number of ways, but even a case of conflicting emotions might be defended as perfectly rational in light of the special relationship between emotions and behavior.

IV

My preceding argument was structured as an answer to the question whether emotions should be identified with judgments; and its upshot was a rough account of how contrary emotions might both be appropriate—what notions of contrariety and appropriateness would make sense of that possibility. Starting with an intuitive treatment of my case of friendly rivalry, I tried to explain the possibility in terms of the way emotions are justified by reasons in a basically rational person. A stronger claim, about some higher rational ideal, was not needed to distinguish emotions from judgments, since holding two judgments one knows to be contrary would seem to be downright unreasonable, besides falling short of "perfect" rationality. Now, though, I want to consider whether the stronger claim can be made as well. The conclusions of my preceding argument should not be affected by this one; but this one should let us see just *how* rational my case of mixed feelings really is, assuming that its rationality is not determined by cognitive criteria. I shall argue that it would sometimes be a mistake to treat emotions like judgments, and reconcile them in cases of conflict, even if one could. On a standard of rationality that evaluates emotions according to their behavioral consequences—which takes into account, for instance, the social value of identification with others —ambivalence might sometimes be *more* rational than forming an "all things considered" emotion that resolves the conflict.[17]

I shall illustrate this point in a moment; but let me begin by explaining two qualifications. First of all, even if it is wrong to treat emotions like judgments generally, there may still be enough similarity between the two to allow for their comparison on cognitive criteria, in relation to a total body of evidence. I have admitted as much above, in effect, by characterizing them both as attitudes directed toward an object, with appropriateness taken as the value of emotions which comes closest to truth for judgments. For example, I have assumed that my happiness at my rival's victory is appropriate as long as he has indeed won and I have adequate reason for sharing his happiness at winning; under these conditions, my emotion can be thought of as fitting the facts, like a true judgment. But "adequate reason" for an emotion need not be sufficient to ground a corresponding judgment—it might not count as "evidence" at all. It is clear enough, for example, that my identification with a friend would not give me adequate (cognitive) reason for adopting his beliefs. I shall not deny, then, that the emotions in my case of mixed feelings are in some sense less rational than judgments; but I shall defend them as perfectly rational relative to the *non*cognitive functions of emotion, with emotions considered particularly as *motivating* attitudes, attitudes with special motivational force.

Second, though my defense of this view must rest on some sort of reference to behavior, I shall continue to ignore the conflicts in behavior that conflicting emotions may or may not give rise to. I shall assume that, though emotions may sometimes motivate (exert a kind of pressure toward) irrational behavior, they need not always disrupt deliberation, even if they conflict. Except in extreme cases, we seem to have some control over how we act on them—*more* control than we have over whether we exhibit them or not. For instance, if I waver between positive and negative reactions to my rival's victory, I might be led in extreme cases—where my emotions are especially strong, say—to alternate between friendliness and hostility in his presence. My behavior toward him might very well be inconsistent and self-defeating, and hence irrational. But this is not a necessary consequence of my conflicting feelings; I would ordinarily be able to control their effects on my behavior without actually resolving my emotional conflict. My question is: supposing that I am under pressure to act on my conflicting emotions in *some* way or other (if only to control their effects), *must* my behavior be any less rational than it would be if I resolved the conflict? Let us approach this question by considering a case where I do resolve the conflict, in the way that we commonly reconcile contrary judgments. I think we shall see that I might lose something important in the process.

Suppose, then, that I do manage to sum my conflicting emotions. We have been assuming that my unhappiness is stronger than my happiness, so perhaps the most likely result would be a somewhat tempered negative reaction to my rival's victory.[18] But then I would no longer participate in his emotion, and share his point of view, though sympathy would have had some effect on what I do feel. From the standpoint of self-interest, then, his feelings might be overridden; and from an impersonal standpoint, on the other hand, they might simply counterbalance my own. A neutral reaction to my rival's victory would also fail to express my identification with his interests—I simply would not care who happened to win—though this solution might well be recommended by some philosophers. The philosopher's ideal of "perfect" rationality is often an ideal of *detachment* from particular points of view. But with emotions taken as motivating attitudes, whose behavioral effects are ordinarily open to control, I think it is clear that conflict between emotional extremes may sometimes serve a purpose that would not be served by moderation. Commitment to different points of view, in short, can motivate behavior unlikely to arise from emotional detachment.

In my case of mixed feelings, for example, how might I exercise rational control over my behavior, in light of my emotional conflict? I think I could best handle the conflict by focusing on my happy feelings in my rival's presence. Assuming that I want to preserve our friendship, I should offer him sincere congratulations, take part enthusiastically in any victory celebrations, avoid dwelling on my own disappointment, and so on. Of course, I could conceivably manage to do all this even if I did not really take an interest in his happiness; but then I would merely be going through the motions, probably unconvincingly: we can often *perceive* the difference between detached and emotional behavior. Genuine emotional identification with others, then, motivates spontaneous sympathetic behavior, behavior that expresses our concern for others' interests for their own sake. I think it should be obvious that such behavior facilitates social relations, and thus promotes an important human end, in a way that detached behavior, or behavior arising from tempered self-interest, would not be likely to. Indeed, even if my conflicting emotions blended to form a positive reaction to my rival's victory, my happiness for him would presumably be weaker than it would be if I failed to resolve the conflict. By allowing the conflict, but controlling its behavioral effects, I can express my strong commitment to someone else's interests without losing sight of my own.[19]

Some philosophers would argue, of course, that judgments, particularly evaluative judgments, also have motivational force. But without taking a position on that issue, I think we can see that the emotions we are discussing motivate behavior in at least one *special* way. Being pleased about something amounts to a pleasurable state, which an agent would naturally act to promote in himself. Positive feeling can itself be positively reinforcing; that is, happiness motivates behavior partly by *rewarding* it, so it is in some ways a more reliable motive than the judgment that something is good, particularly when the judgment is weakened by qualifications.[20] It provides an agent with a further reason for action because it actually increases the desirability (for him) of one of the options he chooses among. Emotions are typically more variable than judgments; but assuming that happiness at others' good fortune is indicative of a long-range tendency, behavior expressing it would tend to be reassuring to others. It would encourage them to think that they could depend on the agent to consider their interests in the future. For even if judgments have *some* motivational force, emotions usually seem to have more; and it usually seems to be easier to change one's mind, and drop a judgment, than it is to alter a pattern of emotional reaction. Thus, emotional identification with others, as opposed to merely including them in one's detached calculations, can lend a special kind of support to social communication. Providing that the agent has control over the behavior it motivates, its behavioral consequences may make it perfectly rational—ideally suited to promoting human ends—even where it involves emotional conflict.

This is just one fairly simple and obvious example of how the emotions can be useful to us, in view of their motivational force. They are "adaptive," let us say for short; for with proper control, they can help us adapt to our social (and material) environment. Since social adaptation serves some chief ends of morality, moreover, we can begin to appreciate the obvious *moral* significance of the emotions, even supposing that emotions and moral *judgments* are quite distinct. Indeed, the emotions very likely have moral significance beyond what I need to argue for here in defense of their rationality. Without any reference to the informational role I am assigning to them, we might want to say that they function morally just in so far as they actually let us perceive the world from other people's different points of view, by "mirroring" them in our own, as it were, instead of merely viewing them all from some neutral standpoint. Does moral motivation depend, in fact, on our commitment to "points of view," as opposed to detachment? Would I support my friend's chairmanship with equal enthusiasm, for instance, if all I could do were to observe his happy feelings from a distance? A kind of Humean moral stress on the emotions, but without any version of the "emotivist" account of morality, may seem to emerge from questions like these about their special motivational force. But we need not try to settle such questions here. The argument from social communication suffices to establish *one rational* purpose for the emotions, whatever their further rational or moral purposes. Even in promoting our selfish ends in society, that is, we seem to rely on emotional behavior for the information it provides about the future.

Someone might maintain, though, that a perfectly rational *person* would not *need* the emotions to reassure others about his future behavior. He could be relied on to act in strict accordance with detached calculations of the good, since (unlike a "basically" rational person) he would never be subject to weakness of will. But I think that this argument holds only for someone assumed to be living among others who are also unusually rational, so that they can be depended on to take his qualified judgments as strongly motivating. Even so, of course, they might take emotional behavior as a particularly useful sign of someone's tendency to act in their interests, since emotions are typically harder to fake than judgments. As I have suggested, emotions exert a kind of pressure on us to act, at least partly, by affecting the very options we choose among. But at any rate, though judgments may have motivational force as well, I would insist that any *realistic* ideal of perfect rationality must take account of the stronger link, as people are in fact constituted, between emotions and behavior. Instead of detachment, it should stress control over the behavioral consequences of emotion; for with such control, emotions play an important role in motivating rational behavior.[21] On any remotely realistic ideal, then, suppressing an emotion may sometimes be *less* rational than controlling its behavioral consequences.

Since this point seems to apply even to a case of conflicting emotions, like my case of friendly rivalry, I think we may conclude that the "logic" of emotion permits ambivalence. In general, there seem to be two phases of our reasoning with an emotion: to it from its object and from it to behavior. We are far from understanding the logic of the two phases, in particular, the special motivational force of emotions needs further explanation, and I have suggested that we need to understand it if we are to make any progress toward explaining the general concept of an emotion. For the moment, however, I think we may conclude that, where both phases are under proper rational control, even conflicting emotions may be perfectly rational in at least one important sense, given the fact that the agent and the others he interacts with are not perfectly rational. Exhibiting the emotions may be the best way of promoting the agent's ends—that is, the emotions may be "adaptive" as well as appropriate—even if (as philosophers often argue) emotions are in some sense intrinsically *ir*rational and impose some *limitations* on rational control. Indeed, the fact that emotions resist control may be part of the reason why they are useful to us, and hence in our sense rational—part of what gives them their motivational force, and thus lets them serve (in my particular example) as a way of binding ourselves to one another.

Someone might maintain, of course, that we would really all be better off with no emotions whatever, and no need for emotions to bind ourselves to each other. Just above, I have dismissed such cognitive ideals of "perfect" rationality as unrealistic; but in fact I think that the problem goes deeper than that. Some unrealistic ideals (utopian visions of society, for example) seem to provide us with a reasonable standard for action, since the attempt to live up to them presumably is likely to have good consequences, even though it can never quite succeed. But on the whole, I strongly suspect that approaching an ideal of complete detachment, in a world where we depend on the emotions for their special motivational force, would be likely to have rather *bad* consequences. Detachment is surely sometimes in order, in those extreme cases (for instance) where our emotions would otherwise be too strong to allow for control of their behavioral consequences. But where an emotion is both appropriate and adaptive, it may be clearly wrong to urge "philosophic detachment" from it.

NOTES

*I am indebted to my colleague Arthur Flemming for his extremely helpful comments on the earlier versions of this paper, including one I presented at a University of Chicago philosophy colloquium in November 1977.

1. This view is attributed to the Stoics, for instance. For a detailed historical survey of accounts of the emotions, see H. J. Gardiner et al, *Feeling and Emotion: A History of Theories* (Westport, Conn.: Greenwood, 1970).

2. See Robert C. Solomon, "The Logic of Emotion," *Nous*, XI, 1 (March 1977), 41-49; also, *The Passions* (Garden City, N.Y.: Anchor, 1976). Solomon does not seem to use "logic" in any very precise (or familiar) sense; but I shall not be much concerned here with the fine points of his argument, which I find both illuminating and obscure. A similar view emerges, though, in Donald Davidson, "Hume's Cognitive Theory of Pride," *Journal of Philosophy*, LXXIII, 19 (November 4, 1976), 744-757, see, e.g., p. 751.

3. For an examination of some irrational features of the emotions, see Amélie Rorty, "Explaining Emotions," *Journal of Philosophy*, LXXV, 3 (March 1978), 139-161, also published in this volume. Also, see Frithjof Bergmann, Review of *The Passions* by Robert C. Solomon, *Journal of Philosophy*, LXXV, 4 (April 1978), 200-208, for a refutation of Solomon from another point of view, which I heard at the meetings of the American Philosophical Association, Western Division, in April 1977. On some points, my argument will overlap with these, as well as some others (especially Solomon's; and also, of course, the classic treatments of the subject in Descartes and Hume). The differences are also important, however, and numerous and complicated, so for simplicity's sake I shall present my argument without much reference to other authors.

4. See, e.g., Solomon, *The Passions*, pp. 166, 283, 406. But see also Bernard Williams, "Ethical Consistency," in *Problems of the Self* (Cambridge: University Press, 1973), for a related treatment of the problem of conflicting desires.

5. I shall give page-references to the *Ethics*, using the translation by R. H. M. Elwes; see Benedict de Spinoza, *On the Improvement of the Understanding: The Ethics; Correspondence* (New York: Dover, 1955). For a classical *rejection* of the possibility of ambivalence, see David Hume, *A Treatise of Human Nature* (Oxford: Clarendon, 1964), p. 278. (But cf. Réné Descartes, "The Passions of the Soul," in *The Philosophical Works of Descartes*, ed. E. S. Haldane and G. R. T. Ross (Cambridge: University Press, 1970), p. 408. Descartes' example—and his account of ambivalence in terms of different reasons—comes close to common sense; but Spinoza's general treatment of the subject contains an important insight, as we shall see.)

6. I shall adopt Spinoza's terminology; but I do not mean to suggest, of course, that the transference of emotions he picks out as "imitation" is meant to rest on any sort of conscious mimicry of others' reactions. I think it must involve *direct* trans-

ference, though, in some sense actually coming to *share* another person's happiness, e.g., instead of merely being made happy oneself by reflection on the fact that he is. With this restriction, however, I shall ignore distinctions that other authors might insist upon, and use interchangeably a range of expressions that in ordinary language do seem to fit the rough phenomenon Spinoza seems to have in mind. Thus, I shall speak of "identifying" with others, "participating" in their emotions, acquiring "sympathetic" emotions, and so forth, without taking myself to depart in any significant way from Spinoza's general notion of imitation, though I *will* sson abandon his account of it in terms of resemblance.

7. Spinoza uses ambivalence in his account of jealousy (or our mixed feelings toward a person whose affections we have a rival *for*); cf. Prop. XXXV with its accompanying Note (pp. 153-154). But it does not seem to come into his account of envy (or our feelings toward the rival himself); cf. Prop. XXIV with its accompanying Note (pp. 146-147). For Spinoza's further examples of ambivalence, see Prop. XXXI (p. 151), Corollary I to Prop. XL (p. 157), the Corollary to Prop. XLI (p. 158), and Prop. XLVII with its accompanying Note (pp. 160-161).

8. Spinoza's ideal applies only to those emotions he picks out as "passive"—cf., e.g., Prop. LVIII (p. 171) and the Note to Prop. LIX (pp. 171-173)—but these seem to cover all the emotions we recognize as such in common life. For some further comments on Spinoza's ideal of freedom (particularly in relation to knowledge), see, e.g., the Note to Prop. LXVI in Part IV (p. 232) and the Note to Prop. IV in Part V (pp. 248-249).

9. I am not assuming that *all* emotions are plausibly made out as "propositional pro and con attitudes," but just that these are. Instead, I shall later characterize emotions in general simply as attitudes, of a sort that we can compare with at least some judgments.

First of all, many emotions, e.g., love and hatred, clearly have persons, rather than propositions, as their objects (and it should become obvious, later on, that the same is also true of many judgments, as I am parsing them; see n. 13). It may still be true that emotions are all in some sense *based on* propositional attitudes; perhaps love and hatred, e.g., could be reconstructed out of hypotheticals about what a rational person *would* feel about various possible facts involving the persons they are directed toward. Some such proposal would let us set up a kind of "logic of appropriateness" for the emotions (cf. n. 14); and it may provide us with a way of making some modern sense of the seventeenth-century attempt to build all emotions out of "primaries."

Second, I am not even sure (though I think it not unlikely) that all emotions can be interpreted as pro and con attitudes, as having some positive or negative "point," as I put it below. Spinoza, e.g., accepts desire as a third primary, besides pleasure and pain; see, e.g., the Note to prop. XI (p. 138) and his summary of his views under "Definitions of the Emotions" (pp. 173-174). But it is questionable whether desire really amounts to an emotion; and in any case, perhaps it *could* be made out as a pro attitude, with aversion as the corresponding con attitude. However, I shall leave such questions open here. Many emotions can be taken as pro and con attitudes, surely; and my argument below will make use of this view.

10. This suggests at least one rough point of analogy between emotions and judgments, but with important limitations. Judgments, too, may be held over time spans including, but not limited to, the times when they are actually *asserted* (whether in speech or just mentally). So perhaps assertion, as a cognitive episode, plays a role for judgments, which is something like the role I have assigned to emotional *experience,* or episodes of feeling. Taken as attitudes, as I take them here, emotions and judgments both may be said to be based on (at least the possibility of) certain mental

occurrences; but clearly we can hold a judgment, or exhibit an emotion, without at the same time—or ever—expressing it in conscious thought or feeling.

On the other hand, I shall expand below on some of the crucial differences between judgment and emotion. For instance, not every expression of a judgment in thought—not every "mental utterance" of it—need actually count as an assertion. There are various possible degrees of assent to a judgment: one can merely "entertain" it, to examine its implications, say; or one can assent to it tentatively, pending further evidence, taking the judgment as merely *prima facie*. Perhaps we can sometimes "toy" with an emotion, try it out, as it were, to see how it fits the situation, and perhaps emotions can sometimes be exhibited without full conviction. But in any case, it is clear that we only have limited control over our ability to take such intermediate emotional positions, and, in general, to "change our mind" about an emotion, so the decision to withhold full assent from a judgment often may have no effect at all on the emotion we take to correspond to it.

Moreover, there seems to be an important analogy (again with important limitations) between contrariety in judgments and emotions. Its details will emerge as my main argument proceeds; but in general, I think we must take contrary emotions, like contrary judgments, as expressing conflicting "points" or "positions," and not just as amounting to conflicting properties or states. It is clearly possible for someone to exhibit two contrary emotions, just as he might hold both of two contrary judgments. But—someone might object—is it possible to *experience* conflicting emotions at one and the same time? I am not sure how this question should be answered; but in any case, I do not think it really threatens the limited analogy I wish to set up between emotions and judgments.

Is it possible actually to *assert* two contrary *judgments* at one and the same time? I have my doubts, but perhaps this point is undercut somewhat by the intermediate degrees of assent to a judgment which I sketched just above. Is it possible, instead, to give some sort of simultaneous mental utterance to two *prima facie* judgments? I still have my doubts, in fact, because of some general questions, also applicable to emotions, about the restrictions on occurrent thought. Perhaps it *is* impossible to experience simultaneous conflicting feelings (though we do speak of "mingled" pleasure and pain, say). But this point (supposing it holds) would not seem to apply particularly to *contrary* feelings. I think it may be impossible to experience any two very *different* feelings, whether or not they are contraries, at one and the same time. Can we actually be said to experience hope and hatred simultaneously, for example? My doubts are even stronger about occurrent feelings which are directed (and often appropriately directed) toward the same object, e.g., love and anger.

In general: how many mental occurrences can take place in the same mind at exactly the same time? Doubtless certain combinations are possible; but those that are ruled out would clearly include many that could not be plausibly taken as contraries, at least in the sense of "contrary" that seems to be relevant here. Later on in my main argument (after bringing in some of the points I anticipate here), I shall try to pin down the relevant sense of "contrary," for emotions, by analogy with judgments. For the moment, though, I think we may conclude that the relevant sense is *not* explained by reference to possible real-world combinations of emotion or judgment.

11. I owe this point (and much of my treatment of Spinoza) to Arthur Flemming. Spinoza takes pleasure and pain as "confused ideas" (see, e.g., his "General Definition of the Emotions," pp. 185-186); and on some interpretations his "ideas" come out as judgments. His characterization of the judgments that amount to emotions seems to depend very heavily, though, on the peculiarities of his overall system; so I shall limit my attention to some simple modern candidates below.

12. Solomon seems to suggest both alternatives in different places. For the first view, with judgments taken as evaluations, see, e.g., *The Passions,* pp. 149, 187; but he also at least allows for the possibility of the second view, with judgments taken as giving the grounds for evaluations, e.g., in "The Logic of Emotion," p. 47. I shall eventually conclude that the first view *is* more plausible, even though the second may give better support to the claim that emotions and judgments always *correspond* (see n. 14).

13. As my parenthetical insertions are meant to indicate, I am not parsing these statements as they are standardly parsed by authors who make out judgments as propositional attitudes. The attitude in question is standardly taken as simple *belief* (not a pro or con attitude), directed toward *contrary* propositional objects which give the content of the two evaluative judgments, as follows:

I think (it is good that he won).
I think (it is bad that he won).

But on this interpretation, my contrary judgments would not seem to be analogous to the contrary emotions ascribed to me above, with contrary *attitudes* taken as directed toward a *common* propositional object. Instead, to exhibit the analogy, I suggest that we take the attitude involved in judgment as some sort of attitude of predication (in this case, "judging good" or "judging bad") applied to an object (in this case, a propositional object) which amounts to the subject of predication. Thus, I would parse the two statements above as follows:

I think it is good (that he won).
I think it is bad (that he won).

These statements clearly ascribe to me contrary pro and con attitudes directed toward a common propositional object. (For a similar interpretation of *non*evaluative judgments, however, we would need to make some changes. They can be taken as attitudes of predication toward a common object; but the attitudes need not be contrary pro and con attitudes, and the object need not be propositional.)

14. Some further "logical" differences between emotions and judgments emerge from an interesting variant of my example, which I had intended to use in a side-argument designed to strengthen the case against emotions as qualified evaluations. In fact, this example may turn out to be in some ways more revealing than the one I focus on; but it is not a case of basic rationality (or even, necessarily, of ambivalence), so it might just constitute a distraction from the main argument presented in my text. Consequently, I shall restrict it to footnotes, outlining it here, and exploring some of its implications for the attempt to identify emotions with evaluative judgments; and then, in n. 15, showing how it forces us to distinguish appropriateness from truth.

My variant case rests on the possibility of conflicts between emotions and evaluative judgments themselves, of having an emotion one does not consider appropriate. Where emotions, like evaluative judgments, involve taking positions pro and con on some object, it seems that our emotional and judgmental "positions" can sometimes conflict. I might actually believe, for instance, that my rival's victory is good without qualification, though simply out of competitiveness I feel bad about it. What if I feel extremely guilty about my competitiveness—so guilty, in fact, that I consider my emotional reaction completely inappropriate? (I think my guilt-feelings *are* appropriate, say.) For I do not really want the chairmanship at all. My negative feelings at not attaining it stem from a lifelong aversion to losing *anything* that I recognize as completely irrational. It seems at least possible, in this variant case, that I do not hold even the qualified judgment: "His winning is bad in that it frustrates a desire of my own.'' (I think it could only be *good* to frustrate *that* desire, suppose.)

Indeed, this variant case suggests that the argument for identifying emotions with evaluative judgments may be trading on an important confusion. In general, it seems that an emotion will be *appropriate* just as long as some evaluative judgment is *true*. Perhaps this means that the belief that one's emotion is appropriate corresponds to an evaluative judgment; but it does not mean that the emotion itself corresponds to that judgment. Thus I have spoken of emotions and judgments just as corresponding "generally" above, though perhaps a stronger claim can be made for cases of basic rationality, where the agent does take his emotional reactions to be appropriate. This, in fact, may be what really stands behind philosophers' several attempts to identify emotions with judgments—what gives that view its initial appearance of plausibility—for we might say that, insofar as they are *reasonable,* emotions have a kind of cognitive "content" which evaluative judgments express. Where an agent's emotions are "basically rational," that is, they involve an implicit commitment to some claim (perhaps unspecified) that would support them as appropriate (We might think of this implied claim as spelling out the *rational* content of an emotion.) This is a suggestion worth looking into, I think, in exploring the logical interrelations between emotion and judgment. But it rests on the (at least partly) normative notion of "rationality"; so I see no way to get from it to a descriptive thesis identifying emotions with evaluative judgments.

More needs to be said, of course, about the various logical terms I am applying to emotions, here and elsewhere: "appropriate," "rational," "reasonable," and the like. I shall say a bit more about them below, but by no means enough.

15. Reflection on my variant guilt case above (see n. 14) has led me to a stronger argument for distinguishing appropriateness from truth. Holding a judgment involves some kind of commitment to its truth, even apart from the requirements of rationality. To hold it *is* just to think that it is true; and to assert it is to say so. But the guilt case seemed to indicate that we can have or exhibit (or even experience) an emotion without any commitment to its appropriateness. (Perhaps, in fact, it is this disanalogy between emotions and judgments which explains those I outlined, e.g., in n. 10 above; it certainly drives a wedge between assertion of a judgment and emotional experience.) Here it seems that appropriateness comes closer to justification than truth (as I suggest just below); for at least in cases of irrationality, we can hold a judgment without thinking it justified. We can cling to it obstinately, as it were, in the face of strong counterevidence; or just blindly, without even evaluating its evidence at all. (Consider, e.g., some people's belief in God.)

On the other hand, we might not want to equate appropriateness with justification, either. Like truth in judgments, appropriateness does not seem to depend on everything we might want to count as a reason for an emotion, but only on reasons that somehow serve to link it to a real-world object. First of all, there may be extrinsic reasons for an emotion, reasons why it is useful in attaining our ends. (I shall touch on some of these—particularly social reasons—in my last section, under the heading of "adaptiveness.") For instance, in a threatening situation in which others are depending on my calmness, I may have reason to avoid exhibiting fear, to keep myself from having the feeling at all, that is (in accordance with my use of "exhibit" throughout this paper), even though the feeling would be perfectly appropriate. For the situation I face may be so extremely threatening that my fear would be too strong to hide from others, if I felt it. So in this case, we might want to say that an appropriate emotion would not be justified, at least on the grounds that seem to apply to emotions.

But second, if I may complicate this discussion further, there seem to be some important differences between the grounds on which emotions and judgments would be deemed justified. A reason that would justify a judgment, presumably, is reason for thinking the judgment true, not just some noncognitive reason for holding it, e.g., in order to please others or to make oneself feel secure. Suppose, then, that I model my reaction to some situation on my observations of another person, not because I identify with him but just because he is generally sensitive and rational in such matters, a reliable guide to emotional appropriateness. In this case, he is wrong, however; so my reaction might seem to be justified but not appropriate. I have adequate reason for thinking it appropriate, say; but I do not have adequate reason for the emotion. (In fact, my way of arriving at it would in most cases seem ridiculous, though it is analogous to a common and legitimate path to judgments.) I can only conclude that appropriateness falls somewhere in between justification and truth, and that the relations between these notions (for emotions as well as judgments) are confusing. But I can think of no notion that comes closer to truth than appropriateness; so I shall continue to suppose here that it is the basic rational value of the emotions. If there is a better notion, my argument can simply be rephrased in terms of it.

16. For a concise account of several such attempts, ending in a Wittgensteinian "paradigm case" view (and thus, in effect, in a rejection of the general question), see William P. Alston, "Emotion and Feeling," in *The Encyclopedia of Philosophy*, Vol. I, ed. Paul Edwards (New York: Macmillan, 1967). It remains a crucial issue, of course—which the "paradigm case" view does not shed much light on—just how emotion is related to phenomena in those other categories (in what sense emotional attitudes, e.g., are "based on reactions to particular facts, as they come into consciousness"—my brief suggestion below). But I think, by now, it is clear enough that we cannot easily make out emotions as identical to any of those phenomena; and if, as attitudes, they must involve various dispositions to exhibit those phenomena, it also seems clear enough, by now, that it is difficult to make them out as simply identical to those dispositions. (It is also clear that the dispositions must be extremely complex, for both emotions and judgments.)

17. My argument for this final point need not be taken, like that in my central sections, as an argument for distinguishing emotions from judgments. Judgments can also be evaluated on noncognitive criteria at times; and in this case, someone might argue that I would be better off stopping at the first stage of their reconciliation, and resisting the urge to decide between the qualified evaluations above. However, where grounds for forming a single judgment are available to me, I think it must always seem odd, at least, to refuse to take them into account. We seem to recognize some rational "push" toward moving on to the second stage of reconciliation for judgments. Though we may sometimes resist it, and refuse to sum them, I think this requires a stronger justification than the one I go on to sketch for emotions. I would suggest, then, that cognitive criteria are somehow more essential to the proper evaluation of judgments; but my further remarks can be made out as independent of this view.

18. There are various different senses in which we may speak of the "strength" of an emotion (e.g., felt intensity vs. force as a motive); and in any case, there may be other factors (e.g., the importance assigned to it as a reason) which determine whether a particular emotion is "overriding." To avoid some difficult issues, then, I shall not limit my argument to any single imagined outcome of the attempt to sum emotional contraries.

19. Losing sight of my own interests—completely repressing my *un*happiness— might in fact be worse than ignoring someone else's feelings. Arthur Flemming has pointed out the dangers of *servility*, for some agents, in this connection. But even supposing that I have no tendencies toward servility, I may have reason to retain my

emotional point of view. Without some counterbalancing reaction, some private disappointment, e.g., identification with a rival might often have damaging consequences, like bottled-up hostility. Even a healthy self, in short, needs occasional reinforcement.

20. This need not hold for every positive feeling, for every emotion "based on" positive feeling (cf. n. 9), in the sense that it involves taking a pro attitude toward some object. Thus, e.g., love need not always be positively reinforcing; in some circumstances, hatred may actually feel better and be preferred. Indeed, perhaps there are even some circumstances in which the "primary" positive feelings I am discussing here would actually be annoying, on the whole (where we really—perversely—were *hoping* to be disappointed about something, say). But I think they must always be to some extent pleasurable, even if the pleasure can sometimes be outweighed by accompanying "pains," and even if it is wrong (as I think) to *equate* positive and negative feeling ("being pleased" and "being pained") with simple pleasure and pain. (In fact, since it is emotional *attitudes* I mean to be discussing here, it would be wrong to equate them with *any* features of experience.)

In general, I mean to suggest, just above, that part of the special motivational force of an emotion has to do with extralogical facts about the nature of positive and negative feeling, granting the "logical" fact with which my main argument began: that like evaluative judgment, it involves some sort of pro or con attitude toward an object. Judgmental pro attitudes may also be to some extent positively reinforcing; and it is hard to say precisely why emotion is generally more so, or more so, at least, than evaluative judgment alone (which is all I really need to grant here). But this point does seem intuitively clear.

21. This claim should hardly be surprising to a post-Freudian era (e.g., in view of the likely effects of repression, which I bring up only briefly in n. 19). For that matter, something not unlike it seems to lie behind Descartes's various comments, and especially his general approach to examples in "Part Third."

Note that control over the behavioral consequences of emotion may also give us some indirect control over their expression in experience. I may be able to restrict myself to happy feelings in my rival's presence, e.g., simply by getting involved in his victory celebrations and refusing to think about the grounds for my own disappointment. We need a more detailed treatment of the relation of attitudes to experience and behavior, to flesh out my many hints in this last section. (I hope to flesh them out somewhat in a forthcoming book, *Emotions and Reasons.* For some initial comments on the question of motivational force, but without much reference to the emotions, see "Behavior Control and Freedom of Action," *Philosophical Review,* LXXXVII, 2 (April 1978), 225-240, esp. 230-233. A fuller discussion of these topics would have to deal with the possibility of identifying emotions with desires; but I have focused here on the attempt to identify them with judgments. Since this paper was completed, I have benefited from comments by Jerome Neu whose recent book on the emotions charts an opposing view; see *Emotion, Thought, and Therapy* (Berkeley, Los Angeles, London: University of California Press, 1977), esp. pp. 148-149. For some later remarks on the subject, emphasizing the distinction between judgments proper and the general category of "thought" which Neu equates with belief (see esp. pp. 36-37), see "Emotions and Evaluations" (unpublished, presented at the December 1979 meeting of the American Philosophical Association, Eastern Division).

X

EMOTIONS AND CHOICE

ROBERT C. SOLOMON

I

Do we choose our emotions? Can we be held responsible for our anger? for feeling jealousy? for falling in love or succumbing to resentment or hatred? The suggestion sounds odd because emotions are typically considered occurrences that happen to (or "in") us: emotions are taken to be the hallmark of the irrational and the disruptive. Controlling one's emotion is supposed to be like the caging and taming of a wild beast, the suppression and sublimation of a Freudian "it."

Traditionally, emotions have been taken to be feelings or sensations. More recently, but also traditionally, emotions have been taken to be physiological disturbances. Accordingly, much of this century's literature on emotions is dedicated to mapping out the relationship between sensations and correlative occurrences. William James, for example, takes consciousness of emotions to be consciousness of physiological occurrences. Other philosophers and psychologists, for one reason or another, have tried to reduce the emotion to a physiological occurrence, or, alternatively, have focused on the feeling of emotion and denied any conceptual role to the physiological occurrence. But these traditional worries should be quite irrelevant to any analysis of the emotions, for an emotion is neither a sensation nor a physiological occurrence, nor an occurrence of any other kind. "Struck by jealousy," "driven by anger," "plagued by remorse," "paralyzed by fear," "felled by shame," like "the prick of Cupid's arrow," are all symptomatic metaphors betraying a faulty philosophical analysis. Emotions are not occurrences and do not happen to us. I would like to suggest that emotions are rational and purposive rather than irrational and disruptive, are very much like actions, and that we choose an emotion much as we choose a course of action.[1]

Emotions are intentional; that is, emotions are "about" something. For instance, "I am angry *at John for stealing my car.*" It is not necessary to press the claim that *all* emotions are "about" something. Kierkegaard's dread may be an emotion which is not "about" anything, or , conversely, may be "about" everything. Similarly, *moods,* which are much like emotions, do not have a specific object. Euphoria, melancholy, and depression are not "about" anything in particular, though they may be caused by some particular incident. We might wish to say that such emotions and moods are "about" the world rather than anything in particular. In fact, Heidegger has suggested that *all* emotions are ultimately "about" the world and never simply "about" something particular. But we will avoid debating these issues by simply focusing our attention on emotions that clearly seem to be "about" something specifiable.

"I am angry at John for stealing my car." It is true that I am angry. And it is also true that John stole my car. Thus we are tempted to distinguish two components of my being angry; my feeling of anger and what I am angry about. But this is doubly a mistake. It requires that a feeling (of anger) be (contingently) directed at something (at John's having stolen my car). But feelings are occurrences and cannot have a "direction." They can be caused, but to say that I am angry "about" John's having stolen my car is very different from saying his stealing my car caused me to be angry. John's act might cause me to be angry "about" something else, e.g., my failure to renew my insurance. It might be false that John stole my car, though I believe that he did. Then it is false that John's stealing my car caused me to be angry, but still true that what I am angry "about" is John's stealing my car. One might suggest that it is not the alleged *fact* of John's stealing my car that is in question, but rather my *belief* that he did. But what I am angry "about" is clearly not that I believe that John stole my car, but rather *that John stole my car.*

Feelings do not have "directions."[2] But I am angry "about" something. The relationship between my being angry and what I am angry about is not the contingent relation between a feeling and an object. (Though it is surely contingent that I am angry at John for stealing my car.) An emotion cannot be identified apart from its object; "I am angry" is incomplete—not only in the weak sense that there is more information which may be available ("Are you angry about anything?") but "I am angry" requires that there *must* be more information available ("*What* are you angry about?"). But feelings have no such requirements. Anger is not a feeling; neither is anger a feeling plus anything else (e.g., what it is "about").

Neither can "what I am angry about" be separated from my being angry. Of course, it makes sense to say that John's having stolen my car is something different from my being angry at him for doing so. But it is not simply the *fact* that John stole my car that is what I am angry about; nor is it, as I said above, my *belief* that John stole my car about which I am angry. I am angry about the intentional object "that John stole my car." Unlike the *fact* that John stole my car, this intentional object is opaque; I am not angry that John stole a vehicle assembled in Youngstown, Ohio, with 287 h.p., though that is a true description of the fact that John stole my car. I am not angry that someone 5'7" tall got his fingerprints on my steering column, yet that is a true description of the fact that John stole my car. Sartre attempts to point out this feature of what emotions are "about" by saying that their object is "transformed"; D. F. Pears points to this same feature by noting that it is always an "aspect" of the object that is the object of an emotion. What emotions are "about," as in beliefs, can only be identified under certain descriptions, and those descriptions are determined by the emotion itself. This does not mean that what emotions are about are beliefs—only that emotions share an important conceptual property of beliefs. "Being angry about . . . " is very much like "believing that. . . . " To be angry is to be angry "about" a peculiar sort of object, one that is distinguished by the fact that it is what I am angry "about." Husserl describes this peculiarity of mental acts in general by insisting that an intentional act and an intentional object are "*essentially* correlated." For our purposes, the point to be seen is that emotions cannot be discussed in terms of "components," by distinguishing feeling angry and what I am angry about. (Pears, e.g., begins by making this distinction.) In Heideggerian phrase, I am never simply angry, but there is always "my-being-angry-about- . . . ."

If there is no legitimate distinction between feeling angry and what I am angry "about," or, to put it in a different way, if the connection between my being angry and what I am angry "about" is a conceptual and not causal connection, then it is easy to explain a feature of emotions that has been pointed out by many analysts. A change in what I am angry "about" demands a change in my anger; if I no longer feel wronged by John, who only bought a car that looks like mine, I cannot be angry at John (for stealing my car) any longer. One cannot be angry if he is not angry "about" having been wronged. Similarly, one cannot be ashamed if he does not accept some responsibility for an awkward situation, nor can he be embarrassed if he does not find the situation awkward. If emotions were feelings, it would be a peculiar coincidence that the feelings were so faithful to our views of our situation, that they did not hold onto us with a momentum of their own after opinions had passed, that they were not so "irrational" as to pay no attention to our opinions at all. But emotions are not feelings, nor feelings plus what they are "about"; the format of an emotion is "... -about-...." And so it is no surprise that emotions change with our opinions, and so are "rational" in a very important sense.

Emotions typically involve feelings. Perhaps they essentially involve feelings. But feelings are never sufficient to differentiate and identify emotions, and an emotion is never simply a feeling, not even a feeling plus anything. Moreover, it is clear that one can have an emotion without feeling anything. One can be angry without feeling angry: one can be angry for three days or five years and not feel anything identifiable as a feeling of anger continuously through that prolonged period. One might add that one must have a disposition to feel angry, and to this, there is no objection, so long as being angry is not thought to *mean* "having a disposition to feel angry." I do not know whether it makes sense to suppose that one can be angry without ever feeling angry. But I do know that it does not even make sense to say that one feels angry if one is not angry. This might seem mysterious, if we accept the traditional view that anger has an identifiable feeling attached to it (for then, why could one not have the feeling without whatever else is involved in anger?). And this might seem obvious on the traditional view that anger *is* a feeling (for then being angry is nothing but having the feeling of anger). But on our account, anger is not a feeling, nor does it involve any identifiable feeling (which is not to deny that one does feel angry—that is, flushed, excited, etc., when he is angry). One can identify his feeling as feeling angry only if he is angry. It is true that I often feel something when I become angry. It is also true that I feel something after I cease to be angry. I am angry at John for stealing my car. Then I discover that John did not steal my car: I cease (immediately) to be angry. Yet the feeling remains: it is the same feeling I had while I was angry (flushing, etc.). The feeling subsides more slowly than the anger. But the feeling, even if it is the same feeling that I had while I was angry, is not a feeling of anger. Now it is just a feeling. Sometimes one claims to feel angry but not be angry. But here, I would argue that the correct description is rather that one does not know exactly what one is angry "about" (though one is surely angry "about" something); or perhaps one is angry but does not believe he ought to be. One cannot feel angry without being angry.

A familiar move in the analysis of emotions subsequent to the discovery that emotions are not feelings or occurrences, is the thesis that emotions are conceptually tied to behavior; that is, the ascription of an emotion to a person is the ascription to him of various sorts of behavior. Thus, to be angry is necessarily to "anger-behave." Of course, it is evident that one can *pretend* to be angry, that is, anger-behave without being angry, and so pretending has become a major topic in the analysis of emotions. (More on this in Part II.) What is generally agreed is that a single piece of behavior is never conceptually sufficient to identify an emotion, or to distinguish emotions from pretense. E. Bedford, for example, suggests that what is always needed is at least "more of the same." Since Ryle's *Concept of Mind,* this "more of the same" is provided by the suggestion that ascribing an emotion to a person is not to simply describe one or more episodes of behavior but rather to ascribe to him a disposition to behave. But there is considerable confusion about the nature of such disposition-ascriptions, and the suggestion is clearly unsatisfactory as an analysis of *my* having an emotion. The behavioral analysis does maintain one important feature of emotions, their intentionality, though authors (e.g., Ryle, Armstrong) who favor this analysis are often intent to reject "intentionality" as well. But for our purposes, we can remain uninvolved in these issues that have become virtually definitive of "philosophy of mind.'' We can agree that it is undeniably true that if a person is angry he has a disposition to anger-behave and leave it entirely open whether this connection between emotions and behavior is conceptual, or causal or something else. The purpose of this essay is to show that emotions are very much like actions, and if it should turn out that emotions are actions in any such straightforward sense, this can only make our task easier. And so, we can simply say of the behavioral analysis: insofar as it is true, it supports our thesis.

"Emotions are caused.'' The idea that emotions are occurrences naturally gave rise to the idea that emotions are caused. Many philosophers would argue that, if emotions are occurrences, then they must be caused, and conversely, that if emotions are caused they must be occurrences. But if, as I am arguing, emotions are not occurrences, then they cannot be caused.

But surely this is wrong. We do speak of the cause of anger, the cause for sadness, a cause for fear. And surely emotions, as intentional, are typically if not necessarily *reactions* to something that happens to us. Sometimes this cause is manifest in what the emotion is "about''; for example, I am angry about your hitting me; your hitting me is the event which caused me to become angry. But sometimes the cause for an emotion is *not* what the emotion is "about.'' The cause of my anger might be too little sleep and too much coffee. The cause of my love might be sexual deprivation. But I am not angry "about'' lack of sleep and hyperstimulation, and I am not in love with my sexual deprivation (nor is my love "about'' a cure for my sexual deprivation).

The cause of an emotion is a function in a certain kind of explanation. The cause must in every case be distinguished from what my emotion is "about'' (its "object''). The cause is always an actual event (or state-of-affairs, etc.). The object of my emotion is always an intentional object. The cause is subject to certain lawlike generalizations in a way that objects of emotions are not. If I claim to be angry because of a harsh review of my book, pointing out that I have not become angry at previous harsh reviews of my book is sufficient to show that the cause of my becoming angry is not (my reading of) the review of my book, but it is not sufficient to show that I am not angry "about'' the harsh review. I am not in any special position to know the cause of my emotion (though only I know, as a matter of fact, that I did not sleep last night, that I have had four cups of coffee); I am always in a privileged position to identify the intentional object of my emotion. This is *not* to say that my knowledge of the object of my emotion is "immediate" or "direct," nor is it to claim that my identification of the object of my emotion is "incorrigible." It is possible and not unusual that I should misidentify—sometimes in a gross way—what I am angry about, or whom I love, or why I am sad. I may identify the object of my anger as John's having stolen my car, but I am really angry at John for writing a harsh review of my book. I may think that I love Mary, when I really love my mother. And I may think that I love Mary when I am really angry about the harsh review of my book. The problem of "unconscious emotions" would take us far beyond our current argument. For now, it should suffice for us to insist that the difference between identification of the cause of an emotion and its object is not a difference between direct and indirect knowledge—as traditionally conceived—or a difference between corrigible and incorrigible identification. The cause of an emotion is an occurrence (state-of-affairs, etc.) of a type that stands in a lawlike connection with emotions of that type. The object of an emotion is simply "what the emotion is about," whether or not it is also the cause, whether or not it is even the case, and whether or not the subject himself knows it to be the object of his emotion.[3]

We have noted that emotions are interestingly similar to beliefs. We can now explain this similarity by claiming that emotions are judgments—normative and often moral judgments. "I am angry at John for taking ("stealing" begs the question) my car" *entails* that I believe that John has somehow wronged me. (This must be true even if, *all things considered,* I also believe that John was justified in taking my car.) The (moral) judgments entailed by my anger is not a judgment *about* my anger (although someone else might make such judgments to the effect that my anger is justified or unjustified, rational, prudent, foolish, self-indulgent, therapeutic, beneficial, unfortunate, pathological, or amusing). My anger *is* that judgment. If I do not believe that I have somehow been wronged, I cannot be angry (though I might be upset, or sad). Similarly, if I cannot praise my lover, I cannot be in love (though I might want her or need her, which, traditional wisdom aside, is entirely different). If I do not find my situation awkward, I cannot be ashamed or embarrassed. If I do not judge that I have suffered a loss, I cannot be sad or jealous. I am not sure whether all emotions entail such judgments; moods (depression and euphoria) surely present special problems. But emotions in general do appear to require this feature: to have an emotion is to hold a normative judgment about one's situation.

The idea that an emotion is a normative judgment, perhaps even a moral judgment, wreaks havoc with several long cherished philosophical theses. Against those romantics and contemporary bourgeois therapists who would argue that emotions simply *are* and must be accepted without judgment, it appears that emotions themselves are already judgments. And against several generations of moral philosophers who would distinguish between morality based upon principle and morality based upon emotion or "sentiment," it appears that every "sentiment," every emotion is already a matter of judgment, often moral judgment. An ethics of sentiment differs from ethics of principle only in the fact that its judgments are allowed to go unchallenged: it is an ethics of prejudice while the latter is typically an ethics of dogma.

We can now see why "what an emotion is about" is not simply a fact; nor is it even a fact under certain descriptions. The object of an emotion is itself "affective" or normative. It is not an object *about* which one makes a judgment but is rather defined, in part, by that normative judgment. The peculiar emotional object, *that John stole my car,* can only be fully characterized as the object of my anger. "That John stole my car" is also the name of the object of my belief, of course, and perhaps of any number of other propositional attitudes I hold. But the object of my anger, that John stole my car, is an inseparable piece of my being angry. This sounds strange, no doubt, if the intentional object of the emotion is thought to be a fact or a proposition. But my anger-at-John-for-stealing-my-car is inseparable from my judgment that John in so doing wronged me, while it is clear that the *fact* that John stole my car is very different from my anger or my judgment. My anger *is* my judgment that John has wronged me.

It has always been recognized that there is some difference between our ascriptions of emotions to ourselves and our ascriptions of emotions to others. I know that I am angry and what I am angry about very differently than I know that John is angry and what he is angry about. (This first person privilege remains the presupposition of, and is not undermined by, either the Freudian concept of "unconscious emotions" or by recent philosophical attacks on "incorrigibility.") On the traditional view in which emotions are feelings, this difference has been explained by appeal to the peculiar "privacy" of sensationlike occurrences. But emotions are not feelings and not occurrences, we have argued, but rather judgments. Yet the difference between first- and other-person cases can still be made out, and in a far more convincing way than on the feeling-analysis of emotions. *You* can say of me, "he is angry because he thinks John stole his car, which he did not." *You* can say of me, "he is angry about the review, which actually was favorable, but only because of his lack of sleep and his having drunk too much coffee." *You* can say of me, "he doesn't really love Mary, but rather a mother-surrogate." But *I* cannot say these things of *myself*. "I am angry at John because I think that he stole my car, which he didn't" is nonsense. If emotions are judgments, then the sorts of "pragmatic" paradoxes that have long been celebrated regarding judgments in general will apply to emotions also. "I am angry about x, but not x" raises the same problems as "P, but I do not believe P." No feeling-account of emotions can account for such paradoxes. But, if emotions are intentional, emotions must partake in conceptual relationships in a way that mere occurrences, feelings, or facts do not. If I am angry about John's stealing my car, there are certain beliefs which I logically cannot hold, for example, the belief that John did not steal my car.

The difference between first- and other-person ascriptions of emotions lies in the realm of the "pragmatic paradoxes." Given that I have a certain emotion, there are certain beliefs which you can have (including beliefs about me) but which *I* cannot have. The most interesting set of beliefs in this regard are those which pertain to the *cause* of an emotion. Earlier, we argued that the cause of an emotion is a fact (state of affairs, etc.) which can be variously ("transparently") described and occupies a role in lawlike generalizations. The *object* of an emotion, however, is limited by certain judgments (is "opaque") which are determined in the subject's having that emotion. But this distinction, we can now add, breaks down in the first-person case. If I am angry *about* John's stealing my car (the object of my anger), then I cannot believe that the sufficient *cause* of my anger is anything other than John's stealing my car. *You* can attribute my unjust anger to my lack of sleep. *I* cannot. If I attribute my anger to lack of sleep, I cannot be angry at all. And this is not simply to say that my anger is "not reasonable." (I cannot say that of myself either, except perhaps in extremely peculiar circumstances, for example, following extensive psychoanalytic treatment, which here, as elsewhere, confuses all distinctions as well as the patient regarding first- vs. other-person ascriptions of emotions, motives, intentions, etc.) I can only be angry so long as I believe that what has caused me to be angry is what I am angry about. Where the cause is different from what I am angry about, I cannot know that it is.

One can argue that the person who is angry (or in love, or sad) is in the worst position to pick out the cause for his anger (or love or sadness) *as opposed to* its object.[4] We can only add that this thesis marks out a conceptual necessity. We earlier pointed out the familiar phenomenon that our emotions change with our opinions and argued that this was not a causal matter and not a coincidence, but a consequence of the thesis that emotions are themselves judgments. We can now add that our emotions change with our knowledge of the causes of those emotions. If I can discover the sufficient cause of my anger, in those cases in which the cause and the object are different (and in which the newly discovered cause is not itself a new object for anger, as often happens), I can undermine and abandon my anger. It is here that Freud's often debated notion that emotions are "defused" by bringing them to consciousness contains an important conceptual truth too often and too easily dismissed by philosophers. Once one becomes aware of the cause of his emotion as opposed to its intended object, he can indeed "defuse" his emotion. And in those familiar Freudian cases in which one mistakenly identifies the object of his emotion (he thinks he is angry at his teacher: he is "really" angry at his father), correcting this identification can, in those cases where the correctly identified object is also the cause of the emotion, also "defuse" it. Where Freud opened himself to unnecessary criticism, I believe, was in his construing this as a *causal* relationship, a "catharsis" of repressed emotional air bubbles in the mental digestive system. But it is not as if my recognition of the true cause of my anger *causes* the easing of my emotion. Rather, my recognition of the true cause of my emotion amounts to a denial of the judgment which is my emotion. When I see that my anger is wholly a result of my lack of sleep and overdose of coffee, I thereby abandon my anger. Of course, the flushing, pulsing, irritable *feelings* of anger may thus be *caused* to diminish by the disappearance of my anger, but these are, as we have argued, in no case my anger.

If emotions are judgments and can be "defused" (and also instigated) by considerations of other judgments, it is clear how our emotions are in a sense *our doing,* and how we are responsible for them. Normative judgments can themselves be criticized, argued against, and refuted. Now if *you* criticize my anger at John by maintaining that he has not wronged me, you may conclude that my anger is unreasonable, unfair, and perhaps unbecoming. But if you should convince *me* that John has not wronged me, I do not simply conclude that my anger is unreasonable, unfair, or unbecoming. *I cease to be angry.* Similarly, I can make myself angry at John by allowing myself to be convinced that he has wronged me. I can dwell on minor behavioral misdemeanors on John's part, building them into a pattern of overall deceit and abuse, and then become angry at any one or any number of these incidents.

Since normative judgments can be changed through influence, argument, and evidence, and since I can go about on my own seeking influence, provoking argument, and looking for evidence, I am as responsible for my emotions as I am for the judgments I make. My emotions *are* judgments I make. Now one might argue that all we have shown is that one can take steps to *cause* changes in his emotions, such as one can take steps to diminish a pain by pulling out a splinter or take steps to prevent being hit by a bus by crossing only on the proper signals. And it is true, of course, that one cannot *simply* choose to be angry or not to be angry, but can make himself angry or cease being angry only by performing other activities. But this is true of judgments in general: I cannot simply choose to judge a situation fortunate, awkward, or dangerous.[5] It is worth noting that I cannot *simply* perform most actions either: I cannot simply assassinate a dictator. I must do something else (pull the trigger of a rifle, let slip the string of the bow, push the button activating the detonator). Yet, although it is also true that I cause the death of the dictator (I do not cause the killing of him), I kill the dictator. Similarly, making judgments is something *I do,* not something that happens to me and not something I simply cause, even though I cannot *simply* make a judgment in many cases. (Legal judgments by an appropriately empowered judge or judiciary should *not* be taken as paradigm cases here.)

I must be in appropriate circumstances to pass judgment, have some evidence, know something of what the judgment is about. Of course, one can make judgments rashly, with minimal evidence and with superficial knowledge of what the judgment is about. Emotions, we can now see, are rash judgments, something I do, but in haste. Accordingly, the evidence upon which I become emotional is typically (but not necessarily) incomplete, and my knowledge of what I am emotional about is often (but again not necessarily) superficial. I can take any number of positive steps to change what I believe and what judgments I hold and tend to make. By forcing myself to be scrupulous in the search for evidence and knowledge of circumstance, and by training myself in self-understanding regarding my prejudices and influences, and by placing myself in appropriate circumstances, I can determine the kinds of judgments I will tend to make. I can do the same for my emotions.

II

Against the near-platitude "emotions are irrational," we want to argue that emotions are rational. This is not only to say that they fit into one's overall behavior in a significant way, that they follow a regular pattern (one's "personality"), that they can be explained in terms of a coherent set of causes. No doubt this is all true. But emotions, we have argued, are judgments, and so emotions can be rational in the same sense in which judgments can be rational. (Of course, judgments can be irrational, but only within the context of a rational activity.) Judgments are actions. Like all actions, they are aimed at changing the world. But, although the expression of a judgment may actually produce such a change, the judgment itself is more like the winding of the mainspring of an intention to change the world rather than the overt activity which will do so. But if emotions are judgments, and judgments are actions, though covert, emotions too are actions, aimed at changing the world (whether or not their expression actually does succeed in changing the world). In other words, emotions are purposive, serve the ends of the subject, and consequently can be explained by *reasons* or "in-order-to" explanations.

Because emotions are usually thought to be occurrences that we suffer, the idea that emotions are purposive actions has not been given sufficient attention. But consider the following very familiar sort of case:

Joanie wants to go to a party: her husband does not. She begins to act bored and frustrated; he watches television. She resigns herself to reading, sighing occasionally. He asks if she has picked up some shirts from the laundry: she says "no." He flies into a rage. He needs shirts (he has hundreds). He needs one of *those* (they are all the same). She is negligent (she was busy). She takes advantage of him (she stays with him). Naturally, she rebels, but she is upset, with mixed guilt and anger. She thinks him unreasonable, impossible, and slightly neurotic. Their encounter is short-lived. She goes off to read; he settles back before the television. The party is out of the question.

What are we to say of this familiar sort of case? It appears to be given that the husband's anger is inappropriate to the incident. His being angry about his wife's failure to pick up his shirts seems unreasonable; and the *intensity* of his anger is most surely unwarranted. To this, the standard response, since well before Freud, has been to suppose that the husband is really angry about something else; perhaps he is redirecting anger from his day at his office—anger which could not be expressed as safely toward his superiors as it could to his wife. Or perhaps the anger is accumulated anger from weeks or months of minor marital frictions. Or perhaps, it might be suggested, the anger is caused by the fact that the husband is tired.

But, in this case—and many other cases—there is an alternative sort of explanation that is available and persuasive. The anger can be explained, not in terms of what it is "about" or what causes it, but in terms of its *purpose*. The husband, in this case, has *used* his anger to manipulate his wife. He has become angry "about" the shirts *in order to* get his wife's mind off the party and in order to stop her irritating reminders. His anger is not a disruption of his activities (watching television, refusing to go to the party) but a part of it, its winning strategy. The best explanation of his anger is not that it was caused by anything (although that is not precluded) and not that it was "about" anything in particular (although that is surely true), but that he got angry at his wife *in order* to continue watching television and in order to insure that his refusal to go to the party would be successful.

But if emotions are rational and purposive, why is it that emotions are so often counterproductive and embarrassing to us, detours away from our aspirations and obstacles blocking our ambitions? Why do emotions so often appear as disruptions in our lives, threats to our successes, aberrations in our rational behavior? We can outline three distinct accounts of the apparent "irrationality" of emotions.

First, it is the situation in which one becomes emotional that is disruptive, a detour, an obstacle, a threat, and not the emotional response. Emotions are urgent judgments; emotional responses are emergency behavior. An emotional response occurs in a situation in which usual intentions are perverted or frustrated; an unusual response is necessary. The normative judgments involved in having an emotion are inseparable from the overall network of our motives, beliefs and intentions. The fact that emotions typically lead to apparently "pointless" behavior is not a consequence of emotions being irrational, but a natural consequence of the fact that emotions are responses to unusual situations in which usual behavior patterns seem inappropriate. The intentions of an emotional reaction are not infrequently impossible. The angry or sad man may wish to undo the past; the lover may want to possess, and be possessed by, his loved one. This is why Sartre calls the emotions "magical transformations of the world." One can always reduce the range of his emotional behavior by developing stereotyped responses, by avoiding all unusual situations or by treating every situation as "usual." These are common but perhaps pathological ways of choosing our emotions. But such common "control" is not the avoidance or the suppression of a wild psychic beast; it is simply the avoidance of situations (or recognition of situations) where one's usual behavior patterns will not suffice. Emotions are rational responses to unusual situations. They differ from "cool" judgments and normal rational deliberate action in that they are prompted in urgency and in contexts in which one's usual repetoire of actions and considered judgments will not suffice. An emotion is a necessarily hasty judgment in response to a difficult situation.

It must be added that the "hastiness" of a judgment does not entail that it is made quickly. For example, one can make a hasty judgment after weeks of halfhearted deliberation. Similarly, although emotions are typically urgent and immediate responses, one can become increasingly angry over a period of time, or one finds that an emotion that is formed in urgency is then maintained in full force for weeks or even years. But what distinguishes emotions from ordinary judgments is their lack of "cool," their seeming urgency, even after weeks of simmering and stewing. There are no cold emotions, no cool anger, no deliberate love. Emotions are always urgent, even desperate, responses to situations in which one finds oneself unprepared, helpless, frustrated, impotent, "caught." It is the situation, not the emotion, which is disruptive and "irrational."

Second, and consequently, emotions are short-term responses. Emotions are rational in that they fit into a person's overall purposive behavior. But this is not to say that a person's various purposes are always consistent or coherent. Short-term purposes are often in conflict with rather than a means toward the fulfillment of long-term purposes. My desire to drink at the reception may tend toward disaster regarding my meeting of the celebrity who is my reason for going to the reception. My desire to visit Peking may undermine my ambition to become an FBI agent. Similarly, emotions often serve short-term purposes that are in conflict with longer-term purposes. I may be angry with John because I feel I have been wronged, but this may be inconsistent with my desire to keep a close, unblemished friendship with John. I may love Mary, but this might be totally inconsistent with my intention to preserve my marriage, to remain celibate, or to concentrate on my writing. Thus, the husband in our example might succeed in staying home from the party by becoming angry, but break up his marriage in so doing. It is in this sense that emotions are "blind"; more accurately, they are *myopic*. Emotions serve purposes and are rational; but because the purposes emotions serve are often short-sighted, they appear to be nonpurposive and irrational on a larger view. For the sake of a passion, we destroy careers, marriages, lives. Emotions are not irrational; people are irrational.

Third, there is an anthropological response to the idea that emotions are irrational. In a society that places taboos on emotional behavior—condemns it in men and belittles it in women—it is only to be expected that emotions will be counter to ambitions. A society that applauds "cool" behavior will naturally require strategies that are similarly "cool." In such a society, emotional behavior appears as "irrational" because it is bad strategy, not because it is not purposive. Perhaps it is not at all difficult to envision a society in which *only* emotional behavior would appear rational—where only short term emotional responses had any meaning at all. But it is surely not Anglo-American society in which "reason is and ought to be the slave of the passions."

Against our view that emotions, as actions, are purposive and that a person chooses his emotions rather than being victimized by them, there is a uniquely powerful objection. A person cannot identify at the time the purpose of his emotion. The husband who uses his anger to manipulate his wife cannot identify the purpose as opposed to the object-cause of his anger. If he were to identify the manipulative function of his anger, the effect would be the destruction of his anger. One cannot be angry and know that his anger has a purpose.

This is much more, of course, than a mere pragmatic claim. It is certainly true that the husband cannot tell his wife that his anger is purposive, for the very purpose of the anger is to distract his wife from that purpose. But the claim here is that the husband cannot even think to himself, "I am being angry in order to. . . ." If the husband is unusually self-aware, he may know that he, in general, uses his anger to manipulate people; but he still cannot entertain that thought at the time of his anger and remain angry. If he does, he ceases to be angry and continues, at most, only to act angry—to feign anger.

One's inability to see the purpose of his emotion is a conceptual matter, just as before we pointed out that one cannot (conceptually) make certain judgments, such as the judgment that what he is angry about is not the case, or that the cause of his anger, where this is different from the object of his anger, is a sufficient explanation of his anger. We can now add to this list of conceptual inabilities the inability of one to suspect the *purpose* of his emotion. Now many philosophers would argue that, regarding intentional actions in general, one cannot fail to be aware of his motives and intentions at the time of acting. It would take us too far astray to argue against this view here, but notice that this inability to notice one's *purpose* is not limited to emotions. Consider, for example, Nietzsche's account of belief in God as a belief whose function is to serve certain purposes (achievement of salvation; a basis for "slave-morality" and self-righteousness; to seek power). Yet, even if a purposive analysis of belief in God is true, this neither denies that people do in fact believe in God nor need it suggest that believers could state these purposes. To the contrary, we can add, if they were to think seriously that their belief was held to serve a purpose rather than because it was true, we would have to conclude that they did not believe at all. (A conclusion that Nietzsche too easily comes to on the basis of an argument from the third person to the first person case.) To believe is not to believe for a purpose; yet beliefs can still be purposive.

Judgments in general, not only emotions, can be purposive but cannot be recognized (by the person who makes them at the time that he makes them) as purposive. If I judge, calmly and deliberately, without a hint of that urgency and intensity that characterizes anger, that John has wronged me by stealing my car again (he does it all the time), I may be rationalizing an opportunity to take out John's wife. In fact, I may even say to myself, "since he has wronged me so, I feel justified in taking out his wife." But I cannot believe that my judgment that John has wronged me has been made for this purpose. I can at most believe that since he has wronged me, I am justified. . . . Similarly, I may judge, calmly and deliberately, that Mary is a magnificent woman, attractive and intelligent, strong-willed and sensitive, but without the slightest hint of that urgency and intensity that characterizes love. But, knowing that Mary is John's wife, I may be so judging as a way of rationalizing an opportunity to run off with John's mistress. Now I may openly judge that John does not need his mistress, since his wife is so magnificent, and so I can feel justified in running off with his mistress. But I cannot believe that my judging that Mary is magnificent is made for this purpose. In other words, judgments, no matter how calm and deliberate, when they are made for some purpose (leaving open the question whether all are so made), cannot be recognized as having been made for a purpose. In this sense, all judgments are "blind." To recognize the purpose for which a judgment is made is to undermine the judgment. One cannot judge that he has been wronged and at the same time recognize that he has judged that he has been wronged only in order to. . . .

One must also consider apparently "unintentional" actions, to which emotions bear a striking resemblance. Some act-types allow for only intentional acts, for example, murder, fishing. Others allow for only unintentional acts, for example, forgetting, slipping, stumbling, tripping, losing, in short, most of those actions that make up the subject matter of what Freud calls the "psycho-pathology of everyday life." Yet Freud demonstrated that such "unintentional" actions function in a remarkable accordance with a subject's overall purposes and intentions. Freud surely does not want to say that these simply *appear* to be intentional (as some authors have argued, e.g., R. S. Peters, A. MacIntyre), but rather that they truly are intentional, the difference being, in his terms, the "inaccessibility" of the intention to the subject. The status of such actions remains a matter of controversy, but we feel reasonably confident that most philosophers and most everybody else would agree that such "actions" are indeed actions and can be demonstrated in at least some cases to be done for a purpose; yet the subject cannot state their purpose. And once again, the "cannot" is a *logical* "cannot," since a man who knows that he is losing his wedding ring in order to show his opinion of his marriage is making a gesture, not losing his ring. And a man who knows he is forgetting to call his office in order to avoid extra work is not forgetting but refusing to call his office. Thus we can see in what senses such actions may appear to be both intentional and "unintentional." They are intentional insofar as they clearly fit into the purposes and intentions of the subject; they appear to be unintentional insofar as they cannot be stated as purposive or intentional by the subject. Similarly, anger is purposive and intentional insofar as it can be clearly shown to fit into the structure of the subject's purposes and intentions; it appears to be "unintentional" and thus differs from many straightforward actions, in that these purposes and intentions cannot be known by the subject at the time. Emotions, when they are purposive and intentional, are essentially devious.

Can one feign anger? One might think, "Of course, act angry

when you are not angry.'' But what is it that constitutes the anger apart from acting angry? The traditional answer to this is simple enough: a feeling. To feign anger is to act angry but not feel angry. To feign love is to act lovingly but not feel love. To feign an emotion would be, in general, to pretend one has a feeling which one does not have, as a child pretends—usually badly—to have a cramp in order to stay away from school. But we have seen that an emotion is not a feeling. This traditional analysis does lend support to our contention that to have an emotion in order to..., is not to have that emotion. But, on our account, the difference is not due to the presence or lack of a feeling. Rather, to have an emotion is to make certain judgments; to feign an emotion, then, is to pretend that one holds certain judgments which one does not hold.

But this makes the notion of feigning emotion much more difficult than has been supposed on the simple ''feeling'' analysis. André Gide has written that feigned emotion and ''vital'' emotion are indistinguishable, and in this there is an often unseen giant of a truth, one that would appear absurd on the thesis that emotions are feelings. Miss Anscombe, replying to J. L. Austin, has distinguished between mock performances and real pretenses. The most obvious difference between the two is that one is intended to mislead others, the other not. Accordingly, the one should be more cautiously consistent and prolonged than the other: a successful mock performance may be announced as lasting only 35 seconds, a real pretense must go on as long as it must go on. But the most important difference between mock performances and real pretenses is the *context* (what we have been calling ''the situation''). A mock performance may be performed on a stage, in any context in which it can be announced or in which it is evident that this is a *mere* pretense. A real pretense, however, requires that the context of performance be appropriate; anger can only be feigned in real pretense if the situation is one in which anger is appropriate. One can only pretend to be in love with someone whom it is plausible that he should love. But the appropriateness of the situation is not a causal determinant of a feeling of love or anger. Rather it is the context in which judgments of the requisite kinds make sense and are plausible. But if to feign anger is to act angry in a context in which the anger-related judgments are plausible, it is easy to see how one could, upon prolonged pretense, come to accept those very judgments. If, over a protracted period of time, I pretend to love a woman whom I have married for her father's wealth, it is more than likely that I shall grow to love her (if I do not first come to openly despise her). And if I pretend to be angry about a political issue in order to be accepted by my friends, it is not at all unlikely that I shall come to be really angry about that same issue. Perhaps there is no better way to choose to have an emotion than to decide to pretend that one has it. As Sartre has said, the best way to fall asleep is to pretend that you are asleep. And here, I think we may say that Gide's theory has a plausibility which cannot be explained on the idea that what one pretends to have is a feeling.

Emotions are intentional and rational, not disruptive and "irrational." Emotions are judgments and actions, not occurrences or happenings that we suffer. Accordingly, I want to say that emotions are choices and our responsibility. Yet I am never aware of making such a choice. Emotions, we argued, are hasty and typically dogmatic judgments. Accordingly, they cannot be made together with the recognition that they are dogmatic and not absolutely correct. What distinguishes emotions from other judgments is the fact that the former can never be deliberate and carefully considered. Emotions are essentially nondeliberate choices. Emotions, in this sense, are indeed "blind" as well as myopic; an emotion cannot see itself. Few things are more disconcerting than suddenly watching one's angry reflection in the mirror, or reflecting on one's anger to see its absurdity *in media res*.

If emotions are judgments or actions, we can be held responsible for them. We cannot simply have an emotion or stop having an emotion, but we can open ourselves to argument, persuasion and evidence. We can force ourselves to be self-reflective, to make just those judgments regarding the causes and purposes of our emotions, and also to make the judgment that we are all the while *choosing* our emotions, which will "defuse" our emotions. This is not to opt for a life without emotions: it is to argue for a conception of emotions which will make clear that emotions are our choice. In a sense, our thesis here is self-confirming: to think of our emotions as chosen is to *make* them our choices. Emotional control is not learning to employ rational techniques to force into submission a brutal "it" which has victimized us but rather the willingness to become self-aware, to search out, and challenge the normative judgments embedded in every emotional response. To come to believe that one has this power *is* to have this power.

In response to our argument, one might conclude that we have only argued that one can choose and is responsible for his *interpretation* of his situation and his emotions. But then I simply want to end by once again drawing Nietzsche to my side and quipping, with regard to emotions, "there are only interpretations...."

APPENDIX

Against Plato and the rhetoricians (e.g., Gorgias), Aristotle defended the view that some emotions were both practical and intelligent (righteous anger, for example), *essentially* involving both goals and cognition.[6] Anger, for example, was a desire for vengeance because of an unjustified offense or slight.[7] Aristotle also developed a theory of the intentionality of emotions and understood the linkage between logic and rhetoric in changing emotions.[8] Centuries later, Seneca defended the view that emotions are judgments, within our power.[9] He then went on to chastise emotions as *irrational* judgments, incompatible with reason, and so promoted his Stoic concept of *apatheia,* in direct contrast to Aristotle who took at least certain passions as essential to moral virtue and the *eudaimon* life.[10] The idea that emotions are akin to judgments and within the bounds of human responsibility is thus a very old theory. How pathetic then that the emotions have been so removed from their cognitive and activist moorings by modern philosophy, from Descartes's "animal spirits" to James's visceral spasms and Freud's "id." How this has happened is not my concern. But what does concern me—passionately—is to resurrect and defend the older view, with a decided existentialist twist.

"Emotions and Choice" (1973) was a polemic. It hit some raw nerves, but it soon became obvious that its bolder claims had to be qualified and defended by a far more detailed analysis of emotions, which I developed in *The Passions* (1976).[11] Subsequent discussions and criticisms convinced me that some of these claims require still further defense and modification, but I remain convinced that no noncognitive view of emotions will ever allow us to understand

them[12] and no view that does not involve the idea of responsibility
will have any but a deleterious effect on both moral philosophy and
psychology. But let me review the arguments:

EMOTIONS ARE INTENTIONAL

In "Emotions and Choice," my defense of the distinction between
the object and cause(s) of emotion had to take priority over a careful analysis of intentionality. At the time, the notion of intentionality was under severe attack, and several articles and books have
straightforwardly attempted to eliminate this notion altogether by
reducing all talk of "objects" to accounts in terms of causes.[13] The
motivation behind this attack has turned in part on well-known historical abuses of "intentionality" and a recent fetish for extensional accounts, as well as a reaction against the still platitudinous
obscurity surrounding that sacramental concept in the writings of
some phenomenologists. But more importantly, it was a reaction
against the now classic account of the intentionality of emotions
suggested by Anthony Kenny in his *Action, Emotion and Will*
(1963).[14] Kenny analyzed emotions as intentional feelings: what he
did not provide was any way of understanding how it might be possible for a "feeling" to be intentional. Kenny argued, following a
tradition that stretches back to Aristotle (if not Plato)[15] that there
must be a *formal* connection between the feeling and its object; but
again, he provided us with no understanding how this might be possible.[16] And, finally, pointing out that some emotions clearly have
"inexistent" objects (for example, emotions concerning the
future), he disastrously concludes that the objects of *all* emotions
must be understood in terms of "a special non-causal sense."
Kenny rightly insists on the distinction between objects of emotions
and their causes, but he gives no adequate analysis of "a special
non-causal sense." Thus he provokes one recent critic to accuse
him of rendering the connection between emotion and object, and
the notion of "object" itself, both "otiose" and "mysterious."[17]
    What is needed is an account of the intentionality of emotions
which avoids these obscurities. Accordingly, the opening move of
The Passions is one of ontological frugality; the distinction between
cause and object is made to be functional, not a distinction between

two types of entities. The traditional emphasis on existence and "inexistence" of emotional objects is replaced by a phenomenological concept of "subjectivity," where the emphasis is wholly on the idea of an object *as experienced*.[18] Whether an experience also provides an accurate account of the world is not part of an analysis of either emotions or their intentionality, although it may enter into discussions of their rationality or their justification. Whether the description of the object can also function as a description of the cause of an emotion, in other words, in a causal explanation, is also something other than the analysis of emotion requires. But this is not to say anything about the identity of cause and object. The notion of intentionality is ontologically innocent.

The simpleminded disjunction between the existence or "inexistence" of emotional objects and discussions thereof has a more disastrous consequence. Consider, for example, the Freudian claim that a certain young man, Dorian, does not in fact love his wife but his mother. Whether or not this claim is defensible in general, whether or not it is defensible in this particular case, it is clear that here we have a critical test case for any analysis of the emotion of love: What characteristics are essential for the love of a particular "object"/person? But what is clearly not at stake is any question about the ontological status of the disputed object, only its phenomenological ("subjective") identity in the eyes of Dorian. In this way, the concept of intentionality opens up a rich field of new investigations: to ontologize is to forfeit them.

To account for the fact that emotions are intentional, I reject Kenny's claim that emotions are a species of feelings and insist that emotions are a species of judgments. This explains, as no "feeling" analysis could, how it is that emotions are "about" the world in a "noncausal sense." It also explains, in a nonmysterious way, why so many authors (Aristotle, Hume, and Kenny, for instance) have felt compelled to insist upon the "formal" connection between emotion and object and the "essential" or "natural" connections between emotions and beliefs. What a judgment is about defines the judgment. Similarly, what an emotion is about defines the emotion.

In "Emotions and Choice," I attack what I call a "components" analysis of emotions, for just this reason. As soon as one distinguishes between the "feeling" of emotion and its object, as Kenny does, for example, there is no way to understand either how emotions intend their objects or how their objects define emotions.[19] In *The Passions,* I counter this "components" view by developing a (quasi-Heideggerian) notion of what I call "surreality," a theory of intentional structures, given conceptual shape by judgments of a number of specifiable types which I there describe in detail. In "Emotions and Choice," the nature of these intentional structures is not discussed, and so my attack on the "components" view and the analysis of intentionality remain dangerously incomplete.

EMOTIONS ARE JUDGMENTS

This is the key slogan of my entire campaign, but as a slogan, it should not be taken as a theory as such. I repeatedly insist that emotions *essentially* involve desires, expectations, purposes, and attitudes. Emotions are motivated by desires, sometimes distinguished by desires, and in virtually every case some desire is essential to an emotion. But I take this claim to be so widely accepted— even by Descartes, to whom I am most vehemently opposed[20]—that I saw little point in defending it. But it certainly does not follow that by so "opening up" my analysis beyond the "emotions are judgments" slogan I am thereby bound to include also dispositions to behave and feelings and all sorts of things.[21] It is the heart of my argument that "feelings" and physiology and, with qualifications, dispositions to behave, do *not* play an essential role in the constitution of emotions and cannot be used in even the most rudimentary account of the definitive properties of either emotions in general or particular emotions. My central claim is that emotions are defined primarily by their constitutive judgments, given structure by judgments, distinguished as particular emotions (anger, love, envy, etc.) as judgments,[22] and related to other beliefs, judgments, and our knowledge of the world, in a "formal" way, through judgments. No alternative theory, it seems to me, has ever made the slightest progress in explaining the central features of emotion, as opposed to their red-in-the-face and visceral cramp symptomatology.

We often think of "making a judgment" as a distinctively deliberate act; to counter this, I argued in "Emotions and Choice" that emotional judgments are essentially nonreflective and prior to deliberation. This was, however, an overreaction, and in *The Passions* I discussed several examples of deliberate emotions, for example, making oneself angry. In the book I also stress the affinities between my notion of judgment and Kant's concept of "constitutive judgment," but what is "constituted" in emotions is not knowledge but meanings. In my more recent work, I prefer to talk more in terms of emotions setting up "scenarios," within which our experiences and our actions are endowed with personal meaning. Each emotion, so characterized, is a specifiable set of judgments constituting a specific scenario. Anger, for example, is to be analyzed in terms of a quasi-courtroom scenario, in which one takes the role of judge, jury, prosecuting attorney and, on occasion, executioner. ("I'll be judge, I'll be jury, said cunning old fury." —Lewis Carroll, *Alice in Wonderland*.) The object of anger is the accused, the crime is an offense,[23] and the overall scenario is one of judgmental self-righteousness. (One might add that the court is almost of the kangaroo variety, with self-esteem taking clear priority over justice.) The scenario helps to explain, among other matters, the tendency to self-righteousness in anger, which in turn can be used to explain the motivation of petty anger and "bad tempers" and provide, in general, the beginning of a functional account of emotions. In the context of "Emotions and Choice," the scenario analysis provides a far more complete portrait of emotional experience than the bald claim, "emotions are judgments."

With these additions, it is possible to map out a refutation of the most common objection to my theory, which is that it is possible to make a judgment, the same judgment that I claim to be constitutive of an emotion, and not have that emotion. If that is true, then emotions cannot be judgments.[24] But an emotion is never a single judgment but a system of judgments, and although one might well make one or several judgments of the system without having the emotion, my claim is that one cannot make *all* of them and not have the emotion. To make all essential judgments is to create the relevant scenario and take one's part in it. Of course, one might simply act *as if* one were taking part, but the distinction between pretending and really taking part is none too clear, as I argued in "Emotions and Choice," and insofar as one is merely acting, the set of judgments, and thus the scenario, cannot possibly be completed. (This example shows why it is so important that the scenario be understood as a way of experiencing a situation and not as the situation itself—as it might be described by others, for example.) Finally, to have an emotion requires not only a specifiable set of judgments but certain desires as well. One might make a judgment—or even much of a set of judgments[25]—in an impersonal and uninvolved way, without caring one way or the other. But an emotional (set of) judgment(s) is necessarily personal and involved. Compare "What he said to me was offensive" (but I don't care what he thinks) and "He offended me!" Only the latter is constitutive of anger. (The first is a judgment about the perlocutionary act potential of a certain utterance; the latter is, in part, a judgment about my own self-esteem.)

EMOTIONS AND CHOICE

My most cavalier move in "Emotions and Choice" was my easy inference from "emotions are judgments" to the idea that we "choose" them. The suppressed sequence of moves was something like this: emotions are judgments and we "make" judgments; ergo emotions are activities, and activities are "doings"; "doings" are voluntary and what is voluntary is chosen. So, emotions are chosen. I agree with my critics that this is much too glib, much of it unsound, and I tried to weaken the argument accordingly in the book. I do insist, even in the essay, that emotions, like many activities, cannot "simply" be done. (One cannot "simply" decide to love someone.) But this is not enough.[26] I still insist that emotions, as judgments, are a species of activity, and thus to be included on the "active" side of the all-too-simple "active—passive" disjunction according to which we evaluate most human affairs. This means too that emotions fall into the realm of responsibility, so that it always makes sense, at least (as it does not, for example, for headaches, heart attacks, and hormones) to praise or blame a person, not just for contributing to the situation that caused the emotion but, in some sense to be worked out, for having the emotion itself, as one blames a person for bigotry, for example, or praises them for their courage. What I now question is the once seemingly innocuous move from "activities" to "doings," and I reject the subsequent moves to "voluntary" then to "chosen." Perception, for example, is an activity: I am not sure that it is something "done," and (as opposed to an activity such as "looking for") I am sure that it makes little sense to ask whether perceiving something is voluntary, much less a matter of choice. Intractable emotions[27] must be treated similarly; they are still matters of judgment, and as such activities and matters of responsibility. But they are surely neither voluntary nor chosen. My account in *The Passions* is in terms of emotional "investments," the "cost" of giving up certain emotions.[28] But what this shows is that the whole question of choice and voluntariness, outside of the overworked realm of intentional action, has yet to be pursued successfully.

In the essay, and even in the book, I say far too little about the sociocultural determinants of emotions, the extent to which the essential sets of judgments and desires are shared, restricted, suppressed, or encouraged within a given society. Accordingly, some of my most recent work has been more anthropological apprenticeship than philosophical analysis.[29] From this, I want to add to my thesis the sense in which emotions are cultivated responses, within whose limits one is responsible even if they were learned in childhood and so seem entirely "natural." This certainly places harsh restrictions on my original "choice" thesis, but I still take the notion of responsibility as inescapably central.

EMOTIONS ARE PURPOSIVE

In "Emotions and Choice," I insist that emotions can be accounted for in terms of "in order to" type explanations. This is suggested by the fact that desires are part of emotions. What I do not do in that essay, but attempt in the book, is to provide an overall theory about the function of emotions. In a phrase, it is the *maximization of self-esteem*.[30] The concept of self-esteem serves two very different purposes in my theory: First, it is part of my characterization of emotions as judgments that they be personally involved judgments, and this can be further elaborated in terms of self-esteem. Second, I offer an empirical hypothesis about the motivation of emotions—emotions serve self-esteem. This is not the place to pursue these claims, since they play a relatively negligible role in "Emotions and Choice." But it is necessary to point out that, (1) to say that emotions have a certain purpose or function does not require that there always be an intention as such. Often, even usually, emotions do include such (implicit) intentions; sometimes they clearly don't. (2) To say that the purpose of emotions is to maximize self-esteem is not to say that they always—or even usually—succeed in this. Resentment and spite, for example, can be easily argued to be desperate attempts at self-esteem, but it can also be argued that they usually fail. (3) Emotions are ready candidates for self-deception, and sometimes the goal of an emotional strategy is exactly the opposite of what it seems to be. Resentment, guilt and depression (a mood) are examples. (4) There are examples that raise difficulties for the claim, for example, grief.[31] A man who loses his son in an accident does not grieve to increase his self-esteem to be sure, but, the difference between an appropriate sense of loss and the emotion of grief may be considerable, and it is in this difference that self-esteem plays a weighty motivational role. After a certain point, grief becomes feeling sorry for oneself, and here the strategy for self-esteem becomes evident.

Much more could be added, but let me just present my minimal claim: every emotion is at least a candidate for a purposive account (which can't even be made sense of on the traditional theories). It always makes sense to ask "what is motivating that emotion?" and, at least usually, part of the answer will involve an appeal to self-esteem.

My preliminary example in part two of "Emotions and Choice" involves a serious error. In the book, I make a point of distinguishing purposive explanations of the *expression* of emotion (e.g., using angry behavior to intimidate someone) and purposive explanations of the emotion itself (e.g., to maximize self-esteem through the self-righteousness of anger). In my example of marital politics in the essay, I conflate the two.

EMOTIONS ARE RATIONAL

Emotions require rationality (the ability to manipulate concepts) but they may be said to be rational or *ir*rational (opposed to *non*-rational) in a second sense, according to whether they succeed or fail to satisfy certain purposes or functions. In the essay, I discuss only the coherence, consistency and completeness of the evidence in the making of emotional judgments. There are also questions about the *warrant* to making certain claims (e.g., a "right" to something in jealousy,[32] or whether something is or is not *worth* getting angry about). What must be added are questions about the maximization of self-esteem: resentment and spite are usually irrational because they fail to maximize self-esteem. Moral indignation, however, succeeds rather well. But one must also add the "external" consideration of social utility; hatred and love might equally raise self-esteem, but the social cost of hatred is considerable—divisive and destructive. Any account of the rationality of emotions must take into account these features as well as others,[33] and by the time we have done this, we will have in effect developed a full-scale moral theory and done a good deal of philosophical anthropology as well.

NOTES

1. Perhaps we should distinguish getting into an emotional state and being in one (e.g., getting angry vs. being angry). But nothing turns on this, for being in a state as well as getting into a state, like God's maintenance of the Universe as well as his creation of it, requires devoted activity. Accordingly, I shall be arguing both that we choose an emotion and that we continuously choose our emotions. There is no need to separate these arguments.

2. I take this to be definitive of the difference between "emotion" and "feeling" as I am using those terms here. Emotions are intentional; feelings are not. I do not deny that the everyday use of "feeling" is broader than this and includes both of these concepts. I find this ambiguity less objectionable than others surrounding "sensation" and like terms.

3. There is nothing in our analysis which is not compatible with an all-embracing causal theory. We might agree with writers like A. I. Goldman, who argues that intentional characterizations of actions (in terms of "reasons") also function in causal explanations of a Hempelian variety. I do not wish to argue a similar thesis regarding emotions here, but I want to be careful not to preclude any such theory. Similarly, nothing I have said here bears on the so-called "free will problem"; I want to show that emotions should be viewed in the same categories as actions, whether or not there are further arguments that might lead us to conclude that not even actions are chosen freely.

4. Freud has a curious way of defending this thesis, which is surely central to much of his theory. Because he attempted to maintain a thesis of the intentionality of the "affects" within a strictly causal model, he obscured the distinction between object and cause. Without crucifying Freud on this point, as Peters, MacIntyre and others have attempted to do, it is important to see that Freud typically confuses first person and third person accounts, and the concept of the "unconscious" as an "assumption" (e.g., see the essay "The Unconscious," *Collected Papers,* Vol. VI) often depends upon the failure of the subject to be capable of applying third person ascriptions—notably, ascriptions of the cause as opposed to the object of an emo-

tion—to himself. Without in the least detracting from Freud's overall conception of the unconscious, we must insist that the subject is never logically privileged with respect to the causes of his emotions, but that he does have some such authority (without infallible authority) with respect to what he is "affected about."

5. Though perhaps I can simply *express* such a judgment.

6. Aristotle, *Rhetoric,* Book II, 1378 ff. See also W. W. Fortenbaugh, *Aristotle on Emotion* (London: Duckworth, 1975), chaps. 1, 4. Gorgias, *Hel.* 10, 14.

7. Aristotle, *Rhetoric,* 1378a30-32.

8. Ibid., 1378a33-34.

9. *De Ira,* esp. Vol. II (Oxford: Loeb Classical Library). Seneca argues that the "cause" of emotion is beyond our power, but whether a cause affects us is not.

10. See Fortenbaugh, *Aristotle on Emotion,* pp. 63 ff.

11. R. Solomon, *The Passions* (New York: Doubleday-Anchor, 1976).

12. Here I still follow E. Bedford, "Emotions," *Proceedings of the Aristotelean Society* 57 (1956-57), 281-304. Where we differ is his (too) strong emphasis on the behavioral expression of emotion.

13. For example, Robert Gordon, "The Aboutness of Emotions," *American Philosophical Quarterly,* 11, 1 (January 1974), 27-36. J. R. S. Wilson, *Emotion and Object* (Cambridge: Cambridge University Press, 1974) and Donald Davidson, "Hume's Cognitive Theory of Pride," *Journal of Philosophy,* LXIII, 19 (November 4, 1976), 744-757.

14. A. Kenny, *Action, Emotion and Will* (London: Routledge and Kegan Paul, 1963).

15. *Philebus* and *Topics* (150b27 f.). See Fortenbaugh, *Aristotle on Emotion,* p. 11.

16. Wilson, *Emotion and Object,* rightly accuses Kenny of confusing properties of the emotions themselves here with properties of their description (chap. 3, sect. iii).

17. Gordon, "The Aboutness of Emotions," p. 27.

18. Solomon, *Passions,* chap. 2.

19. I have defended this cryptic suggestion in detail in my forthcoming "Emotions' Mysterious Objects," *Journal for the Theory of Social Behavior* (1979).

20. Descartes, "The Passions of the Soul" Part First, Article XL and ff. in Haldane and Ross, *The Philosophical Works of Descartes* (Cambridge: Cambridge University Press, 1911).

21. Frithjof Bergmann, review of *The Passions* in *Journal of Philosophy,* LXXV, 5 (May 1978), 208, who insists I either defend *just* my slogan or nothing.

22. Aristotle does this too, using the idea of the efficient causes of different emotions, e.g., *Rhetoric,* 1382a3-7 ff.

23. Ibid., 1378a30-32. Cf. Hume on pride in his *Treatise on Human Nature,* ed. L. A. Selby-Bigge (Oxford: Oxford University Press, 1951), Book II, "Of the Passions," esp. p. 277 f.

24. E.g., Bergmann, review of *The Passions,* p. 204 f.

25. Some of the judgments constitutive of an emotion imply their own personal concerns and desires, for example, judgments of praise and blame, inferiority, superiority, trust, intimacy, and power.

26. See Amélie Rorty, "Explaining Emotions," this volume.

27. See ibid. Also Bergmann, review of *The Passions.*

28. Solomon, *The Passions,* chap. 9, esp. sect. 1.

29. "Emotions and Anthropology," *Inquiry* (forthcoming, 1978).

30. Solomon, *Passions,* chap. 9, esp. sect. 4, and "The Rationality of Emotions," *Southwestern Journal of Philosophy,* Vol. VIII, no. 2 (December 1977).

31. Bergmann, review of *The Passions,* p. 202.

32. The idea that jealousy involves "rights" has been disputed, notably, by Jerome Neu (this volume, Chap. XVIII). But the difference between being merely "hurt" or disappointed, on the one hand, and being jealous, on the other, seems to be a kind of vindictiveness and indignation ("That bastard!") which requires moral claims, not just sense of loss.

33. See Rorty, "Explaining Emotions."

XI

SELF-DECEPTIVE EMOTIONS*

RONALD DE SOUSA

That emotions attend self-deception is a commonplace. Vanity, grief, resentment, apprehension, all induce us to connive in the clouding of our vision. But in recent discussions of self-deception most philosophers' attention has gone to the puzzles it generates for the notion of belief, with emotions confined to a causal or motivational role. That terrain is well trod, and I shall not go over it again.[1] I wish to focus here instead on emotions themselves, and explore ways in which they can be intrinsically self-deceptive.

Deception normally involves cognition. The task I set myself therefore requires that "deception" be extended to a noncognitive domain, or that we think of the emotions themselves as cognitive. My strategy will be to do both, seeking rapprochement from both ends.

Erving Goffman has pointed out that a rough distinction may be made among forms of deception. One kind consists in the deliberate distortion of information that one (explicitly and intentionally) *"gives":* this is lying or "deceit." The other deals with information that one "gives off":

> A wide range of action that others can treat as symptomatic of the actor, the expectation being that the action was performed for reasons other than the information conveyed in this way.[2]

Deliberate misinformation by means of this type of communication is pretending or "feigning." Expressions of emotion are typically treated as "given off." So it may be fruitful to look for a kind of self-deception that bears the same relation to *feigning,* as self-deceived belief bears to *deceit:* a kind where the self-deceiver is taken in not by their own lie, but by their own pretense. This will be one approach I shall take. It would lead to nothing very novel, however, if pretending to oneself resulted merely in having false beliefs. We need to move also from the other side: to show that emotions can admit of an interesting range of error without reducing to mistaken beliefs. The delimitation of such a range requires that we make sense of the idea that emotions have a semantics of their own. This, then, is my first task.

SEMANTICS FOR EMOTIONS

In an excellent and little known paper, C. D. Broad suggested that emotions might be construed as cognitions. He distinguished a "cognitive" from an "affective" aspect of emotion. The latter he called "emotional tone":

> To be fearing a snake, e.g., is to be cognizing something—correctly or incorrectly—as a snake, and for that cognition to be toned with fearfulness. In general, to be fearing X is to be cognizing X fearingly; to be admiring X is to be cognizing X admiringly, and so on.[3]

This scheme gives rise to one range of possible errors which Broad calls "misplaced emotions." These are "felt towards an object which is believed to exist but does not really do so, or . . . in respect of attributes which do not really belong to it" (291). Broad also distinguishes a category of error that concerns one's attribution of motives for an emotion (he thinks he's angry because . . . but the *real* reason is . . .) (289). Errors in both these classes are straightforwardly cognitive, and can directly affect beliefs whether involved in emotion or not. There can be failure of reference to the putative topic of belief, and illusions about the grounding of beliefs. To what differentiates emotions from other "cognitions," however, Broad does not grant cognitive status. He points out that the affective aspect of emotions can be assessed for appropriateness or "fittingness" (in degree or in kind):

> it is appropriate to cognize what one takes to be a threatening object with some degree of *fear*. It is inappropriate to cognize what one takes to be a fellow man *in undeserved pain or distress* with *satisfaction* or with *amusement*. [293]

But while he finds these notions "plainly of the utmost importance to ethics and to esthetics," he thinks they "still await an adequate analysis" (293).

In Broad's terms, my proposal can be simply stated: it is to bring the "affective aspect" into the ambit of cognitive appraisal. I shall define the unique cognitive role of emotions in terms of appropriateness. My starting point will be the suggestion that *appropriateness is the truth of emotions.*[4]

This idea will be met with an immediate objection: Appropriateness is not an *objective* matter in the way truth must be. Its ascription depends on the subject's temperament, situation ("how much they've had to go through"), as evaluated according to the ascriber's sympathy, experience, and prejudice. So there can be no such *fact* as the appropriateness or inappropriateness of an emotion.[5]

I shall charge forth without meeting this objection directly, though I aim to be undercutting it in the rest of this paper. It is enough for the moment to point out that a working semantics can proceed on the basis of a provisional, "as if," ontology. Disputes about appropriateness are *treated* as if they were genuine disagreements, however hard they may be to settle. This presupposes that there are criteria of appropriateness; we can take this presupposition at face value without requiring these criteria to be grounded in nonrelative facts or even always to be clearly decidable. What we do need is a sketch of the "meaning" or "content" of emotions: that which in a given situation determines their appropriateness, as sense determines reference or truth. One way to tackle this is to ask: How are emotions learned, and how do they acquire a content?

In answering this question, I shall take for granted some fundamental claims of psychoanalysis and developmental psychology. Obviously I cannot defend them here. I assume that even skeptics might agree that these claims are widely enough accepted, to make an exploration of some philosophical implications worthwhile.

This, then, is the story. Our emotional repertoire is learned in the context of what I shall call *paradigm scenarios,* many of which are played out in infancy. In the context of such a scenario, a child's instinctive responses to certain stimuli become a part—indeed sometimes acquire the name—of an emotion. In simple cases the instinctive response (smiling, crying) becomes an *expression* of emotion (joy, sadness, or rage): but it does so only in the context of the scenario. Otherwise, it lacks the property of being embedded in the complex structure characteristic of emotions. This structure is variable for different emotions; but typically it involves a *target* (such as the person I am angry at), a (more or less propositional) *object* or ostensible factual focus (such as what I am angry at the target for doing), a characteristic *expression* (an angry tone of voice, etc.), and a *formal object* (the property that the situation must have in common with the paradigm scenario, if the emotion is to be appropriate). All these structural features are learned at the same school, in the complex paradigm scenario. [6]

The semantics this story suggests are relatively simple: we learn our repertoire of emotions, much as we learn at least some of our verbal repertoire—our vocabulary of concrete predicates—by ostensive definition. In the paradigm situation, an emotion is appropriate "by definition." Once learned, it is correctly "applied," like a learned predicate, to situations that are relevantly similar to the paradigm scenario in which it originates.

This preliminary sketch of the semantics of emotion can do much to explain the difficulties involved in trying to articulate criteria of appropriateness. In the remainder of this paper, I shall explore three sources of emotional fallibility offering possibilities of self-deception. The first is "self-feigning": a consequence of our capacity for expression. The second is a special case of the first, and springs from some complications in the relation between the learning scenario and later "applications" of the emotion. And the third arises from the influence on the content of particular emotions of what I shall call the *ideology* of emotions: what we learn, in the process of being socialized, *about* (an) emotion: its moral and social significance, its place in the hierarchy of human states and capacities.

SELF-FEIGNING

An essential outcome of emotional learning is the potential for nonverbal communication. [7] Our expressive repertoire, like any other device of communication, can be used deceptively. [8] There is but a short step from here to the possibility of self-deception as

being fooled by one's own pretense, or "self-feigning." A reconstruction of the James-Lange theory of emotions will enable us to
take that step.

That theory, which identified emotion with the perception of a
bodily state caused by an evoking situation, is almost universally
held to have been refuted.[9] The central argument against it is that
identical physico-chemical stimuli produce divergent emotions
depending on the situational and epistemic context. But if we reinterpret the bodily changes involved to include those that amount to,
or normally determine, the *expressive* motor events associated with
the emotion, we can say that *what we feel* in an emotion state *is the
expressive set of our body.* This is not to say that what we feel is all
there is to an emotion: for that would leave out the semantic aspect
I have been explicating: an emotion means a formal object, that is,
a property characteristic of a paradigm scenario, and ascribes it to
an object. It does imply, with common sense and against prevalent
philosophical doctrine, that we can commonly *identify* our emotions *by* what we feel. Against this version of James-Lange the
standard objections have no force. Now in cases where the expressive set is deceptive, and where the deception is not consciously
acted out, it is not hard to see how one could take one's own expressive state for the corresponding emotion.[10] (This is what is being
imputed when someone is accused of histrionics.) On this account,
we can see how self-feigning is not merely a matter of acquiring
false beliefs about one's own emotions. Rather it *induces* an emotion, which is itself erroneous in its ascription of a characteristic
property to an object. We have then a possible mechanism for emotional self-deception of the type advertised above. But what are the
occasions of its manifestation? A partial answer to this question
will lead to a second form of fallibility.

TRANSFERENCE AND DETACHABILITY

Sometimes a situation or target evokes an expressive response that
is not appropriate to it as a whole, but merely triggered by some
partial aspect. The response has been associated with a paradigm
scenario, defining an emotion which is then *read into* the present

situation. This is what psychoanalysts call *transference*. The classic case of transference, of course, takes place in the analytic situation, where the patient characteristically "falls in love" with the doctor regardless of the latter's lovableness. According to Freud, "the patient does not remember anything of what he has forgotten and repressed, but acts it out . . . and in the end we understand that this is his way of remembering."[11] In other words, transference is not merely mechanical repetition triggered by a stimulus, but has a semantic structure of its own, akin to that of memory. Its defining feature is that it lacks *detachability*—in a sense now to be explained —from the paradigm scenario.

The use of a predicate can be said to be detachable from its learning context in this sense. Suppose I learn a color word from a chart. Once learned, the word no longer refers to the color chart, but to the color. The learning situation does not remain incrusted in the meaning of "red," though for some time it may be more or less vividly remembered and affect the *connotation*—as opposed to the Fregean sense—of the word. This contrasts with the semantic structure characteristic of *symbols*, typified by religious rites and the objects used in them. The worship evoked in the faithful *by* the bread and wine are directed *at* the body and blood of Christ. The sense of the ritual depends on an essential reference to the original ceremony. For the more thorough sects, indeed, the bond of symbolization is strengthened into identity by the power of transubstantiation: the bread *is* the body. So for the patient: (unconsciously) the doctor *is* the parent. The difference is that the average neurotic cannot endorse the identification once its role is brought to full consciousness, and seeks to be cured of rather than sustained in that identification. Detachability seems to emerge as a *norm* for the semantics of emotion, an ideal often thwarted by our tendency to symbolic interpretation.

This account treats symbol-semantics as an undesirable affection of emotions. But perhaps this is only therapeutic prejudice, which should not be taken for granted. The neurotic and the religious do not have a monopoly on transference. As Freud put it, transference

consists of new editions of old traits and . . . repeats infantile reactions. But this is the essential character of every state of being in love. There is no such state which does not reproduce infantile prototypes. [*TL* 168]

The origin of emotions in paradigm scenarios implies the possibility of extending that observation to emotions other than love. Two questions can then be raised: first, whether transference emotions are *authentic*—whether they are the emotions they advertise themselves to be—and second, whether their real object and target are their ostensible ones.

It is tempting, for the sake of simplicity, to take a hard line on both: emotions are always what they seem, and their objects are always the ostensible ones. And if this means that some emotions are inappropriate, then things are just as we know them.

With respect to objects, the story I have told is compatible with this line, so long as we remember that in some cases the *content* of the emotion must be interpreted in terms of a reference to an object or target other than the ostensible one. This is preferable to talking of the paradigm as the "real object," for it allows judgments of degree in respect of the relative role of the present and the past in shaping present content. These are degrees of pathology or self-feigning, in which trouble with the semantical relation to the *target/object* is reassigned to the *content* or character of the emotion.[12]

In respect of content, the possibility of reinterpretation is not similarly dispensable. Freud sometimes appears to think otherwise: "We have no right to dispute," he says, that transference love "has the character of 'genuine' love." But his reason is perplexing: "lacking to a high degree...a regard for reality,...(being) less sensible, less concerned about consequences and more blind in its valuations...constitute precisely what is essential about being in love" (*TL* 168-9). But "less" than what? Freud seems to change thought in the middle of the sentence: he starts out to say that one would expect normal love to be more sensible than neurotic love, but switches to thinking all love equally crazy. If this is so, then the "genuineness" even of normal emotions is bought at the price of systematic inappropriateness—an unwelcome implausibility. Besides, Freud also thinks that emotions, like actions, can be reinterpreted as something other than they seem: transference love is itself sometimes a disguise for resistance (since it can function to distract the patient from the analytic task) (*DT* 101 ff.).[13] And common sense also avails itself of this possibility of reinterpretation.

What are the criteria that guide such reinterpretation? The origin of emotions in paradigm scenarios implies that each person's emotional "dialect" will be subtly different. For the content of emotions for which two people have the same name will depend on their individual temperaments and the specific details of their learning experience. When we interpret one another's emotions, therefore, we have a Whorfian problem of translation: our "dialects" determine different experiences. So when can we place credence in an interpretation?

The problem is solved in much the same way by psychoanalysis and by common sense. But the solution leads to further problems.

Freud's direct answer is confusing, as we have seen. But we can construct an answer on his behalf, by looking at his strategy in a related domain. He thought of the "plasticity of instinct" as an essential and pervasive characteristic of the human psyche, manifested in normal development, involving *sublimation,* and also in *perversions.* What is the difference between them? Ultimately they are sorted out on evaluative grounds: sublimations have redeeming social value, perversions are antisocial or by consensus found aesthetically repellent.[14]

Much the same is true of commonsense judgments of authenticity and appropriateness. We are often content to infer what emotion someone *must* be having from our knowledge of the situation in which they find themselves. Far from granting any privileged access to the subject in this area, if there is discrepancy between the conclusion of such an inference and the subject's declaration, this last is more commonly taken to be self-deceived. Allowances are made for variabilities of individual temperament, reactivity, style, upbringing, and so forth; but ultimately the barrier between the neurotic, intrinsically erroneous emotion and the normal one is drawn along *conventional* lines. And this is—up to a point—as it should be: for intuitively the difference between mere transference and authentic emotion is in whether the ostensible object is actually, in its present relation to the subject, fitting for the emotion that it occasions. Otherwise it is merely acting as a trigger for something to which it is only accidentally connected. Nevertheless, the conventional source of assessments of emotion is also the source of an important category of self-deception in emotions. It will be my main concern in the rest of this paper.

THE IDEOLOGY OF EMOTIONS:
TWO EXAMPLES FROM THE NATURAL HISTORY OF SEXISM

Among the criteria that socialized consensus lays down are beliefs and attitudes *about* emotions, both in general[15] and regarding particular emotions. I shall argue that these attitudes at the *metalevel* have an effect on the *content* of particular emotions, thus offering more opportunities for emotional error. We can think of this phenomenon on the model of the contamination of the content of beliefs by higher-order methodological principles. But there are differences as well as analogies, which I have no space to pursue.

We have seen how different paradigm scenarios can generate subtly different repertoires of emotion. In some cases this is systematized by the process of socialization to differentiate whole social groups. Gender socialization, the deepest level of sexism, provides an example whose importance transcends philosophical illustration. The most vivid case can be made about such general sentiments as *love*.[16] But love, whose characterization involves whole complexes of particular feelings, expectations, long term patterns of intercourse, and social sanctions, while offering all the wider scope for the promotion of sexual inequality, is arguably too complex to be called "an emotion." For this reason, though I shall have a little to say about it in the next section, I shall consider two more specific emotions: *anger* and *jealousy.*

The paradigm scenarios for anger differ between men and women in respect both of its expression and its criteria of appropriateness. An angry man is a manly man, but an angry woman is a "fury" or a "bitch." This is necessarily reflected *in the quality of the emotion itself:* a man will experience an episode of anger characteristically as indignation, a woman as something less moralistic, more like guilt-laden frustration. Insofar as the conception of gender stereotypes that underlies these differences is purely conventional mystification, the emotions that embody them are paradigms of self-deceptive ones. But they illustrate the fact that in what I have been calling self-deceived emotions the self mostly connives rather than originates. We are responsible only to the extent that we are generally motivated to conform to the social and gender roles assigned to us, and that we allow ourselves to be taken in by the feigning that this necessarily requires.

The case of jealousy is more complicated,[17] but exemplifies the same points. A man's jealousy is traditionally an assertion of his property rights: and something of that survives in the emotional tone of jealousy as felt by many contemporary men. A woman's, on the other hand, "is regarded as nearly equivalent to shrewishness, fishwifery" (Farber, 182). It is not taken as seriously (there is no feminine of "cuckold"). Underlying the surface ideology, according to Dinnerstein's persuasive speculations, is the fact that "the symbolic shock value of the other's physical infidelity is far less absolute for her than for him." In the original scenarios in which mother-raised men and mother-raised women have learned both their sense of self and the emotions provoked when it is threatened, girls are able to identify with their mothers more than boys. Consequently a woman is likely to feel "that she carries within herself a source of the magic early parental richness" (42). By contrast, the man's attitude stems "from the mother-raised boy's sense that the original, most primitive source of life will always lie outside himself, that to be sure of reliable access to it he must have exclusive access to a woman" (43). Not only is the very experience of jealousy for men and women tinged with the different consequences of this mystification but the attempt to eliminate jealousy is also fraught with divergent meanings. For a man, to overcome jealousy is to overcome possessiveness. But for a woman, the effort described in the very same terms may simply play into the possessiveness of the male and thus reinforce the sexist mystification. This discrepancy adds yet another level of self-deception, namely that which results from the assumption, fostered by the homonymy of "jealousy," that the task of achieving greater rationality of emotions is the same task for both. Hence the complex emotions that may be tied to an expectation of reciprocity in the elimination of jealousy may once again be self-deceived.

THE DIALECTIC OF FUNGIBILITY

Earlier I suggested that detachability from paradigm situations seems to be an ideal of rational emotions. What this amounts to is that the targets of emotions ought to become *fungible*[19] in the manner of the referents of ordinary predicates. In law, an object is said to be fungible if it belongs to an equivalence class any member of which can substitute for any other in the fulfillment of a contract. Money is the paradigm fungible: individual dollar bills are not material to a debt. On the other hand if you lend me a vase and I return another, I have not strictly paid my debt: though I have perhaps offered an adequate *substitute*. In terms of our earlier discussion, it seems that in the economy of emotions and their objects a transference emotion is a mere substitute; fungibility is an achievement.

Yet at a certain stage and for certain emotions it is nonfungibility that has to be learned. This is the case for attachment emotions. The differentiations of which an infant is capable are qualitative ones, and it is a fact about early psychosexual development, in need of explanation, that general desires for fungible satisfactions become focused on a particular person or persons. There is then a further developmental question about how it is possible to transfer (or replace) this affection, focused on a parent, onto a new and equally nonfungible object. That the new object—ideally the Spouse—be nonfungible is part of the ideology of love in most culture:[18] "Love is not love which alters when it alteration finds." The ideology of love is therefore directly contrary to the general desirability of emotional fungibility. For the properties on which human attachment is based are not qualitative, but *historical*. Must we conclude that attachment emotions are not emotions at all? Perhaps. But we could say instead that they are always transference emotions in a sense different from the one Freud intended: their ideology requires that we generalize not from a fungible scenario, but from an individual *target* as the essential component of a succession of constitutive scenarios. All this generates two sorts of self-deceptive possibilities. One is that a desire for fungible sexual satisfaction, because it advertises itself as "love," should be *experienced* as nonfungible ("I *feel* that I love you forever"). The other is its converse: an ideology constructed out of the desire to avoid the dangers of the former ideology, which denies the need for nonfungible attachment, or even their possibility. But if psychoanalysts are right about the connections between the capacity for attachment and other aspects of human fulfillment, then the zipless fuck[20] may also be delusive as an alternative ideology of love—and delusive in the very same ideologically conditioned way.

I must now face two problems. The first is terminological. Admitting that the phenomena I have described exist, why call them *self*-deception? Are they not rather a form of mystification in which the individual is merely the victim of a socialized ideology? No. For the ideology that infects the content of an emotion can do so only if it has been internalized. It comes from outside myself, to be sure—but so does much of what I call "myself." To attack it requires "consciousness raising," in the sense in which that term is restricted to the bringing into consciousness of facts *about myself* which then come up for endorsement as avowed parts of my identity.

THE PHONY PARADOX

But this answer suggests a graver problem. I have spoken as if consciousness-raising provided an avenue of escape from emotional self-deception. Yet in my account both appropriate emotions and self-deceptive ones have their origin in paradigm scenarios. Some forms of self-deception seem to lodge in the very semantic structure of emotion, or in an ideology that has the same source whether it is constructive or distorting. How then can I leave conceptual room for the distinction between normal, authentic emotions, and hypocritical, self-feigning, or ideologically self-deceived emotions? A theory of emotions that finds them to be learned as social *roles* must still find a place for those that we denigrate as *mere role playing*. When, in short, is an emotion *phony*?

The full resolution of this puzzle would have to raise the whole question of the source and justification of therapeutic norms. I can only hope to point in the right direction, with three concluding remarks.

The access we have to our emotions, in the crucial aspects that have concerned us here, is more difficult than access to either will or belief. Of course, as has often been noted, a change of belief can radically alter an emotion. But this touches only Broad's "cognitive aspect," not that which I have claimed to constitute the idiosyncratic core of emotions as cognitions. We have no more direct access to the content of our emotions than we have voluntary control over the past situations in which we learned them. So one form of the phony is just this: the pretense of complete control, which can be made at various levels of awareness. We do have some indirect control, however: we can re-gestalt even those early paradigms. Sometimes we do it willy-nilly, forced by fresh vision to change our emotional attitudes to our past, now seeing what seemed domineering as protective, what seemed weak as gentle, what seemed principled as priggish.

In coaxing or badgering ourselves into such regestalting, we should note the crucial role and example of the *aesthetic* emotions. Aesthetic emotions are probably an exception to the general rule that paradigm scenarios go back to infancy. I am inclined to think that they constitute emergent emotional structures, which bear witness to our capacity for fresh emotional experience, built on, but not out of, preexisting emotional repertoires. Emotions more or less mechanically constructed in the latter way, out of ready-made atoms, are also phony. Fresh emotions are not necessarily unreflective: on the contrary, the emotions of the unreflective are threatened with cliché.

Some role there is for verbal argument in this process of examination. Consciousness raising largely consists in propositional description and redescription. But we must carefully note its limitations. Verbal argument is not a powerful tool at the level of the immediate content of emotions. It doesn't help much to repeat, like incantations, "this isn't really frightening," "there is really no reason to be angry/jealous/depressed/envious/sad." It helps a bit more to draw out the similarities with other paradigm scenarios, redescribing not the emotion but the situation: "he's being intimidating only because he's shy." But the level at which the effort of rational redescription is most useful is where I have argued much of the harm is done: at the meta-level of ideology. It is in searching out assumptions *about* our emotions; about their peremptoriness; about their "naturalness," about their transparency to the subject; about their identity or "biologically determined" differences between males and females—that we are most likely to transform and reform their experienced content and emerge from self-deception. In this sort of life examination, philosophical analysis merges with psychoanalysis, and each strengthens the other's promise of therapeutic virtue. In the realm of emotions, it is the simple life that is phony.

NOTES

*I am indebted for criticism to Paula Caplan, Hans Herzberger, Marcel Kinsbourne, Kathryn Morgan, and Wayne Sumner.

1. The best treatment to date remains that of Herbert Fingarette in *Self-Deception* (London: Routledge & Kegan Paul, 1969). It takes a more inclusive view than most. I have discussed it in *Inquiry*, 13 (1970), 308-321.

2. Erving Goffman, *The Presentation of Self in Everyday Life* (Garden City: Doubleday Anchor, 1959), p. 2.

3. C. D. Broad, "Emotion and Sentiment," in *Critical Essays in Moral Philosophy* (London: Allen & Unwin, 1971), reprinted from the *Journal of Aesthetics and Art Criticism* (1954). (Page references are to the former.) Attempts to view emotions as cognitive are not new. The most recent is R. C. Solomon's *The Passions* (Garden City: Doubleday Anchor, 1976), in which the cognitive view is intriguingly conjoined with the claim that emotions are subjective. The affinities of my own account are with Plato. See my "False Pleasures in the Philebus," forthcoming.

4. In the course of writing I found that this idea is discussed with considerable subtlety in Patricia Greenspan's "A Case of Mixed Feelings: Ambivalence and the "Logic" of Emotions," in essay 9 of this book. Greenspan's is the best discussion I know of the applicability of the notion of *consistency* to emotions.

5. In the search for objective correlates of emotions, language helps us more with some than others. Some gerundive constructions formed from the names of emotions appear to connote passivity in the subject (depressing, boring); others, cognates of a different sort, apparently imply a passive target (lovable, fearsome, hateful); some objects are referred to by the same word as the subject (indifferent, hopeful); some have clear correlates but no cognate words (unjust [indignant], unfaithful [jealous]). Yet others are referred to by terms awkwardly made up (anxiety-provoking, resentment-inspiring). The list is not exhaustive. There are lessons in it that would be worth pursuing.

6. The role of paradigm scenarios is explored further in "The Rationality of Emotions," essay V in this book.

7. Indeed, we are free to speculate that this may be one important biological *function* of emotion. We unreflectively assume that our capacity to feel emotions precedes both our need and our capacity to express them. But the naturalness of some expressive behavior suggests that, on the contrary, emotions might have evolved for their communication value. On the cross-cultural constancy of some emotion expressions, see Carroll E. Izard, *Human Emotions* (New York and London: Plenum Press, 1977), p. 7.

8. This might be little more than the "injury feigning" of those birds that "pretend" to be wounded, dragging a wing along the ground, to distract an enemy from their brood. See E. O. Wilson, *Sociobiology* (Cambridge, Mass.: Harvard University Press, 1975), p. 122.

9. Especially by W. B. Cannon, "The James-Lange Theory of Emotions: a critical Examination and an Alternative Theory," *American Journal of Psychology*, 39 (1927), 106-124, and by S. Schachter and J. E. Singer, "Cognitive, Social, and Physiological Determinants of Emotional States," *Psychological Review*, 69 (5) (1962), 379-399. For a recent discussion tracing a "facial feedback" version of James's theory to Darwin, see Izard, *Human Emotions*, p. 57.

10. A related view is defended by Kendall L. Walton in "Fearing Fictions," *Journal of Philosophy* LXXV, 1 (January 1978), 5-27. Walton is discussing cases where suspension of disbelief is no real belief, but involves real emotion. But it is not exactly the same emotion as would be generated in the presence of belief. See below on the "ideology of emotions."

11. Sigmund Freud, "Remembering, Repeating, and Working Through," in the *Standard Edition of the Psychological Works, XII* (London: Hogarth Press, 1958). See also in the same volume "Transference Love" (*"TL"* below) and "The Dynamics of Transference" (*"DT"*).

12. In some therapeutic contexts, however, it may be important to insist on the emotion's *reference* to another object: an emotion might be repetitive and neurotic precisely because it has been *spuriously* detached from its target or object, and the first step might be to bring this into focus.

13. There is no implication that we have reached a rock bottom of interpretation. Resistance can itself be a form of transference.

14. This is greatly oversimplified. For an account of some of the complexities of Freud's actual account, see my "Norms and the Normal," in R. Wollheim, ed., *Freud: A Collection of Critical Essays* (Garden City: Doubleday Anchor, 1974). The strategy of supplementing a structural account with normative criteria is found in Aristotle's treatment of *akrasia*. He points out (*NE* VII-5) that if an act is noble, we don't call it *akrasia* even though it might strictly involve the same psychological mechanism. For by definition *"akrasia...deserves blame."*

15. See R. C. Solomon, *The Passions,* for an argument that the general ideology of emotions as "passions" has a distorting effect on our lives. But note that he uses the expression "ideology of emotion" in a sense unrelated to mine.

16. For a brilliant attack on "falling in love" as an inherently self-delusive emotion, based on sexist ideology, see Simone de Beauvoir "The Woman in Love," in *The Second Sex* (New York: Random House, Vintage, 1974), 712-743.

17. For a good discussion of jealousy by Jerry Neu, "Jealous Thoughts," see essay 18 of this book. But Neu does not consider the issue of sexism. Illuminating treatments of that issue are to be found in Leslie Farber, "On Jealousy," in *Lying, Despair, Jealousy, Envy, Sex, Suicide, Drugs, and the Good Life* (New York: Harper & Row, 1976), and especially in Dorothy Dinnerstein, *The Mermaid and the Minotaur* (New York: Harper & Row, 1976). My sketch draws on both of these, with references in the text.

18. But not in all: "Dr. Aubrey Richards, an anthropologist who lived among the Bemba of Northern Rhodesia in the 1930's, once related to a group of them an English folk tale about a young prince who climbed glass mountains, crossed chasms, and fought dragons, all to obtain the hand of a maiden he loved. The Bemba were plainly bewildered, but remained silent. Finally an old chief spoke up, voicing the feelings of all present in the simplest of questions: "Why not take another girl?" he asked." (Morton Hunt, *The Natural History of Love,* quoted by J. A. Lee, *The Colours of Love* [Toronto: New Press, 1973], p. 87.)

19. For an interesting and relevant (but independently generated) discussion of fungibility in love, see Jerome Neu, "Jealous Thoughts," in this volume.

20. The term is taken from Erica Jong, *Fear of Flying* (New York: Holt, Rinehart & Winston, 1973). But the concept was in the air.

The research for this paper was generously supported by a Canada Council Leave Fellowship, 1977-1978.

XII

ON PERSONS AND THEIR LIVES

RICHARD WOLLHEIM

I

Every person has a life of his own, his one and only life, and that life he leads. But some more so than others. It is to this thesis that I devote this essay. I devote it to the nature of this thesis, and to its explanation.

In saying that some persons lead their lives more than others, though each has only one life to lead, I do not mean—at any rate in the first instance—anything to do with the externals, with the outer circumstances, of life. I am not thinking of the way in which, in the leading of their lives, some are able to draw upon resources that for social, for physical, for historical, possibly for quite arbitrary reasons are unavailable to others. My point is different though not unrelated, and concerns the varying degrees to which people, persons, manage to give to their lives a pattern, an overallness, or the different measures of success that they have in making their lives of a piece.

And since it is not strained to recognize in such integration of a life, in the life of wholeness, something that, in many ages, for many cultures, has been in the nature of an ideal—a grace to be cultivated or a triumph to be won—the question arises: What is the connection between this ideal unity (call it that) and the formal unity that a life possesses in virtue of being one and the same life, a person's one (and only) life? How are the two halves of this essay related?

II

Let me start with a philosophical intuition, which must seem to have, at least superficially, a clear bearing upon this question.

The intuition is one which though perceived by earlier philosophers, has been fully exploited only in our day. It concerns the relationship between a concept and the criterion for identity under that concept, and it asserts the intimacy of that relationship. The intuition may be formulated in a number of different ways, but can be seen to best advantage when it is formulated regulatively or as indicating the way forward in much philosophical inquiry. For instance, thus: If you want to understand the concept f, then essential to your understanding it is grasping those conditions under which an individual a, which is f, and an individual b, which is also f, would be one and the same f, and, likewise, those conditions under which a and b would be two different fs. Or to take the relevant example: If you want to understand the concept *person*, then essential to your doing this is grasping the conditions under which, say, a boy who once stole apples from a particular orchard and some general who, years later, won renown on a famous battlefield would be one and the same person, and likewise, those conditions under which the boy and the general would be two different persons. That which tells us whether a and b, both f, are the very same f, that which tells us whether the boy and the general, both persons, are the very same person, are criteria of identity: every criterion of identity is relative to a particular concept—say, the concept f, the concept *person*—in that it fixes identity under that concept: and the philosophical intuition is that concept and criterion of identity relative to it are essentially linked. The former determines the latter.

This intuition can be formulated in different ways, and so can its rationale. But, however formulated, this rationale has something like this pattern: When someone applies a concept—say, the concept f, *apple, piece of gold, person*—to the world, what he does is he confronts the world and he segments or articulates it. "This" he says, and we may imagine him running a finger round the contours of some area he isolates, "This is an f"; and the world as it is presented to him divides into this f and the rest. And this act of segmentation, this process of articulating the world, appears complete in itself. There is nothing that could happen later, or so it seems, that would lead us to reverse this description of what was done within that moment. So it seems—but is this really so?

For now suppose that this same man again confronts the world. What should we expect of him? He should be able, of course, to pick out *f*s if there are such things around: for that is just the ability he has already—or so it seems—exercised. But also he should be able, in principle at any rate, to pick out (if there is such a thing) the *f*, the very same *f*, already at the earlier moment picked out. He should be able to recognize *f*s in general and to reidentify particular *f*s. And there aren't two distinct abilities here, but the first requires the second. We may be able to describe the two abilities separately, but if the man can't reidentify particular *f*s, then he can't recognize *f*s in general: nor, unless something special has happened in the meanwhile, could he ever. For, go back to the earlier moment. His finger moved, he isolated an area, he said "This is an *f*," certainly, but there are an indefinite number of varied types of thing, varying in solidity, consistency, duration, constancy of shape or stuff or color, any one of which might momentarily have conformed to what he isolated—might have occupied the contours all right, might have provided the filling all right—and then, they would have gone on their very different courses: and unless the man had some idea about which of these courses from present to future, from earlier moment to later, the thing that he allegedly picked out was in its nature disposed to follow, we have reason to revise this description of what he did. And this just shows that the act of segmentation, the process of articulating the world, could not be complete at a moment: it reaches into the future. So that if the man could neither find the original *f*, nor declare it lost or destroyed, nor knew how to set about either, then we must believe that his finger moved in vain to pick out a thing of one sort rather than of another: a thing, say that was *f*. The synchronic cut, which is what the application of a concept at a time is, necessitates a diachronic link, which is what the application of the relevant criterion of identity over time effects.[1]

III

I said that this intuition appears to have a clear bearing on the thesis of this essay, or how its two halves are related. We can now see what that is: It drives the two halves of the thesis apart.

For the first half of the thesis the intuition shows to be conceptual. And that is because what we think of as a person's life is just the projection over time, the diachronic expansion, of what we initially or at a time pick out as a person. So a life is the product of a criterion of identity and, more specifically, a person's life is the product of a criterion of personal identity. Accordingly, to know what a person's life is, what it is, for any particular person, for a life to be his, derives from our knowledge of the concept *person*. It is out of this knowledge that we come to know how, given the relevant historical information, we are to collect, to bundle up, those experiences, those thoughts, those feelings, those total momentary states of a person, and only those, which individually belong to and collectively constitute one and the same biography. And conversely, if we don't know how to set about finding out the beginning and the end of a person's life, and how to bridge the gap, then our understanding of what it is to be a person is, at best, incomplete.

If, however, this is accepted and, accordingly, the formal unity of a life is recognized to be a necessary property of that life, then a gap opens up between this formal unity and ideal unity. For, since ideal unity is not possessed by every life—some lives are not of a piece; they do not exhibit pattern or overallness—those that do possess it have it only as a contingent property. This difference seems enough to pull the two halves of my thesis apart beyond repair, but to this difference two more differences must be added. The formal unity of a life does not admit of degree but is absolute, whereas the ideal unity of a life clearly does admit of degree or is relative. And the ideal unity of a life is normative, but the formal unity of a life is not something that a life is superior for having. The formal unity of a life is something that it has, necessarily, absolutely, neutrally: ideal unity is something that a life has contingently, to some degree or other, and for better rather than for worse.

I said that this is how the philosophical intuition about concept and criterion of identity *appears* to bear upon this evening's thesis: or this is its *superficial* bearing and I stand by this. For though it is clearly true that formal unity and ideal unity are different unities, it doesn't follow that what it is for a life to be of a piece has nothing to do with what it is to satisfy the criterion of personal identity, nor, that it has nothing to do with the concept *person*. For there is the possibility that the two unities are related, and related so that one can be explained in terms of the other. I want to consider the proposition that what it is for a life to be of a piece is explicable in terms of what it is for a life to be self-identical, but this cannot be taken very far without making some substantive reference to the actual criterion of personal identity.

IV

Famously, notoriously, philosophers seeking for the criterion of personal identity have divided into two camps over where they should look. Some have sought it in the domain of the physical, generally equating personal identity with sameness of body; others have sought it in the domain of the mental, widely favoring the equation of personal identity with continuity of memory, or with what John Locke meant by "consciousness."

I would want to dissociate myself from this division if it is taken to coincide with a convincing theoretical dichotomy. If only for this reason: that anyone who tries to formulate an exclusively physical or an exclusively mental criterion of personal identity always seems, sooner or later, to cry need and to come running to the rival theorist for assistance. Take the physical theorist. He starts off by equating personal identity with sameness of body. But the body must be a living body. Further, the life that such a body leads cannot be any kind of life: it cannot be (standardly) the life of a vegetable or of a somnambulist. And the question is whether, before the physical theorist is through, he can avoid characterizing the requisite life as that which it takes a psychology to lead: by which time he is something of a mental theorist too.

So I think of the division between the two kinds of theorist as a disagreement where to start, and I incline to the mental theorist: and the crucial consideration here is that an account of personal identity is heavily constrained to do justice, as it goes along, to a person's sense of his own identity. If it is wrong to think, as some philosophers have done, that our identity derives from our sense of it, it is certainly a highly significant fact about our identity that it is such, or is so grounded, that, in all but the most extreme cases, it does give rise to a sense of itself.

Following this lead, then, I contend that somewhere at the core of personal identity—and it is beyond the confines of this essay how it fits into the total criterion or what more is needed to reach either necessity or sufficiency—is a rather abstract property called mental connectedness. If we wish to grasp the conditions under which *a,* a person, and *b,* a person, are one and the same person, we have to see just what it is for *a* and *b* to exhibit mental connectedness and just what follows for them if they do. And if, in bringing to the fore the notion of mental connectedness, I am following in the tradition of mental theorists of personal identity—without, to repeat, subscribing to an exclusively mental theory of personal identity—it is for me a crucial fact, and for the development of this essay a crucial point, that within that tradition the key feature of mental connectedness or just that feature of mental connectedness which makes it such a suitable support for personal identity, has been consistently misperceived. Philosophers of personal identity who have paid tribute to mental connectedness have nevertheless not recognized it as such.

Let me begin by contrasting the surface structure of mental connectedness with the underlying structure.

On the surface mental connectedness is this: It is a relation. Moreover it is a dyadic or two term relation: and the terms that it relates are such things as experiences, thoughts, feelings, sensations, acts of will and intention, total momentary states of a person: mental events for short. Mental connectedness is then a dyadic relation holding between mental events and, of course, if mental connectedness *is* criterial of personal identity, it will follow that the mental events it relates must be mental events belonging to one and the same person. However, it would be quite wrong to go on and *define* mental connectedness as holding only between mental events of one and the same person. For that, by reducing the equation of personal identity with mental connectedness to a triviality, to a mere verbal point, would be evidently against the spirit of the whole inquiry into personal identity.

So much for mental connectedness on the surface. Below the surface more stirs. For mental connectedness is not just any two-term relation between mental events that belong to one and the same person. Mental connectedness *is* that, but it *also* satisfies the two following conditions. One: the earlier of the two mental events that it relates causes the later of the two events. And two: the later mental event is caused by the earlier mental event in such a way that it—the later event, that is—then passes on to the whole person the causal influence of the earlier mental event.

If, then, on the *surface* mental connectedness is a two-term relation, relating mental event and mental event, the *underlying* structure is that of a three-term relation, relating mental event, mental event, and the psychology of the person, and this triadic relation allows causality to occur twice over in the orbit of mental connectedness. When two mental events are mentally connected, a causal influence is transmitted between them—occurrence one—and then —occurrence two—this causal influence is onwardly transmitted. And it is this second occurrence of causality, the onward transmission of a causal influence once generated, that is simultaneously the key feature of mental connectedness as far as personal identity is concerned and that feature of mental connectedness which its advocates have failed to recognize.

Why is this the key feature of mental connectedness? Why is mental connectedness so apt to be criterial of personal identity just because, when two mental events are mentally connected, the later one hands on the causality of the earlier one?

To answer this question let me make use of a distinction. The distinction is between a certain property being indicative of some phenomenon, or revealing its existence, and that property being creative of that phenomenon, or bringing about its existence. And, to allow myself some leeway, I take "creative" to cover "partly creative" as well as "fully creative": a property may be creative of a phenomenon if it helps to bring about its existence as well as if it brings about its existence unaided. And now my answer to the question about the peculiar suitability of mental connectedness to be criterial of personal identity would be this: Mental connectedness is not simply indicative of personal identity, it is creative of it. Or better: Mental connectedness is indicative of personal identity because it is creative of it. Mental connectedness is creative of personal identity because, on each occasion of its instantiation, it brings the person somewhat under the influence of his past: A mental event is assigned to a person because of its relation with some earlier event in his life: and, when this happens, the relation ensures that the later event is a carrier of the influence of this earlier event, an influence that then pervades the person so that his biography is bound together even as it unfolds. The present is tied to the past, a new past is thus constructed under whose influence the future may then be brought, and so the diachronic expansion of the person, his life, gets its unity. And this tells us not only something about the special suitability of mental connectedness to be criterial of personal identity but also something about the singular character of personal identity.

V

I have referred to mental connectedness as "a rather abstract property," and one thing I meant by that is that it can be realized in a number of different ways. I have referred to the fact that mental theorists of personal identity have widely favored memory—or, more strictly, the memory-relation where this is the relation that holds between a memory and what it is a memory of—as criterial of personal identity, and now I want to suggest that, insofar as memory can make a good claim to be criterial of personal identity—and I can't hope to evaluate just how good a claim that is—memory exemplifies mental connectedness, and that is why.

But there are different types of memory, and that to claim that memory is criterial of personal identity on behalf of some types would be ridiculous, and therefore it is essential to get clear the type we are talking about. The relevant type of memory I call "experiential memory," and experiential memory can be distinguished from the irrelevant types by two differential features. The first feature is phenomenological and it is that, if I experientially remember an action or an experience, then I remember that action or experience from the inside. There is, critically, a point of view to the memory-experience. The second feature concerns the way an experiential memory is reported, and it is that, if I experientially remember, say, an action that I did or an experience that I suffered, then, if I report the memory (something that I might or might not do), I characteristically report it by saying "I remember doing, suffering, such-and-such" or "I remember my doing, my suffering, such-and-such"—all in contrast with "I remember that I did, that I suffered, such-and-such," which is more appropriate for the report of an external type of memory or one that does not contain a point of view.

So, if I experientially remember quarreling, my quarreling, with my father at the age of thirteen, then: I report it as I have just done, and I remember the quarrel from my point of view, through my eyes as it were.

In connection, for instance, with the psychoanalytic phenomenon of identification, I have elsewhere talked of a type of imagination—for imagination too has its types—which I have called "centrally imagining."[2] I should like to think that this phrase was sufficiently carefully chosen that it brings before the mind the exact phenomenon that I have in mind. But the only point I need to make now, and to which I shall return, is that the structure of experiential memory, as it is given by these two differential features, totally parallels that of centrally imagining. In centrally imagining, too, I centrally imagine whatever it is that I imagine from the inside, *and* if I centrally imagine, say, an action that *I* do or an experience that *I* suffer, then I characteristically report it by saying, "I imagine doing, suffering, such-and-such" or "I imagine my doing, my suffering, such-and-such."

So: How does experiential memory exemplify mental connectedness?

First, then, on the surface: Experiential memory is a relation. It is a two-term relation holding between mental events: one being the memory-experience, the other the experience remembered. Furthermore, if experiential memory is indeed criterial of personal identity, then, of course, it will follow that the mental events it relates invariably and necessarily belong to one and the same person. But, again, it is not required to put this into the definition of experiential memory, nor for evident reasons would it be right to do so. To define experiential memory in this way would be to trivialize the link between experiential memory and personal identity.

So, secondly, to the underlying structure: Does enough in the case of experiential memory stir beneath the surface? Is there a three-term relation to be found there such that causality can occur twice over in the orbit of experiential memory?

For the first occurrence of causality—that between the earlier and the later of two mental events that experiential memory relates —or for the view that an experiential memory is caused by the experience that it is of, the crucial kind of case is neatly illustrated at the beginning of Goethe's autobiography.[3] There he recounts the earliest event in his life still known to him. It is the famous incident, which occurred just after the birth of a sibling, when the young Johann Wolfgang, initially lured on by some naughty friends of his own age, threw all his parents' crockery piece by piece into the street, and Freud, who devoted an essay to the recollection, interpreted it as Goethe's attempt to regain his mother's love. But the interest of the incident for us here and now lies in the way Goethe prefaces his account by saying that he does not know whether this is really a memory—an experiential memory it would be—or whether he is retailing hearsay, so often has the incident been repeated to him. Now, we might ask, what is it that Goethe does not know? What is the object of his uncertainty, and what further evidence would make uncertainty yield to knowledge? And reflection upon the various possibilities, the various alternatives, seems to force this conclusion upon us: that what Goethe needed to know was how his current knowledge of the past was caused. Was it caused by what his friends and family had said to him, in which case it was not experiential memory, or was it caused by the action, the experience itself, for then and only then would it be experiential memory? Significantly Goethe himself poses the issue by talking of those cases where our knowledge of our past is "a possession of our own derived from what we ourselves have witnessed." Gloss "derived from" as "causally dependent on," and we can credit Goethe with the correct philosophical view that an experiential memory is caused by the action, the experience, that it is a memory of.

To see, however, that causation occurs not just once but twice in the orbit of experiential memory, or that the memory onwardly transmits the causal influence of the remembered event, we must return to one of the differential features of experiential memory: its phenomenology, or that it is memory from the inside. For this can be filled in in the following way: If I experientially remember something that I did or suffered, I will tend to remember, both systematically and liberally, what I thought and what I felt in the doing or in the suffering of it. What "systematically" means here is "as and when they—that is, the thoughts and feelings—occurred in the history of the event." And "liberally" means "rather a lot." Again, insofar as I remember, systematically and liberally, what I thought and what I felt at the time, I will tend to rethink, or refeel, those very thoughts and feelings. There will be a tendency for the original affective complex to set itself up anew in the mind of the rememberer, and I call this tendency "the affective tendency" of experiential memory, and the state that results when this tendency actualizes itself I call "the affective tone" of a particular experiential memory. Now it is, by and large, through its affective tendency or through its affective tone—depending, of course, on whether we are talking generally or in particular—that experiential memory onwardly transmits the causal influence of what is remembered. For the affective tendency, the affective tone, is well designed to have an effect upon the dispositions, attitudes, sentiments of the rememberer. So when I experientially remember quarreling with my father those years ago, I tend to remember also the thoughts I had, the feelings I experienced, all the while, and when I do so, the thoughts, the feelings tend to come back over me. I once again sense the rage, the despair, the self-righteousness, like a bitter taste in the mouth, and those sentiments deriving from the past stay on to affect my whole being and my future.[4]

And here another analogy is to be noted between experiential memory and centrally imagining. For an experience of centrally imagining also tends to have an affective tone, and this tone is well designed to have an effect upon the dispositions, attitudes, sentiments of the imaginer. But, of course, there is this big and for our purposes all-important difference between the two phenomena: that, in the case of experiential memory, the affective tone is causally dependent on an earlier event, the event remembered, and by transmission the effect of the experiential memory is the effect of that earlier event. Through its affective side, the experiential memory onwardly transmits the causal influence of that event which it is of. But there is nothing, there could not be anything, parallel to this in the case of centrally imagining.

Of course, this is not to say that the affective side of an experiential memory would be what it is or would bring about what it does, if it were not for its cognitive side. That would be an absurd view. But it is significant that the affective side of experiential memory has been neglected even by those philosophers who have been keenest for the claims of memory to be criterial of personal identity. For their neglect of this side of experiential memory is absolutely of a piece with their neglect of what I have called the key feature of mental connectedness: the onward transmission of a causal influence once generated, or what might be called the forward-looking side of experiential memory. They are of a piece because it is in virtue of this neglected side that experiential memory realizes the key feature of mental connectedness.

Nor has everything yet been said in favor of experiential memory and its role in the creation of personal identity. For in bringing a man under the influence of some past event, experiential memory also brings him more generally under the influence of the past. It does so in two ways. It does so in an obvious way, which is altogether derivative from mental connnectedness: and that is that experiential memory is such a recurrent element in mental life, it provides such a continuous undertow in the mind, so that a man will, even in a short time, come to remember many many many different events. But experiential memory also serves to bring a man more generally under the influence of the past in a less obvious way and one that does not derive solely from mental connectedness. And that is to do with the fact that memories—supremely experiential memories—get woven into the general texture of our inner life. The affective tendency attached to some memory adapts itself to the rest of our emotional being: at least, normally. The affective tone that a particular memory has derives—true enough—from the event remembered; it reproduces the original affective complex that surrounded that event. And yet it has also compromised, in ways that could never precisely be identified, with the man's remaining feelings, sentiments, dispositions. The despair, the self-righteousness, the rage, that I experience when I remember my adolescent quarrel with my father represent the whole of me up till now as well as me specifically then. It is thus that the affective tone of a memory comes to stand for a man's past as well as for one event in that past, and so when, by virtue of the key feature of mental connectedness, that tone casts its influence over the man, the man is thereby brought under the influence of the past generally as well as of some particular past event.

VI

And now this key feature, pertaining generally to mental connectedness, specifically to experiential memory may be further served by considering briefly no longer persons but creatures of a different kind, whose identity in no way depends on mental connectedness, and seeing how very different their nature or natures would be. Such creatures need not be the inventions of fancy, for it is reasonably certain that, as we descend through the animal kingdom, this is what at some point we encounter.

Such creatures have, let us assume, experiences, thoughts, feelings, sensations, even acts of will and intention: there are total momentary states of them. These mental events are interrelated in a number of different ways. Some of them may be causally connected. But there is just one way in which these mental events may not be interrelated. One such mental event may not cause another such event so that this later event then goes on to transmit the causal influence of the earlier event to the whole creature. That is ruled out, and with it is ruled out (this is what we have to see) a whole way in which the creature might be dependent in his mind on his past. ("In his mind," for my negative claim does not stretch to the creature's body insofar as the creature's body does not directly affect his mind.) It is possible for singular present events in the creature's mental life to be dependent on singular past events in his life, or indeed on groups of such events. But these events do nothing to bring the creature himself under the influence of his past. Every mental event in the life of such a creature constitutes a kind of Verdun to the past, saying *"On ne passera pas."*

The inner life of such a creature is not easy to reconstruct: a fact worth pondering. But it is, as far as I can see, perfectly compatible with the absence of mental connectedness that such creatures should have memories—memories indeed of their own past actions and experiences. But if we try to consider how these memories would be for them, what it would be like for them to have these memories, then I suggest this peculiarity: that insofar as they could learn from these memories, they would do so much as they would from a book or from a childhood lesson. What would be lacking from the memory experience would be any reflection, any intimation, of the fact that this benefit derived from a past experience that they had once lived through. Nor on consideration should this surprise us. For just what these creatures thereby show that they lack is a sense of their identity of a kind akin to our sense of ours. But since they do not have an identity of a kind akin to ours, and since it is peculiar to our kind of identity that it gives rise to our kind of sense of our identity, it is only to be expected that their sense of their identity should differ essentially.

VII

I return to the question left hanging: that is, how are the two kinds of unity which a life can have—the kind it must have and the kind it may be fortunate enough to have—to be explained, and can they be explained one in terms of the other? On the basis of this substantive discussion of the criterion of personal identity, I suggest an answer. The answer, and because of its centrality to this essay I shall refer to it throughout what remains as the Answer, is this: If a person's life is his just because the different mental events that comprise it are so related that later parts of his life are brought under the influence of the earlier parts, then a person's life is of a piece just insofar as at successive moments he is under the due influence of the past. His life exhibits pattern or wholeness to the degree to which the influence of the past, as it bundles up his life through the instrumentality of mental connectedness, is neither excessive nor insufficient. And if this is so, then the two kinds of unity are indeed to be explained one in terms of the other.

Of the many objections that might be raised to, or difficulties found in, the Answer, I shall confine myself to two, and I have selected these because it seems to me that, meeting or trying to meet them more or less assures further progress into the subject.

VIII

The first objection would be that the Answer is too unspecific. It refers us to the "due" influence of the past, to an influence of the past that is neither "excessive" nor "insufficient," and how are these terms to be interpreted, and how is their interpretation to get the necessary concreteness, generality, and objectivity?

If we want an interpretation of these terms that is adequately grounded, it seems to me that there is only one place where we can look. We should look to the actual mechanism whereby the influence of a person's past over his later life is secured, and see if there are general features of such a mechanism in terms of which we can understand what it is for that influence to be too much, too little, or just right. Let us continue to suppose that memory, or more specifically experiential memory, provides the principal mechanism for the onward transmission of this influence: then, can we find certain structural principles governing the way in which experiential memory functions which will allow us to legitimize the distinctions that the Answer requires us to make?

Everything that I have said so far is, I hope, compatible with psychoanalytic theory taken broadly. Nothing presupposes it. But now there will be a change. Accepting that psychoanalytic theory gives us the best available account of psychological development—or does, at any rate, over those areas which it covers—I want to extract from the theory three broad conclusions about the way in which memory brings a person under the influence of his past: now benignly, nor malignly. I shall put them together, and my treatment of them will tend to be perfunctory.

The first concerns the normal functioning of memory: And it is that, though memory does indeed bring us under the influence of the past, this does not mean that each time some past event is remembered and influences us, that influence is unchanged. Nor should the fluctuations in the influence of a past event—basically, the waning of that influence—surprise us. For they result from two very unesoteric facts about the way in which memory secures the influence of the past. One is that memory modifies the man; it does not make him out of nothing. And it was in this connection that Freud liked to emphasize the limits that constitutional factors set upon the pathological. The other is that any man is modified, in the course of his life, by many many different memories. Put these two facts together, and it follows that it is only in deviant or aberrant cases that a single memory, a memory, that is, of a single event, preserves intact and undiminished, on every occasion of its revival, its original vigor.

Incidentally, this point, if duly appreciated, indicates another way in which mental connectedness theory recommends itself. For any concept a criterion for identity under that concept must permit change. It must exhibit how change is compatible with identity. But with persons there is a further intuition that a theory of personal identity should try to grapple with. The intuition is that it is in the nature of persons that they change. As they live, they necessarily change, and therefore it would be a merit in a criterion of personal identity, if it not merely showed how change is compatible with identity, but also predicted change on the basis of identity. It is just this that, I suggest, mental connectedness can make a good claim to do.

And the second thing concerning the way memory functions to secure the influence of the past is this: I have spoken of the undue influence of the past as though it could be further divided into excessive influence and insufficient influence. And that is how we ordinarily think. But theory teaches us that this distinction doesn't cut very deep. Certainly there is a difference to be observed, in behavior and in conscious thought between a brooding preoccupation with the past and a refusal to set store by it. But this difference in attitude to the past does not necessarily correspond to any difference in the causal efficacy of the past. More significantly, when we come to analyze the structure of any particular case where the influence of the past is undue, we appear to find both an excessive influence and an insufficient influence at work, and it could only be a reflection of this same fact that, in his earliest attempts to formulate a diagnostic account of neurosis, Freud seemed to vacillate between an account in terms of reminiscence and an account in terms of amnesia as though they represented only shifts in emphasis. Perhaps the best way of bringing out the unitary character of all those cases where there is a deviant influence is to say that in none of them is the person able to bring the experience of the past to bear upon the reality of the present. The two pieces of knowledge are kept apart: so that he comes to live either in a present denied a past or in a past deemed a present. And the mechanisms of the mind that bring about these outcomes are so interrelated, so serially connected, that it serves no good purpose to think that we have here two different kinds of situation, suitably distinct, rather than one highly articulated and variant. Read the account of Anna O as this is given in *Studies on Hysteria,* with her cramps, her *absences,* her tears and her little rituals, and who can say that her father's deathbed affected her either too little or too much? What can be said is that she could neither mourn it nor recover from it.

And this leads directly to the third conclusion that we can extract from theory, and that is that in each and every case where memory fails to make the past properly available to and assimilable within the present, memory assumes in varying degrees the role of some other mental activity. It takes over from perception, it declines into imagination, it feeds desire, it exchanges itself for action. In each case there is an intermediary: fantasy is the intermediary, and it is the similarity between memory and fantasy, anticipated in the parallel already discussed between experiential memory and centrally imagining, that permits memory to degenerate and the past to take on the character of an alternative life. I reckon it one of the striking virtues of Kleinian theory that by engaging with the nature of internal representations, their content and their mode of appearance, it has managed to exhibit how those transformations come about in which the sense of reality is attenuated or lost.

IX

Once a memory has become the carrier of the undue influence of the past, then on each occasion of its revival this effect is likely to be reinforced. The function or functions that it now takes on, in addition, that is, to recording the past, will be strengthened, and the past will increasingly be placed out of link with the present. But this malign outcome is not the only possibility. A benign outcome is also possible. For, if the memory contains within itself or within its associated thoughts enough information, and if the person is able to avail himself of this information, then on some occasion of its revival the memory may be turned against the use that has been made of it. The person, finding out what it was about the past that incapacitated him from dealing with it, may now learn to deal with it. The memory will be restored to its proper function, and the past will eventually begin to exercise no more than a due influence over the present.

This is the process of "working-through," and it and the malign process that it reverses are supremely topics of the therapeutic session. But they are also exhibited—not surprisingly when one comes to think of it—in a literary genre singularly dedicated to the notion of pattern in life or the ideal of wholeness. Anyone who has led a life is a fair object for a biography. But to be the appropriate subject for an autobiography, a person should have lived his life more than most or struggled to make it of a piece. Autobiography is highly relevant to this essay just because it is poised between the writing and the rewriting of a life; and a life may be rewritten so as to impart to that life a unity that it never had—that is, malignly; or it may be rewritten benignly—that is, so as to achieve, even at a late hour, some reconciliation with the past. If in daily life generally, and in the therapeutic life not infrequently, a memory, as it occurs, has a single function, nevertheless when a memory is first recalled, then held in the mind, then set down, then allowed to remain there unerased, then has a context placed around it, as happens in autobiography, it is altogether convincing that it should represent or stand for something closer to a process that we the readers of the autobiography may hope to reconstruct.

Compare and contrast two passages of autobiography, both of which are immediately intriguing and would repay deeper study. One is from the *Memoirs* of Vittorio Alfieri, the other is from John Stuart Mill's *Autobiography,* and both describe a turning-point in their subjects' lives. Alfieri emancipates himself from what he has come to regard as a licentious and disgraceful mode of life so as to devote himself to the service of the muses and to the love of fame. John Stuart Mill recovers from that "dry heavy dejection" which coincided with the onset of manhood and in which none of the great humanitarian causes for which he had been so relentlessly educated seemed any longer worth pursuing.

Determined to break off a liaison with a woman nine or ten years older than himself, and for whom he felt alternate antipathy and love, Alfieri dresses himself in a large mantle, seats himself at his desk from which several times a day he can observe his mistress, who lives across the street, enter and leave her house, and then he has his servant Elias tie him to his chair with heavy cords, concealed under the folds of his mantle. One hand is untied, the right hand, and with it Alfieri attempts to complete a tragedy on the theme of Cleopatra: a piece that, Alfieri has already told us, he had begun about a year earlier, in a condition approximating that of automatic writing, as he sat by his mistress's sickbed, not knowing whether she would recover. It was only when the tragedy was well under way, and Alfieri judged that he was detached from his passion, that he absolved Elias from the metier of jailer and the cords were put away. Alfieri's literary career had begun, and the succession of chill declamatory dramas that were his life's work began to unfold.

In Mill's recovery a central part is played not by the writing but by the reading of a book. The book was Marmontel's *Memoirs* and, as Mill tells the story, the crucial moment occurred when he (I quote) "came to the passage which relates his [Marmontel's] father's death, the distressed position of the family, and the sudden inspiration by which he, then a mere boy, felt, and made them feel, that he would be everything to them—would supply the place of all that they had lost." Mill goes on, "A vivid conception of the scene and its feelings came over me and I was moved to tears. From this moment my burden grew lighter.'' Gradually Mill began to feel and to find things worthwhile. He could work, and eventually he would love if in an idolatrous fashion.

Obviously these two passages are very different. The men themselves are very different. As two men must be, when for one of them (Mill) the father was so permanently, so painfully, present, whereas for the other, bereaved in actual fact in the first year of his life, the absence of the father is such a desolate fact that, when at the age of eight or so the child Alfieri, now separated from his sister, sees in a nearby church a group of young Carmelite novices saying office, chanting anthems, the light from the wax tapers they were carrying falling on features that ''partook of the feminine nature,'' and, passionately in love for the first time, hurries to his dictionary, looks up the entry ''monk,'' crosses out the word, and substitutes in his handwriting the word ''Father,'' he does this not only (as he tells us) to enhance the standing of the young boys, to aggrandize them, but he also does it (we must believe) to intimidate himself a little or to bring himself under an authority that he had never known.

But we switch attention from the content of these passages—the wishes, impulses, anxieties, set down—to the way in which they contain this content, and a similarity emerges. They not only have to be contrasted but they also may be compared. For what is happening in each case but that the man, struggling with certain feelings, distances himself from the struggle and then gets another to feel these feelings for him. It is through the servant Elias—against whom, incidentally Alfieri's fury had erupted only a few weeks before and he had thrown a candlestick at his head—that Alfieri attempts to suppress his feelings for a woman; it is within the youthful Marmontel—son of a large family where Mill was an only son—that Mill entertains the feelings that his father is experienced as forbidding him.

Now, there is every reason to believe that these memories capture, for each writer, somewhat how the crucial event was lived through. Thus they record the past. But there is also something else, something extra, that the writing down of these memories seeks to achieve. For each memory incorporates a fantasy, a fantasy of projection within which the controlling part of the person, alternatively feelings of loss and mourning, are lodged within another; and now we must suppose that each time the memory is revived, this reordering of the inner world is reasserted, the split-off parts of the person are triumphed over, and the undue influence of the past over the present is fortified.

After the differences, a similarity. And now after this similarity, a further difference. For in the case of Mill but not in the case of Alfieri, it is also possible to discern a further or counter-current of influence. A sensitive reader of the *Autobiography* must take note of the way in which Mill also tries to take back into himself, to reabsorb, the feelings that he has set the orphaned Marmontel to experience for him. Having sent out his feelings for adoption, he tries somewhat to be a father to them: or, in his words "to supply the place of all that they had lost." And this endeavor, we may guess, is not without success. The fantasy that is at the heart of the memory having been worked through, the memory has its proper function restored to it and Mill is thereby returned to reality. At any rate it is to such reconstructions of the reconstruction of a life that autobiography characteristically lures us.

X

And so to the second objection I shall consider to the Answer. And that is that it is now too specific. For if we interpret terms like "due," "excessive," "insufficient" in a way that effectively rid them of their unspecificity, are we not committed to explicating a notion that evidently belongs to common and universal thinking, a perennial ideal, by reference to a particular psychological theory of local and recent cultivation?

I began this essay on one philosophical intuition, and I conclude it on another, also fully exploited in our day, which might seem to provide the material out of which the objection before us could be met.[5] For if it were possible to think of persons as forming a natural kind, and consequently the term *person* as exhibiting the peculiarities of a natural-kind term, then it would be not at all surprising that at least some part of the sense of the term *person* should be explicated by reference to the best available theory true of persons. Apart from the question whether persons do indeed form a natural kind, the outstanding questions would be whether the possible history (or the necessary development) of a person can constitute that part of the sense of the term *person* which is appropriately explicated by reference to theory and whether the best available theory applicable to persons is that furnished by psychoanalytical theory.

These three questions are very big questions, and I shall say something about the first first and then consider the second two together.

It has certainly been no part of the way in which the contemporary argument for natural-kind terms has been generally presented that persons should be regarded as forming a natural kind. That is because natural kinds have been thought of as *physical* natural kinds, and the real essences definitive of such kinds have been required to be *physical* real essences. And since those characteristics that are most distinctive of persons—thoughts, speech, emotions, behavior—could surely have been realized in some other physical way than that in which they acutally are, they cannot be dependent on an inner or hidden structure physically identified. But there seems to be no necessity for the argument to be presented in this way. Indeed, not only does it strike me as arbitrary to restrict natural kinds to physical natural kinds but also it is inviting to believe that a real essence for persons could be located in a psychological structure that could have all the properties appropriate to a real essence. So, one, it would be internal; two, it could be uncovered layer by layer, or would be epistemically deep; three, it could be used to explain the surface characteristics of a person's life; and four, as it was laid bare, it might lead us to revise or enlarge our ordinary or commonsense conceptions of what are or could be persons.

If the first question is properly answered thus, the second two may be considered together. Of course, the details of psychoanalytical theory are one thing, but another is the general character of that theory, and, if it is right to look upon persons as forming a psychological natural kind, then it would seem that at the very least psychoanalytical theory has the right character for a theory definitive (or partially definitive) of the natural kind they form. A theory that was not developmental could not fill the required role. For surely (a point to be argued) a psychological essence must be some-

thing that can be fully understood or interpreted only over time.
But if it is only a developmental theory—which is what psychoanalytical theory is—that will do for the proper explication of the term
person, it is barely surprising that that part of the sense of the term
on which it bears most heavily will be that part which fixes the possible history, or the necessary development, of those things that the
term denotes. It is barely surprising that theory will fix how the life
of a person must necessarily run.

XI

To this last point I foresee an objection: an objection in which the
keyword would be "Naturalism." For there will be some, many,
who will see no objection at all to appealing to psychological laws
to determine questions about—as I have put it—the possible history or the necessary development of a person: they will readily
accept the idea that psychological theory should produce necessary
truths about the person—of this sort. Of this sort: for they will
regard it as a totally different matter, an utterly unjustified extension of this idea, that psychological laws or theory should be in-
voked to settle the issue of what it is for a life to exhibit pattern or
be of a piece. For here we are dealing with something normative.
And the normative cannot be determined scientifically. We must
introduce laws or theory to explicate what it is for the influence of
the past upon a person's present to be undue: but not to equate the
wholeness of a life with one duly influenced. The Answer may be
elucidated by reference to science: but science can give it no
support.

Obviously this must seem so, so long as we continue to reject
Naturalism in all its forms, and I shall simply state baldly where I
think Naturalism comes in legitimately.

A naturalism that deserves consideration is any that can show
how our values, how our norms, derive from certain more primitive
or elementary ways in which we regard those feelings, desires, dispositions that physical constitution and our personal histories have
given us: thereby coming to accept some and to reject others, to
look upon some as belonging to us and others as external to us, to
identify with some and to repress, to inhibit, to deny others. And it
is a naturalism that not only deserves consideration but can com-

mand our adherence, which can further show that these more primary attitudes, and the acceptances and the rejections that they give rise to, are crucial to our development: so that unless we concurred with them, we would be immobilized.[6] And a concurrence with the due influence of our past upon us seems just such a case. It is nothing less than the acceptance of ourselves as the persons that we are: as hard as it is simple, and the foundation stone of human culture.

NOTES

1. Here I am evidently borrowing from David Wiggins *Identity and Spatio-Temporal Continuity* (Oxford, 1967), and later writings, especially "Continuity, Identity and Essentialism," *Synthèse,* 23 (1974), 321-359.

2. Richard Wollheim "Imagination and Identification," in his *On Art and the Mind* (London, 1973), pp. 54-83, and "Identification and Imagination: the Inner Structure of a Psychic Mechanism," in *Freud: A Collection of Critical Essays,* ed. Richard Wollheim (New York, 1974), pp. 172-195.

3. I am indebted to Elizabeth Anscombe for having first drawn my attention to the philosophical interest of this passage in a paper read many years ago at University College, London. This paper in a much revised form has been printed as her "Memory 'Experience' and Causation," in *Contemporary British Philosophy,* 4th series, ed. H. D. Lewis (London, 1976). For the causal nature of memory, see C. B. Martin and Max Deutscher "Remembering" *Philosophical Review* LXXIV (1966), 161-196.

4. Much more has to be said than is said here about the conditions under which a mental state, which has a causal influence and has been causally brought about by an earlier mental state, can be said in its causal influence to transmit the causal influence of its cause. I place no reliance upon any alleged transitivity of the causal relation itself. I am inclined to say this: Given S_1 which belongs to individual I and S_2 which belongs to individual J, and S_1 causes S_2, and S_2 has an influence over J, then S_2 onwardly transmits the influence of S_1 to J (if and) only if (i) S_1 differentially causes that part of S_2 which influences J: (ii) the influence of S_2 on J within broad limits reproduces the influence of S_1 on I: (and (iii) from then onward J cannot be understood without reference to I.

5. See Saul Kripke "Identity and Necessity," in *Identity and Individuation,* ed. M. Munitz (New York, 1971), and Hilary Putnam, *Mind, Language and Reality* (Cambridge, 1975), passim.

6. I have proposed such a form of naturalism in Richard Wollheim *The Good Self and the Bad Self: The Moral Psychology of British Idealism and the English School of Psychoanalysis compared,* Dawes Hicks Lecture on Philosophy, British Academy (London, 1975).

This essay is a shortened version of a lecture delivered in the autumn of 1977 under the same title as the first James Lecture at New York University. I am grateful to Richard Sennett for the original invitation and to Amélie Rorty for encouragement with the present version.

XIII

INTELLECTUAL DESIRE, EMOTION, AND ACTION

MICHAEL STOCKER

I shall argue that desire, emotion, and action are proper and essential to intellect, including scientific intellect. To help put this position, I shall oppose it to one I call the purified view of intellect: the view that intellect, especially scientific intellect, is or should be purified of desire, emotion, and action. I concentrate on scientific intellect because it is taken as paradigmatically "hard and pure." If I succeed in showing that not even it is purified, there should be little interest in claiming that other forms or areas of intellect are purified.

I believe the purified view of intellect is Aristotle's position in the *Nicomachean Ethics* in regard to scientific and other theoretical intellect, as I shall indicate in notes. And I believe it is also the dominant view of intellect in the contemporary English-speaking philosophical world, or so one would be led to believe by leading works on epistemology, philosophy of science, philosophy of mind, and theory of action, which seem to assume, more than argue for, this position. But I shall not be concerned to show that the purified view is Aristotle's or ours. For what is of far more importance is the positive position I urge; and I do not want it lost sight of in historical and exegetical disputes. Indeed, whether or not the position I urge has been explicitly or implicitly rejected, it has clearly received far less attention than warranted by its significance. Because of this, our understanding of intellect, emotion, desire, and action —thus, the mind and the person—is, at the very best, incomplete.

This paper attempts to remedy this situation. To this end, it must be kept in mind that this paper is concerned with the philosophy of mind—or better, the moral psychology—of intellect, especially scientific intellect. It is not concerned with the epistemology or metaphysics of what is sought or known by such intellect—science. In particular, it is not concerned with whether scientific proof, when this is taken as a formal relationship among statements, should be purified of desire, emotion, and action. Thus, it does not canvass recent attacks on this "positivistic" claim made by Habermas, Kuhn, Lakatos, Feyerabend, Putnam, et al. These attacks no more falsify the purified view of intellect than the view they attack establish it. For—as this paper will help show, if it is not already clear— the epistemology and metaphysics of science do not bear in any simple or clear way on the moral psychology of intellect in general or scientific intellect in particular.[1]

The purified view of intellect, taken as a thesis in the moral psychology of intellect, neglects the role of character in scientific and other theoretical intellect and the active nature of that intellect. These are really two aspects of one area; and after dealing with each aspect briefly, I shall continue with a general discussion of the one area.

For any number of reasons, not all mutually consistent, character is thought not to be proper or essential to scientific (and other theoretical) intellect: Character is the "repository" or "location" of desire, emotion and perhaps other "unruly," "lower" aspects of people; character is that in virtue of which people are morally evaluable, for example, as praiseworthy or blameworthy; character is something that develops, but intellect is somehow natural; character develops through training or habituation, but intellect develops through teaching; character depends on intellect for objective guidance; intellect is concerned with means, character with ends. (See Aristotle, N.E. 1102b30 ff.; 1103a4 ff.; 1103a14 ff.)

There are ways of conceiving of intellect—for example, in terms of formal properties of reason; in terms of natural, perhaps even genetic, endowments—which license the exclusion of character from intellect. But this exclusion would have us ignore or deny many essential features of intellect.

In particular, it would have us ignore or deny many of the forms, modes, and styles of intellect and intellectual life. People are intellectually honest, intellectually arrogant, intellectually scrupulous, possessed of intellectual care for and interest in a subject, and so on. Speaking of people this way is speaking of the sort of intellectual work they do and want to do; what they do and want to do with their intellect and intellectual work; how they go about and want to go about their intellectual activities; what sort of intellectual person they are and want to be, and so on. It is to ascribe to them structured patterns of desire, choice, and emotion involved with, and internal to, their intellect, intellectual work, and intellectual life. Thus, it is to say that they have an intellectual character, or less misleadingly that one "part" (or more) of their character is involved with, and is internal to, intellect and intellectual work.

It will be shown below that intellectual honesty, arrogance, and so very many other intellectual features stand to intellectual action and character and evaluations of them and of people in exactly the ways such traditional, "active" features of character as temperance or bravery stand to traditionally-considered action and character and evaluations of them and of people.

For the moment it may be sufficient to point out the following. Developing moral character, traditionally so-called, requires training and developing passions and patterns of desire, choice, and emotion. In exactly the same ways developing intellectual character requires training and developing passions and patterns of desire, choice, and emotion. By this I do not mean simply that if we are always seeking sexual satisfaction, say, we will not get on intellectually. What I am also and more importantly saying is that there are passions and patterns of desire, choice, and emotion in and of the intellect, and that they must be mastered and developed if we are to get on intellectually: We must, for example, learn intellectual discipline, we must master and develop those forces and tendencies connected with directing the mind as opposed to letting it wander; we must learn to recognize and keep to the point; not to stop thinking when the problem is too easy or too difficult; not to be satisfied with just any answer, but to press on for a correct or important answer; not to be too concerned with detail at the expense of the general, nor the general at the expense of detail. And so on and so on. As will be shown, in these and other ways, intellectual character is just like moral character, which after all is not surprising, since they are both part of character.

The second neglected aspect is the active nature of scientific (and other theoretical) intellect. Although it is not denied that science is an activity, is something we do, this aspect of science is often ignored or scanted. Discussions of science focus on science as an articulated body of truths or statements, and on formal patterns of argument, evidence, and proof—on in short, conceptual relations among scientific claims, theories, and the like.[2]

Neglect of the action aspect of science has various dangers. I shall mention only three.

First, we deprive ourselves of a means for seeing that character is important for science. For clearly, character is important for what we do.

Second, we may not see that scientific reasoning—what is done in doing science—is practical, not theoretical. Or more exactly, we may fail to understand the natures, differences, purviews, and interconnections of practical and theoretical reason and reasoning.

Let us grant, for the sake of the argument, that science is properly conceived of as an articulated body of truths or statements, and that the goal internal to doing science is finding or affirming what is known, true, or to be believed. (And let us further grant that science admits of a realist—that is, nonpragmatic, nonidealist, nonsubjective—account.) Even so, doing science involves, and involves from within science, posing and answering such paradigmatically practical questions as "How can this be shown?," "Where should we look next?," "How is this to be done?," "What is to be done?," as well as such theoretical questions as "Does this follow from that?," "Is this true?," "Should this be believed?." Science's being involved with knowledge, truth, or what is to be believed does not imply that it is not also involved with doing. Indeed, it is obvious that such scientific doing is often necessary for scientific knowing. These points are straightforwardly seen if we keep in mind that doing science involves such practical activities as investigating, inquiring, framing and testing hypotheses, considering alternatives, engaging in criticism, using imagination, and so on.

It might be objected that this practical element is a feature only of the context of discovery, not proof.[3] This, however, is only another way to put the formal conception of science. It has us conceive of proof in terms of formal relations among statements or truths, rather than in terms of the activities of proving, of doing the proofs. Proving in science is something we do; it involves, in the ways just sketched, practical reason and reasoning.

The third danger is that because we do not conceive of science as an activity, our characterization of action will be inadequate for scientific action—that is, for the intellectual action of doing science. Consider the following claims that are held, jointly or severally, by philosophers today: choice or desire is the efficient cause of action; intellect, by itself, moves nothing; only when joined with desire or choice does intellect move anything; choice, desire, and character are not essential parts of intellect.[4]

In recent times, often following Hume, philosophers have used claims like these to show that practical, especially moral, reasoning and intellect—which are held to involve choice, desire, emotion, and character—are of a very different, often inferior, sort from the reasoning and intellect concerned with science and more mundane matters of fact.[5] One central argument for this difference is based on the claim that intellect by itself moves nothing. For if intellect by itself moves nothing, then presumably it does not by itself create, arouse, mold, direct, strengthen, weaken, or otherwise control desire. Therefore, so it is held, desire and desiring are, to some extent at least, nonrational. (This is tied up with other conceptions of desire, connecting it to the body, as opposed to the mind, characterizing it in terms of energy, force, impulse, urge, which are in turn often characterized as blind.) Therefore, so it is concluded, practical intellect is, to some extent at least, nonrational. Another central argument for this difference is based on the dual claim that practical reasoning is conceptually linked with acting, and for two reasons action is, to some extent at least, nonrational. First, action has its origin in choice and desire, which are, to some extent at least, nonrational. Second, action is nonpropositional.

Such considerations have motivated many philosophers to hold a purified view of intellect. But instead of sustaining such a view, these very considerations devastate it. They show that we cannot have a purified intellect.

To see this, consider these five claims. First, if intellect by itself cannot move anything, then presumably it cannot by itself move itself. Second, if intellect by itself cannot explain our actions, then presumably it cannot by itself explain our intellectual actions. Third, if desire is needed to help explain our actions, then presumably desire is needed to help explain our intellectual actions. Fourth, whatever is not created, moved, controlled, or explained by intellect alone is thus, to some extent at least, nonrational. Fifth, whatever has its origins in desire is thus, to some extent at least, nonrational.

But our intellect moves. We perform intellectual actions. And our intellectual actions have their origin in desire. This is as true for science and scientific intellect as it is for practice and practical intellect. Thus, the very reasons motivating the purified view of intellect show that there is no purified intellect. Or rather, they lead to this dilemma for proponents of that view: either our intellect, including our scientific and other theoretical intellect, is not purified, or alternatively, if our intellect is purified, it can do, literally, nothing and is of no use to us.

But why take it that the intellect moves, that we act intellectually, and that our intellectual acts have their origins in desire? My answer to these questions is threefold.

First, we clearly do perform intellectual actions. There are, of course, periods of intellectual contemplation when, as it were, our mind or its content remains "perfectly at rest," and not because we hold it at rest. It may be questionable whether this is action, intellectual action. (Indeed, that contemplation may seem not to involve action or desire is one reason it has gained favor as the model of intellect, or of the purest or highest intellect, or divine intellect.) So too, there are periods when our thoughts go as they will, so to speak, when they happen just any which way, without any direction, intervention, or the like, by us. It may be questionable whether this, too, is intellectual action. (There are, of course, similar problems with "physical" acts.)

But there are other—and I would say far more important—forms of intellectual activity which are cases of directed and purposive process, directed and purposive action. These processes, activities, and actions are directed and done by us for reasons, done out of desire, done to achieve goals, satisfy interests, and the like. We investigate, try out solutions, follow leads and arguments, mull things over, form hypotheses, consider alternatives, review what has gone before, use our imagination, engage in criticism, and so on and so on. These activities are what the intellect, including of course the scientific intellect, does: this is what we do intellectually. There is as much movement, as much controlled, directed, purposive, goal-directed movement, and as much desire, force, vigor, energy, drive, urge, and urgency in intellectual action as in physical action.

If this needs to be shown, consider these pairs of actions: Working out an argument in one's mind compared with reading an argument in a book; excitedly exploring a theory in one's mind compared with excitedly discussing a theory with someone. (These examples also raise problems for the view that while the intellect alone cannot explain physical action, it can alone explain intellectual action. For there seems exactly the same need, or lack of need, to go beyond intellect alone in regard to these physical actions as the intellectual ones.)

This leads to the second reason to hold that the intellect moves, that we act intellectually, and that desire is involved in this action. Contemporary action-theorists, in large measure because they hold that the intellect alone moves nothing, argue that actions are to be explained as outcomes of a combination of factors, including beliefs and desires, wants, and the like. (Few, if any, action-theorists hold this of intellectual actions, which are almost entirely, if not entirely, unseen or neglected by them. Instead, reasoning is often explained as the outcome of beliefs, perhaps conjoined with the acceptance of certain rational principles.) Their claim that desires, wants, and the like are needed is plausible only if "desire," "want," and the like refer to the theoretically needed source of energy or movement for the action, as differentiated from what is felt or experienced as desire, want, and the like. For in many actions, such as the ones we do habitually, automatically, without opposition, without excitement, and the like, often there is no felt or experienced desire, no felt inclination, no felt pro attitude. Nothing other than beliefs may be felt or experienced. But there is no need to pursue these matters. For insofar as these action-theorists are correct and actions do require desire, intellectual actions also require desire.

The third reason in support of my contention is an amplification of the previous two and is connected with my earlier comments on intellectual character. For I would argue that not only does the scientific intellect act—not only do we do science—but also desire and choice are essential elements in our doing science, and in our doing all, or most, other intellectual matters. (Since what is true of doing science is also true of other intellectual activities, in what follows I shall often talk only of science.)

Science is done, as an intellectual activity, for any number of reasons. Science, like practical matters, usually so-called, involves "intellect which aims at an end" (1139^{a}36 sq.). Some of these ends are external to science, and internal only to why particular people or groups of people do it; for example, working on a scientific problem in order to keep one's job, to steal a march on a rival, to maintain one's self-respect, to help one's country win a war, and so on.

Some ends are internal to science. Understanding is clearly one of these (*pace* Habermas). Not only do we want to understand in general but also to understand this or that particular thing or system. Very often scientific activity is a response to some quite particular problem: How is malaria eliminable: "Is number theory reducible to set theory?" Often it is a response to a very general interest or problem, whether practical or theoretical: What constitutes health for humans? How are the various physical forces interrelated?

It is clear that desire and choice bear on why we do at least many of the various scientific and other intelectual activities we do. Considerations similar to those advanced above would show that emotion and other elements of character also play this role. In short, desire, choice, emotion, and character play the same roles in accounting for intellectual action as they do in accounting for traditionally-considered action.

It is important that this not be taken as suggesting that the very same desires, choices, emotions, and character sorts are at work in each case. What I have been arguing is that there are intellectual desires, intellectual choices, intellectual emotions, and intellectual character sorts and that these play the same roles in accounting for intellectual action as do the nonintellectual desires, choices, emotions, and character traits in accounting for nonintellectual action. (This amplified below.)

Intellectual desire, intellectual choice, intellectual emotion, and intellectual character also bear on how we do intellectual activities. In this, too, they play the same roles as do nonintellectual desire, choice, emotion, and character in regard to how we do traditionally-considered nonintellectual activities. This can be brought out straightforwardly by considering our own intellectual activities and work.

Scientists, philosphers, and other intellectual workers are involved in doing intellectual work, in acting with the mind. We inquire, think, try to understand, study, write, discuss, and so on and so on. We believe there are ways of doing these activities well and poorly; and we often attempt to get ourself and others to do them well. We evaluate ourself and others for having or lacking the requisite intellectual emotions, intellectual desires, intellectual character traits and sorts, and the like. We evaluate our own and others' work, ideas, styles, interests, and so on for having or lacking these emotions. We take it that having these emotions can importantly affect how we do, and how we do in, those enterprises. Being careful in one's intellectual endeavors, caring for the subject and having care in it, are humanly essential to doing a certain sort of intellectual work and doing it well. Intellectual care plays, that is, the same sorts of roles as do traditional, "active" characteristics like bravery and temperance in doing well in various human enterprises.

Both the traditional, "active" and also the intellectual emotions play the same roles at a societal level, too. It is a commonplace that in a society engaged in constant warfare, such as Classical Greece, martial emotions are valued and others devalued. And this is true also in regard to intellectual emotions. One would hardly expect a traditional society, intent on maintaining its traditions, to value the intellectual emotions connected with creativity, the formation of new ways of approaching problems, and the like. But one would expect just this of a society which was pleased to see itself as making breakthroughs in knowledge, technology, and the like. Such considerations are deeply implicated in different societies' having different ideals of knowledge and intellectual work, having different focuses for knowledge and intellectual work, and producing different knowledge and other intellectual work.

The same is true of disciplines or occupations. For example, the amalgams of intellectual emotions, intellectual character traits and sorts, intellectual affective states, patterns of intellectual desire and choice, and the like which are important for good work by a historian are not the same as those important for good work by a philosopher. Further, one philosopher, say, because of age, ability, experience, times, problematic, and so on, might well require different amalgams than another philosopher for doing equally good work. In this, the intellectual emotions, intellectual affects, and so on are exactly like the traditional, "active" ones.

Just as they play the same functional roles, they play the same dysfunctional roles. One can be involved in intellectual error and failure because one does not have enough of the right intellectual emotion—for example, care and respect for a discipline. So too, by having too much of such an emotion one can go wrong; for example, because one has too much care and respect for a discipline, one may do nothing but march up and down in the same place for all one's intellectual life. So too, a given intellectual emotion may hinder or aid one aspect of intellectual work, at a given time, but not another. And so on. In this, intellectual emotions are on all fours with "active" ones.

This is all commonplace, especially when we consider intellectual character. Even apart from intellectual charlatans, cheats, and the like, some people, because of their intellectual characters, are simply not capable of dealing well with certain intellectual problems. They may have no sympathy toward that problem or way of going about things. They may not take it seriously, as a worthwhile intellectual problem or procedure. They may be too concerned with protecting their own theories and views that bear on the question. They may not care for the subject enough to use sufficient care in examining it. They may have lost interest in that area, that methodology, that style. Their mode of thinking may be far more involved with speculation and kite-flying than the problem demands. And so on and so on. And, conversely, of course.

So far then, I have argued that both the intellectual and also the traditional, "active" emotions, character traits, desires, and the like play exactly the same functional and dysfunctional roles in regard to many different and important functions and dysfunctions.

This should not be surprising. First, almost all, if not all, the emotions, are found in both the intellectual and nonintellectual spheres of our life. This can be shown by considering them seriatim: by noting that for example, arrogance, bravery, care, curiosity, fear, interest, and the like are found in both spheres. This can also be shown by the following, which is a second reason it should not be surprising that the intellectual and the traditional, "active," emotions play the same roles: What distinguishes the intellectual emotions from the traditional, "active" ones is not, at least not typically, that qua emotion they are different. Rather, it is such things as the following: In the one case their object is intellectual and in the other case their object is some traditionally-considered activity or state. Or in the one case, the sort of activity or state they properly perfect or hinder is intellectual and in the other case it is not. (This is not to deny that intellectual traits can bear on "active" states and doings, or that "active" traits can bear on intellectual states and doings.)

In arguing that there are intellectual emotions, and that they are essential to intellectual activity, including scientific and other theoretical activity, I have not "psychologized" such activity. I have not been at all concerned with traditionally so-called psychological reasons, influences, or causes of intellectual activity. What I have tried to show is that there are and must be desires, goals, interests, emotions, and the like within and proper to the intellect, within and proper to intellectual activity, for there to be intellect and intellectual activity.

This way of putting it is important. For just as I have not been concerned to psychologize intellect and intellectual activity, I have not argued that they are subjective or nonrational. One of the major reasons emotions have traditionally been excluded from intellect, or from scientific and other theoretical intellect, was that emotions were thought to be essentially subjective and nonrational and to transmit these characteristics to whatever they involve. Some emotions may well do this. Perhaps letting one's intellect be guided by one's hopes or fears does this. But I see no reason to believe either that the emotions I have been considering do this or that anything I have argued suggests or depends on their doing so.

Indeed, if my arguments are correct, emotions, as such, need not be subjective or nonrational, nor need they transmit subjectivity or nonrationality. Or alternatively, our reasoning, our intellectual action, including scientific and other theoretical reasoning and action, are subjective or nonrational.

In what follows, I shall try to show in greater detail how the intellectual emotions are related to their actions and life, and also that these relations are the same as those between "active" emotions and their actions and life.

Up till now, I have said things like: Without intellectual interest, it would be humanly impossible or very difficult to do well in intellectual enterprises. And I have claimed that the roles of intellectual and traditional emotions, and intellectual and traditional desires are the same. But what are these same roles?

Is it claimed, for example, that it is impossible for a person lacking care or interest in an intellectual subject to do good work in that subject? At the extreme, is it claimed that a machine could not do good work in a subject? Is it claimed that such care and interest are merely useful for most of us to do well in the enterprise? These and similar questions have their strict analogues in regard to the traditional, "active" emotions and their actions. Consider courage and courageous actions. If by a courageous act we mean one done with courage, then that emotion is necessary for that sort of act. But this does not tell us all we want to know: whether acts like standing up to the enemy must be done with that emotion; whether that emotion merely helps in doing them; whether a person's having that emotion means that typically, or typically other things being equal, that that person will in the appropriate circumstances do that sort of act; whether having that emotion must in other ways affect how the person acts, and so on.

These raise extremely difficult, general problems about emotions and their connections with action, character, and life. All I can do here is begin to suggest some answers to them. In doing this, I will, however, be able to support my claim that the intellectual emotions stand to their actions, characters, and lives, just as the "active" ones do to theirs.

A consideration of Aristotle should help us on these matters. He does not hold—indeed, it is central to his doctrine of habituation to deny—that doing a courageous act requires being courageous. Similarly, I do not hold that doing an interesting or good piece of science or philosophy requires any of the intellectual virtues—that is, excellences—I have mentioned. Indeed, machines have, for example, proved interesting theorems in logic. Nor does Aristotle hold that having the relevant emotion or virtue must lead to a successful doing of the sort of act in question. He denies that a brave person must perform better in battle than a less brave person—when this "better" is understood in terms of winning the fight. He writes,

> it is quite possible that the best soldiers may be . . . those who are less brave but have no other good; for these are ready to face danger and they sell their life for trifling gains. [1117^{b}16 sq.]

To put this point more strongly and starkly: the better man, indeed the braver man—for the very reasons he is braver: willing to face danger even though he has more to lose, for example—may be the worse soldier.

Thus, a virtue in light of which we admire a person, or admire how that person does something, may go hand in hand with that person's doing that activity less well than someone who lacks that virtue or that virtue to that degree. This implies that success at good activities does not make a good person. It also implies the possibility of concrete conflicts in the realization of various excellences. It also brings out the important contrast between being an excellent doer of A qua A—that is, getting A done and done well, where the criteria of goodness have to do with A—and being an excellent or admirable person qua person who does A excellently, qua excellent person. This contrast has application even if A is, itself, a worthwhile activity. (I cannot here go into the very complex nature and grounds of these various evaluations and their interrelations.)

Many intellectual virtues are characteristics of a good person, qua good and intellectually active person, and are recognized as such, but which nonetheless need not go hand in hand with intellectual success. For example, great care in and for a subject, great scrupulousness and the like constitute and are otherwise involved in intellectual activity of the most admirable sort, by the most admirable people. But they are neither necessary nor sufficient for intellectual success or good intellectual work.

First, for any number of different reasons, certain people do better intellectual work because of intellectual vices. For example, certain forms of inventiveness and creativity go hand and hand with various forms of lack of care—for example, carelessness about intellectual predecessors or about strict and rigorous proof. Second, an intellectual cheat or charaltan can solve problems, get the correct answer, and the like. And such a person may be "naturally" or otherwise so much more gifted than another that no matter how excellent the latter is in respect of those intellectual virtues, the former will always do better. Third, a person's intellectual successes or failures, or that person's singular appreciation and understanding of a problem may correctly be attributable to his/her particular intellectual emotions, intellectual character sorts, and the like. It might be that but for a given person's strange combination of intellectual carefulness and intellectual stubbornness, some problem would not have been seen, much less solved, at least not by that person. Nonetheless, and as unlikely as this may be, another person with very different intellectual emotions might be able to do the same piece of work, and understand the problem in the same way.

Exactly the same lack of necessary or sufficient connection characterizes the relations between the traditionally-considered, "active" emotions, character traits, and the like and their action, character, and life. Such lack of necessary or sufficient connection, therefore, does not seem strong or even good evidence that intellectual emotions, intellectual character traits are not proper to intellectual action, character, and life. Or alternatively, the "active" emotions are not proper to their action, character, and life.

Let us approach this from another direction, from the standpoint of the person doing the intellectual activity, as differentiated from the standpoint of the activity. Let us look at the matter from a more traditional, evaluative point of view. I contend that a life lacking in the intellectual virtues, emotions, and desires is a life lacking important human goods. To show this fully would require a complete study of how our intellect constitutes and informs our whole life. But for the present purposes, it may be useful to make these four brief, interrelated points.

First, these virtues, emotions, desires are very useful in doing intellectual work and in doing it well. Second, in doing at least some actions, people "take over" and internalize the criteria of success of those actions, for example, the goals and purposes of such actions; they get caught up in and identify with those actions; they see themselves as doers of those actions and want to see themselves as good doers of them. To deny the importance of this is to deny one of the central features of our life, more particularly of our life connected with and constituted by self-assessment and feelings of worth and value. The intellectual virtues, emotions, desires are essential to such assessment, such value and worth, especially for those engaged in intellectual endeavor. Third, there is the related point concerning being able, and the value of being able, to engage in activities wholeheartedly, authentically, unalienatedly. Here one contrary state is not being able to do what one does for its inherent purposes, but rather having to treat activities the way a spy must treat "friends" spied upon. Another contrary state is doing the activities simply for what results from the activities, treating the activities simply as means, for example, of solutions to problems, getting correct answers, finding truths. Another contrary state is doing the activities for no reason at all, without any attachment or commitment to the activities as such, either as means or end. Without the intellectual virtues, emotions, desires, some such contrary state is inevitable.

In regard to the second and third points, consider what sort of life a person would lead, and what sort of person a person would be, if, though engaged in intellectual work, the person did not judge or evaluate him/herself as a person doing such work, who did not care whether he/she did the work well, who did not care for the work itself, but at most cared simply for getting the answers or a promotion.[6] Such a person no more cares for or about his/her doing the work or doing it with the intellectual virtues, emotions, and desires discussed above, than we presumably care about which particular calculating machine does the sums. In each case, the doing is only a means to the end, and insofar as the end can be achieved independent of the means, or independent of the means being of a certain sort, the means is of no particular importance or value.[7]

This leads directly to the fourth point. Intellectual activities done for the goals and according to the criteria inherent in them are among the greatest human goods. They are constituent parts of many—though, certainly not all—sorts of good human life. The intellectual virtues, emotions, and desires are essential to such involvement in and with intellectual activity and life.

My views on these matters can be summarized by three claims: The intellectual virtues, emotions, desires, and attendant action are essential for good intellectual work. They are essential for a good intellectual life. They are essential for a great human good, and many sorts of good human life.[8]

NOTES

1. This is rejected by Aristotle, *NE* 1139^{a}9 sq, and, so it seems, by many who now hold a purified view of intellect.

2. See 1139^{a}21 sq. However, in an illuminating discussion of the *Topics,* "The Place of Logic in Aristotle's Thought," Weil argues that to accuse Aristotle of neglecting scientific activity one—I—must make the common mistake of taking what is translated as "science" and discussion of such science to have application to our

science. Weil argues that this is due to the "modern positivist identification of technique with science" and that those features of Aristotelian inquiry, syllogistic and dialectic, which we take to be scientific or which we take Aristotle to have deemed scientific are held by him to "constitute *technai,* or procedures, and not *epistemai,* or sciences: and they belong to the realm of *poiesis* (production) and not of *theoria* (contemplation)," (*Articles on Aristotle, 1. Science,* ed. Barnes, Schofield, and Sorabji [London, 1975]), p. 100. If this is correct, and if in the *Nicomachean Ethics* as well Aristotle does locate "our science" in the practical or productive, then my criticisms are directed only at a common misinterpretation of him. (They still apply, I would argue, to his views on contemplation. But I shall not pursue this.) Nonetheless, it should be useful to locate those passages which lend themselves to such common misinterpretation—to locate, in short, "our modern Aristotle." In what follows I shall write as if this Aristotle is Aristotle. Whether this is a mistake, as Weil argues and "charity" dictates, I shall leave for others to decide. Weil claims also that Aristotle "is as much interested in the psychological side . . . — in what we are accustomed to call, characteristically, the moral principles or *ethos* of the scientist—as in . . . formal principles; indeed, he would not even understand the separation of these two things" (p. 105). Two points should be made. First, I find this very difficult to reconcile with Aristotle's explicit claim of 1103^{a}4 sq, which excludes the moral even from practical intellect. Second, Weil's "we" does not refer all that obviously to those in the English-speaking philosophical world, who have not profited e.g., from Bachelard.

3. It might also be argued that Aristotle was concerned with the latter, not the former, as indicated by 1139^{b}30 sq and, following Ross, *An Post* 71^{b}9-23. But Barnes argues in "Aristotle's Theory of Demonstration" that "the theory of demonstrative science was never meant to guide or formalize scientific research: it was concerned exclusively with the teaching of facts already won; it does not describe how scientists do, or ought to, *acquire* knowledge: it offers a formal model of how teachers should *present and impart* knowledge" (*Articles on Aristotle 1. Science,* p. 77). This also raises the question of the location of scientific research in Aristotle's framework, especially that of the *Nicomachean Ethics.* Barnes, we might note, ends the above sentence with a footnote to p. 100 of Weil's article.

4. See 1139^{a}31 sq.

5. How Aristotle and Hume differ on these matters need not concern us here. Nor need we be concerned with whether their followers followed them correctly.

6. See Aristotle's claim about truth and science, 1139^{a}21 sq.

7. On the second and third points, see my "The Schizophrenia of Modern Ethical Theories," *The Journal of Philosophy* (1976).

8. I am deeply indebted to all those who discussed earlier drafts with me. I should like to express my special thanks to John Campbell, Max Deutscher, Michael Devitt, Peter Herbst, Genevieve Lloyd, Kim Lycos, and Amélie Rorty.

XIV

RITUAL AND THE RELIGIOUS FEELINGS

GARETH MATTHEWS

> For when men pray they do with the members of
> their bodies what befits suppliants—when they
> bend their knees and stretch out their hands, or
> even prostrate themselves, and whatever else they
> do visibly, although their invisible will and the
> intention of their heart is known to God. Nor
> does He need these signs for the human mind to
> be laid bare to Him. But in this way a man excites
> himself to pray more and to groan more humbly
> and more fervently. I do not know how it is that,
> although these motions of the body cannot come
> to be without a motion of the mind preceding
> them, when they have been made, visibly and ex-
> ternally, that invisible inner motion which caused
> them is itself strengthened. And in this manner
> the disposition of the heart which preceded them
> in order that they might be made, grows stronger
> because they are made. Of course if someone is
> constrained or even bound, so that he cannot do
> these things with his limbs, it does not follow
> that, when he is stricken with remorse, the inner
> man does not pray and prostrate himself before
> the eyes of God in his most secret chamber.
> —Augustine, *De cura pro mortuis* 5.7

I

One smiles and tells the expert chef how good the sauce béarnaise is, not so much to inform him about the sauce (he knows better than we how good it is) as to assure him that we are enjoying it and that we appreciate his efforts. But when one kneels in one's pew and repeats a litany of thanksgiving it is not, it seems, that one means to be informing God of anything—not even of one's thankfulness. For God, unlike the chef, has no need of information.

So why do religious people do all the things they do in prayer "with the members of their bodies"?

The answer Augustine gives in the above passage from his treatise, "On the Care of the Dead," is that the bodily performance of ritual has the effect of intensifying appropriate religious attitudes and affections. ("... in this way a man excites himself to pray more and to groan more humbly and more fervently.") Yet Augustine is puzzled by his answer. "I do not know how it is," he says.[1]

And he should be puzzled. For, as Augustine conceives it, the intensification of a religious attitude or feeling by the performance of a ritualistic act is a case of movements of the body having the effect of moving the soul. ("... when [these motions of the body] have been made, visibly and externally, that invisible inner motion which caused them is itself strengthened.") And this never happens —it cannot happen; for, according to Augustine, the soul, any soul, is superior to the body, any body (*Enarrationes in psalmos* 145.3 and *De musica* 6.5.8) and that which is inferior can never move that which is superior (*De genesi ad litteram* 12.16.33).

There would have been an even better reason for Augustinian puzzlement. Augustine, like Descartes, conceives the soul and the body as two different things of such disparate sorts that the idea of interaction between a body and a soul becomes incomprehensible. Augustine is presumably led to overlook this incomprehensibility by the (to him) very obvious fact that the soul does affect the body (see, e.g., *De genesi ad litteram* 12.19.41). Perhaps a similarly robust sense of fact leads him to throw out his metaphysical principle about the superior and the inferior and to concede that the actual performance of ritual often does intensify the attitudes and feelings that give rise to it.

Sometimes, of course, the reverse is true. A child who is made to say "Thank you" upon receipt of any and every benefaction may thereby be made more thankful; she may also be made more resentful. It all depends.

Some people are annoyed and offended by ritual. Even those for whom characteristically religious attitudes are enormously important may abhor ritual; indeed they may abhor ritual precisely because they feel it encourages the wrong feelings and attitudes.

Augustine can hardly have forgotten that it was Jesus who condemned the Pharisee's energetic recitation of public prayer. Jesus advised praying in secret, where concern with externals could be eliminated, or at least minimized. Perhaps this is a second reason for Augustine's embarrassment and puzzlement in the passage above. Aware that Jesus criticized ritualizers (see Augustine's *De sermone domini in monte* 1.3), Augustine nevertheless finds himself somewhat uneasily suggesting that the behavior of the outer man (*homo exterior*) often intensifies the spiritual motions of the inner man (*homo interior*).

II

Metaphysics and theology aside, it seems obviously true that sometimes and for some people participation in a liturgical rite nurtures certain religious attitudes and affections. But why? Well, if I refer to myself as a poor and miserable sinner often enough, I may come finally to believe that this is what I am. Is this not an honored truth of both pedagogy and propaganda?

Now suppose I bow or kneel. This in itself may have an important effect upon my attitudes (the primary meaning of "attitude" is relevant to this point), even though it does not involve making an assertion.

I suppose we might try to understand the effect of nonverbal gestures and ritualistic movements in terms of what they symbolize—what they "say."[2] Kneeling, for example, "says": "I am a suppliant."[3] Then we could add that the performance of these ritualistic acts, like the repetition of a statement, encourages one to believe what is thereby "said."

Yet this is all much too easy. Not just any old repetition of a statement encourages belief. Not just any old performance of a ritual instills the appropriate attitudes. The mocking repetition of a statement may undermine its credibility. And the self-righteous and hypocritical performance of ritual may discourage the favored attitudes. At most it is sincere, or at least apparently sincere, repetition that instills belief.

Now, however, we have torn ourselves loose from the terms of Augustine's problem. His problem is how what the outer man does can affect the inner man—how the mere "motions of the body," motions that "cannot come to be without a motion of the mind preceding them," can affect the mind itself.

That Augustine identifies the outer man with the body, something merely physical, that "part" of a human being buried at death, is shown in this passage from *The City of God:*

> ...a man is not just a body, or just a soul, but a being made up of body and soul.... The soul is not the whole man, but the better part of a man; the body is not the whole, but the inferior part of a man. When both are joined together they have the name "man," which, however, they do not either one lose when we speak of them singly. For who is prohibited from saying, in ordinary language, "That man is dead and is now in peace or in torment," though this can be said only of the soul; or "That man is buried in that place or in that," though this cannot be understood except as referring to the body alone? Will they say that Holy Scripture follows no such usage? On the contrary, it so thoroughly adopts it that even when a man is alive and his body and soul are joined together it calls each of them singly by the name "man," speaking of the soul as the "inner man" and the body as the "outer man"—as if there were two men, although both together are one man.
>
> [*De civitate dei* 13.24.2]

Now clearly a motion of the outer man (or body), so understood, cannot be either sincere or insincere, mocking or serious. It takes the action of the whole man—body and mind (or soul)—to be insincere. According to Augustine, its insincerity will lie in a certain discrepancy between what the outer man does and what the inner man does.

This means that our effort to understand a physical motion as "saying" something (e.g., "I am a suppliant") is misplaced. For a mere motion of an Augustinian body could not by itself have meaning in the way required.

Thus we cannot explain how the mere motion of the body in ritual inculcates religious attitudes and intensifies religious feelings because it is not the mere motion of the body that has this effect. What may have this effect is the sincere and understanding performance of ritual.

III

So the puzzle Augustine moves on to is a specious puzzle. What about the puzzle Augustine starts with? That is, what about the worry as to why one need pray outwardly when God knows already what is in one's heart? Augustine's answer to this worry—that the bodily performance of ritual may have the effect of intensifying appropriate religious attitudes and affections—suggests that Augustine's question ("Why need one pray outwardly?") is really two questions. One question is "Why pray, when God knows already everything one could possibly tell him?" and the other is "Why pray *outwardly,* with 'the members of the body,' when God knows already one's 'invisible will' and the 'intention of one's heart?' "?

It seems perverse to run these two questions together. Surely one can't make a good judgment as to whether what Augustine offers us is a good reason for praying *outwardly* until one is reasonably clear about what a good reason for *praying* might be. And there is a further point. Suppose the reason for praying were Q. It might actually follow from Q (or perhaps from Q together with certain natural assumptions) that one ought to pray *outwardly.* So an answer to the first question might actually be all, or most, of an answer to the second.

Perhaps Augustine tends to conceive praying inwardly as simply having certain feelings and attitudes without expressing them, much as one might conceive giving alms inwardly as simply having feelings of charity. If this is the way Augustine conceives, or tends to conceive, inward praying, then the question "Why pray, when God knows already?" easily becomes the question "Why pray *outwardly,* when God knows already?"

I think that such is, in fact, the way Augustine conceives inward, versus outward, praying. That this is so can be seen at once from his use of the biblical locution "inner man" to mean simply *mind* or *soul* and "outer man" to mean simply *body*—as in the quotation from *The City of God* in the last section.

Augustine therefore looks upon inner acts and speeches as making up one's authentic mental and spiritual life. Outer acts and speeches, only contingently related to inner acts and speeches, may sometimes manifest the inner ones with a modest degree of accuracy; but they need not even do that. In any case, psychological descriptions (descriptions of one's thoughts, desires, intentions, attitudes, feelings, etc.) are really descriptions of the independent and self-sufficient inner man. With this sort of picture before us it is natural to suppose that the body's only functions are to manifest the soul's thoughts, to help gratify the soul's desires, and to help execute decisions made by the soul. And since ritual serves neither to advance practical ends nor to pass on information to God, the question arises, why engage in ritual?

That Augustine's dualism affords a mistaken basis for interpreting the biblical inner-outer contrast could be shown in detail; but I shall not attempt that here. Instead I shall just say, rather dogmatically, that when (to pick one example) the psalmist speaks of someone as blessing outwardly and cursing inwardly ("They bless with their mouth, but they curse inwardly" [Ps. 62:4]) he is describing the mock piety of an insincere person, not a merely physical movement of a body. As we have already noted, a merely physical movement is not either sincere or insincere.

Moreover, the inner-outer contrast one finds in the Bible, far from rendering problematic the importance of ritual to one's devotional life, in fact underlines its central significance. Corresponding to each inner act or gesture that one may be said to perform, there is a state, attitude, or feeling that all and only those who perform the inner act may be said to have. Thus, "He kneels inwardly" corresponds to the claim that he has contrition, or is contrite, or does something contritely, and "He gives alms inwardly" corresponds to the claim that he has charity, or is charitable, or does something charitably. In making use of an inner-man locution rather than the corresponding abstract substantive, adjective, or adverb, biblical writers remind us of the way of life in which typically religious attitudes and feelings take form.

Two caveats are in order. First, one's participation in this life of worship may be insincere. One's actions may then be said to be merely outward. (But that doesn't, of course, mean that they are merely physical.) Second, one may be faithful and God-fearing though one is either physically or psychologically unable to worship in standard, ritualistic ways. This inability may be only momentary, or it may be long-term. But in saying that one kneels (etc.) inwardly, the biblical writer reveals that it is by reference to the standard ritualistic case that he conceives and understands piety.

IV

Augustine's mind-body dualism may give rise to an even more basic puzzle than anything I have mentioned so far. This puzzle concerns nonreligious feelings as much as religious ones. Take, for example, gratitude.

Suppose my sister has foregone a chance to hear a concert so that I could hear it. Suppose, as would be likely, it is important to her that I be at least minimally grateful to her for what she has done. What exactly is it that is important to her? That I have a certain feeling, a certain mental datum? And how can that be seriously important to her? Or is what is important to her that I act toward her in a grateful way? But acting toward her in a grateful way may not please her at all, may even upset or annoy her, if she discovers that no feeling of gratitude accompanies my actions. So we are back to the feeling of gratitude. And how can it be important to her that I have a certain feeling?

Or take, for example, feeling sorry for having done someone a wrong. Suppose my friend is prepared to forgive me a grave injustice I have done him if he knows I am sorry. How can it be so important to him that I have a certain feeling? Or is what is important to him that I behave in a contrite manner? But if he discovers that I behave as if appropriately contrite but do not really feel sorry, he may be even more upset than before. So it is, after all, my feeling sorry that counts. But how can it be so important to him that I have a certain feeling?

What generates this puzzle is the notion that a feeling of gratitude or sorrow is basically an inner event—what Augustine calls "an invisible inner motion." In fact, other-directed feelings such as these, whether religious or not, are much more complex and interesting than the notion of an "invisible inner motion" would suggest. Gratitude, for example, carries with it the recognition of what one takes to be a benefaction and a disposition to look favorably on one's putative benefactor. There is no such thing as having the feeling without recognizing the (putative) benefaction and being disposed to look favorably on the (putative) benefactor.

What my sister wants, in the above situation, is not simply that there be within me an invisible mental motion, perhaps something like a sensation of warmth. What she wants is that I recognize her benefaction (already something complex and far-ranging) and that I be moved by that recognition to look favorably on her as a benefactor.

Something similar is true of sorrow at having wronged another. Such sorrow carries with it the recognition that one has wronged another and the disposition to behave toward that person in a compensatory way. What my friend wants, in the situation just described, is not especially that there be within me some mental motion (say, something like an unpleasant sensation). What he wants is for me to recognize that I have wronged him and for me to take certain steps toward effecting a reconciliation. (What some of those steps might be I shall detail in a moment.)

These points apply to religious, as well as nonreligious, feelings. But before we can see how they are relevant to Augustine's worry about why one should pray outwardly, when God knows already what is in one's heart, we need to deal directly with the apparent disanalogy between God's knowledge and what any human being could know.

V

It is very easy to overdraw the contrast between being sorry for one's sins before God and being sorry that one has wronged another person.[4] Of course no human being is omniscient. But sometimes a human being knows as much about the feelings of another human being as is relevant to an apology. And then the fact that an omniscient being would know infinitely more is not important to the apology.

Suppose I have wronged you, and I am sorry for what I have done. I may want to bring it about that you know I have the feelings I in fact have. In order to achieve this result I may apologize by saying, "I'm sorry."

But of course you may already know that I am sorry. You may know by the sound of my voice, by the look on my face. Furthermore, I may know that you know I am sorry. In such a case I do not need to bring about the result that you know I have the feelings of sorrow I have. I do not need to bring about that result because it is already achieved. In such a case you are like God insofar as he, too, already knows; and I know that he knows.

Still, there may be a place for me to tell you what you already know, namely, that I am sorry. That is, there may yet be a place for apology. Here are some reasons why an apology may yet be important.

1. I need to acknowledge my wrongdoing. I have done you wrong. I know it. You know it. But unless and until I acknowledge my guilt, there is something important to both of us that has gone unsaid. It needs to be said. Our relationship cannot be put right until I have "owned up" to what I have done.

2. I need to ask for forgiveness. And I cannot ask for forgiveness without owning up to what I need to be forgiven for. Of course you may be able and willing to forgive me without an apology. "He didn't know what he was doing," you may say; or, "He is not aware how his actions strike others." But you cannot excuse me like this as a general thing. Or at least if you do, you will not be treating me as a moral agent, responsible for what I do; you will be treating me as a child, or perhaps as a case study.

3. I may want to commiserate with you. You have been hurt by my misdeed. As your friend, I want to express sympathy for your hurt. But, since it was I who wronged you, I cannot commiserate sincerely, or successfully, without apologizing.

4. I may need to share the burden of my guilt. To apologize is to invite a response from you. By responding in a forgiving way you accept me, wrongdoing and all, and so relieve me of some of the burden of my guilt.

I think it is clear that there are theological analogues to most, if not all, these four points. I shall try to bring them out by reference to the Prayer of General Confession from the Episcopalian *Book of Common Prayer* (1928 version). This is the way the prayer goes:

Almighty God, Father of our Lord Jesus Christ,
Maker of all things, judge of all men;
We acknowledge and bewail our manifold sins and wickedness,
Which we, from time to time, most grievously have committed,
By thought, word, and deed,
Against thy Divine Majesty,
Provoking most justly thy wrath and indignation against us.
We do earnestly repent.

And are heartily sorry for these our misdoings;
The remembrance of them is grievous unto us;
The burden of them is intolerable.
Have mercy upon us,
Have mercy upon us, most merciful Father;
For thy Son our Lord Jesus Christ's sake,
Forgive us all that is past;
And grant that we may ever hereafter
Serve and please thee
In newness of life,
To the honour and glory of thy Name;
Through Jesus Christ our Lord. Amen.

1. The importance of acknowledging one's sins is made clear in the opening statement, "We acknowledge and bewail our manifold sins and wickedness..." It is not enough to be sorry. One must acknowledge one's sins.

2. The connection between being sorry, acknowledging one's sins, and asking for forgiveness is brought out in this sequence: "We do earnestly repent, And are heartily sorry for these our misdoings;... Have mercy upon us,... Forgive us all that is past; And grant that we may ever hereafter Serve and please thee In newness of life..."

3. One might question whether there is any place in the believer's relations with God for commiserating with God. To attempt to commiserate with God might seem to be attempting something presumptuous and inappropriate. Still, there is a recognition in the Prayer of General Confession that one's misdeeds are an affront to the Divine Majesty ("... our manifold sins and wickedness, Which we, from time to time, most grievously have committed... Against thy Divine Majesty..."). To recognize that affront is, perhaps, to offer a kind of commiseration.

4. Finally, the request to share one's burdens is suggested in the lines, "The remembrance of [our misdeeds] is grievous unto us; The burden of them is intolerable." God is conceived as not merely lifting the burden of one's guilt, but sharing it. This is the point of the doctrine of the atonement. ("Surely he hath borne our griefs, and carried our sorrows" [Isa. 53.4]).

It is clear now that our Augustinian puzzle—Why is it necessary to express sorrow for one's sins, when God knows already? Why isn't it enough to have feelings of sorrow?—arises from an oversimplified picture of what it is to have such feelings and of what could be the point in expressing them. Certainly there may be point, even profound point, in saying that one is sorry for a misdeed even when one's hearer already knows how one feels, and one knows that one's hearer knows.

VI

Can something similar be said about other religious feelings? I think so. Consider gratitude to God for one's blessings. Here, as before, it is easy to overdraw the contrast between relations with God and relations with a human being. If A has done a favor to B, other things being equal, this fact needs to be acknowledged by B. It will not, in general, be enough that B is grateful, even if A knows that B is grateful and B knows that A knows. B needs to say, "Thank you."

To get an idea of the importance of Bs saying, "Thank you," we might think of possible explanations for Bs failure to do so.

One explanation might be that B, though grateful, is too proud to admit any indebtedness to A. Another possible explanation would be the very opposite, namely, that B lacks sufficient self-respect to be able to admit any gratitude to A; saying "Thank you" might threaten the little self-esteem B has. In both these situations it will be important to B, as well as to Bs relationship to A, that B say "Thank you."

There are, of course, all sorts of ways that saying "Thank you" may go wrong. The "Thank you" may be grudging, servile, resentful, patronizing or automatic. But it may be appropriately spoken and appropriately received. My point is that saying "Thank you" is not usually simply doing something to bring about the result that another person knows one has feelings of gratitude. It is acting in a way appropriate to the receipt of a gift or favor.

Most of this carries over to the theological case. The believer needs to acknowledge God's blessings. It may be hard to do this, and especially hard to do it in the right spirit. But to do it in the right spirit is to offer a kind of return gift; it is to give thanks, which is an act of worship.

I turn now to feelings of joy. "My soul shall be joyful in the

Lord," says the psalmist. One religious feeling of joy is joy in God. We do not ordinarily think of ourselves as rejoicing or being joyful *in* other people (though we certainly delight in our children, or take delight in them); but we do rejoice in the good fortune, success or happiness of other people. Perhaps an interhuman analogue to being joyful in God is therefore being joyful in the success, happiness, or good fortune of another person.

We often express joy in the good fortune of another person by a celebration. We throw a party. Suppose I have a friend who has just passed a difficult examination. I have shared her ordeal with her. I am overjoyed by her success. Since she is a good friend, she can easily tell how elated I am. And I know she can tell. Yet it would be ridiculous to say there is no need for me to throw a party for her, since she knows already how happy I am at her success, perhaps even how pleased everyone else is who would come to the party. The role of the celebration is in no way usurped by someone's prior knowledge of the feelings of joy it is meant to express.

So it is also with joy in God. The Bible enjoins us to be joyful in God. We are to "make a joyful noise unto the Lord," to "make a loud noise, and rejoice, and sing praise" (Ps. 98.4). Among the many recommended noisemakers are the harp, the voice, trumpets, and a cornet (Ps. 98.5-6). The role of such a celebration is in no way usurped by a prior knowledge—whether Divine or human—of the feelings of joy it is meant to express.

Thus the idea that God knows already the secrets of one's heart does not make it inappropriate to rejoice in God, to express gratitude to him for one's belssings or to express sorrow to him for one's sins. In fact, almost the reverse is true; the idea that God knows already cancels out a range of considerations that might otherwise be thought to justify one in hiding one's feelings. To see that this is so let us first remind ourselves of nonreligious cases in which it might be appropriate to hide one's feelings.

I may want to hide my feelings of jealousy and frustration when I lose a game or contest lest the winner be unable to enjoy her well-earned satisfaction. Again, to express to my child the rage I experience when I learn that he has been slighted, or unfairly dealt with, may bewilder and confuse him; it may be best to hide these feelings.

There certainly are occasions on which one would not express one's religious feelings before others. Thus, for example, it may be wrong to express my gratitude to God for a healthy child in the presence of someone with a deformed child. Or again, it may be inappropriate or wrong to rejoice in God in a public school, lest the religious sensibilities of others be offended.

But there can be no point in hiding one's feelings from God, lest God be offended; God knows already. The idea that God knows already what is in one's heart—far from being a reason for not expressing religious feelings—may actually be a good reason for not hiding them. Concealment has no point when we are dealing with one "unto whom all hearts are open, all desires known, and from whom no secrets are hid" (Opening Collect from the service of Holy Communion, *The Book of Common Prayer*).

VII

I have argued that Augustine's idea of engaging in ritual to enhance one's religious feelings is, in his own dualistic terms, misconceived. I have also argued that the puzzle this idea is meant to solve, is misconceived. But mightn't it still be the case that some people sometimes engage in religious ritual to enhance their feelings toward God? And suppose someone had that project? Mightn't it be a reasonable one, or would it be inevitably phony and in bad faith?

Consider gratitude to God for one's blessings. Imagine thinking that by going to church or synagogue to join in a service of praise and thanksgiving one might arouse or enhance one's feelings of gratitude toward God. Either one now has no such feelings at all or one has them only to degree n. Isn't the project of doing something "with the members of one's body" to arouse those feelings or to enhance them beyond degree n, inevitably phony—phony because one's motivation to join in the service must go beyond any feelings of gratitude one now has?

I am inclined to think that this project is indeed a phony one. (If I am right, that point, too, counts against what Augustine says in the passage from "On the Care of the Dead.") But there is a similar project, one that might easily be confused with the project Augustine outlines, that need not be phony.

I have already mentioned that other-directed feelings, such as gratitude, carry with them the recognition of some truth, or alleged truth (in the case of gratitude, the truth, or alleged truth, that someone has benefited one). Now religious feelings are feelings such that having them carries with it the recognition of alleged truths (e.g., that God is gracious, that one is a sinner, etc.) which are such that one who leads a religious life will think it important to find regular occasions on which to rehearse and acknowledge them. To provide a regular opportunity to rehearse these putative truths is also to provide opportunity to feel afresh the gratitude, the joy and the sorrow that carry with them the recognition of these alleged truths. It may, of course, be the case that on a given occasion, or for an extended period of time, even for life, one in fact feels no gratitude, no sorrow, no joy—no matter how many times one says the familiar words and makes the familiar movements. But one can make a place in one's life for the feeling of religious feelings without seeking to manipulate or force those feelings. One can do this by making a place for the dramatic rehearsal, "with the members of one's body," of what one regards as life's most important truths. Put briefly, that is the justification for religious ritual in the life of a believer.

VIII

Both the puzzle Augustine begins with in the passage cited from "On the Care of the Dead" and the puzzle he ends up with have turned out to be specious. The puzzle he ends up with is this: How can the mere motions of the body in ritual intensify religious feelings and attitudes? This puzzle is specious because it is not the mere motions of the body that have such an effect; what has, or may have, such an effect is (among other things) the sincere and understanding performance of ritual—the dramatic rehearsal of the tenets of one's faith, including the story of salvation.

The puzzle Augustine begins with is then this: Why need one express, as well as simply have, feelings such as sorrow for one's sins, since God knows already what feelings one has? This puzzle is specious because it presupposes that the only (or at least the primary) reason for saying (e.g.) that I am sorry for having done something wrong is to bring about the result that someone else knows (or thinks) that I have certain feelings. But this is not so. An apology may have real point even when the person it is directed toward already knows, and I know that she or he knows, what is in my heart. And so, for that matter, may a banquet. And so may a ritual in which people rehearse, dramatically, the tenets of their faith and in which, as Augustine says, they "do with the members of their bodies what befits suppliants—when they bend their knees and stretch out their hands, or even prostrate themselves."[5]

NOTES

1. In a passage somewhat reminiscent of Augustine, Jonathan Edwards says this: "To instance in the duty of prayer: it is manifest that we are not appointed in this duty to declare God's perfections, His majesty, holiness, goodness, and all-sufficiency, and our meanness, emptiness, dependence, and unworthiness, and our wants and desires, to inform God of these things, or to incline His heart, and prevail with him to be willing to show us mercy; but suitably to affect our own hearts with the things we express, and so to prepare us to receive the blessings we ask. And such gestures and manner of external behaviour in the worship of God, which custom has made to be significations of humility and reverence, can be of no further use than as they have some tendency to affect our own hearts, or the hearts of others" (*The Religious Affections* 2.9). Edwards's suggestion that one reason for gesticulation is to affect the hearts of others seems a natural addition to what Augustine says. It is noteworthy, however, that Edwards, unlike Augustine, shows no puzzlement over the idea that "external behavior" might have "some tendency to affect our own hearts."

2. "No less than words, actions or gestures are also a type of language; they hold a message for us. They have a meaning which the person who sincerely wishes to pray the Liturgy must get to know. Whether used by man for practical or symbolical reasons, gestures or ceremonies help man to express himself better, make his thought and intent clearer and more vivid." (John H. Miller, C.S.C., *Fundamentals of the Liturgy,* [Notre Dame, 1959], p. 188).

3. "In the Liturgy . . . kneeling was usually associated with fasting and was a penitential and suppliant posture" (ibid., p. 192).

4. I owe the idea developed in this section and the next to discussions with Stanley Cavell.

5. This paper is a revised version of a paper called "Bodily Motions and Religious Feelings," which was first published in the *Canadian Journal of Philosophy* I (1971), 75-86.

XV

NATURAL PRIDE AND
NATURAL SHAME

ARNOLD ISENBERG

> You can reasonably take pride in strength, beauty, or intelligence; but you cannot reasonably be ashamed of the corresponding defects.

I

There is a "pride" which is *identical* with the possession of a certain gift—like the proud bearing of the race horse, which is nothing but vitality itself, or like the pride which the birds take in flight. Pride is immanent in the prance of health and of intelligence, as in the employment of any talent or skill. More, the exercise of a natural faculty can be censured as a piece of insolence: the mere enjoyment of the body or the mind takes you across the limits of what someone, rightly or wrongly, considers your proper sphere. To kick up your heels in exuberance is to fling sand in somebody's eyes. To wear bright clothes in the vicinity of a funeral is to offend the mourners—who may resent the very existence of a healthy person as an insult to the dead. The frolics of Panurge and of Pantagruel— entirely apart from the state of mind which shamelessly extols them —are an outrage to the god or man who, in Spinoza's phrase, "rejoices in our want of power." Living is an affirmation and can be taken as an affront.

Such pride might nevertheless be reasonable; but such pride is hardly pride. To pride yourself on a quality means something more than just to have that quality: it implies at least a reflection upon it. A good posture, for instance, is a pleasure in itself; but to *know* that your posture is good is a distinct, a superadded, pleasure; and this consciousness betrays itself, by a slight change, in the posture itself. (Pride is a "swelling." The proud man "swaggers" or "struts." He is "bursting" with pride, and so forth.) So also to be beautiful is to exercise the power of attraction. Beauty brings admiration, and admiration pleases. But to be proud *of* one's attractiveness (or one's riches, one's birth) is still another thing. On this basis Hume distinguished between pride and joy. To have or to get something which you desire is joy. But in pride there is something more —the recognition, the thought: "I have this thing." There is a reference to self and to the attainments of self. Pride is the reflex sentiment which accrues with the consciousness of what is already an advantage.

Now, what are the qualities of which we are proud? They are qualities, first, which are considered desirable; and there is no quality deemed desirable the possession of which cannot be a source of pride.[1] But in the second place it might seem to us that they are qualities by which we win, or believe that we win, social admiration or approval. On this view we are at bottom proud of nothing but a certain standing in the eyes of others. But this social thesis must be rejected, for the following reasons.

It is one thing to receive from society one's standard of good and evil, which determines what is approved even to oneself, and another thing to crave the approval of society. An approved good is one thing; the good of approval, another. No one will deny that the approbation of one's kind is an important object of desire and, in consequence, a source of pride; that it figures to the exclusion of everything else in the love of eminence, rank, decorations, social status; or that this motive may be inextricably mixed with any pride of achievement whatsoever. But a normal person wishes to be esteemed for those attributes which he esteems. The artist and the scientist demand applause on their own strict terms. The shallowness of those who exult in empty praise is inexpressible, for they have sacrificed every other standard and have no longer a conception of what it is good to be honored *for*. Besides, there are people who, having proudly rejected the toleration of society in behalf of some notion of good, are supported in their intransigence by no one but a few dead authors, who cannot make their pleasure or displeasure felt. If the social thesis is to maintain itself, then, it must fall back on the prior influence of society on the very standard of value. It must assume that every taste and desire, from the love of money to the love of music, is created purely by the application of social sanctions; more, that the objects of taste and desire (and of conscience and emotion) *still*, in some definable sense, symbolize approval and disapproval and derive their whole value from what they symbolize. Here, of course, it is supported by a selection of the available facts, because some people have no reason for believing or valuing anything except that it is believed or valued by somebody else and, if they go to the stake, do so because they would rather defy the ruler than disobey a deceased parent. But (to establish only the minimal point) it is impossible to concede that we are primordially sensitive to nothing but the reactions of those around us. If there are natural desires which convention cannot eradicate, there may be latent but ineradicable standards of what is desirable. One thinks, for example, of a woman who "accepts" but violates the code which prescribes permanent virginity for unmarried women. Since she has done what she thinks undesirable, she is ashamed; but since she has done what in spite of herself she may "think" desirable, she is proud—as Héloise was. Even if such an instinctive basis for judgments of value, skulking beneath the conventions, be denied, there is still the rational plane above them: and the rationalist, who *thinks out* his criticism of society and its standards of good and right, may well be proud of himself and of what are, according to his lights, his virtues and achievements. This shows that we are proud when we have what we value, whether society agrees with us or not. And this point is independent of any theory which should hold that there are radically individualistic values, totally uninfluenced by the existence of a social environment.

We can also dispose of the closely related question of *comparative* advantages. We do not doubt that it is gratifying to be first in the competition—wealthiest, handsomest, foremost in anything. Some societies encourage such comparison by distributing their rewards on a competitive basis, as for example in athletics. But that does not mean that one may not equally reflect with pleasure on absolute qualities, such as agility, and on qualities, moreover, which many people have, such as health.[2]

The definition of pride, then, has three parts. There is (1) a quality which (2) is approved (or considered desirable) and (3) is judged to belong to oneself. A word about (3). Even if there were something logically peculiar about judgments one makes concerning oneself, if they did not have the same standing as judgments we make about other people, if they were not formulated and tested by the same procedures that another person uses when he makes a judgment about us, still this sort of peculiarity would have no relevance for any of the issues to be discussed below. Those issues would be illustrated just as well by the fact that you have a good batting average or a long bibliography, which anyone else can see as well as you can, as by the fact that you have a warm heart, which, according to some philosophers, you can know when other people either cannot or do not know about it. The fact that one is both the subject and the object of all judgments concerning oneself does introduce exceptional opportunities for error and distortion. Because a certain quality, such as genius or popularity, is considered valuable, I am tempted to impute it to myself when I do not in fact possess it. And because a certain quality, such as blondness or horsemanship, happens to belong to me, I am disposed to value it much too highly. Hence, innumerable varieties of "false" pride (as well as "false" modesty, "false" humility, and so on). Yet we need not, after all, go to examples of judgments concerning self to discover motives which give rise to illusion: there are forces in the self which distort our perception of many other objects than the self. We deceive ourselves about many things besides ourselves—and for reasons which are, for a theory of cognition if not for a minute psychology of judgment, essentially similar.[3]

Pride, from the psychological standpoint, is pleasure taken in the possession of some quality that one deems valuable—and there is the clue to the position of this paper. A *genuine* and *reasonable* pride, from the ethical standpoint, will depend on a comprehensive and just sense of values.

Now "gifts" are not the basis of pride that "achievements" are.

At first sight it does not seem difficult to distinguish between gifts and achievements. Achievements are the result of purpose and effort. I am in no way responsible for the good looks I may have inherited from my mother or the vigor transmitted by my father; so I am said to "deserve no credit" for them. Yet it must be the intention of this remark not to deprive me of all credit whatsoever but to insist only that such credit should be *less* than the credit accorded for traits of character or acts of will, and should be *different* in quality, as honor, reverence, and admiration are different one from another. For, in a more radical sense of the word *gift,* is not everything in the end a gift? Who gave me talent or kindness or heart, magnanimity, courage, the capacity for self-discipline and self-development? Not I myself. The aptitude for learning is not learned, the ability to acquire is not acquired. My acts are dependent on my will as my stature, for instance, is not. But my will—what is that dependent on? Some people are endowed with the desire for improvement as others with beauty or strength of body; and one is not at bottom more praiseworthy than the other *if it is a question of ultimate responsibility for what one is and does.* It is true that my character has been more deeply affected than my appearance has by decisions which I have taken in the past; but does that explain why it should be more seriously praised or blamed? Does a scoundrel become more lovable if we find out that his character was inherited? It is true, again, that the world is interested not in promise but in performance, and that an element of striving and practice is bound to enter into performance. But beauty and force of body are precisely the exceptions (or nearly so), the cases where the finished performance is turned out effortlessly; and it is hard to see why that should be held against them.[4]

Here we hit upon what is really meant when we discriminate, as moralists, between natural advantages and moral achievements. We mean that certain qualities are humanly more valuable than certain others. We are venturing a judgment in ethics and not in genetics. The will is praiseworthy and blameworthy where the torso is not, not because it had something more to do with creating itself but because the will is the will and the torso the torso. Just as we put taste and musicianship above mere tone in a singer and ability above glamour in an actress, so size and strength and physical charm are inferior to wisdom and moral perfection; and we are not really interested in distinctions of origin as between these things— though such distinctions can of course be made. We are not the less grateful to Mozart for the prominence of the congenital factor in his ability; and if there were a man who acted wisely and justly on instinct alone, we should not withhold a jot of praise. If a woman, on the other hand, is known to have acquired her beauty by hard labor, we do not think any the better of her for it; because the attribute of beauty is consistent with her proving a bane both to herself and to everyone she may know. Some credit, it is true, is given to people who have won their health back by their own efforts or made their own money by arduous toil. But that is because industry and effort are, as it happens, valuable qualities on their own part. Between a man born crooked and one who achieves crookedness there is really nothing to choose.

I shall continue for convenience to refer to qualities like beauty and strength as "gifts" and to qualities like wisdom as "achievements." Gifts, then, are not the basis of pride that achievements are. For pride should be proportioned to the real value of the things of which we are proud. The pride taken in qualities of our own must run parallel to the respect which we should feel for the same qualities in another person, and this respect must in turn correspond to the actual worth of those qualities. You would expect, then, that people who preen themselves on trivial accomplishments (as the boardinghouse keeper on her "respectability") should also worship false gods and make heroes out of crooners and prizefighters. There lies the danger, for any actor or athlete or aviator, of accepting the homage of the crowd. He will soon begin to accept their judgment, and then he is lost. It goes, as we say, to his head.

By the same token, pride which is just and proportionate to the quality or act is reasonable. Now there exist both general and particular objections to this statement. It can be said either (1) that there can be no justification for any sort of pride, or (2) that pride in the so-called natural advantages cannot be justified.

1. The substance of this argument is simply that a reasonable person will give himself very little opportunity for reflection upon what he is or has or has done but will be devoted to purposes and tasks which remain. In other words, he will be "objective," outward-directed; and this comports very badly with pride. But this again is a question of where and when and how much. It can hardly be expected that a person intelligent enough to be sensitive to any merit in anybody should be ignorant of its existence in himself, that while he must be conscious beforehand of what he wants to attain, he should not know when he has attained it. Self-approbation, the pleasure of reflecting upon what one has already accomplished, reinforces the incentive to acts of the same kind; and while it would be wrong to rest one one's laurels, or trade on credit issued long before, it is hardly better to plunge ahead without a stocktaking. So

we find that Aristotle sanctions pride in his "magnificent man" (endowing him even with a slightly ridiculous pomposity) and that Lenin, a tolerably objective personality, could be subjective enough to indulge in a moral review of his life. Spinoza, on the other hand, seems to disparage pride; but that is because he defined it to begin with as "*over*-estimation of oneself by reason of self-love." What Spinoza calls "self-satisfaction," which is "pleasure arising from the contemplation of oneself and of one's power of action," is "the greatest good for which we can hope"—and "self-satisfaction" is of course exactly what I mean by pride.

The defense will be clinched if we can show that a just pride is not opposed to humility. Humility consists in knowing one's limitations as pride consists in knowing one's merits or, as Spinoza would say, one's power. But the knowledge of both is comprehended in the act of knowing one's place. I know my place: I am a distinguished statesman or scientist. But I know my place: I am one life among millions; I am neither omnipotent nor all-important; I am hedged about by a myriad of rights; my discoveries in physics do not entitle me to trample on anyone, to sit at the head of the table, to speak first or longest or loudest. No conceivable human attainment can override the finitude of individuality, that is to say, cancel the rights which every other person enjoys merely in virtue of being human.[5] The "humility of truly great men" is probably something of a fiction; but there is no *reason* why a great man should not also be great in humility—understand his total position as he understands his position in science or government or art.

As a matter of fact, we have been speaking so far only about modesty. Humility goes beneath modesty; for modesty and its opposite, arrogance, are related to the sphere of rights and of claims. Modesty is knowing your place in relation to other men's rights—to their right to breathe, their right to assistance, their right to courtesies and attentions. But humility is knowing your place in relation to their thoughts and affections. Now there cannot exist such a thing as a claim to another man's solicitude or love. One is entitled to consideration, one is never *entitled* to love. The nature of the benefit is such that it comes necessarily as a favor, a free-will offering, a gift of grace; and the appropriate feeling is gratitude. A reasonable person, therefore, conscious of his complete dependence upon other people for this necessity of life, will be conscious of his unworthiness; and he will betray this in the humility with which he approaches those who have it in their power to confer their affection or to withhold.[6]

When Hume says, "It is impossible a man can at the same time be both proud and humble," he is confusing humility with shame. Humility is not the opposite but the complement of pride. Modesty and humility are based on the recognition of inherent and inevitable limitations, whilst shame is an experience of weakness and inferiority. The first is an active withdrawal of pretensions seen to be groundless, while the second is a passive admission of pain, failure, impotence, or vice. You could be proud and humble, like Isaac Newton, through perceiving at once that you had advanced knowledge and that you had not advanced it very far. But you could not be proud and ashamed of the same book unless it contained both truths and errors, merits and avoidable faults.

Pride, then, is consistent with humility. We may even take pride *in* humility, as an achievement of no little difficulty. And this establishes the legitimacy of pride.

2. But we must still ask whether it is permissible to experience pride in thoughts such as these: I am attractive to men—I am exceptionally powerful—I have more than my share of cleverness. We must admit that to allow oneself even a slight pleasure in such reflections is a course beset by the danger of excess—the excess of vanity, of truculence, of conceit. But where there are aberrations, there must be a norm; and the norm in the case of beautiful people or strong people or clever people is *confidence.* But confidence is something desirable, and what is desirable cannot be wrong.

A woman has begun to *plume* herself on her beauty—when? When she is blind to the necessity of other qualities besides; when she acquires a contempt for ugliness; when she considers herself entitled to privileges; when she forgets what a small part of the self the appearance is; when she overvalues superficial admiration and sacrifices the affection which is due only to qualities of mind and heart. Such women are unbearable, and unfortunate,

> for such,
> Being made beautiful overmuch,
> Consider beauty a sufficient end,
> Lose natural kindness and maybe
> The heart-revealing intimacy
> That chooses right, and never find a friend.

But there are women who combine beauty and confidence with humility and show deference to experience and achievement.

The consciousness of strength of body may lead to swagger and the traits of the bully. But it is compatible with gentleness and humility. Pride of physique is at its best when it is functionally related to services and achievement. The strong man, like the skilled man, is grateful for his ability to be useful when called upon and for the place in the estimation of others which that ability confers upon him.

Intelligence which is overproud of itself belies itself: to be conceited on the score of intelligence is to exhibit a want of it. This quality belongs anyhow in a special category, because of all things it is the easiest to be proud of when you have it not. But suppose you have it—who cares? Intelligence is supposed to display itself in results and even the best results are, as we have shown, limited. Nothing is more disagreeable than the smirk of a superior intelligence, addicted to comparisons of itself with other minds instead of being devoted to positive and objective conclusions, and hardly anything more revolting than a congress of able men at which everyone backs his own insight because it is his own. Yet intelligence is intelligence; and that exhilaration, that confidence, which we feel when we know that we see things clearly or do things well is something that cannot properly be decried.[7]

The proposition that every human being has an ego is probably not necessary (logically true). For, even if we ignored the evidence from psychopathology on disintegration or loss of the ego functions, it seems possible to imagine a man, otherwise normal, who should have no need to acquire a good opinion of himself and no feelings which were conditional on that opinion; and it is a matter of fact that some people have "small" egos (a small degree of preoccupation with themselves) compared with others. Whether the extirpation of the ego would be psychologically feasible or morally desirable—this is a different question. And the "conquest of pride" is still another. The destruction of self-consciousness would take humility with it as surely as pride, for humility presupposes the existence of an ego. Let us therefore ignore the question of eliminating the ego with all its feelings, positive and negative, and concentrate on the question of destroying pride. It is religion that provides the evidence on this point, for it is religion that presumes not to control or to normalize but to banish the feeling of pride. When, in one of the *Little Flowers of St. Francis* (not an entirely credible record of the Saint's life or words), we read: "forasmuch as those holy eyes have beheld among sinners none more vile, more imperfect, nor a greater sinner than I, therefore since He hath found no viler creature on earth to accomplish the marvellous work He intendeth, He hath chosen me to confound the nobility, the majesty, the might, the beauty, and the wisdom of the world: in order to manifest that every virtue and every good thing cometh from Him the Creator," we see that the humility is artificial, groundless, false: there is no good reason to think that St. Francis was as vile as anybody on earth. But the pride is concrete, definite, immense—and immensely dangerous: it is founded not only on the actual position of leadership in society which Francis had achieved but on the presumption of a divine endorsement for his particular mission. In Morton Wishengrad's *Chassidic Tale* a certain Rabbi Eliezer is made to say: "I have a greater love for the wicked man who knows he is wicked than for the righteous man who knows he is righteous. The first one is truthful and the Lord loves the truth. The second one falsifies, since no human being is exempt from sin and the Lord hates untruth."[8] This, again, distorts truth in the interest of a strained humility: it confuses the man who knows how righteous he is with the man who thinks he is more righteous than he is. It takes back what it grants: it assumes that one can be in error concerning that which one knows. On this reasoning there would be no difference between smugness and self-respect; and any degree of satisfaction with self, no matter how solidly supported, would be sinful. Yet the very quality which is pronounced wrong is also seen to be inevitable. The discipline of the ego, when conceived with ascetic immoderation, is like any other discipline when similarly conceived. It cannot achieve its object—the extinction of pride or of desire as the case may be. But by refusing to countenance a just pride or a legitimate desire it can forestall the existence of either. It is a notorious fact that obnoxiously complacent or self-righteous people are among those who have obscure reasons for feeling dissatisfied with themselves. Here the ego has been distorted by natural causes. The deliberate attempt to thwart or suppress the cravings of the ego leads, in its own way, just as surely to queer forms of egotism.

II

The analysis of shame runs parallel to the analysis of pride. Shame is the feeling that comes with consciousness of faults, weaknesses, disadvantages—that is, of qualities deemed undesirable. Most of these qualities, like deformity, ugliness, and vice, already entail suffering by their very nature, so that shame is a misery heaped upon miseries. To be ignorant, awkward, poor, impotent or undersized or bald, criminal, homosexual, member of a disgraced family or an oppressed race—these are in their various ways concrete liabilities; and to reflect upon them, insofar as one accepts the standard which discredits them, is to suffer a constraint upon confidence and freedom of action.

This reflexive character of shame must be reemphasized. Take as an example the feeling of loneliness. This feeling is not always disinterested. What you might want of other people when you think you would like to see them is not their company so much as the assurance that you can have their company if you want it—that somebody is willing to kill his time with you. You want to flatter yourself with the thought: "I have friends." Loneliness would not be crushing if it did not induce the reflection that nobody cares for you, that you are abandoned. It is this reflection which makes you feel really small. (The intensity of this feeling depends, of course, on the strength of the ego-requirement which has been created by the previous life history. A proud ego, secure in the belief in its social eligibility, can face periods of solitude or desertion without loss of confidence.) But such a value existing in the ego presupposes the existence of a genuine and disinterested loneliness. You could not think it a compliment to yourself to be sought out by other people unless the friendship and company of other people were first considered valuable. And they are considered valuable because we have social needs. It is not the ego that creates these needs. The ego *superimposes* itself upon these needs—and others like them—and defines itself in relation to them.

Pride and shame have been defined as feelings, and that is what they are in the isolated act of reflection. But reflection is continual, so that the momentary reactions establish themselves as dispositions, affect the structure of personality and modify the life pattern. That is why we can characterize individuals as overbearing, craven, or diffident; and that is why pride can be a permanent blessing and shame an enduring curse.

The qualities of which we are ashamed will vary according to the standard of value. The standard is derived, of course, in a very great measure from the group and has been impressed on us through social sanctions. Moreover, even more than in the case of pride, the feeling of shame is bound up with the idea of publicity. We feel ourselves disgraced by those qualities which evoke the contempt and aversion of others. For instance: sexual inversion, which might otherwise be regarded as (at worst) a handicap, becomes a source of anguish through the fact that it evokes derision and blame. It is hard to exaggerate the degree to which we fear disfavor and are therefore ashamed of the things which bring it upon us. So that Spinoza could incorporate that element in the very definition of shame: "Shame is pain accompanied by the idea of some action of our own which we imagine others to blame." Our difference with Spinoza is only terminological: we must allow for the existence of an autonomous conscience, for the fact that a man may feel himself disgraced by something that is unworthy in his own eyes and apart from any judgment but his own. It would take us very long to analyze the reciprocal play of conscience and public opinion even in a single example, like Conrad's Lord Jim. But it is useful to notice the illusion that is usually involved in the idea of disgrace. We have a tendency to overrate certain qualities because they are ours, instead of rating ourselves according to the qualities, and to impute the complementary error to others. I imagine that people admire me for qualities which in fact they have hardly noticed and do not think very much of. So too, judging by the intensity of my own shame, I imagine a degree of opprobrium which exists in no mind but my own. I am ashamed of my stature, my income, my accent, my clothes, when nobody, in fact, holds them against me and when I would not blame anybody else for the same things. People are more considerate than we think: they do not concentrate upon single qualities but take them into reckoning with other things. Besides, they do not bother about us as much as we suppose: it is a false pride, a form of egotism, which persuades us that they have no way of spending their time but in condemning us. Just as I can look at distinguished men quite coolly and critically while I imagine that everyone must be impressed by my own least attainment, so a scandal in which a friend of mine is embroiled leaves my regard for him unaffected while I imagine (Dostoevsky's example) that the world is pointing fingers at a pimple on my nose. When we see public opinion for what it is, it turns out to be a smaller thing, for good or for ill, than what our fantasy projected. And (though the subject requires a much closer discussion) this seems to point to the existence of sources of shame independent of society. For if we can stigmatize ourselves more severely than others do and impute that judgment to them, if (in Spinoza's terms) we can "imagine others to blame us" more harshly than they do, there must be a spontaneous and factitious element in our sense of disgrace.

An element of comparison enters into what we regard as our disabilities: income and height and status might rarely become objects of shame without it. In itself there is nothing good or bad about being exceptional: the question is whether you deviate in a direction of which you and others approve. The *very* tall man is regarded not with respect but with curiosity. His painful self-consciousness would of course disappear in a community of people like himself; for then the difference would be gone, and it is the difference, not the height, that discomfits him. But it would disappear also in a world in which men looked at him as they look at geniuses and not as they look at freaks. In a community of hunchbacks no hunchback would be ill at ease, both because he would not stand out and because the standard would be different.

But there are absolute liabilities as well as comparative ones.

Now we can discuss the thesis which I have advanced concerning shame. An immanent penalty attaches to anything that we call a disadvantage, a penalty which, like the pain of deformity, it may be impossible to throw off. But shame is the farthest weakness, psychological in type, which the *consciousness* of our disabilities involves. Now it is just as natural to be ashamed of our weaknesses as it is to be proud of our strengths; but that does not mean that it is equally reasonable. On the contrary, it is as reasonable to seek the cure of this secondary malady as it is, say, to consult a doctor about the first.

The following points are made chiefly by way of supporting this last proposition. They are considerations, relevant for an evaluation of shame. They are not, as they may seem to be, primarily proposed as practical "remedies," counsels, exhortations, or cheering reflections. The impression of moral optimism which the reader may draw from them is not intended. A person subject to any of the liabilities mentioned above is not merely ashamed. His reaction is endorsed by his opinion: he says to himself, "This thing is shameful." It is to this conscious judgment, this faculty of valuation, which is accessible to argument even when the shame feelings are not, that these remarks are addressed.

The influence of shame is counteracted by estimating any weakness (assumed to be insurmountable) at its actual importance, that is, by the development of an accurate sense of values. If anything at all be shameful, illness is not as shameful as cowardice nor cowardice as shameful as malice—which is only to say that some things are not as *bad* as others. The decisive consideration, be it noted, is not the deterministic excuse: "It is not my fault that I am feeble, inept, or ugly; I couldn't help it; it was visited upon me," but the moral judgment: "Ugliness is no disgrace, or but a small one; it is I, after all, who suffer from it, and I give no ground of complaint to anyone else; there remains virtually the whole field of action in which I can still win credit." We surround the source of shame with sources of pride and objects of ambition, which may well-nigh overwhelm it. We bring our emotions into correspondence with the actual balance of assets and liabilities. We dispel the illusion of centrality which shame tried to create for its object. We try to see our weaknesses as they are, in relation to everything that is desirable or the reverse, and not in the magnified form in which shame presents them. Needless to say, this is very different from *forgetfulness,* which simply tries to seal off the source of discomfiture, leaving the fundamental value judgment uncorrected. And it is different from *consolation,* which also accepts without criticism the proposition advanced by shame—that the qualities which I lack are the most desirable things in the world—and strives to discover substitutes and compensations, a weak balm for the wound to which no radical treatment has been given.

There are important sources of shame that can be cleared out entirely by this treatment. Social upstarts long for the speech and manners of the class above and are ashamed of their own, though it might be difficult to show that the one were at all superior to the other. The weakness here is not a real weakness; it is not such as a reasonable mind would inevitably pronounce undesirable; it is contingent totally upon the "level of aspiration"; and a good sense of values would resolve it.

So there are weaknesses which, since they are created by estimation, will disappear when the estimation is corrected; and with the weakness goes the shame in the weakness. But there are other weaknesses that are not created by estimation: estimation must, on the contrary, take account of them as real. Though we should not, in our feelings, *exaggerate* these weaknesses, yet they remain; and with them, it appears, a modicum of shame. An accurate sense of values does not abolish it, for it does not abolish its source. Yet it is as unreasonable to tolerate the sear of shame upon the spirit as it is to permit a wound to fester in the body. There is not such a thing as a right amount of shame, as there is a right kind and amount of pride. *Every* shame, however circumscribed, must go. This leads us to our main consideration.

It has hitherto been unnecessary to invoke the distinction between what is *desired* and what is *considered desirable*. An impartial judgment seems to be seated within us, which pronounces on the general value and rightness of things. This we call the moral standard or *attitude* (identical with the "sentiment" in Hume). The term 'attitude' suggests that it is ultimately volitional and affective. The judgment is not impartial in the sense of being a deliverance of pure reason: it is impartial in the sense that it operates in relative independence of what may happen to be our personal desires. Thus I may desire wealth above everything else; but I shall not have the brass to maintain that money is the greatest good (much less *money for me*). And I may be perfectly sincere in this concession. At the same time, the independence of desire and attitude is not absolute— it is obvious that the desire for wealth influences the moral attitude and is influenced by it. One thing more: the attitude is not *necessarily* more "reasonable" than the desire. *Either* may be reasonable or unreasonable, depending on the considerations upon which it is based. People who are relatively sane in their personal morality not infrequently hold wild and prejudiced moral or social standards.

Now the attitude and the desire should be made to agree. Moralists usually conceive this as a one-way process, a capitulation on the part of desire; but it might in fact imply a concession on either side. Sexual desire is a notoriously difficult thing to regulate according

to a standard of what is proper; but if the standard is total absti-
nence, then the standard might be wrong. In any case, standard and
desire must be integrated, so that our normal interests may have the
backing of our total judgment. But I wonder whether there is not a
class of exceptions, a class of cases where there should exist an
explicit separation between the object of approval and the direction
of desire. In the case of a remediable ill, like jaundice, the subjective urge to get rid of it is in full agreement with the objective judgment, that health is better than disease. But take the man with a
hump. He should not be expected to suffer a distortion of judgment. His standard will be the same as our own: deformity is undesirable. But his *desire?* So long as straightness remains a good for
him, he will be consumed with longing and shame; he will develop a
hatred for his very life; he will experience the most futile and desperate of all wishes—the wish to be reborn. There is no alternative
but a total redirection of wish: privately and subjectively, normality must cease to be his standard. And when you lack what you do
not want, there is no shame.

For the situation, albeit more serious, is not entirely different
from those which we meet in normal life, for example, when circumstances force me to relinquish the vocation on which I have set
my heart. Every choice, even the most trivial, compels us to for-
swear the unattainable, to accept the reality, to desire those things
which with available means can be obtained. A special philosophy
of handicaps must commence with the insight that *misfortunes*—
which are never contemplated, never chosen or rejected, but imposed on us from without—do not belong to a completely different
category from those *conditions* which we face in action and which
enforce retreat, compromise, revision of plan. The difference lies in
the order in which things confront us. If you begin by wanting (A)
to be both a good musician and a good chemist and are led to see
that you can hope to attain (B) real proficiency in only one, then B
and not A is your goal and your good. If the same result is produced suddenly and violently by an accident to your bowing arm,
then you are passive to begin with; the choice is made, or at least
shaped, for you without your consent; the readjustment is sharper
and, conceivably, more painful; but the *elements* of the psychological situation and of the moral issue—barring, of course, the factor
of traumatic suddenness itself—are identical with the other case;

and this identity can be ignored only through our failure to acknowledge the relative rigidity of many of the ordinary conditions of life.

The evil of deformity is not a simple evil. It is not the pain alone, nor the pang of comparison, nor the unwantedness, nor the fear of it, nor the sexual impasse, but all these, with their psychic involutions, which surcharge the countenance with the marks of a permanent crucifixion. Yet there have been cripples whose minds were utterly straight; and we observe that if misfortune comes late enough, when the mind is mature, the mind can remain untwisted in spite of it. If there is one natural injustice more hideous than the rest, it is the fate by which afflictions are heaped on children, whose spirit is too weak to cope with them, so that the paralysis of fear and of shame becomes fixed and incurable.

We must now deal with the quality of unintelligence as a reason for shame. Mental disabilities do not present an exception to anything I have written; and it may seem endless even to treat them as a special case. No matter who you are, there are more things you cannot do than you can: what Shakespeare and what Newton did not know and could not say filled volumes, even in their own times. Scientists and artists are not embarrassed by the infinite scorn of their ineptitudes; and most of us behave just as reasonably when it is a question of particular disabilities. When you find that you are slow at mathematics, you take that as a reason not to become a mathematician—and nothing more. A merciful arrangement in our natures makes it the rule (though not an invariable one) that people become interested in things they are good at and lose interest in things at which they fail. It is not otherwise with special qualities like wit, cunning, literary taste, or, for that matter, the ability to speak French, the lack of which may be a material and social handicap in a given time and place. Everyone knows that such deficiencies can be galling; and everyone knows someone who is perfectly accommodated to them.

But what if you are good at nothing? Many people who are not intelligent enough to keep up with the class or group in which they find themselves are quite intelligent enough to perceive their own backwardness; and such discoveries are a source of feelings of bitterness and inferiority. For intellectual gifts, though valuable in themselves, have more than an intrinsic value: they stand for economic success, admission to certain circles, friendship with certain people, and bulk large therefore in the estimate of one's own personality. Hardly anybody is more pathetic than the college student whose perceptive intelligence outstrips his productive powers, so that while he appreciates gifted people, he is not appreciated by them in return. True, there are those, perhaps the great majority, who find that their social environment does not emphasize mental qualifications, and—since shame can exist only when we fail to live up to a standard of our own election—they can be stupid and know they are stupid without being crestfallen because, like everyone else around them, they honor stupidity. But in this case the penalty for peace of mind is an error—the failure to recognize that intelligence is a good thing.

It is time to ask what intelligence and stupidity are. Let us consider a definition long accepted by psychologists and subjected to criticism only in recent years. Intelligence is the ability to learn—an aptitude distinguished in point of generality from the aptitude for lawn tennis or languages. If this is intelligence, it is certainly possible to know that you lack it, by carefully observing and comparing your own and other people's learning performances.

What it means to be good at nothing, then, is that there is a general quality of slowness in your acquisition of knowledge and skills. But you can make yourself *good* at many things all the same, with sufficient incentive and force of will. Now, a man who by working twice as hard as other people has made himself only a little better than they is not going to feel downcast about the inferiority of his mind. The lack of "intelligence," a favor of native endowment, is seen and felt as a special handicap on a plane with those we have discussed already, to be treated morally and technically as they are treated. In the developed personality, which knows many things and harbors many interests, the perception of an incapacity for rapid assimilation counts as a single trait, for which the proper kind of allowance has to be made—not as an overwhelming and insuperable stigma.

In other words, it is intelligence as achievement and not as capacity that poses the only serious problem. The flower of the natural intelligence is the developed understanding. It is this, and not a few degrees of difference in IQ, that creates the qualitative gulf between one man and another. Between genius and mediocrity (a distinction of capacities) the difference may be great; but between enlightenment and confusion (a distinction in point of attainment) the difference is as night and day. A good head is an asset in the pursuit of understanding; but understanding is the end and justification of intelligence. And this, the *result* of experience and learning—not the *ability* to learn—is, on the whole, what people mean when they describe their acquaintances as intelligent or stupid. Henry Ford, with his great congenital endowment, could have acquired an understanding of human nature and society superior to that of many people who would, justifiably, describe his actual outlook as "unintelligent." Now if, given any problem or point of controversy, there are two classes of people, those who admit their lack of understanding and those who do not, then the second kind will never be ashamed of their stupidity—so they do not give us any question to discuss. But the first kind should not be ashamed, because they are not stupid but at worst merely ignorant. And ignorance is not inherently wrong: if it were, we should all of us be *infinitely* embarrassed all of the time. Ignorance of this or that might be wrong at this time or that—when the practical situation impresses upon us the obligation to know a specific thing. But the obligation to know cannot exist for me if I lack the ability to know; and if I have that ability, the reasonable thing is to start learning.

I am aware that my treatment of this topic has been absurdly schematic. But I believe that the scheme, as a scheme, is adequate: it covers the alternatives which seem to exist in all those cases where people are ashamed of their own minds.

So much for the natural disadvantages. They are evil; and they are, by hypothesis, fixed. But the shame and disgrace of them are just as evil; and though equally natural are not, or not always, equally fixed. It might seem that pride and shame involved each other and could not be separated without a convenient but dishonest shift in the standard of value. If you are justly proud of a certain quality because you think it good, how can you *not* be ashamed to lose it unless you resort for the occasion to an attitude of sour grapes: "After all, it isn't really any good"? Superficially, this question is logical; but it ignores the intervention of the practical effort. On the same assumption it would be inconsistent to enjoy the use of money while you have it unless you were prepared to moan for it when you do not. If health is good, illness is evil: a man in his right senses accepts both these judgments, whether he is well or ill. But if health is something to be proud of, it does not follow that illness is something to be ashamed of. Between pride and shame it is the practical will that interposes itself, not to register the static judgment, "X is good" or "X is evil" but to *make* of X as little of an evil as may be.[9]

But now, is there *nothing* of which we can justifiably be ashamed? Not cowardice, nor dishonor, not incompetence or moral failure? No act of will and no trait of character? (Shame obviously merges here with remorse or the sense of guilt.) It seems almost implied in the preceding pages, where we maintained, for example, that ugliness is nothing to be ashamed of, that there must be other things which indeed are shameful. But these things fall within the scope of effort and control, so that they seem to call for resolutions bearing upon the future rather than for reproaches based upon the past.

A man will never be ashamed of anything he has done unless he accepts a certain standard of rectitude. The feeling of shame, therefore, can *bear witness* to an uncorrupted conscience; and such a man, as Spinoza says, is better than one who is both wicked and shameless. But the feeling cannot be sanctioned just because it testifies to something good: the question is whether it accomplishes anything good. Shame and repentance in themselves are painful and to that extent bad. But painful things, like medicine, can sometimes lead to what is good. Can this be said of shame?

Everything that can be accomplished by a passion, says Spinoza, can be accomplished better by reason. But this, as he admits, hardly meets the issue; for if we were *perfectly* reasonable, we should not have erred to begin with, and the very question would not exist. The question for us is, granted that we *have* been cowardly or stupid or malicious, whether shame can serve any useful purpose.

It will never do to argue that just as pride of achievement encourages us toward further exertion, so to dwell upon our failures is to produce a revulsion toward good. I am afraid that there is no "law of effect" which operates in this manner; for if there were, it would follow that to *cultivate* the sense of guilt, to brood over our infirmities, would be tantamount to improvement; but this, on the contrary, is morbidity. Despondency is *weakness;* it reduces the power to act; it confirms us only in despondency, in loathing of self; it indicates no direction in which effort may move: and by its own intolerable weight, by the need we feel to get rid of it, it prompts us, if not to sheer escape in liquor and drugs, then to irrelevant acts of atonement—self-flagellation, breast-beating, the voluntary incurrence of punishment.

On the other hand, it is impossible to dispense with what I have called *reflection;* for it is the reflection upon a fault that enables us to analyze it, and analysis is the first step in treatment. One who, in the interest of moral reconstruction, should ignore his failures and imperfections, would be like a fool: his resolutions are fatuous because they take no cognizance of his problem. We could not endorse a program to abolish the habit of self-contemplation; for though there is no correction merely in looking upon oneself and cursing one's fate (or one's character), there will certainly be no correction without it. A positive morality does not forget the past, but recalls it to consider it; and reflection, in my special sense, is an indispensable phase of moral reflection in the general sense. But we cannot reflect upon errors without exposing ourselves to the attack of shame. Suppose that I let my tongue wag last night and said certain things about *Y*—which I regret. A reasonable person would not regret them because he would not have uttered them; but *I,* for whom it is a question of *becoming* reasonable, have something to reckon with. How should I change unless there were something which I deplore? Yet regret by itself effects nothing: what is more familiar than that we repeat what we have regretted? Shame and regret are literally helpless, for they are concentrated upon what we can do nothing about, on the past. Hence, they are "passive," incompatible with action. But if we *go on* from such feelings to weigh and measure, chart and explore—if, that is, they can instigate us to consideration of the future—then guilt and remorse will be replaced by a purpose, a resolution, one test of whose efficiency is precisely the degree to which the penalty of conscience has been surmounted. Shame, then, is seen as a *price* we may have to pay for our weaknesses and the attempt to cope with them; and morbidity, or the tendency to linger in self-reproach, is the evidence of the failure of that attempt, of the inability to act.

Are there not, finally, vices—just as there are bodily defects—that are incurable? Experience sometimes proves to us that we cannot hope to control certain irregularities of behavior and temper; and we conclude, at a certain age, that we are doomed to cowardice, to laziness, to futility.

Uncontrollable vices border, by definition, on pathology—the pathology of the will and of action. What we mean by a pathological trait is an undesirable trait that defies voluntary control. Every vice and every fault can be represented as an erroneous decision engrained in disposition. Now erroneous decisions are normally subject to review, so that we are not absolutely *fated* to repeat them. But it is the distinction of the "neurosis," or pathological vice, that the circumstances which gave rise to it are not accessible for review. The original motives, with their environmental causes, are buried in the unconscious; and the erroneous decision, once enacted, will bear in relation to the conscious will the character of a compulsion: we are impelled to act, as it seems, not by a voluntary choice but through *force majeure.*

True, it is never to be finally assumed, without a certificate from a physician, that a given trait is neurotic; for there exists the Freudian "preconscious," by which many of our acts are controlled. For thirty years one has hesitated, and felt a slight anxiety, before depositing a nickel in a telephone box. Only to stop and ask the reason for this would be to recall the poverty of one's youth and to see that that condition exists no longer. The motive was unconscious, but it is eminently accessible to consciousness, without the help of any special technique. There are people whose lives are pinched and bitten merely for want of a critical and reflective habit in their conduct, and to them we should recommend the Socratic rather than the Freudian method of self-knowledge. But when this whole area is accounted for, there remain the genuinely invincible perversities. And let us remember that to most men today, as to all of mankind before this century, no form of therapy is available.

I raise this topic not for its own sake but because it seems to stand as the final objection to any general criticism one can bring against shame. To be afflicted with uncontrollable vices is, *inevitably,* to be consumed with shame: indeed, the narcissistic ego formations of which exaggerated prides and exaggerated shames are the double manifestation are themselves, frequently, not to be controlled even by individuals who may be aware and critical of them. What can "reason" possibly have to say about this?

The question reaches into the foundations of ethics and is too formidable to be properly treated here. There is this one point:

We cannot admit that what is not to be altered is not to be condemned. Any analysis of moral judgments must accept as a datum the fact that "Cancer is evil" is a significant judgment, even though it expresses a helpless wish and proposes no course of action. (Such judgments are, in fact, presupposed by all those judgments which do express a resolve or an exhortation, for example, "It would be well to spend more money on cancer research.") By the same token, Spinoza makes good sense when he says that shame, pity, grief, remorse, and so forth, are evil.

But if it *were* necessary to show, for every moral judgment, that it embodies or expresses a practical decision, then we might point out that feelings of guilt and shame are constantly being produced, encouraged, and confirmed by people who *approve* of them. The moral issue could therefore be said to deal not with irremediable passions already existing but with those which are yet to be produced.

POSTSCRIPT I

Both the Greek "moderation" and the Christian "humility" can be interpreted in terms of knowing one's place, if we allow for differences in conceiving the place of mankind in the universe. "Moderation," of which the opposite is *hybris,* pride, was by Aristotle's time a purely ethical conception; but it had a religious origin, which was in turn the projection of a social requirement. The fragments of Anaximander apply the idea of metes and bounds to the very elements: the cosmos itself is a system which subsists only by a kind of mutual restraint. The fate of Tantalus and of Niobe teaches us how men should comport themselves in relation to the powers that rule the world. Prosperity and power are dangerous, since they encroach upon the prerogatives of divinity. Happiness itself is somewhat too godlike and has a Nemesis appointed to dog it. (Jehovah, similarly, could not abide the tower of Babel, which threatened his privacy and supremacy.) Crimes, in particular, are reserved for the gods, who undertake to punish any poaching on this preserve. The gods, however, though they are immortal, are finite. They are subject to limitations of their own. There is an essential proportion between their nature and ours; and, accordingly, there is a middle sphere in which men are allowed to flourish. We are asked only to bring our ambitions into correspondence with our modest status and capacities; and if we are commanded to *think as mortals,* we are allowed to think at least as mortals. Now there can have been but few opportunities in Greek life for a man to trespass upon the "domain of the gods." Impiety no doubt was one, that is, the omission of any sacrifice or observance that was due them; but no one was likely to join the gods for dinner, to compare her beauty to Aphrodite's, to challenge Artemis to a foot-race or Zeus to an exhibition of fireworks. There are, however, a thousand ways in which presumption can offend against one's *neighbor.* I feel, then, that the legends project a set of social demands. How the wicked or dangerous man came to be conceived as the "uppity" individual, how the wrong was identified with the immoderate, the unlimited—to explain this would require a thorough study of Greek society. But this conception, which persists in the great ethical systems, has not even today exhausted its usefulness.

Christianity assumes that man is both vile and insignificant— dependent utterly, like an infant, upon a Father, whose value and power are incommensurate with his own, being infinite; and he is encouraged to regard himself as a worm. One phase of Christian doctrine insists even that there can be no such thing as merit, that no virtue whatsoever entitles a man to the slightest consideration. No depth of self-abasement, clearly, will be sufficient to express this relationship: it is impossible to be too humble. Now the effect of exercises in humility, like the effect of other exercises, is not confined to the situation which gave rise to them; and this doctrine seems to have produced some of the most unpretentious people in the world, men and women who claimed nothing for themselves from other people any more than from God. As an example of modest and unheroic self-effacement I cite the poet and priest George Herbert. But if "nature," according to the proverb, is difficult to expel, it is even harder to eliminate the "self." The self has a way of crawling back into the picture: it can even be found wielding the charm which is intended to exorcise it. I can vaunt myself as the chief of sinners. I can contend for the laurel of unworthiness. St. Augustine treats us to an exhibition of groveling that must fairly have sickened an honest Deity; for a wise God will surely appreciate that there must be a limit to the claims even of the Infinite.[10] Now it can be argued (and has been argued, I think, by Rebecca West) that Augustine was not primarily an egotist. His intellect is too vast and too impartial; he speaks for mankind and not solely for himself. But it can hardly be urged that he was distinguished for *humility*. Manifestly, he makes claims upon the consideration of God even in the act of renouncing them. He seems to see himself already in the position which he occupies in the *Disputà*—can anyone imagine him waking without a shock, say, in Purgatory? Augustine deems *man* unworthy but not himself: his conception of grace has no counterpart in his innermost attitude.

The pride of individuals, then, can invert itself and adopt the channel of Christian humility. But Christianity, like Judaism and other theistic creeds, is also committed, as an institution, to a special form of pride, which its apologists regard as a glorious asset. God may not be indulgent, but He is not indifferent. He made everything for us, and He takes an interest in the least event of our lives. His infinite Love strives to embrace us and is perpetually foiled by His infinite Justice. It is obvious that a life which is singled out for a solicitude of these dimensions will be invested with a great sense of importance. This is the "grandeur of man," complementing his "wretchedness"; and herein lies the pride which man enjoys on taking the theistic view. His role in nature is after all central, after all immense. Unworthy and helpless before the Lord, it is still flattering to him to be the object of such ministrations. Religious man is like a child who craves attention above everything else and would rather receive it in the form of punishment than not to receive it at all.

Here we are naturally confronted by such questions as whether human dignity, and a sense of the meaningfulness of life, are dependent upon the family type of relationship which theism extends to the universe. Is it exalting, and at the same time chastening, to regard ourselves as the children of a Father, to be rebuked, forgiven, condemned, or saved by Him? Does it degrade us from that height, and lift us from that depth, to believe that we have risen from the slime and have not fallen out of favor? Does it render man complacent, and also insignificant, to consider that there is nothing "higher" than himself? Is there no greatness, and no wretchedness, save in relation to a paternal will? Is the nursery the only deeply satisfying model of the universe? Must we be reluctant to grow up and make our way in a world in which we are responsible only to ourselves and to one another?

I do not discuss these questions, for I am interested not in the pride and humility of "man" in relation to "his" place in the cosmos but in the pride and humility of *men* in relation to one another. It may be that certain attitudes are incumbent on the species the moment it adopts a certain conception of its cosmic role. But what limits us fundamentally, as individuals, is not God or the gods or nature but *other men,* with their rights and pretensions and the need that we have of them. I seriously question the value of the humility which comes with the reflection that one is but a man: I think it more important to realize that one is but *one* man. So that the humility which I defined above, though it is closer in most respects to the Greek than to the Christian outlook, is closer still to the Chinese—if we can suppose that the polite tradition of self-disparagement which persists in their speech reflects what is now or was once a living practice.

POSTSCRIPT II

"Pride of intellect" is a sin which divinities must naturally reprobate, since their very existence is endangered by it; but it frequently assumes forms in which mortals can properly be disgusted if not terrified by it too. The claims of intelligence can easily be excessive. Yet whenever we point out that intelligence is encroaching on a sphere where it has not yet demonstrated its competence, we are paradoxically accusing it of unintelligence, since the standard by which any form of pride is judged to be warranted or unwarranted is the standard of reasonableness. The paradox disappears if we make it clear that we are talking about specialized intellectual attainments and of the claims that can be made on the strength of them. There is a false pride which is proper to the theoretical intellect. Its name is error. Error is presumption, because ideally it is always possible to know when you do not know something, to limit your claim according to the weight of the evidence in hand. There is a false pride whose name is confusion, which is the mark of the specialist who does not know that he is a specialist and who extrapolates the criteria which are applicable only within his narrow field. (The classical examples are the mathematician who wanted to know what a certain poem "proved" and the famous argument of the dancing master in Molière.) There is a false pride corresponding to every field in which claims are advanced and evaluated. (Thus when Croce speaks of the "not very great brain of the philosopher Bacon" and when T. S. Eliot refers to Hobbes as an "extraordinary little upstart," they are supercilious if not insolent. If we said that *Croce* had no very great brain and that *Eliot* was a little upstart, we should be much less in contempt of court, simply because our claims are more nearly warranted. The subjective feeling with which the claims are advanced may be the same in all cases; but the objective qualities of the several claims, when submitted to the norms of judgment, prove to be different.) Each form of exaggerated pride is corrected by mind, that is, by a better judgment, if it is corrected at all. And the pride which exaggerates the role of mind within the whole framework of life and society can be chastened only by the practical reason, which is the comprehensive tribunal to which all values must be brought. This faculty is charged with the criticism of its own claims.

It is evident from the foregoing examples that I have not, in the present note, limited the meaning of intellectual pride to the *reflection within the ego* of an attainment or claim of the intellect. I have followed a usage according to which the arrogant individual is "overweening," that is, one who does what he should not. But if we place our emphasis (as through most of this paper) on a man's reaction to his judgment of his own merits (in this case, pride of intellect, in the stricter sense), the moral does not change: it is intelligence which checks the presumption of the ego, permits a due pride and fosters intellectual humility.

NOTES

1. "Every valuable quality of the mind, whether of the imagination, judgment, memory, or disposition; wit, good sense, learning, courage, justice, integrity; all these are the causes of pride, and their opposites of humility. Nor are these passions confined to the mind, but extend their view to the body likewise. A man may be proud of his beauty, strength, agility, good mien, address in dancing, riding, fencing, and of his dexterity in any manual business or manufacture. But this is not all. The passion, looking further, comprehends whatsoever objects are in the least allied or related to us. Our country, family, children, relations, riches, houses, gardens, horses, dogs, clothes; any of these may become a cause either of pride or of humility."—Hume. There is only one thing to be added: that the *opposites* of all these qualities and relationships could also become objects of pride if the notion of what constitutes a "valuable quality" shifted sufficiently.

2. I do not agree with Hume, who says that "goods, which are common to all mankind, and have become familiar to us by custom, give us little satisfaction." See the whole passage in *Treatise,* vol. 2, part 1, chap. 6. Pride, for Hume as for Hobbes, is *essentially* emulous and invidious.

3. The concept of the *ego* seems to contain, first, the normal or regular set of values in its totality; second, a special set of values which can be described as the need to associate the first set (more exactly, the positive values in the first set) with oneself; and third, the set of judgments which either do or do not predicate those values of oneself. (Each of the three variables is determined by factors both of heredity and of life experience.) By specifying constants under each head and introducing a few notions of relationship from general psychology, it should be possible to derive from these terms all the ego concepts, like modesty, vanity, complacency, self-love, self-reproach, self-pity, and so on—except for those which, like conceit, smugness, arrogance, self-abasement, seem to belong as much to ethics as to psychology and involve the application of moral norms by the observer—and to construct a priori models for any typical state of the ego. This would also seem to be a suitable conceptual base for an empirical theory of the ego, that is, a set of laws which, with particular statements of fact, would yield the whole range of ego phenomena. Needless to say, we do not envisage the rapid success of such a project, since (to mention only the most obvious impediment) our scheme presupposes that whole idea of self which is built up from the earliest perception of body and surrounding world. Yet it should be of heuristic value to recognize that the mysterious ego dissolves on inspection into a system of functions.

4. The "natural advantages" are, in fact, the "godlike" qualities which people envy more than they praise. But godlike too are moderation, serenity, poise, the "health of the soul," every quality which makes for happiness. And I draw no distinction in this essay between these latter and the further catalog of "social" virtues, like justice and generosity; for that would be to recapitulate the argument of the *Republic* and raise the whole question about the identity of the right and the good. I assume here that the kind of person one is most disposed to honor would be the kind of person one would care most to be; in other words, that there is genuine inconsistency or conflict between values when one is *grateful* and *reverential* toward Socrates, Christ, or Lenin but *envious* of Napoleon or Rockefeller. The notion that we are indebted to the greatest of men for having *sacrificed their own good* is an interesting commentary on our own conception of good; but it finds no support in the teaching of those men themselves.

5. Jefferson on the Negroes: "But whatever be their degree of talent it is no measure of their rights. Because Sir Isaac Newton was superior to others in understanding he was not therefore lord of the person or property of others."

6. See Postscript I at the end of this article.

7. See Postscript II at the end of this article.

8. Quoted from a review by Daniel Bell of M. Wishengrad, *The Eternal Light,* in *Commentary,* November 1947.

9. It is unfortunately necessary, because of its extensive ramifications, to leave this point for the present largely unproved. In one of Hume's essays, "The Sceptic," there is a brief but devastating critique of the classical theory of the affects. I quote a few sentences: "Another defect of those refined reflections which philsophy suggests to us is that commonly they cannot diminish or extinguish our vicious passions without diminishing or extinguishing such as are virtuous, and rendering the mind totally indifferent and inactive. . . . In vain do we hope to direct their influence only to one side. . . . When we destroy the nerves, we extinguish the sense of pleasure, together with that of pain, in the human body." Now, I believe that every one of the

following propositions, which are entailed by Hume's remark, is false: (1) To overcome the *fear of dying* is to extinguish the *will to live* and leave no incentive for avoiding death or danger. (2) If nothing is *blame*worthy, nothing is *praise*worthy: one cannot experience feelings of gratitude or admiration without being subject to feelings of indignation and resentment. (3) To *love* is to be exposed to *jealousy* and to *grief*. (4) One cannot *rejoice* in good fortune without *sorrowing* over bad. These propositions, and many others like them, which run parallel to the negation of our thesis concerning pride and shame, are false; but Hume's predecessors did not show why. Stoicism accepted them, and argued that the common *objects* of the positive and negative emotions are "indifferent": for this philosophy the choice is between sensibility and insensibility. Spinoza rejected them, but (in my opinion) with no clear justification. Modern psychology must sooner or later reinstate the distinction between the active and the passive affects, providing it with a clearer and solider basis than the classical philosphers did.

10. If it were certain that God exists and that He is infinite and perfect, it would still be hard to relish the spectacle of absolute submission. For on any premises, even pantheistic ones, there is still such a thing as otherness. The individual is separate, he is not absorbed by the Whole. He has a judgment, a mind, a will of his own. Not even an infinite being can logically exact a total abnegation of these proud faculties; and there is something preferable to the author of the *Imitation* (the most perfect example of Christian humility) in the spectacle of Job, who treats with the Almighty as an inferior indeed but one who retains the dignity and independence of a man. Not that a perfectly abject humility is the worst of the religious vices. For in postulating God in the first place, and His commandments, and His rewards and penalties; and in claiming, as he does so often, the sanction of God for his purposes, his animosities, his laws, man does after all exercise his own judgment and will—but a judgment and will that are arbitrary, unteachable, refractory to the discipline of fact. Judged by an objective standard, he is arrogant and unsubmissive in his very humility—even if there were no heretic and reformer to testify by their ashes or the stripes on their backs. And in the last analysis it is this presumption, circumscribing its deference and submission, that constitutes the menace of religion.

XVI

PRIDE

GABRIELE TAYLOR

Pride is one of a set of emotions which seem to me of special interest and importance in our understanding and assessment of human beings as self-conscious agents capable of making value-judgments not only about the world but about their own role in this world. My discussion of pride is therefore part of a larger project dealing with emotions of this type, such as shame, humiliation, guilt, and remorse. These can be regarded as forming a set in that they resemble one another in the nature of the beliefs they each essentially involve and which makes each the emotion it is. The structure they share distinguishes them as a group from less sophisticated emotions like fear, anger, or joy. I do not here explicitly defend the thesis that the analysis of many of the emotions we commonly experience must involve reference to the subject's thoughts or beliefs; this much seems to be quite widely accepted.[1] Little has been done, however, to explore such beliefs in more detail and to draw out their often complex implications. My investigation of pride will be restricted to these concerns.

I

Hume suggests that "everything related to us, which produces pleasure or pain, produces likewise pride or humility."[2] In his view, pride is itself a feeling of pleasure which is parasitic on another feeling of pleasure derived from the perception or contemplation of some object that strikes the agent as agreeable in some respect. This initial pleasure is quite independent of the pleasure that is pride. I may just take pleasure in some beautiful house, say, and not feel proud at all. A further minimum condition to be fulfilled if I am to experience pride is that the beautiful house be in some way mine. This is how the self enters the analysis as part of what Hume calls the "cause" of pride: whatever I am proud of must be "related" to me. The self features again in the analysis as the "object" of pride, as that toward which my pride is directed. So pride on this account can be summed up as consisting of a self-directed pleasure based on a distinct pleasure derived from something that is also mine.

I do not intend to discuss in detail Hume's analysis of pride as one of the indirect passions; his views on the distinction between "cause" and "object" of a passion and the mechanism of association have received a fair amount of attention.[3] Rather, I wish to take as my starting-point an important constraint that he imposes on the principle that everything related to us which produces pleasure also produces pride. All the constraints he proposes are, he assures us, "deriv'd from the very nature of the subject" (290). By this he means that they are all based on and can be explained by reference to the doctrine of the association of ideas, so that, while any mistakes he might make about them may be due to the faults of the underlying system, it is equally true that if he is right in putting forward the points he does this would provide additional evidence for its correctness. It is therefore consistent with the Humean enterprise to examine the proposed constraints in their own right, as contributions to an elucidation of the nature of pride, which of course they are primarily meant to be. As such, although at first sight perfectly plausible, they will turn out to be no more than half-truths that obscure rather than clarify the structure of the emotion. If we can pinpoint what is right and what is wrong in Hume's account, we shall be able to see more accurately what is involved when a person is proud of this or that.

The problem that seems to worry Hume is that it is just not the case that everything that is related to us and produces pleasure also produces pride. The agent may continue to feel joy or pleasure in this self-related agreeable object and fail to make the transition to the second, self-directed pleasure which is pride. So, Hume thinks, we have to impose certain limitations on the relation between the self and that agreeable object, as well as on the object itself as a source of pleasure. The relation must be a "close" one, and the agreeable object comparatively rare, fairly constant, and discernible to others as well as to the agent himself. As Hume presents his problem, it looks as if his search for limitations is a search for a set of conditions that are jointly sufficient for a person to experience pride, enabling him to conclude that if the agreeable object is related to agent A in such-and-such a way and also fulfills conditions C_1 to C_n, then A will feel proud of it. If this is what Hume is trying to establish then his enterprise is doomed from the start, for no strengthening of bond or pleasure can force a man into feeling proud. But we need not commit him to such a fruitless task: his formulation of the problem is naturally dependent on the model he works with, and so he has to think in terms of conditions which should facilitate the move from the initial pleasure to the second, self-directed one. Hume's actual treatment of the constraints, however, lead rather to the contention that if the relation between agreeable object and self is not a "close" one, or if it is not the case that conditions C_1 to C_n obtain, then the agent in question will not feel pride but only joy or pleasure. So the problem he quite properly sets himself to solve is how pride is to be distinguished from other, similar emotions. His framework of various feelings tied together by association allows him to speak of the relevant conditions as merely holding "normally" when some agent experiences pride; but given their function of individuating pride and separating it from other passions they quite naturally present themselves as candidates for a set of necessary conditions that must obtain if A is to be proud of something.

The most important requirement for pride, but not for joy or pleasure, is that the relation between the self and the agreeable object be a "close" one. The only clarification Hume offers of what a "close" relation might consist in appears in the form of an example, and there it is hinted at rather than spelled out. His point is that joy is based on a "slighter" relation than pride and vainglory: "We may feel joy upon being present at a feast, where our senses are regal'd with delicacies of every kind. But it is only the master of the feast, who, beside the same joy, has the additional passions of self-applause and vanity" (290). So while a guest may feel joy or pleasure on the basis of being present at a feast, only the master, who has organized it, can feel proud of it. "Being present at" is not a close enough relation for the purpose. This sounds as if Hume is suggesting that it is possible to enumerate different relations and to pronounce each as close or not close enough for pride, as the case may be. But it turns out that this is not quite what he has in mind, for he immediately produces a counterexample. It is quite possible, he admits, that men by so "small" a relation as "being present at" convert their pleasure into pride, and "boast of a great entertainment at which they have only been present" (290). The suggestion here is that someone sufficiently determined to shine can somehow build his pride on a relation which is not really adequate. Hume, it is clear, regards such people as uncommonly silly and so perhaps as not requiring serious attention, for he concludes: "this must in general be own'd, that joy arises from a more inconsiderable relation than vanity, and that many things which are too foreign to produce pride, are yet able to give us a delight and pleasure" (290/1).

There must be confusion in a story that allows us to accept both that some relation is not close enough for pride and that nevertheless pride can be based on it. Hume has promised to provide us with a feature of pride by means of which we can distinguish it from joy or pleasure. The boastful guest, however, is allowed to be proud of the feast, though we are meant to infer that he is not at all sensible in being proud, that he has no reason for his pride. If, then, a relation like "being present at" will do for pride that is not rational, Hume has after all not kept his promise to offer points that will distinguish pride as such from joy or pleasure. It is *well-founded* pride, it seems, which is now in question.

A crucial mistake in Hume's account is that he takes a wholly external or objective view of the situation; that is, he completely ignores the relevant beliefs of the agent himself. But reference to such beliefs is essential if we are to settle what is involved in pride but not in pleasure, and when pride can be said to be in some sense justified. Hume's own story shows that this is so, though it needs to be a little disentangled for this point to emerge. The "agreeable object" of which the master can and the guest, unless foolish, cannot be proud is given simply as "the feast." Hume's immediate purpose is best served if we interpret him as having just the occurrence of the feast in mind, rather than for example its success; otherwise it is not nearly so clear that the guest's pride would be absurd or foolish. The two characters in the story are given conventional roles, where that of the master but not of the guest has responsibility for the feast built into it. So the master has a basis for his pride simply because his role is what it is, and this precise basis is not available to anyone else. It would indeed be strange for the guest to be proud of the feast on the basis merely of his presence; this alone does not make it "his" feast, as responsibility for it may be thought to make it the master's. But there are two quite different cases here:

1. The guest maintains that he is proud of the feast's occurring on the grounds that he was present at it. He is not in any way responsible for the occasion, nor does he claim responsibility. But this cannot be reconciled with the claim that he is proud of the feast's occurring. We cannot in this case make sense of what he says and will conclude that whatever his feelings about the matter may be, they can hardly amount to feeling proud of *the feast,* though this guest may still be proud of having attended it.

2. The second case is, I take it, that of Hume's boastful guest. The circumstances are the same as before, but the guest manages to persuade himself that somehow he had a hand in bringing the feast about. He believes he is to some extent at least responsible for the event, though as the situation is described his belief is quite unjustified. So this guest, while feeling proud of the feast, has no proper basis for his pride.

Hume runs these two cases together. But we cannot make sense of his boastful guest unless we interpret the situation roughly as I have just done, and this introduces an appeal to the agent's beliefs. In ignoring these Hume left himself no satisfactory way of settling the distinction between pride and pleasure. He was bound to confuse, as he did confuse, two different sorts of conditions, those that have to be fulfilled if the passion a person experiences is to be the passion of pride, and those that must obtain if his pride is to be well founded. While he embarks on a search for the first set, the very telling of his tale leads him to the other: he assesses the agents and their responsibility or lack of it without any reference to how they themselves might view the situation and their own involvement in it, and the question of responsibility is settled simply by conventional role-allocation. It may well be that, as Davidson[4] suggests, Hume thought one must have a reason for one's pride, but if so he is not at all clear about the notion of "reason" here in place. His boastful guest has a reason, namely, his belief that somehow he has contributed to the feast. This sort of belief, whether mistaken or not, is necessary for him to feel proud at all. The master has the same reason, but in his case the belief is based on what is as a matter of fact the case. His belief is therefore not just a reason for his pride, but a well-founded one, the sort of reason that is needed if his pride is to be justified at all.

The introduction of the agent's beliefs has further repercussions. Hume distinguishes between two features in that which we are proud of, in the "cause" of pride, in his terminology; namely, the "subject," as for example the house or the feast, and the "quality": the beauty of the house or the success of the feast. The "close relation" is said to hold between the agent and the subject, whereas the quality is what strikes the person concerned as agreeable. But what we are proud of cannot always be so neatly subdivided. The agent views a whole complex situation, and if we are to use Humean terms at all then it is to this complex he has to be closely related. The guest may not have organized the feast but be, or see himself as being, the life and soul of the party, and so would have a reason for being proud of the *successful* feast, though of course not necessarily a good or well-founded reason. He sees the success of the feast as being largely owing to him, and so it is "subject" and quality" combined which stand in the "close relation" of being his achievement, at least in his own view.

Hume may be telling us no more than that at least one way in which the required relation between agent and what he is proud of is to be established is by the agent being responsible for whatever it may be. Alternatively, having already stipulated that he is always proud of something that is *his* in some way, we can understand him as taking this relation for granted and putting forward the view that only certain other relations holding between the agent and what he is proud of will support the crucial one of his being responsible for it: "having organized it" is alright, and "being present at" is not. But if so, he is again straying from considerations of the features of pride as such and concerning himself with what is rational in pride, with what would count as a supporting and acceptable reason for "I am responsible for it." Of course, we could not list such possible reasons; whether or not an agent's particular belief constitutes a good reason for his pride has to be assessed in the light of the whole situation: a distinguished guest may be perfectly rational in regarding his mere presence as the chief contribution to the success of the feast. It is equally impossible to list relations that can be offered as a reason for pride, whether good or bad. Anything may do here, given suitable (including possibly crazy) beliefs of the agent.

Hume's assumption that the occasions for pride can be discussed from some external point of view involve him, therefore, in a further mistake, namely that the constraints can be put in far more definite terms than is in fact the case. We certainly cannot enumerate a set of close enough relations, as he seems to suggest. Related mistakes occur in the other constraints he mentions. So for instance he tells us that what we are proud of is to be restricted to what is comparatively rare. He says:

> We are rejoic'd for many goods, which, on account of their frequency, give us no pride. Health, when it returns after a long absence, affords us a very sensible satisfaction; but it is seldom regarded as a subject of vanity, because 'tis shar'd with such vast numbers. (292)

The example is not implausible, but the whole story is rather more complex than Hume makes it appear. It is not really the widespread distribution of the good or the frequency of its occurrence which is here at stake. Again, it is the agent's view that matters: it may be that normal people in normal circumstances take health for granted and are not proud of their possession of it. But I or my circumstances may not be normal and I may be proud of my health, and for this to be the case it is quite irrelevant how many normal people there are about. It may be that keeping my health costs me more effort than is normal and so I am proud of it just because for me it is an achievement to be in this condition. Or it may be that I consider myself to be generally below what I take to be normal and so am proud of any possession that puts me into the group of "normal people." In ignoring the agent's view of the situation Hume mistook for a general constraint what is merely one possible instance of it: The crux of the matter is not how rarely or frequently the relevant goods are to be met with as a matter of fact, but how rare or common they are in relation to the particular agent, in that agent's own view. One reason, but one reason only, why possession of some things may be beyond what I can expect is that such things are, as it happens, so rare. But it is quite possible that I regard some good, however widely distributed it may be, as not at all easily within my grasp. If this is the basis from which I start then I may well be proud if after all I find myself in possession of such good.

II

Hume goes wrong in the constraints he wishes to impose on pride. Yet not only is he quite right in thinking that joy and pleasure need to be distinguished from pride but his suggestion that there is something peculiarly "close" between the "cause" of pride and the self is equally correct. He just mislocated this closeness. The discussion of the Humean system has made it plain that an analysis of pride must be in terms of the agent's own view of the situation, where this includes both, how he sees his own role within this situation, and his evaluation of this or that aspect of it. The following set of beliefs fulfills this requirement: if A is proud of x, then of x A believes that in regard of some F

   (i)   A made it true that x is F;
   (ii) that x is F is of value;
   (iii) because of (i) and (ii) A's worth is confirmed or enhanced.[5]

For example, if A is proud of the successful feast then he believes that he has brought about the successful feast, that the successful feast is of value, and that as it is of value his having achieved such a thing has confirmed or increased his merit or importance. Beliefs (i)-(iii) make more precise Hume's point that "pride has in a manner two objects" (292): that object the description of which fills the blank in the formula "A is proud of ——," and A himself. What gratifies A is the boost to his self-esteem alluded to in belief (iii), but such gratification depends on his view of things other than his own worth; hence the need for beliefs (i) and (ii). That A should regard x as in some way valuable I take to be noncontroversial: we could not understand the case of A being proud of something while setting no store by it under *any* description. To be proud of the successful feast he need not value successful feasts as such, but he must then value it as, for example, a duty well performed, or simply as an achievement of his. The present requirement replaces Hume's point that what we are proud of strikes us as pleasant or agreeable (285, section V). But this condition is too weak, as he himself discovers when he sees the need to distinguish pride from pleasure itself. That x being F be valued already provides such a distinction, for it is quite possible to value something without finding it pleasant, and conversely, quite possible to think it agreeable without in the least valuing it. Mere pleasure is here not enough to account for the increase in self-esteem which is so central to pride.

Of course, however much I may value x it can do nothing for my self-esteem unless I can somehow relate it to myself. This is taken care of by A's first belief. "Making it true that" is to be seen as a formal relation that is satisfied by A having achieved or acquired the x that is F. What he is proud of, then, he sees as something he is responsible for or possesses. This does not mean that he must see in this light what Hume called "the subject." If A is proud of his country's football team then he need not think of himself as being responsible for or owning the team. It is rather that by in some respect identifying with his countrymen he can vicariously share their achievement. So he can see their victory as "closely related" to him in the sense that it has a specific role to play in his view of himself. What can have such a role will depend on the attitudes and beliefs of the individual. So a common country of birth, or the mere presence at a feast, may be grounds for pride for the patriot or guest, for to be so connected with the successful or distinguished may be thought by him to bestow glory.

The beliefs given identify the emotion a person experiences as pride and so distinguishes this from other emotions.[6] They reflect the, for pride, essential interconnection between two kinds of assessment, concerned respectively with the x that is F, and with the agent's own worth. It is the implications of the latter which are of particular interest and which will be discussed in the remainder of this paper.

A certain structure if given to a person's life by for example, his job or his various roles in society, but this is merely the framework. He may value one role more than another, and he may think of himself as being more or less capable of dealing with this or that responsibility. He operates not only with certain values (which may be rudimentary and confused) but also has a view of himself as an agent required to make something of his life, to cope with different situations in which he finds himself, to achieve a certain standing. Of course, how he thinks he should conduct himself on various occasions depends again on what he values. Assessments of this sort are essentially involved in pride. As feelings like joy and pleasure possess no such structural complexity we have here a fundamental distinction between two sorts of emotions. We also have here a basis for the distinction between A being proud of this or that, and A simply being proud. Hume is again uneasy on this point: he regards his treatment of pride and humility as a break with tradition: it may surprise those, he says, who are "accustom'd to the style of the schools and pulpit" (297, section VII), and he adds that "considered in themselves" pride is by no means always vicious, nor humility always virtuous. He seems to think that he and the schoolmen are concerned with the same phenomenon when they talk about pride, but that unlike their account his has the virtue of treating pride "in itself." But he is mistaken in assimilating pride the passion to pride the sin.

What A is proud of he sees as boosting his self-esteem by confirming or adding to his worth in some way. So to be proud of anything he must think it possible for his worth to be added to or confirmed. This presupposes that he must think that (in a certain area, at least) he is of worth or anyway capable of acquiring worth, and also that this worth is not something that is permanently fixed. He must not, that is, view the situation as being static in this respect. If he believes that he is not only worthless (in this area) but also potentially so, then obviously he cannot regard anything as adding to or confirming his worth, so that here nothing can present itself as a candidate for pride.[7] The alternative, namely the belief that his worth in some respect is permanently fixed, divides into two broad cases, that of the humble and that of the proud respectively. To be humble a person need not think of himself as of no worth at all, but he will be aware of his limitations, and it is these he may see as unalterable. Little Dorrit, one of Dickens's devoted and self-effacing heroines, while not regarding herself as worthless, thinks little of her worth, and in spending her life trying to improve the lot of others gives no attention to her own role in these dealings. The thought that what she does reflects on her merit as daughter or sister does not occur to her; hers is a case where the setting store by some good (the well-being of her family) does not turn into pride, although she would have every reason to take credit for this state of affairs. She exemplifies one case of a person possessing humility:

> The continued kindness of her sister was this comfort to little Dorrit. It was nothing to her that the kindness took the form of tolerant patronage: she was used to that. It was nothing to her that it kept her in a tributary position, and

showed her in attendance on the flaming car in which Miss Fanny sat on an elevated seat, exacting homage; she sought no better place. Always admiring Fanny's beauty, and grace, and readiness and not now asking herself how much of her disposition to be strongly attached to Fanny was due to her own heart, and how much to Fanny's, she gave all her sisterly fondness her great heart contained. [*Little Dorrit,* Book 2, Chap. VII]

Alternatively, and at the other end of the scale, A may believe that his worth (at least in some area) is so established and so great that it needs no confirmation and cannot be added to. Here, too, he may not give a thought to his own role in whatever dealings are relevant, but this time not because he does not think in terms of the possibility of merit accruing to him, but because he so takes his own merit for granted that no further attention to the matter is required; what he has and does is *of course* the best of its kind. He is the man who is proud in some way. How proud he is will to a large extent depend on over how wide a field he assumes such superiority, what that field is, and perhaps how his pride is based. Lucifer, the personification of pride the sin, says in his heart: "I will ascend into heaven, I will exalt my throne above the stars of God" (Isa. 14:12-13). He does not just think himself distinguished beyond others in certain ways and so the most superior of his kind. He sees himself as transcending the limits imposed upon beings of the kind he is. Not content with being the foremost of the seraphim, he wants to be God himself. In thinking of himself as God he thinks of himself as the source of all value, so that, in his view, there can be nothing valuable possession of which could reflect value upon him. Such a picture of himself cannot be reconciled with the possibility of having his worth confirmed or added to in any way. So Lucifer cannot be proud of anything.[8]

It is the case of pride rather than that of humility which concerns us here, for it is the contrast with the proud man which is to throw more light on him who experiences emotional pride. In taking his own superior worth for granted, the proud man also takes it for granted that certain things are due to him, and such things he does not regard as items to be proud of. The point is illustrated by the very different attitudes of two characters in Jane Austen's *Pride and Prejudice:* a friend of the Bennet family, Sir William Lucas, had "risen to the honor of knighthood by an address to the king, during his mayoralty." His knighthood, therefore, came to him more or less by chance, it was not something he could expect. He is inordinately proud of it ("the distinction had perhaps been felt too strongly"), but he is not a proud man. He gives a great deal of thought to his knighthood, to the difference it has made and, he thinks, should make to his standing and behavior. It had, for instance, "given him a disgust to his business and to his residence in a small market town." Mr. Darcy, the owner of Pemberley and with £10,000 a year, has a totally different attitude: he is a proud man, but he is not proud of his high position in the social scale. He does not ask and need not ask: does my position add to my worth? He does not think of it as adding to him in any way, for he takes it so much for granted that he seems to think of it as partially constitutive of his worth. His social standing is, in his view, intimately connected with his general standing: intellectually and morally he is superior to others as well, and these superiorities are interconnected. Seeing his worth in these terms rules it out that he should think of his social position as enhancing him, for it is part of a whole already perfect. While he feels secure in this belief there is no need to give a thought at all to the value or importance of his social standing; not that he does not value it, but he is so accustomed to taking it as a matter of course.

The crux of the matter is not, as one might suppose, that Darcy is born into a certain social position, while Sir William has his thrust upon him, though this of course helps to explain why the two men have the attitudes they do. But men of Darcy's standing in society may well be proud of it, while a different Sir William might take his elevation in his stride. It is the nature of their attitudes themselves which is of crucial importance. Mr. Darcy, or the proud man in general, takes for granted his superior worth in some respect. On this basis he has a number of expectations over different areas; in these areas he takes the fulfillment of such expectations as the norm. Mr. Darcy expects to be treated in a certain way; (he is surprised when he is informally accosted by Mr. Collins, a man greatly inferior to him in status). He expects to find himself in certain kinds of company; (he is disgusted with the society of local inhabitants at the village dance), and he also expects certain things of himself, for example, to fulfill to the best of his ability the duties of landowner and landlord. The relevant features of his case, that is, those that make him a proud man and distinguish him from those who would be proud of for example keeping such company and looking after the poor, are firstly that he sees himself as the sort of person who just has and does these things; they are essentially part of the person he is. And secondly, the sort of person which these sorts of expectations help to identify is to his mind a superior sort of person. He is then not proud of being in that company, and so forth, because such activities being the norm for someone of his worth they cannot be regarded as being that something extra that is needed to provide the boost to self-esteem. Nor can such boost be forthcoming, for taking one's worth so for granted as the proud man does prevents him from looking for confirmation of his worth, and his activities and possessions being manifestations of his already established worth cannot be taken by him as adding to it.

The point that emerges for emotional pride is that where the agent expects the possession of some good in the way described[9] he cannot be proud of it. Conversely, for A to be proud of it he cannot regard it as constituting the norm of his expectations; in this sense what he is proud of must go beyond what he thinks he can expect. What such expectations are, and what is taken as the norm and why, will of course vary greatly over different situations and for different people. One contrast I have already touched upon in connection with Hume's example about health. We are not proud of our health, Hume thought, because health is such a common gift. But the point is correct only in the case of those who take their health for granted or who take the fulfillment of their expectations of health as "normal," given their situation. There is no reason why for example the businessman should not be proud of keeping so fit in spite of all those heavy meals. On the other hand, that certain things are rare is very likely to be one of the considerations that influences my expectations and determines the degree of confidence I may have in ever possessing such an object. Here my pride is not based on my viewing my situation as in any way abnormal and as yet achieving what others take for granted. It is precisely by starting from what in this context counts as normal that I have shown that I am clever, persistent, or attractive enough to come by a splendid thing which few can hope to possess.

One constraint, then, which is implicit in the characterization I have given of A being proud of something is that possessing or achieving it must in some way go beyond what A himself thinks he can take for granted, and this constraint marks one difference between this case and A just being proud, though he may be proud in virtue of this very thing. Mr. Darcy's social standing certainly has a role to play in his pride, but it is not the role in his own view of himself which is required for him to be proud of it. His social position being a relatively high one, it is partially responsible for Mr. Darcy's conviction of superior worth. And this points to a further distinction between the two concepts: the scales of comparison employed are quite different. It is essential to the proud man's being proud that he regard himself as superior in some respect, and this superiority is relative to others. But the comparison with others is quite secondary to him who is proud of something. The scale of comparison he employs primarily concerns his own position at different times or looked at from different points of view. If I am proud of the recently acquired beautiful house, then I think my worth increased in some respect by comparison with what I was before the house came my way. Of course, my improvement brings with it that a comparison with others is now also more favorable: as house-owner, say, I am now better than some. But such a comparison may not loom large or cross my mind at all. Or, to take a less simple case, I may be proud of some ability of mine which I value, have always possessed, and always known to possess. Here a crude "before and after" comparison is clearly not in place. The only basis for regarding my possessing such an ability as something I cannot take for granted is my discovery that not everybody possesses such a thing. So this view of it is based on some comparison with others, but it does not follow that my view of my consequent worth is of the nature "I am better than you in this respect." Others do not here provide the scale but function merely as the foil against which the value of my possession becomes more prominent. The comparison is between what, owing to this ability, I am, and what, without it, I would have been. It is the function of other, less able people to highlight the importance of what I have, and this is what I realize when experiencing pride. This does not of course preclude that I may not also and as a consequence feel superior to others, but this is incidental to the case.

The man who is proud of various things need not think himself superior to others at all. The basis for the "boost" may be found anywhere, and being proud of many things is quite compatible with

being very humble. This relativity makes it possible that the gratification a certain achievement will give me is by no means unsullied.
I may think that I should not really be proud of such a thing, for a
better, tougher, or more efficient person would do or get it quite as
a matter of course and not think of it as an achievement in the first
place. The mere fact of my being proud of it shows up my deficiencies as a person. In such a case I operate with two scales, my view of
my own abilities and standing in the light of which it is splendid to
have done this thing, and the view of the matter likely to be taken
by a more "normal" person, from whose standpoint doing it is not
splendid at all. None of these considerations are appropriate to the
proud man, at least not in that area where his supposed superiority
lies. On the other hand, of course, he who is proud and therefore
thinks himself superior to others in some respect may still be proud
of many things, for unless he is Lucifer himself he is unlikely to
take his superiority everywhere so for granted that he does not look
for confirmation, and it is unlikely that there is nothing possession
of which he might not regard as adding to or highlighting his worth
in some respect. It may indeed be the case that thinking himself
superior in a number of ways already he is inclined to look for more
areas where his worth can shine. This, for example, is Dr. Sloper's
case:

> Dr. Sloper would have liked to have been proud of his daughter; but there was
> nothing to be proud of in poor Catherine. There was nothing, of course, to be
> ashamed of; but this was not good enough for the doctor, who was a proud
> man and would have enjoyed being able to think of his daughter as an unusual
> girl. [Henry James, *Washington Square,* chap. 2]

Dr. Sloper is unlucky in his search for further areas of pride. However, he can accommodate the situation and make the best of it: he
decides that paternity is, after all, not an exciting vocation (chap.
15) and so presumably not an aspect of his life worthy of much
attention. If one looks for superiorities in an area where one cannot
find them then the obvious way of not shaking one's trust in one's
superior worth is to rule that area insignificant.

The points just discussed, that what a man is proud of goes
beyond what he thinks he can expect, that the comparison involved
is of himself with as against without some good, and that the starting-point for such a comparison may be anywhere and does not

require that he look on himself as either superior or inferior to others, all follow from the crucial consideration that he thinks of the x that is F as adding to or in some way highlighting or confirming his worth. They all relate to his concern with and his confidence in his own role or standing. It follows from what has been said that a man who is proud of many things need not be a proud man, and that he cannot be a Lucifer. Hume is therefore correct when he says that the kind of pride he is interested in, that is, pride the passion, is not always vicious, though this is not a remark that need upset those who preach that pride is a sin. It may, however, be thought that all cannot be well with someone who is proud of many things, for if some concern with one's role or standing is central here then this would seem to imply that such a person pays rather exaggerated attention to himself and his own worth. He may not be sinful or vicious, but he seems morally suspect none the less. But this would be too rash a conclusion to draw. The concern may be fleeting and superficial as well as central and preoccupying. I may be proud of having grown such a beautiful rose but not think rose-growing an important part of my life, nor that having here succeeded shows anything about myself that is of particular significance. What I am proud of may play a quite negligible part in my life. Even where the concern goes deeper, as in the case of Sir William, it need not carry with it an undue preoccupation with one's self. Although Sir William is hardly an admirable character, his pride in his knighthood does not prevent him from being kind and considerate. But maybe he could regard his rise in society as something of a luxury: there is no indication that he needed to take the distinction conferred upon him as proving his worth to himself and to the world. It is largely where there is such a need that he who is proud of many things may be unduly occupied with himself. The most likely candidate here is perhaps the man whose being proud of some achievement is itself the catalyst for other emotions, such as shame or humiliation. The mere fact of his being proud confirms, in his view, that he does not match what he thinks he should be, and the frequent occurrence of such occasions may well indicate that he pays exaggerated attention to his own standing.

There are of course other things that may go wrong with a man's being proud of this or that. The discussion of Hume's constraints brought out a distinction between conditions which must obtain if a man is to be proud of something at all, and those which must obtain if he is to be in some sense justified in his pride. His beliefs about the various pride-provoking situations may be quite unfounded, so that given the beliefs we can at least begin to assess whether a particular experience is well based or not. So it may be absurd for him to be proud of x being F if he really had no hand at all in bringing it about; his beliefs involve some self-deception. Hume's boastful guest at the feast is a case in point. Similarly, the attaching of a positive value to the x that is F may not be justifiable, or even where it is, the move from this belief to that concerning the consequent addition to one's worth may be mistaken. So "ready wit" is quite a valuable property, but as the heroine of *Pride and Prejudice* discovers, her exercise of it has by no means added to her worth. The man who is often proud, then, may be silly or pompous, he may take credit where none is due and so overestimate himself. What he is proud of will indicate what he sets store by as well as what he makes of himself as an agent leading a life, and in either area his views may be totally misguided. The experience of pride may be based on all sorts of failings and all sorts of misvaluations of oneself. But whether a man who is frequently proud is a good or a bad man, whether he is bursting with confidence or given to self-doubt cannot be settled by just an investigation of the emotion itself.

Whether or not a person is proud of something will depend on how he sees himself, on how he regards his position in society and his relation with others. If he is proud of it, then the x that is F will play a very special role in his view of things, and so it could perhaps be said that it is indeed the "close relation" between it and the self which distinguishes pride from mere joy. But it would be misleading to state the point in these terms because it would make the difference appear to be one of degree only, whereas what separates the two emotions is that they have entirely different structures. A mistaken assumption about the kind of distinction here required at least partially underlies Hume's confident assertion that his hypothesis being so simple, and requiring so little reflection and judgment, it applies to every sensible creature, so that "pride and humility are not merely human passions, but extend themselves over the whole animal creation" (326, 328, section XII). But the complexity of thought and assessment in fact involved in pride make that claim highly implausible.

NOTES

1. E.g., in recent literature J. R. S. Wilson, *Emotion and Object* (Cambridge: Cambridge University Press, 1972); R. M. Gordon, "The Aboutness of Emotion," *American Philosophical Quarterly* XI, 1 (January 1974); Donald Davidson, "Hume's Cognitive Theory of Pride," *Journal of Philosophy* LXXXIII, 19 (November 4, 1976); I. Thalberg, *Perception, Emotion and Action* (London: Basil Blackwell, 1977).

2. *A Treatise of Human Nature,* ed. L. A. Selby Bigge (London: Clarendon Press, 1967), Book 2, Part 1, section VI., p. 291 (all following page references will be to this edition. Unless otherwise indicated, they are from section VI.)

3. Most recently by Jerome Neu in *Emotion, Thought and Therapy* (London: Routledge & Kegan Paul, 1978).

4. Donald Davidson, "Hume's Cognitive Theory of Pride," p. 752.

5. (i)-(iii) are not meant to be in any way indicative of any particular view of the logical form of these sentences.

6. In concentrating on the beliefs involved in pride, I ignore Hume's feelings of pleasure which according to him constitute the emotion itself. But no such separate feeling can play an identificatory role; whatever feelings there may be are identified as pride-feelings by the beliefs given.

7. A possible example here is Marcel in one of his recurring moods: "How little joy there was in this sterile lucidity! . . . had fate granted me another hundred years of life, and sound health as well, it would merely have added a series of extensions to an already tedious existence, which there seemed no point in prolonging at all." Proust, *Remembrance of Things Past,* trans. A. Mayor (London: Chatto & Windus, 1970), 12:222.

8. Aurel Kolnai discusses this kind of pride in "Hochmut," *Philosophisches Jahrbuch* (1931), 44. Band, 2, Heft.

9. And only in the way described, i.e., the expectations are based on the already assumed worth of the agent. A man may of course, e.g., on inductive grounds expect x, achieve x, and be proud of having x.

XVII

MASTER PASSIONS

ANNETTE BAIER

Hume's most famous claim about the passions is that they do *and should* rule reason, which "can never pretend to any other office than to serve and obey them." The metaphor that he uses is a social one, the obedience of slaves to masters, and I think it is deliberately chosen. The claims made include both a claim about what is possible, and a claim about what is desirable. Only passions can motivate, so only they can pretend to the office of ruler. But what is the force of the normative claim, that reason should serve passion? Should it serve any and every passion? Hume surely does not believe that reason *should* be controlled by envy and malice, merely that it can be, and sometimes is. To specify the precise normative claim Hume is making, as well as to square this section of the *Treatise* with its other claims about passions, I think we must take the social metaphor seriously. Hume is not claiming merely that passion controls reason, but that some passions can and should *rule* it. Rule, unlike influence and control, cannot be secret, and requires some continuity in the ruler. Were reason's workings either covertly determined by some secret passion, or controlled by a succession of openly avowed but ephemeral passions, then the metaphor of masters and servants would be inappropriate. Unless a passion is sustained enough to determine not merely momentary motivation but a line of conduct, over time, it cannot properly be said to master of anything. To command obedience a passion must last, and for a group of passions, which individually are perhaps only episodic ones, to last, some dependable order must be established among them. As everyone from Plato onward knows, the passions can be an unruly lot, inconstant and in conflict with one another. If they together are to attain oligarchic rule over reason, some unification, or at least some rule of succession, will first have to be achieved among them. It is a reasonable question to ask what account Hume has of how the passions can achieve that internal order which would enable them not only to provide a sequence of whims or urges which supply reason with short-term goals, so determine its short-range means-end reasoning, but also supply it with some longer range policy, some consistency of purpose, some rule. And if only some passions are the ones that can and should, in this strong sense, *rule,* which ones are they, and what qualifies them for sovereignty? I believe Hume has answers to these questions.

To draw out his answers, I must bring into relation to one another several discussions, from different parts of the *Treatise.* I shall look at some general distinctions Hume draws among passions, and I shall also look at passages that are concerned with the passions typical of those persons who command other persons. I assume that Plato was correct in supposing that the psychology of rulers can point us to a correct account of what should rule within each psyche, so that we can learn something about Humean master passions by attending to his description of the passions of masters, of the rich and powerful, of slave owners, of magistrates and princes. In relating these passages to one another I shall sometimes be going considerably beyond anything Hume says in so many words, but my attempt is to find, in Hume's work, and then to develop, an answer to the question of *why* reason should serve passion, and which passions it should serve.

Hume classifies passions in many ways—direct and indirect, violent and calm, agreeable and uneasy, regular and irregular, instinctive and acquired. In my search for features that would qualify a passion to rule I shall focus on two features (which have been less discussed by other commentators), namely on the genetic feature of being a "corrected" sentiment, one which has undergone a process of correction or alteration in its direction (T. 492) and also on the feature Hume calls "purity," which I shall consider first. Hume says of pride and humility that they are "pure emotions in the soul, unattended by any desire, and not immediately exciting us to any action" (T. 307).[1] Unlike love and hatred they are "compleated in themselves" and "rest in that emotion which they produce" (ibid.). This last claim reminds one of Spinoza's account of a free active emotion, one that, like Humean pride, is a self-sufficient emotion and which has, as its object, the one whose emotion it is. But

Spinoza's free emotion, the intellectual love of God, whereby a person both loves himself and participates in the infinite love with which God loves himself, is eternal, is a self-sustaining emotion. When Hume says that pride "rests" in the emotion it produces, does he mean merely that no different emotion is produced, so that pride may be followed by the absence of any passion, or does he mean that pride, like Spinoza's love of self-in-God, rests in its own continuation? I do not find it unthinkable that Hume's proud person might have affinities with Spinoza's free person, despite a recent interpretation[2] of Hume as an opponent of Spinoza, as regards the treatment of the passions. Hume's own references to Spinoza are cautious and ironic, and I think the areas of agreement between them[3] are as important as their disagreements. So although, in the passage concerning the purity of pride, Hume's claim, in its immediate context, seems to mean no more than that pride, unlike love, is not followed by a desire to make happy the person who is the "object" of the emotion, I will pursue the possibility that we can give a stronger reading to his claim that pride rests in the emotion it produces.

In his argument to show the double intentionality of pride, that it has a "cause" (a fine possession) as well as an "object" (oneself), Hume says that, had it depended only on its object, "pride wou'd be perpetual" (T. 288). Only pride's relativization to possessions, which both vary in quality and are of inconstant presence, saves us for total absorption in it, "since the object is always the same, and there is no disposition of the body peculiar to pride, as there is to thirst and hunger" (ibid.). I take this last remark to mean not only that the pleasure of pride is not the pleasure of satisfying a felt lack caused by a state of bodily depletion, but also that there is no natural consummation to pride, no state of repletion that ends the emotion. Humean pride is not a naturally self-terminating passion, like satisfied thirst and hunger. What is more, it is a peculiarly agreeable emotion, so that one in its grip has no reason to switch, even to another agreeable passion, like love. Hume believes that love easily leads to pride, when the loved person in some way belongs to one. Love of a brother passes smoothly into pride in his good qualities, but "pride or humility is not easily transfus'd into love and hatred with the same ease that the latter passions are chang'd into the former. If a person be my brother I am his likewise. But tho' the relations be reciprocal, they have very different effects on the imagination. The passage is smooth and open from the consideration of any person related to us to that of ourself, of whom we are every moment conscious. But when the affections are once directed to ourself, the fancy passes not with the same facility to any other person, how closely so ever connected with us" (T. 340). Pride "engages the attention and keeps it from wandering" (T. 399). There is reason, then, to suppose that Hume does believe that pride rests in itself not by leading to "perfect tranquility" (T. 422) but by sustaining itself.

How can it sustain itself if it is unattended by any desire? Hume's account of the purity of pride pairs its resting in itself with its absence of accompanying desire, but these two features seem at odds with one another, if the self-sufficiency of pride is interpreted as its self-sustaining power. What is the dynamic force, the action, by which it sustains itself, if pride is "unattended by any desire, not immediately exciting us to any action"? There must be some such dynamic element, if pride is to be a violent passion, not even *apparently* inert, like calm passions, if it is to "invigorate and exalt the mind" (T. 391) and, especially, if it is to sustain itself. Desire, for Hume, is usually the desire for not yet present pleasure, or absence from pain, but in one passage he seems to recognize another sort of desire, which *does* accompany pride. He gives us the example of a person who wants a particular fine suit of clothes, comes to possess it and whose pride and pleasure in it is said to "return back to the direct affections and give new force to our desire or volition, joy or hope" (T. 439). This might seem to contradict Hume's earlier claim about the purity of pride, its freedom from accompanying desire. But what exactly is the desire that the proud owner has? It cannot be the desire to *get* the clothes, since by hypothesis he already has them. But it can be the desire to *keep,* the will and the hope not to lose the possessions of which one is proud. Now the desire to keep what one has does, indeed, not immediately excite us to any action. But it may indirectly motivate action, and Hume gives us in Book III a long account of the artifices we create to enable us to keep what we have while simultaneously acquiring new possessions.[4] We can reconcile the claimed purity of pride with the fact that it is attended by the desire to keep if we suppose that such conservative desires, desires to stay as one is, are importantly different from the

desires that flow from discontent, from lack.[5] Hume usually re-
stricts the term *desire* to those latter necessarily restless desires, but
he does at T. 439, and implicitly throughout his account of the
"violent" passion of pride, recognize a dynamic psychological
force whose tendency is to preserve a state of affairs rather than
change it.

Once we see that pride, as a pure emotion, does have its own
impetus or desire, and that this is a self-maintaining desire, then the
two aspects of purity can be seen to be closely related. A pure emotion is attended by no desire except the desire for that which pro-
longs it in existence, and if this desire is satisfied, then pride will
sustain itself, will "rest" in itself. Its rest, however, will be that rest
in self-contained motion which Spinoza attributed to the universe
as a whole, and to a less perfect extent to any self-maintaining complex thing. Pride is *not,* like a Humean idea, inert; it sustains itself
in existence by a self-directed desire, that is one directed at oneself.
Since any master passion would need to be a lasting one, not one
leading to its own demise, this purity may confer on a passion one
feature needed in a master passion.

There are two features Hume claims to be true of all the passions
with which purity might be confused. These are the inertia of the
passions, and their status as "original existences." Hume is claiming more for pride's self-maintenance than simply that it, like any
passion, is "slow and restive" (T. 441), tending to outlive the ideas
that introduced it, and he is also claiming more about its self-direct-
edness than that it, like any passion, is an impression, an "original
existence" which "contains not any representative quality that renders it a copy of any other existence or modification" (T. 415). This
latter claim is made, for passions as such, as "confirmation" of the
immediately preceding pronouncements that "reason is and ought
only to be the slave of the passions," and that only another passion
can oppose passion. It is a puzzling claim, since Hume requires of
any passion that it be "reflective," or "secondary," that is, that it
be introduced by another perception, its cause. Implicit reference
to an "other existence" seems essential to the intentionality of the
passions,, or what Hume calls their status as impressions of reflection. Even if, as he claims, "when I am angry I am actually possest
with the passion and in that emotion have no more reference to any
other object than when I am thirsty, or sick, or five feet tall" (ibid.)

my anger would not be a passion unless another perception were its cause, and would not be the passion of anger unless, on his own account elsewhere, its object were "a person or creature endow'd with thought and consciousness" (T. 411) and one whose injurious action incites the passion. Thirst too, which is one of those direct passions Hume believes to arise from natural impulse or instinct, which "properly speaking produce good and evil and proceed not from them like the other affections" (T. 439), even if it does not need to be preceded by the impression or idea of the *pleasure* of drinking, does require an accompanying thought of what would quench it, if it is to count as an impression of reflection. Does Hume, by the other examples he gives of nonrepresentative existences, mean to suggest that just as sickness *does* refer us to the health which is lacking, thirst to the drink which is wanted, and being five feet tall to the measure used, so too anger has its own reference which is *not the same* as the reference of a representation? One thing it is clear he means is that ideas make explicit claims to correctly represent or copy other realities, while passions do not. But if they require idea-copies of their causes and objects as their accompaniments, they do implicitly make claims to truth-as-accurate-representation, so their claimed independence of other existences seems exaggerated. Whatever we are to say about this difficult passage,[6] the independence it claims for all emotions must be construed as different from that peculiar to pure emotions. Being "possest by anger" excites to action, to moves made to change the situation, but being "possest" by pride is less disruptive.

Stability, then, seems to be what Hume finds in pride as a pure emotion. It has its own dynamic, and it can set reason to work in helping the proud man *keep* his valued possessions, but it does not lead to discontent and unrest. Humility, on the contrary, cannot be given such an analysis, since the man who finds his own possessions shameful will not be content to keep merely them, but strive to acquire better. There may be a deeper level where it is true that humility reinforces itself, as pride can, if the humble person is, by the fact of his humility, deprived of any confidence in his ability to get or keep valuable things, so must remain in an increasingly hopeless state.[7] Hume claims that humility dejects and discourages (T. 391) but his account of it has not shown it to be self-reinforcing. On the contrary one would expect the person who is ashamed of his ragged coat to desire a better one, thereby ruining the purity of his emotion. Hume himself describes humility as unlike pride in being an "uneasy" passion (T. 333). He may, then, have erred in claiming purity for humility as well as pride. Leaving humility aside, then, let us consider the reasons Hume gives for believing that pride cannot merely aim at sustaining itself, but can succeed in that. What are the mechanisms whereby pride achieves its own survival?

Hume says that in respect of the passions in general the mind is "not of the nature of a wind instrument of music, which in running over the notes immediately loses the sound after the breath ceases; but rather resembles a string instrument where after each stroke the vibrations still retain the same sound, which gradually and insensibly decays" (T. 440-1). This is the inertia typical of all passions. What is special in the case of some emotions is that the sound, far from insensibly decaying, is "reverberated" (T. 365). Hume uses this metaphor, of sounds and their reverberation, when he discusses the way a powerful person keeps his self-satisfaction from decaying. The notes sounded by plucking or striking strings will last a while after the stroke, but will last much longer if they tune in with the same note from another source, tuning fork or second instrument. Then the sounds "reverberate." But such prolongation by reverberation is bought at a cost in self-sufficiency. The proud man, on Hume's account of him, sustains his pride by the recognition of his worth which he finds in others. He needs other well-disposed people to reinforce his self esteem, other minds to mirror and reflect his self assessment. Hume combines the reverberation metaphor with a visual one: "the minds of men are mirrors to one another . . . the pleasure which the rich man receives from his possessions, being thrown on the beholder, causes a pleasure and esteem; which sentiments, being perceiv'd and sympathiz'd with, encrease the pleasure of the possessor; and being once more reflected, become a new foundation for pleasure and esteem in the beholder." The mechanism is one of positive feedback, and the source of the feedback is the mind of another. The proud person, then, sustains his pride only if others let him. Purity as the ability of an emotion to sustain itself is in tension with purity as self-containment.

Hume's rich powerful man, however, has other resources. Even if his fellows do not let his pleasure in his possessions spread by sympathetic contagion to them, even if they refuse to be his mirror or his tuning fork, nevertheless his pride can be sustained, since, when sympathy fails, "comparison,"[8] that principle directly contrary to it, can achieve a similar result. Hume cites the reinforcement of pride by sympathetic reverberation in his account of our esteem for the rich and powerful, but in his account of pride in property and riches it is not recognition by admirers, but comparison with those over whom one wields power, which he emphasizes. The rich man's delight in his riches is said to be a delight in power, accentuated by a comparison with the poverty and powerlessness of others, and especially of his slaves and subordinates. "Comparison is in every case a sure method of augmenting our esteem for anything. A rich man feels the felicity of his condition better by opposing it to that of a beggar. But there is a peculiar advantage in power, by the contrast that is, in a manner, presented to us, betwixt ourselves and the persons we command" (T. 316). If sympathetic reverberation fails, then, one can perhaps turn to the less generous feedback from envious and resentful slaves, whose very "irregular" (T. 376) emotions confirm one's own power and self-esteem. This reinforcement of self-esteem from the envy of others, equally with that obtained from the esteem of others, is won at a cost in the self-sufficiency of pride—in both cases it is made dependent on the feelings of other people.

But this induced dependency of the proud powerful person on his fellows is not the only cause he has for self-doubt. There is a tension in Hume's story about the psychology of the powerful master which surfaces only when we look at what he says in the section concerned with "love of fame." There he stipulates both that the esteem we value is *only* the esteem of near equals, and also that envy is felt not of those superiors very distant from one in power, but of those quite close in position. This means that the rich man cannot count on division of function, getting esteem from his equals and envy from his subordinates, he must look, for esteem, to the very group prone to envy. The esteem he *may* get, by Hume's account, is that of the powerless he commands, but that will be useless to him if he is indifferent to their opinions. "We receive a much greater satisfaction from the approbation of those whom we ourselves esteem and approve of, than of those whom we hate or despise" (T. 321). But if those we esteem are our near competitors for power, we will be as likely to get their resentment of our success as their admiration.

Does this matter? Does it now show that the proud powerful man is indeed secure—if his pride is not reinforced by the esteem of others, it will be reinforced by their envy, and even if his subordinates and slaves are so far beneath him that they do not even envy him, he may still compare his power with their powerlessness and reinforce his pride by contempt of them. It may indeed be important to his sense of power that the gulf between himself and his inferiors remain great enough to prevent there being any question of their emulating him: "A man who compares himself to his inferior receives a pleasure from the comparison: And when the inferiority decreases by the elevation of the inferior, what should have been only a decrease of pleasure becomes a real pain by a new comparison with its preceding condition" (T. 377). Hume calls this sense of insecurity, the awareness that inferiors are advancing, a species of envy, although it is strictly an envy of ourselves, in relation to those inferiors at an earlier time, before they improved their position and narrowed the gap between us. So when that gap is narrow enough for them to aspire to the powerful man's position, and envy him, that very fact is also occasion for him to feel the peculiar envy which depends upon "the effects of comparison twice repeated" (ibid.), that is, a comparison of the gap between them before and after the inferiors' advancement. The masters, then, on Hume's account, will be secure in their pride of power as long as they have near equals who are either admiring, and so positively reinforce the pride of the powerful, or envious, and so negatively reinforce it, or underlings whom they can despise and who do not approach them closely enough to feel envy or inspire the peculiar self-directed envy of double comparison.

How good a security is this? Certainly there is a tension between the demand that *equals* confirm one's self evaluation, and the supposed content of that evaluation, namely that one is superior, that is, *better* than they are. To provide oneself with suitable valuers one puts at risk the very superiority one wants acknowledged, and, once one *has* near equals, one may "envy" their advance as well as incur their envy and competition in place of their contented esteem. The latter outcome is not all bad, inasfar as envy confirms one's superiority, but it is an unstable situation, since the envious have motive to harm and outdo one. Hume does not in Book Two spell out these tensions in the master's pride in riches and power, but he does in his account of the choice of magistrates, in Book Three, by implication acknowledge that their situation contrasts in stability with that of the wielders of other forms of power, of slave owners or robber barons. I turn now to his account of the psychology of magistrates.

As early as Book Two, in his account of punishment, Hume begins his portrait of the magistrate and his proper passions. He distinguishes between a punisher "in his magisterial capacity" (T. 410), acting to secure obedience to law, and the angry "avenger of crimes on account of their odiousness" (T. 411). The magistrate does not feel anger toward the criminal, and punishes for purposes of deterrence, not retribution or revenge. In Book Three Hume describes these calm law-enforcers as those who are "satisfied with their present condition and their part in society," so have an immediate interest in upholding it and its rules, and have "no interest, or but a remote one, in any acts of injustice" (T. 537). These paragons are to be entrusted with the task of formulating existing rules and enforcing them on all, that is of contriving matters so that their *own* interest in social conformity is made to spread to others. They, before becoming magistrates, obeyed society's rules because they were contented with their part in society. Once they have magisterial power, their subjects will obey the rules to escape the penalties they attach to breach of those rules.

What sort of assurance of their new power do they receive: public recognition of their office, whereby they are assured of their position of power, and also, if they want it, a comparison of their own position with the powerlessness of their subjects. Since their recognition comes from the public, as such, and from the public conventions and procedures that created them *as* magistrates, they need not rely on individual recognition, which could only come, in the circumstances, from other princes, or from less powerful persons, their subjects. The problem of securing, from an equal, recognition of one's superiority over others is solved by the artifice of authority. The equal that recognizes one is the law, or rather that public will that legislated the common law. The inferiors over whom the magistrate wields power are not the ones he need look to for recognition, although he looks to them in their *joint* capacity, as a public, for self-recognition, while exercising his power over them as individual subjects. Like Rousseau's sovereign people, they in their collective capacity have the power to recognize or refuse to recognize a magistrate, while in their several private capacities they must obey the power which is recognized. This solves one of the problems of the master—how to get recognition without thereby creating a rival power. It does not solve the problem of how to keep superiority, how to prevent inferiors from getting close enough for envy or resentment to get a hold, and to motivate rebellion, and usurpation of power. Hume, I think, has no answer to that problem. All his artifices *aim* at stability, and the institution of government is, for him, the crowning artifice: "Thus bridges are built, harbours open'd, ramparts rais'd, canals form'd, fleets equipp'd, and armies disciplin'd, every where, by the care of government, which tho' compos'd of men subject to all human infirmities, becomes, by one of the finest and most subtle inventions imaginable, a composition which is, in some measure, exempt from these infirmities" (T. 539). But only in some measure.

For all its incompleteness, Hume's account of the progress leading from an unstable situation, a competitive scramble for possessions, to greater stability of possession through the institution of property, greater facility in profitably exchanging it or making it productive, through the institution of contract, greater security in protecting it, through the institution of governing magistrates, is a remarkable story of both social and psychological transformation. He himself insists that men can never change their natures, so he would not call it psychological transformation, merely a change of situation which allows unchanged passions to be exhibited in new ways. The passion that is corrected in the story which leads to the emergence of the magistrate is avidity, not pride, but it is instructive to see how much greater is the self-sustaining ability of pride when it is a magistrate's pride in power than when it was the slave owner's or the rich man's pride. The magistrate is secure in the fact of his power, by a comparison of his state with that of private citizens. He is also guaranteed recognition of his power. The recognition he receives, if it must be not only the recognition of an equal but recognition in the *mind* of an equal, cannot come merely from the law but must come from the public will behind the law. The law itself would be an equal whose very abstractness prevented its becoming a rival. It is his equal in that there is equality of dependency between them. Without the law, the magistrate has no authority. Without the magistrate to enforce it, the law's authority is insecure.

But the recognition the law can give the magistrate will scarcely be that reverberation from other minds which Humean pride demands. A proud official might get a certain reassurance of his power by keeping his certificates of office framed upon his wall, or by rereading the constitution which affirms his status, but this will be a poor substitute for recognition by persons, mirroring fellow minds. Only the people whose will lies behind the law can give the magistrate the recognition he craves, but the citizen as lawmaker may indeed pose a threat of rivalry to the magistrate.

Hume himself did not apply his earlier account of pride to the magistrate's pride in power. Had he done so, he might have seen the inadequacies in his account of political authority and its stability. He sees the magistrate's power to be limited by the laws that created him, and recognizes a right of rebellion in subjects when the magistrate acts against those laws. But he does not see the full implications of his own account of those laws as conventions, created by the intentions of a people who by cooperation become a public, nor of his statement that conventions are changeable by public will (T. 528). It is to this public mind that the magistrate must look for recognition, for reverberation of his self-esteem. From the law alone he may get some reassurance, but not full personal recognition.

Such stability and security as there is in the magistrate's pride in power has been achieved by a long process of "correction," or negative feedback, directed on the passion of avidity for possessions and power, the desire to get things in which one can take pride. That process involved successive moves to facilitate keeping and getting, the two sides of the appropriative passion. They are also two aspects of pride. Although to sustain itself the "pure" desire to *keep* the prideworthy possessions must be satisfied, the prior satisfaction of the impure desire to get is presupposed (at least whenever what pride is taken in is some noninnate good). Humean pride and avidity are both essentially possessive passions, and so Hume's account of the way avidity corrects itself through artifices is also an account of a transformation of the causes of pride, from present goods to absent property and abstract wealth and political power, from the ability to make and get goods to the reputation for honesty and fidelity, obedience to law and magisterial impartiality.

Is it only the magistrate who can sustain pride? So far I have argued that one aspect of the purity of pride, its self-sustaining power, demands a sacrifice of the other aspect, its self-containment. Both for the recognition that allows pride to reverberate, and for the "correction" of the instabilities inherent in that need for recognition, other people are essential adjuncts to the proud person's pride. The magistrate to some degree has other people where he wants them—within his power, yet able, through their collective product, laws, and conventions, to provide him with some sort of recognition by an equal. What of the pride of nonofficials? Is that doomed to be ephemeral? Not if, as Hume claims, every person can occupy a role, which, like that of the magistrate, is public and publicly recognized, and find ground for pride in the fact of occupying this role. The role, of course, is that of moral judge, discerner and approver of virtue in oneself and others.

This capacity, like the magistrate's, is acquired through a correction of natural tendencies, by a series of reactions to the effects of the working of less corrected versions of those forces. Hume likens moral judgment to "judgments concerning external bodies. All objects seem to diminish by their distance: But tho' the appearance of objects to our senses be the original standard, by which we judge them, yet we do not say that they actually diminish by the distance; but correcting the appearance by reflexion, arrive at a more constant and establish'd judgment concerning them. In like manner, tho' sympathy be much fainter than our concern for ourselves, and a sympathy with persons remote from us much fainter than that with persons near and contiguous; yet we neglect all these differences in our calm judgments concerning the characters of men" (T. 603). We are forced into this reflective correction by the need to reach agreement with others. The demands of "society and conversation" force us to "form some general unalterable standard," since others "cou'd never converse with us on any reasonable terms, were we to remain constantly in that situation and point of view which is peculiar to us" (ibid.). It is the shocks of "many contradictions to our sentiments in society and conversation" (T. 583), which fuels this self-corrective process. By reacting to others we eventually reach a viewpoint of optimal distance for viewing character—one neither too remote nor too close, or perhaps more accurately one which is neither merely remote nor merely close. Hume describes this optimal viewpoint as one that is distanced by sympathy, but made close by the fact that the ones with whom we are to sympathize, to see a man's character clearly, are "the person himself, whose character is examin'd; or that of persons who have a connexion with him" (T. 591). The connection Hume is thinking of, which explains the indifferent "or" in that quotation, is not that linking the judged person to his rivals and enemies, since such interested sentiments must be "overlooked" (T. 583), but that linking a man to his companions in business, pleasure, family. What is important is that "his company is a satisfaction to me" (T. 588), that he be "a safe companion, an easy friend, a gentle master, an agreeable husband, an indulgent father" (T. 606). Moral judgments are the sympathy-distanced estimates of the judgments of those close enough to know what sort of company the person provides.

Nietzsche contrasts slavish reactive sentiments with sovereign free ones,[9] and his contrast repeats Spinoza's contrast between free active passions and unfree passive ones to which I earlier likened Hume's contrast between a pure and an impure emotion. But now it is evident that, for Hume, the only way to make a passion really able to sustain itself by its own activity is to allow it to become reactive, to be corrected by its "contradictions" with the passions of others. When thus corrected, when no longer self-contained but sensitive to both the negative and the positive feedback from other persons' passions, both pride and the moral sentiment are self-sustaining passions, passions fit to be master.

Which of them is to rule? It now looks as if there are at least two Humean passions that have that ability to sustain themselves in existence which is a prerequisite of any governing force. It is, I think, quite clear that Hume believes that the dominating passion should be the moral sentiment, but this does not mean that pride must be subjugated, merely that the correction it undergoes, in becoming stable, is a process of socialization or moralization. Once it *is* corrected it is no longer a separate passion from the moral sentiment, but merges with it. Hume claims, in the section where he discusses the purity of pride, that passions, unlike ideas, "are susceptible of an entire union; and like colours may be blended so perfectly together that each of them may lose itself and contribute only to that uniform impression which arises from the whole" (T. 366). Although he says this as a preamble to his account of the blending of love with benevolence, which he contrasts with the purity of pride, nevertheless in Book Three he tells us that virtue and vice *must* give rise to either love, hatred, pride or humility (T. 473). The discernment of virtue by the moral sentiment will occasion pride or love,[10] so there will be a blending of these passions with the moral sentiment that introduces them. Due pride need not compete for mastery with the moral sentiment, since it will complete it, "lose itself," in that complex passion, and rule when it rules. This is especially true when the discerned virtue, in which pride is taken, is one that is an artificial virtue, like honesty, which cannot exist in one person unless others also possess it, so that there is a sense in which the virtue is a community virtue, a necessarily shared virtue in which shared pride may be taken. Hume does not discuss shared pride, but his account of the dependence of artificial virtues, in an individual, on cooperation between individuals, naturally suggests such a development of his views.

The merger of corrected pride with the moral sentiment is seen not only by the fact that pride accompanies discernment of virtue but by the fact that pride may accompany virtue, so that one's own discerned pride in virtue will be a further proof of virtue and a further occasion for pride. Virtuous pride in virtue reinforces both pride and virtue, so that pride and the moral sense become lost in one another. This mutual reinforcement is evident not only when individuals recognize their own virtuous pride in virtue but when the moral sentiment itself, as a general phenomenon, is examined from the moral point of view. Like virtuous pride, it affirms itself. At the very end of the *Treatise* Hume praises it for its agreement with itself and its ability to accept and approve its own origins: "Not only must virtue be approv'd of, but also the sense of virtue: And not only that sense but also the principles from which it is deriv'd. So nothing is presented on any side but what is laudable and good" (T. 619). This success is in striking contrast with the fate of intellect's attempt at self-survey in Book One, and I believe the *Treatise* as a whole is designed to point up that contrast, to show why reason should be ruled by the moral sentiment, in both its natural and its artifice-assisted workings. It is noteworthy, however, that the moral sentiment that does affirm itself, its origins, and its expression, is a sentiment that has merged with pride. It finds itself laudable.

If what is to rule is a merger of pride and the moral sentiment, why does Hume treat the dominating element in this complex passion to be the moral sentiment, rather than pride? For there is little doubt that Hume believes that the passion which should rule is more properly denominated the moral sentiment than pride, even shared pride in shared virtue. The answer is twofold. First, there is a clear sense in which the self-sustaining ability of pride depends upon its correction or moralization, so that it is dependent, for its stability, upon its virtue. In Book Three, Hume emphasizes, as he had not in Book Two, a difference between "due pride" and "overweaning conceit" (T. 597). The pride that can sustain itself and is supported by the moral sense is corrected or due pride. By this Hume does not mean merely pride based on a true rather than a false belief about what counts as one's possessions; he means a pride based on a corrected sense of the worth of those possessions, and also one which can coexist with others' due pride in their possessions.[11] This coexistence is impossible, Hume believes, if each person flaunts his pride, for then "the proud never can endure the proud, and rather seek the company of those who are of an opposite disposition" (T. 596). Hume concludes that due pride must also be duly concealed—"it must be own'd that some disguise in this particular is absolutely requisite; and that if we harbour pride in our breasts we must carry a fair outside and have the appearance of modesty and mutual deference in all our conduct and behaviour" (T. 598). Virtuous pride, he concludes, must be both "well conceal'd and well founded" (ibid.). This is an unsatisfactory outcome of a search for "rara temporum felicitas ubi sentire quae velis, & quae sentias dicere licet."[12] Others may expressly recognize one's worth, but one dare not express one's own self-esteem. It is, I think, unnecessary for Hume to draw this conclusion, and it is partly because of his conclusion that the coincidence of due pride and the moral sentiment is only implicitly recognized by him. A passion that cannot express itself could scarcely be the passion that can claim to rule. If the pride in question really is well founded and if, as he asserts, pride is to be esteemed not a divisive but a social passion, which can unite men (T. 491), since it "gives us a confidence in all our projects and enterprizes" (T. 597), including cooperative projects, then the only restraint that seems in order is one on the expression of ill-founded excessive and uncorrected pride. As

Hume emphasizes, "Tis requisite on all occasions to know our own force" (ibid.), and pride both assures us of that and, when expressed, assures others of it where they need to count on it.

The second reason why it is the *moral* sentiment that gives its name to the complex passion which should rule, according to Hume, is because that sentiment has a structure which parallels that of reason, and which gave what plausibility there was to that false pretender's claim to rule. The special capabilities of reason, relevant to its claim to rule, were its contradiction avoidance, its generality or comprehensiveness, and its consequence tracing power—its ability to make absent things present by relating them to what is present. The moral sentiment has all these features. It "prevent(s) those contradictions and arrive(s) at a more stable view of things" (T. 581); it enables me to "feel the same lively pleasure from the virtues of a person who liv'd in Greece two thousand years ago that I feel from a familiar friend and acquaintance" (ibid.). It considers both what is pleasant, the present good, and what is useful, for oneself and for others. Thereby, in two different ways, it brings the contiguous good into relation with the remote good. To some extent the mutual recognition, through sympathy, which pride requires, also distances the contiguous and brings the remote close, but the moral sentiment ranges more comprehensively, not merely over ones' contemporaries but backward and forward in time. It has all the generality, and the contradiction avoiding power, of supposedly sovereign reason and unlike it has motivational force—has strength, as it has authority. Its calmness, for Hume, is a consequence of its success in reconciling the concern for the contiguous with the concern for the remote. Violence comes about through opposition of passions, and vanishes when the once opposing passions are aligned, and can "shock in a direct line" (T. 442). The calm of the moral sentiment does depend on those structural features that it shares with reason, while its strength depends upon its passional origins.

It may be objected that even if reason, in the philosophical tradition, is a faculty that shares the formal features of the moral sentiment, Humean reason is a more restricted power, namely the ability to discern relations between ideas. But Hume uses the term "reason" in a wider way,[13] and I believe that the common element linking reason in his "strict" sense, with reason in an "improper"

sense (T. 231, E. 26, T. 526) used in causal reasoning, is that both
are the mediated discovery of remoter truths, that they both trace
consequences. Demonstration, or reason in the strict sense, traces
logical links, where reason in the improper sense traces causal consequences or causal ancestry. More generally, "what is vulgarly
called his reason" (T. 419) is the faculty that can "consider any
object at a distance" (T. 536). Reason brings the remote close
enough for consideration, enables us to compare it with the contiguous, overcomes that narrowness of mind, that "infirmity"
(ibid.) which ignores the remote. Hume even uses the term *reason*
for the faculty, whatever it is, which invents the social artifices,
those devices for making remote interests close, and for overcoming opposition between self-interested individuals. In a note he
speaks of human *reason* as supplying the place of the social instinct
in animals (E. 308), where the context makes it clear that it is not
merely causal reasoning but inventive artifice which is here called
reason. Just as he describes our habit of causal inference as a re-
placement for animal instinct (or "reason" in animals), and one
that enables us, unlike the animals, to "comprehend a whole system of objects" (E. 107 n.), so our social inventiveness is also "reason" in the wide sense, a faculty that brings the remote into the
same clear view as we have of the contiguous, and that which produces a social system. If this is Humean reason, in its essence, then
it is understandable that the moral sentiment can be confused with
it (T. 417) not merely because of its calm but because that calm
depends upon the overcoming of both the separation and the opposition between contiguous and remote.

   The moral sentiment then, is as long-sighted as reason and as
concerned as it with system, harmony, and avoidance of contradiction. It can rule reason not only because it supplies motivational
force but because reason is no alien thing to it, but a slave which is
also familiar. Its claim to rule the other passions rests in part upon
its very "reasonableness," its ability to take a comprehensive view,
and in part on that self-sustaining power that it shares with its partner, pride.

   I conclude with a last query about moral pride. Is this pride in
"one's own force?" The moral agent occupies both the position of
judge and of judged, and earlier I suggested that something like a
magistrate's pride in power is available to ordinary persons in their

role as moral judges. This pride is pride in authority and power. But to be a virtuous person, on Hume's account, is not to function well as a moral judge; it is to be found pleasing *by* such judges. Pride in virtue, then, threatens to appear a peculiarly servile "pride," scarcely distinguishable from humility, since it requires accepting the passive role of one to be judged. The threat, however, is unreal. It vanishes once one recalls that the capacity of any to adopt the moral point of view, to be moral judges, depends upon their own willingness to be subject to correction, to the mutual adjustments that make a stable point of view attainable. The virtues found in them, when they are judged, are abilities to function in company with others. The power and ability they exercise as moral judges is itself the outcome of just such cooperative functioning, of mutual contradiction leading to mutual adjustment.[14] As long as the same persons are judged as are judges, their virtues in the subject role will not be discontinuous with their authority and power in their magisterial capacity, but on the contrary will ensure that they are "*gentle* masters," and that their pride in mastery is stable and self-sustaining.[15]

NOTES

1. References throughout are to Hume, *Treatise of Human Nature,* ed. Selby Bigge (T), and to Hume, *Enquiries Concerning Human Understanding and Concerning the Principles of Morals,* ed. Selby Bigge and Niddich (E).

2. Jerome Neu, *Emotion Thought and Therapy* (Berkeley, Los Angeles, London, 1977). Neu contrasts Spinoza's version of freedom as intellect's dominance over the affects with Hume's subordination of reason to passion.

3. Spinoza's intellect is a descendent of the Cartesian will, a faculty that *affirms* things. It is not that passive idea-discerner which Hume calls reason in the strict sense. Spinoza and Hume are in agreement that the ruling faculty must be the active affirming faculty. They are also in agreement concerning the sort of freedom humans can obtain, and on the nonsubstantiality of the human person. Even the undeniable differences between Spinoza's geometrical and Hume's natural-historical method are more stylistic than substantial. Spinoza's conception of deduction is idiosyncratic, demanding more than that mere avoidance of formal self-contradiction which Hume called "demonstration," and which he believed of very restricted usefulness. Spinoza's geometrical method is aimed at reflective self-affirmation, not merely the avoidance of self-contradiction, and Hume's *Treatise,* in its very different way, is also a search for a self-sustaining truth, for a mind that can, not merely "bear" its own survey, but find what it surveys to be "laudable and good" (T. 619).

4. I have examined this in "Hume on Heaps and Bundles," forthcoming, *American Philosophical Quarterly* (October 1979).

5. Plato, in *Philebus,* calls pleasures arising from the satisfaction of such desires mixed or impure because inseparable from the pain of preceding felt lack. Conservative desires and desires for change obviously have differing relations to pleasure and pain. Ronald de Sousa discusses the different sorts of pleasure and pleasure-related desires in "Instinct and Teleology" (unpublished).

6. Hume undeniably has trouble over the intentionality of ideas and beliefs. In one suggestive passage, at T. 106, he equates the representative content of belief with its status as *idea,* and its actual occurrence as a conscious perception is said to make it equivalent to an impression! The idea "consider'd not as the representation of an absent object but as a real perception of the mind, of which we are intimately conscious," is said to "supply the place of an impression," so provide vivacity. Here Hume toys with dividing beliefs into two components, or aspects—one an impression, the other an idea-copy. Just as he seems to find the intentionality of the passions less troublesome than that of ideas, because he thinks he has a causal analysis of it, in which the intentional object of the passion is segregated in a causally connected accompanying idea or impression, so here he wants to separate out the representative content, to treat the meaningful belief as vivacious impression accompanied by its own meaning, in the form of an idea. But if ideas are present wherever there is intentionality, then impressions of sensation too will have to be partnered by accompanying ideas, by pointers beyond themselves.

7. Both Gabriele Taylor ("Pride," this volume) and Jack Norman ("Pride and Self-Esteem," read to 1978 Hume Conference, Banff Springs, Alberta) point out that Hume's version of pride omits an important dimension of it. By making all pride a matter of taking pride in something, being proud of something, Hume neglects to note that there may be preconditions for this sort of emotion, and that pride, in an absolute sense, is a state of person relevant to these preconditions for being prone to take pride *in* an achievement or possession. Norman claims that unless one already has some pride, some *general* sense of competence, one will be unable to take pride in particular things. Taylor points out that the really proud person may be the one least needing to bolster her ego by taking pride in specific things, and it may be the humble person who is more likely to *feel* pride in specific achievements. Hume's version of pride, as always relativized to particular causes, seems to have no room for the assured pride of the confident person, nor for the inability of some to feel pride, even when there is cause for it. It should be noted, however, that the pride Hume speaks of in Book Three, pride as confidence, assurance, a sense of one's own power or force (T. 597) sounds very like that absolute pride which Taylor and Norman rightly want to recognize, and to distinguish from felt pride in some specific thing.

8. Hume's account of the way passions can spread by sympathy is strikingly similar to Spinoza's account of "imitation," discussed by Patricia S. Greenspan in "A Case of Mixed Feelings: Ambivalence and the Logic of Emotion" (this volume). Equally striking is the parallel between, on the one hand, Hume's account of the possibly alternating contrary passions aroused by sympathy and the opposed principle of comparison (T. 594) and, on the other, Spinoza's account (*Ethics,* Book 3, Props. 17, 31, 35) of vacillation between an imitative and a nonimitative affect. Hume, however, has a more complicated story to explain when there will be alteration or time-sharing, rather than coexistence or mutual destruction of contrary passions.

9. Nietzsche, in *Towards a Geneology of Morals,* contrasts guilt, bad conscience, and the sense of injustice which grows out of resentment of the power of others, with the conscience of the sovereign free man, with justice from his perspective, as distinct from the reactive sentiments of mere subjects.

10. The place of love in the complex moral sentiment is a complicating factor which I cannot discuss adequately here. On Hume's account of it, it differs from pride in three ways, in addition to the main way—its having as its object another person. Hume says that it is an "enfeebling" (T. 391) passion, that it is impure because followed by benevolence, and also that its causes are less restricted than those of pride. Although in general he believes that one loves another for the very quality that would, in oneself, be cause for pride, he thinks there are some qualities, such as good nature, which evoke love more readily than they occasion pride (T. 392). It may be significant that these qualities seem to be minimally power conferring. A loved person, in Hume's view, is someone whom we will want to benefit, whereas pride is not followed by the desire to reward oneself. In doing good to a loved person, we will increase their fine "possessions" and so increase the strength of the cause for love. If love can be a sustained passion, it will also, therefore, be a self-augmenting one, since benevolence enhances the one loved. Love, then, will not merely involve a conservative desire for its own preservation, but a creative desire for its own increase. Its dynamic, then, could provide not merely for the stability of the moral sentiment but also for its stable growth.

11. Here again Hume echoes Spinoza's contrast between the pride of overestimation of self, which thrives in the presence of flattering parasites, and that self-esteem based on self-knowledge which is in accord with reason, a noncompetitive good that can be enjoyed in common, by free persons living under a common law. (See *Ethics,* Book 4, Props. 35, 36, 48, 49, 52, 57, 73.)

12. Hume places this quotation, from Tacitus, on the title page of the *Treatise.*

13. Barbara Winters has emphasized the significance of Hume's wider concept of reason, in her paper "Hume on Reason," forthcoming *Hume Studies.* She does not, however, note its inclusion of the socially inventive faculty.

14. I am well aware that the Hume I present sounds not only surprisingly Rousseau-like and Kantian, in my emphasis on autonomy, the coincidence of sovereigns and subjects, but also surprisingly Hegelian, when the emphasis is placed on the way the "contradictions" in avidity, sympathy, and in pride's demand for expression and recognition, lead to a correction of those sentiments, lead toward a more stable outcome in which each person's power can be real, expressed, and recognized by equals. No doubt such a reading of Hume is possible only by hindsight, but what other kind of sight have we of him? I believe it is time that hindsight through the analytic empiricist tradition be supplemented with a more Hegelian look back at Hume's phenomenology of mind, *The Treatise of Human Nature.*

15. I am grateful to Kurt Baier, John Cooper, Paul Guyer, for helpful discussions of an earlier draft of this paper. Only some of their criticisms have been met in this revised version.

XVIII

JEALOUS THOUGHTS

JEROME NEU

If I imagine that an object beloved by me is united to another person by the same or by a closer bond of friendship than that by which I myself alone held the object, I shall be affected with hatred toward the beloved object itself, and shall envy that other person.... This hatred toward a beloved object when joined with envy is called "jealousy," which is therefore nothing but a vacillation of the mind springing from the love and hatred both felt together, and attended with the idea of another person whom we envy.

Spinoza*

The slave revolt in morality begins when *ressentiment* itself becomes creative and gives birth to values: the *ressentiment* of natures that are denied the true reaction, that of deeds, and compensate themselves with an imaginary revenge. While every noble morality develops from a triumphant affirmation of itself, slave morality from the outset says No to what is "outside," what is "different," what is "not itself"; and *this* No is its creative deed. This inversion of the value-positing eye—this *need* to direct one's view outward instead of back to oneself—is of the essence of *ressentiment:* in order to exist, slave morality always first needs a hostile external world; it needs physiologically speaking, external stimuli in order to act at all—its action is fundamentally reaction.... While the noble man lives in trust and openness with himself..., the man of *ressentiment* is neither upright nor naive nor honest and straightforward with himself. His soul *squints*....

Nietzsche*

> . . . normal jealousy . . . is compounded of grief,
> the pain caused by the thought of losing the loved
> object, and of the narcissistic wound, in so far as
> this is distinguishable from the other wound; fur-
> ther, of feelings of enmity against the successful
> rival, and of a greater or lesser amount of self-
> criticism which tries to hold the subject's own
> ego accountable for his loss.
>
> Freud*

Psychological problems are sometimes in some ways logical problems. Our lives do not simply fall apart, they collapse in structured
ways, and the fault lines are marked by our concepts. Our ways of
understanding and describing our psychological states often reveal
(and sometimes limit) the potentials in those states themselves, the
potentials both for development and for disorder. That this should
be so may be explained through considering the roles of our concepts and beliefs in constituting our emotions and other mental
states.[1] In this context, it is especially instructive to consider jealousy: partly because of its internal complexity, partly because of
the richness of its conceptual surroundings, and partly because of
its independent interest. That it has such rich surroundings, that we
make such a wealth of fine discriminations in the area of jealousy
(envy, resentment, indignation, schadenfreude, begrudging, malice, spite, ill will, hatred, ingratitude, revenge, hostility, and so on
indefinitely) is itself a sign of its interest and importance.

By tracing some of the tensions, some of the directions and complexities, built into jealousy, we may see some of the ways in which
the forms and limits of our conceptions in this particular area shape
our lives. Going beyond that, looking to a psychogenetic account
of the origin and place of jealousy, I would like to raise some questions about how far and in what ways understanding our concepts
may enable us to shape (and reshape?) them and so, perhaps, alter
our lives. What are the limits here? What else would have to be different and what else would we have to give up if the possibility of
jealousy were to be eliminated?

In what follows, I shall want to distinguish between jealousy and
envy in relation to the hopes for emotional transformation connected with two types of ideals: communitarian and socialist. (The

personal and the political are sometimes mistakenly assimilated. The ideal of the loving community is not the same as the ideal of the just community, though one might wish for, and work for, both.) I shall be arguing that despite the hopes of social reformers, the possibility of jealousy cannot be eliminated. It is wrong to think that jealousy is always necessarily misdirected, that it cannot have appropriate objects—on the contrary, it can. The presence and persistence of jealousy have more to do with the development of self-identity than with the possession of others; and while the underlying fears may make us prone to pathological forms of jealousy, it is also the case that jealousy is tied to certain forms of love—so the elimination of the possibility of jealousy might involve the loss of much else. On the other hand, the same difficulties do not, it seems to me, stand in the way of the hopes of social reformers in relation to envy. Which is not to suggest that envy can be readily dislodged from its place in human life, nor is it to say that the harmful consequences of jealousy cannot be ameliorated. In subsequent sections I will be taking up the questions of the eliminability of jealousy (I), of the relation of jealousy to envy and of malicious envy to admiring envy (II), and of the relation of jealousy to claims of right (III) and to certain underlying fears (IV), and I shall conclude by juxtaposing the two faces of jealousy: the face turned to love and the face turned to lack of love (V).

I. STALKING THE GREEN-EY'D MONSTER

It was one of the hopes of the sixties (as of many other periods) that by restructuring social relations it might be possible to eliminate jealousy and other painful, "bourgeois," passions. This was the hope that inspired many in the commune movement. It has been largely, I think, a failed hope. Jealousy, envy, and possessiveness reasserted themselves despite the best efforts to keep them down. If this judgment is correct, the question becomes: "Why?" Was the failure a matter of changeable circumstance, or is the possibility of jealousy ineliminable?

It might be said that at the center of the typical commune problems was the fact that the makers of the new world were children of the old, and that they carried their pasts with them into the new institutions. And even their children, brought up under new arrangements, had to face the problem of "socialism in one country"—they had to relate to a wider world the inhabitants of which were not a party to the new arrangements. But these problems, while real and difficult, are merely contingent—one can imagine their being overcome.[2]

I think there are reasons for believing jealousy ineliminable (the possibility remains permanent), no matter what the social arrangements. And these are worth considering in some detail.

First, certain significant differences are ineliminable, and they are just the sort of differences necessary (and perhaps sufficient) for jealousy to get a foothold. Most basic perhaps is the difference between adults and children. It will always be the case that children, in the course of their prolonged dependency, will have needs and make demands which the supporting adults (whether or not they are the biological parents) will, because of needs and attachments of their own, be unable to meet. They cannot be constantly available in all the ways that children demand. The presence of siblings accentuates, but does not essentially change the situation. When loved persons are not available to us and they are (thought or felt to be) available to others, their absence will tend to be experienced as "loss to a rival." (Parents can also come, in this way, to feel jealous of their children; i.e., to experience *them* as rivals.) Jealousy forms one side of the Oedipal triangle because there is a natural (which is to say, biological) hierarchy. So far as the consequent inequalities, dependencies, and mismatches are universal and ineliminable, there must be room for jealousy.[3] (There certainly may be other differences—such as the differences between the sexes, e.g., in reproductive powers—with similar significance, but they may connect more with envy than jealousy, and I wish to come to and treat envy separately.)

Second, the development of children suggests that competitive possessiveness may be an ineliminable phase with permanent consequences. Consider the typical reaction of a two-year-old when it sees another child play with a toy it has just thrown aside. The primitive possessive behavior that emerges is apparently a cross-cultural universal.[4] I do not pretend to fully understand why this phenomenon should emerge just when it does and be universal. Presumably it has something to do with a developing (biological?) need for control.

This primitive possessiveness is certainly an element in mature jealousy, but it needs to be understood that the character of possessiveness is itself problematic. It is too often said that what is wrong with jealousy is that it involves treating people as though they were things. What is more likely to be true in the psychogenesis of possessiveness is precisely the reverse, that is: we come to treat things as though they were people. The psychogenesis of possessiveness, and so jealousy, may perhaps be better understood if we introduce Winnicott's idea of the transitional object. In the beginning, when the difference between inside and outside is still unclear, there are no independent objects in the world of the infant and the notion of a possession has no place. ("The mother, at the beginning, by an almost 100 per cent adaptation affords the infant the opportunity for the *illusion* that her breast is part of the infant.")[5] Gradually, as the child comes to differentiate itself from its mother, it seizes on some object (typically a teddy bear or blanket) which has for it some of the properties of an independent object but at the same time forms an essential part of its identity: it may be given a name (as though it were a thing apart), but if it is changed (e.g., cleaned) or lost, its loss is felt as a loss of self. This transitional object is the child's first possession. The loss of the mother, contrasting with the time when she could be regarded as part of the self, contributes to the development of the child's attitude toward independent objects in such a way that the loss of an object can come to be felt as a loss of self. Identification with objects (so that they become "inside" while remaining "outside"), a process primarily begun and continued with people, gives possessions a special character and gives jealousy, insofar as it involves a fear of loss, a special place and force.

A third set of conditions that help give jealousy a place has to do with the character of love and intimacy. It may be that precisely what we most value about certain relationships also makes them essentially nonreplicable and nonshareable, and hence leaves a place for jealousy. For example, suppose one has a relationship characterized by "absolute openness," by a sharing of everything. Because one finds it so satisfying, one might wish to replicate it, to establish it with a second person. But imagine what would happen in the attempt. The second relationship would inevitably involve one in betraying the intimacies of the first. Thus it is the very thing that is most valuable about the first relationship that makes it impossible to replicate it. In trying to eliminate the possibility of jealousy here, one would be losing much else. Exclusivity is essential to the nature of the relationship.

There are at least two sorts of responses that might be made to this claim: First, that the relationship is replicable but that one must have the figure of a circle rather than a triangle (with unequal sides) in mind. That is, one could have absolute openness with someone and extend it to a second person, provided that that person also has a relationship of absolute openness with the original partner. The notion is that no two people should be any closer than any other two. All share absolute openness. This returns us to the ideal of the commune. And there come the basic problems that currents of human feeling vary, that people are different, that not all are equally attractive to all (though the sources of attraction may have unconscious roots and we may not care to defend the sources of all our preferences—the preferences are nonetheless real), and finally that love has material conditions and limits. (We shall consider this last point more closely in Section V.) We may defend the ideal of human equality and the notion that all have certain rights and entitlements, but can everyone be equally entitled to our love? Is our love something that can be dispensed on the basis of principle? And even if it could, would that be a good thing? It cannot be assumed that the ideals for the personal and the political are interchangeable. The principles of impartiality in distribution and of equal concern and respect that must govern institutional arrangements may be inappropriate if mechanically transferred to the governance of personal relationships. In any case, so long as we are involved (even if in different ways) with a number of people, there will always be the problem of *their* interactions and attitudes toward each other—which will always be complicated by our own ever-shifting needs and desires (and our equally shifting attitudes toward those needs and desires). Any apparent equilibrium (circular or triangular) is expectably unstable. A second response might claim that what is valuable in a relationship of absolute openness that compels it to be exclusive only seems valuable from the perspective of a bourgeois society. But the value may really depend on the value of *choice* in human relationships.[6] And is that value really limited to bourgeois societies? Is it wrong to value different people differently and for different reasons, and to desire different relationships with each of them (including exclusive relations with some of them)? Must we really desire (if we cannot in fact achieve) absolute openness with everyone? (Everyone in our society? in our city? in our commune? in our family? There may be natural limits in even this last, narrowest, category.) And where the value of choice is not at stake, security doubtless is. (That security may not be achieved does not mean that it is not sought.)

There is a third sort of response that becomes appropriate once one accepts the claim that certain valuable relationships have exclusivity built into them. One might wonder whether it is possible to preserve what is good in these special intimacies without having to bear the costs of jealousy. My belief is that one may be able to limit the consequences of jealousy and the suffering it involves, but that one cannot eliminate the jealousy itself. Think here of two special contexts. One is that of a person who has a relationship of (something like) absolute openness with someone, and then becomes the patient of a psychoanalyst. Psychoanalysis too calls for absolute openness. But here the first relationship has not been straightforwardly replicated. The intimacy is confined to a special sphere, and in particular the rules prohibit a full sexual relationship. (This connects with two further complications: what happens to the analytic relationship if there *is* the possibility of physical intimacy? Among much else, the analysis of one's life then threatens to turn into one's life; the isolation of the relationship is broken down. Second, what if one tries to establish a second relationship of absolute openness simultaneous with a first one, but limiting its sphere so that what belongs to the first relationship does not get brought up in the second. This involves, I think, a too narrow notion of "what belongs to the first relationship" and a too optimistic view of the possibilities of circumscribing the influence and connections of what may be the central set of experiences in one's life.) Returning to the analyst-patient relationship, we should note first that it is very special (e.g., the openness is onesided and of limited, if not fixed, duration): social expectations give it a special place, and it would be as wrong to confuse the intimacy of a patient with his or her analyst with the intimacy between lovers, as it would be to confuse the intimacy between lovers with the intimacy between parents and children—they are all, of course, connected, but to confuse them is perhaps to put oneself in the position of a patient, one's problem begins to appear clinical. Second, and most important in connection with our topic, the lover of a patient may always raise the questions: "What is missing?," "What is the analyst providing that I am not?," "Are there things that my lover can say to her analyst that she cannot say to me?," "Do we really share everything?," and so on. To imagine the elimination of jealousy is to imagine the elimination of the possibility of these questions, for these questions *are* jealousy. To have these doubts and worries is to be jealous. (Jealousy is not a sensation or headache, it is in its essence a set of thoughts and questions, doubts and fears.) And these questions cannot be eliminated. They are real questions. What we must do is first recognize their appropriateness and then see that they are not given undue weight. (Which is especially a danger when a relationship is colored by narcissistic fantasies of omnipotence.) To raise a question is not the same as to give a negative answer. And even where the possibility of a gap and a loss amounts to a real gap and loss, we must not confuse something with everything: that there is something between an analyst and his or her patient need not exclude the lover from everything, need not be the end of that special intimacy, which is outside the analysis.

A second context where one might want to test the exclusivity of absolute intimacy might be same-sex friendships that remain different and apart from the intimacy of lovers who are otherwise absolutely open and share everything. Again there is the possibility of questions: "What is it that she can share with her friend but not with me?," "What is it that the friend offers that I cannot provide?" Again the questions are, I think, real and cannot be eliminated. But this need not destroy the relationship. The recognition of the questions in their appropriate place with their appropriate force may in fact help allow a friendship which is not shared to strengthen a relationship that depends on everything being shared. This paradoxical strengthening would come about because a need that might otherwise go unmet gets satisfied outside the relationship it might otherwise disrupt. We may demand too much of ourselves and others if we demand that they or we not be jealous, where this means that we do not raise or contemplate the doubts and questions of jealousy.

II. GREEN EYES AND EVIL EYES

Othello is jealous, Iago is envious.[7] Jealousy is typically over what one possesses and fears to lose, while envy may be over something one has never possessed and may never hope to possess. Going with this, the focus of envy is typically the other person, rather than the particular thing or quality one is envious over (a thing that may not in itself even be desirable to the envier, whatever its perceived value to the present possessor). In jealousy there is always a rival, believed or imagined, but the focus of concern is the valued object. For jealousy, but not envy, the other must be seen as a genuine rival for the object: their gain is one's loss (the evil eye, on the other hand, can be directed at anyone who prospers, it needn't be at the envier's expense). Similarly, schadenfreude (joy at another's suffering), the inverse of envy (pain at another's success), may be impartial in that the other's loss need not involve a material advantage to the person who takes pleasure at it. This (apparent) aloofness of envy may make it more intractable.

There are alternative ways of mapping out the terrain covered by jealousy and envy, but certain features of each may be illuminatingly brought together in the following way. Jealousy is typically over people, while envy extends to things and qualities. If we restrict jealousy to relations with people, the place of the desire to be desired and for affection comes into sharper focus. At the center of jealousy is fear, specifically fear of loss. What is special about the fear of loss that constitutes jealousy is connected with what is special about people: while one could lose possession of a thing, one could not lose its affection—it has no affection to give or to be taken away. Things do not respond to our feelings. People do. And when they do, we may fear for their loss, not just as things (as objects of desire and love), but as feeling agents (as sources of desire and love). At the center of jealousy is insecurity, fear of loss, specifically fear of alienation of affections. At the center of jealousy is the desire to be desired or for affection, the need to be loved.

Envy extends to things and qualities. Because of this, we can see that its real focus is the rival (though, again, the rivalry need not be real—the quality one is envious of may even be nontransferable). In a way, the thing or quality drops out (as we have mentioned, in some cases the object need not be valued by the envier—he need not believe the thing or office or whatever would give him pleasure if he had it—he need only believe it valuable to the person who possesses it, either because he values it himself or because it increases his status or value in the eyes of others). Once the central relation is seen to be between the envier and the person envied (even if the envy is *over* a thing or quality), the alternatives of malicious and admiring envy become clear.[8] In the case of malicious envy, one wants to lower the other (to one's own level or below); in the case of admiring envy, one wishes to raise oneself (to become like the other). (More on this later.) I shall want to suggest that these two types of envy may have different instinctual sources and developmental paths; and that, as a result, malicious envy, unlike admiring envy and unlike jealousy, may not have appropriate objects, that is, the explanation for its occurrence may always involve pathology.

How are we to describe the emotional state of the third party in situations where there are two lovers, one of whom is jealous over the other and fears the encroachments of the third party, while the third party has not made any advances but certainly desires to supplant the jealous lover? (We leave open the feelings of the middle party.) Are we to say he is envious or that he is jealous? Ordinary usage would, I think, allow us to go either way. I think it better to say he is envious (in an "admiring" way—he wishes to have what the other now possesses), though here it is clear that the thing (person) does *not* drop out (and this may be distinctive of "admiring" envy).[9] If we were to say he is "jealous," we would lose the connection with belief in an established relationship that is necessary to "fear of loss." Jealousy is over what one possesses (or has possessed) and fears to lose.

Because of the differences between envy and jealousy, one would expect them to respond differently to different strategems of elimination. Insofar as jealousy is over a *particular,* overcoming scarcity and inequality would leave it untouched, in this way at least: at the center of jealousy is fear of loss, and so long as sharing is felt as loss and exclusivity of relationship is demanded, one is liable to jealousy. One may of course be less likely to feel jealous if there is no scarcity of goods, so that others have alternatives to trying to seize your (particular) good. But the point of the commune movement (in relation to jealousy) will be better understood if it is seen less as an effort to overcome scarcity than as an effort to change attitudes toward sharing: so possession need not be exclusive possession.

Envy has to do with making people secure in their possessions (if at all) in another way. At the center of envy is invidious comparison, the perception of another as better off. It can be over things or even nondetachable (and so nontransferable) qualities: someone can envy another's good looks or intelligence, even though there is no way in which if they were taken away they could be given to the envier. And even where "sharing" is possible, it may not help. Indeed, the magnanimity of the wealthy can be met with ingratitude or accentuated envy: the magnanimity merely magnifying the perceived difference in position. And, again, overcoming scarcity is not sufficient. Everyone having enough is not enough; it doesn't obviate the possibility of relative deprivation, the resentment of the well-off toward the better-off. But, if everyone has the same (perhaps even if too little), invidious comparison of course becomes impossible. The important element is equality. So achieving equality of distribution (or redistribution) should overcome envy, should leave it no place. But this depends on what the sources of envy are, on the relation of objective equality to perceived equality, on whether equality is achieved through overcoming scarcity or by leveling, on what differences are possible objects of envy (are all of them open to equalization? are no goods unique and unopen to redistribution?), and whether the difference between "justified" and "unjustified" inequality also makes a difference to the possibility of envy.

Let us pick up a few of these threads and see where they lead. That magnanimity may be met by ingratitude does not mean magnanimity is futile. It does not follow, as some would have it, that because magnanimous foreign aid might accentuate envy one should not give such aid: people may be ungrateful, but the point of giving aid is not to win their gratitude, but to help solve their problems (at least if aid is given out of magnanimity). If people raise ungrateful children, would it follow that there had been no reason for raising them (were they brought up precisely to be sources of gratitude)?

That envy may be one reason for demanding equality does not mean that demands for equality are unjustified. For one thing, "envy" may be justified. (Where it is, it amounts to "resentment," which is a moral emotion in the sense that a moral principle must be cited in its explanation.)[10] For another thing, there are other reasons, most importantly reasons of justice, for demanding (certain forms of) equality. But from another perspective the real issue is whether envy must form an inevitable obstacle to attempts to achieve justice and/or equality.

One point in the conceptual situation is I think clear: people may feel envy over some difference (some inequality) even if the difference is both justified and ineradicable. Given this, the most pressing questions become why one would feel envy (what are its sources), and whether this allows any remedy. And if it does not allow any remedy, what place should be given to envy in one's personal and political calculations?

Helmut Schoeck, in a substantial recent study of envy,[11] maintains that envy is to be expected always and everywhere. He points to the important influence of fear of envy as an instrument of social control, helping to make civilized life possible. The fear helps lead to modesty and the avoidance of ostentation, and produces concern for the opinion of others when one is tempted to deviate from social norms in pursuit of pleasure or material gain. He also suggests, very interestingly, that Americans are not afraid enough of envy. (This is evidenced in many advertisements that praise a product in virtue of the fact that it is liable to produce envy in friends and neighbors.) But (and this is Schoeck's main theme) it is also possible to fear envy too much. The ethnographic data reveal countless societies where every failure is viewed as due to the operation of the evil eye, and every success as magically achieved by holding others back. If a society is too afraid of envy it can have a terribly inhibiting effect. Superstition can hold back innovation and "progress."

If fear of envy can hold back progress, so (thinks Schoeck) can the desire for equality. Indeed, Schoeck (following a long tradition) tends to treat socialism and the desire for equality as always motivated by envy. He fails sufficiently to distinguish "envy" from resentment and indignation based on a sense of justice (or rather, he fails to give the sense of justice sufficient scope). And he moves too swiftly from (the alleged) ineliminability of envy to antiegalitarianism and antisocialism (or the dismissal of them as utopian). Socialism, unlike envy, calls for the redistribution of goods, not their destruction. Parodies of socialism often achieve their effects by using destruction, leveling, wherever redistribution is not possible. (There are serious questions about which things must and can be equalized and how. But the parodies tend to beg these questions by assuming everything must, in some crude manner, be equalized.)[12] In considering whether it is possible to overcome envy, one must distinguish the effects of overcoming inequality and overcoming scarcity. Schoeck tends to assume that equality can be achieved only through leveling (dragging down the prominent and better off), and that overcoming scarcity depends on maintaining inequality (that growth depends on inequality). Hence he thinks efforts to overcome envy are futile. The best we can do, on this view, is to go for growth. Growth in itself does not, of course, overcome envy (distribution of goods matters more than their quantity). Nonetheless, if one could overcome scarcity, it might be possible (contrary to Schoeck) to achieve equality without leveling. Admittedly, this may not be possible in every sphere (most interestingly, there are the problems of "positional goods"),[13] but the evidence is not all in on the claim that inequality is necessary for growth. (Do we really need monopolies, bigness, everywhere? Is it always more productive and efficient?) Whatever the conditions for overcoming scarcity (do they include inequality?), and whatever its consequences (do they allow for overcoming inequality?), Schoeck counsels that we must in any case accept envy because it is in any case ineliminable.

He offers two sorts of argument. The first is that envy (fear of envy) is a condition of civilized life. But I fail to see why the socially valuable functions of "envy" ("fear of envy") could not be served by the more moral emotions (e.g., resentment and indignation) alone. Criticism of deviance should be limited to those cases where it can be justified on principle. What Schoeck (following Raiga) calls "legitimate indignation-envy" should be enough for the purposes of social control. The argument this leaves for thinking envy ineliminable is that envy is a given feature of human nature, in effect, an instinct.

But is this an argument at all, and if it is, what sort of argument is it? What follows if, as Schoeck insists, envy is an instinct, a basic (and therefore ineliminable) feature of human nature? Even if one were to overcome inequality, it is claimed, the envious man (all of us, in different degrees) would perceive reality in distorted fashion: he would see inequality where there is none and so find new grounds for envy. Certainly very small, seemingly insignificant, differences can be the object of envy. (Freud speaks of the "narcissism of minor differences.")[14] Can any (all?) differences be an object of envy? And even where a category may be susceptible of envy, if differences are eliminated, will people (all? many? some?) still distortedly perceive inequalities and so experience envy?

Presumably, anything may be an object of envy if anything can matter. Some things matter for everybody. Hence sexuality and the erotic provide a central arena for envy (as well as jealousy). What other things matter depends mainly on one's society or group. And perhaps anything can achieve sufficient (symbolic) importance to sustain envy. But this does not make it inevitable that (1) the things that matter cannot be distributed equally or (2) that only leveling can produce equality or (3) that even if equality is achieved in a sphere, some will perceive differences or (4) that all valuable differences will inevitably produce envy rather than themselves being valued.

Much depends on whether envy must be viewed as a basic motive or instinct that will inevitably find an object, whatever the social arrangements (whatever society values and no matter how it is distributed). Schoeck gives us no good reason to believe it is, though he repeatedly makes the claim. There is evidence to suggest that "fear of envy" occurs in every society,[15] but there is some distance from this to the claim that envy itself occurs (and must inevitably continue to occur) in every individual. What is really needed is a psychogenetic account of envy. The best we have so far, that I am aware of, is the work of Melanie Klein[16] on destructive impulses and "spoiling" and some suggestions in Max Scheler[17] about a tie to impotence and a delusion of causal connection. Scheler writes:

"Envy," as the term is understood in everyday usage, is due to a feeling of impotence which we experience when another person owns a good we covet. But this tension between desire and nonfulfillment does not lead to envy until it flares up into hatred against the owner, until the latter is falsely considered to be the *cause* of our privation. Our factual inability to acquire a good is wrongly interpreted as a positive action *against* our desire—a delusion which diminishes the original tension. Both the experience of impotence and the causal delusion are essential preconditions of true envy.

So envy may begin to make more sense if we see that it is tied by an unconscious causal belief to felt impotence (so the other's possession of a good is, after all, seen as at our expense). What happens if we make that belief conscious? It is one of the lessons of Marx that the belief turns out often, surprisingly often, to be true. When that is the case, envy at inequality comes closer to being indignation at injustice.

To sort out the proportions of justified to unjustified "envy" in a given situation, one would need a theory of justice. John Rawls discusses envy in the context of his theory of justice.[18] If someone would be made envious as a result of some advantage being given to someone else, even though the advantage is thoroughly just and justified (according to Rawls's principles of justice: even the worst off would be better off for the advantage being bestowed and none would be worse off), the envy should carry no moral weight against the arrangement. Rawls recognizes, however, that even where envy presents no moral problem, it may present a psychological, social, and political one. How big a problem, and how often, depends again on envy's sources (would it be a wild aberration in a just society, or rather something only to be expected no matter how we arrange our society?), and one feels again the need for a psychogenetic account of envy. What I want to emphasize here is that Schoeck's discussion of envy does not provide such an account, and moreover is dissociated from any explicit theory of justice, indeed, it is tied to a skepticism about the possibility of distinguishing illegitimate from legitimate inequalities, and so legitimate resentment from illegitimate envy.[19] While the latter must be morally discounted, it is a mistake to conflate legitimate resentment with illegitimate envy and then to assume that egalitarianism and socialism must be associated with motives of envy rather than principles of justice. A conservative antipathy to egalitarianism and socialism cannot be properly founded on a (proper) contempt for motives of envy. Even if one must ignore envy to achieve "progress," one must be careful not to ignore legitimate grievances and resentment in the process.

What is left of instinctual envy when we distinguish between justifiable and unjustifiable inequalities and between envy and resentment? Erik Erikson[20] has claimed that people worry about *minimizing* envy when they should worry about *optimizing* it. He argues that a certain amount of envy is developmentally necessary as part of the formation of an ego ideal. I would argue that one has to be careful here to distinguish between *admiring* envy (which may be necessary for an ego ideal, and so beneficial) and *malicious* envy (which the world could do just as well without). When someone *says* "I envy you," they can usually be taken to be saying: "I wish I were like you" or "I wish I had what you have" (admiring envy).

But they would usually not be taken to be saying: "I wish you did not have what you do" (malicious envy), that is usually an unspoken thought. While both these types of thought may constitute envy, they are different, as different as the desire to be like and the desire to destroy (or the desire to have and the desire that the other not have). There is a common element in admiring and malicious envy: a desire to overcome inequality, but the desire comes from different directions, admiring envy involving a desire to raise (the self), malicious envy involving a desire to level (the other). Do these disparate desires really have a common instinctual source? Is it really inconceivable that we might overcome the sources of malicious envy without doing damage to the necessary foundations of an ego ideal?

It is of course a further question whether there is in fact any way to get at the roots of malicious envy. We need to know more about the sources and character of the Kleinian desire to destroy and spoil. Without pursuing that further here, we can ask whether there may not be a subtle, hidden, connection between the envy involved in forming an ego ideal and the malicious envy we should (otherwise) be able to do without. (So the desire to raise oneself might commit one to lowering the other.) The connection I have in mind is via the "delusional" (unconscious/magical/and, as I have said, perhaps sometimes, true) causal belief discussed by Scheler and the notion of self-esteem. Envy and jealousy come closer together if one always adds the assumption that life is seen as a zero-sum game, so rivalry is always experienced as real, the other's having something (*now* in the case of envy, *in the future* in the case of jealousy) is then always seen as at your expense. On this view, the otherwise unmotivated or maliciously envious desire that another be deprived, becomes a part of a genuine competition or rivalry, an intelligible desire to enhance one's own position. Robert Nozick argues that even where a situation is not overtly competitive (someone else's gain is not your loss), the conditions of self-esteem are such as to give envy a proper foothold, and to preclude achieving equality as a way out.[21] His central notion is that self-esteem is *comparative*. Along any given dimension, a person will judge himself in comparison with others. It does not matter that someone's doing better than you is not at your expense: even though your absolute position on a scale is unchanged, the scale is extended by their performance and your relative position on the scale looks worse, so you must think less well of yourself. Moreover, the dimensions themselves are comparative:

> People generally judge themselves by how they fall along the most important dimensions in which they *differ* from others. People do not gain self-esteem from their common human capacities by comparing themselves to animals who lack them. ("I'm pretty good; I have an opposable thumb and can speak some language.")... When everyone, or almost everyone, has some thing or attribute, it does not function as a basis for self-esteem. Self-esteem is based on *differentiating characteristics;* that's why it's *self*-esteem.

It remains unclear to me why self-esteem must depend on being *better* than others (on some dimensions if not all). Certainly we only take *pride* in special accomplishments, but why shouldn't normal self-esteem rest on normal capacities and achievements? Granted we do not take pride in universal powers (e.g., speaking), but one need not be *outstanding* in a field to gain self-esteem from achievement. A person may be a good cook while recognizing that many others are also good cooks. It is not essential to self-esteem that there be none better. (It may be essential that there be some who are worse or at least some who do not engage in the activity at all. This seems to be the truth in the comparative point.) Even where a situation is not directly competitive, Nozick argues it remains comparative (one must use a scale to judge oneself and so another's achievement on the scale can produce an indirect loss) for purposes of self-esteem. But why should self-esteem be destroyed by someone being better? I must count myself as *one,* but why more than one? The place of envy cannot be secured by the need for self-esteem; the conditions of self-esteem are not so grandiose. If envy is not an "instinct" (whatever that entails), there is no argument for it.

III. JEALOUSY AND RIGHTS

Jealousy is not a merely bourgeois passion, it is not confined to societies with capitalistic or monogamous social arrangements. (That it is not confined to a particular class within such societies goes without saying.) Every society that prefers and sanctions certain social arrangements over others, which is to say every *society,* will have room for jealousy: it serves to reinforce and protect the preferred arrangements (in particular, the preferred distributions of sexual affection). As Kingsley Davis has put it:

> Where exclusive possession of an individual's entire love is customary, jealousy will demand that exclusiveness. Where love is divided it will be divided according to some scheme, and jealousy will reinforce the division.... Whether as the obverse side of the desire to obtain sexual property by legitimate competition, or as the anger at having rightful property trespassed upon, jealousy would seem to bolster the institutions where it is found. If these institutions are of an opposite character to monogamy, it bolsters them nonetheless.... Jealousy does not respond inherently to any particular situation; it responds to all those situations, no matter how diverse, which signify a violation of accustomed sexual rights. [22]

While social arrangements may vary, whatever the social arrangements, jealousy serves to reinforce them.

It might seem that this functional view of jealousy nonetheless leaves it bourgeois in another sense, for it seems to depend on a notion of possession and property in personal relations. And it could be argued that such a notion is illegitimate, that property rights have no place in the sphere of human relationships.

The argument might have it that property rights are applicable only to things, and that therefore, insofar as jealousy involves treating people as though they were things (as though we could have property rights in them) it will always be an inappropriate emotion, an emotion we should strive (through correcting the understanding, etc.) to eliminate from our personal relationships. The argument might continue that jealousy must be futile, for the right that is asserted is a right to love (a right to be loved), and such a right (even if it were intelligible—supposing it did not involve the illegitimate assertion of property rights in people) would be unenforceable. Love is not a matter of will, it cannot be given on demand. We cannot decide to love someone because we think they have a right to be loved by us; we cannot make ourselves love someone because we owe it to them. Moreover (and this is one of the many ironies of the human condition), even if love could be given on demand, that would not satisfy the claims of jealousy, for the love that is desired is usually a freely given love—a response to a desire (backed by a need) rather than a demand (backed by a threat).[23] A love that was coerced (presuming something that was coerced could still be regarded as love at all) would be the wrong sort of love. The love that was given in response to the demands of jealousy therefore could never really satisfy those demands. Thus property rights are applicable only to things, while jealousy is typically over people, specifically because of their power (in contrast with things) to respond (and fail to respond) to our desires: the response that can be given to a claim of right will never really satisfy the desire that lies behind that claim.

These are, I think, powerful arguments. They reveal part of what is troubling about the place of jealousy in human life. But I think that they also distort the situation somewhat and that they go too far; they might make it seem as though jealousy were simply a matter of conceptual confusion, as though it should have *no* place in human relationships because the notion of property rights should have no place in human relationships. I would want to argue against these (I think) misleading claims from several directions.

We can start by asking whether the existence of jealousy must depend on belief in a right. I am inclined to think that jealousy may not depend on a notion of rights at all (even a notion distinguished from and broader than that of property rights). At the heart of jealousy is fear of loss (specifically, fear of alienation of affections), and to fear loss all that is required is the existence or the believed existence of a state of affairs or relationship, and a desire that it continue. To be jealous over someone, you must believe that they love you (or have loved you), but you need not believe that you have a *right* to that love; you need not think yourself wonderful and so deserving of love (indeed, the fear of loss is typically tied to fears about one's lovableness), nor need you believe that the other has an obligation built up over time. Having detached jealousy from rights in this way, however, one is left with the question of how to distinguish "jealousy" from mere "disappointment" (or "grief" or simple "unhappiness")—clearly the contrast cannot be based on the presence of a claim of right in one case and its absence in the other. It may be based, however, on the fact that disappointment is tied to resignation while jealousy is tied to hope. That is, disappointment may be more a response to loss and jealousy to *fear* of loss (where one is not yet resigned to the loss, even if the fear is based on its apparently already having taken place). Moreover, jealousy, unlike disappointment, is always a three-party emotion (involving rivalry, hatred of the rival, etc.), that is, the loss suffered or feared is always experienced as a loss *to* someone else. This last point suggests a further possible contrast: jealousy may always involve anger, either at the rival or at the beloved, while mere disappointment may not involve any rival or any form of anger or resentment toward anyone.[24] Spinoza builds "hatred" toward the beloved and (via envy) toward the rival into his definition of jealousy. If a man of *extremely* low self-esteem thinks the woman who is involved with him is about to leave him for another, but feels no animosity toward his rival, and (aside from his fear of loss) feels only gratitude toward the woman for having given him as much attention as she has (for he believes she is in any case too good for him), we may be inclined to say his state of mind is not jealousy. The absence of anger at the woman or rival might make the man's fear of loss seem more like mere disappointment or apprehension. But there is a complication: if anger is necessary to jealousy, it might seem that belief in a right is also. For what is the anger about? Betrayal? An underlying claim of right would give sense to feelings of betrayal and abandonment as grounds of anger. But while something like anger may be essential, irrational anger or anger at loss or deprivation (more like instinctual aggression or a response to frustration than a response to betrayal or violation of rights) may be enough. In the case described, one suspects the anger has been redirected against the self. (Is the man's state indifferent to circumstances, or does it deepen into depression with the impending loss? One wonders how much of even the initial "low self-esteem" is really anger turned inward.) Freud, in describing the components of jealousy, speaks of the "narcissistic wound" and "self-criticism" as well as loss and enmity against the rival. And perhaps anger (even anger turned inward) is not essential. Perhaps the mere existence of a rival may be enough to make the man's fear of loss (i.e., fear of alienation of affections) amount to jealousy. There may even be other ways to mark the contrast between disappointment and jealousy (but note that the difference is not to be looked for in raw feelings or blind sensations, but in the constituent thoughts involved), and in the end I think jealousy can stand independent of claims of right. One need not think one has a right to someone else's love in order to fear its loss: all that is necessary is that one believe one has the love to begin with. What claims may legitimately be made on the basis of jealousy, on the basis of fear of loss, is a separate and further question. For jealousy to exist all one needs is vulnerability, and we all have that in sufficient abundance.

What claims can one person make on the feelings of another? People are not property (indeed, part of the reason we value them is that *unlike* things they can respond to our desires with desires of their own), but that does not mean that claims of right are out of place in human relationships. What has to be said is that it is not a question of *property* rights (in the sense of ownership that allows for transfer, disposal, etc.), but it may be a question of rights nonetheless: there is room for obligations and legitimate expectations, and perhaps even for enforceable and (sometimes) waivable claims, in human relationships and human feelings. Think for a moment of an established couple, a man and a woman who have been together for twenty years. Now suppose that one of the partners suffers a physical calamity, suppose, for example, that the woman loses a limb (or has a mastectomy). The calamity is a shared calamity. The man cannot simply walk off saying: "Oh well, too bad for you. When I loved you, you were different. Thus altered, I no longer find you attractive. I wish you lots of luck in finding someone who is not put off by your new deformity and incapacities." What is most interesting, though much else could be said, is to consider what this attitude would reveal about his prior attitude (which he describes as love: "When I loved you . . ."): it would give the lie to his love, it would reveal it to have been something else (or a different kind of love). Who or what had he putatively "loved"? If it was that particular woman, are we to allow that the (admittedly drastic) change in her condition is a change not just *in* her but *of* her, that is a different person? To suppose one could lose one's identity easily would be to suppose that she was a bundle of properties, the object of his love was not that particular woman but a set lities that she happened to instantiate. One must distinguish two types of love: love of a particular person and love of a ualities.[25] Qualities are fungible in a way that people are are more than the sum of our present attributes. (Which mean we are some hidden mysterious substance, or some le and empty center of consciousness.) One sort of love w and expect the beloved to change in all sorts of ways.

And other, unexpected changes, would leave that love unchanged. ("Love is not love which alters when it alteration finds....")[26] The other sort of love, being attached to a specific set of qualities, can move readily from person to person depending only on who best instantiates those qualities at a particular point in time. The two contrasting types of object may also be associated with different aims. When one is looking for a set of qualities, it is usually one's own needs that make one look and that set the criteria for satisfaction. And so far as those needs do not look to history, the past and future of the loved object are not tied up with the character of the present love. These features may all be typical of erotic desire and attachment. The other sort of object is tied to a more romantic conception of love, where the aim of love is the good of the beloved, and the love is characterized more by consideration and concern than desire (or rather, the desires involved tend to be selfless).

In the happiest situations, of course, all these features may come together. Part of what is disturbing in the case we were considering is that they there fall apart. What looked like one sort of love comes to look like another sort: it appears another woman would have done just as well all along, because it now appears (given the calamity) that another would do better. So the attachment looks like it was more an attachment to a set of physical properties than to a person. People are embodied and their physical properties matter, but there is more to them than that (this is obvious when we think of *ourselves* and how we wish to be thought of when we are an object of love for someone else). A proper understanding of the case would require a closer consideration of what properties are essential to what, and of precisely what changes with what. But for our immediate purpose, the main thing to note is that a man who has lived with and (putatively) loved a woman for twenty years owes her something. Even if their love was originally grounded in physical attraction, involvement over twenty years builds up a commitment. Their past has weight. It creates obligations. She has rights (though it would certainly be misleading to think of them as "property" rights). There remains the question of what she has rights to. Certainly she has rights to care, consideration, and concern. And presumably all of these rights would be granted by any decent man. But if they were not granted willingly, could they be enforced? (Certainly the state could require that support be provided, but can it require that the support be provided out of "concern''?) At any rate, a man who failed to feel concern in these circumstances would be properly criticizable for that failure. What of a right to ''love''? What exactly the woman has a right to expect, beyond care, consideration, and concern, will depend on how far we (and she) believe the will extends in love. One has, I think, to distinguish its different aspects. Action (or at least outward behavior) is generally readily under control. Desire, while perhaps not directly susceptible to the will, may have complex relations to belief and principle. And affection may be even more complex (being bound to both desires for one's own good and desires for the good of the other). Perhaps the notion of ''a right'' does get overstretched here, but that may be because it carries with it a whole legalistic apparatus. Something goes awry when we use principles (and a language) designed to govern relations between strangers to govern relations between friends or lovers; the relations those principles get used to enforce may be defeated by their application.[27] The law reflects the irony of the human condition, where the love that jealousy demands may never be truly satisfactory because the love that is desired is a freely given love, not a love given in response to a demand. (This condition is not, however, universal. For some, the motivation of a response, whether selfish, selfless, or merely self-protective, may be irrelevant.) But what we have seen is that, whatever the problems with enforcement and so whatever the awkwardnesses with the notion of a ''right to love,'' the character of love may require certain attitudes toward change. To be true to one's love (for one's love to have been true) it cannot ''alter when it alteration finds.'' The existence of a certain sort of relationship creates what may be thought of as rights.

There is room for claims of right in personal relations. Sorting out the limits and types of claims that are appropriate is a complex process, but at least we have delineated some of the main dimensions that must be considered. The rights and claims that may be appropriate depend on love's *sources* (are they in the individual's control, a matter of his choice or choices?),[28] its *objects* (particular/set of characteristics), and its *aims* (own good/good of the other). And a full anatomy of jealousy would depend on a full anatomy of love. Jealousy may arise in relation to both types of love object. One can be jealous over a person thought of as a particular, where one's love is characterized by concern and affection. So far as the person is a particular and special, one may be more liable to fear loss or sharing and so more liable to feel jealous. But so far as one's love is truly unselfish and aimed exclusively at the good of the beloved (whatever you may believe about your essential role in bringing about that good), you may be less liable to feel jealous (and while the beloved remains irreplaceable for you, you may not regard yourself as irreplaceable for him or her). One can also be jealous over a person thought of as a set of qualities, where one's love is characterized by desire (in particular for satisfaction of one's own needs). Here one has to balance the countervailing tendencies involved in thinking of a person as a set of qualities. So far as this makes people fungible, one may be less liable to fear loss and be jealous. So far as it makes people more like things, one may be more liable to regard them as property and so more jealous of your possession and rights—though with this your jealousy may be liable to become perverse.

We have already seen in our discussion of the psychogenesis of jealousy that it may begin with our first possession. But the notion of "possession" should not mislead us into thinking that what is at stake is property rights. What is at stake is the self, is an individual's identity. The infant goes through a transitional period in which it recognizes a teddy bear, or whatever, as an independent object, but it does not want the object to change. Any change in the object is experienced as an assault on the self. I think this sort of attitude toward this first possession, this transitional object, is an attitude that begins with people (in particular the mother at the point where she is not distinguished from the self), gets extended to other things, and then comes back again to people. It makes sharing difficult without a sensed loss of self. So I would reiterate my claim that in the development of jealousy what is happening is not that we treat people as though they were things, but that we treat things as though they were people (ultimately, as parts of ourselves). This sort of identification is misunderstood if it is assimilated to simple "ownership."

IV. PATHOLOGY

It is possible to feel the wrong thing or the wrong amount (including too little, as in the case of Camus's *Stranger,* who fails to feel grief at the death of his mother). Othello's jealousy, if it is pathological at all, is pathological in its intensity (in what it leads him to do). His belief about his beloved is false, but that does not (in itself) make it pathological. Whether a false (or even true) belief is pathological depends, most importantly, on the explanation for its being held. Othello's belief is imposed on him by Iago's manipulation of the circumstances; it is at least based on evidence. (What makes Othello susceptible to such manipulation and evidence is a further and more difficult question.) King Leontes's belief in *The Winter's Tale* is pathological on its face: it is not based on evidence. Of course, once one is jealous, anything and everything can be turned into evidence (the exquisite self-confirming power of paranoia).

Othello's jealousy is ill founded, but unlike King Leontes's jealousy, it is not unfounded. There is a difference between having a grounded (though false) belief and having an ungrounded belief (which may, in the end, turn out true). To believe without grounds, to believe in the face of contrary evidence, is irrational. Ungrounded beliefs, unfounded doubts, are characteristic of one form of pathology in jealousy. Why one would delude oneself against one's better interests, why one would seem to want to believe what one should hope is false, requires explanation. Freud, of course, makes some helpful suggestions.[29]

Freud suggests projected jealousy will typically be a defense against acknowledgment of one's own temptations to unfaithfulness, including (in true delusional cases) repressed homosexual desires. Temptations to unfaithfulness are inevitable. Why should the forces and mechanisms that lead one to love one person automatically cease to operate once one has formed an initial attachment? Indeed, adult attachments always have the infantile prototype of attachment to the parents (especially to the mother's breast) to fall back on ("The finding of an object is in fact a refinding of it."),[30] and so an "initial attachment" is really always the continuation of a process begun long before. Once one recognizes that temptations to unfaithfulness are inevitable, it becomes easier to see that the most unfounded jealousy will always have a level of reality to latch on to. A person may come to neglect his own temptations and focus exclusively on his partner's, picking up every sign the unconscious of the other betrays and adding on projected temptations of his own. Why one should succumb to unfounded jealousy will require separate explanation in each case. Another general thought to bear in mind is a remark Freud makes concerning a patient's obsessive-compulsive doubts about a range of topics (including his would-be fiancé's feelings): "A man who doubts his own love may, or rather *must,* doubt every lesser thing."[31]

Another source of doubt can be found in a certain type of object-choice:

> . . . it seems very evident that another person's narcissism has a great attraction for those who have renounced part of their own narcissism and are in search of object-love. The charm of a child lies to a great extent in his narcissism, his self-contentment and inaccessibility, just as does the charm of certain animals which seem not to concern themselves about us, such as cats and the large beasts of prey. . . . The great charm of narcissistic women has, however, its reverse side; a large part of the lover's dissatisfaction, of his doubts of the woman's love, of his complaints of her enigmatic nature, has its root in this incongruity between the types of object-choice.[32]

A person who chooses to love another who loves only himself or herself has set up a situation which by its nature accentuates the liability to jealousy.

Irrational, unfounded, jealousy should perhaps be considered in relation to cases where a person *urges* his partner to have an affair with another (which in turn should perhaps be considered in relation to cases of "making someone jealous," which we will come to in our next section). Where a person urges his partner to have an affair (rather than imagining that the partner is having one and resenting that imagined fact), a number of different things may be going on. First, there is an obvious denial of jealousy. Second, the value of the partner may be increased when desired by or desirable to others. (Consider a husband's display of his wife, his "treasure," at a party—when does fear of envy and loss set in?) Third, it may be a route to a surrogate homosexual affair. (It is worth remembering that identification is a complex process. It may make a loved object seem a part of us and so make the fear of loss more acute. It may also, in the form of projective identification, make it possible for us to act through the loved object. Moreover, it is a process that can take place with rivals as well as loved objects. Indeed, the normal process of overcoming Oedipal jealousy and rivalry, the incest taboo, is supposed to involve identification with the rival.) And fourth, it may make the person feel freer to have an affair himself.

Irrational and obsessive beliefs, while one form of pathological jealousy, are only one form. We have seen that jealousy is sometimes dismissed as the misplaced application and assertion of property rights. (People are not things; they cannot be owned. Affection is not subject to the will; it cannot be owed.) While I want to say that jealousy *can* be normal, that it need not always involve mistaking people for things, it must here be recognized that there are cases of jealousy that do involve the misplaced assertion of property rights. Consider the swaggering bully who goes into a jealous rage if someone so much as looks covetously at his woman, while he regards the woman herself as useless and treats her as trash. While such a man may fear loss, the loss he fears is not of affection. What he values in the relationship is his domination or appearance of domination. Any threat to that is a threat to his "manhood." The fear of loss involved may be enough to make this count as a case of jealousy, but I want to suggest that it is a perverted and derivative case, that is, a pathological case. The central case involves fear of loss where the thing specifically feared is alienation of affections.

That we should fear the loss of valued goods when they appear threatened may not require special explanation. It is only to be expected that if the affection we believe to be ours is given to another we will fear a more permanent alienation of affections. It does require explanation, however, why the giving of affection to another should so often appear to us as at our expense. That depends, I believe, on certain assumptions we shall turn to shortly. It also requires explanation why jealousy (understood as fear of loss, specifically alienation of affections) should be so prone to pathological forms and exaggerations in intensity. I think that at least part of the explanation may be found in the fact that the fear of loss is tied to a deeper underlying fear: fear of annihilation.

The loss of an object is often felt as loss of self. This should not surprise us given what we have said about the development of our relations to loved possessions and people. Those relations are at points better understood in terms of identification than ownership. We are prone to pathological forms of jealousy because we are prone to identification with valued things and people—we are inclined to regard them as parts of our selves. The loss of a valued object may provide objective danger (the character of the danger depending on what was valuable about the object). The loss of affection from a loved person, in addition to the obvious gap it opens in one's life, may endanger one's identity. Spelling out this danger would involve going more deeply into processes of identification and identify formation. But here we can note the simple fact that if others do not love us, we may disintegrate. Who we are depends (in straightforward ways) on how others respond to us; and who we think we are may depend (in deeper ways) on what we believe is within our control. The loss of an affection which we felt to be as reliably at our disposal as the movement of our limbs may make the whole world seem to go out of joint.

As a fuller understanding of jealousy would require a fuller understanding of love, of the need to be loved, and the need to be secure in love, so a fuller understanding of the possibilities for pathology would require a fuller understanding of processes of identification and identity formation (including the contrast between introjective and projective identification), of how we think about ourselves and our love objects, and of the underlying fear involved in jealousy. Throughout, I think it most helpful if we think of jealousy as essentially involving fear of loss; more specifically, fear of alienation of affections; and, more generally, fear of annihilation.

V. THE TWO-FACED GREEN-EY'D MONSTER

Jealousy has two faces. One face is as a sign of love. If a person does not feel jealous, or is incapable of feeling jealous, we tend to suspect that they do not really care. There is even the phenomenon, a staple of situation comedies on television, of "making someone jealous," where the point is not so much to persuade oneself of someone else's feelings as to get *them* to recognize them. What typically happens is that a person, in love with a second, but unresponsive person, pretends to be in love with a third person (who does, in fact, for the sake of the pretense, respond). The upshot is supposed to be that the second person becomes jealous and, seeing their jealousy, realizes that they loved the first person all along. Now this assumes that jealousy is easier to recognize than love (in ourselves). It assumes also that jealousy is a sign of caring. It is this second point that matters here, and as far as it goes, I think the point is made. But we must recognize that life is more complicated than the situation comedies would have it.

For one thing, it is highly questionable whether jealousy is easier to recognize than love in our own case. Jealousy is in fact the typical example of an object of self-deception and repression.[33] For another thing, pretense has an awkward way of slipping over into reality. The more plausible the third person in the "making someone jealous" strategem is as a candidate for love (and so the more plausible the pretense) the more lively the possibility of real love becomes, and the more ambiguous becomes the pretense. And there is a further complication: Suppose that someone is in fact made jealous, does it in fact follow that they must have cared all along? I think there are other possibilities. The jealousy may not be the sign of a love that has existed all along, but rather be attached to a new love that has sprung up in response to the desire of the third person. That is, the fact that the first person is desired by the third person may be enough to make him or her desirable to the second person. The jealousy means that the jealous person covets what is also coveted by another, but it may not have been the case that the object was valued independently of the third party's attitude. (A good test for this is whether the love persists after the third party has left the scene—in situation comedies the thirty minutes are usually up at this point, and the question is not raised.) Another possibility is that the jealousy is not a sign of love at all, neither old love nor new love, but simply a sign of selfishness. That is, the response might be less to the desire of the third party (producing recognition of the desirableness of the first, or simply making the first desirable), than to the (apparent) loss of the affection of the first. The jealous person, the person made jealous, may simply desire to be desired, not caring about the first person (the one who has done the maneuvering) except as a source of approbation (a desiring, not a desired object). (The test mentioned in connection with new but fleeting love won't discriminate between that and this form of selfishness.) Here however we should consider whether taking jealousy as a sign of selfishness (specifically, concern at not being desired rather than concern at the loss of a desired object) precludes or even contrasts with taking it as a sign of love. The answer here would have to depend on the place we give the desire to be desired in our account of the nature of love. That it must have some place seems to me certain.[34]

A full taxonomy of jealousy would require, as I have suggested, a corresponding taxonomy of love. Rather than pursue that here, let me raise another question: can jealousy strengthen a relationship? Certainly that is the point of the "making someone jealous" strategem. And in the situation comedies, where the jealousy is taken as evidence of a prior (real but unrecognized) passion, precisely that happens. The central characters are united and strengthened in their love. But this depends, please note, on the special conditions in which the "making someone jealous" strategem makes sense. The first person is an unrequited lover, not a person who has been involved with a second person and then becomes involved (for real) with a third person. In those, more typical, situations where the person is torn (or at least tied) to two others, the jealousy of the second person gives no promise of strengthening the love of the first and second persons. In the situation comedies, the first person wants to make the second person jealous (and has always been ready to drop the third person). In most real-life situations, the first person wants to avoid the second person becoming jealous (typically through keeping him or her ignorant) and is not prepared to give up the third person. In the sitcoms the ground for jealousy vanishes with him or her and only the original love remains, strengthened because it was never really a conflicted love. In contrast with the special situation of "making someone jealous" and also with the typical conflicted situation, we have seen at least one special case (namely same-sex or nonsexual friendships in the context of an otherwise exclusive relationship) where jealousy may be appropriate and may persist without weakening a relationship. In that case, while the jealousy may not itself strengthen the relationship, it arises in response to features of the situation which in turn strengthen the relationship.

So far we can be sure that one face of jealousy is as a sign of love (though the *strength* of jealousy is more likely to be correlated with a person's degree of insecurity than the depth of their love; the overlap is perhaps marked by the degree of dependence involved in the love, the degree of desire rather than affection or selfish desires rather than selfless ones). Behind jealousy lies love. This side of jealousy is sometimes neglected, but it is extremely important (especially in relation to the question of the eliminability of jealousy). It reflects the fact that "jealousy" includes a positive evaluation of, or attachment or commitment to, the person (or thing or property) one is jealous over or about. One can be jealous only of something that is highly valued. This is reflected in one of the special senses of the word; as the OED points out, *jealous* can mean:

> zealous or solicitous for the preservation or well-being of something possessed or esteemed; vigilant or careful in guarding; suspiciously careful or watchful.

Someone who is "jealous of his time" values his time ("husbands it") and seeks to keep it in his control. The desire to keep implies that one already has (a contrast with envy), which brings us to the fear of loss and the second face of jealousy. Narrowing our focus again to interpersonal relations and love: jealousy can be a sign of lack of love.

Jealousy, in addition to involving an obvious lack of trust, may betray a deeper lack of love, or rather, lack of trust in love. That is, behind whatever personal insecurities (fear of loss, fear of not being lovable, etc.) which may surface in jealousy, may lie (what I will call) a quantum view of love: the amount of love in the world, the amount in any individual, is limited. If we discover or believe that someone we love also loves someone else, that must mean that they love us less. The love for another is given at our expense. Life, or at least love, is a zero-sum game. This is the presumption of the jealous person, and it is a presumption we must now examine. It is one of the fault lines where relations and efforts at social reconstruction break.

The quantum view may seem immediately implausible once stated. In fact, most people are ready to reject it in their own case. That is, they can readily imagine being involved with one person, then meeting and becoming involved with a second person, and not caring any the less for the first person. The difficult thing, however, is to believe others capable of the same feat. There is a natural double-standard (here not between men and women, but between self and other). It may have many roots,[35] but the result is in any case the attribution of a differential capacity for love; and whatever the sources, the position is of course untenable. Why should we believe ourselves capable of what we believe others incapable of, or why shouldn't we believe others capable of what we believe ourselves capable of? Certainly the quantum view must appear suspect insofar as it is a theory that seems plausible only in relation to others. But this does not settle matters. It could as well be true for all as false for all. What cannot be the case is that it be true for others and false for us (where the identity of "others" and "us" shifts with whoever is speaking).

If the quantum view is untenable, then *all* jealousy may seem pathological, even where the particular beliefs involved are true, for the background belief in a zero-sum aspect to love would seem a delusion. Can scarcity and exclusivity in the sphere of love be dismissed with the notion of quantity? I think exclusivity would have a place whatever we may think about the applicability of quantitative notions to love (a point we have seen in our discussion of eliminability), and in any event I do not think the notion of quantity can be so readily dismissed. I think there is something important and true captured in the quantum view of love, the view we are more ready to apply to others than ourselves. To bring it out we should shift the emphasis from "zero-sums" to the notion of "limits." To make the shift, let us run down the path again: in one form at least, the quantum view is patently untenable, that is, if we hold that *we* can love two people without loving the first any less than before the growth of feeling toward the second, but deny that *others* can. Why should our capacity for love be any greater than that of others? But that is what must seem true if we hold, in our jealousy, that the love someone bears toward another must mean less love toward us, while we do not believe that in relation to ourselves. But before we, in our search for consistency, reject a quantum view of love for others as we reject it for ourselves—do we really reject such a view in our own case? Perhaps we believe we can love two people equally (with no loss of strength). But what of five? . . . of twenty? . . . of all mankind? What happens when one follows the Christian admonition and extends one's love to all? What can be the content of such a "love"?[36]

Clearly, there are limits. "Goodwill" may be inexhaustible, but there are features of love (at least the intimate, erotic love most associated with jealousy) that limit it (if not to one or two, at most to a relatively small number). There are material conditions of love. There may be things in the nature of love which allow of infinite extension, but there are also limiting parameters. One is time. Intimacy takes time, not just to grow, but to have the experiences the sharing of which is part of the body of love, of the lived experience.

Shared experiences may be as mundane as going to the laundry together, but whatever their character, time is needed wherever love is to be built on intimacy. (Of course, it does not follow that because shared experience is a condition of intimacy, the more shared experience, the stronger the bond of love. Countless divorces go to the contrary.) Another limiting parameter is attention. One can devote only so much "loving care" at any given moment. (The Oedipal triangle doesn't emerge because parents do not love their children as much as their spouses, but because they must seem, to the child, to turn away when paying attention to the spouse or another, and may seem to the child to be turning away and abandoning for good.)

It is within such limits (whatever their precise character may be and wherever they may come from) that we must build our loves. And while living with our loves we may also have to live with jealousy. Once one appreciates the thoughts that underlie jealousy, their relative independence from claims of right and their attachment to basic fears, one can see that jealousy holds a place in human life as fixed as human vulnerability and the need for certain types of love. If we must live with jealousy, on what terms is it to be: must it persist, condemned but ineradicable, or distinguished from envy and detached from some of its noxious consequences, might we be better able to tolerate it for those aspects that serve to make it a sign of love?

Jealousy, where it is over particulars and has its special ties to love, seems secure of a place in human life. Some relations are essentially exclusive; the development of an independent identity seems to involve denying some people and things an independent identity (they become a part of us in a way that gets perceived by others as possessiveness); and in the course of development we find that we cannot always have what and who we want when and how we want them—people have desires of their own, and even where what we want is a thing, other people are liable to want it too—indeed it is part of our humanity that we are liable to desire and love what others are also liable to desire and love. Within the flexibility of attitudes to sharing, overcoming scarcity and overcoming inequality, we must draw the limits of jealousy as they reflect the limits of love.[37]

458 JEROME NEU

NOTES

*Spinoza, *Ethics,* ed. Gutmann (New York: Hafner, 1949), Part Three, Proposition XXXV. Nietzsche, *On the Genealogy of Morals,* trans. Kaufmann and Hollingdale (New York: Vintage Books, 1969), First Essay, Section 10. Freud, "Some Neurotic Mechanisms in Jealousy, Paranoia and Homosexuality" (1922), *Standard Edition,* XVIII, p. 223.

1. This is a theme I pursue at length in *Emotion, Thought, and Therapy* (London: Routledge & Kegan Paul; Berkeley and Los Angeles: University of California Press, 1977).

2. On communes see Rosabeth Moss Kanter, *Commitment and Community* (Cambridge, Mass.: Harvard University Press, 1972); on the Israeli experience see Melford E. Spiro, *Children of the Kibbutz* (Cambridge, Mass.: Harvard University Press, 1975); on China: would there were something to let us know how it is going.

3. These points are elaborated by me in "Genetic Explanation in *Totem and Taboo,*" in Richard Wollheim, ed., *Freud: A Collection of Critical Essays* (Garden City, N.Y.: Doubleday Anchor, 1974); and in "What Is Wrong with Incest?," *Inquiry,* XIX (1976). Aristotle provides arguments (*Politics* 1260b-1264b) in favor of differentiation and diversity, and against the possibility of total "unity," in the course of his critique of Plato's scheme of communism.

4. According to Jerome Kagan (in conversation in 1976).

It might be useful to consider a child's upset at another child's possession of an abandoned toy in connection with Freud's discussion of a child's game of disappearance and return (*"fort"* and *"da"*), where the need for active mastery and control comes to the fore. Freud, *Beyond the Pleasure Principle* (1920), *Standard Edition* (London: Hogarth Press), XVIII, 14-17.

5. D. W. Winnicott, "Transitional Objects and Transitional Phenomena," in his *Collected Papers* (London: Tavistock Publications, 1958), pp. 229-242, quote, p. 238.

6. Which is not to say that we are jealous only over relationships we have freely chosen. Again, the sources of our preferences are many and various, and often hidden (even from ourselves). And the fact that preferences may be socially prescribed or structurally dictated does not preclude jealousy. Indeed, as Amélie Rorty has put it: "After all, one doesn't choose parents, even to have them. But jealousy is rife there." On the relative contributions of social structure and emotional constellations to patterning relationships, anthropologists have much to say; see, for example: Claude Lévi-Strauss, *The Elementary Structures of Kinship* (London: Eyre & Spottiswoode, 1969; first published in France in 1949); George C. Homans and David M. Schneider, *Marriage, Authority, and Final Causes: A Study of Unilateral Cross-Cousin Marriage* (Glencoe, Ill.: The Free Press, 1955); Rodney Needham, *Structure and Sentiment* (Chicago: University of Chicago Press, 1962); Lounsbury, review of *Structure and Sentiment, American Anthropologist,* LXIV (1962), 1302-10. Again, it is to be remembered that whatever the sources of a particular relationship or patterns of relationship, one may develop a jealous concern to preserve it or them.

7. That is, Iago is envious where he is not merely vengeful (over Cassio's preferment, etc.). I am assuming that Iago himself did not especially desire Desdemona. At the least, his machinations were not aimed at winning her over (if he did desire her, he wanted even more that no one else have her if he did not). Essentially, he was a "spoiler" (in the language of Melanie Klein). See Auden's analysis of Iago in terms of the practical joker: "The Joker in the Pack," *Selected Essays* (London: Faber, 1964).

8. This corresponds, I think, to Aristotle's distinction, in the *Rhetoric* (1388ab), between *envy* and *emulation.*

9. Going back to the case of Iago, we can now see that even if Iago had himself desired Desdemona, his state would remain envy. The question that turns on whether Iago desired Desdemona—or only that Othello not have her or that Othello be lowered—is not whether his state was envy or jealousy, but whether his envy was malicious or admiring.

10. John Rawls, *A Theory of Justice* (Cambridge, Mass.: Harvard University Press, 1971), pp. 479-485, 533.

11. Helmut Schoeck, *Envy: A Theory of Social Behaviour,* trans. Glenny and Ross (New York: Harcourt, Brace & World, 1970).

12. For parodies see L. P. Hartley, *Facial Justice* (London: Hamish Hamilton, 1960); and Kurt Vonnegut, Jr., "Harrison Bergeron," *Welcome to the Monkey House* (New York: Dell, 1970). For a beginning on some of the hard questions about equality (its meaning, which differences need remedy, which are remediable, how, etc.) see Bernard Williams, "The Idea of Equality," in Laslett and Runciman, eds., *Philosophy, Politics and Society,* Vol. II (Oxford: Blackwell, 1962), and also in his *Problems of the Self* (Cambridge: Cambridge University Press, 1973).

13. See Fred Hirsch, *Social Limits to Growth* (Cambridge, Mass.: Harvard University Press, 1976).

14. Freud, "The Taboo of Virginity" (1918), *Standard Edition,* XI, 199; *Group Psychology and the Analysis of the Ego* (1921), *Standard Edition,* XVIII, 101-102; *Civilization and Its Discontents* (1930), *Standard Edition,* XXI, 114-115.

15. Schoeck brings together much of this evidence, though he has a tendency to assimilate all forms of hostility and conflict and aggression to envy (an overcorrection of the frustration-aggression approach). In addition, there is George M. Foster's very helpful survey of ways societies cope with fear of envy: "The Anatomy of Envy: A Study in Symbolic Behavior," *Current Anthropology,* XIII (1972), 165-202. I have found Foster's subtle study useful at a number of points.

16. Melanie Klein, "Envy and Gratitude" (1957), *Writings of Melanie Klein* (London: Hogarth Press), III, 176-235. But see also Walter G. Joffe, "A Critical Review of the Status of the Envy Concept," *International Journal of Psychoanalysis,* L (1969), 533-545.

17. Max Scheler, *Ressentiment,* ed. Coser and trans. Holdheim (New York: Schocken Books, 1972), quote p. 52.

18. Rawls, *A Theory of Justice,* pp. 530-541.

19. The skepticism emerges, for example at pp. 251-253 (Schoeck, *Envy*). An empirical approach cannot dismiss the claims of socialists and egalitarians to moral (as opposed to envious) motivation without confronting their underlying conceptions of justice and perceptions of the social situation—for it is these that distinguish the moral emotions from envy.

It should also be noted that the desire that others not have something thought valuable (by them) may be less an attack on the possessors (either malicious or based on a sense of justice) than on the thought that it is valuable. There is more to the moral psychology of negative desires than just envy and resentment. (The "desire that another not have" may nonetheless play a role in the analysis of envy comparable to the role of the "desire to be desired" in the analysis of jealousy.) A Savonarola may claim to be neither envious nor resentful, but merely to want others not to have or do certain things because it is *bad* for them to have or do them. (This is the standard claim of paternalists—and parents.) To properly judge such denials of envy, one would need, in addition to a theory of justice, a theory of the good. (I am indebted to Jay Cantor for raising the specter of Savonarola.)

20. In response to a presentation of an earlier version of this paper at the Wellfleet Meetings in Summer, 1976.

21. Robert Nozick, *Anarchy, State and Utopia* (New York: Basic Books, 1974), pp. 239-246, quote p. 243. Comparative aspects of envy are discussed by (among others) Aristotle (*Rhetoric,* 1387b-1388a), Hume (*Treatise of Human Nature,* Book II, Part II, Section viii), and Kant (*The Metaphysics of Morals,* Part II, §36). That self-esteem (unlike envy) is not *necessarily* comparative is part of the point of Nietzsche's contrast between the Ancients and the Horde. But, as Amélie Rorty points out, Nietzsche may have been mythologizing wildly, and dangerously ("because to set the ideal of a non-comparative self-esteem before us is to invent yet another way for us to fail...."), and there may be features of language and self-imagery that force us to form our conceptions of ourselves initially (and therefore, to some extent, on some level, forever) through the eyes of the other, so that comparison becomes a *psychological* necessity in self-conception and self-esteem.

There may be a contrast between self-esteem and self-respect that is helpful here. Self-respect, having to do with one's rights and dignity as a person, may be noncomparative. Self-esteem, having to do with one's merits and self-valuation, may depend on the standards of value in one's society and how one compares with other members of that society. Put crudely, of self-respect one cannot have too much, of self-esteem one obviously can. Put more precisely, the idea of too much self-respect is at best problematic, while that of too much self-esteem, like those of either too little self-respect or too little self-esteem, poses no difficulty. (I am indebted to David Sachs for this point. Cf. Rousseau's contrast of *amour de soi,* which is supposed to be natural, noncomparative, and tied to self-preservation, and *amour propre,* which is supposed to be social, comparative, and other-directed—see *Discourse on the Origin of Inequality,* and *Emile,* Book IV.) There remains a problem, the one we have been considering, of just how self-esteem depends on what one's society thinks and on what one thinks about others in one's society.

22. Kingsley Davis, "Jealousy and Sexual Property," *Social Forces,* XIV (1936), pp. 395-405, quote pp. 400 and 403.

23. "If we assume *man* to be *man,* and his relation to the world to be a human one, then love can be exchanged only for love, trust for trust, and so on. If you wish to enjoy art you must be an artistically educated person; if you wish to exercise influence on other men you must be the sort of person who has a truly stimulating and encouraging effect on others. Each one of your relations to man—and to nature—must be a *particular expression,* corresponding to the object of your will, of your *real individual* life. If you love unrequitedly, i.e., if your love as love does not call forth love in return, if through the *vital expression* of yourself as a loving person you fail to become a *loved person,* then your love is impotent, it is a misfortune." Karl Marx, *Early Writings,* trans. Livingstone and Benton (New York: Vintage Books, 1975), p. 379.

24. The importance of anger and resentment in jealousy, of the fear of loss as inimical, was usefully pressed on me in comments by Robert Solomon and Rogers Albritton. So long as the anger is understood as at loss or deprivation (or as a response to frustration rather than to violation of rights) it adds an important dimension to the component of fear emphasized throughout this paper.

25. See Gregory Vlastos, "The Individual as an Object of Love in Plato," *Platonic Studies* (Princeton, N.J.: Princeton University Press, 1973), pp. 3-42, esp. pp. 28-34. Professor Vlastos tells me that he would now prefer to get at the contrast between two types of love "by contrasting the attitudes of desire (which can be—though it needn't be—totally egoistic) and tenderness (which can be—though it needn't be—totally altruistic")—that is, in terms of contrasting aims rather than

objects. He points out that possessive love can be directed intensely and exclusively to an individual: "...when desire is deep and intense it *fixates* on the individual who instantiates the desirable qualities: the individual may then become irreplaceable. This is certainly what happens in the Odette-Swann case. Proust speaks of 'an anxious torturing desire, whose object is the creature herself,' that creature being the "exclusive" object—the exclusivity of the desire being the most marked feature. (The quote is from p. 331 of the Modern Library translation.) The fungibility of the qualities X desires in Y characterizes an Epicurean or, better, sensualist, attitude that may be contrasted with what the novelists and even the philosophers (Lucretius, or Plato in the first two speeches in the *Phaedrus*) call 'love' even when speaking of love-desire rather than love-tenderness. The moment desire becomes deep, fungibility is lost: one is 'hooked' to a particular person. That is certainly the great point in the Odette episode." On this account, what I am calling "love of a particular person" is really tenderness for that person: "the sentiment which corresponds to the attitude of pure good will—desiring the good of that person ('for that person's sake, not for our own sake' in Aristotle's good phrase)." I think, however, that just as love-desire at its extreme can degenerate into exploitation, love-tenderness at its extreme can generalize into an unfocussed goodwill (not directed toward any individual to the exclusion of any other)—so that to understand the most typical experiences of love we might have to acknowledge overlap in terms of aims (desires) as much as in objects. Since, however, as we shall see, jealousy can arise in relation to both types of object, it may appear that the more significant dividing line (in relation to the possibility of jealousy at least) depends on the types of desires involved rather than the objects. Genuinely and totally selfless desires for the good of the other may leave no room for jealousy. But then, sexual passion (arising in connection with instinctual needs) may leave no room for such purely selfless desires—a love without such passion, and so without mixed desires, if not an etiolated love, wins its distance from jealousy only at some cost. The need for mixed desires can also be seen from another direction: "It is the fate of sensual love to become extinguished when it is satisfied; for it to be able to last, it must from the beginning be mixed with purely affectionate components—with such, that is, as are inhibited in their aims—or it must itself undergo a transformation of this kind." (Freud, *Group Psychology and the Analysis of the Ego* [1921], *Standard Edition,* XVIII, 115.) We should perhaps also note that there may be a level at which the distinctions in terms of attitudes, aims, and desires should themselves be understood in terms of differing objects, namely self and other (rather than particulars and bundles of qualities); so the multiple contrasts might in the end reduce to self-love v. love-of-other, egoism v. altruism, narcissism v. object-love.

Steve Kaye has also pointed out to me that "the fungibility factor may be given too much weight unless we take account of both the tendency to project qualities onto a lover and how much the nuances come to matter, i.e., how we come to see uniqueness in the ways our love object instantiates a desired quality." He also brings out another way in which love of a particular and love of a bundle of qualities may be seen to come together. He notes that my example uses physical qualities, and he suggests that we consider what happens when we turn our attention to other sorts of qualities, especially moral ones. If we leave our lover after discovering that he or she is not generous, or is, after all, insensitive, what does our leaving show? Was our love not true (while it lasted)? Is the ideal perhaps unobtainable? The whole matter of breaking-up is especially puzzling because, despite cases of leaving after discovering a mistake or a change in character, we *do* often forgive and accept faults of character in those we love—sometimes there are compensating factors and sometimes it is a part of the commitment we have made. (Cf.: "One of the important factors of a relationship is as a cushion for the jolts of bad fortune—we do not walk out on our spouse because he or she receives a pay cut, we comfort them.'') Whether a change undermines a relationship is not determined, straightforwardly at least, by whether or not the change was in the person's control. While I am leaving out much of the subtle detail in Kaye's arguments, it is clear that at least one has to consider the question of which qualities (if any) are essential to identity, before one can be sure of a contrast (sharp or otherwise) between love directed at a particular person and love directed at a set of qualities.

26. Shakespeare, Sonnet 116.

27. This is part of the tragedy of the "legalization" and "commercialization" of our culture. "Family law" embodies the conflict in the very words used to designate it: the law disturbs personal relations when it intervenes, but if it fails to intervene it may leave the weak to be victimized by the strong, and when that happens personal relations have already been disturbed. But the *possibility* of the law intervening may itself have disturbing effects.

28. Since emotions are importantly constituted by beliefs and desires, much turns on the sources of belief and desire. Certainly we cannot choose our beliefs directly, but it does not follow that they are completely outside our control. Certainly we can be overcome by desires, but it does not follow that they are not criticizable. The questions of the relation of belief and will, and of desire and belief, are as difficult as they are important. See H. H. Price, "Belief and Will," *Proceedings of the Aristotelian Society,* Suppl. XXVIII (1954); Bernard Williams, "Deciding to Believe," in his *Problems of the Self* (Cambridge: Cambridge University Press, 1973); Stuart Hampshire, *Freedom of the Individual* (Princeton, N.J.: Princeton University Press, new edition, 1975); Harry G. Frankfurt, "Freedom of the Will and the Concept of a Person," *Journal of Philosophy,* Vol. LXVIII (1971).

29. See Freud, "Some Neurotic Mechanisms in Jealousy, Paranoia and Homosexuality" (1922), *Standard Edition,* XVIII, 223-232. The other great resource in this area is of course Proust. Among other things, Proust brings out how the freedom of the beloved can, by itself, become a ground for jealousy. The mere fact of freedom, the mere *possibility* of loss, gets experienced as a *probability* of loss. (Cf. how children may initially experience the mere fact of separateness as loss. Children have to *learn* that objects that can go away can also return.)

30. Ibid., "Three Essays on the Theory of Sexuality" (1905), *Standard Edition,* VII, 222.

31. Ibid., "Notes Upon a Case of Obsessional Neurosis" (1909—the "Rat Man"), *Standard Edition,* X, 241.

32. Ibid., "On Narcissism: An Introduction" (1914), *Standard Edition,* XIV, 89.

33. In Freud's classic Oedipal cases (e.g., "The Rat Man" and "Little Hans"), jealousy is perhaps the archetypical object of repression. In those cases the love is acceptable enough, it is the jealousy that cannot be acknowledged.

34. Which is not to say that because some love may have a selfish aspect, all love must be totally selfish. But it is to insist that that love which is the desire for the happiness of the other, perhaps the purest form of love, is not the only form or even the only valuable form. Indeed, mature sexual passion may always involve some variant of the desire to be desired. See Sartre, *Being and Nothingness* (Part Three), trans. Barnes (New York: Philosophical Library, 1956); and Thomas Nagel, "Sexual Perversion," *Journal of Philosophy,* Vol. LXVI (1969). See also Freud, "On Narcissism" (1914), *Standard Edition,* XII; and *Group Psychology and the Analysis of the Ego* (1921), *Standard Edition,* XVIII, 102-103, 112-113.

The wisdom of a fortune cookie (passed on to me by a friend knowing my research interests) has it that: "In jealousy there is more self-love than love." (The fortune cookie fails to credit La Rochefoucauld.) Life, including both love and self-love, is of course more complex than that. In regard to self-love, one ought to distinguish selfishness and self-esteem. One may be quite high while the other is quite low; indeed, the person suffering from jealousy will typically have very low self-esteem (lack of faith in own lovableness, etc.). In regard to love, one should note that the wisdom of the fortune cookie is tied to a very special, romantic, and as we have just said, pure, conception of love: a view under which the true lover always puts the good of his beloved first (whether or not that good includes him). But we do not in general expect lovers to drive their beloved to the airport to help them go off with some other (better) lover. (Humphrey Bogart at the end of the film *Casablanca* is *heroic*—and his decision was made in the larger context of World War II: "Ilsa, I'm no good at being noble. But it doesn't take much to see that the problems of three little people don't amount to a hill o' beans in this crazy world.")

35. What may seem special about "my" case may be that when I am the one with multiple lovers I am sure of my control and that *I* won't desert anyone; or, again, I may be concerned about the shift of quantities in the case of others, while in my own case I have a sense of constant renewal of quantities; and so on.

36. See Freud, *Group Psychology and the Analysis of the Ego* (1921), *Standard Edition,* XVIII, especially 90-99, 134-135, 140-142; and *Civilization and its Discontents* (1930), *Standard Edition,* XXI, Chap. V.

37. This paper has benefited from the comments of a number of people, but especially Norman O. Brown, Ellen Hawkes, Robert Meister, and Amélie Rorty.

XIX

JEALOUSY, ATTENTION, AND LOSS

Leila Tov-Ruach

Otto is deeply attached to Deborah: his sense of well-being as the person he takes himself to be is in part formed by what he takes to be her perceptions of him. But he believes that D's attentions have swerved toward, and indeed to center on Chayim. O knows that D is loyal: she will not abandon him or their children. Knowing her, he suspects that she will be rather more meticulous though perhaps more abstracted in her care of all of them precisely because she has come to be absorbed in C. But O senses that her relation to him will be defined by her own self-respect and her habits rather than by her attentive perception of him. O's days are consumed with researches into the exact character of D's encounters with C, his nights are spent in dreams and fantasies of the details of their joys in one another's company. He envisages scene after scene of their happiness. O is wracked by jealousy; he loses all sense of himself; his steady behavior becomes erratic and arbitrary. He no longer seems the same man.

What does O's jealousy presuppose? In what does it consist? Where does it lead? Certainly O fears a loss: but he need not fear losing D or D's love in order to be jealous. He might, as it turned out, stand in the same formal relation to D as before: she might continue to share his bed and board, his life, as ever she did, and perhaps with more forebearing kindness than before. And yet he is jealous. Is it then the loss of her love that he fears? No, because in some cases O might well have retained D's love, even though her attentions concentrated on C. (And, as we shall see, in other circumstances he might be jealous of someone where there was no love at all.) Perhaps he might fear that the character of D's love would change, that she might come to love him as one loves a kindly friend, rather than in that wholly absorbed way that she loved him when first they came to know each other. Yet O might know that even if D had never met C, the character of her love would certainly have changed from its early youthful form. But yet he might nevertheless fear that her present comfortable love would change still more radically.

With Chayim in the picture, O might fear that D could not retain any continued sense of her life as being intertwined with his. Even when jealousy is a fear of the loss of love, the loss must have a special cause. After all, O might have feared the loss of D's love because she was forced to move away, or because she altered in some profound way, or because she became dangerously ill. Jealousy requires that the loss be experienced as someone else's gain: that there is a direct transfer.

The transfer is characteristically made to another person, but it can also be directed to a cause or an occupation. O might have been jealous of D's relation to her law practice, jealous of her devotion to legal researches, and to the welfare of her clients, thinking that the attention she gave them could only come as a diminution of her devotion to him. But O's jealousy of D's work need not be a jealousy of her *love* of her work, her research, her clients; it depends rather on his belief that her *attention* to her legal practice deprives him of attentions he requires.

Jealousy need not involve love at all. Otto might be jealous that Diana, his favorite chess partner—the person whose regard for his chess playing has confirmed his sense of his unique capacities and style as a chess master—has found a new and favored chess partner. He believes that D now regards Clara with the centrality of attention as a chess player that she once gave him. D's playing with C has cast a pall on O's sense of his gifts: he imagines the delights of their chess strategy session, the elegance of their developing interactive style. If he were envious, he would concentrate on C's gifts, comparing his unfavorably to hers. If he were envious not only of C's gifts but of the attention she receives from D, he would compare his situation unfavorably with hers. His envy is transformed to jealousy, when he considers the transfer of attention as a deprivation of an important part of his personality, one that impels him to obsessive thoughts about the rival relation. The fantasies of envy focus on another person's *properties,* and one's own comparative lack of them, but the other person is not believed to have those properties at one's own cost. Even though one loses by the comparison, one is not the loser because of the comparison. The fantasies of jealousy focus on a person's *relations* to another. Of course such relations can be considered properties, and the pattern of a person's envy shows his beliefs about what properties assure the sort of attention he wants. But the relation became the subject of jealousy rather than envy only when another's acquired relational-property is perceived as one's own direct loss.[1]

Yet the sense of such deprivation does not always generate jealousy: it can also generate sadness, longing, or discontent. A person is jealous only when the perceived deprivation makes him doubt himself, forces him to reasses his style or ability or power in a way that generates obsessive thoughts of the rival relation.

Because the focused attention that recognizes and constitutes a set of aspects that an individual takes to be central to himself is also a crucial feature of love, it is natural, but nevertheless mistaken, to assume that jealousy presupposes love. When we find ourselves jealous, fearing to lose a formative attentive regard, we often erroneously take ourselves to love. Often it is only jealousy that reveals the character of our attachments. But we can become attached to a special sort of attention, an attention upon which we depend, without depending on love. There are, after all, many forms of attention that are not necessarily loving. There is for instance, nonloving sexual concentration, which often also has a strongly obsessive character.[2] One of the reasons that jealousy so often focuses on sexual relations is that sexual attention is just about the most focused and concentrated form of attention we experience. It is, moreover, one that can reawaken our earliest experiences of the sort of physical attention that sustained our existence in infancy and that formed our somatic sense of our selves. It is because intensely focused attention is a central feature of both love and sexuality that they tend to go together and that we often move from one to the other, back and forth. (Those who attempt to free themselves of sexual jealousy may therefore find that they must diminish the importance of individually focused sexual experience as part of their sense of their own identity. Either they diminish the importance of sexuality as such to their sense of themselves, or they generalize sexuality, without focusing on the individuality of their partners as a crucial part of the importance the activity has for them, or they identify themselves as samplers and connoisseurs of varieties of individuals, avoiding sexual bonding with any one of them.)

But why should the extension or diversion of focused formative attention generate a fear of loss? It is because such attention has the psychological and the physiological character that it does, that any redirection is perceived as a loss by the original recipient. Certainly there is some economy in love: one cannot love a great many people all at once, either singly or conjointly. But within the limits of the expansion of attention to the details of persons' lives, a shift of love within a small group does not require readjustment to the whole field. Parents do not find that they *love* their elder children the less, when they have more children, although they certainly find they can give them quantitatively less *attention*. We come to know that we need not lose love, when our lovers also love elsewhere. It may be a difficult lesson to learn, but sometimes we can recognize that we are better loved, because we are not the only persons on our lover's mind. This is not only true for love: the economy of a large number of psychological attitudes shifts at a critical limits between large and small numbers, at just that point where the capacity for detailed attention can expand no farther.

It is a difficult complication in our loves, that while the capacity for loving can grow by its exercise (especially its happy exercise), one of the preconditions for love *is* subject to a zero sum economy. That condition is the 'singling out' of focused attention. It is, after all, not merely any random glancing attention that is at issue, but an attention that has a special focus on the individual character of a person, a concentration on some traits that, by virtue of being attended in a special way, come to be thought of as centrally constitutive. The thought is that the person regards certain traits as centrally defining his personality and believes that he could not retain those traits outside of the particular attentional relation.

In concentrated attention, a person may project some tangential characteristics, or attend some relatively peripheral features of a person's personality structure. But since loving attention also requires an interest in the beloved's real welfare, it requires attempting to discover what the beloved is really like to determine the conditions for the best development and exercise of the person's central features. When the lover's attentions are active in forming and crystallizing the beloved's personality, the lover is also careful to attend to the real structure of that personality, not foisting or projecting an identity that, by becoming constitutive, will so conflict with the rest of the beloved's character that the person cannot flourish. We do indeed help to create those whom we love: but we do not do it from whole cloth. And that is why the lover who is essentially concerned for the welfare of the beloved takes care that his constituting attention is appropriate to the real traits and the tonal character of the person whom he loves.

Because concentrated attention is such a crucial feature of love, it is natural to confuse the two, and to suppose that the presence of one entails the presence of the other. But the economic logic of the two are distinct: a loving care for what is central to a person's flourishing is not an all-or-none activity subject to a zero sum economy. What *is* such an activity is that part of loving which requires completely focused attention. Such attention is a precondition for loving: but it need not accompany every moment of loving activity.

The paradigm for such attention, that sets the model and expectations for later extensions, is direct gazing. That is how, as infants, we first experience attention and that is how we first experience the possibility of its loss, when the attention that was directed to us is turned away. At that level, anyone's gain, must be our loss. We have strong evidence that the development of an infant's ego requires this sort of attention: a child's coming to have a sense of himself as a center of consciousness and of agency depends on his having received attention that centered on him as an individual capable of consciousness and agency.[3] Even more strikingly, some of the detailed characteristics that the developing child comes to take as essentially his, characteristics that define the tonality of his consciousness and the style and direction of his agency are those that centrally attending persons see in him. Gradually, of course, it is not merely parental figures on whose forming attention ego development depends, but also teachers, friends, lovers. "Look at me!" does not stop when one leaves the playground. Nor does that closely related cry, "Catch me if I fall!"

Jealousy need not be experienced as a special sort of feeling, as a pang, or a twinge.[4] An adult may indeed be jealous without feeling so, his jealousy taking the form of obsessive imagistic thoughts of the rival relation, without his being reflectively aware that these thoughts indicate his jealousy. Sometimes there are strong inhibitions against jealousy, not only against its expression but against feeling it. Many parents treat their children's jealousy as if it were a sort of vice, and such children, fearing their own jealousy, learn to deny it in various ways, sometimes by repressing it by 'ostrich behavior' and sometimes by sublimating it. When it is strongly re-

pressed jealousy can be turned to forms of self-destructiveness or
more directly vindictive behavior. When it is sublimated, it can lead
to the development of strong competitive traits that make a person
a visible bearer of characteristics that are likely to attract the sort of
focused attentions they require.

But though adult jealousy need not be *experienced* as such, our
earliest experiences of jealousy did involve painful feelings, sometimes the pain of great anxiety. Early experiences of focused attention were also associated with being-attended-to, and there is a
natural tendency to fear the loss of sustaining being-attended-to
with the theatened loss of attention. Infantile jealousy is an experience of the sort of losses that do in fact genuinely jeopardize the
ego.[5] In their most extreme form, they generate anxieties of being
abandoned by those whose physical attentions are required for the
most basic level of physical well-being. At a somewhat later stage,
they involve anxieties of the loss of that sort of facial-attention and
interaction that is a condition for the development and formation
of the child's sense of its own ego. But early experiences of jealousy
remain latent in us all. If the development of a person's ego suffered setbacks (and for most of us surely it did), then later incidents
of jealousy often evoke undercurrents of unresolved earlier anxieties, even when we are functioning quite well and are reasonably
aware of our securities.

Many fears of adult jealousy are quite realistic: a person may
genuinely fear to lose prized characteristics that depend on the continued attention of others. Even well-formed autonomous adults
can be changed by the loss of characteristics that can only flourish
through the attention of another person, and some through the
attention of another *particular* person. It is difficult to sustain a
sense of oneself as witty or humorous or sexy unless one is continuously so perceived. And there are forms of wit and forms of
humour that require very particular interlocutors for their exercise.[6]

Other anxieties of jealousy—that the loss of even important
traits must involve annihilation or the complete disintegration of
the self—the anxieties that are evoked by reawakened infant fears,
are quite irrational. Nevertheless, irrational or no, jealousy can,
when it is experienced as a feeling, involve intense vertigo, like that
of fainting or a loss of consciousness, or a sense of strong disorientation and disassociation. Sometimes this sense of annihilation is

histrionically magnified by the jealous person, who then seems actively complicit in extending the damage already effected by the transfer of attention. There is a dramatization of the extent of the real damage to other parts and aspects of the ego, and acting out of the sensed destruction. (This often resembles the behavior of children who, devastated by some small damage to a favorite toy, then completely destroy a plaything that seemed still quite suitable for play. This strategy of identifying with the oppressor, taking on the active role of the destroyer to finish off the job, can have the strengthening benefits that any active affirmation of the self can convey; but these benefits are obviously of a not very promising or enduring kind. Such strategies undermine more than they bolster.)

A person might fear the loss of just this sort of defining attention and neither feel, nor be, jealous. He might, without having repressed or sublimated jealousy, directly become depressed or withdrawn or feel self-pity or deny the original relation. The fear of the loss of focused attention is a jealous fear only when the sense of danger to an aspect of one's identity generates a set of obsessive scenario-constructing thoughts. These thoughts generally involve the construction of vivid stories, with the jealous person as a voyeur of an endless series of vignettes that cause him pain.

Jealous thoughts are characteristically (though not necessarily) highly imagistic. Even a person whose thinking is in other contexts not particularly imagistic (consisting rather in phrases, schematic inferences, word associations and relatively abstract thoughts [whatever they may be!]) nevertheless tends, when he is jealous, to construct fantasies of a highly visual sort: he becomes a sort of voyeur even when the content of the imagery is not particularly sexual. The earliest forms of jealousy may explain these later structures. Infant jealousy is experienced when a parental figure, on whose attentions ego development depends, looks away, focusing elsewhere in such a way that the child does not easily regain the original attention. The first experiences of jealousy actually do involve the jealous person as a witness of the redirected focus of attention: we learn jealousy by *watching* that redirection, experiencing it as our loss. If a parental figure is looking at C, he is not looking at O. The child learns of the new relation by *seeing* it take place. It would seem natural that later experiences of jealousy would recreate that structure in fantasy and in thought. Perhaps, too, jealous imaginings tend to be so visual because what is lost is precisely the sense of being *seen* in a certain way. So the content of the fantasies might well involve the visual attentions that the rival received.

Not only is jealous thought characteristically imagistic: it is also highly obsessional. Even persons whose visual thinking does not ordinarily tend to be obsessive do, in jealousy, often obsessively run through scenario after scenario.[7] One might speculate that the obsessive character of jealousy comes from its being an attack on the ego. Whatever strategies a person had developed in the defense of the ego come into play here. There are two ways in which the obsessive character of jealousy tends to exert itself: one is in the *need to know,* the endless tests and investigations and spyings that are so characteristic of jealousy. The other is the *need to visualize.* Both obsessions seem to make the jealous person less passive, less helpless because he is actively engaged in investigating or in imagining. It is as if he joins in the agency of his jealousy, and by being active in it, changes the character of his suffering, even when he actually increases it by doing so. His then becomes an active rather than a passive suffering. Since the fears of jealousy evoke anxieties of infantile helplessness, activity may somehow assuage the sense of annihilation: there is even often a tone of exhilaration that enters into the imagistic investigations.[8] It is one thing to be annihilated by others, quite another to be annihilated as the result of one's own frenzied activity. Even the jealous person's recognition that it is often precisely his obsessive investigations that precipitate a transfer of attention that might not otherwise have developed, does not usually deter him. There is an obsessive desire to bring things to a head, to have the worst revealed and perhaps even brought about. Even when it is also accompanied by ostrich behavior of denial, jealousy can be embedded in, or sometimes trigger off a larger, more general project of self-destruction.

Following a suggestion of Sartre, it seems plausible to interpret the obsessive character of jealousy as a way of attempting magically to return to the center of the world.[9] Both the need to know and the need to visualize appear to allow the jealous person to regain control as playwright, director, manipulator. In his thoughts at least, the rival relation becomes his creation, the work of his mind. By being active in its construction, in the determination of its tonality, he is not merely passive and helpless. But these investigations and imaginings make the jealous person vulnerable to additional pain when he actually sees the rival relation, and sees it as having tonalities and characteristics that he himself has not succeeded in inventing in the course of his jealous imaginings. He then suffers the loss of the magic control that he had temporarily achieved by being the only begetter of his jealous imaginings.

Well, then, there is O, endlessly imagining D and C at kibbutz festivities, gazing into each other's eyes, or O is engaged in envisaging the strong intensity of D's attention to C as he rises to speak at the weekly meeting of the production planning committee. Not every jealous person has the same scenarios, but each person tends to have a characteristic set, a pattern whose variations reveal the concerns that his attachment to the person's attention has served. If that attachment defined the character of his sexuality, he will envisage the rival relation in sexual scene after sexual scene. But it will even be more precise: for what may matter to O is not simply the fact of some sexual situation, but its tonal character as urgent, tender, prolonged, playful, aggressive, or athletic. Indeed, the tonality may in some cases dominate the actual sexuality, so that what comes to be significant to the person's self-definition and therefore the concern of his jealousy is not so much the fact of sexual intercourse (about which he may be relatively indifferent), as the tonality of the psychophysical relation. What can be at issue is not so much the actual character of O's relation to D, but how its (imagined) tonality endangers the focus of O's sense of himself.

For instance, if O's relation to D formed him as a certain sort of intellectual, the two sharing speculative investigations, then his jealous thoughts of D and C will focus on their being engaged in absorbing intellectual discussions or investigations. If O thinks of himself as essentially a truthseeker, his thoughts and fantasies may center on his discovering the truth of D's relation to C. In general, the details of the thoughts and fantasies that are such a large part of jealousy reveal the forms of O's characteristic uses of thought-in-the-services-of-defense, as well as the details of the ways in which O's relation to D have formed his conception of himself.[10]

But surely one might think of all this as overdone? After all, someone can be jealous of a distant person: an adolescent might be jealous of a rock star's attentions to a movie star. One need not be in a real relation to feel jealousy; one need never have had, what one takes oneself to have lost. But when that happens, the person is likely to have fantasied an absorbing relation between himself and the rock star. His jealousy is contained within a fantasy in which he has realized some attentive relation between himself and the distant figure. This sort of fantasy can also occur with people whom one knows. A figure who plays an objective role in one's life can be fantasied as providing a forming attention. The person can be real, and the effect real, but the forming attention only fantasied. The person can then be jolted by jealousy, and even jealous vertigo at the feared loss of something that, although it never existed, did indeed form some aspect of their sense of themselves. If a person has neither had, nor imagined themselves to have had what they feel as a deprivation, their condition is one of longing rather than jealousy. But since this sort of longing generally generates fantasies of attachment, it usually moves toward jealousy. Because medical situations, especially psychiatric ones, involve the sort of concentrated focused attention on traits that the patient regards as crucial to his well-being, patients are often in a fantasy attachment to their physicians. It is this that is thought to facilitate the operations of the mechanisms of transference in psychoanalysis. And it is for this reason that medical practitioners try to protect themselves and (as they imagine) their patients by adopting a formal and impersonal manner.

Some people are especially prone to fantasy attachments, and others especially prone to fantasy losses of either real or fantasied attachments. Such people have generally been deprived of crucial attentive attachments, or suffered their loss at crucial stages of ego development. They come to expect attachment dependencies or to foresee their vulnerability to the redirection of attention. Their sense of their own reality contains a sense of its own fragility.[11]

There are a number of serious objections to our discussion. It might be argued that in order to explain at least some of the phenomena of adult jealousy, it is often quite unnecessary to postulate an elaborate account of the etiology of such jealousy in childhood history. The theory sketched in this paper might be thought to deal primarily with pathological cases, where a person's jealousy is not adequately explained by the situation that engenders it. A person might quite realistically fear the loss of a particular attention, and quite realistically fear that the loss of such attention might cause him to lose important goods. Such losses may affect a person's sense of well-being, without generating a fear of the loss of some important aspect of oneself; and certainly they need not awaken childhood traumas.

On the surface, this objection seems absolutely right. Not every adult jealousy awakens childhood experiences; some adult jealousies are entirely realistic and can adequately be explained by the situations in which they occur. Nevertheless, our account is an account of the etiology of jealousy, and not merely of its pathological forms. Part of our answer is metatheoretical. In general, the explanation and analysis of the pathological forms of an emotion or attitude should not import principles of a radically different character from the explanation of normal phenomena. The pathology of attention and emotions involve an imbalance of just those ingredients that are at work in the normal condition. Pathological jealousy is generally also occasioned by present and real fears: it differs from the normal cases only in that the person has a lower threshold to such fears, and that they also have a lower threshold to the evocation of older fears. Their adult jealousy is more likely to trigger or evoke early fears of abandonment. Our susceptibilities to the pathological evocation of ancient anxieties tends to vary with our vulnerabilities: such thresholds can vary markedly at different times in a person's life, in different sorts of social situations.

The childhood origins of jealousy are of theoretical significance for another reason. While it is true that there are perfectly realistic grounds for a person fearing to lose some important benefits from the attention of another, there is a question about what makes such fears *jealous* fears, rather than apprehensions, predictions, forebodings. Not every fear of the loss of attention which is gained by another person is a jealous one. The roots of jealousy in infant fears of abandonment distinguishes jealousy from other fears: but of course not every case of jealousy activates such fears.

Moreover, childhood jealousy need not be dramatic. A child can be momentarily jealous of the attention received by some sibling, without going through any crisis of identity. Nevertheless, a child's ego—its strength and the directions of its identifications—fluctuates enormously in the processes of its development. Issues of just distribution are the focus of jealousy as well as envy: they give a child the sense of its dependency and vulnerability. A child who has experienced arbitrary or inconsistent attention, especially if favorite siblings are played off against one another, may become chronically jealous or resentful. While standardly jealousy is a reactive emotion, it can become what Rorty calls magnetizing disposition, that structures and sometimes creates the conditions that elicit it.

Etymologically, *jealous* is linked to *zealous:* both involve an attentive regard for what is close to oneself. One can jealousy guard one's reputation, zealously carry out one's duties. Whatever is the subject to jealous or zealous alertness is bound with one's sense of oneself: one's defining possessions, one's uprightness, one's public face.

Jealousy is an emotion that has distinctive varieties: but there are several ways that these varieties can be classified. One is to distinguish the consequences or secondary attitudes that jealousy triggers. Since jealousy is one of the emotions that has a perceived danger to the self at its center, it generates various strategies of defense. Varieties of jealousy can, then, be mapped according to these strategies and their characteristic etiologies.[12] For instance, some jealousies are attended by depression or withdrawal, others by anger or thoughts of revenge. Still others by an intensification of the original attachment; or by intellectualization; others by frantic activity, or with frenzied competitive behavior. The choice among these strategies seems to be influenced by early ego-defense moves in the face of instinctual vicissitudes.

Another way to characterize varieties of jealousy is to distinguish the tonality of the attentive regard that then comes to constitute the character of the person's relation to himself. For instance, early parental attention may be strongly accompanied by anxiety, or by impatient resentment. Even when the attention is loving, its character and direction can be quite variable. The attention can involve joy in the child's activity and alertness; or it can be strongly directive and teacherly; or it can involve an identificatory concentration on traits the parental figures take to resemble their own, eliciting narcissistic reactions, or hostile aggressive ones. The undertones and associated emotional embedding of attention will then also accompany the adult's own expectations: his later attentions will tend to have similar (or opposed) undertones, and he will seek out the attentions of those whose attitudes have similar (or opposed) forms, almost as if he didn't believe that attention was really *atten-*

tion unless it was also accompanied by these other characteristics.

Finally, we can characterize the varieties of jealousy by the varieties in their characteristic causes. So we can distinguish sexual jealousy and its various forms, from jealousy in situations of competition for esteem, and so on.

Each of the varieties would be recognizable by their characteristic patterns of obsessive imagery, by the details and structure of the scenario narratives, by the varieties of expressions in posture and gesture which are manifest in jealousy, and of course by their characteristic consequences. But all the varieties of jealousy depend on a contextually determined state of a person's ego. A set of events that would spring a person's characteristic jealous responses at one time might not elicit them at another, depending on the previous contrast experience, their physical condition, and their expectations. When a person has recently had ego-building experiences, he is less likely to be subject to fears that the transfer of attention requires revision of his own attributes, than he would be if he had just suffered other setbacks to his sense of himself. Unfortunately, we seem to be so constituted that one ego defeat tends to make us prey to more, less able to slough them off. A person who has just suffered inroads on her job, or has been ill, is more likely to be sensitive, if not actually hypersensitive to the directions of her husband's attentions than she normally is when she is in a less vulnerable condition. Of course the contrast effect is not the only operative determinant of threshold: a person's expectations, some of them formed by very early experiences, and many of them culturally fixed and conveyed, would also condition his responses.

Is jealousy always damaging? It seems that jealousy is unavoidable, if only, ironically, from the psychophysical character of biocular focusing and attention. But are the griefs and fears it causes us always and only damaging in our development? The damages are obvious; the benefits less so. In the first place, our patterns of jealousy can teach us what we take to be our central traits. It is such experiences as jealousy and our reflections on their patterns, rather than simple introspection, that are the best indicators of the details of our images of ourselves. By also revealing the forms of our attention-dependencies, jealousy can be the first step toward evaluating their directions and appropriateness. Once we recognize our basic attitudes to ourselves, we can in principle either confirm or

reject these attitudes. Not that such confirmation or rejection automatically affects our emotional attitudes! The principles of the conservation of emotions are too strong for that. Yet the strategies of
self-knowledge can develop a position and a *persona* whose activities as investigator and evaluator can in principle sometimes so
strengthen the ego that it becomes less prey to the vulnerabilities of
the transfer of attention. In any case, the revelations of the patterns
of one's images of oneself through such emotions as jealousy can
also reveal the preferences, needs, and principles that are at work,
guiding our choices and decisions. For the aspects of personality
that are at work in fixing our attachments and fears are not isolated: they are expressed in our ordinary decisions and behavior as
well as in the more regional experiences of jealousy. Unmasking the
structures of our jealousy can show us how we operate in other contexts.

Jealousy can be a great teacher in other ways as well. Sometimes
if a person is thrown back upon himself by the loss of attention he
discovers that he can become autonomous in his self-regard. (Children, for instance, often emerge from sibling jealousy with much
strengthened egos, having discovered that they did not depend on
parental regard as much as they had feared.) At first such autonomy is an internalization of the attentional attitudes of some parental figures, whose modes of attention a person has incorporated
as part of their own sense of themselves. (That is why Freud says
that a man whose mother has adored him is invulnerable for life.)
But ironically, a move toward greater autonomy can only occur if a
person has, in other ways, the basis of a relatively stable ego, capable of taking on the strenuous tasks of being one's own audience.
(But these are extremely delicate matters: a strongly protected
autonomous ego may close a person to the possibility of being further formed by the attentive regard of others. The scars that close a
wound protect it against infection: but they can also cause other
damages to the organism by taking on a feverish growth of their
own.)

At its best, then, jealousy can lead to a person's having a better
sense of what is central in his character structure, and developing a
new form of autonomy. But like other emotions that concentrate
on the self, jealousy raises questions about whether there is, at the
core of traits that are central to us, an irreducible *me* that would
remain even if the most central traits were altered.

Because jealousy is a painful and disorienting experience, whose obsessive character undermines a person's sense of his capacities and destroys what might be saved or salvaged from attentive relations, one might think that we would try to school ourselves against it. But precisely because jealousy does raise crucial issues of personal identity and its survival, there are strong blocks in the way of our overcoming jealousy.

One of these is the set of mechanisms by which threatening experiences tend to evoke responses over which we have very little voluntary control, the most powerful of these being the mechanisms that come into play with anxieties of abandonment that seems to bode annihilation. Recognizing that these may be irrational and unrealistic does not generally help a person slough them off, although it may help them, on another level, to prevent their spinning into a heady regress of more and more dangerous and self-destructive attitudes. Sometimes it is helpful if the person whose attentions have shifted insists on retaining some sort of (perhaps newly defined) bond with the jealous person, especially when he can focus attentively on traits and capacities that are brought into play in the task of "coping" with jealousy. But the vulnerabilities and dangers of jealousy do not usually permit such a benign outcome. It is, for instance, common to say to the jealous person "Well, it is true that I am entranced by Chayim's ways of resolving the problems of the kibbutz, but I regard your steadiness and composure in times of trouble as ever I did." But there is the "Catch me if I fall!" as well as the "Look at me!" aspect of attention. Since our vulnerabilities are ever latent in our thoughts, and not unrealistically so, we are always testing our friends and relations for their reliability in countdown situations. O will wonder whether D's continued regard for his steadiness will assure her returning from a delightful vacation in Ashkelon with C, should O fall ill and require attention. The danger is, of course, that O's latent fears of losing D may precipitate illnesses and disasters that would test or to reaffirm D's devotion to him.

The resistance to the cure of jealousy has another source. Though, to be sure, we often profit from regarding ourselves as composed of distinct and separable traits, recognizing that we can be esteemed for some, while being pitied for others, still we do have a strong pull toward the unification of our traits, the unity of our persons. There is one level—and sometimes it is strongly a physical level, because we are *one* organism, that thrives or languishes as a whole—on which we say: but what about *me,* not this or that trait that I may so wonderfully and uniquely have? Sometimes indeed we test those upon whose attentions our sense of ourselves depends, by taunting them with deviations, violations, and disappearances of just those traits we take to be centrally constituted by our relation to them. It is perhaps an infantile maneuver, and it is perhaps a maneuver that a truly secure adult rarely plays out, but the infant generally lurks just a few layers beneath the skin of even the most secure adult. While it is true that we could defend ourselves against jealousy by consenting to separate our traits, recognizing that someone can continue to attend some, while being detached from others, there is a strong resistance to this splitting or disassociation of traits.

The core of the second resistance to the cure of jealousy really rests on the first ground of resistance: we connect our attentive-relations not only to those aspects of our selves that they define but to our general dependence on sustenance in situations where we are truly vulnerable and helpless. If we protect ourselves against the ravages of jealousy by the strategy of separating our traits, we run the danger of damaging our sense of the unity and the protection of our persons. Now one might indeed have a metaphysical view according to which that sense of unity and the protection that goes with it, is an illusion well lost, if only because such a sense generates jealousy and its kin emotions, envy, remorse, guilt.

Whether the sense of the unity of the self and the protections that sense evokes is an illusion, is a question we must leave for another occasion. It is after all a question which has vast ramifications on the theory of agency and responsibility, on choice and rationality, both in psychology and ethics. Until we discover that the conceptions of the ego that underlie our fears are illusions, we do objectively take ourselves to require the attentions of others for our real flourishing. If such notions are illusions, they seem illusions that beings like ourselves inevitably have, with them go the host of attitudes—jealousy, envy, remorse, responsibility—that are conceptually bound up with them.[13] Even when fears of self-destruction are premature and self-defeating, they are not entirely unrealistic fantasies. Without the attentive cooperation of others, individuality starves, physically and psychologically. Perhaps we would be better off without such an idea of individuality: but the idea that we could do without that illusion may itself be an illusion. The drive to connect our traits in a unified entity (Could you love me for myself alone, and not for my yellow hair?) comes from the fragility of many of our traits (and not merely from the fragility of their unification). The continuity of attention to the core *me* assuages the fears that our traits alter and disappear as they tragically do in just those situations where we need others most, in illness, in age, and in situations of social ostracism. One of the drives toward the bonding of attention to the underlying *me* is the quite realistic sense that when we most need others, we are also least likely to have the traits which on the surface once bound them to us. The impulse to bind our traits together in one *whole* person and to feel threatened in that whole, where there are only regional shifts in attention, elicits all the forces that are at work, for good or ill, to aid and to deter the integration and the unification of personality.

OEDIPAL JEALOUSY

There is no denying that male children are jealous of their fathers' claims to their mothers' loyalty and attentions, that they want desperately to have exclusive "right" to their mothers. But it is implausible to attribute affects whose ideational content a child does not yet have, back into early psychological sets. Jealous, they are; and jealous of some forms of possession, they are. But possession of what? And if that possession has a sexual dimension, what is its ideational content?

In most societies, the one haven that a male child has, the one place where he is safe to be exactly what he is, without judgment or expectation, without the striving, the competition that is the tragic fate of the male in virtually every relation, is his relation to his mother. This bond is cemented even more closely by her physical attentions to him, her supplying his basic physical comforts and satisfactions The male child's fear of his mother's relation with his father is his terror that the father will take her into his domain, the domain of the judges. Through her tie with the father, he may lose the one place in the world where he is wholly accepted: physically and psychologically attended and safe. And in fact, at just about the Oedipal phase, the child's fears are realized. The male child that was attended, accepted without demands, comes to receive (from his mother!) demands, expectations, judgment. His mother's attentive regard entirely changes character. Terror ensues. Perhaps if he could have exclusive rights over her, he could return to himself, his kingdom, his world. But he cannot: and so his bitterness and resentment of his mother's treachery sets an undercurrent that remains latent in his relations to the very women from whom he hopes to regain his original haven.

This explains why men are generally more jealous of their wives' sexual fidelity than are women of their husbands'. Men who live, as women rarely do, in a world of endless judgment and comparison, the universal animal terror of the constant hierarchical orderings—a world in which a person's self-esteem is always at stake in every encounter—suffer jealousy in a special way. With rare good fortune, a man can, ideally, hope to recreate in his marriage the conditions of his initial relation with his mother: the relation of unjudgmental, noncomparative attention that combined unconditional allegiance with physical care—the one secure place in the world. Of course the economic structure of family arrangements make that hope elusive: if the husband is unjudged, the breadearner often is. And the recollection of his mother's betrayal—her joining the world of the judges—leaves a man wary, if not actually hostile to the very woman to whom he is most closely bound. Nevertheless, in a traditional marriage, a man can at least expect exclusive sexuality: if he successfully binds his wife's sexuality, he can hope to win the whole attentive bonding as well. Even if that turns out to be an elusive hope, he can at least expect to be sexually secure, safe from the terrible comparison that is his lot in the world. (It is interesting that prostitutes report that their clients seem to want reassurance of their prowess even more than they want sex.)

But if a man's wife sleeps with someone else, the world returns: there is no haven left. He will be compared, he will be judged in that one place where he was secure, most vulnerable because most himself. What, after all, one might ask, is possession, possession *of*? Why is sex thought to give possession of the body? It manifestly does not: strong sexual ecstasy absents the person. The fantasy is that it may give possession of the person. But what can that possibly mean? It may of course mean the power of control, of physical control, and the control of a person's objective social fate. But why should sexual relations be thought to be the key to such extraordinary power? It is because it is thought to be, and sometimes actually is, an assurance of unconditional, unjudgmental attentive acceptance. The excitement of adult male sexuality comes in part from the hope that sexual bonding will assure him what he had received in infancy from his mother: physical satisfaction from an unjudgmental other. The tragedy is closely related: the satisfaction of such hopes continues infantilism. (This is only one of the reasons that sexual play often also has a strong infantile character.)

But jealous fears are closely linked to the corresponding terror of engulfment. The desire for exclusive possession is paired with a contrary desire: the desire for autonomy and individuality. Most of our basic drives are paired in contraries: the drive to exploration matched with that to withdraw, the cycles of sleep and activity, hunger and satisfaction, the need for companionship and the need for solitude, the cycles of slow and fast pacing of activity. We shall not understand the dispositional character of our motivational system until we trace the self-regulating, self-generating cycles of these paired contraries. To understand how male sexual jealousy operates, it is also necessary to understand its paired contrary fear: the fear of absorption and containment, of engulfment. (The desire— and the terror—of the womb.) There is, then, a cycle in which the male child depends on the nonjudgmental attention of his female; yet fears that if he is absorbed, wrapped in that attention, he will lose his powers, his identity in the father's world. The need for activity and daring, for exploration and testing pulls him away... and into the dangerous world where he is judged. There is a cycle of forays into the world, followed by a return to safety. But the danger of safety is engulfment and debility; and the danger of individual activity is exposure and judgment. The man turns to the woman with conflicting needs: unconditional acceptance on the one hand, and recognition and appraisal of his individual achievements on the other. He wants, and fears, the return to infantilism: and his jealousy bears the stamp of that conflict.

And the girl child? Characteristically, the love she receives from her father comes much later than the love the male child receives from his mother, and the father's love is not unconditional. An important part of a father's love for his daughter is that she does not—as do his sons—pose a judgmental threat to him. The attentive regard that a girl receives from her father gives her the self-image of a nonevaluative, nonjudgmental female. That is one of the ways that she is prepared for being a mother, and it is one of the sources of her later compliance and her fears of competing with males. An initial condition of her father's love is that she never enter into competitive relations with him. (And, of course, no father can secure such assurances from his sons; because he identifies with them, he sets them the general tasks of emulation and striving, even while trying to control their relation to him). A boy comes to regard his mother as a traitress: she withdrew the kind of attention she had once given. But a girl does not experience her father as a traitor: the constraint that marks her relation to her father was part of the initial condition of the relation. And that is why a woman's jealousy focuses, typically, on another woman's ability-to-attract-the-attention-of-the-male, while a man's jealousy, typically, focuses on his wife's-attention-to-some-other-man. It is because a wife's infidelity returns a man to the world of competitive judgment that such infidelity automatically lowers his place in the world. It is for this reason that men are more prey than women to jealousy over sexual infidelity. Because women's social realities are fixed by their dependence on male attention, they are more subject to nonsexual jealousy than men are. They also are more likely than men to suffer envy of the traits and properties they suppose would assure them the attentions they think they require.

Female jealousy tends to be directed to matters of practical dependence. Even when a woman is strongly bonded sexually, it is rare—and this is evident in polygamous societies—that female jealousy is strictly sexual. Women's attentional jealousy arises from their social condition. A woman's well-being in the world depends on her male's continued attachment to her. If she loses it, every detail of her life—the goods and the respect she can command—is subject to change. Her place in her man's world is her place in the world. In societies where widows depend upon their sons for livelihood and status, women are naturally prone to jealousy toward their daughters-in-law, who represent a clear threat, as rivals for the attentions, the goods and services that the son/husband distributes. The daughters-in-law are, in turn, jealous of their mothers-in-law's attempt to control their sons. In such cases the command of attention is clearly a command of sustenance and objective social status.

The asymmetries of patterns of male and female jealousy are closely related to the asymmetries of their affectional bonding. Characteristically, women attach themselves—or, in traditional societies, are attached by their parents—to males who are thought their superiors, by whatever the goods the society trades: power, money, wealth, strength, age. Psychology and practicality go hand in hand. But, as long as a female's status and character is not so low as to bring a man shame that he can command no better, he need not particularly care about the character of his female. What he requires from her is not wealth, cleverness, or status, but competent physical care and children. Indeed, a markedly higher status is, traditionally, a potential threat to his command and control of her. For an ambitious man, there is often a difficult choice: whether to improve his status by connecting himself to a family that will provide dowry, lands, and well-placed patrons (thus running the risk of being a lowly figure in his household, a petitioner where he should be lord) or to assure his dominance in his household by making a marriage that can bring him no advancement. In polygamous societies, the problem is often solved by two marriages: the first, to a person of lesser status whose labor advances a man to the point where he can afford a second alliance to a higher-born woman. Characteristically, the pattern of the male's jealousy will then differ for his two marriages.

These social and economic differences also help to explain some of the differences in the imagistic and obsessional thoughts to which men and women are subject. Characteristically, the male does not, after the first stages of an infatuation or bonding, wish to know very much about his women's thoughts, interests, preoccupations. Because the women are objectively dependent on their men, any narration of their condition and their experiences constitutes or implies a complaint the man might be expected to redress. But it is just this dependence that requires a woman to be closely apprised of her man's moods, thoughts, foibles, penchants. Her well-being depends on her intimate knowledge of his traits—and on her ability to use that knowledge. This difference feeds directly into the differences in their respective jealous thoughts: the man is more likely to concentrate on what the woman *does* and the woman on what a man thinks or feels, as a clue to her own well-being.

It is these political origins of male and female psychological attitudes that Freud and early analysts missed. Virtually all of their analytic patients were thoroughly middle class. But a child who comes to see that the parent, on whose attentive regard his sense of himself depends, is a poor thing in the world, undergoes a terrible and dangerous humiliation. It is, of course, a political social and economic humiliation. But it is also—for these matters are by no means independent—a psychic humiliation that affects development. The patterns of adult attachments, their expectations and fears, their jealousies, are affected by such a child's shame and anger at his parents.

Of course a male child generally sees what a poor place in the world his mother has: the social, economic, and often political limitations on his mother's power. That recognition affects his relation to her: he must of course in any case cut off any identification he had originally made with her. But since she was originally also his source of self-esteem, that self-esteem is jeopardized as he sees that her judgment counts for little in the larger world. In coming to have contempt for her, he undermines himself. And as Lawrence has so brilliantly shown in *Sons and Lovers,* when the son is the bearer of the mother's social ambitions, her desperate hopes and ambitions for him leave him in a whirl of confusion. While she has not joined the father's forms of judgment, she has imposed on him tasks whose shape he cannot understand. And on her part, her identification with him leaves her prey to later ambivalences of pride and jealousy at his having a relation to the world, claims on its attention, that she cannot ever have.

The son who sees that his father is as poor a thing in the world as his mother is, suffers a debilitating form of anguish. If he strongly identifies with his father, he fears the possibility of his own success, and the threat that it may pose to the father. But more frequently, the perception of the father's powerlessness makes identification with the father much more difficult. The son must then prove that he is, as his father was not, a powerful man. That is one of the reasons that one often finds, among the socially and politically powerless, a strong and often desperate determination to male powerfulness, and a corresponding intense susceptibility to the need for exclusive possession of the female, a jealousy often more intense than that suffered by those who sense themselves to have wordly power.

Interestingly enough, a father's social and political powerlessness does not affect his daughters as much as it does his sons. Of course it affects them in important ways, simply because the reality of their lives is affected by their father's ability to command the goods of the world. But it does not affect their psychological development in the same way, because their initial judgment of their father's powers was never in question. A daughter's perception of her mother's powerlessness, especially if she has strongly identified with the mother, would induce depression rather than jealousy, even when she sees a mother suffering from a father's infidelities. If she does not strongly identify with her mother, she is likely to be angry rather than jealous or depressed, and to be angry at her mother rather than at her father. Frequently, since daughters who attempt not to identify with their mothers nevertheless on some level do accept the identification, one generally finds that women suffer anxious ambivalence rather than simple anger.[14]

NOTES

1. Cf. G. Foster, "The Anatomy of Envy," *Current Anthropology* XIII (1972). H. Schoeck, *Envy: A Theory of Social Behavior* (New York: Harcourt Brace and World, 1969). D. W. Winnicott, "Transitional Objects and Transitional Phenomena," *Collected Papers* (London: Tavistock Publications, 1958).

Margaret Gilbert and Gareth Matthews have pointed out that my analysis focuses on what might be called dark and heavy cases. They produced many convincing examples of light and passing jealousy, that do not require strong fears at all, let alone fears of abandonment. A woman might be jealous that her partner spends too much time with someone else at a party; a child might be jealous that someone else gets a slightly larger piece of cake. These cases need not be disqualified as bona fide instances of jealousy because there is nothing strong enough to be called *fear* that provokes them. I think that is right: and yet, in such cases, we are generally puzzled about why the person should be *jealous* at all. Often, it is a serious question whether a person is jealous, rather than piqued or angry. Following the suggestions developed by Jerry Neu, I think that if a person is *disposed* to passing light jealousy, when the occasions seem to present no threat, it is because the conditions for dark and heavy jealousy obtain in the background. A child prone to passing jealous outbursts is one who generally fears some losses, even though he does not fear a particular loss on a particular occasion. A woman need not fear the loss of her husband to this, that, or the other acquaintance made at a party; but if she characteristically requires her husband's attentions at social gatherings, she suffers an underlying fear.

2. Stanley Cavell, "The Claim of Reason," (New York: Oxford University Press, 1979), Part Four, chap. 13.

3. Cf. Selma Fraiberg, *Insights from the Blind* (New York: Basic Books, 1977). Margaret Mahler, *On Human Symbiosis and the Vicissitudes of Individuation* (New York: Universities Press, 1968). René Spitz, *The First Year of Life* (New York: International Universities Press, 1965).

4. Cf. Jerome Neu, "Jealous Thoughts," this volume, chap. 18. I found Neu's paper enormously useful and stimulating: indeed much of my paper is a development of ideas and suggestions contained in his essay.

5. Melanie Klein, "Some Theoretical Considerations Regarding the Emotional Life of the Infant," *Envy and Gratitude* (New York: Delta, 1977); Rudolph Schaffer, *Mothering* (Cambridge, Mass.: Harvard University Press, 1977); Daniel Stern, *The Developing Child* (Cambridge: Harvard University, 1977); Judy Dunn, *Distress and Comfort* (Cambridge: Harvard University Press, 1977); T. Alloway, L. Krames, P. Pliner, eds., *Attachment Behavior* (New York: Plenum Press, 1975).

6. Erving Goffman, *Interaction Behavior* (New York, Anchor Books, 1967); idem, *Strategic Interaction* (Oxford: Basil Blackwell, 1970); T. Alloway, L. Krames, P. Pliner, eds., *Communication and Affect* (New York: Academic Press, 1972).

7. Cf. Ronald de Sousa, "Self-Deceptive Emotions," this volume, chap. 11.

8. Freud, "Some Neurotic Mechanisms in Jealousy, Paranoia and Homosexuality" (1922). Standard Edition, vol. 28; Freud, "On Narcissism" (1914), *Standard Edition*, vol. 22; Michael Lewis and Leonard Rosenblum, eds., *The Origins of Fear* (New York: Wiley and Sons, 1974).

9. Sartre, *The Emotions: Outline of a Theory* (New York: The Philosophical Library, 1948).

10. Cf. Michael Stocker, "Intellectual Desire, Emotion and Action," this volume, chap. 13.

11. Anna Freud, *The Ego and the Mechanisms of Defense* (New York: International Universities Press, 1946). Also, Amélie O. Rorty, "Weakness, Imagination, and the Self," unpublished manuscript.

12. Cf. Amélie Rorty, "Explaining Emotions," this volume, chap. 4.

13. Cf. Spinoza, *The Ethics,* Part II-IV, and Kant, *The Critique of Pure Reason,* The Antinomies and Paralogisms.

14. I am grateful to Amélie Rorty for the hospitality that made the writing of this paper possible. She was kind enough to make available to me a number of the papers published in this volume: stimulated by them, and by her skeptical questions, I was able to work through some problems that arose from Stanley Cavell's interpretation of *Othello.* Discussions with Marcia Aufhauser and Margaret Gilbert were helpful; Genevieve Lloyd contributed many substantive and organizational suggestions for which I am very grateful. Correspondence with Liam Hudson provoked the section on Oedipal Jealousy. As always in such matters, literary sources are the richest, not only *Othello* and *Remembrance of Things Past* but also novels by Henry James, Ivy Compton-Burnett, the Brontë sisters.

XX

AGENT REGRET

AMÉLIE OKSENBERG RORTY

Andrea is the director of a wild animal refuge in Kenya. The animals under her care are thriving; indeed the lions are flourishing so well that their over-population endangers some of the rare species that are their natural prey. After painful deliberation, Andrea issues an order to the park wardens that a certain number of lions must be killed. She herself shoots one of those creatures in whose larger freedom her heart delights. A beautiful animal leaps up, twirls, falls dead. While her regret is terrible to her, she also feels a moment of exulta-tion, a wild sense of her power commingled with her grief at what she had had to do.

Natasha and her daughter Sasha are building a table together. They are nearly finished: there is one more nail around the edging to go. Although the main point of the project had been to encourage Sasha's confidence in her manual skills, Natasha mindlessly leans over and hammers in the last nail. As she ob-serves the fall in Sasha's face, she feels a stab of regret: she has wrecked the whole enterprise, and no amount of celebrating with chocolate cake to inaugu-rate the table will undo what she has done. Regretfully, she reflects on her fail-ures as a mother.

What are the conditions for agent regret? In what does it consist? What follows from it? What are its benefits and dangers? What is its moral worth?

1. If an agent A regrets having done something, having brought about a state of affairs E, then he believes that he has contributed to the occurrence of E, and characteristically, he judges that E is harmful, bad, or undesirable.

Regret is triply intentional; (a) Its object is regretted under a description that cannot be substituted *salva affectione;* (b) The cause of a person's coming to regret what he has done affects him under a description; (c) The norms that govern the proper objects of regret are intentional.

a) An event is regretted under a description; regret need not be preserved when an extensionally equivalent description is substituted. The objects of regret have two components, an event or state of affairs, and the agent's action in bringing about that state of affairs. Characteristically, the agent regrets his action because he regrets the state of affairs to which it has contributed. But it is possible for a person to regret *his* having brought about *E,* without regretting *E.* (He may, for instance, think it is important for someone else to enjoy the satisfaction of having brought about *E.*) Of course *A* may be mistaken about whether *E* has occurred, and whether his action was a contributory cause: but his regret is genuine for all that. Even if he discovers his errors and ceases to regret, still he *had* regretted.

The regretted event is normally in the past or present. But one can regret something that one intends to do, or something one is convinced one is likely to do. It is also possible to regret an event that is the consequence of a conditional, and to regret the whole conditional. A person can regret that if he were to be pressed in dire circumstances, he would act in a harmful or undesirable way. While he cannot now regret something embedded in a conditional whose antecedent he regards as improbable, he can now regret being the sort of person who would, under these circumstances, perform an action of a type he considers regrettable. Such character regret is agent regret if the person also regrets what he did to become that sort of person, regrets his part in the formation of his character. But a person can regret traits over whose development he has no control. (Sometimes such regret becomes more subtle by becoming more diffuse. "The time is out of joint;—O cursed spite that I was born to set it right!" Hamlet regrets that he is so situated that he must act against his nature; and yet what he must do follows from his being the person he is: a loving loyal regal son. Despite his detached ironic character, it falls to him to enact an ancient violent justice. Yet another subtle and even more diffuse form of character regret is shown by Hardy's figures. The situations of Henchard and Tess carry such power because it is unclear to them—and to us— whether they regret what they do, or their natures, their characters, or whether their regrets are more properly directed to the impersonal wind-shift forces of time and chance which again and again bring the course of their lives to tragedy. Dostoyevsky portrays even starker forms of character regret. *Notes from the Underground* presents a figure whose regret is not regional or situational: he regrets being himself. It may be paradoxical to regret every single one of one's characteristics, including the capacity for, and the tendency to regret. Still, there are Dostoyevskian figures who believe themselves to be in that condition, who live out lives of regret, however logically incoherent their attitudes may be.)

b) Genuine regret must have the right sort of causal history. Although the cause of regret can be quite distinct from its object, it must stand in some continuous causal line to the object of regret, and crucial links in that causal line must be intentional. Someone may come to regret an action because he suffers from an action similar to his own; or he can be struck by a novel that describes a similar action. But these can only cause him to regret what he did if he interprets them in a certain light, if he "takes them in" as similar to what he did, and as regrettable.

c) The objects of regret have a normative intentional description. While there are no limits to the range of objects extensionally identified as objects of regret, there are intentional constraints on the objects of regret. There are significant cultural and individual variations in the objects of regret: birth can be regretted and death the object of rejoicing; the Ik are said to rejoice in the wanton and deliberate wounding of a friend and to regret marriages. Nevertheless, although anything can in principle be thought regrettable, it can only be regretted insofar as it is thought to be in some way bad, damaging, harmful. And while there are also cultural and subjective variations in some norms for what is bad, damaging, or harmful, these conditions are open to objective and independent evaluation. They introduce the propriety of a rational critique of individual cases of regret.

There are many intentional attitudes whose objects do not provide grounds or reasons for the attitude. Our likes and dislikes do not have rationales. One can like or dislike the fishy saltiness of anchovies, but neither taste is justified by the fishy saltiness: it does not provide the reason or ground for the attitude. Getting the intentional description of such attitudes just right can be a very important and even a practical matter: but it is not in itself a matter for rational justification. (For manufacturers of foodstuffs from petroleum wastes, it is an important question whether consumers like fishy saltiness of a certain texture, or whether they like the fishy saltiness of *anchovies*. Whether consumers buy and eat petroleum waste fishy saltiness of a certain texture rather than anchovies is subject to rational evaluation: but what is evaluated is what one eats, not what one likes. Because there is a strong connection between what one eats and what one likes, it is rational to give critical attention to one's tastes. But it is one's general health, and not the intentional description of the object of one's tastes, which grounds or justifies one's attitudes.)

It is a matter of contention whether some attitudes—love, for example—have rationales, whether the descriptions of their proper objects also give the ground or justification of the attitude. But (with the exception of Sartre), there is a consensus that there are norms for regret, that it can be unfounded or required, appropriate or unreasonable. Getting the intentional description of the object of regret just right is a feature in determining its rationale; it is a necessary stage in evaluating the attitude for its appropriateness and justification. Of course the simplest norm for regret is assured by the minimal conditions for rationality built into intentionality. If a person's description of an event fails to apply, his regret is unfounded. But even when the intentional description applies, there is a further question of whether a person ought to regret his agency. His description of the event and of his agency in bringing it about may be nominally correct: truth functional conditions are satisfied. But his description may overemphasize incidental features of the event, and relegate central features to the periphery of his attention. The norm governing the intentional description of events and agency goes beyond truth conditions: a person's nominally accurate description may fail to accord with the normic description.

Cultural and moral norms set constraints on the descriptions of actions that justify reactive, evaluative attitudes: for example, pride, indignation, regret. Because the criteria for injury vary even among subcultures, judgments about the appropriateness of regret vary. There are also cultural variations in the conceptual connections that are thought to hold between regret and other attitudes. For instance, in some cultures, regret presupposes fear: regret without fear of divine punishment would in such cultures be not only irrational or inappropriate, but anomalous to the point of pathology. (Of course it remains an important question whether, when some of the norms for its identification and evaluations vary, "regret" remains the same, or merely an analogous, or a wholly distinct attitude.)

There are also moral constraints or norms for regret: a person who fails to see that some of his actions are harmful, or who, while seeing the harm, focuses on his pleasures in performing the action, is morally flawed. While there is legitimate moral disagreement about what is genuinely harmful, there is none about the conceptual connection between agent regret and agent responsibility for wanton, pointless harm.

The proper objects of regret cover a wide range of harmful or undesirable events: there is a wide spectrum between passing light regret to dark and heavy regret. But even the strongest regret might be insufficient for some actions. Someone who pushed the button that began a nuclear holocaust is frivolous if he (merely) regretted what he had done. Conversely, a person who managed to concentrate on the negative features of every centrally joyful event is morose rather than sensitive.

2. A need not be wholly responsible for the occurrence of E. Indeed his contribution need not be voluntary, let alone deliberate. A person might unwittingly be an intermediate cause of an event he regards as deplorable. (A driver whose car was hit from behind might regret having injured a pedestrian.) His thoughts could run in two directions: if he focuses primarily on the event rather than on his agency, his thoughts turn to the *pedestrian*'s pain, to the possibility of his being crippled. If the driver focused primarily on his own agency, his thoughts turn to *his* contribution in the causal sequence: "If only I hadn't decided to go to the movies in the pouring rain.... If only I had had the brakes tightened.... If only I hadn't passed the car in the last block." His rehearsals of scenarios of the effects of his action or scenarios of events that could have shifted the causal sequence are constitutive parts of his regret.

Conceptually, but not analytically, agent regret presupposes event regret; but the event that the agent brings about need not be regarded by him as wholly undesirable, or even undesirable as a whole. Characteristically, there is some aspect or feature of E that A considers in a negative light. If it is E that A regrets, then those negative features are regarded by A as central or essential to E. But the focus of regret need not be E as such; it can be some negative feature that is incidental to E. The agent then regrets E only incidentally: he would regret any event insofar as it had the negative feature that is the primary object of regret. For the occurrence of regret, although not for its justification, it is the perceived, rather than the actual centrality of the negative feature that counts.

While regret presupposes a judgment that an action or a state of affairs is bad, undesirable, or harmful, not every judgment that an event or action has these negative qualities imbeds or entails regret. Someone may wish to produce just these harmful effects in the knowledge of—and even because of—their negative features (Iago). But secondly, also, a person can, without pathology, consider the negative features of an event so intrinsically bound with desirable featues that he does not actively regret the negative features, even though he sees them for what they are. His attitude toward those features is modulated by his view of their intrinsic connection with their beneficial features (an attitude that many women have toward childbirth, and many parents to the rigors of child-rearing).

3. "A regrets his doing E" is ambiguous between "A regrets E and A regrets being a contributory cause of E" and "A regrets his being the person who caused E to occur, whether or not he regrets E."

Parents, teachers, and others engaged in maieutic activities often regret their interventions in a course of action they believe in itself beneficial. A mother making a table with her daughter, a man baking a cake with his niece, a teacher engaged in discussion with students, a physical therapist working with a patient—may regret banging in the last nail, pouring in the chocolate, drawing the conclusion from the argument, reaching down to pick up the book that was dropped. What is regretted is not the action, but the presumption of agency. This can sometimes be quite subtle: it can be the timing, or the place, or the mode or tone that can be regretted. Of course these details, including whose hand performed the motions, can be included in the expanded action description, and it is the action caught by the expanded description that is regretted, and not that described by the rough general schematic outline.

Schematic descriptions of regret can be quite misleading; only when an event is described in considerable detail does it become possible to see the rationale of regret. Sometimes the addition of detail in the description of the object of regret does not significantly change the intentional object, and so leaves the attitude unchanged. For instance, when Natasha regrets having hammered in the last nail on the edging of the table she and Sasha made, she also regrets having hammered in the nail at just the point at the edging where it entered. Her regret would not have been changed had she focused on the nail entering several centimeters to the left. But sometimes the addition of a detail significantly alters the intentional object. A person may not regret an action, but the fine details of the way it was done, the tone of voice, the arch lift of the eyebrow. Sometimes a regret that appears in the schematic outline, the thin description of the event, disappears in the finer-grained description; sometimes a regret that does not attach to the rough schematic description of an action is captured by the net of a finer description.

4. It is not a condition of regret that the agent would undo the action if he could.

A person can believe that he has taken the proper course, a course he would not undo, and yet regretfully takes that course. The easy cases are of course those that the agent regrets under one description and does not regret under another. It is then only nominally, at a very general level of description, that the person regrets the same action that he also underwrites and approves. When the full description of the intentional object is specified, what is regretted is distinguished from what is approved. (Faced by severe financial cutbacks over which she has no control, an employer might regretfully "let go" [i.e., fire; it may be morally important to be clear about what one is doing] a sweet man with five children, an ailing wife, and a senile father, in order to retain an inventive, productive free-lancing young woman who could easily get another job. The employer might regret that she had been unable to prevent having to make such a terrible choice. But she need not regret being forced to that decision: she might believe that even under the best of circumstances the staff was too large, and the man a terrible bumbler, however fine his moral character. So she may regret that the man will in all probability be unemployed, regret his situation, and yet not wish she could have been able to prevent his being fired. She can regret what she does under one description, but not under another.)

Often, however, the separation between the intentional description of the regrettable and the desirable features of a complex action involves self-deception. While the two aspects or features of the complex action may be logically or intentionally distinct, each with its own proper object, there may nevertheless be a strong causal connection between the two aspects or features of the event. What one approves (under one description) and what one regrets (under another) may be so bound together that their separability is only logical or notional. When that is so, insistence on simple rationality can be a piece of moral evasion. When there is a strong relation between the regretted and the approved features—a causal relation, or a relation of subsumption under normic descriptions— it is morally and practically important to attend to the mutual dependence of what is regrettable and what is desirable, to assume the larger responsibility. (If she were to take such an attitude, the employer might for example, try to help the man find another job: her regret for his condition would remain agent regret, rather than becoming event regret. Rather than treating his unemployment as a state-of-affairs, she would recognize it as a state-of-affairs her decision had brought about.)

5. Regret is characteristically felt as a particular sort of painful feeling, a pang, a stab, waves of stabs, relatively low keyed in comparison with remorse or guilt.

It is because the standard feelings of regret are painful, and because we tend to focus on pain when it is present, that regret often swerves inward from the action to the agent. While regret is characterized by certain sorts of thoughts and postures, no particular actions need follow from it. Nevertheless a person can behave regretfully—apologize, take some remedial steps—without being, or feeling regretful. But standardly, if one feels regretful, one is so, even though a person can be regretful without feeling himself so, or even being aware that he is regretful. A friend, observing someone's cast of face and following the trend of his thoughts, can ask, "What is it that you are regretting?" bringing it to the person's attention that he is, in fact, regretful. It is, of course, much easier to recognize that someone is regretful than to determine what he regrets, although very close acquaintance can sometimes assure that. (It is a moot point whether a person who has been unaware of his regret nevertheless had a feeling of which he was unaware, or whether, in such cases, the person didn't have the regretful feelings at all.)

Although regret is often roughly identified by a certain sort of feeling, posture, and facial expression, and although a person can be aware of feeling regret without being aware of what he regrets, the feeling is not sufficient for genuine regret, or its proper identification. To qualify as a feeling of regret, the feeling must have certain sorts of intentional objects, be accompanied by certain sorts of thoughts. If some bizarre accident of digestion produced just the sort of wave of stabs and pangs, just that hangdog posture, vacant sadness of the eyes that are the marks of regret, one would not call the attitude regretful (unless one was regretting having eaten stale bagels). The feeling must be associated with a causal story that connects it to its proper intentional object, in order to qualify as regret.

That causal story essentially includes certain types of thoughts, imaginative scenarios, characteristic sorts of speech, as well as certain sorts of bodily stance. One's friends can diagnose one's regrets, because one's conversations have specific themes, picking out and elaborating the negative features of one's actions. A person can have such thoughts, engage in such conversation at great length and in great detail without reflectively recognizing that the pattern of his thoughts is the pattern of regret. He might simply rehearse, in what is often an obsessive way, the negative features of his action, dwelling on how it would have been better if... and if..., giving voice to regret without realizing it. A person's thoughts about the object of regret, generates a characteristic feeling, which then itself generates further thoughts, scenarios of what one has done, instant replays of this angle and that, how it could have gone differently. These thoughts then cause more regretful feelings, which then again produce yet more scenarios, long range imagined effects, and so on. The thoughts of the consequences of one's action generate painful feelings and the painful feelings generate yet further imaginative scenarios and thoughts, all directed to the negative features of the intentional object. What I have described as a causal sequence can take place virtually simultaneously: the thought and the feeling can be completely interwoven. Nevertheless, regret characteristically lasts over time, and characteristically it is the entire causal sequence of thoughts and feelings that identify it.

(Although it is exceedingly obscure, Hume's account of the double relation between ideas and impressions as identifying certain sorts of passions is an attempt to give a conceptual account of a passion by characterizing the complex causal relation between the feelings and the ideas that are typical of the passion. It is the entire causal sequence described on the type level that identifies the passion. This is quite compatible with holding that the particular ideational content of individual instances of an emotion-type is only contingently connected with the associated feeling. Because particular ideas (token instances) can be associated with, and indeed the subject of different and even opposed passions, Hume thought the passion could neither be reducible to, nor fully identified by the associated idea. Nevertheless, the association between the feeling-type and the idea-type is lawlike. That the feeling-type cannot be identified independently of its place in the causal story presents an epistemological problem for classifying individual token instances of the passions; but it does not invalidate the analysis. Indeed, that problem confirms the analysis: these are exactly the problems we *do* have in identifying emotions.)

6. Although it is often difficult to distinguish regretful feelings from closely allied emotions with similar painful feeling tones—shame, guilt, remorse, self-recrimination—they are distinguished by their related characteristic thoughts.

Shame tends to involve obsessive imagistic replays of the moment of exposure, to be expressed in the focused remembering of the event, as if time were arrested. In regret, the imagination has freer play: the action's long-range consequences are explored, the possible preventive alternatives investigated. Characteristically, shame presupposes regret: but it has an additional condition of publicity: the pain the person feels at the action is that of having been seen to perform it, or being recognized as the sort of person who would perform it. (That is why the physical expression of shame involves motions of hiding oneself.) The condition of publicity can be internalized when the shamed person is his own witness; private shame is derivative from imagined public shame. In cultures or contexts where a person's sense of his agency *is* his sense of how he is perceived, regret and shame can coincide. There is some indication that children acquire regret by first acquiring a sense of shame-before-others. On some accounts there are cultures where shame is the primary moral response: in such cultures, regret is internalized shame, rather than shame being a regret that takes place under special conditions of actual or imagined publicity.

When regretful thoughts are strongly obsessive, they can move toward remorse or guilt, especially when the person focuses so strongly on himself that he becomes the proper object of his attitude. In extreme cases, the physical expressions of guilt are distinguishable from those of regret: there is a tightening of the muscles, a retraction of the limbs, as if the person were trying to make himself smaller. These attitudes are on the dark and heavy side of regret: the person would undo the actions if he could.

Self-recrimination differs from regret in the stance the person takes toward himself as the agent. Regret can (but need not) be quite direct and unselfconscious: the person need not even be aware of himself as judging his action. Self-recrimination is, in contrast, self-conscious. It presupposes a division within the self: a judge holds an accused on trial, determines culpability. One holds oneself accountable, blames oneself. The inner dialogues can be quite complex: one can defend oneself against one's self-recrimination. Characteristically, self-recriminatory thoughts take verbal form: unlike regretful thoughts, the projected scenarios are rarely imagistic.

(But these are highly speculative matters: while the descriptive characterization of these attitudes has empirical implications, it is by no means clear [at this stage] how they could be established, except by appeal to introspection and experience.)

7. Is agent regret a condition for *akrasia?* Aristotle thinks it is (1150b 30-31). And in a way, that seems right. For if someone merely notices, with amused interest, that he has voluntarily acted contrary to his judgment about what is best in a particular situation, we suppose there is more of an explanation in the background. Either he does not really, after all, hold the preferred judgment; or he is deceiving himself in some way; or he is incapable of taking himself seriously enough as a responsible agent to be one, let alone to have failed to be one. (Someone whom Kierkegaard would describe as being in the Aesthetic stage would be incapable of akrasia, because there is no presumption of integrity between his judgment and his action.) Of course in a particular case, a person might have accidentally found unexpected benefits from acting contrary to his judgment; his great delight might well make it diffi-

cult for him to regret what he has done. But if his delight (and only his delight) causes him to revise his original judgment, it would be tendentious to insist that he behaved akratically.

Our intuitions on this issue appear to conflict: on the one hand, it seems quite possible that a person might behave akratically—and even acknowledge that he had done so—without actively regretting what he had done. On the other hand, too easy a detachment, too uniform an amusement, seems suspect: the conditions for responsible agency are undermined. This is not merely an epistemological point about the difficulties of assuring the conditions for voluntary actions, the difficulties of attributing and identifying a person's beliefs and desires. It is a problem about identifying akrasia. Akrasia requires the right sort of causal history, the appropriate sort of agent. The *akrates* must be capable of voluntary action: capable of forming, and being guided by, reasoned judgments. Such a person must also be capable of taking second order attitudes toward his actions: pride, regret, shame, and the like. Of course it is not necessary that a person take second order attitudes toward each and every action, passing out gold stars or black marks.

The apparent conflict in our intuitions can be reconciled. While regret is not necessary for every case of akrasia, it is characteristic for the akrates to regret what he has done. The capacity for taking certain sorts of attitudes toward one's actions is a condition for being the sort of responsible agent who can behave akratically. If such a person does not regret having acted contrary to his judgment, there is a strong presumption that the absence of regret has an explanation.

When regret accompanies akrasia, it must be of the appropriate kind, with the appropriate intentional description. The akrates does not regret his action merely because it was, as it turned out, disappointing, boring, without the delights it promised. The object of his regret must also fall under the description that identifies it as akratic: he must regret it as a violation of his judgment about what is best. His regret is not merely incidental to the primary intentional description of the action as it was performed. Of course all the epistemological problems remain: self-deception, and all the difficulties of attributing beliefs and desires in opaque contexts may make it difficult to determine whether the conditions have been met.

8. "Another sort of false prayers are our regrets. Discontent...
is infirmity of will. Regret calamities if you can thereby help the
sufferer; if not, attend to your own work...." (Emerson, *Self-
Reliance*). Like most attitudes that increase moral sensitivity, especially those attitudes that do not have an action component, or that
do not straightaway motivate to action, regret has built-in dangers.
Among other things, it can become a self-indulgent attitude. Although it is basically a painful attitude for a person to have, it can
also become bittersweet, especially when the focus is on the agent
rather than on the action. For people who are unsure of themselves
as agents, whose sense of their own existence and power is fragile,
regret can be reassuring. A person can savor regret, even wallow in
it, dramatizing its occasions. If he receives comfort and sympathy
for his regret, he can use regret as a way of turning acquaintance
into friendship or intimacy. Confessions of regret can be disarm-
ing, even addictive. "I've done something I regret.... Comfort
me!" Eliciting sympathy can come to be the whole point of regret.
Some people become regret-oriented or of a regretful cast of mind,
and can even develop regretfulness as a character trait, focusing on
the harmful aspect of their actions, even when they are also aware
of the joyful and beneficial aspects. In extreme and pathological
cases, a person may even perform harmful actions for the sake of
being able to regret them.

Nevertheless, despite its addictive dangers, regret has moral significance. Because it is a painful feeling that agents are motivated
to avoid, properly focused regret can conduce to agent respon-
siblity, sensitizing a person to preventive and remedial measures.
But its moral value is not limited to its negative force. It is also
morally important to be aware of the harmful and undesirable features of desirable actions. Too easy a separation of the objects of
approval and of regret can lead a person to become undiscriminat-
ing: keeping alert to the regrettable aspects of even those actions of
which one approves—not dwelling on those features, but also not
denying them—is a way of keeping one's moral sensitivities alert.
The capacities exercised in some forms of regret and the capacities
exercised in moral choice are the same: both involve empathic
imagination, a fine sense of the damaging consequences and tonalities of one's actions. Both require precision of attention, delicacy

of discrimination: their "positive" exercise is inseparable from the "negative" reflection. The attempt to extinguish or dampen the capacity for regret damages just those sensitivities that are exercised in moral action. One cannot be sensitive to possible harms, but ignore them when one has done them.

Nevertheless, regret is not itself strongly tied to remedial or retributive action. It is not in and of itself a practical attitude: its moral value comes primarily from its effects on the habits and dispositions of the agent. The most effective assuagement of the pains of regret is action. A person who becomes absorbed in trying to remedy the negative consequences of his action rarely *feels* regret, because his thoughts and attention are not on what he did, but on what he is trying to do. Regret is in the background, a causal factor in the remedial action. Such action can acquire its own momentum and interest: the original motivating cause is not continuously required to assure the continuity of action. But often it is psychologically easier to direct remedial action to another representative of the same class rather than to the original victim, whose reproachful stance tends to inhibit the agent's good will. We become absorbed in the details of what we do, and that absorption generates its own sustaining motivation. Inventiveness comes into play, and regretful thoughts recede; a person's sense of exercising his capacities responsibly replaces his sense of regret. (Sometimes those who have been harmed find themselves in a dilemma: do they want the agent to continue to feel his regret? Or do they want constructive help from him? Often the two are incompatible.)

9. Rarely, if ever, do we feel only one psychological attitude at a time. Our conditions are defined against the background of a complex field of other attitudes, nestling in a set of presuppositional relations; or standing in contributory and supplementary relations; or in oppositions to one another. Our attitudes are defined in part by the company they keep: we often are quite unable to identify an attitude that appears briefly, atomistically as an isolated episode.

Interestingly, sometimes an attitude receives further determination by coexisting opposed attitudes that enhance and magnify it. For instance, regret is sometimes, but not always accompanied by glee, amusement, exuberance, or even self-righteousness. This is particularly true when the action has been voluntary or deliberate: the motives that led in the direction of the regretted action were, after all, satisfied, and that satisfaction remains side by side with the regret. Characteristically our reactions to actions are: delight, dismay, impish glee, regret, sober reflection, vertigo, a sense of the antic comic, sobriety, pride, self-exculpation-with-self-righteousness, a swirl of conflicted and subtly balanced attitudes. Of course these can be quite muted, almost unnoticeable. Many of our actions so flow from one to another, within a directed activity, that we do not take any particularly noticeable attitudes toward them individually. Nevertheless, the undercurrents of our affective reactions to what we do are the raw materials to our more reflective evaluative stances.

What then is one to make of the claim that one *regrets* what one has done? We hardly have a calculus of pleasures, let alone a calculus for the strengths or dominance of attitudes that have distinct causes, objects, expressions, rationales. They are quite incommensurate. How can I determine whether my regret is stronger than my exuberance, glee, or self-righteousness, when none of these is in itself directly motivating? What absorbs my attention and thoughts, need not be what I approve or underwrite, what I acknowledge as identifying my fundamental motivational set. Regretful thoughts can be nearly obsessive, and yet be considered misplaced and improper by the agent.

Sometimes matters are clear: introspection and friendly diagnosis can discover that some attitudes and their attendant thoughts are most vivid, dominant, wholeheartedly accepted. We can recognize a flicker of glee in what is otherwise a somber cast of regret, or a strand of pride in what is primarily an attitude of dismay, or a stab of regret in what is otherwise primarily joy. When there is considerable imbalance of attitudes, the various measures of dominance need not be distinguished, and their incommensurability produces no problems. But often our attitudes are closely balanced, and there is no internal light meter to determine the strength or the vividness, or the tenacity, or the degree of ramification producing consonant associations among our attitudinal thoughts. Regret may be more vivid but glee more tenacious and long lasting; self-righteousness may set off a wide range of closely associated thoughts. Does the person *really* regret? Sometimes when this happens, there is a stance that serves as a "tie breaker": the person stands behind some of those attitudes, and while recognizing the others as his own, attempts to dissociate himself from them. (But this much honesty in the face of psychic division is often intollerably painful, and self-deception often masks the confusion.)

Many affirmations and expressions of regret are of this second level form: they are not reports about what *is* dominant in the person's attitudes, but affirmations or identifications. Indeed markedly strong expressions of regret, particularly when they are elaborate, effusive and flowery, are good indications that the person does not in fact feel regret as his dominant attitude. What is dominant is the person's judgment that, despite all his other attitudes, regret ought to have greater dominance than it does. (But the floweriness or elaborateness of such expressions is also a function of cultural form: attributions of regret—even self-attributions of regret—are extremely difficult across subtle but strong variations in cultural, and often subcultural forms for its expression. Insincerity is particularly difficult to identify across variations in cultural forms.)

But an agent's judgment about what might be the most appropriate attitude is by no means sufficient to bring about the dominance of that attitude. That a person "stands behind" or "affirms" his regret by no means assures that his thoughts and feelings will indeed weigh primarily toward regret and away from glee or self-exculpation.

There are varieties of cases here. The most obvious are those where the regretted action is the expression of strong and important motives: whatever else the person may judge appropriate to feel, those motives were satisfied. They may be relatively archaic motives of childlike defiance—the pleasures of doing what one thinks one should not do; or they may be quite strong prudential desires and needs; or they may be motives that the agent has for some reason generally forbidden satisfaction, but that have had expression in this action. In such cases, regret is accompanied by glee, or more serious and perhaps quite important satisfaction.

The more familiar but far less obvious cases are those that involve the formal expression of regret in social matters, often couched in a relatively formal apology. "I'm sorry I was late..." "I'm sorry there wasn't time to see you...," "I'm sorry but I had to..." Sometimes we self-deceptively avoid real regret by thinking of our actions and situations as *merely* formal, rather than formal;

or think of them as trivial. But they are not. The harms are often objectively real, as well as psychologically wounding, and if the apology is offhand or falsely effusive, insult is added to the original injury.

Secondary formal regret can also take another turn: the agent may recognize that what is trivial to him is objectively important to others, especially when they are socially vulnerable. The expression of regret can then have unexpected resonance, revealing the layers of the agent's attitudes. The real regret is a second order one: that things being as they are, the first order regret is quite slight. The expression of regret can then carry an air of earnestness that also has a ring of falsity. The weight of almost undue sincerity indicates the agent's awareness of the damage he has done; the ring of falsity indicates that the agent doesn't think the matter of any great moment to himself. If he further regrets the disparity between what is trivial to him but important to others, his expression tends toward the effusive.

There is a normative relation between a person's identificatory attitudes and his future actions. If someone endorses his regret but not his satisfaction, his sorrow rather than his self-exculpation, he is presumed to attempt to redirect his actions, and if necessary to modify his first level intentions. He would try, as far as possible, to situate himself so as to avoid the regretted action, by seeing to it that it is not performed, or at least not performed by him. But this is a normative expectation, not a conceptual connection, let alone an empirical correlation. A person may sincerely express regret at his primary attitudinal identification, without succeeding in changing his habits.

10. There is no direct voluntary control over regret: even second order regrets cannot be commanded. But it is possible for a person to learn to focus on, and to attend those features of his actions which, when noticed, will, on appropriate occasions, elicit whatever capacities for regret the person has. The modification of habits of attention and focusing can then further strengthen or weaken capacities for regret, along with other morally significant attitudes toward one's agency. The focus of a person's regrets can itself affect the possibility of success in such changes. Regret that focuses strongly on the agent tends to lead to a reevaluation of priorities. Such a reevaluation is often integrative: conflicts are brought to

light, and sometimes corrected. But this sort of reevaluation does not always lead to moral improvement. Finding himself strongly conflicted, a person can abandon the pretense of holding himself by standards that have caused him the pains of regret. Sometimes motions in the direction of greater unification can lead to greater moral callousness. Regret that focuses strongly on the effects of one's actions, rather than on one's agency, are more piecemeal, less integrative; but because they do not require secondary (and often defensive) postures they can permit the person to attend more directly to remedial or retributive action.[1]

NOTE

1. Although Hume, Spinoza and Rousseau provide excellent philosophic ground for discussions of the emotions, the best and most extensive discussions of regret fall outside canonic philosophical analyses. The richest, bordering on the indigestible are to be found in Dostoyevsky's *Notes From the Underground,* and in Augustine's *Confessions.* There is some account of related attitudes in Nietzsche's discussion of slave mentality in *The Genealogy of Morals.* Less dramatic but equally subtle sources are the novels of Jane Austen, George Eliot, Thomas Hardy, Henry James, and Iris Murdoch. I am also grateful to Genevieve Lloyd, William Ruddick, and Bernard Williams for their discussions of the issues raised in this paper.

XXI

COMPASSION

Lawrence Blum

This paper offers an account of compassion as a moral phenomenon. I regard compassion as a kind of emotion or emotional attitude; though it differs from paradigmatic emotions such as fear, anger, distress, love, it has, I will argue, an irreducible affective dimension.

Compassion is one among a number of attitudes, emotions, or virtues which can be called "altruistic" in that they involve a regard for the good of other persons. Some others are pity, helpfulness, well-wishing. Such phenomena and the distinctions between them have been given insufficient attention in current moral philosophy. By distinguishing compassion from some of these other altruistic phenomena I want to bring out compassion's particular moral value, as well as some of its limitations.[1]

My context for this inquiry is an interest in developing an alternative to Kantianism, in particular to its minimization of the role of emotion in morality and its exclusive emphasis on duty and rationality. I am influenced here by Schopenhauer's critique of Kant's ethics and by his view of compassion as central to morality.[2] But discussion of the specific views of these two philosophers will be peripheral to my task here.

THE OBJECTS OF COMPASSION

How must a compassionate person view someone in order to have compassion for him?[3] Compassion seems restricted to beings capable of feeling or being harmed. Bypassing the question of compassion for plants, animals, institutions, I will focus on persons as objects of compassion. A person in a negative condition, suffering some harm, difficulty, danger (past, present, or future) is the appropriate object of compassion. But there are many negative conditions and not all are possible objects of compassion. The inconvenience and irritation of a short detour for a driver on his way to a casual visit are not compassion-grounding conditions.[4] The negative condition must be relatively central to a person's life and well-being, describable as pain, misery, hardship, suffering, affliction, and the like. Although it is the person and not merely the negative condition which is the object of compassion, the focus of compassion is the condition.

Compassion can be part of a complex attitude toward its object; it is possible to have compassion for someone in a difficult or miserable situation without judging his overall condition to be difficult or miserable. It is therefore necessary to distinguish the conditions for someone being an appropriate object of compassion from the conditions for compassion being the appropriate dominant response to the person. One might predominantly admire and take pleasure in the happiness of a blind person who has gotten through college, found a rewarding job, made close friends—someone whose life is generally happy and who does not dwell on what he misses by being blind. Nevertheless one can also feel compassion for him because his life is deficient and damaged by his blindness.

It is not necessary that the object of compassion be aware of his condition; he might be deceiving himself with regard to it. Nor, as in the case of the happy blind man, need he think of it as a substantial affliction, even if he is aware of it as a deficiency.

That compassion is limited to grave or serious negative conditions does not exclude other altruistic emotions from being entirely appropriate to less serious states. One can feel sorry for, commiserate with, or feel sympathy for a person's irritation, discomfort, inconvenience, displeasure. Nor are all altruistic attitudes primarily directed to particular persons: they can be directed to classes of persons (the blind) or to general conditions (poverty). In addition, there are altruistic virtues not so clearly involving emotions, which come into play in regard to less serious negative conditions: considerateness, thoughtfulness, helpfulness. It would be considerate or thoughtful to warn an acquaintance of an unexpected detour so that he could avoid needless inconvenience and irritation. Such virtues as these, while not necessarily involving emotion or feeling, do involve attention to another's situation and a genuine regard for the other's good, even when more self-regarding attitudes are conjointly brought into play.

Not all altruistic emotions are focused on negative states. Someone might take delight in giving pleasure to others. Though this altruistic attitude shares with compassion a regard for the good of others, compassion focuses on pain, suffering, and damage, whereas this other attitude focuses on pleasure. The capacity for one altruistic attitude is no assurance of the capacity for others. It is quite possible for a compassionate person to be insensitive to the pleasures of others. A focus on misery and suffering in the absence of regard for others' joys and pleasures constitutes a limitation in the moral consciousness of the merely compassionate person.[5]

THE EMOTIONAL ATTITUDE OF COMPASSION

The compassionate person does not merely believe that the object suffers some serious harm or injury; such a belief is compatible with indifference, malicious delight in his suffering, or intense intellectual interest, for example of a novelist or psychologist for whom the suffering is primarily material for contemplation or investigation. Even a genuine interest in relieving someone's suffering can stem from meeting an intellectual or professional challenge rather than from compassion.

Compassion is not a simple feeling-state but a complex emotional attitude toward another, characteristically involving imaginative dwelling on the condition of the other person, an active regard for his good, a view of him as a fellow human being, and emotional responses of a certain degree of intensity.

Imaginatively reconstructing someone's condition is distinct from several sorts of ''identification'' with the other person. For instance, it does not involve an identity confusion in which the compassionate person fails to distinguish his feelings and situation from the other person's.[6] Such a pathological condition actually precludes genuine compassion because it blurs the distinction between subject and object.

In a second type of identification the subject ''identifies'' with the object because of having had an experience similar to his, the memory of which his experience evokes. ("I can identify with what you are going through, since I've suffered from the same problem myself.") Here no identity confusion is involved. While such identification can promote compassion and imaginative understanding it is not required for it. For compassion does not require even that its subject have experienced the sort of suffering that occasions it. We can commiserate with someone who has lost a child in a fire, even if we do not have a child or have never lost someone we love. The reason for this is that the imaginative reconstruction involved in compassion consists in imagining what the other person, given his character, beliefs, and values is undergoing, rather than what we ourselves would feel in his situation. For example I might regard my son's decision to work for the CIA with distress, while someone with different beliefs and values might regard such a decision with pride; yet this other person may well be able to understand my reaction and to feel compassion for me in regard to it.

The degree of imaginative reconstruction need not be great. The friend in the previous example might find it difficult to reconstruct for herself the outlook and set of values within which my son's decision is viewed with distress. But to have compassion she must at least dwell in her imagination on the fact that I am distressed. So some imaginative representation is a necessary condition for compassion, though the degree can be minimal. Certainly a detailed and rich understanding of another person's outlook and consciousness, of the sort available only to persons of exceptional powers of imagination, is not required for compassion.

Nevertheless, as a matter of empirical fact, we often do come to understand someone's condition by imagining what our own reactions would be. So expanding our powers of imagination expands our capacity for compassion. And conversely the limits of a person's capacities for imaginative reconstruction set limits on her capacity for compassion. Finding another person's experience opaque may well get in the way of compassion. Persons who are in general quite poor at imagining the experiences of others who are different from themselves, may well be less likely to have compassion for them. Yet this failure of imagination is typically not a purely intellectual or cognitive failure; for it can itself be part of a more general failure to regard the other as fully human, or to take that humanity sufficiently seriously. That a white colonialist in

Africa does not imagine to himself the cares and sufferings of the blacks whom he rules cannot be separated from the fact that he does not see them as fully human.

A second constituent of compassion is concern for or regard for the object's good. It is not enough that we imaginatively reconstruct someone's suffering; for, like belief, such imagining is compatible with malice and mere intellectual curiosity. (In fact it is likely to be a component of them.) In addition we must care about that suffering and desire its alleviation. Suppose a neighbor's house burns down, though no one is hurt. Compassion would involve not only imagining what it is like for the neighbor to be homeless but also concerned responses such as the following: being upset, distressed, regretting the different aspects of his plight (his homelessness, his loss of prized possessions, his terror when inside the burning house, etc.); wishing the tragedy had not happened; giving thought to that might be done to alleviate the neighbor's situation; worrying whether he will be able to find another place to live; hoping that he will obtain a decent settlement from the insurance company; hoping and desiring that, in general, his suffering will be no greater than necessary.

The relation between concern for another person's good and these thoughts, feelings, hopes, desires is a necessary or conceptual one; compassionate concern would not be attributed to someone who lacked them (or at least most of them). This concern is not merely tacked on to the imaginative reconstruction as a totally independent component of compassion. Rather the manner in which we dwell on the other's plight expresses the concern for his good.

These concerned reactions must be directed toward the other's plight and not merely caused by it. The distress that is part of compassion cannot take as its focus the vivid realization that I might be afflicted with a like misfortune; for it would then be self-regarding rather than altruistic.

Compassion also involves viewing the other person and his suffering in a certain way. I can put this by saying that compassion involves a sense of shared humanity, of regarding the other as a fellow human being. This means that the other person's suffering (though not necessarily their particular afflicting condition) is seen as the kind of thing that could happen to anyone, including oneself insofar as one is a human being.[7]

This way of viewing the other person contrasts with the attitude characteristic of pity, in which one holds oneself apart from the afflicted person and from their suffering thinking of it as something that defines that person as fundamentally different from oneself. In this way the other person's condition is taken as given whereas in compassion the person's affliction is seen as deviating from the general conditions of human flourishing. That is why pity (unlike compassion) involves a kind of condescension, and why compassion is morally superior to pity.

Because compassion involves a sense of shared humanity, it promotes the *experience* of equality, even when accompanied by an acknowledgment of actual social inequality. Compassion forbids regarding social inequality as establishing human inequality. This is part of the moral force of compassion: by transcending the recognition of social inequality, it promotes the sensed experience of equality in common humanity.

Sometimes the reason we feel pity rather than compassion is that we feel that the object has in some way brought the suffering on himself or deserved it, or in any case that he has allowed himself to be humiliated or degraded by it. But such ways of regarding the object do not necessarily undermine compassion, and they are not incompatible with it. It would be a mistake to see the essential difference between pity and compassion in such differing beliefs about the object's condition. No matter how pitiful or self-degraded one regards another human being, it is possible (and not necessarily unwarranted) to feel compassion and concern for him, simply because he is suffering.

Nietzsche's use of the term *Mitleid* does not distinguish between compassion and pity. Because Mitleid is focused on the negative states of others, Nietzsche saw it as life-denying and without positive value. But insofar as compassion involves a genuine concern for the good of others and a "living sense of another's worth,"[8] it is, unlike pity, fundamentally life-affirming and positive.

A fourth aspect of compassion is its strength and duration. If the distress, sorrow, hopes, and desires of an altruistic attitude were merely passing reactions or twinges of feeling, they would be insufficient for the level of concern, the imaginative reconstruction, and the disposition to beneficent action required for compassion. Though there are degrees of compassion, the threshold of emotional strength required from compassion (in contrast with other altruistic attitudes) is relatively high and enduring. Because well-wishing and pity can be more episodic and less action-guiding, they are morally inferior to compassion. As the etymology of the word suggests, compassion involves "feeling with" the other person, sharing his feelings. In one sense this means that the subject and the object have the same feeling-type: distress, sorrow, desire for relief. But in a more important sense the feelings are not the same; for the relation between their subjects and their objects are different. The focus of my neighbor's distress is *his own* homelessness; the focus of my distress in having compassion for him is *my neighbor's* homelessness (or his distress at his homelessness). This can partly be expressed as a matter of degree. My neighbor suffers; in "suffering with" him there is a sense in which I suffer too, but my suffering is much less than his.

COMPASSION AND BENEFICENT ACTION

When it is possible for her to relieve another person's suffering without undue demands on her time, energy, and priorities, the compassionate person is disposed to attempt to help. We would hardly attribute compassion to X if she were to saunter by on a spring day and, seeing an elderly man fall on the sidewalk, walk right by, perhaps with a sad shudder of dismay, leaving the old man lying alone.

Characteristically, then, compassion requires the disposition to perform beneficent actions, and to perform them because the agent has had a certain sort of imaginative reconstruction of someone's condition and has a concern for his good. The steps that the person takes to ameliorate the condition are guided by and prompted by that imaginative reconstruction and concern. So the beneficent action of a compassionate person has a specific sort of causal history, which distinguishes it from an equally beneficent action that might be prompted by other sorts of attitudes and emotions.

We saw that concern exists at different degrees of strength in different altruistic emotions and attitudes. Hence its corresponding disposition to beneficence exists at different levels of strength also. The stronger the disposition the more one is willing to go out of one's way, to act contrary to inclination and interest, in order to help the other person.[9] That compassion as a motive can and often does withstand contrary inclination begins to address the Kantian charge that emotions, including compassion, are unreliable as motives to beneficent action.[10] As a motive to beneficence, compassion can have the strength, stability, and reliability that Kant thought only the sense of duty could have. As a trait of character compassion can be as stable and consistent in its prompting of appropriate beneficent action as a conscientious adherence to principles of beneficence.

Though compassion is a type of emotion or emotional attitude, it is not like a Kantian "inclination." Acting from compassion does not typically involve doing what one is in the mood to do, or feels like doing. On the contrary the regard for the other's good which compassion implies means that one's compassionate acts often involve acting very much contrary to one's moods and inclinations. Compassion is fundamentally other-regarding rather than self-regarding; its affective nature in no way detracts from this.

Compassionate action may extinguish or diminish compassion itself, most obviously when its object is relieved of the negative condition by the action. But even merely *engaging* in action may involve a shift in the subject's consciousness from the imaginative reconstruction of the object's condition to a focus on the expected relief of that condition, thereby diminishing the compassion (though not the regard for the other's good and hence not the moral value of the attitude or state of mind).

Compassion, however, is not always linked so directly to the prompting of beneficent actions. For in many situations it is impossible (without extraordinary disruption of one's life and priorities) for the compassionate person herself to improve the sufferer's condition (for instance, when one is concerned for the welfare of distant flood victims). In other situations the beneficence might be inappropriate, as when intervention might jeopardize the sufferer's autonomy. Compassionate concern, in such cases, involves hope and desire for the relief of the condition by those in a position to provide it. It does not involve an active setting oneself in readiness to perform beneficent acts, once one firmly believes such acts to be impossible or inappropriate.

In the cases so far discussed a link exists between compassion and beneficent action, through the desire that action be taken by someone to relieve the sufferer's condition. But compassion is also appropriate in situations in which nothing whatever can be done to alleviate the affliction, as for instance when someone is suffering from incurable blindness or painful terminal cancer. In such situations compassionate concern involves sorrowing for the person, hoping that the condition might—all expectations to the contrary— be mitigated or compensated, being pleased or grateful if this occurs, and similar responses.

Because being compassionate involves actively giving thought to the relief of the sufferer's condition, a compassionate person may discover the possibility of beneficent action when it seemed unclear whether any existed. Compassion often involves resisting regarding situations as absolutely irremediable. On the other hand the compassionate person may for this reason fail to see and hence to face up to the hopelessness of the sufferer's situation.

That compassion is often appropriate when there is little or no scope for the subject's disposition to beneficence indicates that compassion's sole significance does not lie in its role as motive to beneficence. Even when nothing can be done by the compassionate person to improve the sufferer's condition, simply being aware that one is an object or recipient of compassion can be an important human good. The compassionate person's expression of concern and shared sorrow can be valuable to the sufferer for its own sake, independently of its instrumental value in improving his condition. Nor does the good of recognizing oneself to be an object of compassion depend on the compassionate person wanting to convey his attitude, though the recipient can in addition value the intention to communicate.

The compassionate attitude is a good to the recipient, not only because it signifies that the subject would help if she could but because we are glad to receive the concern of others, glad of the sense of equality that it promotes. Yet it is morally good to be compassionate even when—as often happens—the object of compassion is unaware of it. For any concern for the welfare of others, especially when it promotes the sense of equality, is (ceteris paribus) morally good. In this, compassion contrasts with attitudes and feelings such as infatuation or admiration which may convey goods to their recipients but which are without moral value because they do not essentially involve a regard for their recipient's good. The moral significance of compassion is not exhausted by the various types of goods it confers on its recipients.

Compassion can hurt its recipients. It may, for instance, cause him to concentrate too much on his plight, or to think that people around him see him primarily in terms of that plight. But these dangers and burdens of compassion can be mitigated to the extent that a person recognizes that compassion is not the sole or the dominant attitude with which one is regarded.

Compassion can also be misguided, grounded in superficial understanding of a situation. Compassion is not necessarily wise or appropriate. The compassionate person may even end up doing more harm than good. True compassion must be allied with knowledge and understanding if it is to serve adequately as a guide to action: there is nothing inherent in the character of compassion that would prevent—and much that would encourage—its alliance with rational calculation. Because compassion involves an active and objective interest in another person's welfare, it is characteristically a spur to a deeper understanding of a situation than rationality alone could ensure. A person who is compassionate by character is in principle committed to as rational and as intelligent a course of action as possible.

NOTES

1. Compassion has a particular cultural history: its sources are Christian, it was further developed by Romanticism, especially by the German Romantics. Though I do not focus on this history explicitly, my emphasis on compassion as a particular moral emotion among others should leave room for the results of such a historical account.

2. Arthur Schopenhauer, *On the Basis of Morality* (New York: Bobbs-Merrill, 1965).

3. In general I will use feminine pronouns to refer to the person having compassion (the "subject") and masculine pronouns to refer to the person for whom she has compassion (the "object").

4. I am taking a conceptual rather than a moral point. The compassionate person cannot regard the object of her compassion as merely irritated or discomforted; but of course a genuinely compassionate person might mistakenly take an inconvenience to be a serious harm. To say that compassion is "appropriate" in this context is, then, simply to say that the object actually possesses the compassion-grounding feature which the subject takes him to possess. I do not discuss the further issue of when compassion is *morally* appropriate or inappropriate.

5. Nietzsche saw this focus on misery and suffering as a kind of morbidity in the compassionate consciousness; this view formed part of his critique of compassion.

6. Philip Mercer, *Sympathy and Ethics* (Oxford: Clarendon Press, 1972), and Max Scheler, *The Nature of Sympathy,* trans. Werner Stark (London: Routledge & Kegan Paul, 1965).

7. This way of viewing the other's plight differs from fundamentally self-regarding sentiment in which the person's plight is regarded as a symbol of what could happen to oneself. It is not actually necessary that one believe that the afflicting condition *could* happen to oneself: one might have compassion for someone suffering napalm burns without believing that there is any possibility of oneself being in that condition.

8. Nicolai Hartmann, *Ethics* (London: George Allen and Unwin, 1932), II, 273.

9. Aristotle recognizes differences in the strength of the disposition to beneficence in his discussion of *eunoia* ("well-wishing" or "good will" in Thompson's translation). Of persons who have eunoia toward others, Aristotle says, "All they wish is the good of those for whom they have a kindness; they would not actively help them to attain it, nor would they put themselves out for their sake." Aristotle, *Nichomachean Ethics,* book IX (Baltimore: Penguin Books, 1955), p. 269.

10. For this Kantian view, see Kant, *Fundamental Principles of the Metaphysics of Morals,* trans. Beck (New York: Bobbs-Merrill, 1960), pp. 6, 14, 28; and *Critique of Practical Reason,* trans. Beck (New York: Bobbs-Merrill, 1956), pp. 75, 122.

XXII

EMOTION, PRACTICAL KNOWLEDGE AND COMMON CULTURE

Roger Scruton

We often distinguish between practical and theoretical reason, and despite the many views that hold one or the other to be primary, the existence of both is seldom doubted. What is more often doubted is that we may distinguish theoretical from practical *knowledge*. Part of the distinction between the theoretical and the practical is that in the former case we are dealing with questions of truth and falsehood, whereas in the latter case we are dealing primarily with something else, with a notion of rightness that is in some way irreducible to truth. And it might seem that notions like knowledge (with its implied background of objective assessment) can be applied only where we may also speak of truth. Perhaps the principal difficulty, therefore, which the notion of practical knowledge presents, is the difficulty in making clear what is meant by ''correctness'' where one cannot speak of truth. But there are other difficulties, and it is with these other difficulties that I shall for the most part be concerned.

There is a distinction, made familiar by Ryle, between knowing that (the object of which is a proposition) and knowing how (the object of which is an action). I know that my bicycle is made of steel; I also know how to ride it. But that distinction is not the one that I wish to discuss. ''Knowledge how'' denotes a skill, and one might say that there is a distinction between true practical knowledge and ''knowing how'' which corresponds in part to the distinction Aristotle had in mind in contrasting virtue and skill.[1]

In the first of these there is more to success than the matching of means to end. There is the right knowledge of the end itself.

Ordinary language is unlikely to provide us with the concept we require. Nonetheless, it is worth pointing out that we do use the term *knowledge* in other ways, to denote what seem to be practical capacities, capacities that cannot be evaluated in terms of the truth or falsehood of some proposition that they contain. For example, we speak of "knowing what to do." Knowing what to do is not a matter of knowing the truth about a situation. In *that* sense one might be as knowledgeable as possible and still not know what to do, perhaps because one is so much the further from making up one's mind (which phrase seems to suggest a more than accidental connection between knowing what to do and deciding). And again knowing what to do cannot be considered simply as a matter of knowing how. For the accumulation of skills may also bring one no nearer to making up one's mind, even though a certain confidence in one's skills for that end may be necessary.

There is also another popular reference to knowledge which seems to have something to do with the practical: knowing what one is doing. A man may be said not to know what he is doing, even when what he is doing is an intentional act, because his activity manifests a practical confusion about his ends or means, rather than because he has the wrong description of his action. We have no trouble in our daily lives in recognizing instances of this confusion, and we cannot always (or even typically) reduce those instances to cases of ignorance over the truth value of a proposition.

Now someone might here wish to point out that when we say, of a workman for example, that he does not know what he is doing, we are referring to a deficiency in *skill*. He does not know how to carry out the given task, even though, in some other sense, he knows quite well what he has to do: what he is aiming at. But that is not the only occasion upon which we would wish to say of someone that he does not know what he is doing. There is the more puzzling case where we might say this of someone who had no deficiency in skill and yet was employed in a task of which he had no proper understanding—as we might say of a politician or an administrator, that he does not know what he is doing.

Simplifying somewhat, we might speak here of a difference between knowledge of means and knowledge of ends, and knowledge of ends has two sides—roughly corresponding to knowing what to do (at the outset), and knowing what one is doing (when one has begun). I say that it is simplifying somewhat to make this division into ends and means for the reason that I do not think that it applies to rational behavior with the neatness that is often assumed; none-theless it is an honored distinction, and one that locates as well as one can at the outset the philosophical problems that I wish to discuss. I wish to say something about what "knowledge of ends" might consist in—something about the kind of practical knowledge that is roughly located by the two locutions to which I have referred, when they cannot be replaced by the simpler notion of "knowing how."

Whatever else it is, practical knowledge in the sense I am considering is the property of the individual and must be understood in terms that—while generally intelligible—make essential reference to his individual predicament. To know what to do (for example) involves knowing what *I* should do. That reference to the first person is, I think, ineliminable from the idea of rational agency. I know what to do not just by knowing what a person answering to a certain description should do (even if it is a description that I uniquely satisfy), but (typically) by making up my mind and acting accordingly. In practical reasoning one is, in the last analysis, always subject, and never object.

Now this might lead us to think that practical knowledge is simply identical with decision—with the forming of intentions. But that is surely not so, either from the objective or from the subjective point of view. If we can talk of knowledge at all it is because decisions can be evaluated, and a man who claims to know may be convicted of ignorance. A false claim to knowledge is refuted by the world, not by the way the world is but by the way it turns out to be. It is surely the main question of ethics to determine what this "refutation" might consist in, to determine, that is, the content of genuine knowledge, when knowledge is of ends.

Moreover, it is too simple to represent even the subjective side of practical knowledge as an intention, for the reason that a man may sometimes know what to do and yet fail to do it. This evident fact is also a well-known problem. For if practical knowledge is to be truly practical (that is, if it is to be connected with a *specific* form of action and not reducible to an act of intellectual judgment, or "holding true"), then its connection with action must be noncontingent. And yet at the same time, because of weakness of will, the connection cannot be universal.

Despite those—by now fairly familiar—difficulties, there

remains a strong tradition in moral philosophy which still sees decision (or "choice") as containing the whole of practical knowledge. Kant would not have approved of the recent representatives of this tradition—of Sartre and Hare— but all the same he endowed it with its fundamental concept, the concept of autonomy. To express the thought of this tradition in a nutshell: decision to act is necessary for practical knowledge (of ends); commitment is sufficient. And commitment means nothing more than a reinforcement of the same decision, either by deciding at the same time on a universal principle (Hare), or by deciding not just to *do* this thing, but also to *be* the man whose decision this is (Sartre). In other words, decision becomes practical knowledge when accompanied by a second-order decision, either a decision always to act likewise, or else a decision to be, in this act, what one "really" is.

Now it is well known that both those views find it very difficult to step out of the subjective side of practical knowledge into the objective world of real assessment. There does not even seem to *be* any objective right or wrong: the only standard is that of autonomy (or "authenticity") and indeed, to speak of "knowledge" is to employ a metaphor redolent of discarded moral notions. In this paper I shall begin by concerning myself exclusively with the subjective side of practical knowledge. But I shall suggest, too, an account of something objective, something that might lead us to accept that there really is such a thing as practical *knowledge,* even when knowledge is not of means but of ends. Indeed, it seems to me that philosophers such as Hare have failed to see the possibility of an objective ethics partly because their description of the subjective side of rational agency is so impoverished.

I

One feature that is left out of consideration by Hare, though not by Sartre, is that of emotion. To speak again in terms of our intuitive notions of these things: just as there is "knowing what to do" so too is there "knowing what to feel." The feelings, like the will, are capable of education. Of course, it is no easy matter to say what we mean by "knowing what to feel," or how that process of education might be brought about. But Aristotle is clearly not the only philosopher who has thought that the important thing if one is to lead a fulfilled and proper life is to feel the right emotion, on the right occasion, toward the right object and in the right degree.

Now if we are to speak of knowledge at all here it must be possible to describe—as in all cases of knowledge—a subjective state, an objective rightness, and some nonaccidental relation between the two.[2] In the case of theoretical knowledge the subjective component is usually described as some kind of belief; characteristically, a *certain* belief. A belief that comes and goes, a belief that is merely probable, a belief in respect of which one has to make up one's mind afresh each time one entertains it—such beliefs fall critically short of knowledge. For they do not enable us to attribute to the subject the right kind of authority. Let us begin by asking whether there is any analogue in feelings for the certainty that may qualify belief. It might be better in this connection to speak of something's "being *settled*" for the agent. But I shall continue to use the word *certainty* in the hope that the discussion will make clear what is meant by it.

We all have some idea what it is to be *un*certain what to feel, as when some sudden crisis overtakes us and we find ourselves bereft of ready emotion. This state of uncertainty might, in its extreme form, bear some relation to the state variously described as "dread" or "anxiety," a peculiar, objectless state, which is normally contrasted with the "innocence" of direct and open feeling.[3] The uncertainty to which I refer comes about because, while we may know what we *ought* to feel—in the sense of what the *good* man would feel—we do not feel it. As a result we feel alienated from ourselves, from our thoughts, motives, and gestures. Something like this might happen at the death of someone close. One knows what grief is but, being overcome by the disaster, grief seems impossible: relief, indeed, seems easier. The experience is recorded by Emily Dickinson in the following verses:

> We waited while she passed;
> It was a narrow time.
> Too jostled were our souls to speak.
> At length the notice came.
>
> She mentioned, and forgot;
> Then lightly as a reed

Bent to the water, struggled scarce,
Consented, and was dead.

And we, we placed the hair,
And drew the head erect,
And then an awful leisure was,
Belief to regulate.

Dr. Johnson referred to grief as "a species of idleness." Clearly, that is not Emily Dickinson's meaning. The "awful leisure" to which she refers is the punishment we must expect when, overtaken by a calamity, we do not know what to feel in the face of it.

Now, knowing what to feel is not a matter of knowing what one ought to feel, any more than knowing what to do is just a matter of knowing what one ought to do. In the normal case, at least, knowing what to feel must involve feeling: it is not a kind of opinion about feeling. If it were just that then we should have—I suggest— no special reason to value it. I think it will be conceded that there are men who know what they ought to do, and what they ought to feel, while seldom knowing what to do, or what to feel. Despite the richness of their theoretical awareness, they act and feel in ignorance. What remedy remains to them?

It is now widely accepted that all emotion involves both understanding and activity and, indeed, that nothing important is left to an emotion when those two have been removed from it. It follows that it is possible to educate an emotion, to the extent that it is possible to educate the understanding and activity that are involved in it. It is perhaps only a vestige of Cartesianism which prevents us from seeing this, and from seeing that a man ignorant of the art of emotion is a man who is in a significant way *confused*.[4] Emotions, therefore, are teachable, for one may teach a man both a way of understanding and an appropriate reaction; together these will constitute a feeling. For example, one may teach someone how to understand another's utterance as an insult. An insult may not be obvious, and becomes obvious only when a man recognizes that he is being treated in a highhanded or contemptuous way; that recognition involves the acquisition of concepts of justice, right, and denigration. The thought involved in recognizing an insult is thus extremely complex and I do not think that any philosopher has succeeded in giving a full account of it.[5] But it is a thought that is, so to speak, publicly available. With sufficient understanding a man can learn to recognize what is insulting and what is not. But he must also acquire the appropriate reaction: how and when to treat the insult with contempt, with aggression, with violence. A man may react violently when he should have been contemptuous, or he might be contemptuous when he should have been amused. He must therefore learn the arts of anger and resentment, so that he can measure his response in accordance with his understanding of its object. There is no doubt that we all of us have, at least in the case of these emotions that arise out of and manifest our perception of social realities, a sense of what is and what is not appropriate. Thus we criticize a man for being unreasonably angry over an accident, or resentful of another's good intentions, or proud of having eaten a hundred sausages. It is a small step from such criticism to the distinction between the man who knows what to feel and the man who does not. The education of the emotions has that knowledge as its aim, and while there is a sense in which I cannot be held to blame for my present lack of knowledge, and for the present confusion of my feelings, I certainly can be held to blame for allowing myself, or another for whom I am responsible, to slip into the uneducated habits which those feelings exemplify. (Which is why Kant's attempt to eliminate feeling from the sphere of moral assessment ought to be firmly rejected.) It is hardly surprising that the principal concern of honest parents is to see that their offspring acquire the proper feelings—sympathy, pride, remorse, and affection. I teach my child not just to avoid fire but to fear it, not just to consort with others but to love them, not just to repair wrongdoing but to suffer remorse and shame for its execution. There should be nothing puzzling in that.

There is a distinction to be made at this juncture that, while not essential to my argument, bears on it indirectly. It seems to me that we ought to be able to distinguish between emotions with a universal or abstract, and those with a particular or concrete, object. A few remarks about that distinction will help to isolate more clearly the emotions that I wish to discuss, emotions like love and grief which have a special place in determining the quality of individual life. These emotions have particular objects. Others, such as contempt, admiration, and indignation, have universal objects. If I feel contempt for James, for example, it is because of something that is true about James; if that thing were true of William then I should feel contempt for William too. The object of my contempt is the particular—James—as an instance of the universal. What I despise is James's cowardice, say, or childishness, and I would feel just the same toward anyone else who showed the same defect. Or if I did not feel just the same, then there would have to be an explanation, an explanation in terms of the intentional object. Merely to say "I despise James for his childishness, but not John, although I can see no relevant difference between them" is either to misuse the words or to speak insincerely.[6] It is not difficult to see how one might educate such "universalized" feelings. Having shown a man what is contemptible in one instance of cowardice, and having brought him to feel contempt toward it, one will necessarily have brought him to feel contempt on like occasions. In educating such emotions one is educating a man's values, and providing him with a sense of what is appropriate not just here and now but universally.

It is more difficult to see how we might educate emotions of the particular variety, emotions like love, hatred, and erotic desire, which impose upon the subject no universal logic, as it were, no obligation to respond likewise on like occasions. Although there is no doubt some feature of James which is the reason why I love him, I am not obliged to love William as well, just because he shares that feature.

The important point about such "particular" emotions is their intimate connection with one's sense and conception of *oneself*. These emotions lack the postulated objectivity of their universal counterparts, which abstract from the individual situation and attach themselves to impartial notions of what is just and right. While it is *I* who feel contempt and indignation, I do so in obedience to an imperative that is applicable beyond my present situation, in accordance with a universal law. Such emotions seem to abstract, not only from the particularity of their object but also from that of their subject: it is only accidentally *I* who am feeling this indignation—the call to indignation might have been addressed to and taken up by another. The emotion is, as it were, impersonal. Learning its proper exercise involves acquiring conceptions of justice, appropriateness, and right which propose themselves as universally valid, and which remove the object of emotion from the sphere of any merely personal resentment or dislike. One might say, therefore, that the education of these universalized emotions is an essential part of moral development.

It is not so with love, liking, and delight. From the point of view of individual existence these emotions are indispensable. I cannot regard the call to love someone as addressed only accidentally to me without losing all sense of myself as an agent in my situation. These emotions—love, hatred, grief, and the rest—are irremediably personal. The obligation to feel them cannot be shifted; if a man tries to shift it, then automatically he puts his personality at risk. It may seem strange to talk of "obligation" here, and of a personal "risk." In using such language I am trying to sum up a very complicated phenomenon, a phenomenon so often explored by Shakespeare in his tragedies and sonnets that it would be presumptuous at this stage to describe it more concretely. But my remarks will become a little clearer if we address ourselves to the question: "What is it, in the case of these essentially particular emotions, to know what to feel: And how is that knowledge acquired?" I shall approach those questions from the subjective side: my interest will be in the kind of certainty that would have to be involved. I wish to describe how the question what to feel can be *settled* for me, in the case of an emotion that is, as it were, inalienably mine.

II

Let us return for a moment to the case of grief. Grief is not an easy thing to feel; every man has a reason to avoid it, and may well try to avoid it, even in the presence of its proper object, which is the death of someone loved. A sort of busying anxiety, a haste to clear away the debris and turn to something new, is a familiar reaction in the face of death. So too is the "awful leisure" that is consequent on that avoidance of emotion. Such anxiety is the natural consequence of not knowing what to feel, at a time when it is important to feel something, and yet when one has, as it were, no precedent: the feeling concerns me, here, now; it is not detachable from the imperatives of my individual life and present situation.

Our account of the general structure of emotions suggests that two things might be required in this predicament: first, a way of understanding the world in terms that invite emotion (I shall call this—for reasons that I hope to make clear—an "intentional" mode of understanding); second, recognized patterns of appropriate behavior. What I have in mind can be understood from considering the anthropological idea of a "common culture"—the system of shared beliefs and practices that tell a man how to see the situation that besets him (where "seeing" is a matter of recognizing the appropriate occasions of emotion), and which may also tell him what to do in response to that perception. Consider—to take an ancient example—Elpenor's plea to Odysseus in *Odyssey,* Bk. XI, 11. 66-78:

> Now I beseech you, by all those whom you left behind, by your wife and by the father who reared you as a child, and by Telemachus your only son whom you left within your halls, that you will, sailing from the Kingdom of Hades, put in with your good ship at the isle of Aeaea. And there my lord I beseech you to remember me and not to leave me there unwept and unburied, lest I should become a cause of divine wrath against you. But burn me there with all my arms and raise a mound for me by the shore of the grey sea in memory of an unfortunate man, so that those yet to be will know the place. Do this for me, and on my tomb plant the oar that I used to pull when I was living and rowing beside my companions.

Odysseus shares a common culture, in my anthropological sense, with his band of *hetairoi,* and Elpenor reminds him of shared beliefs and practices. In the hurry to leave Circe's palace Elpenor (who had fallen while drunk to his death) had been given little of the sympathy that was his due. Now, however, Odysseus can bewail him. There is something that it is correct to do in response to this death. Odysseus can burn Elpenor's body, he can mourn his passing, and erect a monument for the eyes of "those who are yet to be." His doing these things is connected, in a way that is immediate to Odysseus's perception, with Odysseus's own love for his family and respect for the father who had reared him. The common culture embraces these complex feelings and obligations and makes them alive together in the single episode of a servant's death. Indeed, it would be impossible to give a statement of all that is suggested to Odysseus by Elpenor's words: to attempt that would be to attempt to describe the entire common culture.

All this is of course subtly suggested by Homer: but its truth to life is surely unquestionable. It is not simply that Elpenor is asking

to be buried: he is asking too to be mourned. "Do not leave me,"
he begs, "unwept and unburied" (*aklauton kai athapton*). Now of
course I am not suggesting that Odysseus did not know what to feel
when Elpenor fell from the roof of Circe's palace. I wish rather to
suggest that there is an intimate and perhaps inextricable connection between that knowledge and the practical knowledge enshrined
in the practices to which Elpenor refers. If we accept the account of
the emotions that I have been suggesting, then it must be that there
is an intimate connection between knowing what to feel and knowing what to do. So that a practice that intimates to one what to do
might also be instrumental in determining one's knowledge of what
to feel. This is especially so if the practice is, as it were, wholly
occasioned, and wholly exhausted, by the proper object of the corresponding emotion. To explain: the proper object of grief is the
death of someone loved. A practice that tells one what to do solely
and exclusively on the occasion of such a death is a practice that
takes its meaning from the emotion of grief. It exists as an imperative in those circumstances when grief is appropriate. If the ceremony is of the right kind it serves to direct the subject's attention to
those features of his situation which make grief the appropriate
reaction. In telling him what to do, it insistently brings him back to
the point of what he must feel. But, being a ceremony, of universal
application, it reminds the sufferer of his participation in a common lot. It tells him what to feel, while at the same time rendering
his feeling objective, independent of his own situation. His grief
becomes part of a continuing activity in a public and objective
world, and ceases to be a private anxiety to be born by himself
alone. That "awful leisure" of which Emily Dickinson speaks is
overcome. The privacy of grief is removed from it, the subject
becomes aware, not as a theoretical insight but as a practical matter, that this emotion, the grief that he feels, is also something
"universal," something that it is right and proper to feel, that
others too would feel to the extent that they engage in like activities
and obey like ceremonial constraints. This sense of "universality"
is present whenever some idea of the validity of a sentiment becomes an active and serious part of the sentiment itself, informing
not just the behavior of the subject, but the very description under
which the object is perceived. (This is perhaps what Goethe had in
mind in speaking of the "elective affinity" that is felt in the most

particular, and least "transferable," form of love.) In being the complete subject of his emotion, a man feels it also as an objective law.

To participate in a common culture is therefore, one might suggest, to be gifted with a certainty in one's feelings, a certainty which the uprooted, alienated, and disenchanted may not have had, and may not want to have. By certainty I do not mean crass impetuousness: there are occasions when any man must hesitate. Certainty comes when the matter is, in the last analysis, settled for the agent, when he sees his situation in terms of objective imperatives rather than subjective choices, imperatives that record for him the fact of his shared humanity, even in the midst of a predicament that is uniquely his. In this way the question what to feel becomes "settled" in a manner that no mere "authenticity" could achieve. The question is, then, why that certainty should be considered valuable, and also whether it is available not only to Odysseus but also, for example, to Leopold Bloom (which was, I think, the main point of Joyce's comparison).

III

To show the value of practical certainty (or, at least, of certain certainties) is to make the bridge from certainty to knowledge. It is to move out of the sphere of subjective choice into that of objective assessment. To speak of practical knowledge is to presuppose some practical analogue of truth, some basis for assessment. For the purpose of this analogy, the salient feature of truth is that it constitutes a kind of success, success in belief or assertion. (Hence the view, made familiar by Dummett, that assertion *aims* at truth, and derives its nature from that aim.) But if we are to speak of knowledge, success cannot be an accident—it must be the sign of some authority; the man with knowledge owes his success to his own reliability. In looking for the practical analogue of truth, therefore, we must look for a notion of success in action which is at the same time capable of being achieved nonaccidentally.

In the case of "knowledge of means," or knowing how, this is not difficult. Success here lies in the end attempted; and the non-accidental achievement of the end is what we mean by skill. That is all there is to "knowing how." The case of "knowledge of ends" is more difficult to describe: the notion of "success" here indicates a gap in accepted theories of practical reason, a gap that philosophers have been unable or unwilling to fill. The unwillingness stems from Kant, who took so seriously the idea of the "autonomy" of practical reason that he could not acknowledge a validity in practical reason that was not, as it were, internal to it: in particular, he could not acknowledge that the rightness of practical thought could derive from the success of its application. In that he was consciously opposing the "ancient" system of philosophy (meaning Aristotle), which proposes some idea of happiness, well-being, or fulfillment, as the cornerstone of practical reasoning. Roughly speaking, the practical equivalent of truth must be some such idea of fulfillment, of finding satisfaction in what is achieved. Clearly, there is more to rational fulfillment than achieving one's ends, for not all those ends will bring satisfaction: practical knowledge consists in the ability to aim at those that do. In other words, for there to be practical knowledge, the satisfaction that is the outcome of a man's activity should not be accidental (a dispensation of fate) but the natural result of his state of mind and character. A fortunate man is not necessarily a happy one.

This is not the place to describe the kind of fulfillment to which I refer;[7] nevertheless, there may well be a part to be played in it by the emotional certainty that I have described. For it is difficult to imagine how a self-conscious being can be fulfilled when he is at variance with his own emotions. A large part of happiness lies in the vanquishing of guilt, and in the achievement of a proper organization in one's feelings. It is true that not every common culture will provide that freedom and control, but a common culture is the kind of thing that does so, and the healthy culture is the one that succeeds. To partake of such a culture, to be educated in the constraints and perceptions that it embodies, is to transform certainty into knowledge. It will not be an accident that a man who partakes of such a culture will be fulfilled. His sufferings will be external— such calamities as the death of someone loved; he will not also suffer in his own self-opinion, or experience his personal life as something alien and confused. His sufferings, in other words, will be misfortunes not faults.

Now much more needs to be said if that bridge from certainty to knowledge is to be constructed. We should need to know more about the nature of happiness, and more about the character of human emotion. But a small digression may show more clearly why the certainties of culture might in the end be indispensible. Consider then, the view of human nature which sees all human fulfillment in terms of the freedom of choice of the individual, and the subjective side of practical knowledge in terms of the willed "authenticity" of the agent. Of course, the dangers for society which that notion enshrines are by now familiar enough. It is important to realize, however, that the dangers for the individual are equally great. According to the defenders of "authenticity," certainty comes only through the deliberate adoption of an aim or purpose—a sort of ideological imposition of the will, whereby all one's future conduct will be governed. There results from this neither the objective fulfillment that is the aim of knowledge, nor even the subjective certainty that is its initial reward. For, however authentic, a choice can lead to certainty only if it is thought capable of succeeding, only, that is, if it accompanies some understanding of the world as an arena of rational activity, an understanding that enables the agent to envisage how the world might be affected by what he chooses to do. Let us consider what that might involve.

In discussing Elpenor's appeal to Odysseus I referred to an intentional mode of understanding. By that I meant an understanding that represents the world through the concepts that inform our aims and attitudes, concepts that characterize the "intentional objects" of our states of mind. That such an understanding is possible, and that it is not necessarily identical with the kind of understanding fostered by science, should be evident. Consider three strips of material, one of wood, one of an artificial fiber with similar strength and cutting properties, and another of some isotope of the same artificial material, which has none of the plastic properties of wood, being soft and flabby. A scientific classification would assimilate the second to the third. But such a classification would have no part to play in the practical understanding of the jobbing builder, for whom the first and second would fall under concepts proper to his aims, being for practical purposes indistinguishable. Nor is the contrast here merely that between a natural and a functional kind.[8] Concepts that play an important part in practical thinking may have their basis, for example, in aesthetic experience.

It used to be the practice for stone merchants to class together (as "ornamental marbles") such stones as marble (a carbonate), onyx (an oxide), and porphyry (a silicate), while limestone (chemically identical to marble) had no part in the classification. An intentional mode of understanding is one that fills the world with the meanings implicit in our aims and emotions. Not only is it indispensible to us as rational agents, it may also be irreplaceable by any understanding derived from natural science.

The last point is of some significance, I believe, not only in understanding the nature of culture but also in clarifying the feature of emotions that has been called their "intentionality." Emotions are classified partly in terms of the conceptions under which their objects are presented. The object of fear is "something harmful," that of jealousy "a rival," that of envy "coveted success," and so on. These conceptions define what has been called the "formal object" of each emotion[9]—that is, they define the description under which any object of some given emotion must fall (or be thought to fall). To put it another way, they define the "proper" object of each emotion, and to the extent that some putative object of jealousy, say, can be shown not to be a proper object (not to be a rival), then jealousy can be not only criticized but actually *refuted* —for it can be shown to be founded on a mistake.

There remains, however, a further dimension of criticism, associated with the idea of an "appropriate" object. Although Timothy is a rival and therefore a "proper" object of jealousy, there is more to jealousy than the thought that he may be so described. There is also the activity that is based in that thought, and which may be criticized in terms that belong to accepted modes of practical reason. A man may be enjoined to master his jealousy, on the grounds that its object is proper but trivial, or on the grounds that it is unjust or heartless to pursue it.

Now it is tempting to try to understand the intentionality of the emotions simply by following our previous division. On the one hand there is the province of theoretical reason, which provides the thoughts and beliefs on which an emotion is founded: these thoughts and beliefs determine the intentional object. On the other hand there is the province of practical reason, which governs the activity of which that object is the "target." However, the activity will play its own part in determining the content of the accompanying belief. For it may provide the classifications in terms of which that belief is formulated. (It is the activity of the sculptor which gives sense to the classification "ornamental marble"; it is the activity of human competition which gives sense to the conception of a rival). Were we completely to separate the theoretical and the practical, then we might find that much of the emotional life that we need and esteem as rational beings would become alien to us. For, construed in isolation from human practice, a belief is a purely theoretical thing, the essence of which is the claim to truth. To make that claim is to commit oneself to the pursuit of truth, and it is the essence of that pursuit to spill over into theory, and into the consequent classification of the world in terms of natural kinds. Yet there is no reason to suppose that such a classification will provide sufficient basis for all rational activity, just as there is no reason to think that the chemical classification of stones will provide a sufficient basis for the activity of a sculptor.

Consider the most elementary human relations. All the people I know are members of a natural kind—the kind "human being"—and behave in accordance with the laws of that kind. Yet I subsume people and their actions under concepts that may not figure in the formulation of those laws. Indeed, the hallucination of those laws (for so it must be described in our present ignorance) often seems to distract people from genuine human intercourse. If the fundamental facts about John are, for me, his biological constitution, his scientific essence, his neurological structure, all those aspects that constitute the abhorred "empirical self" of Kant, it may be that I shall find it difficult to respond to him with affection, anger, love, contempt, or grief.[10] So described, he may be mysterious to me, for it is not obvious that those classifications make contact with the ruling interests of personal feeling. The intentional object of love, of anger, of resentment, cannot, one feels, be so "neutrally" described.

Suppose that we acknowledge that the intentional object of an emotion is specified by some belief or thought.[11] Then we must acknowledge that the concepts used to formulate this thought may not be the concepts of any theoretical inquiry, and that they may not be wholly "transparent" to the pursuit of scientific truth. They will first have to reflect the forms through which our emotions are enacted, and will bear the stamp of shared human interests. Our emotions lose their certainty when our "intentional" modes of understanding lose authority; and this authority is not bestowed upon them by some act of "autonomous" choice. If I see a special significance in common culture, it is precisely because it provides concepts that classify the world in terms of the appropriate action and the appropriate response. A rational being has need of such concepts, concepts that bring his emotions together *in* the object, which enables him—as the Idealists might say—to find his identity *in* the world and not in opposition to it. Culture, far from creating the separation between subject and object that is (on one plausible view) characteristic of theoretical understanding, represents the world as entirely circumscribed by the agent's sense of what it is like to experience it and act on it.

But of course, precisely because the "intentional" mode of understanding is deeply intertwined with action, it is difficult to delineate the concepts that it involves. Indeed it is often easier to speak of the intentionality of an emotion as though it were a matter not so much of thought as of perception: the object of hatred is *perceived* hatefully. Moreover, not only may we not be able to disentangle the intentional classifications from the culture in which they are embedded but also we might find it difficult to describe the ends of the conduct which they serve to rationalize. Understanding the emotion of another as it is felt—understanding its true intentionality—may require the imagination of a poet. Consider again my example. Elpenor referred to a connection between Odysseus's own longing for his wife and family, and the need to erect a sepulcher to Elpenor. The reality of this connection is not stated: it is *present* in the language that Elpenor uses, and if Odysseus responds to it, it is on account of what is more easily described as an immediate perception than as an explicit thought. The funeral rite is perceived, not as fulfilling a specific aim but as lying at the point of intersection of many existing satisfactions. These satisfactions are to be found *in* human relations and cannot be imposed on them from the outside, as willed external aims. If one were to try to encapsulate the shared perceptions of Odysseus and his *hetarros* in a formula or recipe one would in all probability misdescribe their experience. Was Odysseus performing the rite *in order to* give rest to Elpenor's soul, *in order to* escape divine displeasure, *in order to* appease his own feelings toward his wife and father, *in order to* remember Elpenor—or what? It is the phrase "in order to" that is here misleading: the action is not a means to these ends, but an embodiment or reminder of them. It is chosen, as a work of art might be chosen, as the appropriate sign of ends that cannot all be clearly stated, and which are not, in any real sense, *pursued.* But the motives referred to are not for that reason irrational. On the contrary, we have here an instance of practical knowledge, of the ability to achieve order where there might have been chaos.[12]

NOTES

1. I am greatly indebted here and elsewhere to unpublished work of John Casey on the theory of virtue.

2. The need for this "nonaccidental" relation is established, I think, by the examples presented by E. L. Gettier in "Is Justified True Belief Knowledge?" *Analysis* (1963).

3. The opposition of "dread" and "innocence" is already suggested by Kierkegaard in *The Concept of Dread,* trans. W. Lowrie (Princeton, N.J., 1944).

4. See also John Casey, "The Autonomy of Art," Royal Institute of Philosophy Lectures: *Philosophy Looks at the Arts,* ed. G. Vesey (London, 1973).

5. On going to press my attention has been called to an interesting article on this subject by Adam Morton.

6. To make this distinction between universal and particular emotions fully clear is not easy. I have explored the matter at greater length in "Attitudes, Beliefs and Reasons," in John Casey, ed., *Morality and Moral Reasoning* (London, 1971).

7. But see my "Reason and Happiness," Royal Institute of Philosophy Lectures, *Nature and Conduct,* ed. R. S. Peters (London, 1975).

8. See the discussion of these matters in H. Putnam, "Is Semantics Possible?" and "The Mental Life of Some Machines," in *Collected Papers,* col. II (Oxford, 1975) and also D. Wiggins, "The Stream of Consciousness, etc.," in *Philosophy* (1976).

9. See A. J. Kenny, *Action, Emotion and Will* (London, 1963), and also my "Attitudes, Beliefs and Reasons," in *Morality and Moral Reasoning.*

10. See the excellent discussion in Sir Peter Strawson's "Freedom and Resentment," in *Freedom and Resentment and other Essays* (London, 1974).

11. I say "thought," in addition to belief, in order to accommodate emotions that are not founded on belief, say because they have imaginary objects.

12. This paper is extracted and adapted from "The Significance of Common Culture," in *Philosophy* (January 1979). I am grateful to John Casey, Mark Platts, David Hamlyn, Moira Archer, and Amélie Rorty for comments, criticism, and suggestions.

BIBLIOGRAPHY

The literature on the subject of the emotions is as diffuse as it is vast. Some of it—especially research in neurophysiology, biochemistry, and pharmacology—is highly technical. Important as such work is, it is virtually unavailable to any but specialists. Because the relevant material is complex, scattered, and varied, I have divided the bibliographical items into relatively arbitrary categories: general and historical analyses of the emotions; physiological studies of the limbic and autonomic systems and of biochemical processes associated with the emotions; biological research influenced by Darwin's study of the social function of the expression of "basic" emotions; psychological studies of emotion and motivation; psychoanalytic papers on drives and affects; anthropological discussions of the cross-cultural identification of emotions and emotional behavior; and philosophical analyses of the intentionality and the rationality of the emotions. Since this bibliography is selective rather than comprehensive, I have tried to list work that is not only classical and representative, but also itself rich in bibliographical material. Starred items are especially useful for their bibliographies.

I. *General and Historical Studies*

*Adler, Mortimer, ed. "Emotions." *The Great Ideas.* Vol. 2, chap. 22. Chicago: Encyclopedia Britannica, 1952.
*Gardiner, H. M.; Metcalf, R. C. Clark; and Beebe-Center, J. G. *Feeling and Emotion: A History of Theories.* New York: American Book, 1937. This book has a comprehensive bibliography of the history of conceptions of the emotions.
*Hillman, James. *Emotion.* London: Routledge and Kegan Paul, 1960.
*Shibles, Warren. *Emotion.* Whiteware, Wisconsin: The Language Press, The University of Wisconsin, 1974.

II. *Physiological Studies*

*Black, P., ed. *Physiological Correlates of Emotions*. New York: Academic Press, 1970.

Gellhorn, E., and Loofbourrow, G. N. *Emotions and Emotional Disorders*. New York: Harper & Row, 1963.

*Glass, D. C., ed. *Neurophysiology and Emotion*. New York: The Rockefeller University Press, 1967.

MacLean, Paul. "The Limbic Brain in Relation to the Psychoses." *The Physiological Correlates of Emotion*. Ed. P. Black. New York: Academic Press, 1970.

———. "On the Evolution of Three Mentalities." *New Dimensions in Psychiatry*, ed. S. Arieti and G. Chrzanowski. Vol. 2. New York: John Wiley, 1977.

———. "The Triune Brain, Emotion and Scientific Bias." *The Neurosciences: Second Study Program*, ed. F. O. Schmitt. New York: Rockefeller University Press, 1970.

Pribram, Karl. "Self Consciousness and Intentionality: A Model Based on an Experimental Analysis of the Brain Mechanism Involved in the Jamesian Theory of Motivation and Emotion." *Consciousness and Self-Regulation*. Vol. 1. Ed. G. E. Schwartz and D. Shapiro. New York: Plenum Publishing, 1976.

Pribram, Karl, and Melges, Frederick. "Psychophysical Basis of Emotion." *Handbook of Clinical Neurology*, ed. P. J. Vinken and G. W. Bruyn. Amsterdam: North-Holland, 1969.

III. *Biological Studies*

Darwin, Charles. *The Expression of the Emotions in Man and Animals*. New York: Appleton Press, 1896.

*Ekman, Paul. "Darwin and Cross Cultural Studies of Facial Expression." *Darwin and Facial Expression: A Century of Research in Review*, ed. P. Ekman. New York: Academic Press, 1973.

———. *Unmasking the Face*. Englewood Cliffs, N.J.: Prentice-Hall, 1975.

Ekman, Paul, and Friesen, Wallace. "Non-Verbal Behavior and Psychopathology." *The Psychology of Depression: Contemporary Theory and Research*. Washington, D.C.: Winston & Sons, 1974.

Ekman, Paul; Friesen, Wallace; and Ellsworth, Phoebe. *Emotion in the Human Face*. New York: Pergamon Press, 1972.

Ekman, Paul; Friesen, Wallace; and Scherer, Klaus. "Body Movement and Voice Pitch in Deceptive Interaction," *Semiotica*, 16:1 (1976).

*Gellhorn, E. *Biological Foundations of Emotion*. Glenview, Ill.: Foreman Press, 1968.

Hamburg, David. "Emotions in the Perspective of Human Evolution." *Expression of the Emotions in Man*. Ed. P. Knapp. New York: International Universities Press, 1963.

Izard, C. E. *The Face of Emotion*. New York: Appleton-Century-Crofts, 1971.

Jacobson, E. *Biology of the Emotions*. Springfield, Ill., 1967.

*Knapp, P., ed. *Expression of the Emotions in Man*. New York: International Universities Press, 1963.

Tobach, Ethel. *Some Guidelines to the Study of the Evolution and Development of Emotion*. San Francisco: W. H. Freeman, 1970.

Tomkins, Silvan. *Affect, Imagery and Consciousness*. Vols. 1 and 2. New York: Springer, 1962/3.

*Wilson, E. O. *Sociobiology*. Cambridge, Mass.: Harvard University Press, 1975.

IV. *Psychological Studies*

*Arnold, Magda. *Emotion and Personality.* 2 vols. New York: Columbia University Press, 1963.

*————. *The Nature of Emotion.* Baltimore: Penguin Books, 1968.

*————, ed. *Feelings and Emotions.* New York: Academic Press, 1970. See especially the articles by Richard Lazarus, James Averill, Edward Opton.

*————. *Loyola Symposium on Feelings and Emotions.* New York: Academic Press, 1972.

Averill, J. R. "An Analysis of Psychophysiological Symbolism and Its Influence on Theories of Emotion," *Journal for the Theory of Social Behavior,* vol. 4 (1974).

————. "Anger." *Nebraska Symposium on Motivation.* Lincoln: University of Nebraska Press, 1978.

————. "The Emotions." *Personality: Basic Issues and Current Research.* Ed. E. Staub. Englewood Cliffs, N.J.: Prentice-Hall, 1978.

————. "The Functions of Grief." *Emotions, Conflict and Defense.* Ed. C. E. Izard. New York: Plenum Press, 1978.

Cannon, W. B. *Bodily Changes in Pain, Hunger, Fear and Rage.* New York: Appleton, 1929.

de Rivera, J. *A Structural Theory of the Emotions.* New York: International Universities Press, 1977.

*Izard, C. E., ed. *Emotions, Conflict and Defense.* New York: Plenum Press, 1978.

————. *Human Emotions.* New York: Plenum Press, 1977.

Izard, C. E., and Tomkins, Silvan, eds. *Affect, Cognition and Personality.* New York: Springer, 1965.

————. *Patterns of Emotions.* New York: Academic Press, 1972.

Lazarus, R. S. "Emotions and Adaptation: Conceptual and Empirical Relations." *Nebraska Symposium on Motivation,* 1968. Lincoln: University of Nebraska Press, 1968.

————. *Psychological Stress and the Coping Process.* New York: McGraw-Hill, 1966.

————. "The Self-Regulation of Emotion." *Emotions: Their Parameters and Measurement.* Ed. L. Levi. New York: Raven Press, 1975.

*Levi, L., ed. *Emotions: Their Parameters and Measurement.* New York: Raven Press, 1975.

*Mandler, G. *Mind and Emotions.* New York: Wiley, 1975.

Murray, E. J. *Motivation and Emotion.* Englewood Cliffs, N.J.: Prentice-Hall, 1964.

Plutchik, Robert. *The Emotions: Facts, Theories and a New Model.* New York: Random, 1962.

Schachter, S. *Emotion, Obesity and Crime.* New York: Academic Press, 1971.

*Reymert, M. L., ed. *Feelings and Emotions: The Mooseheart Symposium.* New York: McGraw-Hill, 1950.

————. *Feelings and Emotions: The Wittenberg Symposium.* Worcester, Mass., 1928.

Shand, A. F. *The Foundations of Character: A Study of the Emotions and Sentiments.* London: Macmillan, 1920.

Singer, J., and Schachter, S. "Cognitive, Social and Physiological Determinants of Emotional States," *Psychological Review,* LXIX, 5 (1962).

*Spielberger, C. D., ed. *Anxiety and Behavior.* New York: Academic Press, 1966.

*Young, P. T. *Emotion in Man and Animal: Its Nature and Relation to Attitude and Motive.* New York: Wiley, 1961.

*————. *Motivation and Emotion: A Survey of the Determinants of Human and*

Animal Activity. New York: Wiley, 1961.

*Zuckerman, M., and Spielberger, C. D., eds. *Emotions and Anxiety.* New York: Wiley, 1976.

V. *Psychoanalytic Studies*

Bowlby, J. *Attachment and Loss.* Vols. 1 and 2. New York: Basic Books, 1969 and 1970.

Freud, S. *Mourning and Melancholia,* SE 14. London: Hogarth Press, 1955.

———. *Inhibitions, Symptoms and Anxiety,* SE 20, London: Hogarth Press, 1959.

Greenacre, Phyllis, ed. *Affective Disorders.* New York: International Universities Press, 1953.

Hartmann, H. "Ego Psychology and the Problem of Adaptation." *Essays on Ego Psychology.* London: Hogarth, 1964.

Hartmann, H.; Kris, E.; and Lowenstein, R. *Papers on Psychoanalytic Psychology.* New York: International Universities Press, 1964.

Glover, E. "The Psychoanalysis of Affects," *International Journal of Psychoanalysis,* 20 (1939).

Jacobson, E. "The Psychoanalytic Theory of Affects." *Depression.* New York: International Universities Press, 1971.

Klein, Melanie. *Envy and Gratitude.* New York: Basic Books, 1975.

Klein, Melanie, and Riviere, Joan. *Love, Hate and Reparation.* London: Hogarth Press, 1953.

Kohut, K. *The Restoration of the Self.* New York: International Universities Press, 1977.

Lynd, Helen. *Shame and the Search for Identity.* New York: Harcourt Brace, 1970.

Mahler, Margaret. "Notes on the Development of Basic Moods: Depression Affect." *Psychoanalysis: A General Psychology.* Ed. R. M. Lowenstein et al. New York: International Universities Press, 1966.

Psychoanalytic Study of the Child. Index Volume with abstracts of vols. 1-25. New York: Yale University Press, 1975. See entries for: affect, aggression, anxiety, depression, guilt, mourning.

Rapaport, David. *Emotions and Memory.* New York: Science Editions, 1961.

———. "On the Psychoanalytic Theory of Affects," *International Journal of Psychoanalysis,* no. 34 (1953).

Sachs, David. "On Freud's Doctrine of the Emotions." *Freud,* ed. Richard Wollheim. New York: Anchor Books, 1974.

Schafer, Roy. *A New Language for Psychoanalysis.* New Haven: Yale University Press, 1976.

Schur, M., ed. *Drives, Affects, Behaviors.* Vol. 2. New York: International Universities Press, 1965.

Wollheim, Richard. *Freud.* New York: Viking Press, 1971.

VI. *Anthropological Studies*

Bateson, Gregory. *Steps to an Ecology of Mind.* San Francisco: Chandler Publications, 1972.

Briggs, Jean. *Never in Anger.* Cambridge: Harvard University Press, 1970.

Demos, Virginia. "The Socialization of Affect in Early Childhood." Unpublished manuscript, Children's Hospital, Boston, Mass.

Doi, Takeo. *The Anatomy of Dependence.* Tokyo: Kodansha International, 1973.

Douglas, Mary. *Purity and Danger.* London: Routledge & Kegan Paul, 1966.

Geertz, Clifford. *The Interpretation of Cultures.* New York: Basic Books, 1973.

Geertz, Hildred. "The Vocabulary of the Emotions," *Psychiatry,* 22 (1959).

Homans, George. *Sentiments and Activities.* New York: Free Press, 1962.

Levy, Robert. *The Tahitians.* Chicago: University of Chicago Press, 1973.

*Middleton, John, ed. *From Child to Adult: Studies in the Anthropology of Education.* New York: Natural History Press, 1970. Especially papers by Margaret Mead, Meyer Fortes, Dorothy Eggan.

*Munsterberger, Werner. ed. *The Psychoanalytic Study of Society.* New Haven: Yale University Press, 1949—. Vols. 1- .

Needham, Rodney. *Structure and Sentiment.* Chicago: University of Chicago Press, 1962.

Osgood, C. E.; May, W. H.; and Miron, M.S. *Cross-Cultural Universals of Affective Meaning.* Urbana: University of Illinois Press, 1975.

Wallace, Anthony, and Carson, Margaret. "Sharing and Diversity in Emotion Terminology," *Ethos,* I.1 (1973).

Zborowski, Mark. "Cultural Components in Responses to Pain," *Journal of Social Issues,* Vol. VIII (1952).

VII. *Philosophical Studies*

Alston, William. "Emotion and Feeling." *Encyclopedia of Philosophy.* Vol. 2. Ed. Paul Edwards. New York: Collier-Macmillan, 1969.

————. "Expressing." *Philosophy in America,* ed. Max Black. New York: Cornell University Press, 1965.

————. "Feelings," *The Philosophical Review,* 78 (1969).

Anscombe, G. E. M. "On the Grammar of 'Enjoy,'" *Journal of Philosophy,* 64 (1967).

Arnold, Magda. "Human Emotion and Action." *Human Action: Conceptual and Empirical Issues,* ed. T. Mischel. New York: Academic Press, 1969.

Bain, Alexander. *The Emotions and the Will.* New York: Appleton, 1876.

Bedford, Erroll. "Emotions," *Proceedings of the Aristotelian Society,* 57 (1956-57).

Brandt, Richard. "The Psychology of Benevolence and Its Implications for Philosophy," *Journal of Philosophy,* 73 (1976).

Crane, Milton. "Suggestions Towards a Genealogy of the 'Man of Feeling,'" *The History of Ideas* (1951).

Ewing, A. C. "The Justification of the Emotions," *Proceedings of the Aristotelian Society,* supplement vol. 31 (1957).

Goldberg, Bruce. "The Linguistic Expression of Feeling," *American Philosophical Quarterly,* vol. 8 (1971).

Gombrich, E. H. "Art and the Language of the Emotions," *Aristotelian Society,* supplement vol. 36 (1962).

————. "The Mask and the Face: The Perception of Physiognomic Likeness in Life and Art." *Art, Perception and Reality,* ed. E. H. Gombrich, Julian Hochberg, and Max Black. Baltimore: Johns Hopkins University Press, 1972.

Gosling, J. C. "Emotion and Object," *Philosophical Review,* 74 (1965).

————. *Pleasure and Desire.* Oxford: Oxford University Press, 1969.

Green, O. H. "Emotions and Belief," *American Philosophical Quarterly Monograph,* no. 6 (1972).

Hampshire, Stuart. "Feeling and Expression" and other essays. Reprinted in *Freedom of Mind and Other Essays*. Princeton, N.J.: Princeton University Press, 1971.

Hill, Thomas. "Servility and Self Respect," *The Monist*, 57.1 (1973).

James, William. *The Principles of Psychology*. 2 vols. New York: Henry Holt, 1890.

Kenny, Anthony. *Action, Emotion and the Will*. London: Routledge & Kegan Paul, 1963.

Kolnai, Aurel. *Ethics, Value and Reality*. Indianapolis: Hackett Publishing, 1978.

Lange, C. G., and James, W. *The Emotions*. Baltimore: Williams and Wilkins, 1885.

Lyons, William. "Emotions and Behavior," *Philosophy and Phenomenological Research* 38 (1978).

———. "Emotions and Feelings," *Ratio* 11 (1977).

MacIntyre, A. "Emotion, Behavior and Belief," *Against Self-Images of the Age*. London: Duckworth, 1971.

Mercer, Philip. *Sympathy and Ethics*. Oxford: Clarendon Press, 1972.

Meinong, A. *On Emotional Presentation*. Evanston, Ill.: Northwestern University Press, 1972.

Morris, Herbert, ed. *Guilt and Shame*. Belmont, Cal.: Wadsworth Paperback, 1971.

———. *On Guilt and Innocence*. Berkeley, Los Angeles, London: University of California Press, 1976.

Neu, Jerome. *Emotion, Thought and Therapy*. London: Routledge & Kegan Paul, 1977.

Pears, David. "Causes and Objects of Some Feelings and Psychological Reactions," *Ratio*, IV (1962). Reprinted in *Questions in the Philosophy of Mind*. London: Duckworth, 1975.

Perkins, Moreland. "Emotion and Feeling," *Philosophical Review*, 75.2 (1966).

Peters, R. S. "Emotions and the Category of Passivity." *Proceedings of the Aristotelian Society*, supplement vol. 62 (1961-62).

Piers, G., and Singer, M. B. *Shame and Guilt*. Springfield, 1953.

Pitcher, George. "The Awfulness of Pain." *Journal of Philosophy*, 67, 14 (1970).

———. "Emotion," *Mind*, 74 (1965).

———. "On Approval," *Philosophical Review*, 67 (1958).

———. "Pain Perception," *Philosophical Review*, 79 (1970).

Ryle, Gilbert. *The Concept of Mind*. London: Hutchinson, 1949.

Sartre, J. P. *The Emotions: Outline of a Theory*. New York: Philosophical Library, 1948.

Scheler, Max. *The Nature of Sympathy*. New Haven: Yale University Press, 1954.

———. *Ressentiment*. New York: Free Press, 1961.

Schoeck, H. *Envy: A Theory of Social Behavior*. New York: Harcourt, Brace & World, 1969.

Sheffler, Israel. "In Praise of the Cognitive Emotions." *Teachers College Record*, 79.2. New York: Columbia University Press, 1977.

Solomon, Robert. "The Logic of Emotion," *Nous*, XI.1 (1977).

———. *The Passions*. New York: Doubleday, 1976.

Stanislavski, G. *An Actor Prepares*. New York: Theater Arts Books, 1936.

Stein, Edith, *On the Problem of Empathy*. Nijhoff, 1964.

Strawson, Peter. "Freedom and Resentment." *Proceedings of the British Academy*. Oxford: Oxford University Press, 1962.

Tanner, Michael. "Sentimentality," *Proceedings of the Aristotelian Society*, 77 (1977).

Taylor, Gabriele. "Justifying the Emotions," *Mind*, 84 (1975).

———. "On Love," *Proceedings of the Aristotelian Society,* 76 (1975-76).

Taylor, Gabriele, and Wolfram, S. "Virtues and Passions," *Analysis,* 31 (1971).

Telfer, Elizabeth. "Self Respect," *Philosophical Quarterly,* 18 (1968).

Thalberg, Irving. "Constituents and Causes of Emotion and Action," *Philosophical Quarterly,* 23 (1973).

———. "Emotion and Thought," *American Philosophical Quarterly,* 1 (1964).

———. *Perception, Emotion and Action.* Oxford: Blackwell, 1977.

Trigg, Roger. *Pain and Emotion.* Oxford: Oxford University Press, 1970.

Urmson, J. O. *The Emotive Theory of Ethics.* Oxford: Oxford University Press, 1968.

Walsh, W. H. "Pride, Shame and Responsibility," *Philosophical Quarterly,* 20 (1970).

Watson, Kendall. "Fearing Fictions," *Journal of Philosophy,* 75 (1978).

Westermarck, Edward. *The Origin and Development of Moral Ideas.* New York: Macmillan, 1906-1908.

Williams, Bernard. "Morality and the Emotions" and other essays. *Problems of the Self.* Cambridge: Cambridge University Press, 1973.

Wilson, J. R. S. *Emotion and Object.* Cambridge: Cambridge University Press, 1972.

Wollheim, Richard. "Expression" and other essays. Reprinted in *On Art and the Mind.* London: Allen Lane, 1973.

———. "Thought and Passions." *Proceedings of the Aristotelian Society,* 68 (1967-68).

CONTRIBUTORS

Paul MacLean, M.D., is the chief of the Laboratory of Brain Evolution and Behavior at the National Institutes of Mental Health.

James Averill is a professor of psychology at the University of Massachusetts, Amherst.

Paul Ekman is the director of the Human Interaction Laboratory of the Department of Psychiatry at the Medical School of the University of California, San Francisco.

Ronald de Sousa is a professor of philosophy at the University of Toronto.

Adam Morton is a professor of philosophy at Bristol University.

Georges Rey is an assistant professor of philosophy at the State University of New York, at Purchase.

Graeme Marshall is a Reader in Philosophy at the University of Melbourne.

Patricia S. Greenspan is an associate professor of philosophy at the University of Maryland.

Robert Solomon is a professor of philosophy at the University of Texas.

Richard Wollheim is Grote Professor of the Philosophy of Mind and Logic at the University of London.

Michael Stocker is a senior lecturer at the University of La Trobe.

Gareth Matthews is a professor of philosophy at the University of Massachusetts, Amherst.

Arnold Isenberg was professor of philosophy at Stanford University and Michigan State University.

Gabriele Taylor is a fellow of St. Anne's College, Oxford.

Annette Baier is a professor of philosophy at the University of Pittsburgh.

Jerome Neu is an associate professor of philosophy at the University of California, Santa Cruz.

Leila Tov-Ruach is an Israeli psychiatrist, who writes and lectures on philosophic psychology.

Lawrence Blum is an assistant professor of philosophy at the University of Massachusetts, Boston.

Roger Scruton is a lecturer at Birkbeck College, The University of London.

Amélie Rorty is a professor of philosophy at Livingston College, Rutgers University.